Alan Clark

Books by the same author

Journalism
Norfolk Cottage

Alan Clark, Diaries: Into Politics 1972–1982 (edited)
Alan Clark, The Last Diaries 1992–1999 (edited)

The Hugo Young Papers:
Thirty Years of British Politics Off the Record (edited)

Alan Clark

The Biography

Ion Trewin

Weidenfeld & Nicolson
LONDON

First published in Great Britain in 2009
by Weidenfeld & Nicolson

1 3 5 7 9 10 8 6 4 2

© Ion Trewin 2009

A CIP catalogue record for this book
is available from the British Library.

ISBN: 978 0 297 85073 1

Typeset by Input Data Services Ltd,
Bridgwater, Somerset

Printed and bound in the UK by
CPI William Clowes Beccles NR34 7TL

The Orion Publishing Group's policy is to use papers that
are natural, renewable and recyclable products and made
from wood grown in sustainable forests. The logging and
manufacturing processes are expected to conform to
environmental regulations of the country of origin.

Weidenfeld & Nicolson

Orion Publishing Group Ltd
Orion House
5 Upper Saint Martin's Lane
London, WC2H 9EA
An Hachette UK Company

For Jane

Contents

Part Two

Illustrations

All illustrations are reproduced by kind permission of Jane Clark with the following exceptions:

Alan at Oxford, 1946 *(Lord Montagu of Beaulieu)*
In conversation with Joseph Cotten *(Lord Montagu of Beaulieu)*
With Pam Hart at Zermatt *(Pamela Hart)*
Kenneth Clark with the Turner Seascape *(Cecil Beaton, Sotheby's Picture Library)*
With Colin at Sotheby's, 5 July 1984 *(Topham / PA)*
With Jane at Sotheby's *(Jane Bown / Guardian News & Media Ltd, 1984)*
With Margaret Thatcher at Brize Norton *(Press Association)*
Signing the Anglo-Soviet agreement, February 1986 *(Press Association)*
In the Commons, 9 January 1990 *(Parliamentary Recording Unit)*
News of the World front page, 29 May 1994 *(News International Syndication)*
Signing copies of *Diaries* at Hatchards *(Rex Features)*
Josephine, James and Valerie Harkess, 31 May 1994 *(Press Association)*
With Kenneth Clarke on *Breakfast with Frost (Press Association)*
Campaigning with Jane on the King's Road *(Eric Roberts / Telegraph Media Group Ltd)*
In the Commons, 13 April 1999 *(Parliamentary Recording Unit)*

While every effort has been made to trace copyright holders, if any have been inadvertently overlooked, the publishers will be happy to acknowledge them in future editions.

Introduction

In his wilder fantasies in the 1990s Alan Clark thought of himself as a populist leader of the Conservative Party. Realistically he would have settled for a seat in Cabinet. In the end he achieved immortality as a diarist. Wrote *The Times,* 'Literature and the great British game of gossip will judge him for his diary. For its Pooterish self-assessment, for Mr Toad's enthusiasm for new things, for Byron's caddishness, for its deadly candour, it is one of the great works in the genre.'[1]

A decade or so after his death wherever diaries and diarists are mentioned Alan regularly comes out top of the heap. 'A wonderfully candid commentary on the daily ins and outs of politics in the age of Thatcher,' said *The Independent* in 2008.[2] Although the first volume was ostensibly about being a junior Minister in Margaret Thatcher's governments in the 1980s it is far, far more, beginning with the death of his celebrated art historian father with whom he had a variable relationship. Central to his account is his marriage to Jane, who put up with so much, and his love for his sons. Here, too, is his passion for animals and the countryside, his historical interests (particularly of two world wars), his beliefs (religious as well as political), his enthusiasm for cars, for special places (his homes at Zermatt, Saltwood and Eriboll especially), his knowledge of art (and not just inherited values from his father). Nor is he shy in revealing his weaknesses, not least of the flesh. Scandal frequently circled him, yet somehow with one bound and the often unexpected help of others he managed to escape.

That first volume which he transcribed and edited himself is the centrepiece, supported by two further volumes that he planned before his death: a prequel, when he was first selected as a parliamentary candidate, and the sequel, although he saw this only as portraying 'the wilderness years' after he resigned from the Commons in 1992 to his return in 1997 (as a posthumous work it would end with his cancer and death in 1999). Each volume is different in tone, but as a trilogy they are the memoirs which he never thought of writing.

Inevitably the published diaries are an account seen almost wholly from his point of view; they also only begin when he is forty-four. This is the biography and the whole life. It was suggested by Jane, who never stinted in her co-operation, however difficult she found some of the material. Reading a first draft she commented that, although married to her husband for forty-one years, 'she hadn't known the half of it'.

If Alan and Jane drove in London's West End along Portland Place Jane would notice her husband tense up or even shudder as they passed No. 30, the first family home he properly remembered. In all those years of marriage Jane learnt little about his early life. What he did say suggested resentment, that he felt neglected, that he disliked his schooldays and that it was only when he got to Oxford that he made his first lasting friendships. Perhaps his reticence was because, on hearing her talk about her own happy family childhood, Alan could not compete. No wonder that he was all the more determined that his sons should not suffer a similar experience. He would not repeat what he considered were the errors of his father, who replicated the way he himself had been brought up. He broke the mould. In his late sixties he told one interviewer, 'I regard myself as having "spoilt them" by loving them to death. And yet it didn't turn them into sort of little wimpy sort of poofs.'[3]

On the surface Alan had it all. A brilliant, charismatic art historian for a father; a starkly beautiful mother with a superb fashion sense and a talent for interior design and entertaining. And of assets, if not always ready money, there was no shortage. However, after Alan's death a fragment of memoir discovered at the back of a desk drawer at Saltwood Castle, the Clark family home from the early 1950s, and probably written when he was in his sixties,[4] shows him worrying away at his childhood demons. Here he reflected on loneliness, alienation from his parents, being left on the top floor of the Portland Place house, 'subsisting' on Edwardian books – he mentions H.E. Marshall's *Our Island Story* and the novels of G.A. Henty. 'My parents would be out socialising and the large and ill-natured staff would feed me as early as they could and then retire to the Servants Hall in the basement isolated by four floors of total darkness.' There was never any question of physical maltreatment, but emotional neglect was another matter.

He would not have realised how the Clark family experience was in so many ways repeating itself. 'I sought distraction from ghouls and witches in the dry, factual and still comforting pages of *Jane's Fighting Ships*. In 1936 [when eight] I knew the name, silhouette and displacement of every ship in the Royal Navy and most of those of our potential adversaries'.

His copies of the 1935 edition of *Jane's Fighting Ships* and the 1936 *Jane's All the World's Aircraft* (which he swiftly embraced) are at Saltwood Castle today and show extensive signs of childhood devotion. Officially they were reference books, but Alan was not the only child with a military bent who found them of absorbing interest. In a 1987 diary entry, reporting an unsatisfactory meeting at the Foreign Office, he remembered reading about 'all these white-painted ships on the China Station, which I used to memorise from the *Jane's* of that year, the first in which I was given the book'.[5]

The Portland Place upbringing helped form not just his attitude to his sons, but also his own future thinking on military matters. What he learnt about ships and the politics that changed the Royal Navy so dramatically in the quarter-century between the start of the First World War and that of the Second, led him to reflect: 'I did not know of course the extent of the damage inflicted by Lloyd George and Churchill in the twenties, although I realised something had gone wrong simply by referring to the volumes for 1914 and 1919.' He would draw on the knowledge when elected four decades later to a constituency that abutted Devonport's Royal Naval dockyard; and again in the late 1980s when appointed by Margaret Thatcher as a Minister of State at the Ministry of Defence.

With this knowledge it is hardly surprising, therefore, that he would become both a radical twentieth-century historian and ultimately a politician, whose values and beliefs, although mostly to the right, were never slavishly Conservative. The political writer Simon Hoggart summed him up succinctly, as 'an iconoclastic traditionalist, a revolutionary conservative, a man whose views verged on fascism yet who delivered one of the finest defences of democracy I have heard ... a man who loved the idea of not caring what anyone else thought, yet who actually minded desperately what other people thought'.[6] And Charles Powell, Margaret Thatcher's private secretary, had an evocative phrase to describe the Alan he knew: 'The Lucifer of the Thatcher government: a brilliant, dark, quixotic, bawdy presence.'[7]

Having been used as a child to self-reliance, to making up his own mind, Alan would throughout his adult life be true to himself. He may not have reached the top of the political tree he so desired, but as a diarist he was nonpareil.

The research for this biography began at Saltwood Castle. With room to store box upon box of papers from his two constituencies as well as family private papers, he never had to throw anything away. A succession of

four-drawer filing cabinets in various states of organisation show Alan's
life from early adulthood to his death. One tea chest in a tower attic
revealed his early attempts at making a career as a writer, his mother's
affair with a leading composer, as well as piles of magazines displaying his
passion for cars and motoring.

Alan worked in a number of Saltwood locations. The Green Room
next to the kitchen in the castle's living quarters became a late favourite.
Earlier he had used two of his father's studies, one off the Great Hall and
the other in the Garden House, the extensive bungalow that Kenneth
Clark had built after deciding to hand over the castle to Alan and Jane in
1971. In the castle itself he used the two ground-floor tower rooms, one
known as the winter office (it has a fireplace) and the other as the summer
office (it doesn't).

After his death his parliamentary papers arrived at Saltwood. Jane, with
Lynn her housekeeper, gradually sorted these. When I began work in the
summer office Jane showed me three ministerial red boxes, each identified
by the rubbed gold letters 'Minister for Trade, Department of Trade and
Industry'. When Jane first discovered them hidden behind cardboard boxes
from Westminster she was immediately curious. Two opened at her touch
and proved to be packed with House of Commons notepaper. The third
was locked. In a desk drawer she found a key ring with what looked like
the right size key. She inserted it in the lock and the key turned. Easing
open the lid, she took in the contents – a pile of letters, with many in
their original envelopes. On top of the letters, in her husband's unmistakable hand, was a note, on Commons embossed paper:

> JANE
> Darling, please don't rootle here.
> There are papers that might upset you
> even tho referring to matters
> now long past
>
> Love

The correspondent was a woman known to Jane. She had been Alan's
secretary from the late 1980s until the 1992 general election, when Alan
made one of the biggest mistakes of his career by resigning from the
Commons. Jane had assumed there had been letters between them and

had since Alan's death wondered where they might be. Now they had turned up, the envelopes usually addressed either to Alan at Brooks's Club in St James's or the House of Commons, where she also worked. Nor were they unique. Elsewhere I found a box of letters from the first love of his life, a dancer, to whom he had been close in the early 1950s. But I also discovered the aptness of Simon Hoggart's description: 'a philanderer obsessed with his wife'.[8]

Saltwood Castle turned out to be an Aladdin's cave. As well as his own papers here were hundreds of letters from his father (often unsorted, often undated). A cardboard box revealed the engagement diaries of his mother from the mid-1930s to the end of the Second World War, in which she often wrote up her thoughts. Elsewhere were early diaries of Alan's going back sporadically to his childhood.

All this and much, much more has proved invaluable. For a biographer Saltwood Castle offers the literary equivalent of treasure trove.

Ion Trewin
March 2009

Part One

ONE

Origins and Influences

The first child of Kenneth Mackenzie Clark was born on 13 April 1928. The birth, in a nursing home in London's Lancaster Gate, proved difficult. Labour was long and painful thanks, it transpired, to the largeness of the baby's head, a Clark trait. The baby was named Alan (after his mother's brother) Kenneth McKenzie (both Clark family names).[1] In a letter about Alan's christening his father described a moment where the parents give their word that the son would renounce the sinful desires of the flesh; at that point Alan had hiccoughed.[2]

Kenneth, or K as he was known, had married Elizabeth Winifred Martin, the Dublin-born daughter of an Irish businessman and his doctor wife, in January the previous year. K was twenty-three, his wife (who preferred to be known as Jane) a year older. On his marriage certificate he described himself as 'art critic', although 'art historian' would have been more apt.

To understand his passion for painting we need to return to his childhood. K was an only son, often left to his own devices. His father had joined the family cotton thread business in Paisley on the western edge of Glasgow. The firm had been founded by his grandfather and great-uncle, who devised a form of cotton thread which supplanted silk and linen for general use. Nor did the family inventiveness end there; next came a wooden spool onto which the fine cotton was woven. Thanks in the main to the Clarks, Paisley and cotton thread became synonymous.

When the first Kenneth McKenzie Clark, Alan's grandfather, joined the firm he was twenty-two and the family were negotiating to sell the business to a larger Paisley rival, J. & P. Coats. The eventual sale price in 1896 was £2,585,913, or approximately £150 million by the value of money a century later, which, divided between four Clarks, one of whom was Kenneth McKenzie, left each a wealthy man. As K commented to his father's biographer, 'He thought to himself, if business interferes with your pleasure, give up business.'[3] He eventually retired as a director of the merged firm in 1909. Apart from one business venture in the 1920s he lived the life of a man of leisure.

The Clarks now had extensive shareholdings in Coats, an interest that would continue down the generations. As late as the 1970s Alan in his diaries regularly commented on the share price, particularly its decline to 25½p in 1997. For Kenneth McKenzie Clark, money only became an issue after the First World War when the value of sterling plummeted to half its 1914 value. Before then his pleasures included yachting in Scottish waters in lavish, purpose-built craft, *Kariad* and *Katoomba* among them,[4] shooting and fishing in England at Sudbourne in Suffolk and in Scotland, principally at Shielbridge, where he bought 75,000 acres. In London the Clarks rented a flat in Berkeley Square; on the French Riviera they built a house at Cap Martin; and, demonstrating that tastes were nothing if not catholic after the First World War, with money now tighter, they also owned a house in Bournemouth. In the 1920s Kenneth McKenzie speculated in a Scottish aluminium venture, without success. He had married a distant relative, Alice McArthur, in 1900 when she was thirty-three and he was thirty-two. Their son was born three years later by Caesarean section – a rare and difficult procedure in 1903, which may explain why there were no further children.

Kenneth Clark's parents were temperamental opposites; she reticent, with a horror of expressing emotion, he gregarious and emotionally mercurial. According to K his father had been a ladies' man until his marriage, but afterwards Alice rarely let her husband out of her sight. One trait did not repeat itself. Kenneth McKenzie's other pleasures included whisky – to the extent that it eventually killed him, as it did other members of his generation of Clarks. He also enjoyed gambling, which would, for a time, catch Alan in its thrall. Kenneth McKenzie was successful, several times breaking the bank at Monte Carlo before the First World War. K recalled coming into his father's bedroom early one morning and finding the bed weighed down with gold coins, in the days before the casinos substituted chips.

As an only child living in a huge Suffolk house[5] young Kenneth had little company, being brought up, wrote Maurice Bowra in his memoirs, 'with a callousness which only the rich dare to show to their children'. He had a Scots Nanny, Miss Lamont, who was known by the Clarks as 'Lam',[6] and previously had to endure a German governess, who was dismissed after being discovered by his mother yelling at him. Indeed servants of all kinds generally left as bad a taste in the memory of K as they would Alan. K put it down to the inhuman way the upper-middle classes treated servants.

Before long he took refuge in books; one in particular, he was to recall, 'may truly have started me off in my line of business'. This book, about paintings in the Louvre in Paris, would have as much of an influence on his life and career as *Jane's Fighting Ships* would on Alan. A present 'from Granny, Xmas, 1910', when K was seven, it became his 'most treasured possession'. His basic knowledge of art came from it, and perhaps, sub-consciously, something about life. He recalled sixty years later that many of the pictures were of girls, thereby confirming his belief in 'the close connection between art and sex'.

This childhood solitude had one debilitating side-effect, from which Alan was also to suffer: hypochondria. K wrote in his memoirs about his own experience, which had its origins, he suggests, in what the French call *accidie*. 'For some years I believed intermittently, but with absolute conviction, that I was dying of paralysis. My own hypochondria was deep rooted enough to reappear two or three times in later life.' In Alan it would prove more frequent, but no less severe.

K's education was traditional for someone from the moneyed class: from Winchester, where he won prizes (for art four years running), he went on to Trinity College, Oxford, and read history, although perhaps more important were the many friends he made, not least Maurice Bowra,[7] who would be 'the strongest influence' on his life, introducing him to literature as well as later proving a great friend to Alan, too.

Graduating with a second-class history degree, K made for Florence to continue his studies in art. There he pursued an introduction to Bernard Berenson, the leading authority of his time on Renaissance art. Studying under Berenson helped him become one of the most knowledgeable British art critics on Italian painting. K returned to Florence with Jane after their marriage, when he was working on his first book, *The Gothic Revival*. Five months before Alan's birth he was able to brag a little to Jane about the state of his bank balance – £600 on deposit, 'which will pay for the car and the baby (I put them in order of expense)'. By April 1928, 'I shall have got another £500 from Coats'.[8]

With the publication of *The Gothic Revival* in 1929 – helping in the process to kick Gothic out of the doldrums – K had arrived, and now, with Jane by his side, they had the charisma as well as the means to be leaders of the beau monde of the period. By the following year, when he was asked to catalogue the Royal Collection of Leonardo da Vinci draw-ings at Windsor, his career was firmly in the ascendant. In 1931, aged only twenty-eight, he was invited back to Oxford as Keeper of Fine Art at the Ashmolean Museum. K himself, in what his daughter Colette believed to be an ironical comment, described this period, which continued until the outbreak of war, as 'the Great Clark Boom'.

Jane was pregnant again, this time with twins. In her seventh month, K had an idea: 'If I were rich I would get you busted by Epstein.'[9] The babies were born on 9 October 1932, half an hour apart, the older being a son, Colin, followed by Colette. According to K in his memoirs, when the news came through he was at one of Lady Cunard's cocktail parties. K announced to the gathering: 'It's twins.' 'Boys or girls?' they replied. 'One of each.' To which someone remarked: 'That always means different fathers.' Jane and K had known about the twins since she had been X-rayed two months before the birth when she turned the car she was driving upside down after hitting a lamppost outside Oxford's Radcliffe Hospital. Colin was named after one of Jane's uncles, Colette as the female equivalent, leading Colin to remark that this was one of his parents' 'very rare breaches of good taste'.

Hardly had they settled near Oxford in their fourth home in six years of marriage than the top job in Clark's world beckoned. In 1934, aged thirty-one, he became Director of the nation's premier picture museum, the National Gallery in London. Nor was that all: later the same year his work on the royal da Vincis (Sir Ernst Gombrich judged his catalogue 'a masterpiece')[10] paid a handsome dividend when he was persuaded by King George V to become Surveyor of the King's Pictures.

Back in London, the Clarks acquired an impressive house in Portland Place, south of Regent's Park and just north of the sparkling new head-quarters of the BBC. Portland Place was but one of a succession of houses that Alan lived in. At his birth, the Clarks were in rented accommodation in Westminster; by the summer they had moved to a house nearby bought for them by Kenneth Clark's father. As K made his way spectacularly in the world of art so new homes followed, first to Richmond Green when he was working at Windsor on the da Vinci drawings; next to Shotover Cleve, three miles outside Oxford, on taking the Ashmolean post. And then the return to London.

In size and grandeur 30 Portland Place, on the east side of this wide street (unusual for London in being more a boulevard), was a match for Clark's position. In his recollection it was 'far too big; the whole *piano nobile*, with beautiful "Adam" rooms, marble chimney pieces and painted ceilings, was completely unnecessary'. However, his wife was equal to the challenge; 'a born hostess' and in gowns by Schiaparelli, she was 'often described as the best dressed woman in London'. Just as her mother was one of the first two women to qualify as surgeons in Dublin, so she was a rarity among girls of her generation in going to Oxford, where she read history at Somerville. Unlike her future husband she showed little academic prowess and had to retake her finals, eventually emerging with a Third-class honours degree, not something she confided to her children.

As the wife of a brilliant young art connoisseur and with access to the Clark wealth she soon demonstrated that she, too, had something artistic to contribute: a talent for interior design. As her husband made his way in the world of art so he acquired pictures suitable for the walls of Portland Place's huge rooms. Here the Clarks began to entertain on a grand scale, Jane proving a knowing hostess and able to draw on a large staff. The servants that Alan recalled included a cook and kitchen staff, a butler, a chauffeur and several maids, as well as nursemaids for the twins. Jane, said her daughter, never cooked, never bought food, never did any domestic duties – she relied totally on servants.[11]

Colin judged the marriage turbulent. Colette says that although it was her father who became the public celebrity, for the first twenty years of their marriage they were actually known as Jane and K. 'My mother was a very powerful character. She was the one who had the opinions, who dominated the party, was the brilliant one, original, everyone was paying court to her. Papa was almost the dear old professor in the background.'[12] Alan recollected that he never appeared busy, travelling at 'quarter-throttle all his life'.[13]

As a young child Alan was not particularly close to either of his parents. This was hardly unusual among the upper-middle classes, where servants and governesses tended to have greater contact with their employers' offspring. In the summer of 1938 K wrote: 'Alan who used to be much in sympathy with me is now perfectly silent.'[14] As he grew up, his relationship with both Mum and Dad (as he called them then – Mama and Papa came later) would prove topsy-turvy, not least as a result of the coming of the Second World War which upset their lives in ways no-one could have expected. Alan, in 1994, wrote how difficult throughout his life he and his father found saying to each other what they felt emotionally. 'I only just – just – got to him in time to tell him of my love, on 19 May 1983 when he could still hear and understand but was too ill to talk.'[15] Here was yet another family trait. Colin, in a television profile of his father, said that 'neither of his parents had ever hugged or kissed him throughout his life'.[16]

Colin also recalled, 'it was always impressed on us that we were different from everyone else. This was certainly not because we were "upper class" in the conventional English sense – my parents had a horror of the nobility.

Like many intellectuals, they considered the landed gentry to be boors and philistines. They didn't like the middle classes any better.' It was a sin to be bourgeois, common was even worse – common meant enjoying milk chocolate and waltzes by Johann Strauss.[17] No-one seemed immune to the Clarks' views, not even the royal family and their courtiers.

Following the abdication of Edward VIII in 1936, K was quick to give his opinion of George VI and his wife Elizabeth. Invited to Windsor, he 'found the new King and Queen very pleasant – she just above the average country house type, he just below it'.[18] Jane confided to her diary that 'K has enjoyed Windsor espec two long walks with Queen ... they want to get in touch with modern life in as many aspects as poss but go slow so as not hurt people's feelings'. K was, however, 'shocked at how little K&Q do. She gets up at 11. Hardly anyone at Windsor and just as dreary in evenings as under King G and QM, but at least latter went to bed earlier. He likes the Q *v much*',[19] and soon they were hanging pictures together at Buckingham Palace. Taking K's advice, the Queen started a collection of modern pictures including Steer's *Chepstow Castle* and a 1915 Augustus John portrait of Bernard Shaw – 'the 1st modern pictures of any merit bought since Prince Consort'.[20]

In March 1937 the Clarks attended the King and Queen's first dinner party at Buckingham Palace. Jane wrote: 'I stupidly forget to wear a tiara.' Of her dinner neighbour, Sir Hill Child, Master of the King's Household, she reported – and she was quick to identify a philistine – that 'he asks why the King's Duccio is so valuable – "is it the gold on it?"'.[21] At a Buckingham Palace dinner party the following year, when Jane wore a new Schiaparelli gown in white and silver with just one piece of jewellery, a diamond brooch, she had rather better luck with her dinner companions. She whispered to Geoffrey Dawson, Editor of *The Times*, about the Queen's purchase of the Steer and John pictures, and he promised to run a third leader. In the end just a brief news story, and a picture of the Shaw with his eyes closed, appeared.[22]

The Clarks reciprocated the royal hospitality by entertaining the King and Queen to lunch at Portland Place. Colette, who was only four, remembered the occasion, 'You do remember when you meet the King, don't you?'[23] Alan later recalled: 'I was presented – short trousers and satin shirt – and he was very splendid and he offered me some ice cream, which was extremely good. I was never allowed ice cream. My mother had this puritan side. One shouldn't indulge the cravings of the flesh, and so that made me a royalist for ever.'[24]

The Clarks had well and truly arrived.

TWO

Early Memories

What was Alan's first memory? In his late forties he thought it was Scotland, the smell of peat water, possibly in 1931 when he was three years old. In July his grandmother had written to Alan's father to make arrangements for his first visit to the family house at Shielbridge on the Ardnamurchan peninsula, Scotland's most western mainland land-mass where golden eagles might sometimes be seen.[1]

On another occasion, he recalled 'seeing the two Rolls-Royces that my grandfather had sent to meet us – one for the passengers and one for the luggage – coming along on the far side of the loch, raising dust clouds on the unmade highland roads. It must have been August because we never went there before the twelfth but, unlike my recollections in later life, it never seemed to rain in that month.' Of the Rolls, Alan later recalled that one was 'an early thirty horsepower which had been converted into a barrel-sided shooting break and, as far as I can recall, was somewhat abused by the staff. But the Hooper landaulette was a glorious car and it gave devoted service for over a quarter of a century.'[2]

Alan barely remembered his paternal grandfather. By August 1932 Kenneth McKenzie Clark's addiction to whisky reached its inevitable conclusion: 'his superb constitution had finally collapsed, and every organ simultaneously refused to function,' wrote his son. Jane, heavily pregnant, remained in Oxford while K in Shielbridge watched his father in decline. On successive days that month K told his wife of his delight at hearing her news that 'Alan had gone to bed peacefully in his new room' and then that 'Alan has taken to the idea of sleeping alone'.[3]

Two months later, on 9 October, Jane Clark gave birth to the twins; ten days afterwards Kenneth McKenzie Clark died. He was sixty-four.[4] His wife was left the Ardnamurchan estate. In a letter to her son she noted that a friend had been trying to sell his house – 'evidently feeling the pinch like the rest of us'.[5] Alan had a sentimental attachment to the grandfather he barely new, his interest in art, his success as a gambler, his love of women. A few months before his own death he recorded, 'Read my grandfather's diary for 1912. At Poolewe, fishing, what a lifestyle!' But then added, 'Why drink yourself to death?'[6]

With the arrival of Colin and Colette, Alan now had rivals for his parents' affection. Colin wrote that Alan had been the 'adored and spoiled son of a spoiled couple'. Now 'he was pushed out of the spotlight ... permanently ignored in favour of "the twins" ... From then on, he had to stamp and yell if he wanted attention. If he felt a little ill he had to pretend he was dying; if he scratched his leg he had to say it had been cut off. He had to develop his powers of persuasion, and his charm, to a very high degree. It is hard not to see how the birth of the twins was to influence Alan's life for ever.'[7]

Looking back in 1993 he saw it as neglect: 'Like all children who are abused, I assumed that it was normal.' Did he still feel angry about it? 'It has left a bruise.'[8] Eighteen months later he recalled how his parents seemed remote figures, but his mother was 'very loving when I saw her, beautiful and sweet, but I hardly ever saw her'.[9] Colette (who would swiftly become known as Celly) says that her parents used the French description 'rébarbatif' to describe Alan's manner at this time, meaning 'cantankerous', 'surly', to which she adds in recollection, 'Bolshie'.[10]

From the age of six he was sent to Egerton House, a preparatory school in Dorset Square not far away in Marylebone. This had a reward system. In a letter to Jane, in France visiting the Clarks' great friend, the American novelist Edith Wharton, in her 'dotty, converted convent', K related, 'The best news since you left is that Alan has got a ticket. He whispered it to me on my way out to lunch. It seems that the actual ticket is not given until Monday, but the mistress had confided in Alan today. I am naturally disposed to believe this, indeed it didn't occur to me to question the fact until I began writing to you and remembered how (justifiably) sceptical you are about all Alan's information. However this must be true. He is highly pleased with himself and made a dreadful shindy with the Ostrer boy this evening – pirate noises I identified them as being.'[11]

In earlier letters to correspondents outside the family K expressed concern at Alan's health. Following the arrival of the twins he developed, 'a mystifying distemper' that led one friend to suggest it was a physical response to no longer being the sole apple of his parents' eyes. For more than eighteen months Alan complained of an on-and-off bad chest and high temperature. Such was the family's concern at his apparent illness, which doctors were unable to diagnose, that at one point he was hospitalised. Or could this have been an early manifestation of some sort of hypochondria, which was to dog him for much of his life?

K recalled to his biographer that whereas the twins were idyllic and would often be dressed identically by their mother when appearing in public his elder son was unattractive, tall and gangling. Words such as 'solitary', 'crabby' were also used.[12] Not long after starting at Egerton House he was examined by a Wimpole Street eye specialist because he was 'unable to see the blackboard properly at school'.[13] The specialist wrote to his mother, 'I find unfortunately that he has some astigmatism and will have to wear glasses constantly for the present.' Although Alan continued to own glasses for the rest of his life, increasingly he only wore them when driving, even having a set of driving goggles fitted with appropriate lenses.

While the twins had a governess at Portland Place, Alan spent three years being taken daily (usually by one of the servants) to Egerton House, which boasted that it had been established 'over one hundred years'. With about sixty boys, it had three masters (all Oxbridge) and three trained mistresses (one Froebel). The fees were 16–20 guineas a term. For Alan it had the merit of initiating him in the classics, both history and the first basic steps in Latin. The Clarks viewed Egerton House only as a short-term 'pre-prep' school. Not only was it handy for Portland Place, but it claimed that it trained boys for 'leading preparatory boarding schools', which was the direction K and Jane had in mind for their difficult son. In the spring of 1937 they put their plan into action.

Soon after turning nine Alan was dispatched to an establishment on the south coast at Eastbourne. This was the fashionable preparatory school St Cyprian's, which numbered among its old boys Eric Blair (later known as George Orwell), Cyril Connolly, Gavin Maxwell and Cecil Beaton. Founded in 1899 by Mr and Mrs L.C. Vaughan Wilkes, its success was such that by 1906 it had moved to a large, purpose-built, gabled red brick and tile house set in large grounds in Summerdown Road. Here were a playing field, cricket pavilion, swimming pool, gymnasium and rifle range.[14] From the beginning, although Mr Wilkes was described as head-master, contemporary accounts suggest that Mrs Wilkes, a tiny woman, was the power. By the mid-1930s Mr Wilkes had retired, but Mrs Wilkes was still in control even though their son-in-law, Bill Tomlinson, was now given the title of headmaster.

In his memoirs, K described prep schools in general as a 'curious and objectionable feature of English education ... maintained solely in order that parents could get their children out of the house'. Yet in these memoirs – written in the 1960s with memories more rosy-hued – he professes to have enjoyed his own prep school, Wixenford in Berkshire, where he was sent to board when even younger than Alan, aged only seven. St Cyprian's, like Wixenford, also operated principally as a feeder to public schools, Eton by preference. That would be Alan's destination following the Clarks' discussions with friends including Owen Morshead, the librarian at Windsor Castle, and the industrialist Alfred Beit.[15]

The start of Alan's first term at St Cyprian's came the same week as the Coronation of the Clarks' new friends, King George VI and Queen Elizabeth. K, writing on 15 May 1937, described the ceremony to his mother-in-law, complete with a diagram of Westminster Abbey showing where he and Jane sat. The children had their own coronation, as Celly remembers. Their governess dressed them in long robes and crowns. Alan was, of course, King, Celly the Queen. Colin, in a fictional identification was described as the Prince of Wales. K and Jane knew none of this. In a letter to his mother-in-law K wrote that he was depressed about taking Alan to St Cyprian's. 'Memories of my own discomforts came vividly into my mind, and it seemed criminal to make him undergo the same. However he behaves with such courage and cheerfulness that I was a little comforted, and the school seemed a friendly, bustling place. He has a very pleasant dormitory with a view over the Downs. I think they will take care of him. His manly behaviour was a contrast to the other new boys who were cowering miserably in corners. There is no pleasure like having one's children do one credit.'[16] Jane agreed. To Edith Wharton she wrote: 'So far he seems very happy but we miss him very much.'[17]

Jane was more conscientious in visiting Alan at school than K, particularly in his first year. Her diary entries are often brief. 'December 1937: Alan and Miss Newman* arrive from Eastbourne for lunch. Alan looks very well and good looking. We keep him isolated from twins as he is in quarantine for scarletina.'

The Clarks' Christmases in the latter 1930s were spent in Kent at Bellevue, a house opposite Port Lympne they had begun renting from Sir Philip Sassoon in 1936. Sassoon, whose mother was a Rothschild, had built his own house to the south of Bellevue, with terraced gardens giving fabulous views across Romney Marsh to the English Channel. Instead of a life of leisure, he took up politics, becoming Unionist MP for nearby Hythe in 1912 when he was only twenty-four. K in his memoirs considered

---

* Miss Newman was one of two sisters. Newy was the governess. She taught Celly to read and proved a great friend to all the Clark children. Her sister, known as Newman or Miss Newman, was formidable and less liked.

Sassoon lacked taste and he had no time for Sir Herbert Baker's design of the house or its interior (Honor Channon said Port Lympne was like a Spanish brothel).[18] But Sassoon certainly had style and K and Jane were won round by his charm. He was also important in K's career, being chairman of the National Gallery board at the time of K's appointment. Although politics gave him a career, 'more than the air, he loved the Arts', in the opinion of 'Chips' Channon.[19] He was twice Baldwin's Under-Secretary of State for Air, a form of transport he passionately championed. Having given Alan his first flight when he was only eight, it was no surprise that they quickly became firm friends, even with forty years between them.

Bellevue, or 'Bellers' as it became known in the Clark family, was mainly eighteenth-century, proving capacious enough to house family, guests and servants. To the children, Lympne was infinitely preferable to Portland Place as K lamented to his mother: 'It suits them better. They hardly come here at all.'[20] But to Edith Wharton he portrayed a more positive side: 'The children are all marvellously well – due to the air of Lympne.'[21] In its large garden, the Clarks installed a see-saw for the twins and a huge slide, more suited in size to a children's playground, but Jane rarely did anything by halves. In her diary she reported that it took a foreman and five men the best part of a day to set it up. 'They v. nobly work till 7.30 fixing it,' she wrote, 'then we all drink beer with them in garden. Great excitement for children.'[22] And Sassoon too, when visiting Bellers two days later, delighted the children by going down the slide. Sassoon had his own airfield half a mile to the north and his own aircraft, which particularly delighted Alan. The Clarks would even be flown, sometimes en famille, to his other country home at Trent Park near Cockfosters in Hertfordshire, where K recalled that 'the children were astonished by a platoon of footmen with red cummerbunds'. They would also often leave with gifts of £5 notes.

In the New Year's Honours K was knighted – 'Dady given his TITLE', wrote nine-year-old Alan, on the opening page of a Charles Letts Boy Scouts' pocket engagement diary for 1938. Significantly, in the front he gave his address as Bellevue, not Portland Place. He also used it to draw sleek fighter and bomber aircraft, battleships and racing cars.[23] To his 1938 diary on occasions he confessed to being lonely, and always made a point of noting when his parents did manage to visit. Recollecting the experience to his father's biographer more than forty years later, his account is stark. St Cyprian's he described as a notoriously awful place, with bad food, absurd rules, tyrannical atmosphere and a feeling of being imprisoned, which, he felt, left a permanent scar. To another interviewer, in 1993, St Cyprian's was 'foul. I used to wake up on a lovely summer morning and hear the doves, and I remember thinking it was another day of prison.'[24] And were there long-term consequences? 'Like many who have had an unhappy childhood, I am frightened of being laughed at,' he remarked in his diary. 'Perhaps that is why I like making people laugh with me.'[25]

On 2 January 1938 Jane observed, 'we are called Sir K and Lady for first time and feel rather bashful'.[26] The children were by this time in Switzerland, accompanied by their French governess, Mlle Moise, and the indefatigable Newy. They were rewarded with snow ('twins very excited'), the second day 'buy luge, goes beautifully', by day three Alan was having skating lessons. There was a snowball fight, long walks, skiing lessons, ping-pong with Newy. Alan appears extraordinarily self-sufficient and the love for Switzerland, which this holiday gave him, would last the rest of his life. By now he was a strapping nine-year-old: 4ft 9ins and weighing 4 stone 9lbs.

Back at St Cyprian's he was preoccupied by having to look for his trunk, before football – 'rotten game lose by four goals'. Worse was to follow – 'lose by 13 goals', but 'score first goal' and, without an apparent pause, 'very funny cinema. Get inoculated.' He also noted: 'big boys play rugger' and was thrilled when he was considered big enough and they conquered St Bede's 20-nil. He continued to box, knocking out Watson's tooth – 'feel like a hero' – and took up wrestling – in the final he beat Tristram II. Like most small boys he had an obsession with sweets ('bring back tons', he reported after one Sunday out) and after 'pay day' (presumably when pocket money was doled out) he would go to the school shop. One weekend Newy brought him a book of air stories. When a parcel arrived from home he was quick to note if it contained a copy of *Flight* or *The Airoplane* [sic].

Alan makes no derogatory remarks about Mrs Wilkes, but to others she was an unpredictable personality, even, in the words of one contemporary of Alan's, 'evil' and 'a witch'. The author Philip Ziegler, who followed Alan to St Cyprian's a year later, was terrified of her. He remembers early on being sent a box of chocolates. He thought how lovely, but did not know the school rules. Found privately consuming his feast, he was hauled up by Mrs Wilkes and displayed before the whole school. This was a boy who didn't share his sweets with other boys.[27]

Mrs Wilkes, though, had her favourites. Alan, being the son of *Sir*

Kenneth Clark and destined for Eton, would have been among them, which perhaps explains why once when he was in the school sanatorium he recorded Mrs Wilkes having tea with him. Her grandson later recalled to Alan after he published the first volume of his *Diaries* that 'Mum' Wilkes, as he called her, must have been good training when he came to work for Margaret Thatcher.[28]

Health was a preoccupation for Alan in that early diary. On getting chickenpox, he recorded progress: 'have a sore throat, get spots, sent sick room. Very worried.' Two days later 'spots itch terribly. Sleep badly. Bored.' That Sunday 'Mummy and Daddy arrive!!!!' bearing the gift of an old typewriter.

Meanwhile the twins had their tonsils removed, a less than happy experience for Jane as well as the children. 'Colin haemorrhaging freely,' she wrote. 'They wake up every half hour throughout day and feel dreadful and are sick nine times each. Philip [Sassoon] rings up and is so kind and human whereas I am crying.' Her concern at the possibility of war was now ever present. Reporting that K had enjoyed 'peaceful day with twins', she added, 'Papers full of Nazis' triumph in Austria.'[29]

Alan's spring term report was judged 'excellent'. The Easter holidays that year were made special by a purchase that would prove dear to his heart: 'Alan and I go to London for day. After dull shopping for school we meet K at Ford Co Regent St and buy new open 5-seater car, and arrange for it to be delivered tomorrow. Young salesman disappointed at so quick a sale.' Alan thought it 'beautiful . . . opens streamlined'. Next day was his tenth birthday. Jane lamented, 'K. alas at Windsor'. K first telegraphed him from Windsor, then in time for tea he rang up. One detects guilt at his absence. Jane adored celebrating the children's birthdays. Here was a chance to create a special occasion to show off and shine. This year she indulged Alan's first love by having his cake designed as a landing ground with aeroplanes. Alan wrote in his diary: 'Get so many presents they won't fit in my cupboard.'

A week later the mood darkened as she noted in her diary a 'sudden change' in K's attitude. The evidence suggests that she believed her husband was having an affair. Her body responded with depressions and headaches; she took to her bed. 'Decide no use floundering in a sea of surprise, must try and forget and then see what happens, but this is difficult.' Jane and K had been married for a little over a decade: was the shine beginning to wear off? K did indeed have a woman friend, one of several about whom he would be passionate for the rest of his life. It was a situation over which he and Jane would endeavour to reach an accommodation. As her diary bears testimony, Jane was more and more a worrier about life in general: not only over the state of her marriage, but her children's well-being, a shortage of servants, the possibility of war. K, meanwhile, appeared to shrug off the cares of his world.

Holidays, though, helped. Having taken the children on a tour of the Royal Mint – 'Deafening noise. Children at first frightened, then interested' – they spent a day in the countryside north of London at Whipsnade Zoo – 'Greatest fun is giving ice cream bricks to baby bears'. Alan often mentions playing with the twins, which he seemed to enjoy. The Military Canal not far from Lympne was a favourite – one Sunday after Easter 'Colette falls in – awfully funny'. Two days later it was Colin's turn for a ducking, when he tumbled into the swimming pool. Jane returned Alan to school. He appeared to be a natural sportsman, reporting in one week three games of cricket, when he scored runs, including a six, and took wickets. Philip Ziegler recalls his own first game of cricket. He was batting, Alan bowling. A ball pitched very short and rolled along the pitch towards Ziegler. This was 'a sneak' in school lingo; Ziegler missed and was bowled.[30]

However, in July K, shortly before his thirty-fifth birthday, wrote buoyantly to his mother-in-law: 'Alan, I am thankful to say is going through a very good stage. He is a great success at school and the specimens of his work which we have seen justify his success. Colin is a queer little shrimp ... he has a good nature. Colette is just a little girl.' But then he went on to lament: 'I see very little of my children.'[31] All, though, was not gloom: 'Mrs Wharton's library is installed'.[32]

End of term approached. Alan sailed through exams, getting 97/100 in maths and coming top in history, 'Latin easy'. Jane summed up his results: 'Alan back from school, looks well, but thin. Has won French prize.' 'His headmaster Tomlinson lunched with us.' Jane does not mince her words: 'He v. stupid.' She wanted a congratulatory present for Alan, and went to Hamleys 'to see about bombing aeroplanes'. A few days later Philip dispatched the three children on a flight, his plane diving 'low over golf course where we are playing'.

That late summer of 1938 had pleasures for Alan: he learnt to ride a bicycle, watched cricket with his father and Sam Courtauld[33] at Folkestone (the Australians playing Kent) and spent a week's holiday in north Norfolk with a St Cyprian's master, Mr Cutforth (known as Cutty), staying at the Moorings Hotel, Burnham Overy Staithe, where he recorded very high tides, messing about on Mud Island and fishing from a boat called <u>Dorothy</u> (all very Arthur Ransome).[34] This was by no means the first time the

Clarks holidayed in Norfolk, as photographs show. In 1935 they rented a house at Brancaster. That summer Alan (aged seven) and his father discovered something they could do together – walking. In an undated note Alan remembers that his father had a talent for explaining things to him, but only when he was very young. 'He hardly ever did that once I was at boarding school.'

Sometimes another St Cyprian's boy would be invited for company, more often Alan was alone. In 1938 they returned to Bellers for the King's Cup air race at Lympne, which even Jane, despite an antipathy to aeroplanes, found 'v. exciting'. Alan never forgot that afternoon. After nearly sixty years he was still able to recall in his diary seeing the distinguished air racer Alex Henshaw win in a Percival Mew Gull 'when he dived under the little blue Pobjoy monoplane'.[35]

As the Prime Minister, Neville Chamberlain, prepared to make his first flight, aged sixty-nine, to parley peace with Hitler at Munich in September 1938, Alan flew in Sassoon's plane to friends where he was to stay – 'Alan v. pleased because when P flew them to Hawkinge it was v. rough and he didn't mind a bit.' A few days later Jane 'turned on wireless by chance' and heard Chamberlain speaking from Munich as he left the aerodrome. 'V. clear, beautiful benevolent voice as suits the 1st Bourgeois in the land who had just been we hope putting the Fuhrer in his place with his umbrella.'[36]

Despite Chamberlain's Munich declaration, Jane feared that Lympne and the south coast would 'soon be black with aeroplanes'. Romney Marsh was the obvious spot for a German invasion, as it had been for Napoleon more than a century before, and after the war K saw a copy of the 1940 German invasion map that even showed Bellers. In the event the house was damaged by a bomb and, as K lamented, 'the beautiful barn completely destroyed'. Their friends Arthur and Ruth Lee[37] urged them to move to Gloucestershire, close to their own home, with Ruth recommending a number of houses, among them Gatcombe Park – 'House charming outside, but no good bedrooms and too small' was Jane's verdict, 'would require too much spent.'[38] Half a century later it became the home of the Princess Royal.

At St Cyprian's that autumn Alan found himself helping to dig dugouts, and was deluged with 'piles of cig cards' from the ever-attentive Cutty. Eastbourne also now had a roller-skating rink, which Alan adored. He boasted in his diary of dancing on skates, but ordinary ballroom dancing was 'very boring, very feeble'. His parents seem increasingly shadowy, making even fewer visits to Eastbourne. As school term ended he returned first to Portland Place, and then, on 22 December, 'hope to go to Bellers'. They arrived next day in thick snow. 'Lovely toys in stocking,' writes Alan on Christmas Day, 'make snowman and shoot at it with my bow and arrow set', a gift from Sassoon. He also had his now annual copy of the new *Jane's Fighting Ships* from his parents.

The probability of war was increasingly a preoccupation. By March 1939 Jane noticed that Alan, who was a month off his eleventh birthday, had become 'V. interested in all the news and reads all the papers and then asks intelligent questions. Wonder if he will be interested in politics later and perhaps have a public career?'[39] Celly recalls that even at the age of five she was shocked that when the Spanish Civil War was discussed, Alan, still not in his teens, said he supported Franco and the Fascists.[40]

Philip Sassoon's declining health was, however, never far from Jane's mind. He had had a series of infections following the removal of his tonsils in 1931 and as the Clarks prepared to go to the United States, Jane, in her diary, was not convinced at his protestations that he 'hopes to get better'. They returned on the *Normandie* with the film star Mary Pickford and her husband Bunny Rogers among the passengers. During the return crossing the Clarks received a telegram. Jane was stunned – 'Philip is dead,' she wrote on 3 June. 'Dear Philip, who was fairy prince, godmother and magic carpet to us all.' Nearly half a century later Alan agreed. To James Lees-Milne, next to whom he sat at lunch at Brooks's in October 1985, he recalled Sassoon's 'smooth face', how 'he looked incredibly young, walked on the tips of his toes and impressed one as being a person of importance'. Alan added that he thought his mother 'learnt the social graces from him, having been without them at the time of her marriage'. Lees-Milne remarks, 'Strange thing for a son to say.'[41]

Port Lympne was to live on, indelibly, in Alan's memory. Sassoon's executors let his creation remain unoccupied for more than three decades (apart from wartime requisition by, appropriately, the RAF). In 1976 Alan drove across from Saltwood to what he called his 'favourite spot in the whole of E. Kent – one of the most evocative in the world . . . I sit on the terrace where one would occasionally get tea *limone*, and indescribably thin cucumber sandwiches before being sent back to Bellers. Can still look through the glass doors at that marbled, Moorish interior, black and white floors and arched ceilings. Totally still outside, but trees now grown enormously, hemming it in, better even that in Philip's heyday. The place has <u>slept</u> for thirty years, no-one lived in it since Philip died, nothing disturbed. At any moment Philip could come out and call – to this day I can hear his drawl.'

Alan had a concern that the house and grounds would be 'over-run, damaged irretrievably by the tramping public with their toffee papers and Kleenexes.'[42] Happily, he was wrong. He alerted his friend John Aspinall, who eventually bought the house and its 275 acres for £360,000. Port Lympne became the companion to Howletts, Aspinall's original wildlife park near Canterbury. Not long after Aspinall started restoration work, Alan and his wife Jane acquired two old Edwardian-style wash hand basins with chrome legs and taps that had been dumped outside; one is now installed in the ground-floor cloakroom at Saltwood. Alan had a plan – unfulfilled – to list all the names from the Port Lympne visitors' book and have a plaque made to show who had washed their hands in the basin.

While the Clarks had been in the United States, early on Sunday morning, 14 May 1939, fire broke out in St Cyprian's school hall. The alarm was raised just before 5 a.m. Although the seventy pupils were led to safety a maid, aged sixteen, lost her life. The local press showed photographs of the boys, one playing a salvaged upright piano, another 'searching for their belongings among salvaged goods'. In a third, Alan is clearly visible, indeed the cutting that has survived at Saltwood has an inked 'X' to identify him.[43] It was four weeks before the Clarks visited Eastbourne to see for themselves. By then the school had moved to buildings lent by Eastbourne College. 'Not really as nice,' wrote Jane. 'Alan v. well, but thin. Fire did not seem to have upset his nerves, but they all had extraordinary escape. Look at St Cyprian's. Whole centre gutted by fire. Terrifying.'

With Alan safe, other matters became the headlines in the Clarks' lives. They understood the significance of the German blitzkrieg in the Spanish Civil War and what it would mean if repeated over London. K began organising the removal of the National Gallery's collection to Wales, eventually when bombs threatened, to a safe if unexpected haven, a series of caves in a vast, abandoned slate quarry deep in the hillside at Manod, near Blaenau Ffestiniog. Jane, meanwhile, bore the brunt of everything else. Portland Place, which they agreed was too big for their needs, was to be sold. One of their final dinner parties was for the Prime Minister and Mrs Chamberlain at the end of June. With Lympne, regretfully, also considered unsafe, Jane was forced to start serious house-hunting. Her preference remained Kent, but the Lees kept putting the case for Gloucestershire.

The final ten days of July were mayhem. St Cyprian's moved to more permanent quarters, Wispers, near Midhurst in Sussex, home of the late Duchess of Bedford.[44] When Jane set off to see that Alan was properly ensconced, she failed to change trains at Petersfield for the Midhurst branch line and was carried on to Portsmouth. 'Arrive at school $1\frac{1}{2}$ hours late, arrange to bring Alan home with me as term so nearly over and send for luggage later. He v. pleased and looking very well.' But, as so often, the Clarks' social life took over. Alan, who was now eleven, was still put to bed at 7 p.m. so that Jane might change quickly, 'as Beits etc arrive for dinner at 7.45 and we go to the ballet'.

Next day Alan was dispatched with K's mother to Lympne, while Jane looked at another Gloucestershire property recommended by the Lees. This was Upton House near Tetbury. A thunderstorm interrupted a picnic lunch, 'hailstones like marbles, whole lawn white outside. House itself charming and garden could be made so if we planned it or spent some money.' She preferred Kent; 'feel gloomy, but know it would be sensible to take this in case of war and then children and pictures would presumably be safe'.[45] Minds had to be made up, and within a few days, 'Decide to take Glos house and write hoping to give up Bellers.' But they still needed a London home, and quickly settled on a top-floor flat amidst the legal fraternity of Gray's Inn, which they had first looked at a year before as a possible home for K's mother. Now they planned alterations, while earmarking furniture and books from Portland Place that would fit. Jane traipsed back and forth from Lympne; she and Alan went to a Will Hay film, played cricket and picnicked with the twins. 'Glad to be at Lympne in spite of aeroplanes, soldiers etc. If only there were no aerodrome Bellers would be an earthly paradise.' On the final day of July, the Queen rang K to say goodbye before she went to Scotland. The lease on the Gloucestershire house was settled, but in early August sadness fell as their great friend Edith Wharton died in France.

Jane's many admirers included Air Chief Marshal Sir Cyril Newall, Chief of the Air Staff since 1937. K and Jane used to invite him and his very social New England wife Olive to ballet and opera, but Newall was often too busy to accept. As war approached he came into his own, promising K and Jane over dinner that he would take Alan flying in August with his son Francis, who was two years younger – 'so we are in the right set for Alan!' wrote Jane. When the day came Newall, Francis and Alan went to Biggin Hill aerodrome in Kent, which would, little more than a year later, be at the centre of the Battle of Britain. 'Alan had a marvellous time, lunched officers mess and impressed everyone with his knowledge of planes.' They had also been filmed by a cinema newsreel and allowed to sit in the RAF's new fighters. Francis, remembering the occasion more than sixty years later, thought this referred both to Hurricanes and

Spitfires.[46] Newall was certainly determined to please, afterwards buying presents for the boys at Hamleys before taking them all to see *The Spy in Black*, about a German suicide U-boat sent to the Orkneys to sink the British fleet.

August may have been traditionally holiday time, but not this year as their new homes took precedence. Upton required an enormous amount of work to be done – more than the Clarks realised – and 'if there isn't a war it will all be v. nice till we can find a perm home'. But just in case, Jane went on a shopping spree – a suitcase for K, blankets, food, a portable wireless, flashlight, candles, shoes for Alan, winter coats for the twins. There was also her own packing to do, Portland Place to close up, and at Bellers she gave the servants their wages and board for five weeks, plus return fares. 'Glad Philip cannot see the house now.'

Next morning Newman was left to clear up Bellers as the Clark caravan set off for Gloucestershire, with 'Sylvia [servant] driving children and me and lunch in small car; Sandford [chauffeur] following in van with Bogey [the Clarks' dalmatian], bantams, 2pr rabbits and the white kitten. After 100 yards shrieks from children because one milk bottle is upset over Alan. Stop both cars and we clean up. Start off again. Whole journey an increasing nightmare. Colette behaves badly all the way. She is bored and has nothing to do and quarrels with boys. Only cheers up when Sylvia and I almost in hysterics with the continuous traffic, heat and thunder and screaming children stop for beer.' Celly remembers that drive vividly. She didn't believe she had behaved that badly, but her mother wasn't used to it and was 'absolutely livid' with her. 'She became an enemy for the next ten years. A major enemy.'[47] Jane's rows with her children, and with those around her, would become a feature of life in Gloucestershire.

In her diary Jane mused on their future. She was gloomy, the outbreak of war affecting her deeply. The glamour of London was temporarily forgotten as she wrote that she longed 'to take in refugee children, grow veg and help generally'. Those who knew her in the metropolis might have found this Jane hard to recognise, but, as her daughter commented on her mother's character, 'she had every virtue, every vice – she could be kind, she could be cruel etc'.[48]

Towards the end of August when Jane visited Upton to see how building works were progressing she found holes in the main walls and half-finished drains in open trenches across the garden. Some furniture stacked in main rooms had to be moved out as dry rot was discovered in the floors. Naked electricity wires disfigured the walls. Jane despaired: 'Do not see when it will ever be ready, as men taken away each day.' With Upton uninhabitable, she and her family were forced to stay in a pub, the Hare and Hounds at Westonbirt to the south-west of Tetbury.

On Monday, 28 August Jane and the children explored Tetbury, where she opened an account at the chemist's and bought wool to knit blankets for children when evacuated. The following Friday, as Jane shopped in the town for a new term's supplies of school clothes for Alan, they heard that German troops had entered Poland and were attacking on all fronts. War was now inevitable and she arranged for car lamps to be darkened for night driving. Work at Upton stalled as more workmen were called up. 'At least five weeks before we can move in.'

K remained in London, supervising the evacuation of the National Gallery's contents. He wrote to Jane, saying how he understood her plight: 'You sounded rather sad on the telephone this evening. I do hope you are not feeling ill. I can well believe that the joint burden of the children and the confusion at Upton is very disturbing.'[49] The following day, Sunday, 3 September, all their worst fears were realised when Britain declared war on Germany. Where one was, what one was doing, were remembered, even fifty-five years later, although for Alan, inevitably, it was a military memory.[50] HMS *Courageous* had been sunk by a U-boat in the Bristol Channel 'and to my private dismay I could not remember what class of boat it was'.[51]

Jane listened to the Prime Minister's statement from Downing Street, and wrote: 'We are now at war with Germany . . . we can only pray that it will be short and end with a change of government in Germany rather than our entry into Berlin.'[52]

THREE

Worlds at War

In the space of a few months Alan's life – he was still only eleven and a half – had been turned upside down. His school had been destroyed by fire. His familiar homes, in London and Kent, had both been vacated. In London the family would soon be living in a flat at Gray's Inn Square, very different from the grandeur of 30 Portland Place. The variety of temporary accommodation – including not just the Hare and Hounds at Westonbirt, but also the Lees' house at Avening – was inevitably constricting, making them feel, as Celly recalled, 'like evacuees'.[1] Even the promise of Upton House and its substantial grounds lacked for Alan the potential daily excitement at Bellers with its airfield just up the road.

One further, significant and unpleasant change was in his mother's temperament. With K based in London, Jane had to cope not only with bringing up Alan and the twins in an unfamiliar environment, but also with restoring the Georgian and neglected Upton House and making it habitable. Not surprisingly, the strain of wartime existence began to tell. To her diary Jane confided that she missed K very much, but 'the two worlds of K and London and the workmen and house and even children here are so different. If only I could always count twenty before I spoke and not be cross with the children.'[2]

Celly's experience on the car journey to Gloucestershire was only the beginning, as she told K's biographer: her mother could be a bully, scathing and sarcastic, who wanted total obedience. Celly, even aged eight, was a strong personality. As a result, the clash of these two powerful forces could be titanic. Long afterwards Celly – and Alan, too – dreamt of their mother's anger. 'Her fists would be clenched and her face distorted with rage. She'd say, "You are a spoilt, stupid, selfish girl and I wish you were dead."' Even forty years after the war Alan remembered that his mother was capable of 'a screaming rage' for something as minor as a raincoat not hung up in the hall. 'Anything would do to send her off.' To a boy not yet in his teens this had the long-term effect of his mother becoming the enemy, as she had to Celly. 'I flinched when she touched me,' he recalled.[3] If he tried to defend Celly, who was often the subject of Jane's ire, 'he got into so much trouble that it was hardly worth it'.[4]

Looking for reasons for her mother's rages, Celly's view sounds the most likely: K adored his daughter and when she was at home Jane became jealous. She liked having K to herself and was at her best when the children were away at school. Equally she could be marvellous with the children when K was elsewhere. She just appears to have found it increasingly difficult, particularly with the stresses brought on by the war, to operate as a family unit. Celly remembered: 'As a measure of how bad it was, I don't think we had one meal in a month when someone didn't leave the dining room in tears.' Colin, though, suggested that it was not all one-sided. In Alan's case it was because he inherited much of his character from his mother, 'that he would fight her all the time. His independent attitude drove her to distraction.'

There were antidotes to her rages – illness (if Jane had sought a profession, she would have made a splendid nurse) or, more readily manufactured, tears. Colin, very much the favourite, would weep and his mother's anger would immediately evaporate. Celly, however, was made of sterner stuff. As she told her father's biographer, 'it was outrageous to be treated unjustly and then forced to capitulate'. She recalled her father asking her what was going to help, and her answer, 'Perhaps when the war ends?'

In one respect K, Alan and Celly were co-conspirators. Deep down Jane was angry with K over his mistresses, angry at Celly for loving her father so strongly, angry at Alan for trying to defend Celly against her. Is this perhaps why K so rarely intervened, or was he essentially weak? To his biographer he said he tried to stop his wife being 'beastly' to Alan. But Alan had no recollection of his father or indeed anyone else taking his part. The relationship with Dad was distant then on an emotional level and would remain so right up until his father was dying, although on a practical, non-confrontational level their relations would generally prosper, especially in the written rather than the spoken word. When Alan was editing the first volume of his *Diaries* he remarked in one interview that his father 'remained a mystery to me'. He thought of him as 'a gentleman in Lord Chesterfield's definition – someone who never allows his innate self to show'. And that, he concluded, was how he appeared 'even in his relations with his family'.[5]

Both Meryle Secrest in her biography of K and Colin in his memoir dwelt on Jane's change in demeanour after the birth of the twins. To tackle sinusitis in 1935, she consulted Harold Bedford Russell, a well-known Australian-born throat specialist at London's St Bartholomew's Hospital, who was already treating the children for various upper respiratory disorders – Alan had his sinuses washed out on more than one occasion to combat chronic catarrh. In the First World War, when he served in France and was awarded the Croix de Guerre, Bedford Russell had worked among the wounded. Now, from Harley Street rooms, his clientele was more usually the moneyed class. For Jane he provided a 'puffer' into which had been mixed a cocktail – Secrest suggests ephedrine and possibly cocaine, Colin says morphine and cocaine – which would be sprayed onto the sinuses.

The puffer certainly did the trick for her sinusitis, but, as Colin related, its contents also turned out to have 'a very welcome calming effect on the nerves'. And 'nerves' were increasingly Jane's problem. The puffer was, however, also addictive. Early in the war Russell's cocktail ceased to be available. Colin says alcohol became the only alternative and 'its effects were much worse'.

Secrest writes that where K's extra-marital dalliances were concerned Jane gave her tacit approval, being 'determined to behave properly'. She loved her husband and she seems prepared to have allowed him his mistresses as long as they remained together. Colin says he never minded which of his beautiful ladies was with him at any given time, adding that it was like his paintings; 'he could get equal pleasure from his Renoir *Baigneuse Blonde* or his Turner *Seascape: Folkstone*'. To avoid hurting any feelings he would write 'half a dozen intimate letters every night to keep them all happy'.

Tacit approval in public was one thing, but Colin remembered hearing voices raised through bedroom walls as his mother chastised his father when she thought no-one else could overhear. It did not help Jane that Gloucestershire was too far from London for a daily commute for K, who, at best, was only at Upton at weekends. On 2 January 1941 she contemplated her situation. 'So it is another new year. No use taking stock. The last year has been more important than any other for many years and not only because of the war – much of it however the result of the war which has separated K and me and broken our family life as with so many other people.' She felt happier after a long talk with K and hoped that a winter in Dorking (a house they intended renting, being nearer London) might prove beneficial. But she also admitted to depression: 'It is unfair on the children that I should be so unhappy.' And then, 'K turns up very cheerful and gay ... I happy to see him, but wish he had written less casually.'

Jane, not yet forty, was still an attractive woman, and the composer William Walton had fallen for her in a major way. Like Air Chief Marshal Newall, he was also a friend of K's. Did Newall have time for extramarital passion? Alan thought so, although Newall's son Francis disagrees.[6] Newall did not forget Alan's interest in aircraft. K noted on the back of an undated letter that he 'sent round some magnificent trophies for Alan – a German machine gun and a paddle used by a German airman baling out'. The crudely fashioned aluminium paddle survives at Saltwood to this day.

The relationship with William Walton was far more serious. Saltwood Castle's archives have revealed two compositions of Walton's, one in the form of a St Valentine's musical heart and the other on the notepaper of the Nethy Bridge Hotel, north of the Cairngorms in Scotland: 'I'll be there at twelve . . .' which ends, 'I'll bet you're late'. In January 1941 Jane had written, 'W in love with me'. That new year, after seeing out the old year at the film-maker Gabriel Pascal's farm near Denham, she, K and Walton drove to London. K had to go to work, but 'W & I shop and pub-crawl and meet K at Carlton Grill. W gives me a beautiful green and gold 18th c. vanity box with musical emblems in the gold detail. He asks K first as he took it on appro.'

While K stayed in London, Jane and Willie, as she often called him, caught the 1.55 train from Paddington back to Gloucestershire. That evening at Upton, Jane reported in her diary, 'Willie and I play marriages with children and Grannie C[lark] with usual bath of screaming. When Alan goes to bed Willie plays me the Ravel "Daphne and Chloe" he has just given me and shows me where he stole from it for the montage in *Major Barbara* [Pascal's film of Shaw's play] and where Ravel stole from Scriabin and Stravinsky.' Sixty years later it appeared to be accepted that Jane and Willie would have run off together, but for pressure applied on Walton by his benefactor, Lady Wimborne, a wealthy scion of the Grosvenor family. According to Walton's wife Susana – they married in 1949 – Jane and Willie had 'a passionate affair' of which K was aware.[7]

In the autumn of 1939, getting Upton House in a fit state for the Clarks, for their servants and for a host of evacuees they invited into their midst, was not a role for Jane alone, even though K was so often absent in London. The house itself attracted the Clarks because of its central salon, with double-height ceiling and walls big enough for some of their Portland Place pictures, and also a library, so vital to K who in addition to his own books also had to house Edith Wharton's. Jane was fortunate that one friend, the music critic, Eddy Sackville-West, was of an artistic bent and available to help, even if at times he could be eccentric. He was rewarded with the offer of full board and lodging. Celly remembers his sensitivity; if put under pressure he invariably suffered a nosebleed.

Within hours of war being declared, K, who could never resist writing letters, was putting pen to paper to Jane: 'Tell Alan we have a *terrific* balloon barrage here. I counted 57 out of my window this morning. Now they have all come down, but I suppose will all go up tonight.' Two days later he for once acknowledged Jane's concerns: 'You sounded rather sad on the telephone this evening. I do hope you are not feeling ill. I can well believe that the joint burden of the children and the confusion at Upton is very disturbing ... Give hugs and kisses to the twins and my best love to Alan.'

On 15 September Jane telephoned and poured out her troubles. K, typically, responded in the way he knew best, by letter. He was seeing people from 9.30 to 7 every day, he wrote. 'Camouflage and artists generally take most of my time. As I am so busy I am quite happy, or would be if I wasn't separated from you and continually thinking of your unhappy state.' On this, it must have been bad enough for Jane to be 'away from everything with the brats when they were well, and perfectly miserable now that you all have colds'. It was hardly tactful of him then to mention their London friends, even if they were 'full of sympathy and longing to see you again'. He did, though, suggest that 'as soon as Alan has gone back to school you must leave the twins for a night or two. A visit to London for you is absolutely necessary as a tonic.' The first fears of bombing had passed: 'It has actually become quite gay again.' On another occasion he wrote: 'I know you hate feeling so isolated, but you must try to think I am in the Navy. I will write often. The children must think of me as in the fighting forces and not worry.'[8]

Jane, who had a very different view of letter-writing – 'wish letters were forbidden by law', she remarked in exasperation at one point – had to keep the children occupied. One day in August 1939 they bicycled along Gloucestershire's lanes. The Lees, perhaps feeling some responsibility at bringing the Clarks to the county – their house, the Old Quarries, being only two miles up the road from Upton at Avening – could not resist offering advice, or, as the Clarks saw it, interfering. 'Uncle Arthur' and 'Aunt Ruth', although a childless couple, had strong views on how their friends brought up their children. In Alan's case Arthur thought that he should be withdrawn immediately from St Cyprian's and sent to the junior school of Cheltenham College (his alma mater).

By November 1939, with the Phoney War continuing, Jane was buying Alan war maps, food and a torch. In the Gray's Inn flat they were at last able to hang pictures and drawings, and find ways of using some of the Portland Place curtains by the fashionable designer Marion Dorn. 'It will all look lovely,' wrote Jane, 'and we can live there with the children if when the war is over we cannot afford to live in the country as well.'

Although St Cyprian's was accessible by train, visits to Midhurst to see Alan were now less frequent. On one occasion Jane, but not K, managed the cross-country journey and found 'Alan waiting at school, looking very well and much taller. He loves the school but says since the war they get v. little to eat. No eggs, ham or bacon and only jam or butter. Will try and arrange something extra for next term. He is v. intelligent about the war, the new planes etc.' He had been given a copy of the *National Defence Pocket Book*,[9] which contained details of enemy aircraft and ships as well as those of the RAF and Royal Navy.

K, having settled the National Gallery's treasures in north Wales, was at a loose end. As a civil servant he was exempt from being called up, which relieved him, as the prospect of the Army and the idea of 'going back to school' and being in the company of men with whom he had little in common, did not appeal.[10] The Navy, though, would be different. To Jane he had written, with the war only a few days old, that he would go into the RNVR tomorrow 'if he could get a commission, failing that a minesweeper, which gives one lots of time for reading'. The Gallery, meanwhile, took on a fresh role, offering lunchtime concerts with the pianist Myra Hess that proved a huge success, the Queen attending on several occasions. K developed a plan to commission war artists, which resulted in magnificent work by, among others, his friends Graham Sutherland, John Piper and Henry Moore.

The government, meanwhile, had set up the Ministry of Information, which included a film division. K was invited to head this – and accepted, and later became Controller of Home Publicity. His time there was not happy. Jane wrote in her diary, in January 1941, 'Wish K could get away from the Ministry of Information where he is not appreciated except by the underlings.' Despite his original role at the MoI, K had little to do with film-making, although later that year he did take to the screen himself, appearing in some shorts, one about the National Gallery concerts, another in which he spoke to camera on paintings by the war artists. This last, if he did but know it, was a dry run for *Civilisation* a quarter of a century later.

In Gloucestershire, Upton House had at last become habitable. As well

as Eddy Sackville-West, others offered rooms included the Sutherlands
and the Moores. K's mother, Alice, now living in some style in a Cheltenham hotel, came to Upton when Jane was in London. She was,
however, puritanical according to Sutherland, who remembered water
and herrings on the menu when she was in charge.[11] Jane, who had for
most of the 1930s been used to entertaining on a grand scale, managed a
country-house version, often inviting the Lees, William Walton, John
Piper, his wife Myfanwy and their family, and a remarkable entrepreneur,
Hiram Winterbotham, who lived close by. K noted that Hiram 'did much
to cheer us up for he himself was always cheerful'. All, though, at various
moments at Upton witnessed Jane's rages.

As the end of 1939 approached, the family began to settle down to
their new and dramatically altered existence. Alan would be twelve next
birthday; the twins had just had their seventh. Although there were four
and a half years between them they were good friends and played together.
Alan enjoyed being the leader. Colin recalled his 'fantastic imagination',
how he thought up escapades – 'wild, improbable places to go and things
to see and say'. Colin, however, likened him to his grandfather or at least
the family accounts he had heard – 'he would suddenly get bored . . . he
would simply vanish, without telling us why . . . He certainly kept the
whole household on its toes.'

In Gloucestershire Hiram Winterbotham became as much part of the
children's lives as their parents'. In a way he proved, as Alan recognised, a
substitute Sassoon, rich, although by no means as wealthy. Whereas Sassoon's sexuality was never determined, Winterbotham was a homosexual.
His link with K came through the National Gallery. Such was his good
humour that K would send any member of his staff who seemed overcome
by the gloom and fear of the times to see Winterbotham.[12]

Alan viewed Hiram – as he was soon encouraged to call him – as his first
mentor. Celly thought he was even a little in love with Alan. Early in the
war he had also taught Jane to drive in less than two months – the Clarks by
now being without a chauffeur; later, as the end of the war was in sight, he
helped teach Alan. Hiram had read medicine at King's Cambridge, and in
the 1950s became executive chairman of London's St Thomas' Hospital,
where he tested its competence by undergoing minor and unnecessary
operations. Alan was particularly proud in 1969, at a time when his only
public reputation was as a military historian and he had yet to be selected as
a parliamentary candidate, of being asked by Hiram to join the St Thomas'
board as an executive governor, a position he gave on his CV.

Thanks to his wartime job looking after aircraft manufacturing personnel across the country, Hiram had legitimate access to petrol. Thus he was often the driver when the Clarks went to London, as well as for what became annual holidays to Wales, on the coast at Portmeirion, where the architect Clough Williams-Ellis had built his eclectic village.

By then the Clarks had finally followed the Lees' advice and in September 1940 they moved Alan from St Cyprian's to Cheltenham Junior School. Jane was concerned at Alan again changing locations, and hoped that before long they would make him a prefect. With him they sent Colin (a month away from his eighth birthday), while Celly started at Cheltenham Ladies' College, where she would remain throughout her school career, ending up as Head Girl. Hitherto the twins had been educated by governesses. On the day term started they had tea with Granny Clark at her Cheltenham hotel and then came the moment when Jane had to wave her children goodbye: 'Colin v. brave and looks sweet but v. small. Alan will look after him. Hope he will be all right.'

For a time the war, and particularly the Blitz, did not impinge too seriously on the Clarks' domestic lives. No. 5 Gray's Inn Square proved a delightful London home until one night in September 1940 when their block was hit. As K recalled, 'we were blown out of bed (we had got bored with sleeping in the cellar) and landed, unhurt, on the other side of the room'.[13] They were extraordinarily lucky, as the bomb had destroyed the two floors beneath. At this moment they heard that 30 Portland Place, which they had been unable to sell, had been requisitioned by the government.

The effects of that autumn's Luftwaffe onslaught on London were recorded by K in a letter to Jane written from the Ministry of Information.[14] Communications were breaking down, telegrams had ceased to function (even in London) and half the telephones were out of order. 'If you don't hear from me at all, don't worry.' London, he reported with understatement, was 'rather a mess'. He thought there was no point in Jane coming to London, 'as one can't go out at night'. Districts were closed, not only through destruction, but also the risk of time bombs. He concluded that 'the threat of invasion is v. close now'.

By new year 1941 the war had well and truly reached Gloucestershire. Jane recorded standing at Kemble Junction in the dark waiting room filled with soldiers, 'one of which looks like Murillo beggar in half light'. A friend told her how shocked she was in taking a train over Christmas and hearing soldiers boast about thieving and withholding 35s Christmas ration allowance from their wives.

At the end of January, being able to relax without the children, she spent some time in Oxford staying at Wadham College, where she had 'Breakfast alone as usual with Maurice Bowra, who is always grumpy till after lunch.' Two days later: 'Maurice in v. good form, but he has changed ... since becoming Warden. He is mean, ungracious and inhospitable at intervals.' Next day she went to London where she and K stayed at Claridge's and after a long day 'dine in bed together. V cheerful and content.' The only fly in the ointment is the MoI – 'wish K could go somewhere where more appreciated'.

When the children returned for the Easter holidays they 'enjoy first lunch at home as school food is dreary'. Then off to London, where Alan saw an oculist for his eyes, was given a prescription and told to return in four months. Jane's spoonful of sugar followed – a trip to Hamleys. But back at Upton Jane was horrified to discover that 'Mrs M has used fifteen eggs this week and potted none. Staff getting twelve a day. When I protest she bursts into tears. Servants don't realise there's a war on.'

On Alan's birthday (13 April) they went for a walk through 'new and lovely valley. Peaceful happy day – Colin paints himself like a late Renoir for Alan's birthday tea.' She noted that in north Africa Benghazi had fallen, and on 17 April 'hear on radio worst raid London has had since war. K up all night. Left Russell Hotel after it had been hit ... shelters too full and noisy ... top floors blazing fiercely – was stopped going upstairs and told roof had fallen in so went to MoI where greeted by row of corpses from house opposite and spent night helping the wounded, so sleepy but unhurt. We have lost everything in his room, but nothing matters if K is safe.'

News of the war produced conflicting emotions. The sinking of the German battleship *Bismarck* she greeted in her diary with a single word, 'Hurrah'. News from the Mediterranean was less good as the Germans invaded Crete by a glider-born force, but on 27 May Colin Coote[15] said better news might shortly be expected from Crete, so Jane wired the information to Alan. She need not have bothered as Coote's information proved inaccurate. Next day, Oliver Lyttelton[16] announced clothes rationing. 'Poor K ordered two suits Friday and will now have to give one up ... Glad I bought the children's winter pyjamas already, also lots of handkerchiefs and jerseys for them.'

As the summer term at Cheltenham came to a close Colin contracted measles, with a temperature of 103° – 'v. ill poor boy, but spots well out'. Jane lamented that this would come just when she and K were alone together on a 'precious holiday' for the first time since they had had

Upton. Four days later K's mother, Alan and Celly arrived from Cheltenham – 'lovely to see them, but can't help feeling sad that our ten
peaceful days alone together are over – it was so lovely in spite of Colin's
measles, my headache etc. We have seen so little of each other since the
war and when we are with children and his mother we can never talk to
each other privately or feel carefree however nice they are.'

To help occupy the holidays, Jane, Alan and Celly started reading
Hamlet. On 1 August Colin came out of quarantine and Jane reported
how pleased the twins were at being reunited. *Hamlet* was alternated with
a book on the Crusades. Alan had taken to gung-ho fiction. As well as
G.A. Henty, whom he had begun at Portland Place, he now gulped down
the thrillers of Dornford Yates, Sapper's 'Bulldog' Drummond stories,
and the adventure novels of John Buchan. To this day the Hentys with
their decorated board bindings and the Yates, many still with their original
jackets, occupy several shelves of Saltwood's Great Hall library. In his final
year at Eton Alan discovered P.G. Wodehouse.

Until now the Luftwaffe had passed Upton by. Then on 7 September,
at 11.15 p.m., they heard the sound of bombs – so familiar from London –
quite near. To K and Jane's surprise the children did not wake. Next
morning, wrote Jane, 'Children bicycle off to find out where bombs fell.
Return much excited as there are large craters in fields between gasworks
and Tom's house ... windows blown in, but no-one hurt. A cow was
killed in the field and cut in two Bob said, but we can only find one half
... all Tetbury, too, until "an officious policeman more like Germany than
England" moved everyone on.'

Arrangements were now in hand for Alan to go to Eton in the new
year. Meanwhile in November K and Jane moved briefly to Dorking,
where they were visited by E.M. Forster, who 'discusses "art and order"
with K'. It was a sign of war shortages that for the first time in seven years
Jane was unable to buy a 1942 Smythson's diary in its regular red leather
binding, with the year embossed in gold and a chrome lock. Instead she
used a spare 1941 diary, altering the day of the week before each entry.
January 1 saw them house-hunting. 'Go to Hampstead and look at more
houses, but none as suitable as Capo di Monte. We offer £6,000; it would
be lovely to get it settled for at least the end of the war – or till it is
bombed.' In the end they had to pay £500 more. 'Feel very pleased and
hope it all turns out well.'[17]

They (and a future mistress of K's, the artist Mary Kessell) went to the
Sadler's Wells ballet and then K and Jane returned to Tetbury. 'Grateful
that the Christmas holidays are short.' She had had a row with Alan, yet

another about a coat. 'Shot at cars [wrote Alan] with bows and arrows on
the road.' Colin Clark recalled that Arthur, the gardener's son, was the
only boy, other than Alan, with whom he was sometimes allowed to play.
He says he was 'common', taught Colin how to 'cock a snook and run
away' and let him read his copies of *Beano* and *Dandy*. 'Arthur and I used
to climb the apple trees that leant over the walls and try to pee on people
coming up the drive. This did not present too much of a danger to our
visitors, given the size of our bladders and the difficulty of aiming off for
wind, but one day we did score a direct hit on the local farmer, and he
made the most frightful stink (literally). Poor Arthur was banned for
ever.'[18]

For his new engagement diary – Letts The Air Force Diary, price
1s 9d, Purchase Tax extra – Alan devised a code. Entries were divided,
before lunch // and after. At the end of each entry he wrote a single,
circled word – 'my feelings as to what the day was like'. These were Alan's
final holidays before Eton. On 3 January: 'Shoot at Arthur, drive him off.
Feel depressed . . . stay up for foul dinner. Resolve not to again. (BAD)'

On 7 January, Jane was increasingly concerned about the war – 'Japs
still winning in Malaya. Can't bear to read the papers till they can be
defeated. Libya and Russians very successful – end of war would be in
sight if it weren't for the Japs.' Alan meanwhile was delighted that Lam,
Nanny to his father and a friend to all the children at Portland Place, had
come to stay. She was now working at the Prime Minister's country home,
Chequers. As well as joining a hunt for a nearby farm's cat which had
mange, 'hatch plot about Chequers with Lam'. Next day they went to
London for a pantomime.

Alan left his diary behind – a failure that he would worry about
repeating down the years – so 'entries from here to 12th may be inaccurate'.
His plotting with Lam paid off. They went to Chequers – 'see all over
house and cellars // then see AA guns with Lam'. Next day Alan reported
that he had been allowed to stay on and that Frank Sayers, Churchill's
valet, bought him sweets in Aylesbury. '(V. good)'. In London the rest of
the family looked over Capo di Monte and were even more pleased. Back
at Upton – Alan returned first via London 'by car 80 m.p.h.' – he found
a present of an RAF calendar awaiting him. He occupied himself by
acting commandos at the farm, started a new war map, and in the evening
played the gramophone. Next day it snowed. In the morning he walked
with Uncle Arthur, who 'confides in me', and in the afternoon he went
sledging.

That weekend Jane reported a meeting K had in London with one of his war painters, Feliks Topolski, who had been to Russia – 'all intellectuals are Trotskyites and there are concentration camps, one five miles long, of people who don't want to fight'. The weather was bad. 'Terrific snowball fight with Arthur and Col,' wrote Alan, who also admitted to a stiff neck – 'worse'. '(Medium)'. Jane wrote about chores – packing for Alan and Colin, 'the collection of gasmasks, identity cards, ration books and health cards is always the final triumph'.

Only two days left before Eton. Jane, though, was more concerned about the Japanese 'nearer Singapore every day. Terrible stories of German soldiers' sufferings in Russia – their feet come off with their boots. Wonder if they will ever turn against Hitler?' Alan was allowed one final treat, a family visit to London – 'decide to take Col (medium)' – where they all saw the Disney cartoon *Dumbo*. There was another overnight stay at the Great Western Hotel, Paddington, before a visit to the oculists. 'K and I depressed at Alan's entry into public school world tomorrow.'

Not so Alan! On Wednesday, 21 January Jane sorted out Alan's glasses and had a final lunch with him and K at the Carlton Grill, remarking that he was 'v. cheerful' about Eton, but that K 'v. gloomy' remembering his first day at Winchester. No wonder. On arrival he had been caned by his head of house for daring 'to speak to your seniors' as he had at the station as he waited to board the school train. 'In the twinkling of an eye,' recalled K, 'I became a silent, solitary, inward-turning but still imperfect Wykehamist.'[19] The day after Alan's departure for Eton K lunched with Colin Coote, who, reported Jane, 'caps K's stories by saying he was sent to Rugby at twelve with a label tied round his neck'. They caught the 2 p.m. train from Paddington – 'taxi from Slough skidding all way to Eton on the frozen snow. Warmly greeted by Jaques [housemaster] who invited Alan to tea. All his clothes and his room, new curtains etc. up and v. nice, blazing fire and Mrs Turnberry ready to unpack . . . leave Alan v. cheerful going with m'tutor to sign book.' Alan's verdict: 'Nice boy called Tenant.[20] Get fairly settled (medium).'

Next day, at Upton, Jane was exultant. Colin had been seen back to Cheltenham by the invariably reliable Newy. 'First day of my hols and very agreeable! Have hair and face done, but feel v. aged and depressed about Christmas hols – had made so many good resolutions – the children behaved so much better than I did. I just cannot manage to be everything . . . and have leisure to devote to children and be as sympathetic as I want.'

On hearing this remark Celly was surprised only that her mother had been able to find someone to do her hair in the middle of the war.

FOUR

New Home, New School

Alan was a late starter at Eton in January 1942, being only three months off his fourteenth birthday. This was a time of more upheaval in the lives of the whole Clark family – they were moving house once more. The eighteenth-century Capo di Monte in Hampstead would soon supplant the rented Upton House in Gloucestershire as the family's principal home. Jane confessed that she would miss Upton. 'We shall probably never have a house big enough to enjoy again.' How wrong that was to prove.

The children knew that when they returned from their schools for the Easter holidays life would be different; for one thing they would have a new London home, and one close to Hampstead Heath's wide and in places wild expanses. Capo di Monte was on the west side of Judges' Walk. Local history suggests that this cul-de-sac, which ends dramatically above the Heath itself, owed its name to the time in the seventeenth century when the judiciary fled the plague in the city and settled on the clean and wholesome air of Hampstead's heights, then no more than a village. Capo, as the family were quick to call it, was the home in 1804–5 of the actress Sarah Siddons, attracted to Hampstead by the health-giving qualities of what she called its 'strong air and quiet surroundings'. Her time at No. 3 Judges' Walk is memorialised by an 'S' over the door.[1]

Capo had a garden from which one could look across Hampstead's West Heath. With narrow, winding staircases and small rooms – the exception being a twentieth-century single-storey extension into the garden at the back and an Anderson shelter occupying the garage – this new home could hardly have been more different from the spaciousness of their Georgian country house in Gloucestershire.

For Alan his new life at Eton was, for the moment, far more to the point. He did not try for a scholarship so there was no question of his being in College, but he was not dim either. As a new boy in the Lent half, 1942[*] he was placed in Middle Fourth, one of nine new boys there

---

[*] In Eton parlance a term is a half and there are three halfs in a year.

who, in addition to Anthony Tennant, included Robin Leigh-Pemberton, who became Governor of the Bank of England, Marcus Kimball, a future Conservative MP and fellow Scottish landowner, and Lord Montagu of Beaulieu, who as well as sharing a passion for cars would also be a contemporary of Alan's at Oxford. His housemaster, Leslie Harrison Jaques, was both his house tutor (M'Tutor) and his classical or modern tutor. Jaques's house had forty-eight boys. His wife Mary, known as 'Mrs M'Tutor', or affectionately by some boys as 'Bloody Mary',[2] was head of lower boys' table in the dining room.

The Jaqueses' daughter Celia – her brother Nigel would become an Eton master himself – recalls the new boys' tea parties on the first day of the half. The boys themselves were usually shy and not sure of the form, the Jaques family endeavouring to put them at their ease.[3] Alan's priorities were quickly evident. 'No beating as too much red tape attached', he told his mother. In his pocket diary he mentions other boys, prep, playing L'Attaque and winning, but 'first school (nasty)'. The high spot of his first weekend 'opening tin of grapefruits (v. good)'. He learnt that at Eton one referred to other boys by their surnames; indeed Alan was to write some forty-five years later 'that it was thought "unhealthy" to know other boys' Christian names'.[4] Meanwhile Jane worked with Nellie, one of her maids, on which of the surviving Marion Dorn curtains from Portland Place and Gray's Inn would be suitable for Capo. Jane took time off to phone the Clarks' friend, Owen Morshead, the Windsor Castle librarian, who, being based so close to Eton, had agreed to keep an eye on Alan. Morshead was due to take him out to tea, but in the excitement of his new life Alan had forgotten. Morshead, though, was able to report to Jane that, on eventually tracking down Alan, it was 'top hat on side, red locks on forehead, laughing and chatting with four other boys'.

And so his first half progressed; he was obviously feeling his way. He got 'het up' losing the top off his watch, but was delighted to 'get letter from Mum'. That weekend his parents visited – 'great fun. They bring me things.' Work went well, except for construe. The following weekend he joined a group having tea with the Provost. A week later he started fagging 'in real earnest, hard and strenuous, but nice'. At the beginning of March life took a turn for the worse. He was concerned at the war news from all fronts, but also 'feel a little unpopular . . . knife falls to pieces . . . headache all afternoon'. Then someone stole Alan's stamps, and it was three days before 'F.C. at last admitted taking them and hands them back.' For the last entry for the term he concludes: 'Getting more popular.'

Alan's time at Eton was insufficiently distinguished either academically or in sport. He appeared to have made few close friends, although this was not untypical. Richard Ollard, in his study of Eton,[5] points out that although Eton had a complement of more than 1,100 the only boys from other houses one encountered were in the classroom, in the Corps, on the sports fields or if one went beagling.

Every boy at Eton had a room of his own. One Eton contemporary, who wishes to remain anonymous, but who was also in Jaques's and who messed with him,* remembers Alan's room as 'philistine. Some of us tried to be a bit arty. He never did that, no pretensions. The only picture he had in his room was a very good watercolour of a Gloster Gladiator, might have been two Gloster Gladiators. Given him by his father and I have no doubt by the best painter of Gloster Gladiators around.' He also always had hordes of *Life* magazine, 'something one hadn't heard of, but attractive to teenage boys being full of girls and film stars. Was his source parental?'

After Alan's death in 1999 a rumour went round – and was published in *The Spectator* – that he had also put up a picture of Adolf Hitler.[6] 'Total lie,' says his mess contemporary. 'I spent more time in Alan's rooms than in anybody's else's. No picture of Adolf Hitler and there wouldn't have been one in his desk, in his burry as we called them. If he had had one he would have said come and look at this. No, total lie.' Marcus Kimball (later Lord Kimball) remembers differently. Their interests could hardly have been further apart, Kimball being a past Master of the Cottesmore Hunt. In an unpublished diary entry when Kimball announced that he was standing down from the Commons,[7] Alan recalled him as 'a bright intelligent boy, quite handsome, but even then cruel ... Right up to the end Marcus continued to kill animals and obstruct anything in Parliament that was designed to relieve their plight. We clash from time to time on animal legislation – he spoke his mind.' It was mutual. When Kimball and I talked, he said Alan was 'the most unpopular boy in the school. He was very unpopular at Eton because he was a Nazi; no question about it. He supported the Nazi party.' Did he actually say that? 'No, No, No. He went about saying the Germans had better tanks, which of course was true, and had smarter uniforms. That's how he behaved.'

This may well have been the time when Alan first began to focus on the notion of generals as donkeys leading soldiers, who were the lions (what became, in *The Donkeys*, his first military history, some twenty years later). His mess contemporary was incensed that the same *Spectator* article had also said he went around telling the sons of fathers killed in the war

* 'to mess with' – have tea with.

that they were fighting on the wrong side. Kimball remembered this. 'The Seeley boys' father was killed. Alan Clark went up to one of them and said you do realise don't you your father wouldn't have been killed if it hadn't been for those donkeys and generals? He was a shit. Please quote me, because he was absolutely awful.' In fact, his mess contemporary remembers it differently: in Alan's words, it wouldn't have happened if the generalship had been better.[8]

With Alan's knowledge of militaria generally gained from successive volumes of *Jane's Fighting Ships* and *Jane's All the World's Aircraft*, like many others in the school, he also had *Daily Telegraph* war maps pinned up in his room. 'The only thing apart from the universal gossip was about how the war was going; one rushed out to the part of the house called the slab where the morning papers were and you wanted to see whether you were still in Tobruk or whether we had gone back to wherever.'

This being 1942, German bombing raids to Britain remained frequent. New boys therefore had to know that the shelter for Jaques's house was across the garden. When the air raid sirens went off boys would make for one end, the Jaques family and staff to the other. There were times – particularly with the German flying bombs, the V-1s, targeting southern England in the summer of 1944 – when, as Douglas Hurd, a Colleger, recalled in a letter home from Eton, 'we were down the shelter again for nearly ten hours last night, not coming out till after eight'.[9] Marcus Kimball recalls the doodlebugs from another perspective. 'We had to take it in turns to sit on top of the college chapel and press the warning button when one was coming our way.' Kimball never had to press the button.

Eton itself suffered from bombing. The chapel lost stained-glass windows from bomb blast early in the war. Alan's contemporary recalls one boy from Jaques's leaving in March, joining the Navy and by Christmas losing his life when the battleship *Prince of Wales* was sunk by the Japanese in December 1941. 'The school was at the lowest possible ebb. It was pretty dreadful. One or two masters got killed.' As Adrian House, an exact contemporary of Alan's, but in a different house, recalled, 'perhaps the most moving experiences at Eton were the evening services of Intercession in College Chapel to pray for any of our families or friends, for the old boys who were fighting, and for the souls of those who had been killed'.[10]

Alan in later years did not remember Jaques with affection. On New Year's Day 1990, he recalled having his card marked by the Chief Whip, Humphrey Atkins, when the Tories were in opposition in the 1970s: 'he gave me a dressing down, for smashing one of the House telephones. Just like Jaques at Eton, "We don't do that sort of thing."' On another occasion he was caned for bursting a paper bag in chapel and writing 'not dusted' on some untouched furniture. 'These were not the worst things I did,' he confessed later.[11] In his diaries he added a footnote that he and Jaques 'were not in sympathy with each other'.

His contemporaries do not remember Alan as clever at Eton; he just 'chuntered along'. Looking back at wartime Eton, at copies of the *Eton College Chronicle*, it is clear that sport was important if a boy wished to make his name. Although he rowed (which made him a 'wet bob', whereas a cricketer would be a 'dry bob'), it was not with great prowess. As his mess colleague remembers: 'We were frightfully hierarchical in those days. You wanted to get your house colours at football, which I think most people did, but Alan didn't.[12] He was below average at games I would say – it always surprised me how in later life he became this great keep-fitter. He wasn't at all a games player.' He did, though, return to boxing. His mess colleague again: 'I think he was very brave about it because he was a big fellow physically and there was a frightfully good boxer who was captain of boxing, a chap called Peter Blake. I remember poor old Alan being the same weight as this older boy who had been boxing since he was seven and it wasn't a very nice thing to happen.'

Meanwhile, for Alan's mother in Gloucestershire the spring of 1942 seemed less fraught even though, she wrote, it followed the coldest winter for a century. On 8 February she recounted from Upton spending 'a peaceful and v. agreeable day walking in sun and snow with Tor [the West Highland terrier] and choosing pictures for Hampstead'. But she could not ignore the 'v. bad war news – fall of Singapore seems imminent'. The new Hampstead home, like Upton two years before, needed major refurbishment. One half had to be rewired, and, as a result of bomb blasts, collapsed ceilings replaced. Jane was determined that it should be fit for occupation before the children returned from their schools. By the middle of February she was told it should be ready in a fortnight: 'we cheered – it all begins to look so nice'.

Finally, on 6 March furniture started arriving at Capo, but as the stairs were winding and narrow, the only alternative was to winch up the larger items into the house via the first-floor windows. Next day she reported leaving the Great Western Hotel with her last nine cases, boxes and umbrellas, adding, as ever, 'everyone is tipped'. In Hampstead, however, 'Chaos at Capo, more windows have to be removed – too much furniture and too big. Removal men inexperienced, slow and bad. Servants arrive from Upton with Tor and the canaries and are v. sniffy about the house.'

If the servants failed to approve, what would Alan, Collin and Celly think? She need not have worried. Within a few weeks K reported to his mother: 'You will be glad to hear that all the children, even Alan, approved highly of Hampstead, and if the war permits I think we are settled at last.'[13]

When K returned from a journey to Sweden arranged by the Foreign Office, a problem arose at the National Gallery as Arthur Lee had been interfering with K's decisions. She was, however, cheered on 23 March by Hiram Winterbotham, with his access to petrol, first driving Alan on an exeat from Eton to Upton, and then Jane and Alan to London. 'Hiram is a *beautiful* driver,' remarked Jane.

The Easter holidays began early in April. Alan had not seen the twins for three months. He found Celly, as his mother put it, looking thin after 'a term more or less in the san', having had measles and then mumps. Jane, though, was proud of her older son, for once. 'Alan turns up from Eton in time for breakfast. The first time he has ever had to transport himself home from school – get his ticket, taxis etc.' That Easter holiday was spent in north Wales, which became a Clark favourite. They found Portmeirion's creator, Clough Williams-Ellis, 'pleasant', but Jane had reservations: 'like a baby, full of uncritical ideas'. His wife Amabel, however, she found '*very* tiresome'. Alan, though, discovered that Williams-Ellis had served in the First World War – they now had something he wished to talk about.

Their wireless broke down and Jane was distressed that even in nearby Port Madoc it could not be mended. Without her servants Jane had to do the chores. On 10 April she reported, 'Wash children's and my hair and all their underclothes.' The holiday was doing what holidays are meant to do: 'After lunch we walk by the sea – very warm and lovely. All enjoy ourselves very much. I feel so well and have never seen the children look better.' The only cloud on the horizon had been the failure of the postman to deliver a parcel she had been expecting. Finally, on 11 April, 'Alan's stamp album has arrived which is a relief as *Jane's Fighting Ships* will only be published six weeks after his birthday.' But Jane was still concerned that she had 'v. few visible presents. Was so rushed before leaving I couldn't buy the usual oddments.' For his fourteenth birthday, Alan could hardly complain. Jane reported that he was 'pleased with his stamp book and 10/- I give him plus 10/- from uncles and we arrange to have it bound at Maltbys with AKC like K's KMC. Post doesn't yield much alas except £1 from Granny C, but he knows others are coming.'

Stamps became a hobby for a time. Indeed the only office he ever held at Eton was secretary of the philatelic society. His mess contemporary remembers that a cousin, a keen stamp collector, handed over the secretaryship to Alan, and said that his collection was 'just an ordinary schoolboy's collection'. But, as with so many schoolboys, his enthusiasm for stamp collecting did not survive growing up. Air Chief Marshal Newall, now Governor-General and Commander-in-Chief in New Zealand, kept Alan supplied with stamps from Samoa, Tonga, Fiji and even the Cook Islands. Newall, incidentally, in a letter accompanying one package of stamps also very gently corrected Alan's spelling: 'A secret Alan! Marshal has only one "l" and not two, but the majority of people spell it wrong and I am sure you would like to be one of the exceptions.'[14]

The children's reports also arrived. On what was Alan's first from Eton K commented to Jane in a letter, 'It is honourable without being brilliant. I am glad he is a slow developer.' But K had also forgotten his son's birthday. 'I am so ashamed about Alan. I will get him a decent present.'

This holiday Alan was allowed to camp out in the mountains above Portmeirion. He took Tor for company, cooked his own food, collected wood for a fire. He wrote to Granny Clark that at one point K joined him and they went for 'a lovely walk in the mountains, up a lovely little stream with trout in it and wonderful waterfalls'.[15] He also discovered an old Roman road built, he reported, for the miners and merchants who journeyed up into Snowdonia to trade and explore – 'it is terribly overgrown and in some places invisible but in others there are still stretches of Roman paving. It winds its way through the most desolate country.'

On 17 April Jane took 'Colin alone for a long walk and he says he would like to be a scientist. He is a very intelligent and sweet companion.' Next day she followed up this thought by taking Celly for another long walk. 'She is not full of ideas like Colin, but is very sweet and tries her best. Like Mother she blossoms more with the opposite sex.' For once whist was substituted for vingt-et-un after tea. 'Dine and walk with A as usual. He has become very frank and friendly.' Jane concluded, 'Would always like to have each child alone.'

Before the new Eton half, K, in a letter to his mother, stood back for a moment and offered a character study of his Alan, now that he had turned fourteen. 'He is a great boy – very amusing, a great character, but still intellectually lazy and colossally obstinate ... he will do very well if once his interest is aroused in something worth doing. He is now a good deal taller than Jane and as strong as can be.'

Hampstead Heath had its own excitements. At the beginning of May K wrote to his mother that he continued 'to be delighted with Capo ... Alan and I have just come in from sailing [boats] on one of the lakes.'[16] He has been a very pleasant companion and it has been interesting to see something of him now that the twins have gone back to school.'

Was K continuing, as he had when Alan was at St Cyprian's, to write what he thought his mother would wish to hear? In interviews Alan often reflected, as he told Graham Turner in 1992, on never getting close to his father. 'It went from him telling me stories in the woods at the age of five until I bid him goodbye on his death-bed without us having a single talk.'[17] Alan's mess contemporary at Eton had views about the relationship: 'I don't think he was happy at home. I really don't. I don't know why I knew that at the time; it wasn't talked about ... I honestly don't think he was unhappy at school. But I didn't like the look of his parents. My cousin said he always felt so sorry for Alan because his father was such a vulgar character. I said what do you mean? He said, well, he would have a yellow Rolls Royce and he would break a rule in Jaques's, an extremely sensible rule as it was a very flammable house, that visitors to the boys did not smoke, though Kenneth Clark, just to show I'm here and I can afford Havanas and cars, would be puffing a cigar. Harmless enough, but a bit tiresome with discipline enforced by the boys. You can't go up to another chap's father and say "put that light out" can you? And the housemaster wouldn't have been there anyway. He was a bit of a flaunter.'

Capo di Monte, while delightful and romantic, was inconveniently small, or, as K recalled in his memoirs, 'a pretty deceiver'.[18] But from the first-floor windows it was possible to see over the boundary wall of a large house opposite. This was Upper Terrace House. 'We began to cast lustful eyes on this almost too obviously "desirable" residence.' The owner had quit in the early days of the war and was now living in Barbados. The Clarks decided to try and buy it, but their offer was turned down. The Clarks thought again, revised their offer in May 1943 and 'were able to buy it for a sum that then seemed large, but would now [he was writing in 1977] be considered ridiculously small'. Quite how much neither K nor Jane confided. They moved across the road later that summer.

Upper Terrace House would be the Clarks' for a decade. It proved a true home to all the family, even though its eighteenth-century, possibly Queen Anne, origins had been modernised with a staircase, hideous, but sufficiently solid to sit under, thought K, 'during the occasional air raid warning'. Jane, as ever, was responsible for the interior design, and also delighted in working in the large walled garden. K wrote warmly about the house in his memoirs: its walls were extensive enough to take his big pictures from Upton, which they gave up in 1943. Renoir's *Beigneuse*

Blonde was hung in the sitting room on the chimney breast – 'the tutelary goddess of the house'. The Clarks returned to entertaining with a lavishness (wartime rations allowing) that they had not indulged in since Portland Place in the 1930s. Relations between Jane and her children improved, at least a little. Celly was delighted that her parents invited friends from the ballet, which had become her own passion. Alan and Colin heard stories from itinerant G.I.s, who pleased K by wanting to look at his pictures ('no English person ever does').

Five

Eton and Onwards

Alan's time during his final two years at Eton was one of progress without distinction. Not untypically of students of any age, he was good at what he liked, history, English and languages. In addition to French, where, thanks to the twins' Mme Moise, his parents' relative fluency and what he learnt at St Cyprian's, he had a head start, he now began to learn German and would later add Russian. Not that he wrote much about work in the two 1944 diaries he started (but did not complete). Finding his mother's new Smythson's, which she was not using, he began on 3 January, at Upper Terrace House and three months away from his sixteenth birthday: 'In the morning we had a waterfight with squirters.' Then to the entertainment: 'The chief event of the day was the pantomime, *Humpty Dumpty* at the Coliseum, 'the best I have seen in my life'.[1]

During holidays meals in the West End figured largely ('enjoyable lunch at Wilton's'; 'an excellent lunch at the Carlton'). Celly, too, now twelve, was keeping a diary. 'I am the only daughter of Sir Kenneth and Lady Clark. I have two brothers. We live at Upper Terrace House – it is a lovely house. I go to school at Cheltenham Ladies' College ... We have lots of friends and know the King and Queen and lots of famous people. We are very well off and very happy ... Also a dog called Tor.' On the Carlton lunch she gave greater detail: 'Alan showing off trying to balance a glass; it falls and breaks.'[2] The guests were listed: Anton Walbrook, Ivor Novello, Sibyl Colefax and 'a funny little man called Binkie Beaumont'.[3] The Clarks had introduced Saturday night galas at home, when the children were invited to dine with them. Early in January Alan recorded: 'Soirée de gala. Argument about whether one is more excited old than young.'

And so the holiday continued: 'biking on the heath, travelling at phenomenal speed. Afternoon in sham pantomime, fights with Pin [like Col, a lifelong nickname for Colin] as "tough midget" etc.' A more serious entry on 12 January: 'Wonderful day in every way, but it was rudely shattered in the evening. For some time I had noticed that Dad was getting slightly "fed up" with me, perhaps it is my lack of interest in things of beauty that irritates him, but it is definitely there. Still let us turn to the enjoyable part of the day; in the morning we had a cushion fight and I persuaded Gran [Clark] to get out of store two rods and a .22 rifle, we discussed Coot Club.[4] My cup of happiness would be full but for the sudden rift with father.'

Sad news is presaged on 15 January that Granny Martin [Jane's mother] 'is getting worse I fear and will not live much longer'. Gran [Clark] came to lunch, 'but she thaws ... then Mr Blunt comes.[5] Dad goes to bed and there is an air raid. I finish supper in his room with twins as there is gunfire.' The following day a sudden fog descends. The children come in from playing gangsters – 'and drink port. John Sparrow to tea'.[6] With the return to school approaching they had their hair examined for bugs. Alan reported – does one detect glee? – that 'Celly has them'. Then Tor is washed, before a walk on the Heath with Dad where they saw 'strenuous efforts by bren gun carriers to climb slope'.

19 January: back to Eton. '... little did I know what black treachery he [unidentified] was contemplating! Go to bed as usual hard mattress. Boo! Hoo!' Whatever old boys from Jaques's remembered of Alan sixty years on, his diary does not make him sound lonely. 21 January: 'Hilarious evening playing Monopoly and finishing with Parker knocking over photo of Higgins, Kimball laughing and Higgins-Kimball fight enjoyable ... I think I can hold my own though provided things remain as they are.' Next day he reported being moved down a 'set'. 'Go to M'tutor he deals out extras – beaten at chess by McWatters. M'tutor reads us *Esmond* [Thackeray].' The Lent half, 1944, included a visit by Major Bernard Fergusson, not long out of Burma where he served under the already legendary Orde Wingate. Appropriately, he lectured on jungle warfare. Alan would later recall this 'as one of my earliest introductions to tactical thory'.[7] Now, in an exercise book, he wrote his longest diary entry so far. It is in reflective, even depressed mood.

1 April: This half I have failed. I am forced most reluctantly to admit defeat; the only compensating factor is that the cause of the defeat lies with me and not with my adversaries. It is thus more easily remediable. Must in future make such efforts as to prevent such a disgrace occurring again. Never more must I own a defeat of such magnitude to personal failing. I will not record the circumstances which led to athletic failure. I shall never forget them.

On the intellectual side I propose to make a few notes: my failure in this sphere can be ascribed to one terrible, dominating fault: laziness. Placed among stupid boys in a low division I was top with very little effort. I read nothing other than the textbooks set; for my weekly essays which I wrote at great speed, I relied on nothing but my latent ability. I would jeer at boys who laboriously searched in books for 'ideas'; only this morning I boasted that I 'never read books'. This state of affairs is a very dangerous one, and I am glad that I have been made to realise it with such force.

Such introspection would prove a feature of his adult diaries.

Part of the Easter holidays were spent at Portmeirion, where The Coot Club (now adorned with the definite article) came formally into being. Alan, at sixteen, might have thought himself too old for a nature club with the twins, 'for the purpose of obtaining natural history information and also for sport', but as is shown in the immaculate club records – inscribed by Alan and Celly with headings in red ink – he played a major role, even if its existence, typically, was short-lived. Celly was president 'with charge of the funds', Colin vice-president, chief naturalist and chairman, and Alan secretary. The family's West Highland terrier, Arthur Tor Clark, is described as 'chief hunting member'. When on expeditions – the club's *raison d'être* – 'the select committee reserve the right to assume the names of Lord Lansdowne, Sir Colin Princeton, and Lady Colette Princeton'. In addition there were visiting members. Bizarrely, Jane is listed as Lady Elizabeth Clark (the name she disliked using: did Celly see this as a way of getting her own back?). Francis Newall and Robin Douglas-Home (vice-naturalist) were also named. Two pages of rules follow in Alan's handwriting.

At the end of the holiday 'club activities lapsed due to the unfortunate illness of the President' and then on 26 April the secretary recorded that the club had been adjourned until the August recess, when they expected to stay at Woodchester, Hiram Winterbotham's home, and undertake a foraging expedition. 'In September', the secretary concluded, 'the members will move to the Coots nest by fast car and will spend three weeks there before the season closes.' In his published *Diaries* there is a memory of Portmeirion. Alan refers to an au pair installed by his step-mother at his parents' house. He chatted her up; 'she's not pretty,' he writes, 'but is sexual. Dairymaid. Reminded me of Portmeirion.'[8]

Alan's own 1944 diaries were not totally neglected. In the Smythson's, Alan crossed out 12 and 13 July and started: 'After a long pause I resume once again writing my diary which I hope I will maintain for ever now.' Such optimism! It would be eleven years before he managed to keep a regular diary, an essential prop to be maintained for the rest of his life.

A new excitement after lunch the following day: 14 July: 'BASEBALL GAME! Enthralling, makes me a complete convert.' He was also set 'vast amount of work for weekend'. The following morning, 'March about, convinced we're all going to be killed by 18th, but no chapel, so ring up Mum'. Compulsory chapel had been temporarily abandoned because of the unpredictability of the V-1s. With V-1s now commonplace, most nights were spent in the Jaques's garden shelter. This was hardly conducive to exam preparation, and according to his diary, Alan 'Rang up Dad about shelter'. Presumably K then spoke to Jaques. Certainly the night before trials began he was delighted to be allowed to stay indoors. 'Sleep well that night between blankets in my room.'

This 1944 diary is almost at an end. 26 July: 'Well trials are over now. They began well and I was confident of a 1st, but the maths papers, the slackly prepared French and the hideous ... Xenophon may have queered my pitch. I went out to an excellent lunch after a foul Arithmetic and a passable verses paper. The siren went, however, and I made off after lunch. Packed a little in the evening. M'tutor came in and told me reports were good. I hope I've got a 1st. It would cheer him up.' A day of tension follows, 'wander around, in and out of school library etc plan journey to Portmeirion ... tons of cleaning up to do'.

The family spent the summer holidays 'in a different, much pleasanter house' at Portmeirion, wrote K. 'Family talk is fairly ferocious – sometimes deafening. Being an only child I cannot accustom myself to these boisterous arguments which I am unable to distinguish from real quarrels.'[9] And to Jane, again undated, 'dearest wife ... Alan met us looking really marvellous – ever fitter (and considerably fatter)'. And to his mother, also undated: 'the children bathe and climb all day. You know how I love being with them.'

That holiday K and Jane received welcome, if surprising, news of Alan's academic progress at Eton. To his mother, K wrote: 'You will have heard that Alan did well in school certificate with seven credits and five distinctions.' He went on to tell his mother how proud Jane was, but all the same 'shocked that such a lazy, thoughtless boy should get away with it!'. K next made a forecast that, like the earlier conclusions drawn by Jane and Celly, would turn out to be extraordinarily prescient. 'He has a good head and should do well if he can find any occupation to bring out his qualities. I think he would do well in politics if he weren't – my profound conviction – a fascist. That will never do in this country though the rest of the world may ultimately require it.'[10]

★

Alan does not appear to have written about the ending of the war in 1945. One diary entry exists from January when, on the 13th, he reports hearing on the 9 p.m. news of Russia's 'great new offensive – the last winter one of the war I trust. It seems inconceivable that the German army should survive another year's campaigning.' At Eton he moved steadily upwards so that by the Michaelmas half his class or modern tutor was now A.K. Wickham. In the summer, as the *Eton College Chronicle* recorded, Churchill's brief, post-war, pre-general election government included twenty-five Old Etonians in office. It was not a record that would be bettered.

K was invited to a party given by Lord Rothermere (owner of the *Daily Mail*) at the Dorchester Hotel on 26 July to celebrate what he anticipated would be a Conservative victory at the general election. As the school holidays had just started, K took Alan along. Half a century later, Alan recalled, 'As we came up the stairs we were almost bowled over by the Viscount Moore [later Lord Drogheda] rushing down them. White as a sheet he said, "it's a landslide, a landslide". He and Brendan Bracken were the bosses of the *Financial Times* and he was heading back to the city to sell the market. When we got into the room we found that most of the guests had left and the atmosphere was sepulchral.'[11]

Just before Christmas 1945, K wrote to his mother: 'Alan and Colette are in great form and we have great fun together, especially at meals. Alan is really a most intelligent youth, and I believe he will go on developing slowly for a long time till his interests draw level with his natural powers of understanding.'

When Alan returned to Eton for the 1946 Lent half, his mess contemporary noticed something. 'Until then he wasn't particularly convivial, but to my mind he underwent almost a character change. I don't know whether it was a woman who did it, but he went home one Christmas holidays and came back an extrovert. Quite amazing ... It was quite peculiar. He went home one holidays as a really quiet little bloke and came back an extrovert and shouting around. You've only got my word for it. It really was one holiday. One almost wanted to say come on Alan why are you putting on this act? Maybe it was that he had suddenly become rather clever and he was getting on well with A.K. Wickham. I always imagined his father had said, come on, push yourself old boy.'

Celly thinks this change might indeed be explained by what she calls 'Al's first experience of falling in love'. At an Upper Terrace House dinner over the Christmas holidays, Nancy Mitford was one of the guests.[12] Not yet celebrated as an author (*The Pursuit of Love* had only just been published), Mitford was working in London at the Curzon Street shop of the bookseller Heywood Hill. Celly remembered that 'Al came in and was absolutely enthralled by her wit and intelligence.' His father was 'amazed'. Alan sparkled. K told his daughter that he never knew his son could be like that. Nor did it end there – the following month, Celly remembers, he sent Nancy a Valentine card.

His handwriting at this time was not unlike his father's. In later life it became much discussed following the publication of his *Diaries*. For this present volume, Renata Propper, a graphologist who lives in the United States, analysed his handwriting (and that of his parents) at various stages of his life. She was familiar with the Clark family, but says that knowing the writer is irrelevant to her study of his writing.

The first example she studied was by Alan in his final year at Eton, where, she reported, 'one can see his anxious adherence to the system while at the same time he is trying to strike out on his own. On the one hand he wished to please his father who was his role model, on the other hand he wished to liberate himself. Too sensitive and not sufficiently confident, he must have had difficulties maintaining an emotional even keel. Intellectual maturity and talent stand in contrast to his emotional chaos and isolation. *Weltschmerz*, self-doubt, and anxieties were weighing on him, as he tried to find his own identity. However, while he was searching for his own *raison d'être*, he was painfully alone and vulnerable.'

Alan's only school reports that have survived – and even then they are incomplete – cover the 1946 Lent half. By this time Alan had joined the Household Cavalry's Territorial training regiment at its barracks in Windsor, which was considered several steps up from Eton's Officer Training Corps. But A.K. Wickham, writing from Hawtrey House, was only interested in his pupil's academic prowess. He reported to Jaques that Alan had come out first in his division, 'which looks like a piece of tutorial nepotism, but I think he deserves it'. He was fortunate perhaps that their enthusiasms coincided. Wickham pointed to Alan's 'obvious' interest in history. 'He shows a greater power of analysis than most boys, and he has a fairly sure flair for the essential of a situation. There is no padding in his writing, and almost all that he says tells. He has the great merit of being clear. He has been active in mind, as in body.'

Not all, though, was praise. Wickham took strong exception to two of his weekly essays: the first, on 'England's Place in Europe Today', because it was 'crudely told, bad and cynical', the second, on the English counties, because it was 'entirely an outpouring of sentiment about the Highlands of Scotland'. Little did Wickham, or Alan for that matter, realise the significance of both: over politics Alan was never a pro-European; and his love of the Highlands would eventually lead to his acquisition of the Eriboll estate.

Wickham found him insular. In languages it was not any lack of ability but his manner that upset his masters. The German report is missing, but Wickham tells Jaques of 'his German instructor's protests. I have had to make them at times myself. Masters, like others in authority, like all the conversation in their neighbourhood only to be addressed to themselves. It is his impetuosity which leads him to offend against this very human desire, but in his own interests, he must curb it, like some other of his impetuosities.' His French report – and this was one of his specialist subjects – is tougher. 'If he did not adopt this almost casual manner,' it opened, 'and whisper irrelevancies to his neighbour with a wan smile I should be inclined to give him a good report.' Russian was an Extra Study and had been Alan's own choice. Alan would find the language useful a decade later when he first visited the Soviet Union for a youth festival and then again in the 1980s as a Trade Minister.

With these individual reports to hand, Jaques wrote to Sir Kenneth.[13] He mentioned Wickham's 'candid account' of Alan's 'merits and demerits'. Jaques, though, remarked that he 'couldn't help wishing that a boy with such a keen edge to his wits did not appear rather higher up'. He was, as he put it, 'less kind than Wickham – I wonder whether a little more ambition might have provided what was not forthcoming in the luck of the masters'. Jaques was, however, even-handed. Alan, he wrote, was 'using his wits and they are rapidly increasing in range and effect'. Looking ahead, Jaques proved shrewd. 'I can see him as a first rate leader in a crisis, but in a life of more humdrum routine it may not always be clear to him that trouble must be taken to see what is wanted and to get it done.' Successive editors of Alan's books would confirm this early diagnosis.

In a sporting résumé, Jaques noted that fortune did not favour Alan in his boxing – he was runner-up in the middleweight division – but as for next half, 'we shall need his strength and zest for rowing, and I hope he will give all he can to improve the rowing from junior wet bobs'. Jaques also observed that there would be two Clarks in the house in the summer half as Colin was leaving Cheltenham for Eton. Alan would now be identified as Clark major.

With the ending of the European war not quite a year past, foreign travel was still a rare experience. The Clarks' destination that Easter was Sintra in Portugal, which would become a family favourite. While there Alan indulged in a childish prank, which upset his mess friend. 'He sent

me a postcard of his hotel and rather awkwardly he wrote on the back
that this hotel was designed for illicit sexual intercourse. I'd rather he
hadn't sent it c/o Corpus Cambridge where my father was a fellow. We
were quite innocent in those days.'

Alan also kept a diary. At Northolt, he thought the BOAC Dakota 'so
makeshift and ramshackle' that his experience may explain his later fear
of flying. On 13 April he wrote: 'My 18th birthday. I am constipated,
angry weather, thundery. Shop. I have recieved [*sic*] nothing today except
belated good wishes from the family. I had been promised a car. We had
the best dinner I can remember this evening with Gulbenkian.* He toasted
me, went to bed very late.' He found travelling en famille 'cumbersome
. . . never has the shilly-shallying and dilly-dallying been so apparent over
such a prolonged period. It has wrecked me. I hope my at all times ill-
concealed rage has not been too apparent to my good kind father. I am
not ashamed at my mental aversion to the continual (or so it seems) surfeit
of art education, but I'm sure it must wound him terribly when it comes
too rudely to the surface . . . I shall not go abroad with the family again.'
But it was not all bad. 'The only time I have been really happy was when
I went off alone with Papa.' The last Tuesday in Lisbon was a particular
success. 'I felt grand, and dad stood me a very good watch (Omega
Oyster).'[14]

Alan and Colin overlapped at Eton for only one half. K wrote to his
mother: 'Just got back from a day [there] . . . Col getting on very well . . .
looks remarkably fit, far better than he ever looked at the Junior. Alan
seems to be looking after him well, as Colette said he would. He, Alan, is
in tremendous form, full of humour and vitality. He is a most delightful
companion.'

James, Alan's elder son, wrote after his father's death, 'Outside the family,
I truly believe, cars were my father's greatest love.'[15] Alan bought his first
car in 1946 when on 'long leave' in his final months at Eton.[16] He did not
possess a driving licence. His choice was a 1926 two-seater Bentley with
a dicky. It weighed nearly three tons. His account of its purchase survives.[17]

'I was young, and pretty idiotic, I suppose, and showed it. At any rate
the dealer sank his teeth in and gave me the full treatment, even down to
telling me the mileage was 33,000 – "It's not run *in* yet, old chap" – when
in fact the odometer read 83,000, but the car was at the back of a dark
garage and the light was such that shadow obscured the first and last digits.

* The oil baron Nubar Gulbenkian, a friend of the Clarks.

Of course he refused to allow the car on the road for a trial, feigning monstrous indignation at the thought: "My dear good fellow, the man who is going to buy that car has only to set eyes on it. He'll hand me the money in pound notes right here at this office before he even walks across the garage floor to start her up."'

Alan later recalled that prices were spiralling and that he paid £350. It proved to be the most uneconomical car he ever owned. Celly, back from school for the summer holidays, remarked in her diary that Al's Bentley was 'a lovely car. Like a red and green enormous racing car. Play around with it.'[18] Top speed was 73 mph and Alan wrote that it stood up to his driving for several weeks. He remarked that he never took a driving test. 'At the end of the war there was some kind of procedure whereby you could get a provisional licence with a demob certificate and then after a bit it got upgraded.'

He remembers his driving being entirely self-taught, although there is evidence elsewhere of guidance from Hiram Winterbotham.[19] 'I was long on theory, short on practical experience.' He believed that the clutch had only two positions – 'either the engine was connected to the transmission, or it wasn't'. This made manoeuvring the Bentley in confined spaces such as the garage at Upper Terrace House 'somewhat abrupt'. His driving technique had come from '*watching* other people. Watching them fiddling about with the pedals and gear lever, that is, because as far as roadcraft went I knew all the answers. The whole thing was to accelerate, wasn't it? Particularly around corners?' Driving the Bentley provided his early experience: 'At low-speed man-oeuvrability, however, I wasn't so hot, never having mastered the principle of slipping the clutch. When the pedal was pressed down nothing happened. OK, but when I took my foot off, the engine often stalled. Very humiliating. So the answer, it seemed, was to give the engine lots of gas just before letting go. This meant that the old car ... fairly heaved about in traffic.'

As Alan approached his eighteenth birthday, a question was posed: what next? Several of K's closest friends, among them Maurice Bowra and John Sparrow, he had known at Oxford, where K himself (a Trinity man) had just become Slade Professor of Fine Art. That seemed the obvious destination. K took him to reconnoitre, and in a letter to his mother he wrote: 'It was a great pleasure to see his surprised delight at the beauty, calm and spaciousness of the place. He saw the Censor of Christ Church, but the interview was really a farce as the Censor talked all the time and at the end of ten minutes said that Alan was accepted. Maurice [Bowra] was away so we could not stay with him.'[20]

Alan failed to tell his friends. His mess colleague remembered that he only found out on returning to Eton in September. 'Jaques said he had gone up to Oxford, which was peculiar because the natural thing at that stage was one stayed on. I had had my eighteenth birthday in September 1946 and then towards the end of that term one took a scholarship exam, in my case it was Trinity College, Cambridge and then you left at Christmas and you got your call-up papers if you were lucky at once.'

Did Alan enjoy his time at Eton? In 1993 he was interviewed for Michael Cockerell's political documentary, *Love Tory*. Cockerell put it to him that he hated his time there, but that as a grounding for life at the top of the Tory Party his Eton experience was uniquely valuable. Alan agreed, 'Very brutal'. Eton taught him about deceit and cruelty, 'the essential components about adult life. Enjoyment about the pain of others that's a very familiar element in politics.' He also recalled the 'extreme physical hardship' of Eton at that time.

However, the occasional references to Eton in his *Diaries* are mainly favourable, with a sometimes wistful air (28 June 1988, House of Commons Terrace: 'It is humid ... The river boats going back and forth, always with some drunks, who jeer; the smells and breezes still, after forty-three years, evocative of "Rafts"', which, as he explained, were the rafts and sheds on the Thames used by the wet bobs). He did not, though, send either of his own sons, James and Andrew, to Eton. Jane says that although they put down James's name Alan never seemed passionate about the idea, and anyway they could not afford the fees. Once when the subject of Eton came up Jane remembers James suddenly burst into tears: 'I don't want to be eaten!'

SIX

Oxford, Prague, Cars and Girls

Oxford in the autumn of 1946 was unlike it had ever been before. Some undergraduates, Alan among them, came straight from school and were still in their teens. Another group – they were few in 1946, but grew in number the following year – had gone from school into the Forces during the war, but had pledges from colleges that guaranteed them a place once they were demobbed. A third had gone up to Oxford before the war, had their education interrupted by war service and were now returning, often in the second half of their twenties, to complete their studies (wing commanders, half colonels and naval captains were not unknown). One such was the writer and broadcaster Ludovic Kennedy. He left Eton in 1938 for Christ Church (the same destination as Alan), and wrote of his post-war return that 'the priorities of a student of twenty-six who has just been released from the services are not those of a boy of nineteen tasting freedom for the first time'.[1] Not surprisingly, these different groups did not always mix.

By 1946 it was possible to defer National Service (as military service was renamed) if one had a university place. Paul Johnson, later a historian and journalist and born the same year as Alan, recalls that most potential undergraduates chose deferment on the optimistic grounds that by the time they had graduated National Service might have been shortened, or at best abolished.[2] However Alan's brother Colin, by then in his first term at Eton, remembered Alan telling their mother he would go up to Oxford rather than do his National Service. She was incandescent. In her opinion it was not deferment, but avoidance and 'an act of virtual treason'.[3] His sister Celly, too: 'How did Al *not* do National Service – Mama was always very cross about this; she would keep bringing up the matter.'[4] His Etonian mess contemporary wrote to Alan from Northern Ireland in the exceptionally cold winter of 1947 and received a letter back saying 'you are a mutt because if you've got any wits you don't do things like being called up'. 'I remember repeating this to my father who absolutely went through the roof that anyone should suggest that you should get out of these things.'

It is odd that Alan was so adamant about not doing National Service, having been passionate about military matters from an early age. He, though, would say that he did in fact have Army service to his credit. In the winter of 1946, while still at Eton, he took advantage of the Household Cavalry's training regiment based at Combermere Barracks, Windsor, within walking distance of the college. The records show that he 'joined the colours' on 28 February 1946, although, confusingly, the same day transferred to the Army Reserve. His Army number was 306795. The date of his final discharge was 31 August 1946, little more than a month after he left Eton and not long before he went up to Oxford. On his service papers his period with the colours is given as just one day, service not with the colours 184 days. Rank on discharge: trooper. Cause of discharge – and here the papers cite Territorial Army regulations, 1936 – 'services no longer required (remaining at College)'.

The Household Cavalry records include a letter to Sir Kenneth Clark, dated 4 September 1946, saying that 'War Office authority has now been received for your son to be released from his present engagement'. It adds that the regiment was sorry he would not now be joining them.[5] Two decades later Alan had no inhibitions about varying the facts. In one of many CVs Alan prepared when his name went forward as a possible parliamentary candidate, he stretched the truth by saying 'on his 17th birthday [he] enlisted in the Army and served in the Household Cavalry'. That would have been 13 April 1945.

Those who knew him at Oxford offer various theories. Michael Briggs believes that he first applied for the Navy, then for the Guards – each thought he was joining the other and he joined neither. Lord Ashburton (as John Baring, he was another Old Etonian who went straight to Oxford) recollected that 'Her Majesty's Government were reducing the armed payroll and in April 1947 had told a number of us who had recently been modestly ill, to go to university and forget National Service.'[6]

Without doubt he enjoyed the Household Cavalry training regiment. Euan Graham recalled Alan talking about surviving mountain warfare training with the Household Cavalry in north Wales. In a letter K wrote to his mother, undated but probably around Easter 1946, we learn that training conditions were harsh: 'Alan has just come back unexpectedly from Wales – the cold was a bit much even for him, and the orange juice froze on the table.'[7] (On holiday in Wales many years later he stopped the car to ask the way, and surprised Jane not only by speaking in Welsh – but by being understood. It was also where he learnt to cat-nap – Jane relates that he could go to sleep instantly and awake ten minutes later totally refreshed.) Graham also remembered that on the front of one of his many cars at Oxford he had attached, with pride, a Guards' armoured division motoring badge.[8]

Alan was eighteen and a half when he arrived at Christ Church, the Oxford college known as 'the House'. With entry in this immediate post-war period made comparatively easy, the intake was mixed academically. Being neither a scholar nor an exhibitioner he roomed in college only briefly. From his Household Cavalry papers we learn he was now six feet in height with hazel eyes and brown hair; and a complexion described as 'fresh'. His weight is not given, but contemporary photographs show him to be well-built, less wiry, less lanky than in later life. At Oxford he gradually blossomed, revealing a hitherto undetected confidence. Roger Pemberton, a contemporary at the House, who had also been at Eton, reflects that 'like a lot of OEs he had a kind of built-in arrogance. I was very conscious of him. He was a colourful, exotic figure. Obviously he had a lot of money pretty swiftly the way he behaved.'[9]

Alan's arrival at Christ Church coincided with the quatercentenary of the college. The King, Visitor of Christ Church, attended the celebrations and, as the actor Norman Painting recalled, he would never forget the look of 'delighted amazement' on George VI's face when at the end of dinner 'all 400 of us rose to our feet, grabbed our glasses and following a short trumpet call played by the Honourable Francis Dashwood, burst into spontaneous, carefully rehearsed, singing of "Here's a Health unto His Majesty"'.[10] Meanwhile the new undergraduate, with paper still in short supply, began work using his trusted 10ins x 8ins cloth-bound Denbigh exercise book that had first recorded the rules and proceedings of the family Coot Club. But this had used up fewer than ten pages. At Oxford, Alan turned it upside down and on 10 October 1946 it became his history notebook. He lists his weekly programme with tutors Feiling, Masterman, Talboys, Hancock and Falls. On the Saturday: 'clean up'. Opposite: 'The restoration 1660–1815'. In handwriting neater than it became he wrote the key questions, and notes for an essay.

Typically, he kept up these notes only for a few weeks. Turn the page and there is nothing, and then a further page and life has moved on several years as the Denbigh becomes his law studies notebook.

At Oxford he began to make lasting relationships. Euan Graham, also an Etonian, but four years older than Alan, went up to Christ Church in

1948 having served five years in the RAF. Their initial friendship was based on a shared passion for cars. A quarter of a century later, when Alan entered the Commons, Graham, by now Principal Clerk of Private Bills in the House of Lords, 'showed him the Westminster ropes'.[11] It was also Graham whom Jane Clark asked to deliver the address at Alan's memorial service half a century later. Graham and Pemberton both recalled that Christ Church attracted female camp-followers, which suited Alan.

Michael Briggs was at Merton, next door to Christ Church, and says 'He was attractive, frivolous, full of beans, witty, amusing, made you laugh, terrific fun to be with, lively, challenging.' Both enjoyed 'going to the dogs'. Not everyone remembers him so warmly. Paul Johnson ran into him at parties: 'I didn't know him very well. I didn't think much of him. I thought him a cad and idle bounder. What he was interested in was motor cars, he was absolutely obsessed by large fast motor cars.' However Ethne (but known as Ena) Fitzgerald, who would marry Anthony Rudd, another Oxford man (later one of Alan's stockbrokers), agrees with Briggs. She was reading history at St Anne's, having arrived at Oxford a year ahead of Alan's sister Celly, whom she knew from Cheltenham Ladies' College. 'He was funny, so amusing.' Alan became very fond of her.

Along with Euan Graham and Michael Briggs, Malcolm Napier was Alan's closest Oxford friend and for a time they shared lodgings in Bath Place. Napier was from a wealthy shipowning family. Graham recalls that he wrote 'very bad poetry' and had a London flat in Mayfair, possibly North Audley Street ('quite a grand place'). One summer Napier became 'progressively quieter and quieter and tagged along with us, and just before our examinations, I said the best thing to do, you have got to get away, don't revise'. Alan, Graham and Napier drove to Cornwall, where they found the Carlyon Bay Hotel near St Austell and played croquet, swam and generally relaxed. Cornwall and Carlyon Bay would become favourite territory for Alan after Oxford. According to Graham, Napier slowly lost his mind, supposedly, says Briggs, as the result of a late attack of mumps, and disappeared from active life. He died young.

The first winter Alan spent at Oxford coincided with the Great Freeze of 1947, the Shinwell winter. With a shortage of coal to heat the rooms, hardly a pipe in Oxford remained unfrozen, and sleeping in one's clothes became the norm. In these drab times, with rationing still in force, undergraduates often compensated by drinking heavily and dressing extravagantly in whatever clothes they could lay their hands on. Clothes rationing was particularly tough on girls when Dior's New Look came along. However an Army depot announced a sale of surplus parachute silk. The girls made frocks, although all, perforce, were white. The sets divided into politics and the Oxford Union (Jeremy Thorpe, Shirley Williams, Edward Boyle), the arts (John Schlesinger, Kenneth Tynan, Tony Richardson) and the partying-gambling-girls crowd of which Alan was a minor cog. It was a far wilder side of life than he had known previously.

Like many Old Etonians at Oxford, he became a member of the Bullingdon Club, often recollected as hard-drinking – not that Alan was, although he had his moments. In 1928 the Bullingdon was satirised by Evelyn Waugh as the Bollinger Club in his first novel, *Decline and Fall*. Waugh drew on a notorious occasion when Bullingdon members went on the rampage in Christ Church's Peckwater Quad, leaving hardly a pane of glass intact. In Alan's time the club proved only slightly less raucous. In a motoring memoir,[12] he described a revel, known as the Napoleonic dinner, held at Oxford's Roebuck Inn on 11 June 1948. This involved a procession of intoxicated students, a few in cars, some on horseback. All the riders were mounted with real swords (the bill from Nathan's, the London costumiers, was over £300). 'At dinner, as wine flowed, so, in some cases, did tempers rise. Blood was drawn among the guests and a waiter who tried to intervene was lanced on the cheek.' Alan's last coherent memory of the evening was the arrival, as he put it, 'quite independently', of Lord David Cecil, the newly appointed Goldsmiths' Professor of English Literature, who was told by the manager of the inn: 'We don't want any more of your sort here.'

Alan enjoyed an allowance from his father with which he indulged his motoring enthusiasms, but he was never a match for those undergraduates who gathered at 167 Walton Street. Brian Masters in his biography of John Aspinall called the house the 'centre of Oxford's gambling fraternity and a magnet for all kinds of eccentric'.[13] One floor was occupied by fascists, another mainly by homosexuals including John Pollock, who became a friend of Alan's. The third was for the gamblers, whose daily schedule could begin with cards in the morning, followed by a race meeting in the afternoon, dog-racing in the evening and cards again into the small hours. The building was run by a landlady named Maxie who had appeared in music hall and drank gin.

The key gambler was Ian Maxwell-Scott, who was ostensibly reading law. If he wasn't playing poker he went racing. At Walton Street he thought little of raising the stakes to £5 or £10 a time (a huge sum when one considers that Aspinall's government grant was £70 for an entire term). Aspinall learnt his gambling skills by watching Maxwell-Scott. Paul Johnson visited Walton Street for the 'nice girls there', but never gambled.

Alan went, too, making friends with Aspinall, a friendship that would endure. Cards, however, were never a major enthusiasm.

As Alan was reading history he swiftly came into the orbit of Hugh Trevor-Roper, who had not long become the college's Junior Censor (the Censors, junior and senior, being principally responsible for discipline). Trevor-Roper would achieve fame and fortune early in 1947 with the publication of *The Last Days of Hitler*,[14] leading one commentator to call him the 'young Christ Church don who at the moment has the attention of the whole English-speaking world'.[15]

Trevor-Roper was another of Alan's mentors or father figures. His wartime work included military intelligence and SIS (Secret Intelligence Service), which led to friendships with influential people such as Dick White, later head of both MI5 and MI6. In the autumn of 1945 White suggested he undertake the interviews of former Nazis in Allied-occupied Germany that became the basis for *The Last Days of Hitler*. And it was White who encouraged him to publish his book and smoothed the way past objectors. Trevor-Roper, the historian everyone wanted, was soon writing for *The Observer* and *The New York Times*. Alan's own interest in history, ultimately as a writer, would be much influenced by Trevor-Roper.

Trevor-Roper was one of five tutors at Christ Church who supervised Alan's work (the others being Rollo St Clair Talboys, Paul Jacobsthal, Daniel Bueno de Mesquita and J. Steven Watson). Commenting on his first year St Clair Talboys was quick to offer his opinion on what he saw as Alan's state of mind: 'He is rather temperamental; he writes well and there is always zest in his work — and I think that as he becomes more reconciled to the life here he should do very well.'

Alan gained a firm friend in Trevor-Roper. Oxford was proving enormous fun. He was doing just enough work to get by. He had discovered girls in a big way, made loads of friends and, thanks to his love of big cars, became known as 'Klaxon Clark'. This love of motoring led him to become involved in a remarkable journey immediately after Christmas 1947 and into the new year.

In Europe communists were seeking control in the countries the Red Army had released from Nazi tyranny, leading Churchill to adopt the phrase 'iron curtain'.[16] As that curtain began to come down around what would become known as the Soviet bloc, Trevor-Roper contemplated a visit to Prague before the Czech border was closed to the West. Perhaps he was still keeping up his connections with the Intelligence services.

Prague was especially interesting as the communists vied for control with the socialists and liberals. Officially, witness a letter to his new friend, the art critic Bernard Berenson, Trevor-Roper remarked that he simply desired to visit Prague, 'that famous baroque city, the Cisalpine Rome'.[17]

Perhaps it was just a desire to impress that prompted Alan to become Trevor-Roper's chauffeur. His parents invited Trevor-Roper to lunch at Upper Terrace House on 2 December – presumably to look him over and show him the car they would lend, a 1939 Lagonda drophead coupé.[18] Photographs were taken. One has Alan proprietorially standing alongside the open-top car, his elegantly trousered left leg on the running board, with his tutor looking on indulgently. A second has Alan, now wearing a trilby, behind the wheel and Trevor-Roper in the passenger seat.

Before the journey itself all kinds of formalities were necessary. Trevor-Roper had learnt how to pull strings from his own time in MI5 during the war. Now, he approached Frank Pakenham, Chancellor of the Duchy of Lancaster in Attlee's government.[19] They were acquaintances of long-standing. Pakenham's time as a student of politics (1932–6) at Christ Church had overlapped with Trevor-Roper's period as an undergraduate there.

Alan already had a passport issued in March 1946 in readiness for the family's Easter visit to Portugal. At a time when few Britons were venturing into Europe, he was, in fact, much travelled, having in the preceding eighteen months also holidayed in Italy, Switzerland and Spain. On a fresh right-hand page of his passport the Czech Embassy in London stamped and dated a three-month visa. Then on 14 December 1947, Trevor-Roper wrote, on Savile Club notepaper, but actually from Oxford, asking him to run some errands in London. Money for foreign travellers at this time was a problem, exchange controls being severe, but Trevor-Roper's new connections with the The New York Times helped and Alan was instructed to visit its Fleet Street offices to collect a book of travellers' cheques for $750. Both also received cards that accredited them as New York Times correspondents in the occupied zones.

Until the last moment Trevor-Roper was uncertain if their plans would succeed. If Pakenham 'doesn't perform an Irish volte-face, I now think all obstacles will be safely surmounted; but the nervous expenditure entailed has been quite disproportionate'. Time was at a premium. As Junior Censor at Christ Church, he had somehow to find the time to write thirty-nine letters to headmasters who had pupils who wished to be admitted, 'telling them that their boys wrote trash'. Trevor-Roper, though, feared that the results of his letters would be 'sand not oil in the social machine'. No matter. On 27 December Alan's passport shows a 'pass-poorten controlée' stamp at Antwerp. They were on their way. Yes, but ... as Trevor-Roper related to Charles Stuart, a Christ Church colleague who had worked with him on Intelligence matters during the war,[20] even the comparatively short hop across the North Sea from Harwich to Belgium almost failed to happen.

The problems began before Christmas with what Trevor-Roper called 'the incompetence of the RAC, who lost those essential documents, the *triptych* and *carnet*, without which it is quite impossible (they said) to move a car across any frontier anywhere'. The RAC then closed down over the holiday, 'merely sending us a wire that they would send direct to Harwich for me to pick up on our way abroad'. When Trevor-Roper and Alan arrived at Harwich on Boxing Day, of the *triptych* and *carnet* there was no sign. 'Cold wait on quay as no papers', noted Alan in his pocket diary.[21] Trevor-Roper reported that 'the only advice we could get was to wait five days for the next boat, when a new set would be prepared'.

Trevor-Roper rejected this out of hand. 'In spite of the protests of the Port Officer, I ultimately prevailed (by a feat of diplomacy which I cannot now understand) on the Lading Officer at Harwich to write out an authorisation for "temporary export", on the basis of which we were ultimately able to get the car on to the ship.' Alan added one line to his diary: 'Apprehensively to sleep.' Next morning on the other side of the North Sea fresh problems arose, the Flemish customs officials at Antwerp being 'less easy to talk to, and quite inexorable', wrote Trevor-Roper. No sooner had the Lagonda been winched ashore than the officials 'firmly padlocked it into a necessarily capacious cage; and after a whole morning's argument, they only yielded so far as to agree to release it provided that the sum of £600 was deposited, in Belgium currency, as a pledge of its return'. Quite how Trevor-Roper managed this is a testament to his persuasiveness. He told Stuart that he found a rich shipping magnate who, by touting round his business friends on Saturday afternoon, raised the £600. 'Thereupon the iron bars creaked open and we were able to drive on to the German frontier.'

Alan supplied more detail. 'Pouring rain all day ... Customs trouble. Ghastly drive via Liège to Auberge.' The elaborate political rules that governed the Allied occupation of Germany were nothing if not bur-eaucratic. The travellers had discussed their plans for crossing the frontier the night before over a dozen oysters in Antwerp's Century Bar. Trevor-Roper reported: 'Rightly deducing that no British official would yet be on duty at such an hour, we craftily drove up to the frontier at 7 o'clock

on Sunday morning, having previously taken the precaution of flying a
union jack from the bonnet, thus suggesting the presence of a British
general within ... A few sharp words in German to the German on duty
had an electrical effect on the condition reflexes, and we floated effortless
into Germany.' Alan gave the route: Cologne, autobahn to Frankfurt.
Trevor-Roper's military subterfuge in the American zone got them as far
as the Bohemian frontier, where, once more, he turned on his patrician
manner, and 'thanks to the complete ignorance of the English tongue
which disabled the Czech customs officers from detecting that the details
which I gave them rested on no authority whatever, we slid through the
iron curtain – much I hope to the chagrin of the RAC, who still protest
that we must necessarily be waiting at Harwich'.

If all this seemed like plain sailing, one incident in Bavaria almost ended
their adventure before they reached Prague. Alan summed it up in three
words: 'Crash in snow.' His tutor was more loquacious. 'Veracity compels
me to admit that after a head-on collision with the chauffeur-driven
limousine of the Minister of Labour for Land Gross-Hessen on top of the
snowbound Spessart, no other word is strictly applicable. Fortunately, at
the time of this mis-encounter, we had slowed down slightly from the
optimum cruising-speed recommended by the makers of the car (104
mph) so that the impact was less disastrous than it might have been, and
we inflicted rather more damage than we suffered.' The garage was, in
Alan's view, 'lousy'. Luckily Alan had a camera with him. Finally arriving
in Prague on 30 December, Trevor-Roper thought the city delightful;
'the absence of other travellers makes it particularly attractive'. He also
commented how cheap everything was. Although the bank rate for the
dollar was 48 crowns, he found that he could always get 270 crowns for it
on the black market. Although not identifying Alan, in a PS Trevor-
Roper added: 'you should not deduce from the above narrative any
reflections on my chauffeur. He is above praise.' The details of their return
Trevor-Roper did not relate, but Alan's passport shows border stamps for
both the British and American zones, with petrol purchased at Würzburg,
Koblenz and on 13 January at Antwerp.

In a letter written from Christ Church on 15 January, his thirty-
third birthday, Trevor-Roper remarked that 'Certainly the mere law of
probability could not have found me a more efficient and universally
cooperative driver, or a more tolerant and congenial companion; and
I would not like to seem unappreciative of such undeserved good fortune.'
Trevor-Roper enclosed all the documents concerning the unfortunate
rencontre of 29 December, together with a fair copy of the translation of the

German Minister's confession, which he hoped (with Alan's photograph) would prove sufficient for the insurance company. Trevor-Roper was also able to pass on some especially good university news from a letter which awaited him. 'It says you have passed in French and Latin. As I have now experienced your proficiency in both tongues, this is hardly even interesting and I suppose you have taken it for granted too. I confess that food parcels from two American admirers, being unexpected, caused me more exhilaration.'

If Alan wrote about this adventure nothing has survived. However he did note in his diary of 18 March 1956, when driving a Chevrolet in Germany, that a ridge overlooking a frozen canal with skaters on it 'reminded me of that view of the confluence of the Oder and the Moldau in Czechoslovakia with Hugh'.

Later that spring Trevor-Roper asked if Alan would like to chauffeur him to Italy, where he would be seeing Berenson. Alan refused, apparently less enthusiastic than Trevor-Roper had assumed. Certainly in 1964, when invited to undertake a journalistic assignment in West Germany, he wrote, 'Sounds pretty dreary and exhausting – rather like 1947–8 only with a German photographer instead of Trevor-Roper.'[22] Trevor-Roper left for Italy on his own and wrote to Alan on Easter Sunday from Palermo.[23] 'I hope that you, in the cool and peaceful county of Glos' – Alan was staying at Hiram Winterbotham's – 'which from this stifling and darkened closet I so envy you, are reading some books. I may find that I shall try to insist that you go to someone who knows more about that subject than I do; but if you come back without having read at least that great work Bertrand Russell's *Freedom and Organisation*, I shall, with a sad but decisive stroke of the pen, farm you out to Keble.'

On his return to Oxford Alan found himself being judged by Daniel de Mesquita at the end of the Hilary (Lent) term. 'His work is interesting and well expressed. But too often stops just short of the essential point. In discussion, too, he raises intelligent problems but is always ready to drop them. Should do well when he finds something capable of arousing sustained interest.'

Trevor-Roper, also, with Oxford niceties put to one side, showed no hesitation in identifying his pupil's weaknesses. To Bernard Berenson, who had fast become a friend and correspondent, he confided that he thought Alan took after his mother: 'He isn't a serious intellectual character. Though he likes intellectual company he will never make an intellectual effort, & suffers (in my opinion) from always – in consequence of his family background – having had it too cheaply. The clink of intellectual and aesthetic currency has always sounded easily in his ears, and he has effortlessly spent the small-change of it as if he had earned it. He never will earn any, nor wants to, nor will realise that it must be personally earned.'[24]

Trevor-Roper was unmarried when he and Alan first met. It has been suggested that at this time he was uncertain of his sexuality. A few years later, when Trevor-Roper was courting his future wife, Xandra, via an extensive epistolary exchange, she wondered if his taste wasn't for men, and if that was why he spent so much time in the company of his pupils. Trevor-Roper responded: 'I like (some) undergraduates because they're not deferential, and not for the reason you think; also they're energetic, willing to "rough it", and interested in learning and in experience; all this "makes them good travelling companions".'[25]

Euan Graham had no doubt that Alan preferred girls, but Trevor-Roper he believed to be 'a very suppressed homosexual', and recalls Alan saying that 'he made a pass at him, up in some moor they sat in the hollow together, some laying on of hands, which I am sure Alan resisted'. Graham himself was 'flattered to remember' being asked by Trevor-Roper to go with him to Seville to an exhibition, to which 'my father said "I wonder why?" I can see why his report on Alan would have been especially favourable.' Blair Worden, Trevor-Roper's literary executor, makes no such judgements: 'I think Hugh did indeed prefer the company of younger people to that of his contemporaries. He, who could be so scornful of people's failings, was always indulgent to the failings of youth.'[26]

As Kenneth Clark was now Slade Professor of Art he turned up regularly in Oxford, not that he and Alan saw much of each other. The artist Shirley Hughes, then at Ruskin College, thought K's lectures 'wonderful . . . word perfect. Students flocked to hear him.'[27] Paul Johnson considered him 'an amazing man. He was the best lecturer I have ever heard by far. People who knew him only through the *Civilisation* series don't know how wonderful he was in front of a live audience. I went to two of his series, one on Tintoretto, or Tintorett as he called him, and the other on a person he called Rumbrundt. Both absolutely marvellous. Packed, so difficult to get in. They had charm, brilliance, elocution, oratory asides and jokes. In those days there were lots of very good lecturers at Oxford. A.J.P. Taylor of my college, C.S. Lewis, he was brilliant too. There was terrific competition. K. Clark was far and away in front of the field.' Did he detect similarities between father and son? Johnson, like Trevor-Roper, thought that 'Alan had a lot of his mother in him, but partly also that Kenneth

Clark went to Winchester not Eton. Alan absorbed lots of that Etonian, White's Club, Tory Party braggadocio.' Tony Rudd remembers Alan as 'very sharp, exciting to be with, but you had to get him in a good mood'. He did wonder, though, if he recognised truth.

For his living quarters Alan moved around Oxford. At what Michael Briggs recalls as 'nice digs' in Oriel Street Alan joined various friends, Robin Warrender, Julian Pitt-Rivers and Richard Cochrane among them. He spent some time in Bath Place in a house owned by a Miss Walklett and close to the home of Lord David Cecil, another Etonian and Christ Church alumnus, who knew K. Elsewhere Alan's landlady was Mrs Treece, whom Jane Clark remembers Alan always talking about with great warmth. She was the mothering kind, which was a fresh experience for Alan.

Briggs shared a flat – one of the few with a telephone – in the Woodstock Road with Nicholas Ridley (later a Tory MP and Minister in Mrs Thatcher's government). Alan used to come in from time to time on the pretence of looking for Briggs, but really just so he could ring a girlfriend in New York. This did not go down well, particularly with Ridley, who bided his time, but finally got his revenge, it is said, when he was Environment Minister in the late 1980s. Legend has it that Ridley, having to decide the route of the new Channel Tunnel, instructed his officials to make sure it surfaced as close as possible to Saltwood. It starts less than two miles away.

Ethne Rudd recalls Alan at this time as a complex and sometimes confused person. Had Eton repressed him? He was, she felt, certainly a virgin when he first went up to Oxford, but 'desperate to sleep with me'. Tony Rudd believes that Oxford was his emancipation. It helped that he was perhaps one of a dozen undergraduates who had cars, another being Billy Wallace, the wealthy son of a Conservative MP and Minister, Captain Euan Wallace, who attracted girls in such numbers that they became known as the 'Wallace collection'. (Later he would become a regular escort of Princess Margaret.) Whereas an American undergraduate, Burt Todd, imported a 'huge chrome rich drophead Buick/Oldsmobile', as Lord Ashburton recalled,[28] Roger Pemberton remembered that at one point Wallace and Alan were more sophisticated, both the owners of matching Bristol 2-litre sports cars; they became known within Oxford as Castor and Pollux, the inseparable twin brothers of Helen of Troy.

While at Oxford Alan acquired a Jaguar, a 1936 black SS 100. It was to prove a favourite marque. A photograph shows him behind the wheel, its long, louvred bonnet and huge headlights all very Dornford Yates. The photograph may have been taken soon after he purchased the car as it still has a white border around the coachwork, indicating that it was used in the wartime 'black-out' when cars were driven with minimal lighting. He remembered buying it with funds from a brand-new overdraft at the Clydesdale Bank.[29] In another fragment of motoring memoir he recalled driving it back to Upper Terrace House in the rain, and accelerating on the approach to Hampstead where Fitzjohn's Avenue leaves the Finchley Road. The woodblocks which at that time were the road surface became greasy in the rain and Alan found himself in a spin – a full 360°. He wrote that 'passers-by cheered. That was generous of them.' He never again spun a car – at least right round.

As Europe opened up once more to the British after the war, so the SS 100 was Alan's vehicle of choice. He remembered a race with some locals in Portugal when he 'left the road'. They were driving a brand-new 1948 American Ford and 'very sportingly' towed him out of the ditch. Portugal was the scene of a second race, from Estoril to Sintra, and this time with Nubar Gulbenkian, of all people. Gulbenkian was in the back of a Buick Super, 'with the hood down and a very ornamental lady by his side'. Alan wrote that the chauffeur 'wasn't really up to it . . . Anyway we almost dead-heated to the cathedral square in Sintra.' In Britain around this time he drove the SS100 from London to Skye in a day, 'helped by the midnight sun'.

His SS100, with its snarling exhaust note and one of only 314 built, he described as 'the most *obviously* charismatic of all the sports cars built in the 1930s and 1940s'. At Oxford he kept it in the Morris Garages for 7s 6d a week. Even sixty years after it was built, its acceleration could cope with contemporary traffic conditions, as Alan would testify from personal experience. He called its engine 'understressed . . . completely reliable . . . you have the perfect toy for a rich, but slightly retarded male'. For a time he owned two.

When Euan Graham recalled at Alan's memorial service their first meeting in the coffee shop opposite Balliol College in 1948, a girl and a car were inevitably involved. He was asked by Alan to drive him to Stroud (where Hiram Winterbotham lived) in the Buick Roadster convertible owned by Burt Todd, as it transpired that Alan had lost his licence for the 'relatively trivial offence' of allowing a girl to drive the car while sitting on his lap, leaving him to work the pedals. Ethne Rudd says Alan also 'impressed many a girl' who did not realise that the car he was driving was often borrowed from a garage on approval for 'a test drive'. Contemporaries recalled him in different cars in widely varying hues – one was bright yellow and another bright red. Even with petrol rationed in the 1940s Alan managed enough coupons to roar up and down the A40 between Oxford and London. Ethne remembers the first time he took her to Upper Terrace House, she was told to go on ahead while he parked the car. The front door was opened and 'there was Lady Clark in a passionate embrace with M. Massigli, the French ambassador'. She told Ethne, 'you go and wash your hands'. Massigli pretended he didn't speak English.

Ethne felt that Alan was still insecure and uncertain of himself. One way he showed it was by being uneasy about going into a hotel where he did not know the staff. Did this have something to do with growing up in a home run by servants? He was, she says, mean in small ways, like standing a round of drinks – yet could be generous, but never quite knew when to. In Oxford he used to eat at the George, and sign the bill 'Malcolm Napier'. At one meal the trifle was so awful that rather than complain he simply put it in his jacket pocket.

While at Oxford, probably in 1948, Alan organised a holiday to Portugal with Milo Cripps, later Lord Parmoor, David Tennant (then eighteen and at Eton), and Ethne. Their destination was his favourite Sintra. At that time strict exchange controls meant that the maximum sum an individual could take out of Britain was £25, which Ethne handed over to Alan. They drove in a Lincoln Continental, stopped in Paris and at Bordeaux ate in Le Chapon Fin, where the three-Michelin-star food was so good that Milo licked the plates.

In Spain they ran out of money; also sterling was in crisis, which did not help. Milo suggested 'let's sell Ena'. It was a case of 'Who knows who? Who can we phone?' Alan was shy of using the family friendship with Gulbenkian. Then a man in a restaurant coughed up some petrol money. They drove on, but the border into Portugal was closed with tank obstacles. Alan was finally persuaded to contact Gulbenkian, who got the chief of police to remove them. The sight of these young Britons in a huge American car so impressed the mayor of Bragança in north-eastern Portugal that he gave them a grand dinner, where Milo recalls they all drank too much and behaved less than generously to their host. In Lisbon Alan went to thank Gulbenkian. Then finally on to Sintra. The holiday's adventures continued with Milo being arrested in a nearby resort for aggravated indecency because he had worn bathing trunks with no top. The charge was 'aggravated' because the local police had already explained to the party that it was illegal not to cover the top half of the male torso and he had gone along the beach and round a headland where he thought no one could see him.[30]

In preparation for his finals in 1949 Alan joined a winter reading group at Wengen in Switzerland – 'a great success in so far as a lot of work has been done as well as a lot of skiing', he told Trevor-Roper in a letter.[31] He said he adored skiing, but was no good at it. He also suffered a cracked ankle bone as a result of falling over at about 40 mph, and told his tutor that he now hobbled about 'using the lift and generally being senile'.

In Alan's final year at Christ Church one of his tutors, J. Steven Watson, highlighted weaknesses in Alan's character: 'I confess I cannot agree with the unanimous opinion ... that he is a man of considerable intelligence with minor faults he may yet correct. I found him a man of many prejudices and little energy. He has a jaunty way of refusing to see awkward facts or arguments. Instead of thinking he tries to grasp at any generalisation that is extreme enough to be indefensible. Then he need only reiterate instead of having to defend it.' To Hugh Trevor-Roper in 1960 Alan remarked, 'Yes I must come to Oxford this term. I have avoided it on account of its unhappy memories – *how* I wasted my time there.'[32]

Alan, like his contemporary, another future Conservative politician, Edward Boyle, graduated with a Third, much to the disgust of his mother, who was always quick to find fault. Only later did Alan, Celly and Colin discover what degree she had left Oxford with two decades earlier.

Twenty-five years later when Alan, now a successful historian, was first invited to appear in *Who's Who*, his entry makes much of his Territorial experience – Household Cavalry training regiment and then the Royal Auxiliary Air Force 1952–4 – but nothing more. Colin put forward a theory in his memoirs, that on coming down from Oxford and following his mother's goading, he first offered himself to the RAF, but they turned him down saying that according to their records he had done his National Service in the Household Cavalry! If inquisitive journalists had dug deeper this might have proved a fertile field, particularly when Alan was a Defence Minister from 1989 to 1992.

As he ended his time at Oxford in the summer of 1949 a card reached him from the local office in Reading of the Ministry of Labour and National Service. Registration CCK30204, addressed to Christ Church, informed him that according to the National Service Acts he was obliged to submit to a medical, and offered an appointment: 1.15 p.m. on Thursday, 16 June, at St Michael's Hall, New Inn Hall Street, Oxford. If he was called up he would receive a further notification giving him at least fourteen days' notice. 'You should accordingly not voluntarily give up your employment because you are required to attend for medical examination.' He was also asked to bring his glasses.

This sounds as if all along his National Service had been deferred, whatever he said. But what happened next is unknown. If the National Service rejected him, perhaps it was due to poor sight? As a child he had been prescribed glasses in order to see the Egerton House blackboard; in his twenties Celly recalls that he was still so short-sighted that when there was a girl about he would ask, 'Is she pretty?' But if his sight was the reason he would never have been accepted by the Royal Auxiliary Air Force the following year. In any event none of his friends remembers him using poor sight as an excuse.

Without a doubt the experience of Oxford, regardless of his lack of academic achievement, gave him the maturity he had previously lacked. Renata Propper, studying samples of his handwriting from 1950, has no doubts. 'Oxford must have done a good job, giving him some confidence and polish, stirring his ambitions. He has started to harness his considerable intellectual abilities, learning skills, directing them more consistently towards his high aspirations. His talent, his education and social status propelled him to the forefront, but how does all this translate into concrete achievements? While we know that he achieved a lot, the handwriting tells us that he was not really satisfied.'

Propper, however, believes, unlike Trevor-Roper, in Alan's intellectual capabilities. 'Articulate and perceptive, his talents point towards a writing career. He had flair, a certain conservative creativity, and the ability to express himself with elegant language. A man of some brilliant ideas, he was more of a thinker than a doer, although he had some enterprising spirit and motivating ambitions.' She also detected weaknesses. His 'ambitions were not sufficiently backed by strong resolve and toughness, therefore often exceeded his natural potential'. Propper identifies from his handwriting that this lack of resolve and toughness generated stress. She concludes: 'He lacked the driving force and the methodical discipline of his father.'

Once more this would be borne out a decade later by his work as a historian.

SEVEN

America and Possible Careers

Alan came down from Oxford in the summer of 1949. As early as 1945 his parents had been saying that he ought to do something safe, like read law, but Alan wasn't sure what he wanted. As for a roof over his head, he lived 'all found' in London at Upper Terrace House.

Where the idea came from is unclear, but Alan had often thought of social work, particularly with young people. In Alan's post-university vacuum his parents asked their friends for suggestions. One who responded was the poet John Betjeman. During a vacation in his first year at Oxford Alan had been taken by Betjeman to a boys' club at Yarnton, the home to the north of Oxford of 'Colonel' George Kolkhorst, an Oxford don in Spanish with less than wholesome sexual proclivities. He was known as the 'Colonel' because, according to Betjeman, he was so little like a colonel.[1] Today there is no way that Kolkhorst would have been allowed near boys let alone run a boys' club. Betjeman, however, often stayed at Yarnton, it being close to Oxford. The artist and caricaturist Osbert Lancaster later remarked that Betjeman 'liked large girls and the Colonel liked small boys'.[2]

In a letter to K – they were friends of long-standing – Betjeman suggested 'a *temporary* solution for Alan. You say he is a Christian and likes adventure. Why not get him to stay, if he does not do so already, at the Trinity Mission or any other mission in [the] slums of London, Liverpool or Glasgow. All the adventure possible, all the outlets for energy are there. Also one gets first-hand evidence on crime. Also the regular, almost monastic life in a mission house, is a sure steadying effect and stabiliser of true social sense. I tried it myself for some months at the Magdalen Mission after leaving Oxford. It was valuable to me. I remember how marvellous Alan was in the Boys' Club at Yarnton which he visited for about two minutes, joining in *boxing* – the greatest asset for a "social worker" – with terrific success. If you approve the idea, I will get a mission to write to him and ask for his help. It's in the jungles of our barbarism at home that most adventure lies.'[3] Nothing was to come of the suggestion, but Alan did not forget; in spring 1950 he told Trevor-Roper that he was working at a youth club in London's East End,[4] as late as Christmas 1956 he was still mentioning the possibility of becoming a youth leader, and the following summer he took part in, of all unlikely gatherings, a communist youth congress in Moscow.

The Clarks had taken a family holiday in 1949 in Venice. Part of a letter from K survives in which he mentions that they were joined by Hiram Winterbotham, that Mama, who had been ill, went bathing at the Lido daily and that Colin (now seventeen) was becoming 'a well-known local character . . . a boulevardier'. With post-war exchange control regulations still in operation, money was tight, although K also had a legitimate business allowance based on researching and writing a lecture on the painter Bellini. However, the deficit 'more or less righted itself' thanks to a 'notable contribution' from Alan's friend Malcolm Napier. Alan later recalled that Napier received a telegram saying he had failed 'schools'* and they went off in an Austin Sheerline to Yugoslavia.[5] The rest of the family stayed on.

Back in London, K continued to represent his son's interests, witness this diary entry by Cynthia Jebb, whose diplomat husband Gladwyn Jebb was about to become permanent British Ambassador to the United Nations. The Jebbs gave a dinner shortly before Christmas 1949, which had its origins in K telling Gladwyn at their club that Alan was interested in Yugoslavia. The Jebbs therefore invited Fitzroy Maclean, who knew President Tito, to meet him. 'Except that the champagne was uncorked with the loudest of reports, like birthday guns going off, the dinner was a good one.' On Alan, however, she did not mince her words – 'an ambitious, opinionated young man'. As for his parents, 'K and Jane are both hard nuts who could do with a crack, though Sydney [daughter of K's friend Sam Courtauld] says that when K is without Jane he becomes at once a much nicer person.'[6]

With no clear idea in New Year 1950 of what he would do, although he was beginning to try his hand at writing about cars and motor sport, Alan now took himself to the United States. Today this might be called a gap year, even if it did take place after rather than before university. If one believes what he said in an interview with Ginny Dougary in The Times forty years on, he had fond memories of the experience: 'one of the happiest years of his life . . . an anonymous "limey" in America, working as a waiter during the day and sleeping on the beach'.[7] Alan added that

* University as opposed to college examinations.

part of the freedom was that 'no-one knew, or cared, that he was the son of a distinguished man'. In a note compiled in 1954 for a CV, he wrote: 'I was also in the USA for six months as a "bum" in the course of which I drove a truck, worked in a road gang in Alabama and was employed for a season as a "bell-hop" in a luxury hotel in Florida. The only incontrovertible fact which I learned from my US experiences is that, as Ogden Nash might put it, "it's a bore to be poor".'

These memories, however, are at odds with what he wrote at the time in letters to Hugh Trevor-Roper. By February 1950 he had crossed the Atlantic and was in Venice, Florida, his tone suggesting he was not enjoying the experience. He tells his former tutor that he arrived in January with the intention of travelling and earning his living. He had the family Lagonda 'to carry me about' and a 'sinking fund' of $400. Alan relates that the Lagonda 'exceeded its worst Central European form and cost me over $200 in repairs in the first two weeks'. In a motoring article forty years on he recalls having to drive it with the bonnet open all the way from Washington DC to Orange, West Virginia, and leaning out of the driver's window with a jack handle to tap a sluggish fuel pump every forty seconds or so.[8] He then put the Lagonda back on a ship for England. The overall expense left him with $26.83; he had done not a stroke of work and described himself as 'a humbler, slightly forlorn hobo, in an old jersey and carrying one grip and a rolled-up sleeping bag'.

Without an unreliable car to worry about he found work and earned a living. He even managed to save $30. Not that he paid all his bills. Evidence surviving at Saltwood points to unsettled accounts with RCA and the American Cable and Radio Corporation for cables and long-distance telephone calls. He admitted that he could not pretend it had been 'an entirely or even mainly enjoyable experience', but it had been 'highly educative', not least in his view of the United States and Americans. 'I confess to finding the population slow witted and doltish, their customs primitive and tedious, their food expensive and unappetising.'[9]

In his next letter Alan gave Trevor-Roper a graphic description of the American way of life. He had moved a few miles north from Venice to another Florida resort, Sarasota: 'Life here is awful. The prospect everywhere depressing. Myriads of luckless businessmen, unable in this torrid climate to conceal their disastrous bellies ... parade cackling, guffawing, backslapping along great acres of snow white sand. A naturally perfect beach is ruined by the continual deposit of holiday sediment. Strata upon strata of discarded Dixie [paper] cups, empty Coca-Cola bottles, comics, Kleenex tissue, paper towels and sundry newsprint are left untouched and festering by the unbelievably corrupt city administration.' If that was not enough, his diatribe continued, influenced perhaps by Trevor-Roper's caustic views, 'The unattractiveness of the population is heightened by their complete uniformity. All the men in any given age group are completely interchangeable and equally worthless. The women, too, are alike in style, appearance and mannerisms. This is not the result of unconscious impulses – they positively do <u>try</u> to look like one another.'

Enough of Americans. Trevor-Roper must have then turned to Alan's beliefs and future. Alan responded forcibly. 'I don't know why you think I will take to religion. It is one of your ideés fixe, but wrong.' Within a few years – as his diary from 1955 shows – he had made a volte-face. God, prayer and devotion would become an important part of his life.

Alan moved to less controversial matters, reporting to Trevor-Roper news of his Oxford contemporaries. 'I get distant whinnying from the herd: migrations are beginning early this year for most of them are now down, and, not having anything to do <u>at all</u> decide to pick up a little culture and sun tan. Spain is a favourite objective. They can't stay abroad for very long though, as they are insufficiently competent in their black market money arrangements, relying, usually, on a vague spoken word from an American undergraduate or a tiny dago at some 2nd class embassy.'[10]

Alan stayed in the United States for little more than three months. His next letter[11] to Trevor-Roper showed signs of relief at his return: 'Long may the Atlantic stand between us and barbarism.' But his tone is now infinitely more cheerful. 'You will be amused to hear that the American expedition has done my prestige a lot of good. The cry "that young fellow's got guts" is much heard.'

What follows is unexpected. 'I am training to be a young Tory.' He had just missed the February 1950 general election when the Conservatives had clawed back Labour's massive lead in 1945 to single figures. Now he told Trevor-Roper, 'This is a full-time occupation and involves periodic attendance at parliament and the accumulation of such data as current affairs, reading of white papers etc.' He added that the *pièce de résistance* occupying most of his time was research on the international socialists, 1864–1914. But I can see you making the Trevor-Roper gesture of dismissal, that flap of the right hand.' However he insisted he is 'very serious about it all, and a lot of people are serious about me, which helps'.

A further surprise followed. 'I have a bedroom in Oxford because I do not like living at home and I cannot bear London under any circumstances, so I commute in a car, transatlantic fashion, three days

a week.' With petrol still rationed one wonders how he managed it.
His renewed stay in Oxford led to a significant purchase at City Motors
in Oxford on 18 November 1950. For some time he had been following
in the motoring press the development of a new model of Jaguar, the
successor to the SS100, the XK120. Now he was an exceptionally
proud owner of one. In the years to come he never tired of extolling
its virtues. As he wrote in 1996, he doubted if there were many people
who still owned a car they bought forty-six years ago. 'And I would
bet money that in no case is the car an XK120.' In austerity post-war
Britain it was remarkable, 'so soft and silky; the power just went on
and on pouring out'.

Alan did not absent himself from London for long. His serious interest
in politics was but a passing fancy (at least until the second half of the
1960s). Having agreed with his parents' suggestion that he read for the
Bar (at one point joining another future politician, Ian Gilmour, and his
Oxford friend Michael Briggs at the crammers Gibson and Weldon off
Fleet Street), he lived 'quietly', he told Trevor-Roper, 'doing a large
amount of work at the Bar, which I find both interesting and enjoyable.
I take my first exam ahead of schedule, on 4 December.'[12] But how many
other law students of the early 1950s drove an XK120 into the Inner
Temple, and 'raspingly sharpened up the lawyers' aural senses'? He used it
to cross Europe to Monte Carlo (where Pam, a girlfriend, was dancing
with the London Festival Ballet) – 'it seemed to be the only XK in the
Principality and made (I don't doubt) a pretty mixed impression carving
round the streets at all hours with three and sometimes four dancers
squeezed into the front seat. Coming up the hill from the harbour you
could just peak in second before braking for the Hotel de Paris right-
angle.'[13] Nor did he sell the SS100. Here was the beginning of his
collection of cars, a collection that would swell down the years, invariably
outgrowing any garage accommodation Alan could provide.

Officially he was undertaking law studies, but he kept allowing cars to
distract him. Much of Alan's early writing was for motoring magazines.
Some correspondence survives from the summer of 1947 – Alan was not
yet eighteen – when he congratulated the editor of *The Motor* on the high
quality of his magazine. The editor responded to this enthusiasm. 'We
would be delighted if you would care to write to us from time to time on
the various topics mentioned.'

In 1951 he wrote to Mr Kyd, Editor of *The Motor*, asking him to publish
his article 'British sports cars are obsolete'. He hoped this would bring

reactions ('They usually rise like young salmon to this sort of thing') from two leading manufacturers, John Aldington of Frazer Nash and Sydney Allard, whose J2 model with Cadillac motor, he reminded Mr Kyd, was third in the previous year's Le Mans. Alan showed off his expertise: 'If it had had a Cadillac gearbox, it might have done even better, but I have a hunch that that was its high water mark. The Cadillac is a wonderful motor with 92 square inches of piston area.'

At one point Alan thought of racing a specially modified Jaguar in Mexico in the Carrera Panamericana, which from its beginnings in 1950 on the country's open roads rapidly built a reputation as a thrilling, but hugely dangerous sports car racing event (in its original form it was stopped for safety considerations in 1955). By this time Alan was writing for an American magazine, Road & Track, which he had 'bamboozled' (his word) into appointing him as its European correspondent. In 1952 they gave him the go-ahead to write a piece on the Carrera Panamericana from behind the wheel. Alan talked Jaguar into modifying his XK, with – and he spared no detail – 'a special engine, light flywheel, cylinder head, cams, big carburettors, a short-shafted competition gearbox with wonderfully close ratios, a multitude of short-shafted chassis improvements, club, torsion bars, rear springs and a forty-gallon fuel tank'. In the end, embarrassing Jaguar in the process, he 'chickened out'. Perhaps this explains why a letter he drafted to Sir William Lyons, Jaguar's chairman, asking about job prospects with the firm, was never sent.

Alan's growing reputation as a specialist writer meant that when Rover produced their experimental gas turbine car in the early 1950s, Alan wrote 'the first complete road test'. Over three pages, with photographs showing him at the wheel and wearing a white fur hat, he admitted that he had never experienced such a thrill, that the acceleration was 'quite fantastic', and after several columns of technical details, concluded 'Altogether a memorable day.'[14]

Alan coupled his work for Road & Track with a commercial venture called Autextra. Road & Track, he confessed, was valuable to him more for the free passes to Le Mans and other events than as a money-earner (they paid three cents a word, 'pocket money' he called it). Autextra cashed in, as he had forecast when writing his article for The Motor, on American enthusiasts' need for European extras that could be added to their home-grown production-line cars. Special gear boxes were a favourite one year. On the letter heading Alan was listed as a director, along with, for a time, Peter Blond, the younger brother of Alan's Eton and Oxford contemporary, Anthony Blond. Peter was as keen as Alan on cars and racing.

In the 1980s, when he ran a specialist division of Sotheby's which dealt in classic cars, Alan was a director.

He also began trading seriously in cars, initially in 1951 from Warren Street off the Tottenham Court Road, where Bernie Ecclestone, who would become the chief of Formula 1 motor racing, also worked. Charles Howard, who moved into cars from antiques, recalls that Alan 'loved Warren Street'.[15] In the 1950s it was where dealers cashed in their part-exchange cars. Alan was a useful contact; he knew graduates and under-graduates with perhaps a couple of hundred pounds to spend. A good traded-in vehicle might prove just the car they were looking for. For Alan this led to buying and selling cars as a means of augmenting what he saw as his insufficient income from a Clark family trust. But some purchases proved irresistible and would be kept, at least for a time. Since purchasing his first car while at Eton he had become extraordinarily knowledgeable about the finer points of cars and down the years would become totally absorbed tinkering with his ever-changing collection. (He collected cars in the same way as his parents did pictures, Jane Clark recalled, but 'they did not see them as art'.)[16]

Anthony Blond had become one of Alan's close friends. Blond had left the family firm (which made underwear for Marks & Spencer) to become an author's agent in 1952 and then a publisher in 1958 (and would publish Alan, but only once). In his memoirs he tells a number of scabrous stories about Alan at this time.[17] If Blond is to be believed Alan was the villain ('an all too accurate portrait') in The Blackmailer, the first novel by Isabel Colegate, who had been Blond's business partner in his agency and later married Alan's Oxford friend Michael Briggs. She, however, vigorously denies this.[18] Kenneth and Jane Clark had sold Upper Terrace House in 1953 and were moving to Saltwood Castle in Kent, but Alan wanted a London base. At one point Blond took a short sub-lease on B5, the Clarks' apartment in Albany, Piccadilly. 'At Home' cards were printed in their joint names, but Captain Adams, Albany's secretary (Blond describes him as 'sour'), disapproved of their partying and their guests (Alan's girlfriends often stayed overnight). Later they moved briefly into a house Blond owned in Netherton Grove, off the Fulham Road and opposite the incinerator of St Stephen's Hospital.

Alan, meanwhile, kept up an erratic correspondence with his former Oxford tutor. Alan thought of him as a friend. So what should we make of the following extract from a letter Trevor-Roper wrote in 1953 to his future wife, Xandra? 'Late last night I was visited by Alan Clark, Kenneth

Clark's son, once my pupil, now an unemployed *roué* in the smart-crooked sub-world of the metropolis. (Really the Clarks are awful! It is entirely and obviously due to their upbringing that the children are all going to turn out quite worthless.) Well, Alan Clark, whom I deplore, seems devoted to me – rather in the way of a weak-minded rake who every now and then goes to confess, with exemplary piety, to a grave, respectable old priest.'[19] Correspondence over the next three decades suggests that Trevor-Roper actually had a soft spot for Alan, whatever he did or wrote.

There would be hectic times ahead, and then he met a young dancer with the London Festival Ballet.

EIGHT

First Love and the Law

If girls first entered Alan's life at Oxford, he met his first true love two years after he graduated and in his first year reading for the Bar.

Pamela Hart was eighteen when they spied each other in front of a Thames-side inn. She was a classically trained dancer with the London Festival Ballet. Alan was twenty-three and busy doing very little, although he had agreed, reluctantly one suspects, to acquiesce to his father's wish on a law career. In the next four years they were enormously close. There would be girls aplenty after Pam, but no-one meant as much to him until he met Jane Beuttler, who would become his wife.[1]

Pam recalls her first meeting with Alan as if it were yesterday. Born and brought up in Harrogate in Yorkshire – her father was managing director of an electrical engineering company – she trained at the Arts and Education school at Tring in Hertfordshire, where from the age of twelve she learnt all kinds of dance, not just classical. One Sunday afternoon in June 1951 she was cycling by the Thames with Judith, a school friend and also a London Festival Ballet dancer, when they spotted Judith's aunt and uncle coming out of the restaurant of the Bray Inn. They were swiftly followed by a suave, good-looking young man and an elegant young woman. She remembers that as they walked over to a car he put on dark glasses.

Judith and Pam got on their bikes to return to Judith's home not far away. The young man and young woman, they were to discover, followed in his car, but initially they went the wrong way as Judith and Pam had turned left. 'Then we stopped, I genuinely had a fly in my eye. Suddenly a car drew up; it was the young man, who came across to me, introduced himself and said, "You are the most beautiful woman in the world".' This was Alan and the woman turned out to be Celly. 'He's all right,' she said. Pam recalls thinking that the car must be his father's. 'Then Alan asked me for my name and my address. I just gave it.' It was a seminal moment for Alan – in his engagement diary he circled the date and wrote 'see Pamela for the first time'. Next morning there was a letter from him.

Pam had recently joined the London Festival Ballet, a company created by Anton Dolin and Alicia Markova in 1950 with the forthcoming Festival of Britain in mind. As Pam was dancing six nights a week her first meeting with Alan – he was always Alan to her, not Al – had to be lunch. This was on the following Friday, 8 June. The Festival Ballet was based that year at a barn of an old theatre, the Stoll, in Kingsway (now rebuilt as the Peacock). On the day in question Pam did not know what time she would get away from rehearsals of *Prince Igor*. The choreographer eventually said they would finish late, but the company would not be required again after lunch. Alan, she recalls, didn't appear concerned, just sat languidly outside the theatre in his car. Pam's fellow dancers had helped her with clothes, 'they kitted me out, including high heels – not me at all. I didn't feel pretty.'

Alan took her to Le Caprice, then as now a top London restaurant. 'He told me what I would eat – vol au vent and chips! And to drink he ordered me a "White Lady".' This cocktail of gin, Cointreau and lemon was completely new to her. 'I had nothing to say; I was tongue-tied. I just couldn't make any conversation.' After lunch, into his car and across the Thames, probably to Richmond and a drive through the park before returning via Hampstead and Upper Terrace House. 'I live there', he said nonchalantly. She thought it 'magnificent'. Finally he drove Pam back into town, just in time for the evening performance of *Prince Igor*. 'I was so late everyone thought I'd been abducted.' Pam later heard back via a mutual chum that Alan had said 'She's a pretty girl, but is she dumb?'

Whatever he thought of Pam's conversational skills he had no hesitation about immediately asking her out again, and she about accepting. His diary entry for Sunday, 10 June: 'Pamela down to Oxford.' The following Wednesday, they went to Battersea pleasure gardens. It was clear that Alan was smitten; he could not see enough of her, as his diary records. Pam's feelings for Alan were more complex. She had been in love with someone else and at first would not so much as let him touch her. But with the London Festival Ballet continuing to be based at the Stoll Theatre it was easy for them to meet regularly. By mid-July they were sleeping together – Alan circled each occasion and her initial in his diary.

So began their relationship, which became serious to both of them. Pam was different from the young women Alan had met at Oxford. She was true to her Yorkshire upbringing, being down-to-earth and standing no nonsense. She was also self-supporting financially. Each January, if she could get time off from the dance company, she would go with Alan to Switzerland. On one occasion they drove across France to Zurich in his

XK Jaguar. 'Incredibly cold and great roaring winds,' he recorded.[2] Some photographs from this period survive, including one of them dancing together in a Zermatt bar. In another, she has just won the title 'Miss Zermatt' and was encouraged to get up on the stage and dance. After some quick thinking she persuaded the band to play 'I'd love to get you on a slow boat to China' and danced, she recalls, in the musical comedy style of Jessie Matthews On returning to England to work, Pam would receive letters and postcards from Alan, who stayed on, ostensibly to work at his writing. Typical were photographs of the two of them that had been turned into postcards: 'God, who's that <u>divine</u> little number dancing with that awful man? What a waste, she only looks about 16, too. Love xxxxxx "awful man".' A card to his brother Colin shows three girls frolicking in the snow, one of whom was Pam – 'Zermatt improved if anything as you can readily see,' he wrote. 'Bring new Kingsley Amis.'[3]

Alan was very self-conscious about his looks, she recalls. In the alpine glare his eyes reduced to slits, which, combined with his broad, high forehead and his thick hair swept back, led him to complain of an oriental look, hence his comment to Pam on a picture of him skiing: 'That well-known figure, the balding chinaman'.

She noticed a number of other character traits. He declared his love; he was always honest (even telling Pam when he had been seeing other women). In her hearing he never lost an argument. She also remembered: 'Never put him down' – and wonders if anyone ever did? He was the boss, which suited her: 'I like my man to be in charge. It's tribal, it's natural.' In one letter, from the Empire Theatre, Liverpool, she remarks on a spell they spent together in Bath when Alan was 'very sweet and we didn't even have a slight quarrel'. She mused about this: 'I think it's only when I haven't seen you for a long, long time that we quarrel and then it's due to nerves and excitement.'

Alan would sometimes call Pam 'Bluebie', a nickname which started in the bar of White's Club in Oxford where they met an American who remarked on Pam's blue eyes. As well as Celly and Colin, Pam had by this time got to know and like many of his friends, including Michael Briggs and his wife Isabel, and the Blond brothers, Anthony and Peter. A Zermatt postcard addressed to Peter, showing Alan and Pam in deckchairs, is inscribed: 'Film stars on holiday, rather!'

Little more than a year after Alan and Pam's first meeting the Clarks decided to sell Upper Terrace House and buy Saltwood Castle, near Hythe in Kent, for £28,000. Before the sale they turned down an offer of £53,000 from Charles Chaplin who, thanks to the attentions of the

McCarthyites in the United States, wished to return to England. The Clarks' London apartment at Albany had the old maid's quarters in the attic, which Alan quickly adopted. Pam remembers this well as she often stayed overnight. When Captain Adams, who had administered Albany since 1930, discovered what was going on, he made it quite clear to the Clarks that he did not approve of her staying there and Pam was 'thrown out'.

Saltwood was less to Pam's taste, simply 'too large'. She was often a visitor, being billeted in a turret room, she recalls. Staying there made her nervous, giving her stomach cramps. Once she had Sunday supper with all the family. It was a buffet with a whole salmon. K motioned her forward to help herself. This being the early 1950s, and even though rationing had come to an end, many choice items were not widely available. 'I don't think I'd seen a whole salmon before,' she recalls. She hesitated, but remembers that neither K nor Alan stepped forward to guide her, a point of manners which still rankles. 'I simply picked up the servers and cut across the middle of the salmon, through the bone and all.' If the Clarks as a family looked on askance, all she remembers is Kenneth Clark saying, 'That's a bold stroke, my dear.' The family now took their turn, each delicately easing away pieces of salmon in the approved manner.

As for Alan's writing, which at the time she knew him was mainly fiction, she was never convinced. 'I didn't think he really meant it.' She was with him as he struggled with short stories and drafts of his first novel. When, long after their relationship had ended, this was eventually published as *Bargains at Special Prices*, she was 'not very impressed'. She told him that he should be writing about what he knew, particularly history. All this time Alan was meant to be studying for the Bar.

The London Festival Ballet mainly toured, but Alan had a habit of turning up unannounced at a stage door. Otherwise they kept in touch by post. Pam reckons Alan wrote at least one hundred letters to her, but in a clear-out at her parents' home her mother burnt them. However Pam's letters to Alan have survived, a box full, with other later ones slipped into his first narrative diary. They reveal just how widely travelled she became, including annual seasons in Monte Carlo, which coincided with the Monte Carlo rally – like Le Mans, a fixture at the time in Alan's calendar. Not that Pam was that interested in cars. One particular tour meant missing the anniversary of their first meeting by the Thames – 'just think of me and I will think of you too,' she wrote. 'What a shame we won't be together for it, but we must have a little celebration when I come back.' As neither ever stayed in the same place for long, her letters to Alan would often have to be forwarded. As part of his law training he worked as a judge's marshal on the south-east circuit, as an aide-de-camp to Mr Justice Hallett. The envelopes containing Pam's letters are like a gazetteer of Alan and his judge's progress.

In the early 1950s being chosen as a judge's marshal had a certain cachet, even with Mr Justice Hallett, who – if one was being generous – was viewed as a character, although he was not widely liked. Half a century later Lord Hoffmann (a Lord of Appeal) knew of Hallett's reputation not for the quality of his judgments, but as a man who couldn't stop talking.[4] Alan toured with him in 1952 and by Christmas had regaled his father with the experience. K went on to tell a friend, the American Supreme Court judge, Felix Frankfurter. As a result Alan was commissioned to write 'a Lytton Strachey portrait'. He took Frankfurter at his word, describing Hallett as 'an enormously selfish man, "selfish" in the most comprehensive sense, that is mounting to egomania'. He was also short-tempered and in Alan's view could be extremely rude.

Alan combined his profile with a report on an Appeal Court decision in which the Lord Chief Justice quashed the conviction of the accused on the unusual grounds that the defence counsel's speech was continually interrupted by Hallett, the trial judge. At the time Alan accompanied Hallett, 'this formidable machine' was sixty-six, 'a tall, stooping man with long thin legs and a large stomach of which he is not ashamed'. Alan confessed that he had admired Hallett at first, but 'finally grew to dislike him quite strongly', even if he enjoyed his periods in court with him. As for his propensity to talk, Alan recorded that Hallett was 'extremely fond of his own voice because, one feels, it is His voice, and must therefore be talking sense at least on any subject'. 'As a bore, he is rendered the more formidable by a prodigious memory which allows him to recollect, with unfailing accuracy, the smallest detail.'

Six years later Hallett experienced further criticisms in the Court of Appeal, which led the Lord Chancellor, Lord Kilmuir, to take the rare step of asking for his resignation. By then Alan had long abandoned any thoughts of practising at the Bar.

While the rest of the country was celebrating the Coronation of Queen Elizabeth II in June 1953, Alan sat his Bar exams – and failed. K wrote from the Arts Council offices at 4 St James's Square (he had become its chairman that spring), that the news, which he only discovered from *The Times*, did not cause him 'much surprise (or resentment) as you didn't seem to have been working up specially for it'.[5] K went on in that letter to think of Alan's career: 'Although you have done so well in journalism it is rather a precarious occupation.' He looked forward to seeing something of his son — 'we must try to arrange a short expedition together'.

Alan decided to retake his Bar finals in June 1954. In an undated letter from the Hôtel de Crillon, Paris, where his parents were staying, Mama warned him about 'overwork just before your exam ... we shall be thinking of you and hoping the papers aren't too unlikely and depressing'.[6] But he failed again. Pam told him, 'you do nothing but chase girls'. The family, however, oozed compassion. Mama sent a postcard: 'Saltwood will cheer you — the future is long and this won't matter soon. Poor darling Alan — I have failed many exams in my day so couldn't sympathise more. Come home as soon as you can — all we want to do is to help you as we may. No despair and no recriminations.'

Mama, as she had shown in the past, was surprisingly far-sighted: 'Probably you don't want to try the bar again, but you may decide to and not practise and meantime follow a different career. I think it is a help to have a bar degree. However we hope to see you soon and hear your conclusions — you must come home soon and tell us what you think.' Alan, however, decided that Zermatt would provide the necessary balm for his wounds, not least his pride. Papa wrote to him once again from St James's Square: 'It is terribly unkind of fate that after all your hard work this spring and summer luck should have turned against you.'

Alan decided on one more attempt. Pam was about to go to the United States with the Festival Ballet and remembers him saying that he did not care about the law, having been offered a job on *Motor Sport* magazine. 'I was very firm. I told him, "no, you're not taking that. You must take your finals again."' His tutor, by happy coincidence, turned out to be a Mr Hart. Pam returned to Britain in the luxury of a transatlantic liner. On 8 December 1954 she wrote to Alan from Harrogate saying he sounded 'rather depressed — how do you feel now that your exam is over? Relieved I suppose. One week today and I will be with you again. I am looking forward to it so much because except for that one day it has been ten weeks which is longer than any other time we have been apart ever.'

Awaiting the results meant five weeks' nail-biting. Pam had a postcard — Alan is photographed on the slopes above Zermatt moving downhill: 'caught in the middle of a turn, I'm afraid, hence the style looks awful. Also making a face — the tall unrecognisable chinaman, rather! But the big news is I PASSED BAR FINALS!! M & D very pleased.' And surprised — Pam remembers that he had not even told them he was retaking the exams. Telegrams came first. Colin, on behalf of himself and Celly:

CONGRATTERS OLD BOY – TWINS'. Papa and Mama's was traditional: 'LOVING CONGRATULATIONS PERFECTLY DELIGHTED AND FULL OF ADMIRATION – PARENTS'. Not surprisingly, letters followed. Mama gushed: 'We couldn't be prouder or more excited – I can't help it if you find this letter embarrassing!'[7]

Papa's was more formal, but for once the pleasure and the affection at his son's success shine through: 'You have done splendidly, my dear. To keep yourself and to do the work for the Bar must have involved a heroic effort. I must say that both Mama and I have been much impressed during the last months by the helpful, thoughtful way in which you have contributed to family life. We have been really grateful; and I can see that in fact you were making a great moral effort, which affected everything you did. I must say it didn't seem to be making you unhappy. Well, you have certainly deserved your present holiday, and I hope it continues to go as well. All my congratulations, once more, dear son, and may it be the beginning of a long ascent.'

Would he now practise as a barrister? The question of a job, with a regular income, at times obsessed him, but his attitude seems to have been that of his mother: that it was good training, 'a good discipline' as he noted in his diary forty years later,[8] but as a career it was not for him, although Pam remembers that his pass led to an undisclosed job offer. His obsession with cars was another matter. Pam recalls him once again thinking of the motor industry as a career.

By 1955 Pamela was being paid £20 a week at the London Festival Ballet, or, as Alan pointed out, £1,000 a year. His income at that time from a family trust was £10 a week, although his wheeling and dealing with cars and accessories brought in extra sums. He was also playing the stock market, with mixed success. She knew he was a gambler, but he never managed to emulate even a fraction of his grandfather's success at Monte Carlo. One night he lost £40. 'I was so cross. I'd never seen £40.' Pam did, though, confess in one letter to Alan from Monte Carlo – he was in Zermatt – that 'we've all been gambling like mad, and so far I'm just about even. I keep thinking of you.' She even tried Alan's system (picked up in Walton Street, Oxford) of 'doubling upon a dozen', but lost £5. 'If we had just had a little more capital we'd have won a terrific amount as it came up on the last go.' Although she too remembered him as mean when it came to paying his round, he was always prepared to loan money to Pam, and equally 'I always paid him back'.

Alan's brother Colin was, she says, 'quite different'. She got to know him when he was in his final year at Oxford and she was on tour, incidentally getting him a walk-on role in an Arabian Nights ballet, *Scheherazade*, and helping, she thinks, to propel him into a theatrical career. They met again in Paris when Colin was working for Laurence Olivier. A London Festival Ballet season there coincided with Olivier and Vivien Leigh appearing in their triumphant production of *Titus Andronicus*. He took her to nightclubs such as Maxim's and the Crazy Horse. 'With Col it was no expense spared, unlike Alan – money no object.'

Alan did not appear to see contraception as his responsibility. For women in the early 1950s – before the pill – it was still primitive and unreliable. Half a century later it seems remarkable that it was Alan's mother who organised these matters for Pamela. A little more than two years after they first met Pamela was in Cardiff with the London Festival Ballet when she thought she might be pregnant. Alan arranged for pregnancy analysis at a laboratory in Great Portland Street – no over-the-counter test kits in 1953. He gave his name as 'Dr A.K. Clark'.

Pam recalls that he drove to Cardiff from London with the test result in his pocket. 'We're going to have a baby,' he said. Pam was pleased, and then he went on, 'but we don't have to.' She remembers more than fifty years on that she was only nineteen, naïve and had her career to think about. In a letter to Pam that Alan never sent, but which resided for years in an rusty steel filing cabinet in Saltwood's archive room, he wrote:

> Dearest Pam – need I say that I have spent the whole day in a blue panic! On the other hand I kept thinking to myself that it must be all right as I don't see how it can have happened. Every time I get worried I promise to myself not to do it again, as you know, and you always make me. I don't know, I'm in a terrible dither.
>
> I got a little extra money from Autextra the other day and I thought we might slip down to Switzerland for a very short little tour, but of course all this makes it impossible to think. If only it comes alright we must go abroad to celebrate. But what we will do about love-making I just don't know. I can't bear these panics, they literally make me sick.
>
> I've been thinking about it all day. You know I feel we can't, mustn't stop it again. And yet it would be so awful for you and what about your parents?
>
> I suppose we could keep it from them if you came to live in London, but then what about the ballet? You would have to stop dancing after a bit and you couldn't start again for months.
>
> And then what about it?

Alan's next sentence is revealing:

We'd have to keep it if it was a baby boy.

This is a fine way to go on after my saying that 'it <u>must</u> be all right', I know, but just the way I'm thinking.

I know Bluebie. I am a cad for not asking you to marry me. Please forgive me for that. No-one is nicer or sweeter or more lovable or means more to me, and everyone knows that when I see your photos on all the presents you've given me I want to cry. But I just think how solemn those marriage vows were when I went to Michael's [Briggs] wedding and the Parson who confirmed me told me never to marry a girl immediately because she was going to have a baby and I think it would be a mockery if we had a rush marriage after all this.

I'm afraid all this is a meaningless ramble and reflects very badly on me.

Please forgive me for everything Bluebie and whatever way this ends I will stand by you.

all my love xxxxxx Alan[9]

In the end the Clarks organised everything. In those days it was necessary, if an abortion was to be legal, for the patient to be seen by two psychiatrists. At nineteen, consent had to be given by an adult. Pam remembers she had gone in to see one of the psychiatrists with a view to saying she was 'nearly twenty', but she got in a tangle and made herself out to be younger than she actually was. In the end Alan's mother signed the consent form. Her parents never knew. She went into the Bentinck Clinic near Harley Street to have the abortion. An undated letter from Alan's mother has survived – she was writing from the Wentworth Hotel, Aldeburgh. 'Hope you enjoyed Le Mans and have good news of P. on your return. Sorry I couldn't get in to see her again on Thursday before I left.' The pleasantries over, she became stern. 'In case you see P. before we see you I assume you will only behave as a <u>friend</u> until you and I have had a further talk – which won't be possible till Thursday when I hope we'll all have an evening at home.'

Thirty years later Alan showed how his views had changed over what he called 'convenient' abortions. In an 'Extremely Private' letter to Hugo Young, then a *Sunday Times* columnist, he had no hesitation in describing such abortions as 'sinful'.[10] As a newly appointed junior Minister in Margaret Thatcher's government, he was writing to Young – a Roman Catholic – in response to a column he had written about sex discrimination.[11] This followed Alan's controversial presentation of the Equal Opportunities Order to the Commons (see Chapter Twenty-five). Alan explained his position: 'You hold strong views on discrimination, whether racial or sexual. I don't. I know that the strength with which one holds views can lead one to impute a moral stigma to those who don't agree or worse, oppose them and my own experience in this regard is relevant to what happened last week.' He had twice sat on the committees of Private Members' Bills attempting to reform the law on abortion: 'sat all night, all week, that is while those dreadful women (the same gang) have filibustered the thing to pieces. I don't know whether you talk to your priest about this. I don't recall you writing on the subject. But if you will allow me the strength of feeling here which you yourself undoubtedly feel on discrimination, you will more easily understand how I enjoyed getting level with the Medusas. The subject may have been different, but the enemy was the same.'[12]

When Jane Clark first heard of Pam's experience it became clear why her husband held such strong 'pro-life' beliefs. These were not to dim. In a later diary entry he doesn't mince words in a reference to a Private Member's Bill to reduce the maximum age at which babies could be 'legally murdered from six months to three'.[13] Pam's abortion remained on his conscience. Nearly twenty years after the event he wrote again in his diary about still dreading retribution being visited on his sons. 'Filled with remorse and sadness for Pam and the aborted child.'[14]

Their relationship now became more up and down. For her twenty-first birthday party in October 1953 Alan gave her a present from Asprey's, a scatter pin chosen by Peter Blond, who was always fond of her. Alan drove her home and then said, 'I think we ought to part.' Pam burst out crying. 'How could you possibly say you loved me and say that?' Indeed. 'He'd turn up like a bad penny, as if he'd never been away.' Pam remembers saying, 'Alan, this can't go on.' But they were soon back seeing each other. Before Christmas 1955 he wrote in his diary of Pam: 'I wish I could love her and marry her and be "settled", with at least half of me I wish that.' By April 1956, while speculating on the stock market and hoping to make a killing, he wrote: 'And then perhaps I could marry dear Pam.'

Pam remembers when Alan moved to Rye in the summer of 1956. One Sunday evening they went to a local cinema. A gaggle of schoolgirls sat behind. Thinking back, she wondered if Jane was perhaps among them? On another occasion she had arranged to visit Alan for the weekend. After the Saturday evening performance in London she rushed to Charing Cross Station to catch the last train. Alan was due to meet her at Hastings, but when the train arrived there was no sign of him. Then he appeared around the corner. 'I just wanted to imagine I was seeing you for the first time,' he said.

Why Alan finally decided to end the relationship is not clear. Certainly he did not have the nerve to do so to her face. Pam responded by registered post to Rye. 'My dear Alan – your letter didn't come as a great surprise to me and yet it still managed to hurt me a great deal, mainly because it was cold and to the point. Also because you must have felt that way on Monday morning and it would have been less cowardly to tell me straight away – you know I have got past the stage of crying and making scenes now.' With the letter she returned a Cornish pisky which Alan had given her. Pam ended: 'He did his job very well and I think I will be more free without him.'

Unfinished business remained between them. In autumn 1956, the Soviet Union allowed its Bolshoi Ballet Company to visit London. Alan arranged tickets, but this was before the final break-up with Pam. She now addressed the situation. 'I do so want to see the Russians as it is too wonderful an opportunity to miss. Please don't ask me not to come because I need not even see you if you wish, I can meet Celly in the foyer before the performance if she has the tickets. If you don't want to write again Celly could let me know when to meet etc for the ballet. All my love always, Pamela.'[15]

Alan was embarrassed, as his diary entry testifies: on 3 October he refers to 'a sad encounter with dear Pam, real Pam. It is firmly in my mind and although trivial in detail had the stamp of finality and is too painful to record.'

NINE

Words, a House and More Words

Alan loved writing from an early age. Although his parents hoped for a safe job for their often difficult elder son, when he came down from Oxford he really wanted only to write. At that time his style was stilted, not that this mattered in the one area where he had any success: technical articles on cars and motor racing, 'which I can always sell when I can be bothered to sweat them out'.[1] What he wrote about cars in those days was worthy, rather humourless, but full of knowledge – he had a young mind's ability to assimilate information very quickly.

In the autumn of 1950 on his return from roaming the United States, as a sideline he decided to try writing fiction and began with short stories. He thought crime fiction might be his forte, and also westerns, where he could draw on his knowledge of America. Sometimes he used his own name, for others he devised pseudonyms: Louis Dellatrez Brand for romantic crime, and Lane Ford for westerns. Although his parents had given him his first typewriter while at St Cyprian's, Alan wrote his stories in longhand and then handed the manuscripts to a Hampstead typewriting and duplicating agency, Sybil Rang and Ap Simon. In the age before photocopiers and computers the Rang-Simon agency would have manuscripts immaculately typed with as many carbon copies as were legible.

For inspiration he used to read *Argosy*, a short-story magazine. Well-thumbed copies survive at Saltwood. On the back cover was sometimes an advertisement: 'How to succeed as a writer'. To Alan, it seemed like a lifeline. Although many ambitious writers looked askance upon correspondence courses for training – little better, it was thought, than vanity publishers – the Regent Institute was no fly-by-night, having been in business for more than thirty years, helping, as its literature put it, 'new writers . . . to make the most of the profitable openings in writing for the press'. Alan wrote asking for further particulars and received the standard cyclostyled reply. All Alan had to do was submit a story and his cheque for the course and back would come a critique, suggestions on how it might be improved and potential markets he might try on both sides of the Atlantic. But Alan did not respond – and struggled on with his writing.

With his parents selling Upper Terrace House and preparing to move to Saltwood Castle, Alan for a time adopted as his poste restante 114 Wigmore Street, which was also the home of the Autextra business and the London office for *Road & Track*. In the autumn of that year he corresponded with Panther Books, an independent publisher of genre fiction – crime, science fiction and westerns – which published directly into paperback. Most of its titles were priced at one or two shillings and would be found on railway station bookstalls, the larger newsagents, but rarely in bookshops. Panther knew its markets and, given its rock-bottom fees, was constantly on the lookout for new writers. Alan had been attracted by the firm's circular, although to his surprise he learnt that motor racing novels were not to include sex. Feeling sure they would not apply that principle to crime stories, he now enclosed the opening and synopsis for *The Man Who Wouldn't Know.*

Panther Books responded by return.[2] Fashions were changing and what they now wanted were westerns. 'It seems you have style', they wrote, 'that could be adapted to western writing, and we wonder if you would agree to submit to us a Western novel of 47,000 words.' Their rates were £1 per thousand words for all rights. Alan no doubt thought £47 a poor return for the work involved, as there is no evidence that he wrote the novel. In the United States at this time, according to the Regent Institute, 'regular' westerns were paying between $10 and $40 a thousand words (£3 10s and £14), with *Collier's* magazine at the top of the market offering $750 a story.

Alan, though, did nothing further until January 1954. With only motoring journalism producing regular commissions, he was now desperate. Remembering the Regent Institute he wrote an apologetic letter. 'I am afraid I proved singularly idle as a pupil, completing none of the exercises nor answering any of your letters ... On the other hand I did read the lesson and I have been grubbing away on my own, partly because I enjoy writing, largely because I want to commercialise any latent talent that I may have.' He enclosed a short story, 'Choice of Victim', one of several Lane Ford westerns, and asked for criticism. 'How bad is it? How do I put it right? Could it sell, and where?' The Regent Institute responded with a detailed critique of his story, which his instructor thought was 'certainly worth trying, after a little revision'.

At some point in 1954 he sat down and composed a *cri de coeur* about his writing ambitions. 'I am 26 years of age,' it began. 'I have not yet devoted myself full-time to writing, tho' I have been keeping my eyes open and have collected a good deal of story material. Inspiration of one kind or another has floated down over the years, but I never seem to work this into a coherent, saleable entity. Occasionally I like writing things because they amuse me, or because I think they might sell (they never do).' He referred next to *Road & Track*. 'But now I must try and write quite seriously for I do not propose to end my days as a career motoring journalist, I am not getting any younger, and if it is established that I really *can't* write then I must look round for an orthodox job.' Alan continued: 'I know that authors often go for years without adequate recognition – poor Proust carting round the huge manuscript of *Du Côté de Chez Swann*, Henry James trembling in the wings of *Guy Domville*[3] – but in my case, being ill-read and a sensational rather than an intellectual author, I must hope for earlier results on a more commercial basis, to give me confidence.'

Alan was also corresponding with a second organisation, the grandly titled British Institute of Fiction-Writing Science Ltd. Only one letter survives, its notepaper weighed down with two governing directors, a business manager, a secretary and the name of the controller of studies and head examiner, Martin Walter. Alan now submitted to Walter a short story under the *nom de plume* of Louis Dellatrez whose speciality was for mildly sexy crime fiction. In 'She Made Me Wear Breeches', the wife of a wealthy businessman sleeps with the attractive young chauffeur and then together they decide to murder the husband. It was not alone among Alan's stories in being set in a thinly disguised Upper Terrace House, complete with chauffeur's cottage and its own petrol pump, ('a pretty Queen Anne house set behind a mellow brick wall. One could see the upper windows from the street, but the ground floor and the goings-on in the garden were hidden from view'). Martin Walter was tactful in his criticism.[4] He thought it 'an effective fiction', with the writing reaching 'quite a high standard at times'. However, he identified a fault, not uncommon, known as 'author talking', which in more modern parlance might be summed up as 'telling not showing'.

For a long time Alan found it difficult to talk to his father about his writing. K was, nevertheless, encouraging and in an undated letter (probably in the early 1950s) written from the Villa Mauresque at Cap Ferrat, the home of the writer Somerset Maugham, tried to be helpful. 'I needn't tell you, dear Al, how happy I am that you at last feel able to show us some specimens of your work. I always expected that they would be good, but they are far better – more gripping ... more professional. Now what you need is to gain confidence in your own ideas.'

Early in 1955, in a wide-ranging thank-you for Alan's Christmas letter from Zermatt and after a page worrying about Colin's drinking and Mama not being well, K mused further on Alan's writing. 'I hope that the wares you intend to market on your return include some general articles and stories. You are a born writer, and you really mustn't let that advantage slip: it is much rarer than you think (if you don't believe me, read Celly's articles).'[5] On another occasion K goes into considerable detail about Alan's writing, particularly an 'experimental story', which 'comes close to doing what you outlined to me as your aim over a year ago'. He could see 'where your gifts lie ... not in sympathetic character drawing, but in the direction of the evocative macabre'. He admired Alan's ability 'to convey the mounting horror of a situation through strange natural phenomena'. K's one concern was the denouement, which had to be told 'without disclosing the source of the fear'. Alan felt that at last he was being treated as an adult.

On his twenty-seventh birthday in April 1955 at Zermatt, Alan began keeping a regular diary. Whereas his earlier diarising had been haphazard, he now wrote regularly, sometimes daily, but more often once a month. Entries would usually begin on a right-hand page, with the location and the date. He wrote fluently with very few corrections – he had inherited his father's talent for clear thinking.

From the start it was a real journal. Reading the first volume as he gets into his stride one wonders what prompted him – and for whom. At the most mundane it is a record of what he was doing, his investments, cars as well as shares, but that's just the beginning. Alan soon used it as a comforter, a confessional and an opportunity to ruminate on his thoughts and his beliefs. Many an entry ends: 'Thank God'. Given that girls play a significant role, does he, perhaps, see himself as a Casanova? The entries show little sign of inhibition, which suggests that he never thought that anyone else might read it. When he meets Jane Beuttler, the nature of his writing quickly indicates the seriousness of the relationship.

Alan's manuscript diaries would continue in many forms. At first he used some rugged loose-leaf ring-binders, bound in blue cloth.* The paper was plain and all these years later its high quality is obvious, hardly a brown tinge at the edges, even if the rust on some of the metalwork of the hinges is witness to where the diaries languished for many years (in a drawer in the first house he and Jane bought, Town Farm at Bratton-

---

* The first extant diary – blue, cloth-bound National Loose Leaf Ring Book, of approximate A5 size – covers the period 1955–8.

Clovelly in west Devon). When early in 1972 he was upset that the ring-binders had gone out of production, he turned to an heirloom. He and Jane had only just moved into Saltwood Castle, where in the library he discovered a visitors' book, bound in crimson-lake leather with the single word 'Katoomba' stamped in gold on the front. His grandfather had given the name to three of his steam yachts, but this volume had been barely used.

After Katoomba he found a hardback A4 notebook, with lined paper and each page numbered in red. Thanks to its binding it was known as 'the black book'. The A4 format became his standard, as a succession of lined-paper notebooks of the kind used in government departments testify. The paper, though, was coarse and he named the first one 'horrible "austerity" book'. As for pens, he now tended to use whatever was closest to hand – but green, as he noted on 4 June 1999, when recovering from major surgery: 'Green ink! Originally reserved for holidays (Zermatt or Eriboll).'

On entering the House of Commons in February 1974, the diary soon became his prop. He would be seen scribbling away in otherwise boring committee meetings, the uninitiated thinking he was taking minutes. But word soon got round. Each volume was marked REWARD IF FOUND, and Jane recalls only one occasion when one was mislaid, and returned by a civil servant. The level of reward was not mentioned. His writing rate increased, particularly when the Commons was sitting. Politics never dominated, except during a spell where he augmented the manuscript volume with entries dictated to his secretary. Otherwise the familiar mix continued: Jane and his family, money (never enough!), girls and cars, the outdoor life, playing backgammon for money (until the 1980s) and, rarely absent, the state of his health.

His diaries, as with his published books, show how the quality of his prose improved. Even when under considerable pressure, professionally or privately, he kept writing. If the current volume was not to hand he would use his day diary or own parliamentary notepaper, very occasionally stapling the entry into the appropriate place. Alan maintained that, on completing an entry, he closed the notebook 'and seldom turned to that page again'. One wonders whether a rereading prompted him to remove pages from the back of his 1992–3 diary. The chronology is not affected, but the period coincides with an infatuation that was preoccupying him.

When did Alan begin to imagine that he might one day publish extracts? A clue comes from late 1979 when, safely back in the Commons with a majority doubled to 11,000, he started adding putative footnotes. Diarists rarely do that unless publication beckons. In an unpublished entry on 18 February 1983, he wrote, 'Over the last two or three years at any rate, I have assumed that these diaries would be published at some time – though this has never, in the slightest degree I believe, moderated the spontaneous rage, greed, slyness etc with which I have recorded my feelings as events unfolded, my hopes and apprehensions, judgements and (often wildly wrong) predictions.'

To return to 1955 and his writing. Style concerns him. At one point he starts writing 'she has that fantastic ...' then strikes through ~~fantastic~~ – 'I must try and avoid this awful *loose* choice of words'. He asks himself whether it is better to write 'precisely and risk in reconsideration to allow the escape of fleeting recorded thoughts which may never come again to the surface, or write slackly, hotchpotch, as they bubble out'. He then provides his own answer: 'Possibly, the disciplined mind records everything in orderly fashion, files automatically so that nothing is lost. Hugh's [Trevor-Roper] journal, if he keeps one, would be like that.'

In May he was in Ischia: 'This evening is wonderful. Conditions are perfect and at the golden hour of 6.30 I feel it all inside me again. The words come rushing out. If I could only be like this every evening I know I could produce something. I must read more in the daytime and study technique.' On 2 June – 'almost too ashamed to recall the last ten days. Real decay, like "let it come down" – not a stroke of work done (one good idea). I get more Paul Bowles every day.'[6]

Back at Saltwood he was in self-flagellatory mood. 'It is no good kidding myself, really get going as if in Hart's chambers all over again. I've got to work about ten times harder, really get it going. As I lay in bed last night I listened to the water music, thought it *could* be done. Real perseverance ... lucky to have germ of a gift, which I know is there.'[7]

On 23 October 1955 he referred for the first time to a novel, which he calls *Guilt Edged*. He admits to being spurred on by Kingsley Amis, whose first novel *Lucky Jim*, with its 'angry young man' hero Jim Dixon, had been an instant hit the previous year. Now Amis published as his second novel *That Uncertain Feeling*. Both books had sexual frustrations on the part of the characters with which Alan identified. But the more he read the more he also wished he could emulate Amis's satirical gift. Perhaps he could do so in *Guilt Edged*, he thought. He had listened to the view of Pam, to write about a world he thought he knew something about – in this case the Stock Exchange. For advice he had the knowledge of friends such as Tony Rudd, who had married Ethne Fitzgerald and was making a career in buying and selling stocks and shares. He also had an idea for a plot with all kinds of shenanigans.

In the new year, 1956, he stayed not at Zermatt but with the family at Mürren, at the Palace Hotel. Work had so far 'found no place in the regime' of skating, skiing and girls. He showed his parents a story about a girl and a gypsy and 'was surprised and delighted by their reception, which was very good'. Confidence returned. 'I haven't been happier for years – certainly not for a year when I passed my bar finals.' But, typically, it did not last. He and his father had been in correspondence about writing. Now on 28 February from the Cafe Burgener, a favourite Zermatt hotel, he typed a note to K (whose sentences were usually immaculate). 'I find that once I start to think of grammar I become so nervous that I can no longer put pen to paper. It is like thinking about your feet when running down stairs, or the phonetic oddness of words generally, when making a speech.'

Papa had presumably been cautioning his son about submitting his work. Alan concluded: 'I agree with you about bombarding editors. When you come back from the US we will have a look at the armoury and decide on the targets.' In England in April Alan gave his father two stories. K responded: 'I read them with great admiration. Your power of telling a story is most unusual and in each of them the crescendo of fear and horror is splendidly done.' He then proceeded to offer 'a few criticisms or, rather, suggestions'. Alan should stop writing about Americans 'for the time being'. He found the dialogue 'becoming too stylised – "Christ, jeez, scram" etc'. Papa thought that as it was a while since Alan had been in the US his ear had forgotten some of the cadences; he had relied on reading – 'art made out of art leads to mannerism'.

K continued with a larger criticism, that 'what your stories need is more direct experience. In your very proper determination to get away from piffling reportage, you have gone too far in the opposite direction.' He thought 'Mr Benedict's Motor Drive' a 'very masterly affair, without a false note (by the way those elliptical descriptions of the repulsive Americans are rather too rich)'.[8]

Alan was disappointed, confiding to his diary that his father's letter was 'only a medium reception, although I feel "Mr B" is really v good – the best I can do at the moment, and Col loyally takes this view also'. He now dispatched 'Mr B' and two further stories to John G. Murray, known to all as 'Jock' and the head of K's publishers, John Murray. Like all publishers Murray was snowed under by submissions. He did, however, respond on 9 May, with a letter of rejection, but with helpful comments, not that

Alan saw it this way, preferring to describe the letter as 'bolshie'.[9] The stories, thought Murray, were written 'more with intellect than with the heart or with feeling'. He suggested magazines he might try, but to no avail. The rejection letters mounted up.

That first volume of his diary recorded another significant moment, when he first became a homeowner. Encouraged by Papa, he started the search and in early April 1956 found something he liked in the hill town of Rye, not too far from Saltwood. This was No. 11 Watchbell Street. K now wrote, 'Great news about your cottage. I have always wanted to live in Rye, and if it is not actually collapsing I should close with it.'[10] K was in London, but would be returning by train the following day. 'If you and Mama will meet me [at Sandling Station] in the Bentley, we can motor over to Rye immediately.' Alan, meanwhile, was having doubts about 'the expense and angst of moving in', when he could be 'quietly soaking up the sun in Ischia'.[11] The purchase price was £1,800. 'Dad finally came across with £2,500 and the workmen are working away there now.'[12]

The name Watchbell is unique in English towns. Given Rye's position overlooking the English Channel, it was an ideal vantage point in Napoleonic times when an invasion by the French was feared. A bell was hung at the west end of the street and would be rung if the worst happened. The stuccoed No. 11, with shallow-bowed windows on three floors, originally had an 'L-shaped' garden and a back entrance that could be reached from a lane running to the west. Perhaps forty minutes' drive from Saltwood, or less if the level-crossing gates that crisscross the A257 from Hythe were not closed, Rye was admirably placed for a bachelor, far enough from home for Alan to assert independence, but still near enough for mundane matters such as laundry or seeing his family over Sunday lunch.

Alan rapidly adopted Rye. He would own several houses there, but it soon brought about an event of far greater significance that would transform his life: meeting Jane Beuttler. His writing had also freed up. Perhaps it was the keeping of a regular diary that did it. Although he did not stop writing short stories, he concentrated more and more on the novel *Guilt Edged*. By late autumn, he wrote that he must finish it before going to Zermatt after Christmas. In January 1957, at Zermatt, 'the more I feel it could be a success. I must have its back broken by February.' At the end of February he was fantasising on a favourable reception for *Guilt Edged*, to give him the financial wherewithal for an American trip.

Alan already had a second novel under way. Called *Summer Semester*, it owed something to Evelyn Waugh's *Decline and Fall*. With his own hypochondria 'rumbling' he looked forward 'to working in these wilder hypochondriacal fantasies'. He desperately needed to earn money. If he were to visit Ischia again that summer he had 'to sell something'. A rhythm of work was essential and he vowed to get what he called Etonian time-tallies. 'Nothing less than 1,000 words and two hours typing a day.'

And before long the idea for a non-fiction book erupted in his mind. Alan's primary period as a writer was over. The apprentice years beckoned.

TEN

Meeting Jane

Jane's first sighting of her future husband was at long range. She and her family were picnicking on the beach at Camber, a couple of miles south-east of Rye. 'I remember seeing this person walking along in the distance with this huge dog behind him, a great dane. I remember this person mincing along, I remember thinking I don't think I've ever seen anyone with such a conceitedly pompous walk. That was the very first time.'[1]

It is not clear whether Alan also noticed Jane that day. It was almost certainly mid-August 1956, Alan having neglected his diary for more than two months as a result of a visit to Italy and then France. On 26 June, probably at the behest of his father, he had dined at I Tatti in Florence where Bernard Berenson was celebrating his ninety-first birthday. He then travelled to Antibes, ostensibly to work on *Guilt Edged*. By the time he resumed his diary on 6 September Jane was already at the centre of his thoughts and for the next eight weeks his entries are devoted to her, to the exclusion of just about everyone and everything else. Not since Pamela Hart had one woman so consistently captivated him.

Jane was the only surviving daughter of Bertie and Pam Beuttler. Bertie, or to give him his full name, Leslie Brindley Bream Beuttler, was a regular Army officer who had by 1956 risen to the rank of Colonel. He and Pam, who married in Malta in 1937, when she was only twenty-one, also had two sons, Mike, the older, and Nick, who was sixteen months younger than Jane. The Beuttlers had a second daughter, but she died in infancy. Not long after the Beuttlers married they were transferred to Aden, where Bertie contracted polio. Everyone assumed he was going to die, a coffin was ordered, but slowly the crisis passed. The only sign in later life showed itself when he was tired – 'his left eyelid would droop'.

By the second half of the 1950s Mike was away at boarding school, Jane and Nick being educated in Rye. Indeed Jane says her education was not brilliant because of the huge number of schools she went to. 'I was just not meant to be a learner. I failed all the exams to get into an Army school that girls go to so they decided I might as well traipse around with them and the boys went to boarding school and came out and joined us wherever we were.' Every time Jane's father was posted she would miss a year or so and when they returned to England and she met up with her friends, she found she had missed what they were doing and had to start all over again.

At one point in her childhood, Jane and her brothers accompanied their parents to Malaya, where the British Army were endeavouring to put down the communist insurgency. During this posting Jane learnt to swim. 'We were all out there. I remember quite well snakes falling out of trees. That's when my brothers said they were going to pinch some cigarettes in those lovely round metal drums they used to have. I must have been about nine I think and I remember they lit one, but no-one told me what to do so I can't tell you how much I choked, I presumably just sucked in. I have never smoked since. Which is very, very effective. Give children a cigarette at a very early age, but don't tell them what to do.'

Jane was sent to a convent, which was 'absolutely horrible, a Catholic convent. You had to bend down and say your Hail Marys and the nuns used to pinch your cheeks in that special way when they twist it. You weren't allowed to have a bath or shower unless you still had your shift on, even though we were all girls.' The convent was upcountry. 'I remember we were taken by escorts – you had to go by escorts because of bandit trouble. On one occasion I arrived a day early from half-term. I made them take me back. They were a bit uneasy because they had been told to drop me there, but because I was the Colonel's daughter they couldn't actually say you're staying. I made them drive me back with this armoured escort. My parents were absolutely furious, then had to arrange for the escort to take me again the next day. I wasn't going to stop there longer than I needed to. I don't have happy memories of Catholics.' Despite the convent, it was, she recalls, 'a very happy time', even if 'you don't appreciate being abroad, do you, when you're young? You're not into plant life or vegetation, you're just a child.'

Back in England, her father was sent to work at the War Office, 'which he absolutely hated – hated being cooped up. He was a soldier not a deskman. He hated the War Office, which meant he was confined like an animal.' In the early 1950s the Beuttlers had bought a British house as a permanent base. Rye in those days seemed reasonably cheap. Now when the family returned on leave they no longer went to Downton in Hampshire, Jane's maternal grandmother's home near Lymington, where all Pam's children were born in the same first-floor room. If Rye's houses generally appear huddled together, theirs, Jeakes House in Mermaid Street, stands out, being double-fronted, with, in the Beuttlers' time, a blue-painted door. Jane's and Nick's bedrooms were in the eves, reached by a ladder. When they were abroad the house used to be closed up, rather than rented out.

Alan had only recently moved into Watchbell Street, parallel to Mermaid Street, and barely a stone's throw away. Jane remembers the distances seemed very small. She can still recall the summer evenings before they were married, when there wasn't much traffic and she could hear 'the wonderful note' of his Jaguar XK120, from probably halfway across the marsh. The note would change as it hit the cobbles at the bottom of Mermaid Street and then there would be 'the slow rumbling roar' as it passed the Beuttlers' on its way to his house.[2]

Even though Alan knew Jane was only fourteen and therefore half his age, the diary makes it clear how rapidly she became his sexual obsession. According to the law of the land she was a minor, a point that Alan would worry about right up until her sixteenth birthday. In the diary entry for 6 September he is quick to make up for lost time: 'This is very exciting. She is a perfect victim, but whether or not it will be possible to succeed I can't tell at present.' He has been seeing Jane, he writes, for two and a half weeks.

Now even his prose was affected. 'Our first contact when I slid my fingers between hers when we held hands walking back across Rye Green after dinner the day we took our first walk by the lakes.' It was still the school holidays and although Alan had promised himself that he would work on his novel, his obsession with Jane excluded just about everything else. 'For about a week we would walk in the afternoon and end up at the island where I would kiss her hand and stroke her neck and calves. Finally there came the high point so far, as one lay by the shore of the little promontory, out of the wind, and I studied her high thighs through her thin yellow striped summer frock, and she, half mesmerized, pretended to retaliate by pricking my face with a thistle.'

In his diary update of 6 September he is not slow to record developments. 'She comes straight to Watchbell Street in the evenings. Coming through the back door, but as she only stops for about five minutes it has not been possible to make much progress. I have mismanaged it a bit in the last two days, going neurotic after she told me that two people had tried to kiss her before.' Jane thought him 'absolutely super'. Looking back at herself she says: 'My natural thing was flirting. Just flirt, it didn't mean anything, just the way I am. It got me into trouble.'[3] Alan was, as he wrote, 'a bit afraid of her mother clamping down, or worse, catching us one evening on the sofa at my house. Already there is gossip.'

In the 1950s Rye, rising on a hill from the marshes on the southern Kent–Sussex coast, was made for talk. The town's handsome church was, and remains, the centrepiece, the clock tower's gilded pendulum swinging mesmerisingly over the chancel. With few tourists, just about everyone knew everyone else, tending to meet at the Union public house which was like a club. It was still possible to visualise E.F. Benson's memorable characters, Mapp and Lucia, from forty years before, and based on people he knew in Rye. He, like Henry James before him, lived at Lamb House off Church Square.

Jane did not keep a diary, yet half a century on she has a special reason for remembering the detail. Of that first sighting on Camber Sands and south towards Dungeness (where now, thanks to the Ministry of Defence's firing range, it is no longer possible to walk) she recalls: 'There was this click – Al used to say later that I had magic powers – it sounds absolutely dotty if you mention it, a voice inside me saying "that's the man you're going to marry" and it was most extraordinary because at fourteen I was so not into the opposite sex, not into anything like that.'

If these were magic powers they ran in Jane's family. Her grandmother, who used to do the Ouija board with the writer Dennis Wheatley, had it, she says, her mother also: she literally saw people, refusing to join Jane at Saltwood after Alan died, because she said there were too many people there. 'I said what do you mean, only Lëhni and me?' 'No, no. No, they're not, very seriously, they're not. I can see people and there're too many people.' As a young girl Jane was already aware of this family trait so although her extraordinary feeling on Camber Sands was peculiar she knew it had to be taken seriously, even if she was to tease Alan dreadfully before finally agreeing to marry him. Their first meeting? 'I think it happened as it does with everybody who has got dogs.' Her Labrador, George, had a reputation in Rye for wandering up the street, knocking over milk bottles and then drinking the milk. The Great Dane she saw with Alan that first time was owned by Colin; although his real name was Marshal, he was usually known as Big Dog or Plato.

In his diary Alan provides soundbites, of what he called 'the serial', as to how his relationship progresses: at the beginning of September, 'Flower show, she blushes, hug on leaving.' Jane thinks that he was much keener actually on another girl, Pat, who also lived in Rye and was 'an incredibly good pianist. Bit like Sophia Loren. Big cheeks, sensual mouth.' Unlike Loren she had sensible swept-back hair. Jane used to go round to Pat's home in Church Square and knock on the door. More often than not she would be rebuffed. No you can't see her, she's practising, she would be told. Hours and hours and hours; her ambition was to be a concert pianist.

By the second half of September the relationship with Alan was becoming serious. Bertie's Whitehall job kept him in London during the week – the Beuttlers rented a flat in Greycoat Gardens, SW1, which Pam particularly liked as it was close to the Royal Horticultural Society's halls in Victoria; being a keen gardener she would go to its fortnightly shows. In Rye, Jane's younger brother Nick started to follow them around. Alan was convinced this was at the behest of Jane's parents, who, understandably, must have been worried at their fourteen-year-old daughter going out with an attractive unmarried man twice her age. Worried? retorts Jane at the suggestion. 'They were absolutely furious.' As for Alan's age, she says, 'he behaved more like he was twelve, he was permanently juvenile'.

Alan's frustration leaps off the pages of the diary. Jane was so attractive in every way, he wrote, but when he tried to assert himself she continued to be resistant. Alan recounted the dialogue:

'I'm sick of you,' she said.
'You don't want to see me again, then.'
'Not much, no . . .'

Did she mean it? Alan drank beer and waited till 10 that evening, 'but she never came – perhaps because there was a thunderstorm. Slept badly, kept thinking she was coming.'

Towards the end of September, a development in her father's Army career changed everything. 'TERRIBLE NEWS of their impending departure to Malta. Oh God.' That Sunday Alan was invited round to Jeakes House 'for drinks with her Ma'. Bertie was not at home. 'Went quite well and then met her Ma again in Tradesmen's Passage after waiting for her for a long time. Got on well.'

On 4 October Alan resumed his diary after a week's absence. He now related interesting, even intriguing developments: 'I do know that in the last few days of the last week in September I was thoroughly depressed and felt Jane was completely lost. On Thursday her mother came round at 1.30, when I was just about to begin a fish lunch, with *Miss Mapp* [E.F. Benson's 1922 novel], I offered her a drink, and finding there was no gin we opened a bottle of champagne (I, jocularly, having heard she was fond of drink).'

The moment was nigh for the Beuttlers to leave for Malta. An air of melancholy coloured Alan's brief account of Saturday, 6 October. 'A last walk and hug. She was wearing Hugh's coat and Col had gone back with

Big Dog. The tide was coming in fast and we were out of the wind with the sun on us. Then to Saltwood to lunch and back in time to take her to the station.' As ever Alan fantasises: 'She would almost have run away with me.' And then the farewell: 'We didn't kiss goodbye, but she waved till the train was out of sight.'

Alan kept busy – and occupied – for the next six months. Jane's departure, though, struck home, giving him 'a bad period of depression and *accidie*' – the Clark hypochondria. He did, though, discover the 'beneficial effects of thinking on to the typewriter, particularly in clarifying and reviving interest in *Guilt Edged*'. But he was 'still very frustrated, almost like early days at Oxford with the bells striking in the damp evening air'.

It would have been untypical of Alan if Jane's departure meant he had lost all interest in the opposite sex. In his diary he described driving from Saltwood through Hythe on the way back to Rye 'very much on heat this morning'. He mentioned a string of girls, but 'in each case momentary distaste overcome by retrospective consideration'. His mind, though, also turned to writing. 'I had an agreeable rush of thoughts last night as drafted a rough for "The Lehdo Clinic" for *The Observer* story competition.'

On the girl front he noted 'a pleasing shift of fortunes the other night when Vere Harmsworth's girl, Pat Brooks, fell for me,[4] but experiences with Sylvia and Jill had been sterile and depressing, really'. Cars, though, were more reliable and did not answer back. He bought 'a nice VW convertible, red'. But he foresaw a financial problem over a Cadillac. 'A nasty overlapping crisis will, I hope, be solved by my forthright letter to Mr Brown [his long-suffering Westminster Bank manager].'

Into November he became concerned by the political situation: first the Suez crisis, now he was 'upset and frightened by the Russian crushing of the Hungarian revolt'. He had 'a perplexed walk round Saltwood' contemplating what he could do. 'Possibility of going out to Vienna in the VW, with Jack Russell's cheque [for a car he had sold]. Mama and Papa more worried about it, shown it by Mama being very nice, Papa uneasy, talked to him on the phone this evening and he said he thought of me in church.' K followed it with, inevitably, a letter: 'Needless to say I hope that some circumstances prevent you from going to Hungary – not only because it is dangerous, but because such experiences can be withering. If you don't go write some stories like the last.'

Alan's diary now included a line which once more demonstrated a need that had been there since childhood: '*Dear* Papa, if only I could make him proud of me.'[5]

Girls were suddenly everywhere. Pat came to tea. They arranged a further meeting, the following evening at 6 p.m. Hardly had he returned than Mary rang, 'and, feeling randy, I dated her for supper tomorrow'. It promised to be a crowded night. In fact he saw them both and went to a party, which left him tired and depressed the following morning. 'But the fact is, and it is being increasingly brought home to me, that I am too lazy. I didn't dance once and spent the entire time guffawing with men friends.' The dinner with Mary wasn't a success either. 'I became so sleepy (shades of poor Pam) and couldn't quite raise the necessary enthusiasm. *I cannot turn back the pages*, that's my trouble, a trouble anyway. With Pat on the other hand, I could take serious trouble, and she excites me.'

Alan's reputation with girls was increasingly well-known in the locality, as Sir Jeremy Hanley, later a Conservative MP, recalls. His stepfather John Davis, the chief executive of the Rank Organisation, and his mother, the actress Dinah Sheridan, lived at Monks Horton Manor, not more than four miles from Saltwood. About this time Davis told his three daughters that Saltwood Castle was being made out of bounds; they were to go no nearer to the castle than one mile, thanks to the antics of Alan Clark, whom he called Vlad the Impaler. Not surprisingly, Hanley recalled his sisters circling the castle grounds and chalking 'x' on the trees that marked Davis's exclusion zone.[6]

By November his financial news was better, even if the Hungarian situation meant 'mauvais markets'. He sold the Cadillac to Jack Barclay for £2,000 and £200 credit against a future purchase. 'Doing, I think, the right thing, although the news this evening is a little better, "cease-fire" at midnight.' His political antennae, so astute in later years, were at this point off-beam. 'We may get away without it this time, but it is Munich and the real war cannot be far away. Plato barked this evening and I went out on the steps and smelt it, all seemingly gone, it's very bad.' He was once again planning an American expedition, 'constantly veering towards the concept of self-preservation'.

Christmas approached. If he and Jane corresponded it was inter-mittently. 'I wasn't that bothered, I suppose,' is how she remembered their separation. But she did write occasionally, including one letter to her Rye friend Delia, who showed it to Alan. In it she told how she was putting on weight, trying her hair in a bun and dancing about in pyjamas. Alan turned maudlin – 'made me very sad at missed "it might have been"'. He had responsibility for the Beuttlers' dog George, 'who was uncertain of his quarters. I took him for a short walk, down to the Salts, it was high tide and I looked back at Rye and thought how much the prospects had changed since I used to walk there in the evenings in the High Street.' On the writing front he was delighted to have Papa's approval of another short story, 'The Ableman's Tide'.

On Christmas Eve, from Saltwood, he was in anything but seasonal mood. 'Really depressed; and yet it has a sort of depth and quality of pain that make it almost enjoyable. Very tired, bags under the eyes, blue spots and (now a disturbing phenomenon) red ones, in front of them; looking older, looks going.' He was so down in the dumps that he wondered what was the use of writing, 'isn't it a pretence?'. He observed the progress of his friends and contemporaries. 'Euan earning £1,400 a year at the House of Lords, even Col as Laurence Olivier's right-hand man.'[7]

A letter from Pam Beuttler had arrived that morning, written from a beach in Malta, where 'the young are bathing'. Although the family was due to return some time in the new year when he would be at Zermatt, Pam added, 'probably won't see you!' as they expected to be off again in May. Alan now remembered, 'Oh dear, there is Jane's little riding hat in the kitchen in that wire basket – to think of her out there maturing in that hot climate tempting other young men.'

He was in full reflective mode. 'Still, I never really grudge the workings of poetic justice and divine irony, and, in a way, find them stimulating. Paradoxically, and almost inexplicably, they give me hope of a massive burst of acceleration, which will enable me to outstrip the softies in front. That is why I feel, as noted before, that I owe it to myself and to my deity to have one more go at the US.' He once again considered taking a training course to become a youth leader. But for the first time, at least in his diary, he confessed to thinking of a political career, 'stand for parliament, or rather get a constituency'. His thoughts were everywhere. 'Mein Kampf, a book on Bevin, possibly. Action, violent, the skies the limit, with no turning back; or inaction, complete, somnolent, self-indulgent.'

For the new year Alan travelled, as usual, to Switzerland. His pre-Christmas angst hung over him at Paris-Nord as he awaited a train. 'All that dissipated promise, the Bar, Autextra, *Road & Track* . . .' He remembered an earlier time at Zermatt, the summer of 1953, 'the great year – since then it has been an on and off decline'. His diary mentions of 'great years' tended to vary – 1955 was another favourite. Once more he was staying at the Café Burgener. He was increasingly interested in acquiring a Zermatt property or even, perhaps, some land on which to build a chalet.

His first entry for 1957 has him mentioning an evening of debauchery. As so often in the diaries, he mentally makes plans. He really will visit the United States, and, not least, 'the novel must be finished'. He goes on to cheer himself up by noting 'what I look forward to: a nice house, adjacent to Rye with walled stabling for the Cadillac and some vintage machinery. Country house living, better clothes, more space, resident maid, boarding dogs? Tutoring lightly? Youth leader training in the autumn? – But first there must be ten months of travel.'

Meanwhile he tried to find some time for writing, and actually acknow-ledged 'a considerable though, of course, *relative*, increase in the amount of work done. The more I do on *Guilt Edged* the more I feel that it could be a success. I must aim to have its back broken by 16 February.' But, 'this brings me to another, vexing, problem'. 'Problem' was an odd word to describe the fact that the Beuttlers would soon be back in England. Jane had, he said, started writing, but he was not responding.

For the rest of his stay in Zermatt the weather was glorious, with plenty of good powder snow at night and bright sunshine during the day. Financially he made one of his periodic promises to himself to clear his overdraft, but then spent £2,150 on the Caddy before reselling it only a few weeks later – without loss, he noted. 'A wrench to see it go, but after re-experiencing its pleasures and doing a considerable mileage I was unable to resist the temptation to "put my affairs in order".' In its place he wrote about buying a Citroën 2CV or a Minor 1000. 'I may yet shuffle them round to a swap for a new 2CV if (a) the initial depreciation weren't so severe, (b) it weren't possibly *too* eccentric.' Citroëns were the one French make he (and Jane) would admire down the years His new travel plans included a trip to see John Pollock and his patronne, Constance Mappin, in Ischia, and then back to Watchbell Street as no tenants had signed up. The US would be postponed until the autumn.

He returned to England at the end of March, and on 13 April he wrote a longish entry to mark his twenty-ninth birthday – 'no comment, really'. Twenty-nine and what had he achieved? *Guilt Edged* was still not com-pleted. 'Almost in a panic.' In London he had been to see that summer's new theatrical smash hit – John Osborne's *Look Back in Anger* with Kenneth Haigh as Jimmy Porter and Mary Ure as Alison Porter – 'thought it pretty good at the time, still better now on looking back'. He was, though, 'depressed at the party by Mary Ure; all done up in white, living with successful Osborne; also by pretty little waitress in black. Went to bed thinking what the hell.' Ure would marry Osborne the following year.[8] Even the arrival of new cars failed to raise a smile. The Morris Minor disappointed him – 'uncomfortable and has a tiring driving position'.

The next entry, for 17 April, should have been a red-letter day. Margaret McKenna, a neighbour, told Alan that the Beuttlers had returned. What she actually said was: 'Jane's back and she's as pretty as a picture.' Would Alan and Jane pick up where they left off? For the moment he was hardly in a state for romance, having been 'ill – semi gastric – fluctuating temp of 99°–95° more or less' for a fortnight. He was feeling sorry for himself. Some friends who called left a note, describing his house 'as a complete pig-sty', with unwashed plates and his bed unmade. He didn't seem to mind. As for writing, only 'a few paragraphs of *Guilt Edged* left to be done'; he had sold the 2CV profitably – he thought it 'excellent and the greatest fun, but universally loathed on account of its appearance'. He now bought a new VW – 'back where we started'.

On Easter Monday, he and Pat went round to Jeakes House to watch the racing on the Beuttlers' television. It was, as he put it, 'an unfortunate visit'. Jane was 'looking *so* attractive it's agony. Came back pretty depressed. I know I must end this, but she is so attractive this annoys me.' He added a PS: 'No more, ever, with either of these two.' The lesson: 'stay *blander*, more controlled, at all times'. Alan was not entirely on the defensive. 'Broke it to "them" about going to Ischia on Friday.' He made no note if 'they' reacted. But hypochondria rose again. He wondered aloud if the spot, or 'place', on his right cheek might be skin cancer.

His 1 May entry was from the Villa Cavolina at Forio on Ischia. 'A grey day; low heavy clouds on Epomeo and some rain. Yesterday was sirocco, but sunny and I got a little too much on my back.' As if writing a novel, Alan first offered 'a note of the characters; John and Constance – very far gone in drunkenness and estrangement, almost hopeless it seems at present – they will have to be "written off" (so now virtually no inducement to leave Rye at all, except in the winter at Burgeners). A great pity, very sad and depressing, gives one a sense of aging, how far downhill things have gone since those gay, golden days of May '55.' Celly was nearby, staying at the house of William Walton, who was now married. To his surprise he found that John Pollock had written a novel. This fired up Alan to start final corrections and additions on *Guilt Edged*. The weather turned filthy – 'I want to go home.' And he did.

Back in Rye his mood changed with the novel virtually finished and ready for retyping. Hypochondria over, 'temporarily at all events'. Jane was 'Friendly and eager, status-quo-ante almost, except that my own position is stronger in that I don't crave for her in the way I used to.' By early June, the weather was glorious and 'I'm pretty brown'. The relationship with Jane was also in top gear once again. 'Relations with Bertie and Pam pretty ok now, cemented really at the curry lunch last Sunday week. Jane is just *fabulous* to look at these days with her lovely plumpish little legs and ultra-prim breasts.' If other girls in his experience threw themselves at him, Jane was different. If she played hard to get, this was even more of a turn-on for Alan. On the financial front, all was not well. 'However much I seem to make with them [Bache, his brokers] I never get any actual *money* (well-known life-situation).'

Guilt Edged was now, for the first time, on submission to a publisher. Not having an agent, he chose the firm of Victor Gollancz, which had launched Kingsley Amis. An 'amusing expedition' to London, where he spent 'money like water', led him to plan for the future. Over dinner a friend, the accountant Rupert Loewenstein, gave him a pep talk about getting a job and suggested J. & P. Coats with its Clark links ('wasted talents again, it never fails to disturb me'). In the train returning next day 'I thought I really might. However there is no doubt that it would be more *agreeable* to have *Guilt Edged* accepted, finish *Summer Semester.*'

When in doubt Alan increasingly calls on the Almighty, as Hugh Trevor-Roper had predicted he would. 'I hope God will guide me a little, if he hasn't already given up in despair at my sloth and failure to respond.' A week later he noted Trevor-Roper's Oxford appointment as Regius Professor. It made him think – 'You *do* make it if you deserve it. But you must work as well as having the innate qualities.'

Although he no longer acted as *Road & Track*'s correspondent, he still managed to get a prime spot at the 1957 Le Mans 24-hour race. From the Café Hippodrome, 'sitting in a most *excellent* position by my personal window overlooking the street,' he observed that the 'last three days have been very agreeable – good food and sleep (no nerve stress)'. He had only been woken by the loudspeakers 'blabbing'.

Back in Rye 'a delicious evening walk out over the sands with Jane and the dogs. We crossed the river at its mouth, she was wearing a new blue poplin dress and pulled it high up over her thighs, holding it there afterwards as her legs were wet, and got her feet and ankles covered with black slippery mud – very provoking!' And he noted, but then failed to write about it, that the Queen Mother was visiting his parents at Saltwood.

In London that August he saw – and swooned over – a 'beautiful silver Eldorado Caddy – how I wish I had £4,750'. Although he had barely mentioned in his diary plans for his trip to Moscow, it now beckoned. This 'sixth world festival of youth and students for peace and friendship' was to prove an intriguing interlude. Before leaving on Monday, 27 July, he made one last reference to Jane, and a drive to Camber Marshes in what he called the Bullnose, actually his Morris Minor. There was no other girl like her, even if the up-and-down nature of their relationship continued to worry him. 'My lust for her has waned, though this may give rise to a position of strength — cf Christina. Also she seems to make me "nervous", although whether this is causal or associative I couldn't say as yet.' On reading this, Jane recalled that he used to say he was frightened of her.

What would a month apart do to the relationship?

ELEVEN
Moscow Nights and Days

In August 1957 – the height of the Cold War – Alan visited the Soviet Union to take part in the Sixth World Youth Festival, and at the opening he, and perhaps 50,000 other delegates from 122 countries, paraded in Moscow's Lenin Stadium itself. With peace and friendship as its themes, this World Youth Festival was the 'brainchild of Communist ideologues', wrote Olga Fyodorova.[1] These 'awe-inspiring forums of socialist-minded young people moved around Warsaw Pact capitals. Now it was Moscow's turn.'

Reading a letter he sent his father[2] from Moscow and an account that Alan wrote after his return – an article, rather than a diary entry – it is difficult not to wonder at his involvement. Here is a future Conservative politician, who within ten years would be a leading light in the right-wing Monday Club, joining in an elaborate Soviet propaganda exercise. Was he reporting back to British Intelligence? At Oxford he would have talked to Hugh Trevor-Roper about his war experiences with MI5. In 1957 visits to the Soviet Union by UK citizens were rare. Given Alan's previous interest in youth work, an official youth congress was the perfect cover for seeing behind the Iron Curtain – and, perhaps, reporting back.

As one former spy explained to me: 'It would have been impossible I think, any old spook will tell you the same, for a man of his class and provenance who was going under Soviet auspices to engage in festivities in Moscow not to have had a reporting responsibility.' A whole office near London's Victoria Station was devoted to finding what were called 'legal travellers'. Those going to an interesting area would at least have been asked to look out of the window of the train. And Moscow was such a destination. A keen eye might notice something that had previously been missed or had recently changed. Certainly the CIA instructed American students attending youth congresses 'to report on Soviet counter-intelligence measures and to purchase a piece of Soviet-manufactured equipment'.[3] On his return Alan showed no interest in Intelligence as a career option, although he had many of the attributes of James Bond.

Alan's account, which he wrote in the hope of publication – it was, however, turned down, *Punch* saying it was not funny enough – shows that he was under no illusions. The British delegation of 1,650 included a large number of professed communists, not that he used the description in any pejorative sense. The organisation from London, although never referred to as being 'Communist Party', was definitely far, far left. But the festival was about youth, which fulfilled Alan's long-standing, if never realised, ambition that he might make a career in youth work. He had also studied Russian at Eton.

His only diary reference to the trip beforehand was brief: 'Early to Russia on Monday morning. Very much an unknown adventure this, but worth doing from so many points of view. Will my health stand it only real fear?'[4] The journey out was 'ghastly' – ship to Ostend and then a 'long, dark green, filthy train' to the East German frontier, and across Poland to Brest-Litovsk. Wooden seats and not enough of them, but his supplies did include a jerrican of Malvern Water in his rucksack.[5] Any idea of sleep was forgotten, except up front in the Leadership Coach; there Party members – naturally – had kept enough room to lie down.

To demonstrate that paradise was to be found east of Brest-Litovsk, the Soviets made sure that the welcoming bands became louder, the children gayer, the flowers more profuse, the snacks tastier. And the filthy train was exchanged for a spotless and clean Russian express consisting of brand-new wagon-lit coaches, which, Alan was told, 'had never been used before'.

On the first evening in Moscow, he told his father, he went out with Russian students, 'wild, impulsive, enthusiastic and, latterly, drunk'. They disclaimed any affection for communism, 'at the tops of their voices and filled one with hope for the future of the world, for they seemed representative of their generation and just as the fiercest resistance in the Hungarian rebellion took place at the New Government Youth Town, so it seemed that this enormous echelon of technical students which the communists are raising will eventually devour them'.

Alan reported that 'nothing was too good for us, or so, to begin with, it seemed. Breakfasts of caviar, smoked salmon, omelettes, fresh goats' yoghurt – no Hauser Institute in America could have put on such a menu.' If, meanwhile, he wondered about the diet of the Russian peasant he failed to mention it. Olga Fyodorova wrote: 'Never before had the Russians seen so many foreigners who were so surprisingly different in their tastes and manners, were more open and relaxed, who dressed, sung and danced differently.' The festival famously introduced rock 'n' roll to the Russians –

and it took fire. In Red Square, wrote Alan, the moment a delegate was identified, 'one became the centre of a large benevolently inquisitive crowd'. He was intrigued by how many could speak a few words of English; equally they were delighted to find any visitor who could understand Russian and thrust forward autograph books or pieces of paper for signature.

For the official opening of the festival the British contingent, led by a full pipe band with drums and playing 'Scotland the Brave', 'marched' into the Lenin Stadium packed to the gunnels with screaming Muscovites. Alan found the huge crowd overbearing.[6] Certainly he can never have experienced so many people in one arena. Reports talk of 100,000-plus; in Britain at the time only Wembley Stadium could hold as many, Hampden Park even more. There followed, as he reported to his father, an 'interminable demonstration of an orthodox Party kind' with MVD internal security police[7] watching every move. The long day was rounded off with an impressive display by 5,000 gymnastic students. During what he called 'the pauses' he amused himself by mingling with the crowds – 'I'm a fascist spy, don't forget.'

The Kremlin, 'with magnificent gold Czarist bric-à-brac', impressed him, but the Lenin Museum, with its elaborate descriptive labelling, was 'massively boring even if you can read Russian'. He was cheered by the sight of Lenin's Silver Ghost Rolls-Royce 'in excellent state of preservation', but he puzzled over how it had been manhandled into a room on the second floor. He tut-tutted that no-one had thought of taking the delegation to the Pushkin Museum. Alan hunted it out for himself and saw its collection of French Impressionists and Flemish paintings. Here was a chance to brag a little back home. Even though his father had visited the Soviet Union, this, he believed, was not something he had seen.

The Youth Festival programme was largely sporting and artistic, the latter participants betraying their political colours. The British contributions had a mainly socialist or working-class bias (*Macbeth* from Joan Littlewood's Theatre Workshop, two early Lindsay Anderson film documentaries, an octet from the Black Dyke Mills Band). The sport was eclectic: weightlifting, table tennis, water polo, wrestling, rugby and, surprisingly, a coxless four from Pembroke College, Cambridge.

Alan thought the 'genuine warmth and enthusiasm of the Muscovites was quite incredible from a people who have been fed for the last two generations an unwavering line of propaganda about Western Imperial Ogres'. And he was impressed by the 'terrific strength and vitality of the Soviets, in spite of everything'. After the oppressive decades of Stalin's

RIGHT:
Alan, not long past his first birthday, with his father, aged twenty-six, whose career following the publication his first book, *The Gothic Revival*, was in the ascendant.

BELOW:
The arrival in October 1932 of twins, Colin and Colette (known as Celly), changed Alan's position in the Clark household. Swept to one side, he became the outcast. Here the three children are on holiday in the summer of 1933 with their mother. Jane made a habit of dressing the twins alike for the rest of the decade.

BELOW: The north Norfolk coast was a regular holiday haunt in the 1930s, from Hunstanton and Brancaster in the west to Cromer and Sheringham in the east. Alan recalled walks with his father, a rare moment of bonding, although more often the children were cared for by a nanny.

ABOVE: On 15 May, 1936, while his parents attended King George VI's Coronation at Westminster Abbey, the children enacted their own ceremony, with Alan as the King, Celly (centre) as the Queen. Colin (left) is described in the caption in the family album – with no sense of historical accuracy – as the Prince of Wales.

LEFT: Alan, probably aged four, 'displaying the family's well-known dislike of weddings' according to the accompanying caption. The wedding is not identified.

BELOW: Driving his first car.

ABOVE:

The fire that destroyed Alan's prep school, St Cyprian's at Eastbourne, in May 1939. In this surviving cutting from the *Eastbourne Gazette*, a cross was penned identifying Alan among the seventy boys who were saved.

ABOVE RIGHT:

The large slide that Jane had installed for the children at Bellevue, or 'Bellers' as the Clarks called the house they rented opposite Port Lympne in Kent. Colin, in the front, was a sickly child and always smaller than his twin sister.

RIGHT:

In Switzerland in January 1939. The three children were entrusted to 'Moise', a much-loved governess. Alan in his pocket diary reported that the luge (or sledge) 'goes beautifully'.

Alan, early on in the Second World War at Upton House, Gloucestershire, pulling a face, which became a habit. Mama looks on unamused.

Alan enjoyed reading from an early age.

ABOVE: A picnic at Eton in the summer of 1946, when for onc half Alan (far left) became Clark Major, and Colin (in Eton collar) Clark Minor. The poses are not untypical: Mama has a glass to her lips, Papa is enjoying his lunch. With the Clarks are the Earl of Crawford and his son Lord Balniel (Balniel and Alan became colleagues in the House of Commons between February and October 1974). Lady Crawford sits next to Jane. The car is the Clarks' unreliable Lagonda.

Dressed up for the camera at Eton, which in later life he invariably maintained he did not enjoy.

Alan was eighteen when he went up to Christ Church, Oxford, in 1946.

Alan, elegantly trousered leg on the running-board, his fur-collared and fur-lined wool overcoat inherited from his grandfather adding a sophisticated air, seen in December 1947 with Hugh Trevor-Roper outside Upper Terrace House, the Clarks' home on the edge of Hampstead Heath. He was to chauffeur Trevor-Roper, one of his Oxford tutors, across Europe to Czechoslovakia in the Christmas vacation. The car is the inevitable Clark Lagonda.

Alan looks on at a conversation in Oxford that includes the American actor Joseph Cotten (left), in England to film *The Third Man*.

Double-breasted jacket and a rakish hat on holiday at Sintra in Portugal in 1947. Alan is with Ethne Fitzgerald (later Rudd), an early girlfriend from Oxford. The party also included David Tennant and Milo Cripps (later Lord Parmoor).

Alan's first published writing was motoring journalism. In this picture taken from the American magazine *Road & Track*, he is seen road-testing an experimental jet-powered Rover. 'You'd wear a grin like this after doing a standing quarter of a mile in twelve seconds,' he remarked in the caption. The hat, he wrote, came from a Russian air force officer.

Pam Hart, a dancer with the London Festival Ballet, was Alan's first love. Here, in the early 1950s, he is seen with her at Zermatt, where they spent two New Years together.

Alan first spied Jane on Camber Sands. She was fourteen and recalls him striding across the beach with a great dane who had various names, Big Dog being the most appropriate.

Jane, the daughter of Bertie and Pam Beuttler (LEFT), married Alan on 31 July 1958 at the Grosvenor Chapel, with the reception held at the Arts Council's offices in St James's Square. Their honeymoon was spent driving across Europe, taking in the First World War trenches of Flanders, the Nurburgring Grand Prix, the Mediterranean at Positano and Zermatt, which Jane visited for the first time.

dictatorship, Nikita Khrushchev was now undisputed Russian leader, and already 'adored'. In the Kremlin gardens Alan was among a group who 'surprised' Khrushchev. 'He seems to have a highly developed sense of humour and a quick, alert mind.'

However, despite Khrushchev's pledge of greater openness, the official side of the festival, Alan complained, was obviously staged. To utter or exchange any political 'truths' was, he said, impossible. The Soviet secret police were easy to identify and the most disagreeable, 'partly owing to their consistently belligerent expressions' but also because of their blue or brown pin-stripe suits, 'of quite considerable ugliness'; they had slung small cameras round their necks to give them, they hoped, the appearance of tourists 'and the excuse for loitering. Everyone else in Moscow was smiling and cheering, but these men had nasty cruel faces.' He was to experience their cruelty a few days later.

In more private surroundings he found the Russians, particularly students and the young, 'amazingly indiscreet and critical of their government'. Alan also took advantage of indiscretions of a more overtly personal nature. A folder of Moscow colour postcards at Saltwood, very much of the mid-1950s as the cars pictured testify, is inscribed 'Alan from Nelly'. Indeed after it was all over Nelly tried to keep the relationship going. In one undated letter she gets straight to the point: 'What has happened to you? Why do you keep me in a state of constant worry and despair? . . . You did not answer my letter. Have I insulted you somehow? . . . Maybe, you simply don't want to keep up the ball rolling any more?'

To his father he told a frightening story of the communist state's power over the individual. One morning he walked into Red Square and there, 'lo and behold, sitting on the steps of the mausoleum, was a young, extraordinarily pretty, blonde!'. Naturally he introduced himself and after a short tour of the university brought her back to his hotel for lunch. 'My Russian was taxed to the uttermost as she knew no English.' In Gorky Park that afternoon he discovered that she was returning to Leningrad after staying with an aunt near the Black Sea and had stopped off in Moscow for a day between changing trains. 'She was shy, innocent and gay, and held simple and optimistic views on political, as on other subjects.' Her train didn't go until 1 a.m. so back they went to Alan's hotel. He disappeared to wash before supper and on returning found her in an agitated state conversing with one of the MVD men he had seen at the Lenin Stadium. She was arrested, taken away and Alan forbidden to follow them or leave the room.

Alan was devastated. 'The whole thing was done very quickly and discreetly, but was ghastly and sinister and nightmarish to a degree which I have never experienced up until now.' To his father he worried that 'they could very easily make her disappear and no-one will ever know what happened. Her parents expect her in Leningrad; her aunt saw her on the train in Sevastopol – it is not unheard of for attractive girls to disappear in capital cities. Really the subject is too appalling.'

What was the outcome? Alan's letter was written that evening. He said he intended going to the British Embassy first thing next morning. He had the girl's address and would write to her father to say what had happened. But it is obvious that his conscience was getting to him: in theory he wondered if he should have made a great fuss and roused the delegation, but justified his inaction on the basis that (a) no-one would have believed him; and (b) 'they are all communists themselves, it now turns out ALL.'

He had, however, spoken to one of the interpreters – 'I know most are spies but I was simply backing my judgement of human beings' – who, naturally, first of all tried to convince Alan that it didn't happen. But the poignancy of the situation got to him. He helped Alan write a letter to her in Russian involving the complicated subjunctive sentence 'mention to me something we did together so that I know it is you who are writing'. The interpreter was so frightened that his hand shook, but Alan blackmailed him into addressing her envelope in a fluent Russian hand.

'"The lady vanishes", but in real life, and ghastly,' he wrote. 'Why take her? She was so innocent and silly.' He concluded that the weather was glorious (of course) and the food excellent, that he had won the Festival Gold Sports Badge for strength, and that there was a gymnasium nearby. 'Ideal conditions in fact, but only interesting now, no longer enjoyable.'

Towards the end of the festival, he began to notice that 'things tightened up a lot. We had a great many more obvious spies hanging round the hostels, listening in to conversations and observing generally.' Several arrests were made – for what, he does not say – but no-one got more than a 'dressing down in the local police station'. At the same time 'the atmosphere became undeniably more sinister, and Stalinist'.

Alan was determined to see – and the authorities equally determined that he should not – the notorious Lubyanka prison. When he asked the way people professed not to have heard and hurried on. Taxi drivers simply drove off, traffic policemen shrugged their shoulders. In the end Alan made it by 'the brazen expedient of getting into a "ZIM"[8] as a Colonel of the Red Army was getting out and telling the driver to go to the Lubyanka as quickly as possible, as "I am in a hurry"'. Alan's Russian was good enough for the driver to obey.[9]

The Lubyanka, wrote Alan, 'is an ominous looking building'. Its black marble base and first floor of black granite bricks he likened to a Borgia palazzo in Florence. He was surprised at the lack of guards outside its polished teak doors with handles of wrought brass hammers and sickles. The doors swung open gently and he found himself in a small, tight maze of bullet-proof glass that led into a hall of orange marble, discreetly lit and carpeted. Was this really the notorious Lubyanka? 'Two MVD men and a corporal, very smartly uniformed in knee boots and breeches, sprang to attention and saluted.'[10] The storyteller in Alan at this point failed his reader. 'Unfortunately it proved no longer possible to bluff and improvise any more and to avoid labouring the anti-climax I will not give details of my summary ejection.' Later he endeavoured to photograph a friend standing in a suitably insouciant attitude outside the gates, but this was 'also powerfully discouraged'.

Alan did, though, get his own back on the MVD men at the hotel by identifying them, noisily, and confronting them with the fact of their occupation, 'which they would deny with ill-grace'. And he added, 'This flippant behaviour was very badly looked on by the English communists', one of whom told Alan that the man he had just abused was a student at the Institute of Foreign Relations – 'he told me so himself'.

Alan was quick to blur evidence of his trip to the Sixth World Youth Congress. Even his own incompetence with a camera helped, as none of his colour photographs came out. He did bring back a peaked Russian military cap complete with red star on its brim, but did not wear it in public. A biographical paragraph on the jacket of his first book, published less than three years later, creates a fiction: that he had attended Moscow with the 'British Amateur Wrestling Team'. A decade later, when he set his sights on becoming a parliamentary candidate, he made no mention of the Congress. After all, a candidate who had cavorted behind the Iron Curtain for a month, who had been inside both the Kremlin and the Lubyanka, might have induced 'Lenin-Stadium' in his prospective constituents.

TWELVE
Courting Jane

When Alan restarted his diary on 24 August 1957 from Saltwood, he realised what a difference a mere month can make. 'A certain inertia after the *wholly* worthwhile trip to Moscow, arising partly from a sort of what-now? after-the-war-type feeling, also no real base (no. 11 let and half with Beuttlers, half at Saltwood).' Nothing was happening with his writing, either. As far as his health was concerned, 'No nervous angst, or substantially none anyway', but financially he compounded a stock market mess by deciding to move into the property market. For £2,685 he could buy a house that could be converted into flats, which would produce income.

On cars he considered reverting to the Morris Minor after enjoying the use of 'Mama's well-kept example'. And then to the women in his life. 'Girls? Smiles on all sides.' Shirley, '*I* wouldn't miss you, anyway.' Liz, 'chucked me last night. Stray blonde in Folkestone soda fountain – walked away. Christina, *won't* write. Tired of Jane and her cock teasing, so there!' Christina, though, was a stayer. Some of her letters in fractured Italian-English have survived at Saltwood, including one air-letter addressed to 'My dearest and nice master'. She would materialise once more in Alan's life in the most unlikely situation.

Jane, however, was increasingly to dominate his life – and his diary. This still being the 1950s, the explicit sexual revolution had yet to take place. Alan was a man of the world, a man of varied sexual experience. They had known each other for more than a year now, but she was still only fifteen, little more than half his age, and had to make up her own mind what she wanted. No matter how much Alan wished to take Jane to his bed, his diary entries are clear that consummation in defiance of the law was something that frightened him. 'I know what a mistake it would be,' he writes at one point. Of course, he then argued to himself, if they did, he would only get found out if Jane were to become pregnant. However it did not ease his frustration, although one wonders whether writing about it helped.

Autumn approached. His finances were disastrous, yet 'in some mysterious way the angst has been exorcised.' It would be thirty years or so before he could boast of living off the interest of the interest. He toyed once more with the idea of going into property. 'Anyway I will record a real determination to live more methodically, more by the timetable.' Thursday, 25 September was, however, a black day. 'Blind panic in the morning from which I am only just now beginning to recover. Rupert Loewenstein told me on the phone that I still would have a deficit of $800 on realisation of remaining "long" position with Bache [brokers]. This together with the cost of the Ford [he was buying a Zephyr saloon] and the Autextra overdraft would leave me – broke. Capital all gone (it had already been substantially diminished by the sales to redress my personal o.d.).' But later he remembers that there's a car credit possibly coming through, a legacy from Aunt Cassie.

He is, though, pleased to report 'Great progress with Jane, on the verge one might say, as about a fortnight ago she suddenly took to deep kissing.' The following day, he 'understood that Bertie was "getting shifty". When I questioned Pam about this she, too, seemed shifty. So there we are. Bad day.'

Any thought that with Jane so important to him monogamy might now seem attractive can be dismissed on reading the next entry where names of new possibilities trip off the page. But girls are briefly eclipsed by an event in Brighton. Not since the Russians had put down the Hungarian uprising the year before had Alan commented on the greater world outside his own life. Now on 4 October, from Rye, 'I just ought to record a good, happy morning. Opened well with Bevan rejecting H-bomb renunciation at Socialist Party conference.'[1] Then the diary reverts: 'a fabulous walk-run down at petit Camber, a still, warm day of late autumn with the sea like glass. I took off my track suit and plunged in, naked, delicious, and felt invigorated now. Thank God.'

Thursday, 10 October was what he called a 'B' day. 'B' standing for Banks and Brown, Mr. The inevitable had happened, Brown telephoning to say, in effect, that Alan's overdraft was no longer covered by securities and therefore his cheques would no longer be honoured. 'Sweated terribly.' Alan's short-term answer was another run on the beach – 'glorious weather we've been having, of course, as during terrible war years'. He thought first of asking Colin for help, after all Colin had so often come to him when in financial trouble, 'but now, at the time of writing, feel that it may be better to steel myself to approach Papa'. His run left him feeling pretty good: 'good health is priceless – and when Jane came round

I thought that I might have her that afternoon. If I don't it will be due to the more sinister atmosphere generated by Bertie, of late.' Afterwards they went for a walk. 'I was silent with the effort, and thinking of my financial worries.'

He had revised *Guilt Edged*. The new novel, *Summer Semester*, was 'going quite well'. He was philosophical once again, the need to 'sustain the mood', but he was 'contented in this nice little house, putting my feet up after tea and looking at the television'. (He had bought his own and was 'a great convert.') On the financial front he reported a slight, if relative improvement. He would be 'just about O.K.' now, particularly if G.W. [George Weidenfeld] liked *Guilt Edged*.

With Jane the problem, as he put it, had 'advanced sharply'. He now had, he was sure, 'an absolute mastery over her' and felt himself becoming overpowered again by 'massive lust for her.' Looking for ways round 'the problem' he sought advice about 'safe periods'. He then added: 'What I ought to do is concentrate on my work and sublimate my lust in exercises. But who knows what these pages have yet to tell?'

A fortnight went by. It was now late November. As well as Jane he also had to cope with Mama, 'somewhat confused', but 'all mad about my book being rejected by George Weidenfeld; no, she was that last night, the night before about Aunt Cassie only leaving me £100 instead of £200!' The manuscript he recirculated to Secker and Warburg and Heinemann ('succulent little Jewess receptionist'), but it had, he wrote, 'to a rather alarming extent destroyed my confidence in *SS*, which had been maturing, in my mind at any rate, in the promising way.'

The diary was the place for another *réflectif*. Could he now have 'a real, disciplined, Trevor-Roper period?'

> I will say this for my 'wasted' life and speculative money losses; I now feel very much more integrated, wiser – whatever you like. If, but it is a big 'if', but if with God's help I can start on a new phase of industry and self-satisfaction, I feel much more experienced, and capable of 'handling my affairs' with a sense of balance, than before. This may all sound pure gibberish on being re-read, but I don't think so.
>
> Of course if I'd followed the lessons apparent from earlier entries and reflections in these journals my position would be different from what it is now. Anyway here I am with good health (thank God) diversified interests, unmarried, still goodish looking and with, at last, the knowledge that you don't get anything for nothing and that a certain distinctive self-discipline works wonders. Of the future what? I mustn't have Jane until she's sixteen.

It was no longer a case of Alan alone; they had managed, just, to keep their passion under control. He had 'made my pact with God at early service at Saltwood Church that Sunday'. He had tried what he insisted was one last stock market gamble, and failed going short on 200 C.A. Parsons at 53s.

America beckoned. 'Before I finally settle down I think I must have one more return and see what it is like on the bum, travel more, get that out of my system.' Perhaps, he pondered, he might become a salesman on the west coast? Then again, 'the chief objections: (i) basic vulnerability physco-wise of salesman's position (ii) insecurity in States without cash reserve (iii) San Francisco a long way away, eh?'. He ended the entry wondering about a job in television, on *Panorama*, perhaps, or something 'very humble, some arse-licking job with E. Sussex education committee'. He had a bad session with the Westminster Bank; Colin had been 'wonderfully supportive. I wish I could pay him back and sack Mr Brown, and not so much snub as prove to him that I'm not a complete ne'er-do-well.' But all was not gloom. He thought positively. 'There is much hope left. I still seriously think of marrying Jane.'

A week later, 15 December, his mind 'clouded with lust. Very occasionally the clouds part for a second and I can see things clearly – the reverse of the mental state which obtains when one is busily occupied with day-to-day affairs with an occasional flicker of lust arising from one's subconscious.' It was a question of how far could they go without consummating the relationship. Alan went away for a few days and on his return Jane came to Watchbell Street, 'pretending to exercise George, and for a few seconds we embraced with real passion in the hall'. Writing up his diary on the Sunday, 'I am sitting in the study waiting for her to come round. It's 4.15 and she said she'd come at 3. I don't know what can have happened. I always suspect the worst.'

The 'worst' was a meeting at Watchbell Street with Bertie and Pam. From Alan's account it is clear that they had had enough. They had had a heart-to-heart talk with Jane and now they wanted to know from Alan what he thought he was up to. After all, their daughter was still only fifteen. As a result, Bertie, wrote Alan, was 'shaking with rage', but Pam, to Alan's surprise, took his side. 'Anyway I coped as best I could with Bertram who threatened police, publicity, ringing up Papa etc – and this sparked off by Pam telling him that I wanted to *marry* Jane. I rang him when I got back to Saltwood and apologised, but the whole affair left me very shaky.'

When Jane failed to have her period on time, Alan 'absolutely panicked,

dry mouth, not joining in the conversation, etc. Driving over this afternoon I thought I might be wrecking everything through that one vow
that I took in Saltwood Castle, hopes of marriage, settled life, the chalet,
writing, *everything*. But thank God, and I mean thank GOD she started
after lunch today. Happily I went round with her and paid my bills in the
town. Bertie rang up at 4.45, but a fig for him.'

Alan took refuge by playing the Saltwood musical box; the first tune
was <u>Tannhäuser</u>, appropriately enough.[2] 'How grateful I am for God's
forgiveness.'

As ever, the new year 1958 was spent in Switzerland. Success in his writing
was crucial, so *Guilt Edged* had to be accepted, and *Summer Semester*
finished on time – 'I must stick to five pages a day from today onwards.'
He regretted that there was no Cadillac to go back to. 'Oh fabulous dark
green car, how I miss you! What madness possessed me to sell you! Will
I ever reach that summit of independent material prosperity?'

By the end of February he was accusing Jane of not writing. His diary
contains the draft. 'I wish you would send me something – just a small
letter, my darling, because I think of you all the time, and I have so little
to remember you by, not even a photo.' Then good news. 'I had been in
a bit of a panic and as I opened the letter I was full of good resolutions for
work that evening, but, as often happens, elation kept out diligence and
I wasted time chatting to Col.' But was it a waste? Colin, younger brother,
into scrapes and drinking too much, now behaved more like a Dutch
uncle, and Alan did not like it.

'The conversation took a nasty turn: I said my trouble was that I wasn't
worried enough about my position (ie, no money, no publication accept-
ances, debts, what now?). He turned all sort of tough and clipped: "it is
bad, you just don't realise how bad it is old boy. The point is old boy,
you've just never had to do any work, you don't know how nasty and
boring it is to work every day. You've always been able to do *exactly* what
you want, and now you're going to find it very nasty. This is your last
holiday, you know. You'll have to sell the Volks, of course, and the XK." –
that stung one a bit, he had got through my guard there, momentarily.'

Alan was philosophical. 'It is extraordinary how much antagonism
"*Getting away with it*" causes in everyone even, particularly, one's nearest
and dearest. Oh well. I still feel it'll all be all right. God, dare I say it? He
will look after me. That's not hubris, is it? But still, there will be some
tricky passages, I feel. How grateful. How grateful I am to him for what
he has given me, health, looks and a secret, inner, determination and sense

of judgement of which nobody knows except possibly, at intervals, Papa.'
If only, one feels, father and son could have talked, really talked.

That conversation the previous autumn with Rupert Loewenstein had
not been forgotten. A proper job. An advertisement in the *Daily Telegraph*
about working with young people, an idea which he had first discussed as
he left university, led him to draft a letter and claim that he was 'at present
occupied in teaching skiing out here'.

Jane was on his mind. Marry in the autumn? he wondered.

Alan returned to England, and Saltwood, at the end of March where
he wrote of 'a delicious balmy day with the scent of spring everywhere.
Sitting on the roof, stripped to the waist for the first time this year.
Enjoying that relaxed, randy, restlessness that comes over one at this time
of year. But what now? If it weren't for this confounded money shortage
(" – our terms are 48% per annum")³ I would be more than happy to
continue as usual.' It would be a quieter summer this year, with no Stock
Exchange, and Jane always available. He had finally finished *Summer
Semester*, 'but *very* weak I'm afraid.'

Sunday, 13 April approached. 'My 30th birthday. Ouch! I can't at the
moment manage the sort of philosophical review that is needed as my
mind is clouded with lustful anticipation.' In fact nothing happened. This
set him musing about Jane's upcoming sixteenth birthday in May. 'After
that at least one serious threat is lifted,' he wrote. 'Though I really would
like to be actually married to her, that's what is so ridiculous and ironic.'
As for money, 'I really need about £850 to meet all debts.' The fantasy
side of Alan then erupts in his diary: 'Anyway what now? It's not that bad
really, is it?

Big man potential
Pretty little mistress
Nice VW
House in Rye etc'

As summer approached he urged himself on to find 'some sort of part-
time job and work harder, also at writing, *produce*'. He wondered what
next: 'Bondish novel?⁴ A *Pride and Prejudice* or revise *Summer Semester*? Or
short stories? ... I must get some more money. I would like to have
enough to go on a sort of Caribbean-Central American tour with John
Pollock in late autumn.'

He closed the entry thus: 'Is it bad for me always to have everything
I want?'

With Jane there had been a momentous advance, what he – they – had been wanting for so long. She had passed her sixteenth birthday. A fortnight later he wrote of 'a very satisfactory lunch with Mum and Dad at Saltwood who both took to her', but suddenly his health, which had recently been good, blew up. 'Intermittent attacks of hypochondria, symptoms yellow tongue (bilious yesterday), blood in the mouth suddenly from time to time, in small quantities admittedly, and from the back of the nose, I believe – but none the less disturbing. I can't have cancer of the stomach *and* throat/lungs simultaneously, surely?' Jane had earlier been taken to Saltwood, where she recalls upsetting Alan terribly. 'He brought me over. I can't remember whether his parents were there or not. I remember walking in front and he being incredibly put out that I wasn't more bowled over. "You don't seem very impressed," he said. But I said why should I? It's just a big house. Presumably every other girl he had sneaked across here had gone "wow!" I just didn't. It never occurred to me.'

She found herself telling Alan that in hereditary matters her family may not have had the cash, but on her mother's side they had a much better line. To put no finer point on it, Alan's grandparents were in trade, whereas Jane could trace her family to the Ogilvie-Grants, the family name of the Seafield earldom created in 1701. 'He was quite cross actually. You've either got it or you haven't. You can't explain it away.' Each time *Debrett's Peerage* sent Jane proofs for a new edition Alan would be sniffy. She was there in the Seafield entry along with her family. Alan was merely included as her husband. Was this an indication, in George Eliot's phrase, that 'spots of commonness' survived in his make-up?[5]

His hypochondria took a turn for the worse. Over his writing he felt 'depressed and nervous, unable to get started, get my teeth into anything fresh'. But his relationship with Jane had taken a highly significant move forward. Once more he proposed to her.

'Very characteristically outside AFN cars,' as Jane recalled. This specialised in Porsches, which they had gone to look at. 'Why won't you marry me?' he asked. This time she said yes; after all, she believed that their life together was destined from the moment she had first spied Alan with Big Dog on Camber Sands. Later he said: 'You made me marry you,' to which Jane responded sharply, 'I did *not* make you marry me.' She laughs as she speaks. The first ring he gave her was a love token, a tiny forget-me-not ring.

Agreeing to get married was one thing, but they needed the blessing of both sets of parents. Would it be possible to rush through the marriage before everyone started going on holiday in August? A Hythe friend of his mother's having seen the engagement announcement (3 July) wrote how impressed she had been on meeting Jane on a visit to Saltwood, 'such a sweet and attractive girl'. On 8 July, Alan's diary entry began with a laconic opening line: 'A lot has happened.' Indeed! A second visit to Saltwood with Jane 'went well', he recorded. His parents 'suggested getting married soon and offered to meet and persuade Pam and Bertie. Half to please them, half because I vaguely liked the idea − after all she *does* suit me − I consented.'

The Clarks organised a lunch at Saltwood and the Beuttlers were persuaded. Pam settled for 31 July, which meant they had less than a month to send out invitations, organise the dresses for Jane and the bridesmaids, indeed everything a big wedding demands. 'I am amazed at my luck in getting this lovely girl to marry me,' he said some thirty years later.[6] The engagement ring, the Clark diamond, he placed on her finger in the garden of the Natural History Museum in South Kensington.

All, though, was not plain sailing. Jane's father now wrote to Kenneth Clark about his concerns. Whatever Bertie may have felt, he and K did not discuss the emotional questions. His letter was primarily concerned with money. It cannot have been easy. K after all was a millionaire, with a castle as his home, great works of art on the walls. Bertie, by contrast, lived on his Army officer's pay of £2,000 a year.

From his desk at the Amphibious Warfare HQ in Whitehall, he 'thought it better to write initially in order to give you time to consider these things and avoid too direct a shock!'. What, he asked, would happen to Jane 'should this business go adrift in the future?'. He 'quite naturally' did not want to see her, left 'perhaps with a flock of infants, if Alan ever got tired of her'. She would be without any means of providing for herself and any children. Ultimately she might expect to come into about £20,000, but several people, including her parents, would have to die first. Bertie then made a proposal: 'I would, therefore, like to see something settled on her to meet such a situation. I also consider it only fair, should something be possible, that any such arrangement would automatically be void if Jane decided at any time to leave Alan for someone else. This may all seem somewhat pessimistic, but I think you will see what I am getting at.'

His second point was 'more awkward ... and you may well take some umbrage, but I feel you must know about this.' It was still the norm for the bride's parents to pay for the wedding. However, as Bertie wrote: 'At present, we exist on my pay. What capital there was has gone on children's education. It is in fact in this connection that we are trying to sell Jeakes House in order to clear off the mortgage and finish with the youngest's schooling. You will see, therefore, that an income of £170 a month, makes the question of the cost of a wedding a problem which is practically financially insoluble.' Writing in a neat, flowing hand, he did not 'find all this exactly pleasant to have to admit: you are of course at liberty to confirm what I have told you with Coutts, my bank'. Although he and Pam had explained the position to Jane and Alan, he thought that 'neither has absorbed it'. And he concluded: 'These then are my worries about this marriage. You may be somewhat startled by all this, but I feel that you should know the form. I have not told anyone of this letter except Pam.'[7]

K's very practical solution was to offer to hold the wedding reception at 4 St James's Square, which had once been the home of Nancy Astor, the first woman to take her seat in the House of Commons, and is now the home of the In and Out Club. But in 1958 it was the headquarters of the Arts Council, where K had been chairman since 1953.

As far as money was concerned, Alan's diary entry recounted what he called the 'BLOW – when Papa, pretty grim-faced told me just after crossing the disused railway line on a walk to the enchanted valley that he was giving me – *no* money. Simply setting up a trust of 25,000 Coats shares.'[8] Alan's distress wafts up from the fading pages of the diary. 'Irony! I've never had such an awful night I tried everything to make me sleep.' He refers to 'the shattering disappointment and possible wild solutions' that went round and round in his mind.

Alan next tried to enlist the support of his mother. 'I sat on the garden bench and seriously aggravated a cold-in-the-head while I tried to persuade her to let Papa give me 5,000 "free" and 20,000 in trust (successfully, it turned out, thus assuring a bare adequacy). That was the Sunday. The following morning, strongly fortified by support from Col and Celly I tried straight out to say it wasn't enough but was rebuffed. Mama, "drunk all night, put it off, let us all down as usual, etc." Papa, nervous with his fingers together, on the lawn. "I can't afford to give you any more," and "Many of my colleagues have got married on less".'

Interestingly, Alan compares his feelings with those of Pam Hart, 'perhaps, some idea of the degree, though not the type of misery that sweet Pam, Bluebie, must have suffered when I told her the news of my engagement, and afterwards so speciously tried to comfort her'. Pam remembers Alan's letter, this 'bolt from the blue'. She wrote back, 'congratulations, hope you will be very happy'. However that wasn't the end of the story. Pam was sharing a house in Chelsea with two girls. One morning she was driving a car through Eaton Square towards Sloane Square, when one of the girls said, 'I don't want you to have a seizure, but I think I've just seen Alan Clark driving the other way.'

Pam, without so much as a glimpse in her rear mirror – 'one could get away with that in those days' – remembers doing a U-turn, giving chase and eventually catching up with him in Piccadilly outside the St James's Club. 'He looked up at me, registered "mock horror", put his hand over his face, and said, would I like to go to the Caprice "for old times' sake?" He was getting married the following Thursday.' Pam was 'dying of curiosity' to learn about Jane and over dinner she recalls asking him 'what's she got that I haven't?' Alan, once again put his hand across his face: 'I can mould her. I know she is pliable. You are too strong.' Pam burst into tears, 'and that was the end of it'.

Engagement, then marriage – it had all happened so quickly. Jane says now that once Alan had decided what he wanted he could see no reason to delay. Nor indeed could anyone else. Rye was less chi-chi than today. Jane recalls stopping at a house in Watchbell Street, the home of an elderly lady who was seated in her doorway enjoying the sun. Alan introduced Jane as his fiancée. The old lady congratulated them and then leant across to Jane, 'Does he smell nice?'

Their decision to marry immediately raised eyebrows among friends. Were they *having* to get married? This was, after all, the 1950s. 'Everyone assumed she was pregnant,' recalled Alan. But they knew exactly how to demonstrate otherwise. Her wedding dress, deliberately, would show off Jane's 'very, very narrow waist' to advantage. Jane recalls proudly that it measured only twenty-two inches. The dress was made in Beauchamp Place by Miss Terry's, where Jane had worked as the office junior since leaving school in the spring. One newspaper described Jane as 'not old enough to be a débutante', and quoted her as saying, 'I'm not even nervous. I intend to have a lot of fun in my married life.'[9]

The marriage took place in London on Thursday, 31 July 1958 at the Grosvenor Chapel, South Audley Street, with Archdeacon Cecil Matthew, Jane's great-uncle, officiating. The newspaper coverage was considerable, both the formal (in *The Times*) to the more salacious (typically in the London *Evening Standard*). Relations of Alan's mother were thrilled to spot a paragraph in the New Zealand press, where it was described as 'the only big society wedding in London this month'.

On its court page *The Times* reported: 'The bride, who was given away by her father, wore a gown made of Swiss muslin embroidered with orange-blooms motifs, over silk organza, and cut on Edwardian lines. The skirt was pleated at the back giving a bustle effect and forming a short train. Her short bouffant silk net veil was worn with a chignon encircled by a chaplet of real orange blossom and lilies-of-the-valley, and she carried a posy of matching flowers. She was attended by two children, Hew Blair and Louise Morton. The page wore the kilt of Blair tartan and the child bridesmaid wore a dress of Swiss muslin embroidered with garlands of pink flowers, and a pink organza sash, and she carried a basket of pink and white flowers. Mr Colin Clark (brother of the bridegroom) was best man.' Alan, of course, wore traditional morning dress and looked, he recalled, 'an absolute prat'.[10]

Peter Blond, who had a mutual interest in cars, was one of the ushers. He remembered that the guests were an odd mixture, the Clarks' posh friends on one side, and on the other Jane's school friends, whom he imagined might still have had satchels on their backs. One of them described Jane to the *Evening Standard* as 'awfully grown-up for her age'. Jane, even though she was still a teenager, in Blond's view, 'understood Alan. Not a silly little girl. Hard and calm. Mature beyond her years.'

The wedding had been organised with such haste, it was hardly surprising that several loose ends remained untied. When Euan Graham arrived at the reception he was met by Kenneth Clark, who said, 'I am looking forward to your speech.' Graham showed surprise. 'I'm not going to make one, am I?' to which K responded, 'Oh yes, you are.' And so Graham did, the first time he had been asked to speak in public. Tony Rudd recalls Alan admitting in his speech that 'due to the industry of his grandfather and the generosity of his father he had no need to work.' But Rudd also remembers that K had told him that because Alan was rich enough not to have to work, it was important that he did something with his life and not waste it.[11]

As a social event the wedding excited not only the press. Movietone News showed shots of Alan and Jane entering the church, leaving it and at the reception. The *Evening Standard* made the wedding front-page news, showing in its later editions a photograph of Jane outside the Grosvenor Chapel. K may have been comparatively well-known, even if he had yet to become a famous television face with *Civilisation*, but what mattered more to the press was the age of the bride. Under the headline, 16-YEAR-OLD CONVENT GIRL IS MARRIED IN LONDON, they named her throughout as Caroline. Both Alan's and Jane's parents were quoted. K said: 'Caroline is a remarkable young woman. I don't think of people in ages or categories, but as human beings. People become what they are going to be very young and as intelligent as they will ever be.' As for Alan's mother: 'Too young? Nonsense. She has great natural dignity.' And Bertie Beuttler said: 'I don't mind what age my daughter gets married. She has known Alan for two years. It is not as though they have only just met.'

Naturally reporters asked the bride's mother what she thought. 'Caroline has travelled a great deal with my husband and me and this has given her great poise.' Pam then added: 'After all Juliet was only fourteen.'

THIRTEEN
Marriage and a Son

'A new book, a new life, eh?' Thus Alan opened his second volume of diaries on 14 October 1958. He looked back at the wedding, ten weeks before, and wrote that it 'went off very well, really, in a blaze of publicity; not really ill-natured – and that dear old Archdeacon smiling benignly. A final convulsion of nervous dyspepsia while signing the register and then to the reception at Arts Council offices, very sleek in new L&R[1] grey suit, Jane's white luggage, and the *spanking* clean Volks.'

After the reception they made what Alan recalled was 'a terrible early start', taking the little grey Volks across the Channel to Calais. He was determined to visit some of the scenes of the British Expeditionary Force's engagements in Flanders in 1915. The newlyweds spent the first day of their honeymoon trekking along the Ypres Salient, which as an interviewer later remarked he could think of as no more convincing proof of his wife's attachment.[2] The significance was brought home to Jane by a farmer, who gave her a strand of rusted barbed wire.[3]

Next stop was the Nürburgring Grand Prix. This also enabled Alan to show off his motoring connections going back to the days of *Road & Track*. Afterwards they drove on to the Mediterranean and Positano, where they stayed with John Pollock and Constance Mappin. Then Christina, the Italian girlfriend of Alan's who had been flitting around him in England for two years, turned up. She had been living at 11 Watchbell Street at the time of the wedding.

Sometimes Constance was broke ('waiting for War Loan') and 'when the tables were unkind' ('she was a raging gambler'). Alan saved the day by buying from her a turquoise and diamond ring which Jane still wears. In the *Diaries* Alan refers to the strange situation that then arose. Other guests included Milo Cripps and his boyfriend Barry. 'The farcical sub-plot', as he called it, had Barry falling in love with Christina, 'which certainly put Milo out', recalls Jane. 'We used to take a boat round to nice little bays, with gritty sands. I remember Al saying, "look at Milo" and he was eating the sand, self-flagellation, as Barry hadn't come but had gone off with Christina. Something bizarre about it all.' Otherwise 'a pleasant routine of boat to the middle beach, 11–1 p.m., lunch, prosciutto and melone and spaghetti, siesta, and tea at the orangerie, then a little reading, supper with Madame Mappin, a walk and cards'.

The final stop was Switzerland. Jane had never been there, but to Alan Zermatt was the second-best place in the world (after Saltwood). Jane has no trouble in remembering this first visit. They left their car at a garage in Brig before taking the train. 'The whole way up he was incredibly nervous. He kept leaning forward – we were sitting opposite each other on either side of the window – patting me on the knee and saying, "I do hope you like it because you've married a man who loves Switzerland." He needn't have worried, I did love Switzerland. You couldn't not, could you? Zermatt was wonderful. In those days it was so empty.'

Alan had bought a plot of land some time before from Seiler, a local hotelier, but it was only when he and Jane married that they set about raising the money to build, eventually borrowing from a Swiss bank. Seiler, she recalls, was the big man in the local hotels, the grandest hotels, but he also owned property on this, the unfashionable side of Zermatt. 'In those days it was laughable that anyone wanted to build there. It was nothing, but is now just as chic as the main part. People used to stand on the top and talk of this mad Englishman who had bought this pigsty. The river wasn't in its concrete channel as it is now. When I first saw it in summer it was just a beautiful winding romantic stretch of water. But it was very different in the spring. When everything thawed the water came thundering down and sometimes it flooded and it went through the pigsty which is why the pigsty was there so that it would be washed through.'

Alan found letters waiting, inevitably several from his father. The first, dated 2 August, was brimful of enthusiasm for the wedding. 'A colossal success. You both looked enchanting.' K said that the Great British Public was 'beside itself with joy' and that an evening paper-seller told one guest that they'd 'seldom had a sell-out like this'. Mama, he added, was particularly moved by the 'sweet and proprietorial way you looked at Jane'. Television news covered the wedding, 'but alas, we didn't anticipate it, and were asleep'. K concluded that he was 'touched and delighted by the service, exactly what we hoped for, but the C. of E. doesn't always produce'. His final line was music to Alan's ears given how often he had felt parental neglect. 'I feel so proud of you, dear Al, and also confident, as I have always been.'

In a second letter K mentioned that Graham Sutherland had given Alan and Jane 'a masterpiece of its kind' – his interpretation of a blue octopus on a rock – which they took to Zermatt and which now hangs in the chalet. 'He wanted you to have one of his best works, and you have certainly got it.' Of K's other painter friends, 'by a sad chance John Piper has given you almost exactly the same picture, painted with talent rather than genius'. He goes on to suggest 'that it will look ok in a different room'.

Alan and Jane returned to England in the Volks at the beginning of September to set up home at 11 Watchbell Street. With Bertie permanently in London at the War Office the Buettlers had left Rye. For Alan it was a question of earning a living and supporting his wife and, he hoped, very soon, children. But first he looked back over the past few days and wrote about his writing. His fiction had yet to find a publisher, *Guilt Edged* being still out with Frederick Muller for a £500 prize judged by a panel including his hero Kingsley Amis; and also with what he called the 'Hutchinson new writing department'. However, financially things were looking good. His Granada shares, in which he had 'invested' the balance of his father's 'free £5,000' left after paying off the overdraft, were showing a substantial appreciation. Even so he kept an eagle eye on the prices pages of the morning papers. Within a few days things had changed for the worse: his Granada investment was now down. Troubles never came singly: *Guilt Edged* had come back from Muller – 'did not reach the minimum standard required by the selection committee'. No wonder he complained of being in 'a lowish state' at Evensong at Saltwood that Sunday, 'yet the words of the prayers, psalms and hymns are so beautiful and the sense of peace and tranquillity are strong enough to give me still a sort of infinite hope'. He was not a regular churchgoer, although he always knelt by the bed every night and said his prayers.

Here was just one of the things Jane learnt about her new husband as she adjusted to being married, to being a wife. What did Alan expect of the new Mrs Clark? 'My job was absolutely everything while he was writing. I remember once, we hadn't been married all that long and I had the tea towel ready to hand to him to help dry up. He looked at me and looked at the tea towel, "I don't expect you to do my job and I don't expect to do yours." I remember going "Oops!" to myself. Now I know where I am.' Not, she says, that there was anything cruel in his attitude. 'But that was the way he had been brought up, I suppose. He didn't at all make me feel that my job was the kitchen. Women's lib wouldn't like it would they? But that was just the way it was. No, actually I felt my job was to look after him. My job as a woman – that's the way I think you are brought up: to make life easier for your husband. In fact at the time we married he couldn't change a plug or a light bulb.'

For any bride, but for Jane, still only sixteen, all this took some getting used to. Her husband's hypochondria was something again. Indeed as she discovered its extent it was, to put it mildly, 'a bit of a shock, but I realised I just had to accept it. Like anorexia it gets hold of you and you really can't get out of it.' Expert medical opinion says that 'the cause of hypo-chondriasis is uncertain',[4] that it can be 'secondary to depression and anxiety'. That certainly fits Alan's own observations in his diary. Practically this meant always having a thermometer and a sick bowl by the side of the bed just in case, gastrointestinal disturbances being common. 'Where's the sick bowl?' he would cry. But Jane did not remember him actually being sick, ever, even though he was always taking his pulse, taking his temperature. He often used to go to Rowntree, their doctor in London, to get medicine to settle his stomach. He was convinced he was going to be ill every night. 'I was one of those irritating people to him. I never had a temperature, unless I was really ill. Al could run a temp just by looking at a thermometer.'

Money was perpetually a problem. Alan was playing the Stock Exchange, despite earlier promises to himself not to. Nor could he resist buying cars, usually to sell again, but not always with profit. After London's Motor Show in October 1958 Alan gushed about a Caddy, 'lovely to sit in, but spoilt outwardly'. The Mark IX Jaguar, 'delicious – I must have one'. Not surprisingly Jane remembers that they were 'permanently broke, absolutely really broke we were. We used to drive over to Saltwood for lunch. My mother-in-law would sit at the table and say I've just given Pamela, or whoever the member of the staff was, the fridge because we've just bought a new one, or a carpet or something. We'd drive back saying why didn't she ring us up and ask us?'

Alan was never short of ideas for making money. He had long wanted to find a book subject that would draw on his enthusiasm for motoring and motor sport. He now drafted a proposal for what he called *The Duel Between Hawthorn and Moss*. The 1958 Formula 1 world championship had been one of the closest ever, an all-British battle with the two British drivers, Mike Hawthorn and Stirling Moss, fighting it out to the last, Hawthorn emerging ahead of Moss with only one point in it. If he had found a publisher the book would probably have been a huge success for the most ghoulish of reasons: Hawthorn would be killed in January 1959 in a car crash on the A3 Guildford bypass.

★

Their first married Christmas at Saltwood 'didn't go off badly. Jane and
I got some terribly nice presents.' A telescope (his, for bird-watching), an
easel and paints (for Jane), silky shirts from Celly. But the best Christmas
present of all was the news that Hutchinson had offered him a contract
for *Guilt Edged*. Meanwhile he had found a particularly attractive Rolls.
As so often with cars he fancied, he couldn't resist buying it – indeed
Rolls-Royce in its test and report pronounced it 'terrific', to which Alan
added, 'and very splendid it is too. I can't decide whether to alter the
body to open 2–4 seater. Tempted simply to have the sides painted pale
grey and keep as a big, gracious, quiet saloon – I would do that if Jane
would become pregnant and one would have to be transporting baby,
nursemaid etc.'

They were thinking ahead and looking for a bigger house. They saw one
they loved, but it needed much work doing to it. 'I don't think either of us
could bear to leave Rye – what I would really like is Mrs Gilbert's, with
garage to keep my cars in.' Margery Gilbert's house was also in Watchbell
Street, where over the years they would own three different houses.

This being the year end, Alan indulged in a summing-up, admitting,
but not explaining, that 'I'm not quite at rest about being married yet.'
As for girls, a married man of all of five months he may have been, but he
could not resist observing 'Julie Stafford at Col's party and that young girl
with a fringe and head scarf opposite me in Canterbury Cathedral this
morning'. He concluded on a different tack: 'I rather miss those moments
of solitary depression necessary for creative work (I believe). The test will
be Zermatt and how things go there.'

That January 1959 in Zermatt they stayed in a flat belonging to Paula,
another of the Burgener daughters. By Clark standards it was a mite basic,
with washing arrangements based on a hip bath. Alan worked in the
kitchen. As for skiing, he was making progress and was pleased to report
despite foul conditions 'a good fast run in successful pursuit of a "good"
English family with a ludicrous father with knapsack on his back'. Jane
was to learn skiing from Alfons, the mountain guide who doubled as a ski
instructor in winter. She took to it immediately and soon proved more
adept than her husband, much to his chagrin.

Alan's diary at this time is dominated by his marriage and getting used
to what this meant. There is no doubt that he adored Jane, but monogamy?
The idea of one sexual mate, the woman he had married half a year before,
is something he found hard to concede. Jane, however, believed in her
wedding vows. The clashes ahead would sometimes prove dramatic. *The
Times* of 20 January reported the death of Canon Jenkins (of Canterbury

Cathedral) which reminded him that Jenkins questioned the advisability of marriage – 'he had an equal horror of matrimony and cats'. In Alan's view, 'on the whole I think it is better. There is more fulfilment, particularly if one can have children.' Jane was 'sweet and sympathetic'. All he required at thirty was to age gracefully, stay broad-shouldered and fit. As for the future he wrote of being an eccentric, semi-reclusive, but with 'intermittent spurts of lechery'.

By early February they were back in Rye. Driving the Rolls over to Folkestone was 'delicious'. He was keeping fit with exercise, but yearned for 'a little <u>excursion</u> to Hastings'. The double underlining needs little explanation: this nearby resort was for him the 'sin city' of the south coast. On 1 March, 'the good note is sustained . . . although it is alarming how quickly one loses that feeling of boundless vigour and energy that follows the return from skiing'.

Alan recorded that all his worries, with the exception of Jane's non-pregnancy, were now of a constructive kind. And he added one further anxiety, 'namely a mild recurrence of the old war-threat-fear (cf Suez 1956) occasioned by Khrushchev's rudeness and brush-off of Mac in Moscow on his tour'.[5] Relations with his parents were poor, 'doubtless largely rising from the disappearance of the Renoir' and his father's proposal to give his children just £10,000 of the proceeds. The Renoir *Baigneuse Blonde* was one of his father's favourite pictures. At Upper Terrace House he had hung it in the drawing room over the fireplace. But K had quite irrational thoughts at times that he was broke, that the poorhouse was just around the corner. Selling the occasional picture sweetened not only his bank balance, but let him sleep easier at nights.

That evening Alan had a telephone call from Colin, who was out of work. 'We talked for ages about money, cars etc. I must say how wonderful a transformation has come over the scenes since those days when he helped me out. How quickly fortunes can shift! To think that less than a year ago I was penniless, shiftless, illish, neurotic, unpublished and hypochondriacal. I only pray to God that I don't miss the opportunities of my present good fortune, and "stick to it".'

Just how easily he would be tempted by girls is illustrated by the next entry. He and Jane had bought 'some pleasing Victoriana, prints etc at the Old Forge'. On the way back 'I saw Anne (little blonde from Adams) looking very sweet and she gave me such a charming smile'. Alan stopped in at the Union for half a pint – 'it made me feel quite drunk and very randy'. He now had no compunction in writing: 'How pleasant to have an affair, secretly, with her, perhaps make her pregnant (!sh). How delicious to have a succulent little mistress. I must get one somehow this year.' This sounds like Alan's reaction to Jane not yet becoming pregnant – if she were, 'my cup of happiness would be almost full, and I thank God'.

Saturday, 21 March was the day of the Grand National. Not that Alan cared. 'In really *vile* mood – Jane cutting her finger, Hawksfield's diesel thumping in the street, etc.' His depression was not helped by reading Andrew Sinclair's well-received novel *The Breaking of Bumbo* – he envied his fellow Etonian's success – and the massive rise in the price of Jaguar shares to 38s 3d – he had sold at 5s less.

Every mood swing was subjected to self-analysis. That day had been 'one of those shifts in outlook'. He was feeling distinctly sorry for himself. 'I can't have children. I've got no freedom to chase girls ... and Dad, of course, won't pay up the £10,000 ... will probably get worst of both worlds, ie the Renoir sold but no money.' Even the weather – 'A really glorious spring-like afternoon, with buds and blossoms opening' – made him restless. Just how much he disliked being left out was indicated by his reaction when his friends Isabel and Michael Briggs were asked by his other old friends the Grahams to stay in Michael Wishart's house. Alan was petulant: he now felt 'very lonely'. Was it that he didn't 'drink enough in the evenings and that Jane is not sufficiently sophisticated'? (At a time when many of their friends drank quite heavily, Jane was an exception – she did not drink at all.) He would not let go of this imagined slight and a few days later reported that he and Jane might spend the summer in a house 'adjoining the Wisharts''. He also had a longer-term solution: 'a bigger house, where I can entertain more, uncork more bottles of white wine and so on'.

Seven weeks separated this and the next entry, but the all-important news was Jane's pregnancy. 'So basic is this, with its promise of serenity and calm lechery etc that it has revived as a reaction the fear of war, need for retreat, Ireland? Etc.' Protecting his wife and unborn child was one thing, but where should they live? They would need something bigger to accommodate the baby, which they nicknamed 'Crumb', as well as a housemaid and woodshed. Woodshed? His financial situation had improved thanks to car sales, including the Rolls and a complex deal with Desmond, an acquaintance, over a new XK150. Alan got £900 and in part-exchange Desmond's own 3.4, which he had 'bent' during the course of 'a most enjoyable five days' at the Nürburgring circuit for the 1,000km race – 'itself the most exciting race I have seen with the exception of the pre-accident phase of the 1955 Le Mans'. With some of the profit, although he had yet to see any of the actual cash, he bought 'an exceptionally pleasant' American car, a 1950 Oldsmobile '88'. This was a vintage year for Olds, when 'they were still high, rough, and without unnecessary power accessories'. Immediately they made plans to use it on a summer trip to Elba.

Alan also added a footnote: 'was happily randy this evening after a day on the beach at Hastings. The combination of sun, steady exercise, regular means, peace of mind at *dear* Jane's pregnancy and, particularly, excitement at this evening's prospect of "getting off the leash", expedition to Hastings!' Once more his eyes were wandering, as they were again in mid-July when he found Hastings' Fun Arcade with 'those lovely little teenagers doing rock 'n' roll by a juke box. The two in suede coats were very exciting.'

His up-and-down financial relationship with his father took another twist when K allowed Alan 'a discretionary selection over half the trust'. Next his father divulged 'most welcome news' on the Renoir, which had finally fetched £120,000, from which K proposed giving Alan, Celly and Colin £7,000 each.

One cloud, though, disfigured the horizon. His deal over the XK150 had depended on a part-exchange for the damaged Jaguar 3.4, but the RAC, who were charged with bringing it back from Germany, reported a problem – they could not find it. This paled with the news at the beginning of July that Desmond, the buyer, had totally destroyed the 150 in a crash with a Ford Consul which killed two people. Desmond's legs were also broken. Alan worried that in some unexplained way he might be to blame. 'I do feel uneasy,' he wrote. In church the following day he prayed for those killed.

With their first child due in the new year Alan and Jane began house-hunting in their blue Oldsmobile. Come mid-July they were in Devon and one morning 'we found Town Farm at Bratton-Clovelly'. They had been looking for something 'large, rambling and remote' in which they could install housemaids. 'This would also help to exorcise a certain mild feeling of social deficiency with big rooms, open French windows, impressionist paintings on the walls, fitted violet carpet and big gin-and-tonics, white wine etc.' The tumbledown Town Farm, with water from a pump in the yard outside, was anything but this fantasy; it did, however, have outbuildings and potential. The price was £2,600, which they hoped with council grants and the sale of some of the land – three fields went with the property – might prove the overall sum even after renovations.

Not long afterwards they were staying at the Clovelly Hotel, Bratton and 'working like beavers to get the very wilderness-like garden of Town Farm in some condition for priority planning'. Like so many West Country houses without ready access to stone or brick, it was built of cob – a mix of clay, gravel, straw and dung. The closest town and railhead was Okehampton, not far from the county boundary with Cornwall and in the pre-Beeching days still a major railway junction. Alan expected the move there and its redecoration would take all of twelve months. Jane wanted somewhere where horses could be kept, he told one correspondent, 'not necessarily *well-bred* horses'.

Alan's next diary entry became lyrical. 'Feeling wonderful, well and "big-man", stripped to the waist, sweating, washing down at the pump, wandering through the empty house planning – a woodland frieze in the nursemaid's room, a pleasing anticipation of helping pigs up into the hayloft gripping them ruthlessly, right up round one's thigh. Really this place is so perfect and just what I have always planned with all that garage space, barns, the cottage and so on. Darling Jane is being wonderful too, she loves it and works away almost too hard. She is very plucky and good – what a wonderful little find!' They were getting to know the Bratton villagers, among them Hortop (to whom they eventually sold the fields – Alan thought his West Country accent 'bogus') – and the Lintons who ran the pub, Linton himself 'pretty stupid in belt and braces, but not as big a fool as it seems, I suspect'.

By the end of September they were holidaying in Elba, Jane with a terrible cold and much coughing. Alan had not forgotten his thermometer and registered 99° late one afternoon and evening. The weather was filthy. Their holiday was 'proving to be an absolute shambles – marooned on the island by towering seas, and both of us in and out of bed with an obscure but tenacious flu-cold'. Next, he added eyestrain and headache to his symptoms, blaming a 'voracious consumption of newsprint – all of which forecast the same story, namely a Labour victory' at the forthcoming general election on 8 October. He also worried about 'the Jasper affair', a City scandal to do with takeover malpractice, rules on disclosure and the misuse of building society funds. With echoes of the plot of *Guilt Edged*, he even conjectured in one particularly dark moment that it might cause the suppression of his novel altogether. In the diary he listed his assets and his indebtedness. Among the latter he noted two outstanding loans (£700 each) from a Mayfair money-lenders, with interest still at 48%. His reading included *Lolita*. Perhaps he recognised in Nabokov's novel a connection with his own attitude to young girls. All he says is that it 'certainly didn't raise my morale, though made me realise once again how lucky I am to be married to Jane'.

They returned via Zermatt in time for Alan to vote in the general election (Jane at seventeen was still too young). Not that Alan, a firm Conservative, need have worried. For the first time he watched the results unfold on television, 'with Dimblebee [*sic*] plumply satisfied and some of the *Tonight* staff (notably Alan Whicker) pretty puff-faced the following morning'. Despite the newspaper forecasts, the Conservatives under Harold Macmillan gained 365 seats to Labour's 258, thereby increasing their overall majority from 59 in 1955 to 100.

Alan's indecisiveness over his shares while in Elba paid off. The markets moved ahead on news of the Conservative victory (his stockbroker, Raybeck's, holdings to £6,000), although to his eyes, inevitably, not enough. He and Jane were attracted by a second property in Rye, Studio Cottage at Rye Harbour, but this would create liquidity problems and push up his overdraft to £2,600. Ever wishful-thinking, he now wrote: 'if the total Raybeck could really go above £7,000 I would cash it, regardless'. And Christina wrote a postcard from Positano asking if he was yet a daddy – 'I am longing to have one myself, but the conventions say one has to get married first.' Christina went on to bemoan the men she knew – impatient bachelors, men with funny thoughts, men engaged or married. Only one man understood her – 'you . . . before I understood myself'.

Colin turned up at Bratton in early November, 'very hung over after winning £700 at Aspers'. His drinking was a continuing worry. So, too, was Town Farm – 'such a lot needs to be done to it'. For a moment Alan had the wild idea of turning it into a luxurious nursing home, and fantasised about a staff of neat little trainee nurses. Good sense prevailed as he looked into the new year, the birth of the baby ('Jane rather big with child now') and then moving into Town Farm by his thirty-second birthday in April.

He had an eye now on a Rolls-Royce Silver Cloud, the epitome of the marque at that time – which 'we can now, miraculously, *almost* afford – choose the colour, James Young upholstery, and all that. Question is – dare one? It would be wonderful from my point of view – prestige, comfort, seductions etc, but risks grave parental disapproval (they could hardly fail to notice, surely?) and would be straining the exchequer just that extra point, perhaps.'

Christmas was spent at Zermatt and on their return to Rye in early January 1960 Alan devoted his diary to a resumé. Another house in Watchbell Street was coming on the market; Alan wondered if they might live there and slow down the development of Town Farm – 'just going there in the summer for work out of doors'. But, even with the sale of investments, this would, he realised, mean sacrifices, not least at Zermatt where he had just signed the contract for building to take place in the spring. Nor was this the end of his housing ambition. He needed, he felt, something of his own in London, Chelsea, perhaps, a *garçonnière*?[6] He concluded: 'Not enough wit and reflection in this entry, I'm afraid, but it records the crowded scene.'

Alan had not written about his state of health for some time, but on 26 January 1960 he ruminated on 'a strange pinkish wart on my side which suddenly was noticed/appeared in Zermatt and has done nothing since except (perhaps) grow more prominent. This accompanied by acute, it seems, impotence.' Meanwhile, he reported that the chalet would not be completed until October. It was something he had looked forward to for years; now it was in reach. He and Jane contemplated alternating between there and Town Farm, where Jane 'is longing to get in'. With the baby due in February she needed the knowledge of a permanent home. 'I do hope Papa produces the promised £3,000 on the birth – it would be an immense help', giving them 'complete independence and a secure feeling'.

Alan's fidelity to Jane was about to be tested. He took a woman called Divina out to dinner and wondered if anything would happen. He found her attractive, but worried about his 'apparent impotence', adding that 'lack of locale/opportunity' might cripple the whole thing. He could not decide whether she was a virgin, and concluded: 'I think not (she's twenty, after all).' And then, as we shall see, publication of his novel had to be postponed for legal reasons. Life was suddenly complex.

Far more important was Jane's delivery of their first child at the London Clinic. 'Jane produced a son on Saturday, 13 February at 3.18 p.m. This was wonderful, I was so happy. I broke down when I went to see her at the Clinic.' He then wrote what fathers have said since the beginning of procreation: 'He is the most beautiful baby, and gives me a real thrill of pleasure whenever I see him.' They called him James Alasdair.

The date of the birth was enormously important to Alan. The baby had, if possible, to be born on the 13th. It was a Clark tradition – no nonsense about 13 being unlucky. Jane remembers Alan driving them very fast round London 'to hurry the baby up as the dates they had given us were the 11th 12th, but first babies are notoriously late. Al said it had got to be the 13th. I was blissfully unaware of this connection.'[7] Jane was unwell with a mysterious illness after James's birth and had to stay in the London Clinic for 'a long time, a boringly long time. James was 9lbs 5oz. Big baby and not a very big mother.' Jane recuperated at Saltwood, where the full complement of the castle's servants helped take the strain.

By now Alan and Jane had a nanny for James. Nanny Greenwood, a Scot, had looked after many babies; a previous employer had been Edgar Astaire, of the stockbrokers Raybeck. Jane recalls interviewing her at Albany. She was a woman with strong views about how children should be brought up, and would work for the Clarks for the rest of her life. This appealed to her keen sense of social standing, says Jane, 'and she was very fond of my father and mother-in-law'. Indeed the relationship with Lady Clark was fostered over a mutual liking for whisky. In retirement Nanny Greenwood lived at Quince, a cottage on the Saltwood estate.

Alan's religious beliefs now came to the fore in an unexpected way. After the birth of both his sons, he insisted that Jane went through the by now archaic ritual of being 'churched'. Jane recalls: 'I think this was really old-fashioned even then. I was not allowed to come straight into the house until I had gone up to the church.' 'Churching' was the Christian ceremony of thanksgiving following childbirth. There was a sense of purification too, a woman being thought unclean after birth, according to the book of Leviticus. Some sources say it was not considered lucky for a woman to resume normal life until being churched around the fortieth day following the birth of a child.

The Times reported James's christening on 13 April, not only Alan's birthday, but appropriately at the Grosvenor Chapel, where Alan and Jane had married, and with the same clergyman officiating, Jane's great-uncle, Archdeacon Cecil Matthew. The godparents included the historian Basil Liddell Hart, 'Aunt' Ruth Lee and Alan's Oxford friends Michael Briggs and Euan Graham.

Just for once everything seemed to be going well. Alan not only had a wife, but a son and heir. With Bratton not yet ready 11 Watchbell Street became the new family's home. Spring turned into summer. Jane recalls getting up in the middle of the night to nurse her baby and looking out over the moonlit marshes. These were happy times, whatever was to follow.

FOURTEEN

The 'Bargains' Affair

'My, what a hubbub,' wrote Alan in his diary on 8 February 1960. If he had ever thought *Bargains at Special Prices*, as *Guilt Edged* was now titled, would finally appear to some discreet publicity and reviews he could hardly have been more wrong.

Publication did indeed begin with a review, what he called 'a good pre-pub notice in the *Sunday Times*'. Leonard Russell, the Literary Editor, wrote, 'I fancy that Mr Clark's very funny and at the same time instructive novel will be gulped down like a glass of champagne by the army of newcomers to stock market speculation.'[1] What Alan had not expected was the '*colossal* pre-pub injunction-type fuss' that followed. Edgar Astaire, then an employee at Raybeck, took grave exception, claiming that the firm could easily be identified as villains in Alan's satire. Astaire also remembers the novel as anti-Semitic, with 'nasty drawings' on the cover.[2] Alan summed it up in his diary: 'Edgar blubberingly palefaced out of that taxi — which I had to pay for — and all those lawyers and will it have to be reprinted and if so cost one £600 and the delay will cock-up the reviews and what to do now or look for and SO ON.'[3]

The withdrawal of *Bargains* was to Alan at the very least a bore. As his first published book, it had had a lengthy gestation and in the best traditions of fiction demonstrated that no author should be put off by publishers' rejection slips. He had been working on the novel since 1955. His idea from the beginning was to write a satire about the stock market, which was attracting increasing interest from a post-war public with income to invest, drawing on his own knowledge of share-buying and stockbrokers — he had recently spread his favours between Bache and Raybeck to manage his portfolio. In the novel, as Alan outlined it for the jacket blurb, 'a firm of stockbrokers endeavours to gain control of the Dunchester Hotel, a decidedly unorthodox company. The principal shareholder, an eccentric retired colonel, has just put the handling of his financial affairs into new hands ... the resulting melée involves lesser City personalities and spectators on the make.' In fact *Bargains*, 'a frisky, witty, cruel little book' in the opinion of Anthony Blond,[4] was a savage satire, with a cast of financial crooks who used what loopholes they could to manipulate share prices to make money for themselves.

Was it now going to prove to be five years wasted? If Hutchinson declined to publish as a result of the hubbub there was hardly anyone else left to approach as *Bargains* had been on submission to just about every first-division publisher in London since Gollancz in the summer of 1957. The responses included printed rejection slips from Martin Secker & Warburg and William Heinemann. At Weidenfeld & Nicolson, a director, none other than a Christ Church contemporary, Nicolas Thompson, summed up his colleagues' views: lack of conviction in the Stock Exchange background, the fact that all the scenes were farcical (giving the book 'a slightly hectic atmosphere') and the unsympathetic nature of all the characters with the exception of the Colonel.[5]

His brother Colin had read *Guilt Edged*, and offered 'helpful advice ... must make big effort to revise family sections'.[6] He gave himself a month, but inevitably took longer. Financially he desperately needed a publishing contract. But it was not yet to be. Alan sublimated his disappointment by concentrating on the completion of his second novel, *Summer Semester*.

Not until the new year of 1958 did Alan pull the *Guilt Edged* script out of the drawer. His next try came at his father's suggestion. K, who had gushed to Alan that it was the funniest novel he had ever read,[7] 'knew Nicolas Bentley, a director at André Deutsch, like Weidenfeld a firm founded by an émigré. Bentley, better remembered today as a caricaturist, was one of the triumvirate – the others were Deutsch himself and the incomparable editor Diana Athill – who ran the firm. 'I'm not sanguine there really, I'm afraid,' confided Alan to his diary.[8] He was right. In his rejection Bentley also used the word 'farcical' and was concerned, in particular, at the ending, which he felt 'tends to come to pieces'.[9] Next Jonathan Cape, a distinguished firm now beginning to make a fortune from the success of Ian Fleming's James Bond, kept it for what Alan thought 'a surprisingly long time' before saying no.[10]

Hutchinson's New Authors proved the perfect home for *Bargains* and if Alan had had an agent from the beginning they might have been shown it earlier. The imprint, the idea of Hutchinson's chairman, Robert Lusty, had been announced in autumn 1957. Authors were offered a standard advance of £150, but also, unusually, in addition to royalties they operated a profit-sharing arrangement across the whole list in proportion to the sales of the author's own book.[11] In mid-January 1959 Alan signed the contract, which included the publisher's standard libel warranty. His original editor left soon after the novel's acquisition and was succeeded by Raleigh Trevelyan, who nearly half a century later recalled Alan's cavalier attitude.[12] Alan, drawing on his barrister's training, might have realised that *Guilt Edged*, with its factual Stock Exchange background, was not without potential legal problems. Within days of the contract being signed, Trevelyan focused on the key questions: would any character be recognisable by a real-life individual, and if so would their portrayal carry risk of defamation? And was there any malice in the writing? On 9 February 1959 he told Alan he would be sending the manuscript to the firm's solicitors for a legal reading. Alan had asked about money, but Trevelyan pointed to the contract: no money now, but £150 on publication by way of an advance.[13] Mr Brown, his bank manager, to whom he dedicated the novel, would have to wait.

A week later Trevelyan, himself a distinguished memoirist and historian,[14] pre-empted the solicitor's report with his own points, which included the name of one of the novel's principal characters. Alan had called him Timmy Lazarus. 'You really must change this name,' wrote Trevelyan. Alan's marginal note on the letter was firm: 'No'.[15] Trevelyan countered: 'I agree that Timmy Lazarus is a wonderful name but there *is* a Lazarus on the Stock Exchange.'

Hutchinson's solicitors, Rubinstein Nash, were well-known in publishing circles. Harold Rubinstein, the senior partner, in responding to Trevelyan, thought it crucial someone within the Stock Exchange with an intimate and up-to-date knowledge of its operations should read the script. None of Alan's unpleasant characters should be identifiable with real people. The Stock Exchange apart, he worried about less than favourable references to real-life businesses such as the Berkeley Hotel and West End shops, Simpsons and Turnbull & Asser. Rubinstein concluded additionally that there remained 'a risk of some coincidence – e.g. some member of White's having a name resembling that of the doddering Colonel or some actress named Susan May complaining of references to her'. Given that Alan had called the Colonel George Justin Bad-Barratt, this seemed less likely than an actress by the name of Susan May.

As a result of the legal to-ing and fro-ing, early in April Alan finally wrote to G.J. Lazarus at the Stock Exchange and received a polite if tart reply by return: 'I do not see how I could give you permission to use my name without at least knowing considerably more about your book and its contents. I therefore suggest the simplest solution is for you to alter the name throughout.'[16] But Alan chose not to show this letter to Trevelyan. Trevelyan's next letter included a further list of queries, one from a Stock Exchange expert and a second from a lawyer. Trevelyan added his own final sentence: 'I am unhappy about the Lazarus situation still.'[17] As well as legal matters, a new and unexpected problem arose: a printers' strike. The October publication date would have to be postponed.[18] The strike lasted a month and publication was now moved to 11 January 1960.

By early September Trevelyan dispatched a set of proofs, giving him a fortnight to read and correct them. The matter of possible libel was raised again. Trevelyan added, 'do search your conscience once more while going through the proofs'.[19] At proof stage a further item was added, a disclaimer that warranted that 'all the characters in this story are entirely imaginary'. It concluded, 'The author is pleased to assure the reader that it was not his intention to suggest that business on the Stock Exchange is really carried on in this manner.' Like all such disclaimers it meant little.

Just before Christmas promotional plans were being finalised. Alan was impressed on hearing that 120 copies had been sent out for review and publicity purposes. Immediately after the holiday Trevelyan was writing again: 'Don't have a fit when you read the beginning of this letter, wait until you get to the end.' Robert Lusty had seen an early finished copy and been unhappy with the jacket, 'not nearly good enough and not funny enough'. His word was law – 'we therefore decided to scrap the whole design and start again'.[20] 'The end' meant good news as the *Daily Express* (with a circulation at that time of over four million copies daily) wanted to interview Alan.

The cheer that Alan enjoyed from Leonard Russell's early enthusiasm for *Bargains* in *The Sunday Times* lasted less than a week. The following Friday, Trevelyan, having failed to reach Alan by phone, wrote him a brief note – 'Please ring me at home urgently over the weekend.' The urgency was necessary because Hutchinson had been told that a firm of stockbrokers had 'identified themselves and are hopping mad. Solicitors being consulted. Legal action threatened ... Evidently they were once your stockbrokers.'[21] All Trevelyan's worst fears were being realised. Had he not asked Alan to consult his conscience? And why, oh why did Alan not show him the letter from Mr Lazarus of the Stock Exchange? In the end, though, it was Raybeck and Edgar Astaire who raised Cain. Alan, despite every legal query, had given his fictitious and exceedingly 'sharp' firm of stockbrokers Raybeck's address at Copthall Buildings, EC2.

Robert Lusty followed up immediately with a stern, headmasterly letter. 'We had been anticipating a very considerable success for *Bargains at Special Prices* and are greatly concerned at the last minute problems of alleged libel which – I must impress on you – with a little more care and thought on your part could so easily have been prevented.' If Alan felt the ruler hitting his knuckles, Lusty had not finished. 'Both our solicitors and ourselves stressed to you the vital necessity for avoiding precisely the pitfalls into which you now seem to have fallen. A publisher can do so much, but the responsibility is in the last resort that of the writer and of the writer only, and this is why publishers have to be indemnified against such costs as we are now having to incur in order to publish your book at all.'[22]

Alan immediately responded with a hand-delivered fulsome apology to Lusty, who acknowledged it by return, his tone suggesting that Alan's contrition had done the trick. Wrote Lusty: 'Despite the exhaustion which libel difficulties always bring I really am extremely grateful for your very nice letter. As a matter of fact I still think your book will make some money for you although not quite as much as it might have done. I also have a feeling that if this wretched rail strike comes off the later publication date will be much to our mutual advantage.'[23]

Hutchinson – and Alan's – settlement with Raybeck was straight-forward, if painful. The hubbub had come early enough for books not to have reached the shops. Thus all 3,500 copies were withdrawn and pulped and a series of amendments agreed. Lazarus was expunged, the stockbrokers had their names changed and their offices moved to the fictional Breadenhall House. Revising and reprinting cost £434 14s 8d, which was charged to Alan – which meant that even after his publication advance of £150 he still owed Hutchinson £284 5s 4d. Edgar Astaire has another reason to remember Alan – he 'stole' the Astaires' maternity nurse, Nanny Greenwood.

The pluses outweighed the minuses. Rae Jeffs, Hutchinson's ebullient publicist, used the row to advantage. The *News Chronicle* ran an account of the book's withdrawal, with Alan quoted as saying he should have covered himself for libel insurance. 'It's all been very hectic,' he added, 'particularly as my wife expects her first baby any minute.'[24] Reviews were mainly favourable. J.D. Scott (*The Sunday Times*) called it 'shockingly knowledgeable, ludicrously funny', the *Evening Standard* 'amusing and as up-to-date as the latest Throgmorton Street sensation', V.S. Naipaul (*New Statesman*) observed that 'his dialogue is delightful' and the *Observer* critic noted that he had 'a briskly original wit'. The BBC's *The Critics*, 'heard by Mum and Dad', he recorded, 'just loved it . . . their intellectual, well-bred welcome set the seal on its success'. [25] One exception was *The Times*, where an anonymous reviewer (actually Dudley Carew, otherwise the cricket correspondent) thought it 'formless, a fatal flaw in this type of novel. There is, however, scattered up and down the pages evidence that Mr Clark can do better and be funnier than he is here.'[26]

It was a sign of the times that no-one seemed concerned at the implicit anti-Semitism within *Bargains* that Edgar Astaire today recalls. Nor would the Alan of 1960 have worried. Describing a character as a 'Jewboy' was no different then to using the word 'nigger' for someone whose skin was black.

Alan appeared on radio and also on television, describing his performance on a programme called *The Book Man* as 'a substantial triumph'. He enjoyed the milieu, the extravagant hospitality (two free dinners on one trip), even a cigar. Among those he met who were to be valuable to him in the future were J.W. (Jack) Lambert of *The Sunday Times* and his Oxford contemporary Paul Johnson, then a writer on the staff of the *New Statesman* – 'so intelligent and controversial'. *Bargains* was the success Robert Lusty had forecast, and within days Hutchinson had ordered a reprint, which so delighted Lusty that he wrote to Alan to tell him so.

Sales of *Bargains* were healthy for a first novel – 2,345 at home, and 446 overseas. But when his first royalty statement came in he still found himself out of pocket by £43 2s. One final accounting reached him the following year: sales revenue for *Bargains* fell short by nearly £200 of total costs. New Authors Ltd showed an overall loss for the year of nearly £3,000, nearly double that of the year before. 'The harsh economic climate of publishing' that Robert Lusty referred to in his New Authors credo was getting no easier.

Nevertheless *Bargains* had done well, and Alan had made his name as a writer. Not surprisingly Hutchinson swiftly followed up with a contract for Alan's second novel, *Summer Season,* previously titled *Summer Semester* (a word Hutchinson found too American). Alan had touted it around for eighteen months. Set in a boys' preparatory school, it was more obviously Evelyn Waugh, a lineal successor to his *Decline and Fall*. Reviews and sales were, however, a disappointment. Here was an example of 'second novel syndrome'. In retrospect Alan would have done better to have stowed it away in a bottom drawer. He would return to fiction many years later, again with unhappy results. Researchers perusing his *Who's Who* entries, even from the first in 1970, will find no mention of his novels.

Before the hubbub, but just as the book trade press news of *Bargains* was breaking, he noted in his diary: 'Sissons of A.D. Peters literary agents sent me a glowing letter. Appointment with him on Thursday, but I bet he won't be very good.'[27] In fact they hit it off immediately and the relationship would have far-reaching implications.

Alan, though, was now a father. Robert Lusty tried wit, offering his congratulations, 'that despite everything you, or rather your wife, has managed to produce for you a very good Bargain at a very special price!'.[28]

FIFTEEN

The Young Historian

Alan Clark's career as a historian had a startling debut. Despite the controversy that still surrounds its title, its content and Alan's own views, his account of the destruction of an army – the old professional Army of the United Kingdom, as he described the British Expeditionary Force that ventured across the English Channel in the autumn of 1914 to do battle against Germany – has remained in print ever since.

The Donkeys was the book that led Basil Liddell Hart to call him 'a white hope' of the new generation of military historians.[1] Liddell Hart, like Hugh Trevor-Roper and to a lesser extent Robert Blake, was a mentor to Alan, but more than thirty years later it was Liddell Hart who was the 'fondest remembered'.[2] When Alan gave the Liddell Hart lecture at King's College, London in 1990, he reflected: 'Basil was my tutor in Military History, and in much about life, as well. He . . . nurtured me when I was young and obstreperous and made mistakes. But he always had faith in me.'[3] In particular he contributed valuably to the gestation of *The Donkeys*. The book would divide the critics, yet the title and the quotation from which it is derived, no matter what its origin, are now part of our language. It would also play its part in Alan's decision two decades later to turn to a political career.

Many of his father's close friends had served in the First World War, and by the time the second instalment was under way they found themselves being cross-examined by Alan. One in particular was 'Uncle Arthur', Lord Lee of Fareham. Lee, born in Bridport, Dorset in 1868 the son of a poor clergyman, and married to the daughter of a wealthy New York banker, had been a trustee of the National Gallery at the time of Kenneth Clark's appointment as Director. His extraordinary career included service in the Royal Artillery, acting as a special correspondent for the *Daily Chronicle* during the Klondyke gold rush in California, as British military attaché during the Spanish-American war, and being mentioned in dispatches twice with the British Expeditionary Force in France from 1914.

Although a Member of Parliament (for Fareham), in the autumn of

1914 Lee had been recruited by the Secretary of State for War, Lord Kitchener, as his personal 'Commissioner' to watch and report upon the work of the Army medical services, which soon after their arrival in France had been heavily criticised in the press for the way they dealt with the BEF wounded. Lee had complete freedom of movement behind the lines. In spring 1915 he witnessed what he described as 'the futile slaughter at Neuve Chapelle'. Kitchener was not best pleased when his Commissioner moved away from merely medical matters and tried to impress on him 'the tragic consequences of hurling men's bodies against uncut wire entanglements and batteries of machine guns'. Later in 1915, following the battle of Loos and the upheavals this caused in the High Command, Lloyd George, newly appointed as Minister of Munitions, gave Lee a key role in ensuring more efficient arms manufacture.

Lee never forgot what he saw as the shambles of the BEF. He developed critical views on Haig, initially First Army Commander when Sir John French was Commander-in-Chief and then his successor. He saw himself being used by Haig to convey his views about French to Kitchener and the Cabinet. Soldiers, he felt, were as bad as many politicians, 'as much taken up with their personal jealousies and cravings for advancement as are the legislators whom they profess to despise'.

A quarter of a century later, in the early days of the Second World War, the Lees and the Clarks were living close to each other in Gloucestershire. The childless Lee, by now in his seventies, would give Alan a pound note before he went away for the new school term, and, as Alan recorded in his 1942 engagement diary, they would go on walks together. With British forces doing as badly in the early years of this second world war as they had in the first it was hardly surprising that Alan would ask Uncle Arthur about his own experiences as well as his views on the military.

In the late 1950s, having no luck with his fiction, he began to wonder if something historical and military might be better. In June 1958 he wrote about being absorbed by a war memoir, *Stand To*, an account of the Leinsters in the Ypres Salient, which he found 'depressing, then fascinating'. 'The author, Captain F.C. Hitchcock MC, had served with the 2nd Leinsters through the fighting at Ypres, the Somme and on Vimy Ridge. Alan was particularly moved by Hitchcock's calculation that a junior officer's life expectancy in the middle of the First World War might be no more than six weeks.[4] In fact although this may have been Hitchcock's experience, six months would be a more accurate figure.[5]

Alan and Jane's extended honeymoon in July across Europe had included First World War battle sites. Jane, too, with her family's military background, found them intensely moving. Already an artist, she agreed to draw the maps for her husband's as yet unwritten or untitled book (her intertwined initials in the corner of some of the maps in the published edition of *The Donkeys* being the only clue to their origins). As Alan started work once again, he added: 'Now as to the present situation, on Thursday things really seemed very promising; my Ypres book full of hope as fresh sources opened and inspiration flowed.' There was, however, one fly in the ointment: 'I saw on Saturday night, a glowing review in *Time* of a new book [by Leon Wolff], *In Flanders Fields* (!) villain of the book – Haig.'[6]

Alan rapidly realised he needed guidance; 'Uncle Arthur' had died in 1947, but who better now than Basil Liddell Hart, whose writings on the First World War were already well-known? Liddell Hart had personal, direct if brief experience of the BEF, and initially believed Haig to be a great man. But he altered this judgement and by 1930, in *The Real War: A True History of the World War 1914–1918*, he decided that Army generals, if they had been sufficiently far-sighted and imaginative, would have drawn earlier on new inventions and materiel rather than rely on trench warfare, even though this was inevitable under the technological conditions of the time. In the 1930s Liddell Hart advised Lloyd George when he wrote his memoirs. These took a strong view against Haig and the Army High Command. He wrote later: 'Haig was an honourable man according to his lights, but his lights were dim.'[7]

Alan had met Liddell Hart in August 1946 at tea while on a Clark family holiday in north Wales. Liddell Hart and his wife, Kathleen, brought with them Lloyd George's widow, Frances, while the hosts, Rodney Forestier-Walker and his wife Mollie, a portrait painter, also invited Bertrand Russell from what he called 'quite a galaxy of talent in the neighbourhood'.[8] Alan, who was eighteen and due to start at Oxford in October, was delighted to learn that Forestier-Walker (who came from a distinguished military family) owned a 1920s Hispano, with 'still no more than .005" wear in the cylinder bores'.[9] When Liddell Hart was contemplating replacing his pre-war Rolls-Royce Wraith with a Jaguar, Forestier-Walker, who had sat in one, dissuaded him, remarking that the view from it was poor – 'rather like driving a double bed'.[10] This so delighted Liddell Hart that he was still repeating it a year later.[11] The subject of Liddell Hart's style of driving was recalled by Alan as 'a strangely exhilarating experience with Kathleen from the back seat telling him when it was safe to overtake other traffic'.[12]

Alan wrote to Liddell Hart on 21 October 1958, reminding him of that tea party and recalling 'vividly your account of a meeting with Guderian'.[13] Alan was at his most beguiling. 'I should very much like to see you and discuss in general terms the battles in the Ypres salient 1914–17. I have been collecting material for a book on this subject and, naturally, have found your own works invaluable, but I would very much appreciate a personal meeting. After all, you are, if I may say so, the dominant Military Intellect of our time, and I ought to have consulted you long ago.'[14]

Liddell Hart was not slow to rise to the bait and replied on 24 October, 'I was very glad to hear from you again, for I well remember your inclination to throw Bertrand Russell down the hillside when he started arguing that "cowardice" should be taught in the schools.' Liddell Hart would enjoy the social cachet of being close to the Clark family; Alan, in turn, had found someone sympathetic to his own views. Liddell Hart invited Alan to stay the night and look through his historical files and have a talk.[15]

Alan explained to Liddell Hart on 28 October that he had had a conference at Collins (publishers) that morning. 'I am going to have to change the form of the book slightly as Wolff has stolen a good deal of my thunder; this isn't a very serious problem though his book is coming out [in Britain] in March, but I've got one of the American editions here and could bring it over . . . I remember being cross about Bertrand Russell now you remind me – Alas, age has made me less dogmatic now.'[16]

In an undated letter in November Alan thanked Liddell Hart 'for having me to stay – I'm afraid I must have seemed very unsociable, but there was just *so* much to read in such a short time'.[17] On 17 November he followed this up: 'I found the World War I files completely absorbing and was filled with admiration with the way in which you had pin-pointed every flaw, or clue, and rejected all the ordinary historical padding. It will take me some days to digest all the notes which I scribbled so hastily that Sunday morning.'

Observing his mentor led him later to recall 'his almost inaudible grunting speech . . . his consumption of matches, at least one Bryant and May boxful per pipe bowl'.[18] Nor had this first visit all been work. 'I don't want to stress unduly the tremendous pleasure that I got out of our game of L'Attaque in case I seem to be frivolous, but I have in fact been thirsting for "La Revanche" since the moment of my surrender and would have happily played all night.'[19] Alan was by no means the first young historian to sit at Liddell Hart's feet and seek his advice.[20] But the great man didn't hand out everything on a plate. When Alan asked for something to read, 'or if you can be bothered, your own opinion of Smith-Dorrien', Liddell

Hart's response was to point him to an essay he had written twenty years previously.

Alan's next tactic was to invite the Liddell Harts to Saltwood for a weekend. 'My own house at Rye . . . is very humble and I don't think you would be comfortable enough – even the hardiest of my contemporaries sometimes complain after a winter week-end!' He then added in pen, 'We've got a Rolls now, older than your own naturally, but quiet and comfortable. All part, I believe, of a sort of subconscious influence, which I am absorbing from you through reading <u>all</u> your books for the last three months.'[21]

Liddell Hart was delighted that Alan had joined 'the brotherhood of Rolls owners – which is testimony to good taste, except in the higher income groups! The only drawback of joining it is that once you have acquired the taste, it spoils one for anything else.'[22] Liddell Hart was working against time to complete his history of the Second World War. Perhaps in the spring? Alan was not to be deterred. 'I have just about finished the draft and chapter scheme of my own book. I am calling it *The Donkeys* in the light of the judgement on the English armies – "Lions led by Donkeys" and the awful thing is I can't remember who pronounced this. Can you? I always thought it was a German, but lately I have been getting a feeling that it dates from the siege of Badajos.'[23]

It was clear that the relationship had moved to a different plane as the next letter opened 'Dear Alan' where previously it had been 'Dear Clark'. 'Looking forward to "a meal, a talk and a return game of L'Attaque." So far as I recall the phrase "lions led by donkeys" is usually ascribed to Napoleon – but at a hurried glance through reference books I have not been able to find it.'[24] The question was left in abeyance, and Alan's solution would have unfortunate repercussions.

His father, who was in Florence visiting Bernard Berenson at I Tatti, wrote on hearing Alan's good news about *Guilt Edged*, but his real enthusiasm was for *The Donkeys*. He had, he wrote, '<u>great</u> hopes' for it and thought the title 'excellent'. He added that he had told B.B., 'who was delighted . . . with the whole idea'. K, who had a dozen books under his belt by now, also offered sage advice. 'Of course the amount of dull preparatory work is what has kept the subject free. But personally I never find reading documents *real* work compared to writing. I can well imagine what you feel about poor old *Guilt Edged* – whatever its merits, it wasn't the sort of thing that you expect to work at for years, and then it was associated with so many frustrations . . . The novels can wait – you will come back to them with a burst of joy which will give them élan.'[25]

Returning to Rye, Alan reflected in his diary on a 'delicious period of great happiness ... the only flaw is that I haven't yet been able to really get down to *The Donkeys* again – too busy cleaning up here'.[26] A week later Alan provided Liddell Hart with a list of material he had borrowed, including 'War Council Notes (ssh!)'.[27] And three weeks later, 'Work is going well, though not fast enough on *The Donkeys*.' His new deadline to deliver four chapters would be 20 March, which he noted was the old publication date of *In Flanders Fields*, 'which got a very good review from Robert Graves in *The Observer* this morning',[28] under the evocative headline 'The Butcher and the Cur' – meaning Haig and Lloyd George.

In the end Alan delivered five draft chapters of *The Donkeys* in person to Collins and a month went by in 'an atmosphere of uncertainty'.[29] K read the five chapters and according to Alan's gnomic diary entry, his comments were 'helpful but too valid'.[30] As May dawned Alan looked forward to the Liddell Harts' stay at Saltwood – he was depressed as Collins 'seem to think that it is not sufficiently objective! I started impartially enough when I first approached the subject, but became indignant and am showing it now, I suppose.'[31] At some point that summer Collins finally rejected *The Donkeys*. Liddell Hart, though, was encouraging after his visit, 'one of the most delightful and refreshing weekends we have spent anywhere for years past – with the combination of good food and good conversation, in a delightful setting, plus croquet and L'Attaque. I was also glad to find your book shaping so well and shall all the more eagerly await further instalments. When they are ready Jane and you must come and spend a night with us to discuss them.'[32]

It is a sign of the up-and-down nature of Alan's demeanour that on Thursday, 14 June he wrote in his diary: 'I am failing badly in my application to *The Donkeys* whether, because of or in spite of Liddell Hart's encouragement I don't know. I must stick to it. It's monstrous even to ask God.' A fortnight later he was more cheerful. 'Work on *The Donkeys* has gone well, with "winter" done, "Aubers Ridge" nearly finished, and all the dates ready on Neuve Chapelle. This leaves only 1st and 2nd Ypres to do and the Epilogue (the Somme) ... Perhaps I really will get it done by the time we leave for Elba – which would be incredible!'

Letters between them continued. While pleased to hear about Jane's pregnancy and the house purchase, Liddell Hart also referred to a row that had erupted in public about the casualty figures at Passchendaele in 1917. At one point Liddell Hart put off posting a letter to Alan in order 'to carry out a further re-investigation of some of the points'.[33] This became an article, 'The Basic Truths of Passchendaele', in which he criticised John

Terraine, then working for the BBC, who was rapidly emerging as a trenchant historian of the Western Front. Terraine, as well as others, had been misled over German casualty figures, wrote Liddell Hart, and 'only a fantastic juggling . . . could make the total German casualties larger than the British in the three and a half months' Passchendaele battle'. Alan found Liddell Hart's response 'lucid, compelling, and beautifully expressed'.

On Terraine, Alan quickly formed an opinion. He lacked 'an inquisitive or scholarly mind, but is a toady who supports established views with an occasional timely pastiche'. They would soon be disagreeing in public. As for the argument, wrote Alan, 'Apologias for Passchendaele, part of the offensive-defensive kind, always infuriate me and I try to steer clear of them . . . suffering as I am from too much indignation already.'[34]

Half a century on one wonders if Liddell Hart, and indeed Alan, would have been so critical of Terraine. He was in the vanguard of those who rehabilitated Haig, a defender of the strategy of attrition dominant on the Western Front. Later commentators have questioned the validity of his views, but his work was far from pastiche. On the contrary it was highly original in being against the grain. Meanwhile Liddell Hart kept encouraging. 'I hope you will push on with *The Donkeys* for such a book seems to be badly needed to explode some of the fresh myths that have been arising.'[35]

The next alarm came from his publishers, Hutchinson, the day before he and Jane set off. Alan visited its offices to discuss *Bargains at Special Prices*, but Trevelyan had earlier written that he would also be delighted to see the script of *The Donkeys*. Now while in the offices Alan learnt, as he told Liddell Hart, that 'a "new" biography of Haig was scheduled for 1961 by, wait for it – Terraine (!!!) Some moustachio-ed idiot there told me that the "new view" was that Haig had been "much maligned by the politicians" (presumably Ll G and Winston).'[36] Alan was being intemperate: the 'moustachio-ed' figure was Iain Hamilton, editorial director of the Hutchinson group, and previously a journalist on the *Manchester Guardian* and *The Spectator*. Hutchinson had moved quickly. Terraine had been to Bemersyde, the Roxburghshire home of Dawyck Haig, staunch upholder of his father's reputation, and was 'determined to put things right'.

On returning from Elba Alan had to juggle. With substantial legal queries on *Bargains* unresolved, Alan could no longer single-mindedly concentrate on *The Donkeys*. Leon Wolff's *In Flanders Fields*, with its evocation of Passchendaele, was, Alex Danchev has noted, 'very much in the vanguard of fashion'[37] and on its publication in Britain had gained high praise. As Alistair Horne, the historian, and a friend of Alan's, says: 'this particular book had an enormous effect on his generation of young historians'. In Horne's case it inspired his book *Paths of Glory*.[38]

Now Alan worried about the journalist James Cameron's *1914*, a more straightforward narrative of that seminal year, which, he felt, 'will have narrowed still further the market, or field of operation or whatever one should call it ... *The Donkeys* still not ready, oh God please help me find some strength of will here, I must get it finished, and offered around, soon.'[39] He asked Liddell Hart if he 'could bear to look at it again and let me have some more comments. As it is a rather fragile unit with maps, photographs etc, attached, I could drop it in ... I had meant to ask you, if you like the book, to write a short introductory note explaining how you allowed me to use your files. But I remember overhearing you and Papa at Saltwood on one occasion swapping hard-luck stories on the "Introductions" that you were plagued with. It would give me such pride and pleasure that I don't want to let it go without *asking* – but equally I don't want to presume to any degree on our friendship.'[40]

A rapid-fire exchange followed. Liddell Hart politely explained why he would not write an introduction – 'my publishers complain that I have written too many in recent years ... but I might find a way round the publishers' veto in the form of a comment they could quote in advertising the book or even put on the jacket'.[41] Liddell Hart had, however, been reading Alan's script – along with all his other work – and in a letter dated 3 December pronounced, 'Just a line to say I think the new chapters well maintain the standard of the previous chapters and that the whole makes a very vivid and stimulating book.'[42]

New year 1960 began well. Alan had used his connection with Hutchinson, who were due to publish *Bargains at Special Prices* in February, finally to press the completed *Donkeys* on Raleigh Trevelyan, who says that it was in 'an appalling state – the worst script I could ever recall'.[43] There are those since who have assumed that as the son of Kenneth Clark Alan enjoyed an open sesame with publishers. This was not so, even though Robert Lusty, Hutchinson's chairman, was a sometime neighbour of the Kenneth Clarks at Albany. Alan remained jittery. In his first diary entry for 1960 he reported on a Sunday lunch with the Liddell Harts, followed by a run-through of *The Donkeys*. 'Although I must record certain misgivings and detect faint though positive signs of a radical retreat on the part of Liddell Hart so that he won't really have to write anything for the cover. Anyway we'll see. I've been awfully slack about work lately.

Must get Liddell Hart corrections done and into Raleigh's hands before *Bargains* appears and flops.'[44]

The next few weeks were hectic, with Jane giving birth to James and then the furore of libel allegations over *Bargains*. Alan did not know that Hutchinson had decided to have *The Donkeys* read by an expert. Trevelyan, however, thought better of telling Alan, and asked Liddell Hart to read the anonymous report and give his comments; 'Naturally they will be completely in confidence.'[45] In a game of double-bluff he did not reveal the identity of the author (Liddell Hart later thought it might be Captain Cyril Falls, former military correspondent of *The Times*, Chichele Fellow of the History of War at Oxford and a Fellow of All Souls). Alan's view in due course was caustic: 'He's a dull writer I've always thought (he was a dull lecturer at Oxford)'.[46]

The archive copy of the report includes Liddell Hart's marginal comments.[47] As he read, one imagines his pencil poised. The report opened with a statement as to the book's intent and did not question the use of 'the donkeys' to describe the Army High Command, whose 'asininities are demonstrated in loving detail in this exposé of the western front in 1915'. LH's marginal note was simply two delighted exclamation marks. After further description came comment. 'As an exposé the mss is successful for his targets are sitting ducks. Thanks to notes furnished him by Liddell Hart of the latter's conversations [LH's note adds: '+letters'] with General Edmonds (the official British historian of the war, and one of Haig's staff officers) Clark is able to give some new information.' The report continued: 'The tactical descriptions of the major battles are accurate though hardly graphic.'

So far so good. 'But when Clark goes on, as he must, to discuss the strategic and political background of these battles, or to generalisations on the military history of the war as a whole, his lack of general knowledge leads him to serious errors of judgement [LH added a marginal '?']. If published, these sections must be rewritten.' The report then gave one complete page of what the reader saw as wrong opinions, errors and omissions, particularly of AC 'not even using' material on the 1915 Calais conference 'listed in his own bibliography'.

The report next said something about why the British fought their 1915 battles so badly, and made the point that lack of men (one million; the French had double), rifles and cavalry could not overcome enemy machine-gun fire; and that 'the pre-war British army did not attract competent and intelligent men as officers. This in turn was in part due to public neglect and contempt for the military. These truths need saying and Clark does not say them.

'Is this report from a "publisher's point of view"?' concluded the writer. 'I am not sure. What the book offers is a careful, though incomplete description of the major operations of the British Army during 1915 and a glimpse of the disaffections within the High Command. Let me compare the manuscript with two recent bestsellers. Unlike Majdalany's *Cassino*,[48] the strategic background is inadequate and erroneous; unlike *In Flanders Fields*, the style pedestrian. I happen to agree with the view that the high command were donkeys; but wish to read it so argued with greater elegance and knowledge.'

Liddell Hart wasted no time and on 18 February wrote to Raleigh Trevelyan. 'It would seem that the typescript that was sent to your reader was an early uncorrected one. A number of points your reader raises are the same as I made to Alan Clark – which he was going to correct.' He suggested that as Alan was doing the revisions it would be helpful if he were sent the report. 'When your reader takes *In Flanders Fields* and *Cassino* as a basis for comparison he is certainly setting a high standard. Yet, although these books are outstandingly good, they contain a number of errors and oversights that are quite as important as those which occurred in Alan Clark's book – and which I hope will now be corrected.'[49]

Trevelyan was a team manager, referee and linesman rolled into one. To Liddell Hart he now wrote that Alan had been called in to Hutchinson to discuss the specialist report. 'Do you mind if I tell him that you have seen the report and that you say that the specialist's comments are all those that you originally made?' Trevelyan added that Alan was perfectly prepared to revise and had in fact accepted those suggestions made by the reader.[50] Next day Liddell Hart agreed.[51]

Despite the criticisms in the report, Hutchinson were convinced, and on 24 February Robert Lusty signed Alan's contract for *The Donkeys* for an advance of £150, the same as for *Bargains at Special Prices*. In an accompanying letter, Lusty pointed out that this agreement, unlike that for *Bargains*, included the 'usual option clause, which I hope means we shall continue to be your publisher for a long time to come, and that the association between us will be agreeable and successful, unmarred by any difficulties of libel in the future'.[52]

Preparations went ahead fast (publication was set for only twelve weeks hence, on 23 May). Trevelyan drafted a jacket blurb drawing on Alan's Introductory Note to the book, which he shared with Liddell Hart. It included the following: 'Mr Clark's generation did not fight in the First

World War.' As he said, 'to many of us the First is as remote as the Crimean. For so young a writer such a vivid and brilliant piece of reconstruction is all the more remarkable. Whilst it may affront some to whom the events are less remote than they are to Mr Clark, it is nevertheless of the utmost importance that the interpretation of history should begin to be made during a period when it can be illuminated and scrutinised by those to whom such history is a part of their lives.'[53]

Alan continued to multi-task. To Liddell Hart, on 27 February, he wrote that his son James was 'huge and, in our eyes at any rate, very beautiful'. Jane was running a temperature. But the main purpose of the letter was a thank-you. 'I think it was a bit thick to refer to you behind my back, as it were ... Anyway it was absolutely splendid of you to come out so strongly in my support, and I am deeply grateful.'[54]

An aside from work was a letter from Trevor-Roper, which surely made Alan smile. Two and a half years previously Trevor-Roper and his fellow Oxford historian Alan (A.J.P.) Taylor had been rivals for the Regius Professorship of History. Alan had written complaining that 'in spite of the fact that you did not acknowledge my telegram of congratulations on your Regius appointment, or utter even a muffled grunt of conventional good wishes on my engagement, marriage, or birth of a son, I still have a very soft spot for you.' Now his former tutor was having to confess that he had confused the two Alans. Trevor-Roper's letter began, 'I am terribly sorry: I thought I had answered all messages of congratulation – I always do; and I should greatly have appreciated yours. But the fact is – and I have kept all messages and have rediscovered yours – that I didn't know it was from you, and I acknowledged it to the wrong Alan!' He continued: 'and he didn't repudiate the generous gesture which I had ascribed to him!'. He asked Alan to accept his 'now belated thanks, which I appreciate even more through accumulation of interest'.[55]

External pressures were certainly getting to Alan, although he delighted in his son – 'fabulous, divine baby James – so beautiful and rounded and eager and fresh'.[56] The police had been ringing 'about those bloody traffic cases' (there was rarely more than a few months when he was without a speeding case or suchlike pending). He couldn't put The Donkeys out of his mind; bills had been lost, his stockbroker was chasing him, but he was attracted by an invitation to a ball at Buckingham Palace to celebrate Princess Margaret's marriage to Antony Armstrong-Jones, even though this worried Jane ('wouldn't know anybody etc'). 'All this superimposed on a massive, blind, aimless lust.' He described himself as 'always poised, pantherlike, cultivating one's looks and energy. Ready to smile and seduce etc at a moment's notice. Thank God I still have my assets left. If I have patience, bide my time, play my part, an opportunity will come.'[57]

At Bratton he and Jane had a 'wonderful hardworking Easter weekend' and at Zermatt workmen were on site, 'without, so far, any money changing hands'. The Buckingham Palace ball was better in realisation than anticipation and followed 'a boeuf diane flambé and several Americanos at the Vendôme with Celly'. He recorded 'Dukey making a pass at Jane, who looked fabulous in pink with turquoises'.[58] Jane thinks this an exaggeration, although she certainly remembered the Duke of Edinburgh circling around. Later that month, with Jane staying at Bratton, he came to London. In Chelsea he found himself frustrated by 'all those pretty girls' in the King's Road – 'just resisted'. However he concluded, 'Must have someone soon.'

Work pressed. His thoughts for his next book now turned to the 1941 German invasion of Crete and he wanted to be done with *The Donkeys*. He was in confessional, self-flagellating mood: 'I will, I'm afraid, deserve it if I get a "basting" on publication. It may yet be the old story of cocking things up, then relying on money to get you out – i.e. practically rewriting it in galley. I will have been given this last chance and I must take it, get advice from different quarters – if I don't get it right I will never be able to write another history. I will be laughed off the stage.'

SIXTEEN

A Steady Nerve

Basil Liddell Hart was showing his age (he was in his sixty-fifth year), having suffered a recurrence of severe conjunctivitis. But he was saved financially by Terence Rattigan's play about T.E. Lawrence, inspired by his biography. In July 1960 Alan observed that *Ross*, as it was titled, appeared to be 'running on very nicely' at London's Theatre Royal, Haymarket, having opened there in May with Alec Guinness in the title role. He hoped this meant that Liddell Hart would be able to afford to trade-up his Rolls for the Silver Cloud model.[1]

Liddell Hart's eye trouble had put him severely behind, but to 'fall back on dictation', as Alan suggested, did not appeal: 'Detrimental to writing – as the looseness of Winston's style, compared with his earliest books, has long shown. Moreover I take in things through the eye rather than the ear ... while experience has shown me the drawbacks of relying on data produced by other people's investigation of the evidence, in contrast to examining it and checking it for oneself.'[2] He added, however, that the success of the Rattigan play was hardly enough for a Silver Cloud.

Alan's next letter (undated, but almost certainly written in August) contains some unexpected news. Grumbling that *The Donkeys* would now not be out until the new year he told Liddell Hart that 'Hutchinson had another attack of cold feet and sent it for a report to – of all people – Robert Blake!' As the editor of the Haig diaries, Blake was inevitably seen by Alan as *parti pris*, although in the event he could hardly have been fairer. Alan continued: 'They did this without telling me, or to be more accurate while pretending to me that it was at the printers. However, to everyone's surprise Blake is in favour of the book and his report, though long and somewhat hair-splitting, is friendly. All the same the effect of this manoeuvre by Hutchinsons has been, as I said, to delay its publication.'[3] Blake described it as 'a controversial but in general well substantiated account of some forgotten campaigns whose history is worth resuscitating. But it does need maps [which Jane was drawing] and tidying up, and some reconsideration of the "indictment" which the author disclaims, but has in fact delivered.' Blake also pointed out the need for thorough acknowledgements. Alan was not good at giving references. '*The Donkeys* is the sort of book that might well be attacked fairly heavily by some people [who would be given the book to review]. This makes it all the more important that you should be quite unassailable as regards facts.'[4]

Alan, in his diary, reported a busy day in London at the very end of August, which included some time at Hutchinson. 'Raleigh shiftily apologetic.' Alan also worried at seeing newspaper placards 'vaguely clamouring about worsening international situation',[5] and the fact that he had a 'terrible money shortage'. But the news wasn't all bad. Having read Blake's report he concentrated on the good points, finding it 'a great encouragement', even though there were some specific criticisms. 'Now come on,' Alan added in his diary, 'I must pull myself together. The position is still pretty excellent if one stays calm, and applies oneself . . . God after all has given me such a lot I must do something to help him.'[6]

Alan had earlier had an article titled 'The Dismissal of Sir John French' accepted by *History Today*. Hoping it might raise a hackle or two in Establishment quarters, Alan distributed copies, including one to Hugh Trevor-Roper, who had married Haig's eldest daughter Alexandra. They had earlier spoken on the phone. As Alan deduced and wrote in his letter: 'you referred, in a voice so quiet and tremulous as to make me think that Alexandra must also have been in the room, to your father-in-law as "the great man". Now quite honestly my dear Hugh I started on this subject knowing nothing about it at all and with a completely open mind and after three years' work I really can't call him that, myself. However I have only stuck to facts and nowhere in the book is his name coupled directly to any adjective, if I may express myself in inelegant West Indian.'[7]

Trevor-Roper, quick to respond from Chiefswood, his home at Melrose in Scotland, said he had read the article with pleasure – 'How well you write!' But he was torn: 'Of course, largely, I agree with you. If I used the phrase "the great man" on the telephone that was not indeed ironically, but certainly not seriously; it was a convenient, neutral, anonymous formula, in invisible inverted commas, inspired by the fact that the study-door was open and Xandra in the next room, and proper names are always overheard! I am regarded as "anti-Haig" by the family, although I only consider myself to be objective; and so, for the sake of peace, I keep very quiet on the subject. That is why I am so craven about being too openly brought in on it.'

The letter, like so many of Trevor-Roper's, is a delight. Clear-headed, full of insights, displaying wide knowledge, it is a pleasure to read. Alan was grateful for his overview, something that Liddell Hart did not give him as he was almost always obsessed by details. The central section is worth repeating here, not least for its influence on Alan's thesis.

I believe that a great work could be written on the politico-military drama of the first war, on both sides, by someone who could get out of the futile spiral of personalities. Lloyd George behaved abominably to Haig, going behind his back. Agreed. Haig behaved no better, going to the King behind Lloyd George's back. Agreed. Lloyd George conspired against his political, Haig against his military colleagues. Agreed. But do not these facts simply illustrate a larger problem? Winston Churchill told Bob Boothby that he was determined, in the second world war, not to be put in the position of Lloyd George in the first, afraid to sack his generals. But what was this larger problem, and why was Lloyd George afraid?

Trevor-Roper had an answer. It seemed to him that 'in the period 1870–1914 the British generals had got inflated reputations cheaply' overseas and been allowed to return as national heroes.

Think of the scenes when Gordon was killed, and the British public and Queen Victoria (that faithful mirror of its most vulgar prejudices) howled for Gladstone's blood! In 1914, it seems to me, the myth came home to roost. Generals with inflated colonial reputations and immense power through popular support, suddenly found themselves fighting a war which they were incompetent to win, being no longer against fuzzy-wuzzies but against the greatest military and industrial power in Europe, but over whose conduct they had a monopoly which the politicians could not openly break. Hence an insoluble dilemma leading to the morally tortuous behaviour.

The generals, convinced by the myth of which they were the beneficiaries, genuinely believed that they and they alone could win the war. Within their caste-bound limits they were honourable men. But when they found that the war did not respond to their treatment, they had to grope and plunge outside those narrow limits. Hence their unedifying excursions into politics. Similarly the politicians found themselves faced by a political problem (the independence of the Army) which they could not control. So they too groped and plunged, in an unfamiliar world, and resorted to tactics which, when afterwards exposed to the light of day, looked pretty bad.

He thought the same point could be made about the other side.

The German generals were also confident. Had they not, by Blitzkrieg in 1864, 1866, 1870, made the empire? They too had great prestige and believed themselves indispensable; but the difference was that since their wars had been in Europe they could be a much more real threat to the civilian government. And they too, when they proved incapable of a Blitzkrieg in 1914, entered into politics and floundered and intrigued in that strange world. In the end, since there was no Lloyd George, they triumphed in politics though they failed in war.

Altogether I see the first world war as a tremendous drama in which human beings, faced with problems beyond the range of their capacity or conventional ideas, were driven into desperate expedients quite outside their conventional patterns of behaviour; and I feel that if this formidable background, which dominated the merely human background, is recognised, it should be possible to treat the whole subject in a way in which the personal controversies, which can be so tiresome, find their place.

Perhaps this is what you are doing. I hope so. Anyway I greatly look forward to seeing the book, though I shall have to be very careful with 'the great man's' family – except my stepson, with whom I can discuss these matters and who has also read and enjoyed your article.[8]

Alan recognised the value of Trevor-Roper's thoughts and told him so. To be praised by his former tutor gave him enormous pleasure. 'My own book is a humble little affair . . . I feel simply that war is generally – I don't mean "usually", but in a general sense; commerce, sex, administration etc – taken by people at all levels as an excuse for behaving badly and the first world war being very big, and bad, gave rise to correspondingly twisted and unscrupulous behaviour by those who were trying to run it. Also I must admit that I rather enjoy the personal squabbles. I like to think of emotions seething behind those honest red faces and fine white Edwardian whiskers.' On the matter of the title he added a postscript: 'English soldiers, lions led by donkeys etc – can *you* remember who said that?'[9]

American publication also now seemed a possibility. He had Liddell Hart to thank for recommending *The Donkeys* to Frances Phillips, who scouted for the New York firm of William Morrow, where she had once been editor-in-chief.[10] Alan's article also produced a 'fan letter' from Lord Beaverbrook, who separately allowed Alan to quote him about the shell shortage that bedevilled the British execution of the earlier stages of the war. Alan supplied a footnote in which he made the connection between the situation in the First World War and that in the Second when Beaverbrook himself was Minister of Supply. Beaverbrook approved. An epistolary friendship began.

Alan's relationship with Hugh Trevor-Roper, so happily renewed, was about to be threatened. In mid-October he stayed in Oxford with Trevor-Roper and his wife. 'We were both delighted to see you,' wrote his host.[11] 'Do come again.' The question of his father-in-law remained the major if not the sole topic. 'I'm sorry I was so frightened about the book. The fact is I suffer a good deal from those Haig controversies. My in-laws regard me as unsound, and as I can't change my views, I keep quiet. When your article came, I gave it to James [his stepson] and he thought that it would seem too sharp for Xandra. So we decided not to say anything about it. Of course if I had known you were coming to stay, I would have told her and let her digest it, and explained it away first. But in fact, owing to my absence in Greece, I only got notice of you coming to stay the day before you actually came, and I couldn't separate the two announcements. So I decided to leave the difficult matter of the book till after you had been and gone. In fact, as was only too clear, I handled the matter unskilfully.'

The tangled web that Trevor-Roper wove quickly unravelled, as he went on to relate. 'As a matter of fact the matter became complicatider and complicatider; for just after you had gone, I saw the seating-plan of a dinner we were attending that night, and found that Xandra was sitting next to her hereditary enemy Liddell Hart. So I knew that it would be impossible to keep any cat within any bag longer and told all, and was much blamed for not having told her before and for not letting you tell her, etc., etc. Anyway, I took <u>all</u> the blame: you are free of reproach (so far!).'

Three days later Xandra Trevor-Roper entered the fray:

I am <u>wild</u> with Hugh for making you conceal the fact that you are writing about World War I when you were staying here! I thought it rather odd that you seemed to have come to Oxford to write letters in Hugh's study in Oriel!! Robert Blake thinks Hugh is quite dotty to have prevented you from telling me you were writing about something that was connected with my father. I was bound to find out anyway and it is extraordinary to have stayed in our house and not told me what you were doing. But I know it is entirely Hugh's fault and I am <u>extremely</u> angry.

Hugh and I never agree about matters connected with my father. In fact he almost always sides with Liddell Hart, so I suppose that is why he did not want the matter raised. He himself is not in the least interested in military history, but I am, naturally, interested in anything that concerns my father.

The sting, however, was in the tail:

> The day after you left I happened to sit next to Liddell Hart at a dinner party. He told me that my father was the greatest general in World War I. I told him that he did not give this impression. I am afraid I thought he was a conceited poseur.[12]

Eight years later the Clarks invited themselves to Melrose. Xandra refused to meet them, and skulked out of sight in the kitchen.

Alan continued tinkering with *The Donkeys*. In New York William Morrow followed up Frances Phillips' recommendation, agreeing to pay $500 for an option without seeing the manuscript – 'so you must have cracked me up pretty high'.[13] Liddell Hart was impressed, indeed he thought it 'remarkable'. The relationship with Morrow would continue until 1970, but with many ups and downs.

If Alan was disappointed that his *History Today* article solicited only one public reaction, from a retired Army captain, all was to change when he was asked by the editors, Alan Hodge and Peter Quennell, to comment on an explosive letter the magazine had received from none other than John Terraine. Here was a massive attack on Alan that would be spread across a page and a half of the January 1961 issue. Alan was given the letter to read before publication and provided half a column of riposte.

Terraine ticked off Alan for 'a number of inaccuracies', then turned to 'matters of substance', and his method of 'character assassination', which he maintained was by selective quotation. Alan in his response naturally disagreed on matters of fact, alleging that Terraine himself in his letter made factual errors. On Terraine's 'points' they seemed to be 'questions of interpretation'. He also reminded readers that Terraine was working on Haig's biography and was thus 'currently the official custodian of Haig's reputation'. He ended: 'Mr Terraine finds my presentation systematic. Whether it has also been misleading I would prefer to leave to the judgment of students less deeply committed.'

Meanwhile, Alan was correcting his page proofs and to Liddell Hart admitted that he found indexing 'a real eye-strainer. I still like parts of the book but on rereading it in print for the first time it seems horribly young and polemical. I am afraid that it will get some really vicious reviews, although I've laid on a few friendly ones as well and with any luck the Beaver will lend his support.'[14] He then had an hour on the phone with Liddell Hart adding his corrections – 'there certainly were one or two howlers, though' – but took comfort in concluding, 'But not quite as many, if I remember correctly, as those that you corrected in *The Desert*

Generals [Correlli Barnett]. What the younger generation of (so-called) historians owe to you!'[15]

Proof copies went out from Trevelyan to, among others, Liddell Hart and Robert Blake. Liddell Hart responded with a quote: 'It is a striking and valuable study of the British Command performance in an early, but key stage of World War I.' He next tempered his praise: 'If too severe in some respects, it is none the less an important contribution to the further exploration of that war, which had such a far-reaching effect on the future.'[16]

If Hutchinson thought their troubles were nearly over they reckoned without the Haig trustees, no doubt spurred on by the *History Today* exchanges and sight of *The Donkeys* in proof (presumably via Blake?). Towards the end of February Lord Haig put the matter in the hands of his solicitor at Hawick, Haddon and Turnbull, who dispatched to Hutchinson 'a fairly extensive memo' of six single-spaced foolscap pages.[17] The covering letter complained of Alan's biased tone, that certain extracts were inaccurate and abbreviated, which 'in particular cause distortions . . . So far as Mr Clark has found it expedient to refer to the late F-M in his book we find that he has constantly done so to his detriment. This must be one of the main purposes of the book. Nothing is said about the F-M's high ideals of service, but personal ambition is referred to again and again. This the Trustees deplore; they consider the accounts of the battles to be manifestly unfair to the F-M, and the derogatory comments made against him personally, and against members of his family, to be quite unjustified.'

The letter continued: 'Your clients may consider that this venomous attack on the F-M is opportune in view of the possibility of its publication coinciding with his centenary and the British Legion centenary celebrations [in June 1961]. Nevertheless we must appeal to your clients to delay publication until the end of the summer. Publication of this persuasive [*sic!*] and biased account could otherwise do the Legion a grave disservice.' Nor was that all. *The Donkeys* was described as 'this diatribe . . . although we question what value, if any, this book, will be to serious history students . . . It is clearly impossible for the Trustees to request the entire rewriting of the book, and for much of it they will be content to allow material to stand.' The memorandum, it alleged, 'contains comments on many statements in the book, which are erroneous, and they must request alteration and rewriting of these statements to conform with truth'. It was 'the accounts of the battles which will require most rewriting'.

Hutchinson thought a legal response was needed. Michael Rubinstein of Rubinstein Nash was adamant that Alan should amend his book in accordance with the trustees' wishes except where he could quote chapter and verse to refute the trustees' contentions.[18] At this moment support for Alan came from a valued quarter, Hutchinson's chairman, Robert Lusty. On 2 March he wrote to Lord Haig, 'I am sure you will agree that publishers have a considerable responsibility in ensuring that every point of view, whether agreeable to not, is put forward, and no publisher can possibly be expected to support every expression of opinion in all the books he publishes. The first world war is history and historians must be permitted to regard it as such, and clearly young historians looking at all the circumstances with fresh eyes are going to form very critical opinions. These opinions must, I think, be respected and published. On the other hand facts and references should be correct.' Lusty, who would go on to become chairman of the BBC, continued: 'You can rest assured that the Memorandum of the trustees will be most carefully and meticulously considered.'[19]

On 6 March Alan wrote to Raleigh Trevelyan that he believed only two of the objections were questions of fact (which he would amend); and he thought the accusation of intending to harm the British Legion 'ludicrous'. He went on: 'The burden of my book is a tragic one', what he called 'the squandering of heroism', the 'lions' are, after all, the very people represented by the Legion. 'I have not attributed a malevolent inspiration to this tragedy. But I believe it was largely due to the obstinacy and conceit of the senior commanders, and in that belief I have not been taken in by the Haddon and Turnbull memorandum.'[20]

In his diary, from Zermatt, he admitted: 'I was so depressed the day the Memorandum arrived that I wrote a great marathon mass of documents and sent them all off to the "Beaver" – danger of suddenly becoming a bore.' In his letter he was more dramatic – 'the situation has deteriorated alarmingly'.[21] Beaverbook responded: 'I would think that you are unlikely to write anything about Haig which is worse or more damaging than his own Diaries.' He added the caution that, of course, he must not distort Haig's sentences, break them up or in any way lift them out of their context. But he was impressed.[22] A few days earlier in a letter, Kenneth Clark, who was visiting Somerset Maugham at the Villa Mauresque, related to Alan how Beaverbrook, 'who is very thick with Somerset', had been boasting to Maugham of 'his new discovery, brilliant young writer etc'. K added that 'Somerset and Alan [Searle, his companion] are both terrified that you will make a contract with him which will do you harm. I tell them that you are an author, and have no intention of being turned into a journalist, but they are frightened of Beaverbrook's power of persuasion.'[23] Alan took the memorandum seriously: on the first page of Chapter One of *The Donkeys* he added a footnote which began, 'I have been asked by the solicitors to the Haig Trustees . . . '. Perhaps his changes were not done with the best of grace, but they were made.

Alan was now concentrating on his Crete book, but in June, with publication of *The Donkeys* only weeks away, he regurgitated to Liddell Hart its troubled gestation. Liddell Hart, however, had little interest in raking over these particular embers. He had shown enormous patience with Alan over more than two and a half years. Now he finally flipped. The occasion was the centenary of Haig's birth on 19 June. Liddell Hart wrote an article for *The Sunday Times*, Alan one for Beaverbrook's *Evening Standard*. As was now usual, Alan sent his draft to his mentor. On 16 June Liddell Hart complained that a letter Alan had written to him on 12 June was 'obviously not written on that date as it refers to my letter of the same date'. The schoolmaster in him rose to the surface: 'Accuracy is the basic virtue.' (Not that Alan paid any attention: in October he wrote a letter to Liddell Hart simply dated 'Saturday'.)

Liddell Hart continued: 'I would be interested to know your reasons for not employing a secretary, since you can well afford it. This remark is prompted not only by some of the indecipherable yet obviously interesting comments in your letters, but also by the typescript of your piece on Haig where I found it impossible to decipher some of the handwritten additions and insertions . . . sometimes your comments seem to me too severe or sweeping – but I sometimes wonder whether age is not making me too charitable.'[24] There followed a page of comments and corrections.[25]

An advance copy of *The Donkeys* had now gone to Liddell Hart. He told Alan that although most errors had been corrected, 'in reading it through again, rather quickly, I have already spotted a number of unfortunate slips, some of them due to want of care – and even shocking carelessness. I am left wondering how many more there may be undetected.' Three pages of corrections followed. (Trevelyan also received the list – 'if it is reprinted, which I hope it will be, we will certainly get him to put them right'. It was and they did.) Liddell Hart could not stay angry for long. 'Having fired all my rockets I am now glad to tell you that the book, as a whole, seems to me much more striking than when I first read it in typescript. Except for the doubts you raise by intermittent carelessness it would be a most impressive contribution to history. It is a fine piece of writing, and often brilliantly penetrating.'

Another, less amenable letter now reached Alan's publishers. Just prior to *The Donkeys'* publication, Robert Blake entered the field once more. In a letter to Iain Hamilton, the editorial director, he referred to the trustees' February memorandum 'correcting certain errors in the book. Some of these were really matters of opinion and Mr Clark is of course entitled to hold to his own opinion if he remains unconvinced. Some, however, were not and there are in particular some highly misleading omissions and misquotations from Haig's published diary. Although a certain number of these have been corrected, by no means all have – and some are serious.'

Alan responded on the eve of publication.[26] 'Dear Robert, I appreciate your points concerning "omissions" when quoting from DH's diary, although I cannot accept the fact that there have been any actual "misquotations" and I realise that you, or perhaps some lesser nominee, will have to do a demolition job in, presumably, *The Times* or the *Lit Supp* ... After three years work I came to the conclusion that, quite honestly, DH was a pretty bad egg, and I use the diaries to support that contention.' To Trevor-Roper in an undated letter he referred to a 'terrible stink or stench' brewing.[27] But with Hutchinson finally going ahead and pressing the button at the printers, Alan was told that publication had finally been fixed for 17 July 1961.

Leaving Jane and baby James, with Nanny Greenwood in attendance, Alan in June took a Mediterranean cruise with John and Richard Pollock, ostensibly researching his Crete book; then went to Zermatt, where he was interviewed about *The Donkeys* for the *Daily Express* by one of Beaverbrook's protégés, Charles Douglas-Home, a future Editor of *The Times*. Two decades on Alan recalled: 'As a reporter he was (then) completely useless. We parted, but I had second thoughts and, stopping the car, dictated the whole article for him from a pay-phone in Martigny.'[28] The piece duly appeared hugely displayed.[29] Back in England he jumped straight into the publicity round, talking about *The Donkeys* first on his local ITV station, Westward, in Plymouth.

Two days after his return Jane had what he called 'a mock miscarriage' and was rushed into hospital in the middle of the night. To his diary, following publication, he confessed, 'the only thing that keeps me going is the success of *The Donkeys*. How ironical that this, exceeding my most optimistic expectations – should coincide with this period of confusion and misfortune.' And he recorded a visit from one of his literary heroes, Henry Williamson, whose fifteen-volume sequence *Chronicle of Ancient Sunlight* he was particularly attracted to, telling as it did of one man's life through two world wars.[30] Williamson lived in north Devon. 'Rather mad and rambling, but power there. Gave me a certain amount of remorse over DH. I sucked up to him.'

Intention in Alan's diary is so often not met by realisation. As if to bolster his own self-belief he now wrote: 'Well, a steady nerve and "decide what you're going to do and then do it". We shall see.'[31]

The response to *The Donkeys* was to be as mixed as views on Field Marshal Haig had been after the First World War and particularly following his death in 1928. But there was one controversy that had little to do with Haig himself. Alan would soon have to face up to the origin of his title. Who *was* the source?

And in a theatre in east London something else was soon to spring into life and fan the flames surrounding those lions and donkeys.

SEVENTEEN

Facing the Music

Before his Introductory Note to *The Donkeys* Alan Clark placed an epigraph:

> Ludendorff: 'The English soldiers fight like lions.'
> Hoffmann: 'True. But don't we know that they are lions led by donkeys.'
>
> Falkenhayn, *Memoirs*

In an advertisement in *The Times* on the morning of publication under the heading 'Monday sensation' Alan's publishers stated that this Ludendorff-Hoffmann exchange was a 'famous quotation'.[1] None of the original reviewers questioned it. Perhaps, as to Liddell Hart two years before, the notion of lions led by donkeys was familiar, even if not immediately identifiable. No-one went back to check whether Falkenhayn, at one time Prussian Minister of War, had even published his memoirs.

The reviews were many, but mixed. One of the unexpected positives came from Lord Beaverbrook. *The Donkeys*, he wrote, was 'a brilliant piece of work. Your grasp and understanding of war conditions of 1914–18 is a most remarkable demonstration of the art of the historian.'[2] As Max Aitken, Beaverbrook had been with the Canadian Expeditionary Force in 1915 and retained firm links with his native land. 'I am going to send the book to all the libraries in New Brunswick with a recommendation to the young students in history there to read it.' Not surprisingly, Alan was delighted and immediately told Beaverbrook about his troubles, enclosing a copy of Blake's letter and his reply. The old man (he was now in his early eighties) immediately offered his advice. 'Don't reply to any criticism. You have had your say. Malicious and injured persons will, of course, attack you. I read your letter to Robert Blake. I can't see that he has any reasonable complaint against your use of the diary. But I would not have advised you to answer him. You have had a wonderful press, an immense reception and a splendid triumph.' And he added a postscript that particularly pleased Alan: 'I sent a copy of your book to Sir Winston at his request.'

Churchill responded two days later, thanking his old friend and saying he was reading *The Donkeys* 'with interest'.[3]

The 'wonderful press' was concentrated – but not wholly so – on Beaverbrook's Express group of newspapers. As the historian Dan Todman has commented, Beaverbrook, a one-time political ally of Lloyd George, had 'a long-term involvement in denigrating the generals of the First World War that went back to 1918'.[4] He encouraged his editors to publish opinions which coincided with his own. Thus George Malcolm Thomson, a former secretary of his, but also a well-thought-of author and journalist: 'Eloquent and painful', he wrote in the London *Evening Standard*. 'Clark leaves the impression that vanity and stupidity were the main ingredients of the massacres of 1915. He writes searingly and unforgettably.'[5] The left-wing weeklies were also in favour, not least Paul Johnson in the *New Statesman*. 'Mr Clark writes with verve, venom and real feeling for the men whose lives the brass hats squandered.'

However Bernard Fergusson, with no Beaverbrook connections, accused him, in *The Daily Telegraph*, of 'monkeying with the evidence . . . A regrettable book – and not history.'[6] John Terraine, unsurprisingly given their earlier crossing of swords in *History Today*, said Alan's attack on Haig was 'squarely founded on inaccuracy and distortion'.[7] A.J.P. Taylor reviewed *The Donkeys* in *The Observer*, a paper diametrically opposed to Beaverbrook in every way. Taylor could hardly have been more damning, saying that Alan had time and time again twisted the sense of his sources, 'suppressed the limiting phrase, added a slant of his own'.[8] Michael Howard, then Reader in War Studies at King's College, London, was equally critical. 'As history it is worthless,' he wrote in *The Listener*. Alan had accepted without question 'a popular stereotype of brave British lives being squandered by stupid generals'. He criticised Alan for his 'slovenly scholarship', for failing to consult any sources in France and very few in Germany. His 'sustained malevolence' towards Haig 'does nothing to increase our understanding of that complex and controversial man'. And yet, despite these criticisms, Howard commended its readability, adding that Alan's descriptions of battles and battlefields are 'sometimes masterly'.[9]

Meanwhile *The Times*, which might have been expected to take exception given that Haig's youngest daughter Irene was married to Gavin Astor, chairman of The Times Publishing Company, maintained its traditional editorial independence. Its review (unsigned, as was *Times* policy until 1966) referred to the 'excellent narrative' and concluded that 'Mr Clark's book amounts to an indictment even of Haig, sometimes ironically directed, but almost everywhere with force of judgement'.[10] Alan would surely have been thrilled if he had known that the reviewer was the poet Edmund Blunden,[11] who was commissioned in 1915, although he did not join his battalion in France until the following May. What he wrote would have meant so much more if *Times* readers had been told his name.

Alan also heard in 1966 from one distinguished Field Marshal (retired, reluctantly), Montgomery of Alamein, who cut his teeth in the First World War. Alan did a lengthy interview with him in 1966 and also wrote an introduction for a new edition of Alan Moorehead's biography in 1967. When Alan discovered that Montgomery had not read *The Donkeys* he forwarded a copy. Montgomery was impressed. 'A dreadful tale,' he wrote. 'You have done a good job in exposing the total failure of the generalship.'[12]

The Clark family had rallied, too. Alan's mother sent a copy to her good Hampstead friend Meriel 'Mu' Richardson, wife of the actor Ralph Richardson. Back came a letter in August: 'I suppose already 1915 is history, but it is still too near for one to be anything but appalled and conscience-stricken, and so ashamed that such men died so. I am very grateful indeed to have read it. I hope he will continue writing, I hope to continue reading him.'[13] Eight years later Ralph Richardson would appear as British Foreign Secretary, Sir Edward Grey, in the film version of Joan Littlewood's *Oh What a Lovely War*, which was to owe a great deal to *The Donkeys*. J.B. Priestley, who served in Flanders, wrote to K that Alan's manner and style, 'seems exactly right'. His only criticism, 'it isn't long enough.'

Looking back at Alan's work nearly half a century on, Alistair Horne, whose own book on the later First World War battle of Verdun is considered standard, agrees with the judgements of Taylor and Fergusson. 'It was quite slapdash, not very well researched, not a particularly distinguished piece of work. I thought he was too unselectively rough on the Generals.' It did, however, have the merit of being 'provocative, saying things people hadn't said before'.[14]

The public voted at the bookshop tills, identifying what Michael Howard had called *The Donkeys'* 'entertainment' rather than its historical value. By October it was in its third impression and even in new year 1963 reprinted yet again.[15] In the same month Alan was delighted to tell Liddell Hart that Frances Phillips, his friend at William Morrow, which had put down an option of $500 earlier, had now confirmed the firm's purchase of the American rights for $1,000. Morrow would publish in January 1962. And in Milan the distinguished house of Longanesi acquired Italian rights, eventually publishing its translation later in 1962 under the title *I Somari* in a handsome small format.

★

The Donkeys, despite the contrary reviews, was the making of Alan's name as a historian. He was already reviewing books for *The Sunday Times*, having made a friend there in J.W. Lambert of the book pages, at the time *Bargains* was published. At the paper's weekly editorial conference when the Berlin crisis was at its peak, Lambert mentioned his name as a young historian not frightened of speaking his mind, with the added ability that he wrote well. He might, Lambert suggested, have an interesting view on the present crisis. Alan found himself commissioned to write the main leader-page piece for that weekend.

Everything he touched now seemed to attract controversy. Next to his photograph it stated, 'Alan Clark, one of the post-war school of young historians, sprang into prominence with the publication in July of his brilliant and controversial analysis of the battles of 1915 – *The Donkeys*. Aged thirty-two, he was a pupil at Christ Church of Professor Hugh Trevor-Roper. Here he presents his own interpretation of the Berlin crisis as seen in the perspective of history. His views are not necessarily those of the *Sunday Times*, but we believe they express the feelings of many, particularly younger, readers on the Berlin impasse.'[16] This prompted Robert Blake to write to Trevor-Roper, 'Can nothing be done to stop Alan Clark misusing your name? It was done (of course HE may not be to blame) in a particularly scandalous way in the *Sunday Times*. He is a vain and silly young man; as King George V observed about writers in general, he should be "stopped".'[17]

Alan could not now resist renewing contact with Trevor-Roper. Like an itch that must be scratched, he put fingers to his typewriter. 'I wonder how you are, and if the radio-active dust cloud that was aroused by *The Donkeys* has now subsided sufficiently to allow us to communicate. I never sent you a copy – I thought that you would probably prefer not to read it, or, I should say, to have read it.' Trevor-Roper now responded.

The fact is you wrote a book about my father-in-law. I have no personal feelings in the matter, but Xandra is devoted to him and to his memory. For her sake, I asked you two things only, viz: (1) that you should make it fair; (2) that you should not involve me. You made it very unfair – even Alan Taylor, no lover of Haig, pointed that out, and you must know that in a great number of places you chose demonstrably untrue, but damaging interpretations of character; and you published everywhere – not only in that book, but in other articles – that you were my pupil, in such a way that the Beaverbrook Press, that perpetual seed-bed of ancient rancours, was able to suggest that I was involved in the subject or the tone of your book. When all this was cooking, but before we would know the full nature of the concoction, you invited yourself, as a friend, to stay in our house and thus made things even worse when Xandra ultimately saw the book. Really, how can you regard our relations as unaffected by this?

Criticism of *The Donkeys* has not died down. In 1996, in his Foreword to the final volume of his magisterial history of the British cavalry, the Marquess of Anglesey described Alan's work as 'contemptible'. Anglesey thought Alan 'perhaps the most arrogant and least respectable of writers on the war'. *The Sunday Times* in its account of Anglesey's attack failed to mention that the two men had 'form'. Reviewing an earlier volume of the Anglesey history in the *The Daily Telegraph*, Alan had dared to ask, 'Is it not true that, in a practical military sense, cavalry are nearly always a disaster, a waste of space, and resources?'[18]

The Sunday Times solicited quotes from other historians. By now the pendulum of history had moved in favour of Haig. Commented Peter Simkins, senior historian at the Imperial War Museum: 'It is frustratingly difficult to counter Clark's prevailing view. But Haig was a bit like a football manager who suddenly takes over a big club, has a catastrophic injury list in the first season partly as a result of his own tactical failings, but by the third season gets it right and wins the European Cup. There were incompetent generals, but the British did not have a corner on the market. After all, the Germans lost the war which seems to suggest that their generals were as incompetent as any.'[19] Alan remarked in his own defence that *The Donkeys* was still selling, being reprinted twice, in 1993 and 1994.

On its American publication in March 1962 *The Donkeys* was widely reviewed, and praised. *The New York Times* (then as now the most influential American newspaper for book reviews) saw *The Donkeys* as 'controversial' and 'startling', comparing it with Cecil Woodham-Smith's *The Reason Why*, seeing the First World War generals as 'like the incomparable little lords she impaled' in her account of the Crimean War.[20] *The New York Times*'s Sunday edition, in its 'Book Review',[21] called on the British historian D.W. Brogan. Would he be an A.J.P. Taylor or, worse, a Michael Howard? Alan need not have worried: 'This is a savage, angry, intolerant, but impressive, convincing and deeply distressing book.' To Brogan, Alan Clark convicted the donkeys – although he felt 'mules' would have been a better name – out of their own mouths and concluded: 'The case against the British High Command of World War I is proven.'

The matter of the epigraph was not, however, forgotten. No-one was suggesting that the phrase itself, 'lions led by donkeys', was Alan's invention. When he and Liddell Hart had discussed the matter several years earlier they both thought that it probably had its origins in Napoleonic times. Researchers have since found a Crimean War reference in *The Times* where the British were led by asses. In the Franco-Prussian war it was *The Times* again who adapted the phrase, substituting donkeys for asses. Inevitably with a phrase that hits the spot it was also in the vocabulary of subsequent war commentators. Indeed, in 1927 P.A. Thompson wrote a book about how in the war of attrition that distinguished the First World War the side that made the fewer mistakes triumphed. He explained his title – *Lions Led by Donkeys*[22] – with the following apologia: 'The words that form the title ... were used early in the war, at the German Great Headquarters, to denote the English,' but Thompson fails to provide a source.

Some two years after the publication of *The Donkeys* Liddell Hart returned to the subject, which had obviously been worrying him. 'Where did you get the Falkenhayn quote?' he asked Alan. 'It was new to me.'[23] For once Alan did not reply to his mentor. In 1968 Liddell Hart was approached by the Imperial War Museum, who along with the Library for Contemporary World War Literature in Stuttgart had been asked by a *Daily Telegraph* reader for a definitive answer over the origin of the exchange. They had no record in either of their archives, and it was not to be found in biographies of Ludendorff, Hoffmann (who, incidentally, served for the entire war on the Eastern Front) or, for good measure, Falkenhayn and von Moltke. In 1989 Justin Wintle, in compiling *The Dictionary of War Quotations*, attributed the exchange simply to Alan Clark and *The Donkeys*, but did not mention Falkenhayn.[24]

There is an intriguing possibility: that the quotation comes from an account written during spring 1918, when the Germans launched their last great offensive. The memoirs of Princess Evelyn Blücher, published in July 1920, were a bestseller, going through eight impressions in five months. The Princess, although born in Brighton, had in 1907 married Count Blücher, great-grandson of the famous Marshal who turned the tide at Waterloo. Evelyn and her husband lived in England, but on the outbreak of war the Count's nationality forced them to return to Germany. They made their home with other 'internationals' at Berlin's Esplanade Hotel. Her memoirs were a private journal which she kept for her mother, a daughter of the twelfth Lord Petre. Although a detailed record of the war from the German side, it is seen through English eyes, and as she met everyone of note, and was in a position to see and hear all that went on in the military and political world, it was judged unique.[25]

On 9 April 1918 she wrote from Berlin: 'We hear universally that the pluck shown by the English was almost superhuman when they were taken by surprise . . . Even Ludendorff, hard, stern man that he is, confessed that he would take off his hat to the English for their absolutely undaunted bravery. He said they never lose their heads, and never appear desperate; they are always cool and courageous until the very moment of death and capture. I will put it exactly as I heard it straight from the Grosse Hauptquartier [GHQ]: "The English Generals are wanting in strategy. We should have no chance if they possessed as much science as their officers and men had of courage and bravery. They are lions led by donkeys."'

Alan had ignored correspondents on the subject for three decades, but in 1995, as John Baynes recorded in *Far From a Donkey: The Life of General Sir Ivor Maxse*,[26] 'A more recent direct approach to Alan Clark has been swiftly and courteously replied to. He states that "the quotation was given to me by Basil Liddell Hart. (I worked with him for two years while I was preparing *The Donkeys*.)"' Given Liddell Hart's question to Alan in 1963 this does, however, seem unlikely. But by 1995 he was no longer around to argue, having been dead twenty years.

It is hard now not to conclude that Alan, recognising that 'Lions led by donkeys' gave him an evocative title, created the dialogue and the source to justify it.

The story of *The Donkeys* had an unexpected musical coda. Some twenty months after its first publication, the radical theatre director Joan Littlewood, who was having enormous success with the Theatre Workshop company in east London at the Theatre Royal, Stratford-atte-Bowe, directed a musical entertainment under the title *Oh What a Lovely War*. From the late 1950s it seemed that everything Littlewood and her partner Gerry Raffles touched turned to gold: Shelagh Delaney's *A Taste of Honey* and Stephen Lewis' *Sparrers Can't Sing*, plays by Brendan Behan *(The Hostage* and *The Quare Fellow)*, the Frank Norman-Lionel Bart musical *Fings Ain't What They Used to Be* — and then in March 1963, *Oh What a Lovely War*. Joan Littlewood recalled in her autobiography, *Joan's Book*,[27] that this musical entertainment began with the songs of the First World War. It is clear that the idea came from a radio compilation by Charles Chilton, hitherto best known for his serial, *Journey into Space*.

For his new venture, Chilton was inspired by his father, who died in the First World War aged nineteen. In 1958, on holiday in France, and at the request of his grandmother, Chilton visited Arras to photograph his father's grave. Instead he found only his name inscribed upon a cemetery wall along with '35,942 officers and men of the Forces of the British Empire who fell in the Battle of Arras and have no known graves'. In his Theatre Royal programme note he wrote: 'What could have happened to a man that rendered his burial impossible? What horror could have taken place that rendered the burial of 35,942 men impossible and all in one relatively small area? The search for the answer to this question has finally led to this production, in the sincere hope that such an epitaph will never have to be written upon any man's memorial again.'

In 1962, nearly half a century after the British Expeditionary Force first crossed the Channel, the origins and conduct of the First World War had become a subject of debate. As so often happens it was the written word – by Barbara Tuchman, Alan Clark and Leon Wolff – that set the ball rolling. Joan Littlewood and Gerry Raffles were in fact particularly influenced initially by Tuchman's *Guns of August*. On the style that their anti-war play should take, Littlewood and Raffles considered and rejected formats by the playwrights Gwyn Thomas and Ted Allan, but the notion of the popular song particularly appealed to them.

The morning after Chilton's radio programme was broadcast, Raffles telephoned the BBC and asked for a copy. Chilton later recalled meetings at the Theatre Royal around Christmas 1962; next Raffles and Littlewood produced a treatment and by early February a script combining Chilton's material and their own. The final show was worked out by the beginning of March. For his radio programmes, Chilton identified an astonishing number of songs – 800 in all – including the well-remembered 'Roses of Picardy', 'Pack up your troubles' and 'Keep the home fires burning' as well as many that had been forgotten, but which *Oh What a Lovely War* would revive. It was Joan who, according to her memoirs, came up with the notion of the Pierrot show format.

Oh What a Lovely War may have been 'a musical entertainment', but it was also meant to be instructive. 'The war play', as Joan called it, had no script when they assembled their cast from Theatre Workshop regulars – among them Victor Spinetti, Murray Melvin, Brian Murphy, Ann Beach, Fanny Carby. Using factual material, it was gradually improvised in rehearsal. After early problems Joan encouraged Victor Spinetti, as the master of ceremonies, to extemporise. The mood changed; audiences, including many who had relatives who had served in Flanders, began to identify with it. There was still no formal script, but as Joan recounted to

Raffles before the official opening, 'it's rough, but it works'.

And work it did. The first public performance at the Theatre Royal, on 19 March, 1963, was swiftly followed by an Independent Television programme on Sunday, 21 April under a title that attracted Alan's interest – *Lions Led by Donkeys*. He appears, though, to have already been alerted. Indeed the morning after the television presentation, Alan's editor at Hutchinson, Graham Nicoll, wrote to say that having requested a script from Theatre Workshop, he had heard from Raffles that no script was available – one of the consequences of improvisation – but 'they were preparing one!'. Nicoll, meanwhile, had spoken to the Hutchinson lawyers and suggested that Alan take a shorthand writer to a performance to record the passages that 'spring naturally' from *The Donkeys*.

The correspondence trail that followed involved not only Alan, Hutchinson and Theatre Workshop, but his agent, Michael Sissons, as well as A.D. Peters, the eponymous chairman of the agency. Peters had produced plays between the wars, and now in his seventies still knew his way round the theatre.[28] His counsel was to prove invaluable. Within weeks the saga, inevitably, also encompassed lawyers for both sides.

The original Theatre Royal programme for *Oh What a Lovely War* had conflicting credits. The programme cover said it was 'based on an idea of Charles Chilton', inside that it was written by Charles Chilton with 'members of the cast'. There followed a note that authorship was based on 'factual data in official records, war memoirs, personal recollections and commentaries including those of . . . '. Hardly anyone of note in the history of the First World War was left out – from the Kaiser to Lloyd George, Ludendorff to Haig. The list of authors included Liddell Hart, Barbara Tuchman, Leon Wolff and the poets Siegfried Sassoon and Edmund Blunden – but not Alan Clark.

Alan first refers to *Oh What a Lovely War* in his diary, 4 May 1963. 'May get something out of Theatre Workshop.' He recounts being shown up to Gerry Raffles' office by 'a neat little East End blonde'. What he writes next would prove key: 'We negotiated. He seemed quite nice, agreed to pay £100.' They lunched in a pub with Joan Littlewood – 'I took to her. She's spontaneous and sincere and far from stupid.' Alan maintained afterwards that he extracted a confession from Raffles, and that the £100 was not in full and final settlement, but to pay off Hutchinson's bills to him over outstanding copyright claims on his book. Alan reported Raffles as suggesting he join them – 'I don't know if they were fooling me or not, but anyway have rewritten last scene for them.'[29]

Something, though, worried him and he decided to put the matter in the hands of his agents. Peters and Sissons saw Raffles on 27 May and quickly realised that they needed to attend a performance. Peters, the realist, warned Alan that the situation was tricky. Legally he doubted if there was much of a case because so much of Alan's material was available elsewhere, such as Hitchcock's own diary used in *Stand To*, the book that had originally inspired *The Donkeys*. 'Our chief hope', concluded Peters, 'lies in the fact that they admit that *The Donkeys* was one of their main sources, and that they would like you to do some work on improving the play, and on a film if there is one.'[30]

Peters, having seen the production with Sissons, wrote to Raffles that rather than finding Alan's claims exaggerated, he had come to the opposite conclusion. While it was true that much of the show consisted of traditional songs, 'the remainder is very largely based on *The Donkeys*'. Peters was firm: 'Clark is clearly entitled to be described as part author with Charles Chilton and to receive not less than one-third of the normal scale of royalties wherever the play is performed, plus a reasonable share of motion picture and other rights.'[31]

Raffles disagreed. *The Donkeys* together with a number of others 'was a source of considerable inspiration to us'. He also recounted a very different version of his meeting with Alan. The figure of £100 was, he said, suggested by Alan; Raffles agreed to pay him this in the hope that it would encourage him to feel involved and 'to give us the benefit of his brains and technical knowledge'.

Raffles ended his letter by asking Peters to be specific about any points taken from *The Donkeys* − 'if you are correct we will remove them from the show'.[32] Peters rebutted this as not 'practicable', and quoted from a letter that Alan had sent him on 8 May, that although there had been talk of £100, what he had in fact asked for was a down payment of £250 (or perhaps £200) immediately, proper acknowledgement in the programme and billing and a settlement for the future use of his material on stage and in film.[33]

As Peters put it to Alan, 'we seem to be at a deadlock'.[34] Alan: 'I don't want to press Theatre Workshop, whom I admire, for remuneration on account of work used at Stratford, but when they move on to the West End, and start putting on foreign performances, talking of movie rights and so on, then I think it only equitable that I should be allowed some share of the royalties.' He was generous in its understanding of *Oh What a Lovely War*: 'I sincerely believe that Raffles and Littlewood have not "pirated" my work in a brutally commercial sense, but have carried on my theme and given it a fresh and vivid impetus.'

He asked Peters to put his feelings to Raffles, seeking a gesture of appreciation – 'I hope and believe that he will respond . . . and we should accept this.' In return he wanted acknowledgement in the West End programme – it had just been announced that the production would be transferring to the Wyndham's Theatre.[35] On 20 June Alan and Jane took his parents to the West End first night. When Joan Littlewood introduced Tom Driberg, the Labour MP, to Kenneth and Jane Clark as 'Alan Clark's parents' it was a first, as he chortled in his diary, 'a very good moment'.[36] Relations between the Clarks senior and junior had been at a lowish ebb over money – according to Mama, in a 'vicious' phone call to Jane, 'Papa is having to sell shares to pay for all your children.' Alan resisted composing in response 'a shell-burst of a letter'.[37]

Enter the lawyers! On 28 June Oscar Beuselinck for Theatre Workshop offered 'a once and for all payment of £200' and to include a programme acknowledgement.[38] Peters was disappointed, but not defeated. 'I should very much like to fight on, referring the matter to the Arts Council first.' Here Peters was being canny. Theatre Workshop, who had been well supported by the Arts Council, were now coining in revenue. A lull ensued, but Raffles and Littlewood were not idle. Before the transfer to the West End they changed the Theatre Royal programme. Charles Chilton was written out of the credits inside with authorship given solely to Theatre Workshop, and to the list of authors of the factual data had been added the name of Alan Clark.

At the end of November a writ seeking an injunction, damages and costs was issued in the High Court Chancery Division in Alan's name against Chilton, Littlewood and Raffles. If the Plaintiffs had expected the Defendants immediately to cave in they were disappointed, but the new year brought interesting news and a crack in their defences. Chilton's solicitors revealed to Nicolas Cooke, representing Alan, that he had been 'persuaded to take a reduction in royalties on the grounds that the other two defendants were to make payments to us'. Meanwhile Beuselinck had now written to say that as the cost of the action in court would far exceed the benefits to anybody, it would therefore be advisable to see if 'we could arrive at a settlement'.[39]

Nicolas Cooke had it in mind to widen the fissure still further between Littlewood/Raffles and Chilton by negotiating not to continue proceedings against the latter. To Peters he reported a further interesting conversation with Chilton's solicitors: that other people had brought proceedings against Raffles and Littlewood and that in an affidavit it was

stated 'that parts of the play were taken from Alan Clark's book'.[40] Cooke
wished to keep the pressure on the other side, not least because of news
of a forthcoming American production of *Oh What a Lovely War*, to be
presented by Raffles and the legendary New York impresario David
Merrick, using much the same cast as in London but with the addition of
Barbara Windsor, who would prove Theatre Workshop's most enduring
star.[41]

Meanwhile Cooke and Beuselinck were jousting over terms of a possible
settlement. With average weekly takings in London of about £3,000 he
reckoned the royalty amount at stake for Alan was a minimum of £750. But
he was adamant that any settlement must also include future productions of
Oh What a Lovely War. He also added a warning that 'unless a settlement
is reached our client proposes to take proceedings in the United States'.[42]

The New York production opened at the Broadhurst Theatre on West
44th Street on 30 September. The programme is instructive, the cover
referring to 'Joan Littlewood's Musical Entertainment' and the credits
inside now reading

by

Theatre Workshop & Charles Chilton & The Members of the Cast.
(Military Adviser: Raymond Fletcher)
After a Treatment by Ted Allan

By the new year 1965 Sissons made a calculation that gross box office
receipts by Christmas amounted to something approaching $400,000 – at
half per cent royalty Alan would therefore receive $2,000.

The due processes of law ground on. Alan, as required, compiled a
detailed comparison of the stage script and *The Donkeys*, although as he
wrote to Cooke, 'what we ought to have got discovery of, and they have
concealed, is their own working copy of *The Donkeys* (and Chilton's also),
because that would really give the game away as it would be covered in
pencil marks'. He was also delighted by two other documents, one 'a
panicky letter' from Chilton's solicitors saying that '"the plaintiffs' allegations are substantially correct" and the other an affidavit sworn by Raffles
in connection with the action for copyright (settled) brought by Ted Allan
... in this Raffles frequently defended himself by claiming that *The
Donkeys* was his primary source – and not some script/treatment which
Allan had earlier submitted'.[43] So a settlement *had* been made with Ted
Allan! Alan ended his letter to Cooke: 'If Raffles & Littlewood had been
co-operative from the start and openly acknowledged my book as a source
of inspiration it would have had a very positive effect on the sales of the

book during the currency of the show, and I would have benefited from the general favourable publicity which was generated at the time.'

By February *Oh What a Lovely War* had come off in New York after a run of fewer than four months. Raffles and Littlewood had their fingers severely burnt, having mounted the production without a backer. Beuselinck continued to bluster over any possible settlement, maintaining that the events of the war were common knowledge. Meanwhile Alan was once again under pressure from his bank and needed a letter regarding the cash terms of a settlement to show his bank manager.

With April the likely month for the trial, it was no surprise to Nicolas Cooke when the Defendants capitulated. On 28 April he was finally able to write to Sissons that £1,000 would be paid as damages for breach of copyright in past stage performances.[44] The agreement with Chilton, Littlewood and Raffles also gave Alan five per cent of the gross proceeds of the film rights[45] – and these would be acquired by Richard Attenborough, who made the film in 1968. Len Deighton, also an uncredited producer, wrote the script.

The die, though, had been cast. Newspapers invariably now referred to *Oh What a Lovely War* as being based on *The Donkeys*. But Joan Littlewood's death in 2002 aged eighty-seven provided the opportunity for a corrective. Caroline Radcliffe, writing in *The Independent on Sunday*, reminded readers that credit must go to Chilton, even though Littlewood 'took both the glory and most of the financial rewards'.[46] Just how true this was can be seen from the published playscript which, while reflecting the involvement of everyone except Ted Allan, is copyrighted 'Joan Littlewood Productions Ltd'.[47]

The final letter in the file was from Cooke to Alan enclosing a copy of his letter to Beuselinck with the full terms of the settlement. 'I think this should satisfy the bank manager.'[48] Not that there was much left after the lawyers had taken their fees.

Alan rarely looked back. At the time he was pleased to have won the case, but the reception of *The Donkeys* left a shadow over his memory. He did not write a fresh introduction for a new paperback edition in 1991 (as he had with successive editions of his later work, *Barbarossa*) but simply placed the 'author's copies' from his publishers on a Saltwood bookshelf. That introduction could have been a useful vehicle to come clean over the Ludendorff-Hoffmann epigraph. Shortly before his death in 2007, Euan Graham, who was a friend of Alan's for fifty years, recalled a conversation over lunch in the mid-1960s. The legal action against Littlewood and Raffles had not yet been settled. Graham remembered Alan saying, 'It's a bit awkward, actually,' to which he responded, 'Well, give the provenance.' At this point Alan paused, looked sheepish, and finally said, 'well, I invented it.' Graham responded, 'If you invented it you will get the copyright. They can't argue!' The saga demonstrated Alan's essential lack of discipline where historical detail was concerned, and, as Graham commented, just how 'sly, just how devious' he could be.

His future work would show what he learnt from the experience.

EIGHTEEN

Tackling the Second World War

As progress on *The Donkeys* inched its way forward in the spring of 1960 Alan was already thinking ahead. To Basil Liddell Hart he wrote: 'I am very taken with the idea of . . . the Battle of Crete.'[1]

The battle for Crete in May 1941 was something that Alan remembered. He was thirteen and taking a keen interest in the war, even receiving telegrams from his mother about the progress of the German invasion with advance, if not always correct, information from her seemingly well-connected friends. Writing now to Liddell Hart from Bratton, where an 'enormous number of tasks daily present themselves here in this strictly "undeveloped" farmhouse', he confessed to being 'quite fired up by the Crete idea. What an incredible operation that was!' And here he was writing about the war to Liddell Hart exactly twenty years after the Battle of Britain. 'Does it not make one reflect on the possible result if, in July and August of 1940, the Luftwaffe had concentrated solely on the fighter aerodromes in Kent while scraping together every Ju 52 they could lay their hands on for a really big lift in early September. Brr!'[2]

Alan's links with Beaverbrook now bore spectacular fruit. On the strength of his Sir John French article in *History Today* he was approached by Charles Wintour, Editor of Beaverbrook's London newspaper, the *Evening Standard*, who had heard about the Crete project and immediately offered Alan £900 plus £100 expenses to write a series for the paper. It would be published in May the following year, the twentieth anniversary of the German invasion of the island.

With the provisional title *The Loss of Crete* he gave his synopsis the subtitle 'an inquiry into one of the more spectacular defeats suffered by this country in WWII'. At the start of the battle he pointed out that the enemy force was outnumbered by over thirty to one, but this numerical inferiority was compensated for by its bravery and an extremely high standard of training. In ten days the Germans gained mastery over the island, 'inflicting losses that were militarily calamitous and, to the Navy, irreplaceable'.

At the time he wrote his account one strand of information was still secret: the operation at Bletchley Park (known as Ultra) that broke the Enigma cipher encryptions within the German High Command. F.W. Winterbotham, who was responsible for the organisation, distribution and security of the vital information that resulted, later wrote, 'when Ultra informed us that Crete was to be taken by an airborne invasion and followed it up by also supplying all the detailed plans, there was some hope that we would inflict a defeat on the airborne forces, even if we had to evacuate afterwards'.[3] Antony Beevor, whose *Crete: the Battle and the Resistance* was published almost thirty years later in 1991,[4] thinks it unlikely that Alan was unaware of the Ultra information even though he was unable to refer to it.[5] Certainly it would be one reason why he was critical in his synopsis of the many command failures 'at the highest levels'. He was also incredulous that from the time the British first occupied Crete seven generals held the command in rapid succession (one for only two days), hardly a recipe for rallying the Allied forces. The final commander, the New Zealander General Freyberg, was, he judged, 'a bad choice'.[6]

In a letter to Liddell Hart, Alan could not resist bragging about the *Standard*'s fee before adding, 'I have got an agreeable competition going on over my head for the hardback rights, the German rights and the US rights. Really it is too ridiculous – I put far more into *The Donkeys*, and got an advance of £150.'[7] Liddell Hart thought the synopsis excellent and agreed with Alan's view of Freyberg, whose reputation, he said, was 'over-inflated'.[8]

If it all seemed comparatively easy, the contractual situation swiftly turned tortuous and convoluted. Anthony Blond, who now ran his own eponymous publishing house, wished to publish Alan's Crete book and in November 1960 offered him £750 for world rights, which he claimed to be 'the highest advance we have ever paid'. Blond went on to suggest that 'due to your own persuasiveness' the services of Alan's agent Michael Sissons would be redundant; instead they would use a contract devised by solicitors Rubinstein Nash.[9]

This would not be the last time Sissons and Alan clashed over Blond. Sissons, who had negotiated Alan's *Evening Standard* contract, was determined to earn his commission on the book deal. 'Blond's letter gives the impression of complete confidence that he will get the Crete book,' wrote Sissons. 'I hope you haven't given him this impression.' He had talked about the project to Hutchinson, who had an option on Alan's next book dating from *The Donkeys* contract, and had offered his editor, Raleigh Trevelyan, British Commonwealth volume rights for £1,000. He was awaiting a response. If Hutchinson said no, then Sissons would offer it for the same sum 'to one or two other first-rate non-fiction publishers before we go back to Blond'. As comparative new boys on the block the firm of Anthony Blond had yet to earn that rating in Sissons' view. 'There is already considerable interest in this book and you are quite entitled to capitalise on it to the fullest possible extent.'[10]

Sissons' caution appeared to have considerable merit when Blond confessed to Alan the following week that the firm had financial problems. Under the agreement with Alan he was due to pay him £500 on signature, but 'we are temporarily without £500. Apparently as this is a seasonal business we will be flush January and February – business is very good at the moment.' A solution was suggested by the firm's accountant: instead of £500 now and £250 on delivery Blond would pay Alan the full £750 in February.[11] By now the contractual situation was bad-tempered. Alan having confessed the Hutchinson situation, Blond responded, tersely, 'There can be no question of your dealing with any other publisher as this commitment will be honoured.'[12]

Alan remained in Zermatt with his head down. For once he could not get out of a deadline. 'The Crete book is turning out to be an absolute back-breaker,' he told Liddell Hart. 'There is a very great deal more research than I had bargained for when I allowed the *Standard* to make delivery by 15 May a condition!' He was, though, absorbed by the subject – 'turning out even more interesting than I thought'. He had been reading Churchill's history of the Second World War, the discussion in volume three about the use of tanks – 'Tiger-Cubs' as Churchill and General Wavell called them.[13] 'Of course the tanks would have clinched it, but on my reading of the evidence it could even have been won by an infantry battle if the New Zealanders had been properly handled, and what a victory it would have been!' Alan now went into some detail.

While grand strategy always interested him as a historian he also had a penchant for uncovering tactical detail and working it into his narrative, as the remainder of his letter to Liddell Hart testifies. 'The facts which I did not know were that the Germans themselves (a) were so uncertain about the outcome of the battle that it was not even mentioned on Berlin radio until D plus 5 and the following day OKW [the Wehrmacht High Command] threatened to institute an "inquiry" into the failure of the Cretan operations and (b) insisted on the early withdrawal of Richthofen's VIII air fleet in preparation for "Barbarossa" [Hitler's attack on the Soviet Union]. Inter-service rivalry may partly explain this tendency to crab what was really a Luftwaffe operation, but the source seems reliable

enough, the testimony of Baron von der Heydte, who commanded the
1st battalion of 3rd Parachute regiment, and took the surrender of Canea.'[14]

Meanwhile Sissons was trying to resolve the contractual impasse. Blond
had sent Alan his firm's cheque for £750, and asked in a PS if he might
come and stay at Zermatt and learn to ski, adding, 'Please arrange an
instructor as I don't want to be bottom of class. Will there be snow?'[15]
But contracts with Hutchinson had also been agreed for £1,000. Sissons
told Alan to sign, otherwise Hutchinson might change their mind, particularly as there was rumour of a rival book. 'If you are still keen on the
book I can't advise you too strongly to get it firmly tied up now.'[16]

Blond refused to give up – 'just let it glow – we can certainly sell our
book in the USA – we are getting rather good at rights'. But Alan had to
deliver a first-rate script. Blond demanded 'a "classic", not solemn, not
"gimmicky journalese"'. As a concession, and to avoid problems with
Hutchinson until the matter had been resolved, Blond agreed to avoid
inflaming the issue and took the book out of the firm's catalogue. 'Please
tell Peters this and to hell with him anyway.'[17] Hutchinson was not prepared
to back down. On 10 February its cheque arrived at the Peters office.
Sissons wrote immediately to Alan, asked him to sign and return the
contract and then he would send the money.

Someone had to give way. Sissons wheelered and dealered. Blond
would have only British Commonwealth rights (as had been offered to
Hutchinson). He would get round the terms of the Hutchinson option
by treating it as a commission from Blond. Alan, too, had to accept paying
the full A.D. Peters commission of ten per cent (Sissons explained to Alan
that he had been prepared to act for him over the *Standard* for five per
cent as this entailed handling only the contract).[18] Two weeks later Blond
had agreed in principle, and Sissons wrote a wrap-up letter to Alan. The
key element was delivery by 31 May, although Sissons acknowledged that
Blond was 'in a rather weak position' having paid up on signature.[19] If
only it were so simple!

A further fortnight went by. Blond was unhappy at the terms of the
contract he was now being asked to accept. It was Alan's turn to get tough
with his friend. Writing from the St James's Club, he told Blond that he
was 'concerned to hear that you were making difficulties over the contract
for *The Loss of Crete* ... I must make it clear to you that your original
letter to me a copy of which I returned cannot be considered a contract
as I did not accept the specific terms which you suggested therein. In any
case these "terms" depended on your paying on signature which you did
not do. I have always told you that A.D. Peters were my representatives

and empowered to settle a contract. And I am afraid that the task of negotiating subsidiary rights must be left in their hands.'[20]

On 6 June Blond, from his new Doughty Street offices, sent a one-word letter: 'Enough.'

Alan managed to keep the *Evening Standard*'s 15 May deadline. He had given the paper a foretaste six weeks earlier, leading Charles Wintour to remark that he was delighted, but 'My God! Watch out for libel.'[21] On 13 May Alan had picked up from the Howard Street Bureau in Jermyn Street three copies of his typed 56,000-word manuscript. After the extracts, which ran over five days, Wintour wrote again: 'Everyone I have spoken to agrees that your series is most fascinating.'[22] What he called 'the fall of Crete' had also attracted scores of letters. Blond adopted *The Fall of Crete* as the book's title, but any thought that he might publish it in the anniversary year was quickly forgotten. Alan was juggling revisions to *The Donkeys* and, having picked up his £1,000 from the *Standard*, let the new book simmer. His one concern was a rival, John H. Spencer, who was also writing about the Crete campaign.[23]

Alan certainly had more work to do. He made contact with Dan Davin, a New Zealander working at the Clarendon Press, Oxford, who had written the official history of New Zealand's forces in the Second World War. Not only did he loan material to Alan, but he also offered to read the proofs. In Britain, the months immediately before the eventual publication of *The Donkeys* in July 1961 were so crowded that it is hardly surprising that Alan neglected *The Fall of Crete*, even if he excused to himself the Mediterranean cruise he took with John and Richard Pollock as a research trip. He did however write enthusiastically to Blond, having seen the jacket proof showing a German parachutist with a Luftwaffe transport aircraft in the background.[24]

On *Crete* Alan had few expectations for foreign editions. However he was pleasantly surprised that William Morrow made an offer. With no Americans involved in the Crete campaign, it was not a major book for the firm, but they had had considerable commercial success with *The Donkeys* and wished to keep in with this talented young British historian. After all, who knew what he might do next? They paid an advance of $500, a contract negotiated by A.D. Peters' New York associate, Harold Matson. Nor did foreign sales end there: French rights were snapped up by Laffont for £150, a good price, and Italian by Garzanti.

Blond wished to publish early in 1962 but, as Sissons had anticipated, with the full advance paid Alan had no incentive as he had with the

Evening Standard. The firm dispatched his proofs in mid-January, with instructions from Blond's business partner, Desmond Briggs, to 'return in one week'. Meanwhile Alan should 'steam ahead with the index all save actual pagination'.[25] Five weeks went by and Blond himself scribbled a postcard: 'Urgent you attend to proofs. Now a week [*sic*] overdue. Otherwise, no index'.[26] Neither Blond nor Briggs knew that Jane had delivered her second child on 2 February or that the complications that followed the birth had taken Alan's mind off such mundane matters as proofs.

The Spencer book, which had a similar image on its jacket, beat *The Fall of Crete* to the bookshops, but Alan reviewed it, unfavourably, in the *Evening Standard*, alleging that the author had made full use of the material that had appeared in his *Standard* series the year before. To Liddell Hart he remarked: 'I only hope some intelligent reviewer does them both together.'[27] He must therefore have been pleased that *The Observer* gave both books to Anthony Verrier, who judged: 'There is no doubt that Mr Clark's book is the better of the two.'[28]

He felt that *The Listener* – reviewer Monty 'something-or-other' – gave him his one bad review. To Hugh Trevor-Roper he quoted the relevant sentence: '"it all seems rather bad luck on the eminent professor under whom Mr Clark is <u>said</u> to have read history"'. Alan didn't end there. 'That worried me at the time as I somehow imagined it following your gentle dismissal, raising one hand, when asked by him about me at a high table. But then persecution mania is an adjunct/subjunct of egomania, which I definitely have.'[29] Trevor-Roper did not let Alan get away with this. 'You state your suspicion, indeed conviction, that a critical review of your book by Monty Woodhouse was inspired by me at some high table. This is indeed persecution mania. I have never even met Monty Woodhouse, who has nothing to do with Oxford university . . . Your suspicions are absurd.'[30]

Alan was obviously desperate not to lose Trevor-Roper's friendship. 'Honestly Hugh, I could <u>never</u> be cold towards you although I might (I suppose) be querulous. I have a tremendous admiration for you; avidly search out, read and enjoy everything which you write; and regard you as <u>the</u> historian, doyen or whatever-you-like, who towers above all the other dabblers in our own and other countries.'[31]

The Times criticised the haste with which *The Fall of Crete* had been published, and 'the absence of needed maps'.[32] The paper was by no means alone, Alan himself being furious with Blond. 'Little Toby [as he called Blond] has done it <u>without</u> the Maleme and Galatas maps <u>or</u> Contents. My God.'[33] He wrote to the main newspapers and journals which were

likely to review his book asking them to pass on his apologies to reviewers –
'this makes it almost impossible to follow the details of the fighting which
I describe'.[34]

In sending Liddell Hart his copy, which he inscribed, he was more
forthright: – 'that fool* [the asterisk indicated a footnote: '*not strong
enough a word'] Blond allowed himself to be stampeded by the appearance
of Spencer's book and has made a very slovenly production of mine in the
interests of speed'. With the lack of those crucial maps he felt his book
'forfeits any claim which I had hoped for it of being the authoritative
work on this short but interesting little campaign. I am concerned at the
damage it may do to my reputation.'[35] His shared his concern in a letter
to his American publisher, as Morrow had arranged to import copies
printed in Ireland alongside the Blond edition. John T. Lawrence, Morrow's president, was quick to respond: 'I found your letter both disturbing
and frustrating . . . I only wish we had known about their sins of omission
in time to have done something about them.'

Alan's complaints against Blond did not end there. He could not find
copies in the shops. Blond in his response went on the offensive: 'The
whole affair which may easily end modestly well was initially wrong footed
by your having kept the proofs so damned long.' But the book sold,
allowing Blond to reprint. However the maps and the contents page
remained absent.

Given that so many survivors of the Crete campaign were alive and
quick to comment on any account, particularly by someone who was not
'one of us', Alan was gratified by their response. As well as Dan Davin,
Alan had consulted another New Zealander, Geoffrey Cox, by now Editor
of Independent Television News. Cox had served with the 2nd New
Zealand Division in Crete, and wrote: 'I think you have done a very good
job. I agree by and large with your analysis of what went wrong – even
though I think you have been a bit harsh on those who did go wrong.
But that is the privilege of one generation writing of another – and I have
the feeling that I muttered many similar views to myself at the time.'[36]

Overall the reception for *The Fall of Crete* pleased its author. To Liddell
Hart he wrote: 'The critics have taken the book, and me, seriously and
recognised it as a contribution, which is what I wanted – being anxious
to avoid repeating the slightly "sensational" *Donkeys* at too short an
interval.'[37]

Four years after the original publication Alan received a letter from an
RAF participant. 'Magnificent,' he wrote to Alan; '. . . told in such a way
that I at any rate even read the full stops and the commas.'[38]

NINETEEN

Barbarossa *and Family Man*

Of Alan's three major war histories *Barbarossa*, his account of the Russian–German conflict that raged from 1941 until the war's end in 1945, stands head and shoulders above the others. More than forty years have elapsed since its first publication, yet it remains in print on both sides of the Atlantic. Inevitably, a good deal of its content and source material have been superseded. As Alan wrote in a fresh introduction thirty years after the book's first publication, 'many millions of words have since been written on and around the subject by survivors, participants and commentators'. But what attracts the reader still is Alan's appreciation of the German military mind and his talent for telling a story. In all its ultimate horror it remains a vivid account, a page-turning narrative, but written with a distinct point of view.

There are two versions of *Barbarossa*'s conception. If one believes the memoirs of Anthony Blond,[1] it was he who suggested that to follow *The Fall of Crete* Alan should tackle 'the really serious and bloody conflict' between Russia and Germany. According to Blond, Alan then sold the idea to Hutchinson for £7,000 – a sum, he said, obviously beyond his own firm's means; he retaliated by commissioning Ronald Seth, 'a brilliant hack', whose account pre-empted Alan's by a year. It did not, however, make waves. In Alan's account he had the idea for *Barbarossa* while working on his Crete book. He was intrigued by German uncertainty over the outcome of its airborne invasion and the early withdrawal of Richthofen's VIII Air Corps in preparation for the invasion of Russia. Searching for some background reading to 'Barbarossa', he failed to find a satisfactory account. Was this then 'the big subject' he was looking for?

By Christmas 1961 he had made up his mind and told Liddell Hart that in his writing plans *Barbarossa* had taken over from a book on the fate of the Fifth Army as he did not wish to be typecast as a First World War historian. 'Barbarossa – *what* a subject! I don't see how it can come out at less than 600 pages.'[2] At Bratton, Jane recalls that money was tight; thus whether *Barbarossa* would actually be Alan's next book depended on the money he could expect on both sides of the Atlantic, particularly from America. In February 1962 Hutchinson snapped up British rights for, as the contract shows, an advance of £2,500, not £7,000 as Blond states, but still substantially in excess of anything he had previously been paid. In the United States he hoped to receive at least the same from William Morrow, who were about to publish *The Donkeys*. Liddell Hart admitted that this was a larger sum than he had ever been paid for a military history – 'Who's your agent?'[3]

Jane was pregnant again. However, matters did not progress simply. Early on she nearly miscarried, and recuperated at her parents' near Salisbury before returning to Bratton, where Alan had been completing *The Fall of Crete*, with Nanny Greenwood in charge of James who would soon be two. When her waters broke Jane was rushed by ambulance the twenty-five miles to Freedom Fields Hospital in Plymouth. She recalls: 'Still the baby didn't come; there was endless getting into baths. Nanny threw a tantrum, said she couldn't possibly look after the house and baby and cook. A prima donna; she had to have a nursery nurse, the old school.' She thought of Bratton as a backwater with nothing to do, so Alan had to drive her and James back to Saltwood. There Alan rang Freedom Fields where the gynaecologist, when asked 'How's Jane?', replied 'Not good at all.' Nothing was going right: Alan went to Saltwood church to pray, but it was shut. When Andrew was eventually born on 2 February 1962 he didn't breathe. Like James at birth he was, remembers Jane, 'huge, 9lbs; they had to whisk him away; then I started bleeding. I just heard a nurse say "she's not clotting". There was panic. I was lying in a warm lake of warm water, but suddenly realised not water, but blood. Interesting, I never slept properly after that. Every time I was dropping off I had to turn over. Panic stations, drips, blood, glucose, the lot – I remember I thought that I never wanted to see Andrew again. Nurse came in next morning and the whole place was like a battlefield, blood everywhere. I was so tired, absolutely shaking like mad; not enough blood to go round. I told the nurse, I just want to sleep; no, I do not want to see the baby. Take it away. They knocked me out. I did that thing you read about: I couldn't sleep, but also I couldn't move to ring the bell. I could hear what was going on, people leaving the room next door. But I couldn't sleep. Then the nurse came in about 6.30 – "You've had a lovely sleep." "I have not been asleep." "Oh yes, you have." They'd given me this huge injection. I had a rotten time.' Nor was that the end of it. 'Al didn't come for ages; he didn't come back down to Plymouth. I can't remember when he actually appeared.

The father not appearing, lots of muttering, not turning up. He might well have turned right round and driven back again. He couldn't take illness; he couldn't face anything like that.'[4]

With Jane still in hospital Alan indulged himself, beginning a new volume of diaries. It was 18 February. 'The first sniff of spring and summer evenings in the air, a smell of stirring within the leaf mould, of rising sap, a faster-beating vein.'[5] He spent 'a very pleasant three days' in London, visiting the Establishment nightclub, then at the height of its 'swinging sixties' fame, with Michael Briggs, also the Colony Club, where the painter 'Francis Bacon very funny,' and chasing girls. His mind was also on cars. He was taken by a new Mercedes 300SE cabriolet, 'but those SS men on the staff!'.

Only after Jane left hospital did Nanny Greenwood take over, although she was upset on discovering that the Clarks had also advertised for an au pair. Alan meanwhile was complaining of having to be 'a sort of permanent nurse-maid'.[6] On Jane's return they went to Zermatt, leaving Nanny to follow on with the baby (who had to have his own passport). Andrew's christening at Saltwood church on 10 April had Tony Rudd, Graham Sutherland and Celly as godparents, and James, now two, looking 'beautiful and happy in his long breeks and "prickle pin" boots'. However Alan reported an incident at Saltwood that left a bad taste. 'Mama "whine-sneered" and reduced Jane to tears. I lost my temper with Mama – "I've always known you've loathed me" etc. So it is (a) obvious that we can't come here again this year, (b) obvious Nanny, who is being extremely tiresome, needs substantial bolstering by (i) nursemaid (ii) cook. Well one can't get a cook alone so that means a couple.'

Finances were never far from Alan's mind. With the purchase of the larger Watchbell House (No. 31) and associated expenses he needed a chunk of capital. At some time in the past his father had promised him a Pissarro. When Alan saw that an identical one from the Somerset Maugham estate had gone for £28,000 this seemed the answer. On 13 April, his birthday, he recorded a conversation. 'Papa, in one of those strange clairvoyant flashes of his said on a walk (shades of a reversal of that terrible pre-marriage settlement walk), "of course I don't know how much it is or where and what arrangements you are making, and so on, but remember you'll always get the Pissarro(!!!)." Incredible isn't it?' Alan, so critical of his father's neglect of him when he was growing up, now remembered a similar act of generosity from twenty years before. 'What a marvellous man he is. I felt much the same as that time at Eton when I wrote and told him that I thought of selling my stamp collection to buy some binoculars and he sent me the cheque – "a pity to part with such an old friend".'

Sotheby's could not put the Pissarro into auction until October, but were prepared to make an advance of £11,000. Typically Alan recorded that this was more or less swallowed up transferring £40,000 to UBS in Switzerland and by buying 'Miss Dawnays', as he called the pink-washed Studio Cottage at Rye Harbour which he had always wanted. Jane looked after the completion and impressed Alan by seeing it through 'in seven days flat', having advised a bid in cash. The price, with contents, was £1,300. 'A good buy,' he thought, and once done up proposed letting it at twelve guineas a week.

Alan used Studio Cottage as his base for 'working hours' and a 'drive on *Barbarossa*'. But he confessed to his diary, 'only trouble, getting screamingly frustrated sexually … but this would be a wonderful place to lead a bachelor existence'. In August he bought a Thunderbird, 'sexual frustration at the bottom of it, I suppose … preferable even to a Porsche or E-type'. He thought it a classic car of the future. *Barbarossa* excited him. 'I just need time,' he wrote in September 1962. Frances Phillips from William Morrow was passing through London. He wondered how he could impress her. In October in London he found it 'really marvellous to be recognised as a young historian – Gladwyn [Jebb] nodding etc, to me and expecting a work of serious scholarship'.

The outside world interfered in October with what he called 'this bloody Cuban crisis'. He had no time for Kennedy and what he saw as 'direct confrontation with Soviet power'. With missile sites being built in Cuba, and with the US threatening military action against Cuba if American interests were threatened, nuclear war did seem possible. Alan recorded Liddell Hart on the phone: 'You will know in a few days whether your children will still be alive'. Alan commented that a bad night followed, and he wondered if he and Jane and the children should head for Bratton, or Zermatt or where?

Would the 'war scare' wreck the price of the Pissarro? But all was not gloom. His American agent's tactics of showing the *Barbarossa* synopsis around had brought an offer of $12,500 from another US publisher, World. 'That's the stuff!' When Liddell Hart immediately asked for further particulars one detects a touch of envy.

On 28 October the international crisis ended with an agreement between the US and the Soviet Union: the missile sites would be dismantled. Alan commented, 'The Russians backed down totally and victory for JFK. Funnily enough Khrushchev doesn't seem to bear any ill-will.'

But Alan had another concern. Jane washed his hair and told him she thought he was going bald. 'Have I lost vitality. Or is it just nervous (apprehension) lassitude?'

How apposite, he noted, that contemporary and historical Soviet affairs should now overlap. William Morrow topped the World offer for *Barbarossa* with an advance of $17,000. Alan told Liddell Hart that he felt particularly lucky that 'military history seems to have become highly fashionable'. He added that the Americans didn't know what they were getting – 'one of the conclusions which is emerging is that the Russians could have fought the Germans to a standstill on their own, without any aid. H'm.'[7] And yet 'great difficulty in getting down to work', he added on arriving at Zermatt for Christmas. But once there he read John Wheeler-Bennett's *The Nemesis of Power: The German Army in Politics, 1918–1945*.[8] 'Of course the double German revival after each war shows everything is possible from an industrialised country if the leadership is inspired. But two things required. First, elimination of the democratic process to give security and continuity to the leadership; second, some sort of overall global threat which allows you to get away with it (communism in each case). The Hegelian tension must exist to produce a perfect synthesis.'

He thought afresh about a political career, starting at the foot with Rye Council after completing *Barbarossa*, before trying for Parliament. Academe was another idea – if *Barbarossa* was well received, a chair of military history at Edinburgh? Sell up everything in exchange for a big house in Scotland? His reading also included Gavin Maxwell's *Ring of Bright Water*, about bringing an otter back from Iraq and rearing it in Scotland, which he was 'enjoying, yet being a little unsettled by . . . never forget, nature is also "red in tooth and claw"'.

After Christmas he returned briefly from Zermatt – escorting Nanny home for Hogmanay – but ostensibly for a session with Liddell Hart. Although staying at Saltwood he drove to London for a New Year's Eve fancy dress ball in Chelsea given by Michael Alexander and Bunty Kinsman. Alan chose a medieval outfit at Nathan's – tabard, chainmail helmet and tights – 'looked pretty good'. To this he added a pikestaff. He was definitely on the make, but with a girl in tow he became involved with a rival outside Crosby Hall in Cheyne Walk. '"You forget I'm armed," I said mock grimly. My God, he wrenched that pike from my hands, took two swipes at me – I'd have been unconscious and needed several stitches if they'd connected.' The assailant threw the pike, which broke in two – 'a pity as it comes from the Saltwood undercroft'. Alan resorted to skills honed at Eton and used his fists, a left and a right on the jaw, then landed

blows on the mouth and the side of the head. Alan's friend Euan Graham
and others arrived. His rival 'went all magnanimous, shook hands, "She's
all yours"'. And she was.

The new year and being back in Zermatt led to a *réflectif*, encouraged
by reading his early journals from the mid-fifties. 'The first fine, spring-
like day. A real shining day and Jane, who went up, said there were shirt-
sheeves at Sunegga.' He thought about his achievements – 'a lot really
with my lovely family and my books and income'. But he speculated on
how it might be if he were still a bachelor, 'and successful as I am'. He
would, he thought, be living at Rye, but would he be happy? 'I'd probably
have been driven to marriage in the end, and got someone very unsuitable.
Or been outmanoeuvred by Col's prior marriage to Violette.'[9] He concluded, 'I have so much to thank God for, and particularly that there are
so few regrets in my past life.'

As spring turned to summer so Alan needed to get on with *Barbarossa*, but
there were distractions. Girls, yes, and one in particular, very much 'the
succulent little mistress' he had hoped for at the end of the 1950s. Now
he was writing of 'the complete sexual emancipation dear little Jane allows
me'. As for houses, he and Jane and the boys had settled happily back in
Rye, but Bratton remained a summer delight, even if, as he recorded over
Whitsun weekend, it needed several licks of paint.

Alan sweated it out, writing mainly at Bratton. By 1 August 1963
he had reached Chapter Six, which triggered payment of a further
portion of the Hutchinson advance. He also reported that Morrow
were 'very enthusiastic' from what they had read. Could he complete
it by Christmas? Then his back started playing up (had a disc slipped?),
and suddenly a major health scare took over with difficulty in swallowing,
a semi-sore throat, and strange intermittent stomach cramps. 'Totally
out of condition.' He would institute a tough regime – 'Alan Clark
becomes a monk!' Then panic. 'Really thought I had got Hodgkins;
really thought it, I mean and had planned the whole thing out, down
to getting the Public Trustee to deal with my estate and send my letters
to the boys on their birthdays etc etc.' Once again his hypochondria
had taken hold. In Saltwood's library he looked up 'lymph glands' in
the *Encyclopaedia Britannica* – and found 'exact symptoms. I was in a
blubber.' A visit to the Tony Richardson film of *Tom Jones* was
'delightful', but a frightful night followed before he drove the family
to London next morning. 'God that drive, nearly fainted about three
times due to sheer screaming nervous tension.' He had a 'crazy

depersonalised lunch with Vinnikov' (a contact at the Soviet Embassy) and then 'something made me go via [doctor] Rowntree. I steeled myself to ask him and the whole thing exploded in a second when he told me my blood count. No sensation of relief has ever been so sudden or (therefore) so absolute.'

He had been reading the collected and connected essays of the novelist Simon Raven,[10] which caused him to reflect on the pleasures of being a writer – 'how I envy him his freedom and regime! Yet, I regret nothing really. How could I with sweet, darling Jane ("You're my Tom Jones") and the fairheads. All I wish is that I shall find time to take off on a great "ton". Italy, Venice, Greece, the Balkans – drinking, raping, sentimentalising, meandering. That and a lecture post at an American university are the two things I want mildly for myself.'

As year end approached he was behind with *Barbarossa* and heard from his American publishers of a rival book, *Russia at War 1941–1945* by Alexander Werth[11] – 'definitely a race'. Spending Christmas at Bratton, he caught Euan Graham's cold, which went straight to his tonsils. There had been talk earlier in the year of a tonsillectomy, which he now thought inevitable. Worried next about the colour of his urine, he convinced himself that he was incubating jaundice, 'a horrible disease ... general sign of a real crack-up, deeply ill'. And what if the boys caught it? And what if he died? 'I can't bear the idea of them suffering, of being deprived of our company and resonance.'

By Easter he was on the verge of completing *Barbarossa*, but his tonsillectomy was fixed for his thirty-sixth birthday on 13 April 1964. He and Jane had decided to look for a house closer to London. Then Michael Sissons put on the pressure for delivery of *Barbarossa* as he hoped to sell serial rights, but scared Alan on learning about his tonsils – 'oh watch out ... there's a 48 per cent chance at your age that it will make you impotent'. Alan wrote a long account of being in University College Hospital, but chiefly noted his first reaction on coming round. 'I thought I was in some country house weekend; then could see the blood coming out of my nose onto the pillow'. He had his first proper food twenty-four hours later – 'triumphant at having eaten a boiled egg for breakfast' – and enjoyed good music on the radio.

In Devon he forgot Jane's birthday and was mortified when she wept. Was it to make amends that he now bought her a red E-type Jaguar? This was all very well. 'I hadn't even got my driving licence,' she remembers. One day at Bratton she was reversing the E-type under Alan's instructions into one of the cob barns. 'We had the pony trap there. I caught it on the pony trap, a scratch down one side. We had it resprayed, but everyone thought it had been in a crash. We should have left it.'

Monday, 22 June, the anniversary of the Barbarossa invasion, Alan delivered the typescript to his publishers on both sides of the Atlantic. Not surprisingly he wrote, 'last night felt so well'. It was, in every way, the big book he had been hoping for. 'Barbarossa' being, he wrote in his preface, 'the greatest and longest land battle which mankind has ever fought. Its outcome recast the world balance of power and completed the destruction of the old Europe, which the Great War had begun.' His text set out to justify that. His relationship with the *Evening Standard*, which had begun so profitably with a week of anniversary articles on the fall of Crete in 1961, was now renewed. Charles Wintour did not need the prompting of Lord Beaverbrook, who had died on 9 June, but acquired serial rights for £3,500 to run that autumn.

Hutchinson sent the script to the soldier and Eisenhower's former Military Intelligence chief, Major General Sir Kenneth Strong, who reported favourably on 20 July. 'You have on your hands a potentially most readable book ... especially good description of the battle of Moscow ... better than any other I have read.' Whereas with his previous books Alan awaited with trepidation Liddell Hart's judgement it was a sign of his maturity that he now saw him as but one authority. During his research and writing he had kept in touch with Trevor-Roper, whose understanding of Hitler, his generals and others around him proved influential, and who sent him an early copy of *Hitler's War Directives 1939–1945*, which he had edited.[12]

His American publishers, William Morrow, this time took the lead in editing Alan's unruly typescript. Lawrence Hughes, who went on to become president of the firm, played a key role. He recalls that it needed 'a great deal of work (sloppy!), and because the delivery was late and time was taken to get the thing organized with maps/photos index/notes we published about a year or more later than we had expected'.[13] Morrow still wished to publish that autumn because of Alexander Werth's rival book, which had a quote on the jacket from William L. Shirer proclaiming it to be 'the best book we probably shall ever have in English on Russia at war'.

Some of Hughes's letters from the time survive. Trying to get Alan to concentrate on the minutiae of editorial work was impossible. Airmail letters were dispatched from the US to Bratton, to Zermatt or even Saltwood – and often had to be forwarded from one to the other, thereby delaying matters still further. Morrow agreed to finance two-colour maps so that advances and retreats by both sides could be more clearly shown. Hughes also needed author photographs as well as an author biography: 'I agree that we should stay away from the fact that you own both a Jag and a Bentley. I cannot resist asking if you paid for them with our advance? Nicholas Monsarrat [author of *The Cruel Sea*] once showed up here with a Rolls which had been specially built and ordered by a Shah of Persia, but whom I believe was shot before taking delivery. Every time I looked at the car I got ulcers thinking of what he would ask for the next book. O please behave yourself!'[14]

Like Hutchinson, Morrow sought commendations from distinguished authors. Hughes was particularly pleased when the American historian Henry Steele Commager wrote of *Barbarossa* that it was 'an enthralling reconstruction of the most neglected chapter in the history of the Great War – the titanic struggle between Germany and Russia which was in the end decisive. It combines a finished scholarship, judicious inter-pretation of complex materials, and narrative vigour in a masterly fashion. It will, I am confident, take its place among the classics of WW literature.'

Antony Beevor, author of *Stalingrad*, says the strength of *Barbarossa* is its readability.[15] Here was the sort of narrative account that certainly had not previously existed, giving the reader a sense of what had happened little more than twenty years before, but without the academic niceties. It did, though, have weaknesses, which had much to do with the time it was written, Russian material, with a few exceptions, proving inaccessible. The official Soviet history of the war, so Alan reported to Liddell Hart in February 1964, was still available only in German, and even the translation into English – when it came – dealt only to January 1942. John Erickson had yet to emerge as Britain's premier historian on the Eastern Front in the Second World War, with his *The Road to Stalingrad* (1975) and *The Road to Berlin* (1983) laying the groundwork for accounts of the war from the Soviet side. Alan, though, had made contact with Erickson, and valued his advice.

Barbarossa is essentially a campaign seen from the German point of view. To use a contemporary phrase, Alan might have been 'embedded' within the German forces from 1941 to 1945. 'Alan had a very good understanding of the mentality of German generals, almost better than anyone else,' says Beevor. Their accounts – Manstein and Guderian among them – had all been translated. Beevor identifies in *Barbarossa* 'a certain affinity of attitude'. Alan respected German professionalism, whereas he always thought the British were 'a load of bloody amateurs'.

If Alan had been writing *Barbarossa* thirty years on he would certainly have linked the German Army to Hitler's Final Solution. But in the early 1960s Alan did not question the received wisdom that laid the blame for the atrocities on the SS, not the Wehrmacht. Beevor also feels that Alan should have explained how the German generals 'got themselves into that totally subservient position' to Hitler. He believes it was due to 'an astonishing moral cowardice'. As Sebastian Haffner reminded us in *Defying Hitler*, 'Bismarck once remarked in a famous speech, moral courage is, in any case, a rare virtue in Germany, but it deserts a German completely the moment he puts on a uniform'.

Alan's preface, in praising Adolf Hitler, even twenty years after his death, was controversial. 'I have tried to suggest a reassessment of Hitler's military ability.' In the Hutchinson edition he added here, 'No truly objective historian could refrain from admiring this man.' Subsequent British editions of the book have used the American typesetting, where this sentence does not appear.[16] Alan wrote: 'His capacity for mastering detail, his sense of history, his retentive memory, his strategic vision – all these had flaws, but considered in the cold light of objective military history, they were brilliant nonetheless. The Eastern campaign, above all, was his affair, and his violent and magnetic personality dominated its course, even in defeat. Since the war Hitler has been a convenient repository for all the mistakes and miscalculations of German military policy. But a study of events in the East will show that occasions when Hitler was right and the General Staff wrong are far more numerous than the apologists of the German Army allow.'

Another historian, Andrew Roberts, as part of his research on the Eastern Front, reread *Barbarossa*. He thinks it 'astonishing how a book from the mid-1960s is still tremendously useful. It is very good.' In his view it contains within it the seeds of its own critique. 'When he says that no objective historian can truly doubt the genius of Adolf Hitler I think that was written entirely to shock and provoke reviewers, because as you read the whole of the rest of the book in fact he does blame Hitler again and again for the appalling errors that were made.'[17] In the years that followed, Alan's stated admiration for Hitler as a military leader was often over-simplified to admiration for Hitler. Frank Johnson, a great friend and former Editor of *The Spectator*, became convinced that Alan, as Roberts puts it, had a *tendresse* for Hitler. But Alan also enjoyed winding people up, even to the extent of showing off Nazi relics to visitors at Saltwood.

Antony Beevor remains impressed at how Alan identified 'the capacity of the Germans in the face of disaster to reorganise themselves and to get back on their feet very rapidly, indeed far more rapidly than their enemies ever give them credit for'. Beevor cites the retreat from Moscow in December 1941 and how they saved themselves from disaster in 1943 (largely Manstein's genius), as well as, at a much lower level, the way that they would put together groups of remnants of battalions into instant battle groups just to keep fighting. 'The British always got it wrong every single time in underestimating the German ability to do this. The Russians learnt their lesson rather more rapidly in that particular way. Stalin of course didn't.'

The British and American publication dates of *Barbarossa* coincided in May 1965. As a result of the Alexander Werth book the previous autumn, Morrow told Alan that the quantity of American reviews was unlikely to be large, but he was gratified, nevertheless, to be noticed favourably by *The New Yorker*. 'The best book on the worst – or at any rate, biggest, war in history ... his thoughtful judgements on such controversial topics as Hitler's military ability and the quality of Russian matériel are convincing and original.'[18]

The judgement that mattered most to Alan appeared in *The Sunday Times*. The headline gave no clue to Michael Howard's opinion – 'The war in the East' – but from the second paragraph it was clear that his review was 'a rave'.[19]

'It is not the least of the merits of Mr Clark's splendid book that it will, for a reading public brought up on Chester Wilmot and Arthur Bryant, firmly set the record straight.' He then quotes a key sentence of Alan's – and agrees with him. 'For the German nation "The War" meant the war in the East. The bombing, the U-boat campaigns, the glamour of the Africa Korps, these were incidentals when over two million fathers, husbands, brothers were engaged day and night in a struggle with the *Untermensch*.' Recalling that Russia lost twenty million lives, three million of them prisoners of war in German hands, Howard continues, 'For three years their western provinces were the scene of what Mr Clark rightly calls an "orgy of sadism and misgovernment" at the description of which one's stomach still turns over in disgust. It was their armies, as Sir Winston Churchill generously recognised, which tore the guts out of the Wehrmacht and made possible the victories in the West. It is refreshing to find a British historian who once again has the courage to admit it.'

Howard reminded readers that with *The Donkeys* Alan showed himself to be a powerful writer whose feelings tended to cloud his judgement. 'From that unfortunate beginning he has made a brilliant recovery. The power of his writing is not diminished – there are evocations of Russian landscapes and seasons which catch one's breath – but it is tempered by wry irony and relieved by wit. The indignation has not diminished either, but is used against more worthy targets than the muddled but honourable British commanders of 1915. The villains for whom Mr Clark reserves his thunderous anathemas are the grotesquely evil satraps of the occupied areas, Greiser, Pruetzmann, Koch, Loehse, Wirth, Dirlewanger, many of whom, as Mr Clark grimly reminds us, remain comfortably in our midst. We are unlikely to see any revisionist historians coming to the rescue of their reputations.'

He concluded: 'So compelling is the sweep of Mr Clark's narrative, so Gibbonian is his irony, that it would be pedantic to strain at the occasional gnat.' But Howard was not pedantic in his criticism of Hutchinson's proof-reading and index. 'The book deserves very much better than this.' Later Alan told paperback publishers on no account to use the Hutchinson version, but to offset from the American edition. Alan sat down and wrote immediately to Michael Howard: 'I must tell you how overwhelmed I was by your review today. There is no-one really no-one from whom I could value such compliments more.'[20]

His mentors agreed with Howard. Liddell Hart sent a preliminary comment, having read only the preface and the first two chapters. 'That is enough to show that it is superbly well written, and the presentation of events masterly.'[21] A month later, he was even more enthusiastic. 'The book is a tour de force – a brilliant panoramic survey of the war on the Russian front that is a most striking contribution to the lit on WWII.'[22] Alan awaited with some trepidation Hugh Trevor-Roper's reaction. He need not have worried. 'I have been reading Barbarossa with great pleasure. Come four corners of the world in arms, I will maintain that you really do write very well! And I think you are right and the critics ... wrong about Hitler. He has to be taken seriously, and to take him seriously is not, as all those sheep say, to admire him!' Trevor-Roper, however, renewed an old complaint that even now Alan 'couldn't resist an (irrelevant) fling at my father-in-law'.[23]

Alan enjoyed Barbarossa's success, both critical and commercial. In 1978 in a letter to The Guardian, as an aside, he wrote, 'As one who researched and wrote what is recognised as the definitive history of the Soviet-German conflict I remain a Russophile.'[24] Despite Morrow's concern, Barbarossa found its audience in the United States. Unlike Alexander

Werth's *Russia at War 1941–1945*, it has reprinted regularly. Alan especially enjoyed the American paperback edition of 1984, which described him on the back cover as 'currently Secretary of State in Margaret Thatcher's cabinet'.[25] If only . . .

TWENTY

Changes in Direction

'Quite exciting prospects,' Alan wrote from Bratton at the end of October 1964.[1] For once everything did seem rosy-hued. A lovely new home in Wiltshire, *Barbarossa* just serialised for three weeks in the *Evening Standard*,[2] debts reduced, Jane 'sweet and industrious', the boys 'an eternal delight'. But Alan wouldn't be Alan if he wasn't also thinking about girls (they had just hired a new au pair) and concerned about his health (although what was actually wrong remained unclear, even to him – symptoms of occasional face swelling, pain in little finger joints and back 'very lumbago-y – probably due to strain').

After a lengthy search across the West Country, contracts had just been exchanged for Seend Manor, a Georgian house in a Wiltshire village, a few miles to the west of Devizes. It seemed perfect – friends nearby, less than two hours from London, add another hour or so for Saltwood, a choice of good schools (with James now four and Andrew two they were thinking ahead); enough space for cars (in need of funds, they had sold the garage space at the back of their Rye house). But Seend required work – not least the addition of central heating, as Alan discovered that winter when briefly back on his own from Zermatt – 'uninhabitable and freezing cold. Only the Gents working so had to make many night-shambling descents there.'

His buoyant feelings continued in early December at Zermatt. 'Impressed by how tremendously *nice* it is here . . . more time for everything . . . feeling just enough cut off and protected. In theory, it couldn't be better, to be shut away in Switzerland, everything paid for, toying with a new novel.' He calculated, 'pleasingly' (a current Clarkism), that *Barbarossa* ('sent off the typed back-matter notes . . . totally finished!') had earned him £12,400 in advances over two and a half years. He was even thinking of sensible housekeeping, however minor: '*Times* air edition coming out so as to cut down on money-spending at paper stall.' He also confessed to 'a slight nagging concern at paying out all that money in weekly envelopes' to Nanny and staff at Seend.

As so often at Zermatt, Alan used his diary to muse on events and the future. 'Cannot completely divorce myself from current affairs.' Following the general election in October, Labour, led by Harold Wilson, had been elected into government for the first time in thirteen years, but with a majority of only five. Alan allowed his invective free rein: 'Constantly seething at that prickarse Wilson, layabouts, leftists, liberals, reformers, barbarians etc and would like to express myself in print and start nosing around Parliament.' Although not the first time he had thought about a political career, the change in Britain's political colour made him think it over anew. A few months later he was to recall that Joe Kennedy gave his children $1,000,000 each 'to set them off in politics' and wished that 'Papa could give me one-thirtieth of his fortune. Not that he hasn't given me a lot already, the dear. We'll have to see what happens, but please God don't let me just let this political thing slip away by default'.

Friends who came out to Zermatt for Christmas included the Briggses and the Rudds. Attending a Christmas Day service, he noted 'how adorable and serious Jolly [James] looked when praying and standing during the hymn'. He praised Jane's cooking, but recorded that at dinner things took 'a quasi-nasty turn when Michael [Briggs] said (I paraphrase slightly) "If you go on being malicious about everyone, the Grahams and the Rudds will all turn on you." I said, unguardedly, "Well, I wouldn't mind, I'm so marvellous." "Oh, but you will, and do," he said, "you've gone very peculiar sometimes."'

He woke next morning 'feeling pretty depressed'. This led to the 'thought of a bleak year with no earnings' and how would they cope given forthcoming expenditure on, amongst other things, Seend Manor and the new Mercedes – or 'perhaps even a Ferrari SF 4.9!'? What would 1965 bring? The breakthrough he had been longing for? Massive royalties from *Barbarossa*? 'Still more exciting – the assault on Jaguars.'[3] He even contemplated the alternative, consolidation and retrenchment, selling Studio Cottage at Rye, letting Bratton and in Britain living solely at Seend – 'calmly Evelyn Waugh in my manor house'. (Jane recalls that they had indeed looked at Waugh's home, Combe Florey, after his death the previous year, as well as another Somerset house, Ston Easton, later bought by William Rees-Mogg, Editor of *The Times*). David Cornwell, better-known as the author John le Carré, who came to know the Clarks around this time, believes Alan wished 'to buy the shell of some writer and get inside'.[4] Alan also reflected back ten years to 1955, when he began his serious diary-keeping. 'Look how far one has climbed.' As ever, he thanked the Almighty.

Future writing plans now included the possibility of a return to a First World War subject for an American publisher, but Alan declared it had to be for a minimum $10,000 guarantee. Without a major book to research and write the next three years proved to be marking time. He briefly contemplated a life of Hermann Goering, as well as compiling a Hitler anthology (some work was done), researching an account of the Second World War in the Pacific, and entering new territory with a study of the Crimean War. However, after his experience with William Morrow in New York he found his British publisher, Hutchinson, indecisive and wished 'to shift my centre of gravity to the States and enjoy their vigour and on-the-ball character'. But the ground proved stony. He was also thinking again of fiction, a semi-pornographic novel and a thriller, Lawrence Durrell crossed with John le Carré. This latter was inspired by the enviable success (the previous year) of le Carré's *The Spy Who Came in from the Cold* and on hearing that *The Ipcress File* and *Funeral in Berlin* (by Len Deighton) had been sold for films. His thriller would be about SS men and German rocket specialists in Egypt and if he could raise advances on his non-fiction he vowed to write fiction in the summer.

By spring he and Jane, who 'had her hair cut off, and looks a real little peach', were beginning to grasp Seend Manor's potential, with decoration all 'historical' colours and *famille rose* mooted for the drawing room. But money, as ever, was short, which meant, he thought, finally putting Studio Cottage at Rye on the market, and then what about his car fleet? – so many treasures to contemplate. Was it time for a cull? The E-type that he had bought Jane – 'sorry to see it go. The Bentley is a classic, although it represents a lot of money, I am going to try and hold on to it.'

The critical success of *Barbarossa* on both sides of the Atlantic was gratifying but more, he felt, a *succès d'estime*, especially in America, 'certainly no outstanding financial gain'. Alan had reached a crossroads. He dithered. Today we might identify this as a mid-life crisis.

Liddell Hart, who had guided him through his historical writing, was by this time increasingly unwell, having suffered prostate problems, and the last occasion he and Alan met was over dinner, with their wives. By then Alan had made his life-changing decision to seek a career in politics, as he later recalled to Kathleen Liddell Hart: 'You and Basil were the very first people we told of my change of course, it was at the dinner at L'Etoile just after *Barbarossa* came out and Basil saying ". . . well Alan you may well succeed because you don't really *care*".'[5]

Alan had worked as a canvasser at the 1964 general election in the North Devon constituency (appropriately close to Bratton), where the

Conservatives tried to unseat the Liberal and future Party leader, Jeremy Thorpe. To become a candidate he needed sponsors. In mid-1965 Papa approached a friend, the Tory MP Sir Edward Boyle, a Christ Church contemporary of Alan's, who had been Minister of Education in Alec Douglas-Home's government. Alan was 're-fired' when he said yes and went on a long walk on Salisbury Plain with the beagles to think about it.

Alan was now offered a journalistic assignment for the *Weekend Telegraph* in West Germany to 'look at' the Iron Curtain. He went immediately. The assignment began at Lübeck, in Schleswig-Holstein on the east-west border, where, he recalled, he landed on his feet – 'fireproof as always'. Staying at the same hotel was David Cornwell, who was researching *The Looking Glass War*. Cornwell remembers the telephone ringing in his room. 'A voice said, "My name is Alan Clark. Your father ripped off my brother."' From that unlikely opening a friendship began. Cornwell descended to the hotel lobby. 'There was this tall, handsome, to me from the start very vigorous, violent looking man with a Mercedes 600 parked outside. I was spare, deeply spare. I was hunting for this book. I was separated from my first wife. I was available and quite lonely. So Alan and I sort of met and talked and bonded.'

According to Alan, Colin had been conned by Cornwell's father, Ronnie. Thirty years later, with Ronnie Cornwell dead, Colin gave his account across three pages in his memoirs.[6] He called him the best con-man ever. In essence, having been entertained at Royal Ascot and enjoyed several good dinners, Colin was shown a derelict property by Ronnie – which, of course, he did not own. If Colin would invest in it, Ronnie promised to double his money in three months. In fact he took the lot. In the Lübeck hotel bar that evening Alan pitched this connection to David Cornwell, 'and was enormously amused by it. Whatever his relationship was with Colin, anyone who conned his brother was his friend.'

Alan's diary entry on the meeting is brief. 'Triumphant, half drunk evening.' Later Alan, but not Cornwell, went on to a casino, where he met some Swedish shipowners and lost 'a lot of *Telegraph* expenses'. Next morning there materialised at breakfast 'darling, plump, pert, red-haired little Inge'. Alan was delighted to discover from her that 'my lust was so strong and radiant that when she first saw me she wanted to kiss *me*!'. After that, the relationship went substantially further than a kiss. As well as Lübeck Alan and his photographer traversed the border, 'some of the most beautiful and romantic countryside of central Europe'. He described the wooden watchtowers, one of which he ascended in twilight, as 'the harsh image of twentieth-century repression, height 40 feet, crew of three with small arms and binoculars, a machine-gun, two searchlights, a radio telephone and a kit of signal rockets'. The towers were built to the original German specification drawn up in the thirties by the *Generalbevollmächtiger für den Arbeitseinsatz*. 'Their dread silhouette was the last image on the dying retina of hundreds of thousands in Dachau, Auschwitz and Belsen.'[7] Both Alan and Cornwell missed being away from their families, but it was especially poignant for Cornwell with his marriage breaking up. 'I was that kind of spare. Ringing home every night talking to my children and feeling awful.'

Jane and the children were at Bratton. They had been apart for ten days and caught up with each other on Exeter station. 'I felt the tears welling up inside me when I saw Boy* on the platform. Tuppy† so good-looking, too, in his high grey polo-neck jersey.' But the pleasure was superseded by Alan's gum playing up viciously over the weekend. He was now convinced he had cancer and spent a page of his diary speculating on its spread, the 'lingering, agonising decline' and why some people would commit suicide; the fact that he would miss Boy getting graded in maths, French and skiing; and to a lesser extent the enforced cheerfulness that would be necessary at Christmas. He went to early service that Sunday and prayed. Was it a miracle, but next day the 'place' started to go down? Two days later, however, he discovered another swelling on the gum and the downward spiral started all over again. It was too late to get to the doctor that evening. 'In some trepidation,' he wrote before going upstairs where Jane was going to cut his hair. 'I'm scared stiff of cancer, just as as an adolescent I used to be of TB. Not at all of a coronary stroke.' It was in fact an abscess.

Back in England the friendship between Alan and David Cornwell blossomed, Cornwell particularly remembering the way Alan talked, 'the excitement of him; he had a homo-erotic quality. He exuded that. Much more a man's man than a woman's man. Women were the enemy for him I think.' Cornwell understood the Etonian ethos espoused by Alan, having taught at the school. Alan saw in his new friend someone he could confide in, someone, too, whose writing success he envied. Perhaps Cornwell might also enjoy sharing some of his shenanigans in London?

Over the following months, when Cornwell had half a foot still in his first marriage, half a foot in a family house in Somerset, he would go over

---

* James.
† Andrew, who was also known as Tip or Tup.

to Seend alone. 'I was in that peculiar position of knowing how Alan was living when in London and then presenting myself to Jane as Alan's friend. You joined the con really of Jane not knowing anything, of you all being frightfully nice people.' Nor was he enamoured of some of Alan's 'appalling' friends from the far Right. He also recalls Alan's interests as a potential collector of cars that belonged to the Nazi regime, including being part of a syndicate that was out to buy Goering's Mercedes. 'It was from my socially worms-eye view a kind of repetition of what I had observed at Eton of the upper classes at play. Rather like *Remains of the Day*,[8] the further you go the further to the right you go. All of a sudden you are among the right-wing chosen and you are very, very close to fascism. That's where Alan was, that's what fascinated Alan. He was always pondering not whether Hitler was good or bad, but whether Hitler was a good general.'

Cornwell was by then living mainly in London, in a flat in a new block in Maida Vale, receiving children, with Alan as his 'cautiously engaged Mephistopheles'. Indeed, looking back Cornwell thinks he was 'a Mephistopheles for quite a lot of people'. It was Evelyn Waugh once again, getting inside the shell of the writer. He believes 'it is impossible to separate Alan's wealth, Alan's unreconciled anger, and the licence that Alan enjoyed all the time, from his later political views. No-one checked Alan except Alan himself, when he felt like it.' The friendship lasted for two years, with Cornwell on occasion lending him his Maida Vale flat for his assignations. 'I eventually found him too rich for my blood. I couldn't deal with it. There were too many confrontational issues. If it was his turn to take us to dinner we would go to L'Etoile or L'Escargot. He never tipped. I always found that embarrassing. He hated waiters. He treated them like shit. He had in that sense all the wrong Etonian tendencies, the absolutely worst ones I had identified among my pupils. He just offended the last of the Puritan in me.'

Looking back at Alan at this time, Cornwell thinks 'he fascinated people because he actually had a potential for evil which was very unusual. He was also extremely resourceful. He would never have told me . . . and God knows I never asked him. I always thought he had an SIS link, he had a reporting responsibility, when he went to Russia. He wasn't just a rake. I think he had a capacity for violence. He definitely had a kind of Geoffrey Household perception of his role in life. If somebody had told him to get a good rifle and shoot Hitler he'd have done that. Buying the land in Sutherland, wanting to die outdoors a soldier's death – he had all these self-images of himself and I think what fascinated him briefly was, as it

were, *The Spy Who Came in from the Cold* and that stuff and he thought
he was joining my army.'

In his end-of-year review for 1965, written from Zermatt, Alan expressed
sorrow that *Barbarossa* 'did not rampage', meaning top bestseller lists on
both sides of the Atlantic and earn huge sums in royalties. He was open
about his failure to go further 'in the project to get into Parliament'. He
had, he wrote, lost a lot of confidence, and 'now really quite gladly would
vegetate, retire, with occasional spurts of Buchanlike activity'. Buchan,
Dornford Yates – it is moments like these when Alan yearns for being
part of an earlier generation. And yet, the topsy-turvy nature of his mental
state meant that on another occasion he thought of branching out and
'really getting into the stratosphere'. As for sex, well, he was older; as he
admitted, it wasn't going to be as easy as it used to be not least as he
worried about spells of impotence. He records Jane catching him looking
at one girl on New Year's Eve and ticking him off in bed that night. 'With
anyone else, yes, but not with her parents knowing mine. I don't want
them to know you're like that.'

In March 1966 a new project emerged, a novel. After referring to the
Weekend Telegraph at last publishing his Iron Curtain article – 'not so much
of a failure as I feared' – he wondered if the Editor, John Anstey, might
commission him to write about Saigon, its 'black market, cafés, brothels,
arms sales', which he could link to research for 'VCN' – this is his
shorthand for Viet Cong Novel. As early as 1965, as the United States
began bombing North Vietnam and increased its forces in South Vietnam,
Alan felt instinctively that he was not on the American side. That summer
he told Basil Liddell Hart that he had become attracted to writing about
Vietnam – 'I am passionately pro Viet-Cong'.[9]

Among significant visitors to Zermatt in spring 1966 was Vivyan
Naylor-Leyland, an Old Etonian and Christ Church alumnus, who was
responsible this holiday for teaching Alan how to play backgammon.
Within weeks he was contemplating adding a backgammon room at
Zermatt and had already started playing for money – and losing. In
new year 1967 he forecast playing against Jimmy Goldsmith, who had a
considerable reputation as a player.

Julian Amery, distinguished Conservative politician and former Minister, turned up in Zermatt (he was a skier), gave Alan an inside track on
the Macmillan/Hogg succession in 1963 and asked him about politics:
would he go in? He also said that standing in a hopeless seat first time
round was no bad thing, and would add to his experience. Back at Seend

he was approached by *The New York Times* (recommended because of *Barbarossa* by Hugh Trevor-Roper) to write about 22 June 1941 to coincide with the twenty-fifth anniversary of Hitler's launch of his invasion of the Soviet Union. 'Morale-boosting, and useful too, I should think.' He was working on VCN, but admitted difficulty with American dialogue ('seems second hand . . . must relook at *Catch 22*, but be careful to avoid pastiching it').

Alan kept abreast of political developments, noting that Harold Wilson was calling a general election for 31 March. Alan forecast a huge Labour majority – 103, which would mean 'considerable financial stringency *(again)*'. He was uncannily accurate, Wilson's actual majority being 97. Alan's throat – his 'Jack Hawkins throat', as he called it, after the British actor with military bearing recently diagnosed with throat cancer – was troubling him and would do so for several tense months.

The helter-skelter of Alan's financial life was 'in some amazing way still holding' and once more he found a historical analogy, 'white Russia in 1944'. Matters looked up in April 1966 when his father talked of a handout of £5,000 – 'the last one . . . to beat the gift tax' (a proposal from the new Labour government). But, just as he thought he might be out of the red, he added a new expense – the backgammon room would increase his Swiss overdraft. Enter a Degas. The bronze of a dancer had come to him via a Clark uncle, his grandfather's brother, known as 'Fat' Norman. The Lefevre Gallery in London offered him £10,000. In the end he 'had to sell it', having decided to buy 'a very good-looking Rolls'. Throughout his adult life, once he had money in hand he rarely resisted the urge to use it to buy a car.

William Morrow were keen to sign him up for his next book. But what? Vietnam was not a commercial subject for British publishers, so to please both sides of the Atlantic Alan contracted to write an account of the Yalta Conference of 1945. But he was not alone. When Morrow and Hutchinson realised there were rival accounts and that Alan's would not be the first, the project was put on hold. Instead he offered his novel. *The Lion Heart* (as VCN became) was about a US Army battalion led by a young Special Forces captain which is cut off and ultimately sacrificed because it would be too costly to rescue. It demonstrated the ruthlessness of the Americans and, with a scene in which an Asian girl is raped, their soldiers' brutality as well. In an author's note Alan wrote: 'Literary custom, and the exigencies of the libel laws, oblige me to declare that all the characters in this book are imaginary, and bear no relation to any living person. And so they are. I can assert this with a clear conscience. But of the *incidents* the reverse is true. Everything depicted in this book actually happened, and only the dictates of structural harmony have altered, slightly, the context of their happening.'

Alan had not written fiction since the ill-fated *Summer Semester*, published in 1963. Not that *The Lion Heart* was intended as a novel. Like Thomas Keneally's *Schindler's Ark*, which won the 1982 Booker Prize for fiction although commissioned as a biography of the good German Oscar Schindler, Alan recorded that *The Lion Heart* was 'originally conceived and commissioned as a general historical work, but I found that the points I wished to get across could only really be made in a fictional setting. If you put it out as truth, people wouldn't believe it.'[10]

Alan had been worrying for some time about his fertility. He desperately wanted another child, but if Jane was not becoming pregnant, was it, possibly, his fault? In the autumn of 1966 he had undergone tests and was miserable to learn from Rowntree that his 'sperm count [was] right down'. Now in May 1967 a further blow: 'I'm in bed with (horrors!) mumps. Only slight discomfort from swellings.' Would this prove the final blow to his hopes for another child? He managed to complete *The Lion Heart* and sent it off to Michael Sissons, who rejected it – 'this virtually tantamount to defeat of Kursk offensive'.

He tried to cheer himself up by planning a trip to India (to look at interesting cars, not least several ex-Maharajah-owned Rolls) and then on to Saigon, where research might inspire him in the further rewriting of *The Lion Heart*. He had enjoyed being flown from Port Lympne to Trent Park as a child, but now the very idea of a commercial flight in a 707 frightened him. 'Claustrophobia (being trapped) and the extreme alternatives offered – speedy arrival or burning, or being smashed, to death.' Twice in the next fortnight he packed his bags and at the last moment flunked it, despite Jane's 'lucky half-penny' which persistently turned right way up.[11] Not until he became Minister for Trade in the mid-1980s – when overseas 'flying the flag' trips were part of the job – did he manage to conquer this particular demon.

That autumn he began to play backgammon seriously at the St James's Club in Piccadilly, but he admitted to 'not being rich enough to keep up with the boys at the Clermont', where, he had heard, stakes could be as high as £140 a point. Even so his backgammon debts often topped £500 a month, one beneficiary being the socialist millionaire and politician Harold Lever. His fragile finances were helped by a cheque for £700, French royalties from *Barbarossa*.

Christmas Day 1967 at Seend began when 'the boys opened their stockings at 10 past 12!'. After church, where he took Communion, he brooded on the future. 'I've got to have a go now at the Party.' Thanks to Hiram Winterbotham he had been appointed an executive director of London's St Thomas' Hospital, which he knew would be a useful line on his CV. Edward Boyle's promise to Papa now materialised in his formally signing Alan's application to go on the Conservative candidates' list. His co-sponsors could hardly have differed more: Hugh Trevor-Roper, and the engineer and inventor of the Moulton bicycle, Alex Moulton, whom Alan had met via Winterbotham. In March 1968 he heard from Conservative Central Office that his application had succeeded. The following month *The Times* Diary column reported that he was 'to go into politics'. It was a mite premature, but the piece continued, 'He has, I learn from a close source, been offered the Tory candidature for a seat now held by Labour, but under present conditions, easily winnable.'[12] The close source was, of course, Alan.

Lady Mancroft, 'a rather fabulous woman' and an important figure in the Conservative Party hierarchy, now entered his life and he thought, 'must try and suck up to her could be useful'.[13] He wrote that she offered him Poplar – was it in her giving? – 'but we must do better, surely?', and suggested he gain experience by canvassing in the borough elections that spring.

In spring 1968 he impatiently awaited news of *The Lion Heart*'s fate in New York. 'I've got accustomed to the assumption that it's going to save our bacon – but if I stop to think about it I'd rate the odds at 60–40 at best.' He thought he might 'do full tax immigration (residence) [in Switzerland], unless reasonable chance of adoption and seat'. He was fascinated by the newly published diaries of 'Chips' Channon, an influential and well-connected Tory MP between the wars and into the 1950s.[14] 'Of course the upper classes were absolutely hopeless – though compliant. A really shrewd operation could have played off Germany and Russia and stayed on top. Just as we could have done over Russia and USA in the last decade – though the chance has probably gone now. Thought gloriously how Chips was my age when war broke out and now he's dead.' Then came news that *The Lion Heart* had finally been accepted and would be published early in 1969. But the devil was in the detail: there was much work to be done.

The report by Morrow's reader (anonymous) ran to two thousand words. 'I agree that Alan Clark can make military operations and combat scenes sound authentic, but that is all I got out of my first reading.' It continued, 'I found it hellishly confusing and had to go over it a second time to make any sense out of the bewildering welter of characters – far too many, I think.' The reader then went on to suggest remedies, chapter by chapter. If by the final page Alan was dispirited his heart must have risen at the reader's final paragraph: 'Even after all the carping, I still think we should do this book. It is strong and vivid.'

In Britain Hutchinson showed little enthusiasm, making a modest contract; but towards the end of the 1960s, with cash flow under pressure, they cut back their publishing programme. *The Lion Heart* was one of the titles axed. Only a tattered jacket proof survives. Relations between Hutchinson, which had hitherto been Alan's principal British publisher (two histories, two novels), soured further when the firm demanded the repayment of £600 they had advanced in expenses. Nor was it just these expenses; there was also the question of £1,500 paid by Hutchinson for the abandoned Yalta book.[15] Hutchinson's letter crossed with one from Alan in which he gushed an apology: 'I have been very hard up recently, and just don't seem to be able to raise that much money, however, I will send it to you as soon as I possibly can.'[16] To Sissons he remarked in a letter of the same day, 'Fortunately the Etonian education allows one to keep one's creditors in the air in a kind of juggling act, more or less indefinitely.'[17] Sissons, however, helped out with a loan for the expenses repayment. Alan ultimately repaid him.[18]

Sissons failed to find another British publisher for *The Lion Heart*, but he and Alan had something else to worry about. William Morrow were also demanding repayment of the *Yalta* advance. 'We've now reached the point where I can't fob them off,' wrote Sissons.[19] Alan understood and responded by return: 'Yes, I am really on my bicycle at the moment.' Realising that Sissons might not understand the reference, he added as a footnote: 'Boxing ring expression for fast retreat away from the opponent.' If Alan thought Morrow were bluffing, he was wrong. He ignored their letters and eventually allowed the case to be heard in a New York court which found judgement in the publisher's favour. Very reluctantly, and slowly, he paid what was owing.

TWENTY-ONE

Banking with Publishers

Once he decided to make politics his career, it looked as if writing would take a back seat. Alan was never short of ideas. But the books contracted rarely got any further. He was happy to take the publishers' money, but delivering the typescript was another matter.

The long-suffering Michael Sissons stopped counting the number of times he had to arrange a cancellation letter and get Alan to return – not always an easy task – the portion of the advance paid on signature. Two major books from this period did finally emerge, but not without a struggle. The first was brought to him by his father: to edit the autobiography of Alan's honorary uncle, Arthur Lee, who had figured in the Clarks' lives from the early 1930s. Lee had privately published the autobiography in 1939 in what K described as 'three stout volumes', under the title *A Good Innings*. As K explained in 1968 to his old friend and publisher, Jock Murray,[1] only ten copies were bound. Lee died in 1947 aged seventy-nine, but K, his literary executor, would not allow the book to be reissued during the lifetime of his widow, being 'afraid that it would arouse a good deal of unfavourable comment'. The noted historian Donald Cameron Watt had been denied permission even to consult it. Lee, K explained, was 'not a popular or even a very likable man, and this comes through fairly clearly'. On the other hand he was at the centre of affairs during the second half of the 1914–18 war and the middle section, in which he tells how he and Lloyd George got rid of Asquith, is 'of considerable historic interest'.

K added that he was under some pressure from Lord Lee's executors, Mr and Mrs William Hardcastle, who felt they had a duty to see the book published – Lady Lee had put aside a sum of money to help this happen. Mrs Hardcastle, now an invalid, had been Lee's secretary, and Mr Hardcastle, his bank manager. K had been firm. 'I have told them that there is no point in publishing a book that no-one will read, and that the book in its present form would have no sale. But I have said that if the book were cut down by about a third and introduced by some intelligent young historian of the epoch, it might be of interest, and even have a certain success'. Would Murray care to have a look at it?

So began a saga that took nearly six years, involved Alan (as the 'intelligent young historian of the epoch'), and helped turn Jock Murray's already thinning hair, grey. K, who suggested Alan as editor, took his literary executor duties seriously, reminding his son that he had to make a decision 'without any thought of the financial implications . . . I gather you would like to do the job if the pay is adequate'.[2]

Two months passed before Alan wrote to Murray, asking for a meeting to 'discuss and possibly codify our business relationship . . . how you and I carve it up we can argue enjoyably between ourselves'.[3] In early January 1970, Alan wrote from Zermatt that Murray had referred several times to the task of 'pruning', 'shortening' and 'annotating'. But Alan did not see it like that. 'I prefer the word "edit"; which allows me to select and write round and set in context the passages I choose.' Murray soon realised that Alan required being kept up to the mark. He had been talking to Frances Phillips of William Morrow. In one of his file notes Murray reported her saying that Alan was 'very difficult indeed – but a good writer', adding with bitter feeling 'that he was terribly slow in finishing anything and didn't stick at it because he didn't need the money'. It was finally agreed that Alan would deliver the fully edited typescript with linking material on 1 March 1971.

All went quiet. Indeed, summer turned to autumn with Murray writing 'almost in despair' to Hardcastle,[4] 'no answer or visit from Alan. I will continue to battle, but it might be a good idea for you to write to Alan to say how impatiently you await the result.' Alan calmed everyone down, explaining the problem of 'sheer technics – ie squeezing three pints into a quart pot'. Hardcastle was unhappy about a 'vindictive' passage in the introduction on why Chequers had been given to the nation. However in a follow-up letter he thought that overall it was 'a literary gem'.[5] Murray sighed with relief and wrote a masterly editorial letter to Alan[6] suggesting that where in the introduction he made it clear that Lee was a disagreeable man, he might temper this – 'I am trying to hold the balance between accuracy, generosity and your interpretation, the finding of as many readers as possible for the book for our mutual benefits as well as for Lord Lee's, and the comfort of Mr and Mrs H (not an easy ploy).' He sent a copy to K, as Lee's literary executor. K responded to Murray[7] that he agreed with Hardcastle's concern on the gift of Chequers. Alan's suggestion that Lee had done so as quid pro quo to advance his political career, K found 'malicious' – he would have a word with his son.

With Alan's editing generally agreed, in October Murray hired Herbert Rees, a freelance copy-editor who was also the author of a valuable textbook, *Rules of Printed English*. Their correspondence reveals the same problems that editors at Hutchinson and William Morrow had previously endured. Alan enjoyed the broad brush, but was bored by the detail. Rees, however, was not going to be defeated. 'In spite of all the wides Alan sends down the pitch, we are going to see this Innings through between us – you and I.'[8] The editorial process continued with Rees often at explosion point. Alan of course knew when to turn on the charm. To Murray he wrote of Rees that he had never worked with anybody 'so thorough and painstaking and who as a delightful bonus combines with these qualities a most agreeable dry sense of humour and a deep fund of literary scholarship. I hope very much he will cooperate with me when my book on Lloyd George and the Tories finally comes to completion.'[9]

The winter passed. Murray, meanwhile, was having to cope with a world paper shortage. When finished copies arrived in June 1974 all concerned were delighted by it. Publication followed in July, but the reception was critical. Colin Coote, a former Editor of *The Daily Telegraph*, who had known Lee, asked why there was not one word about Baldwin's speech at the Carlton Club in October 1922, which really brought down the coalition.[10] Kenneth Rose in *The Sunday Telegraph* thought Alan's editing of the text 'skimpy'.[11] Sales, too, were disappointing. Hardcastle offered some of the modest royalties towards advertising. In the end John Murray opted for a leaflet.

Not long after Alan first became involved with *A Good Innings*, a second project was put to him which took him back to the First World War. *Aces High* was conceived in 1970 as an illustrated account of aerial warfare across the Western Front, the world of von Richthofen and Albert Ball, the evolution from 'stringbag' bi-planes to the more sophisticated tactical machines of 1918. As so often with Alan's writing his original draft was but a sketch, but an expert reader thought 'a good book can be made out of the material', even if 'it does need a lot of work'.[12] Any chance that it would be published in 1972 – the intention not only of his British publishers, but also those in the United States, France and Germany – was to be dashed at Christmas 1971 with satisfactory revisions still outstanding. Alan had been hoping for a further tranche from the £2,000 advance, but Michael Sissons was frank: 'It's clear that unless you're prepared to do some pretty rigorous work on it very quickly, so that they can, as they

must, go to press by the end of January, we're in for a bad scene with
them.'[13] Certainly there's no chance of getting the next £500 out of them
until they're satisfied.' With Alan's agreement an external editor was hired
to pull it together and give it shape – he agreed to pay the bill of £250 –
but all this took time. *Aces High* was eventually published in 1973 and was
to prove profitable. Alan, though, felt cheated by the system, with everyone
taking a slice of commission before he received his share. Dissatisfaction
with this principle would rankle and manifest itself spectacularly two
decades later.[14]

As royalty income accumulated during the next two years Weidenfeld &
Nicolson looked at the increasingly satisfactory figures for *Aces High* and
thought about a sequel. What became *Bomber* started with a letter in
November 1975 from Christopher Falkus, the firm's managing director,
who suggested another illustrated book of 60,000 words, this time on
aerial combat in both world wars. Here again was an approach that Alan
swiftly embraced while giving it his own minting. Rather than aerial
combat, he wrote, it would be specifically about the bomber, concentrating
on each famous type. 'There is a kind of lay view that the bombers were
really rather dull, just droning about bullying the civilian populations,' he
wrote. 'But in fact there is much drama here, the bravery required was of
a different order to that in the single-seaters and the ordeals much more
protracted. When the fighters got in among them it was really nasty.'[15]
His enthusiasm was such that when he did not hear from Sissons he wrote
again immediately after Christmas asking if his letter might have gone
astray. In the new year Sissons pressed Falkus to pre-sell the idea to an
American publisher so that Alan could see 'the package of the best possible
British and American offers'. Falkus said he did not require a formal
synopsis, 'just a mouth-watering letter of intent on why the subject excites
you'. Sissons was excited, too, and when nothing turned up in February
he wrote to Alan: 'sorry to press you, but ... I know I can get a damn
good contract if you'd just deliver yourself of a short statement on the
subject'.

On 18 March 1976 Alan did just that. Sissons called the synopsis
'superb'. He would begin in the Spanish Civil War with Guernica and
then Abyssinia – the Ju 52 and Savoia 'operating almost unopposed'. Then
chronologically through the Stuka in Poland and the Battle of France;
'first major setbacks against fighter opposition (Battle of Britain) with
withdrawal of Stukas from operations and switching of Heinkel and
Dorniers into night operations'.

Alan's knowledge – and passion – were revealed as he continued:

The German night offensive of the winter of 1940/41, the start of Bomber Command's retaliation and the build up through the first 1,000 bomber raid on Cologne to the development of the Lancaster force, the Hamburg fire storms and the second phase of the German defences drawing ahead of our capacity; the loss level finally rising above even what Harris would accept in the Battle of Berlin and the offensive being brought to a dead stop in April 1944 following the disastrous raid on Nuremberg. In parallel with this there is the development of the daylight strike by the Americans, the Flying Fortress and the Liberator, the Balaclava-like operations against Schweinfurt and the gradual extension of daylight fighter cover with Lightning, Thunderbolt and Mustang in which total air superiority over Germany was achieved. The book would end with the B29 fire raids on Japan and, finally, with the biggest bang of all.

He knew how he wished the book to be structured, tying chapter titles to aircraft types, or variants of aircraft types, 'but the real essence would be, as it was with *Aces High*, on the character, background, practices and morale of the air crew'. Alan next shared some facts, not gung-ho *Dam Busters* stuff, but actual matters of life and death.

Did you know that more British air crew were killed in Bomber Command than were officers in the trenches in WWI? In terms of casualties the whole operational strength had to renew itself every three months. The analogy with the trenches is valid in many other ways, notably the tension of waiting around for attack orders that seemed utterly pointless and would lead, statistically, to a 5:1 likelihood of being killed before your 'tour' was finished. But of course instead of waiting in the squalor of the front line, the crews would return every morning to the peace and tranquil contrast of Lincolnshire and Norfolk. I would hope to illustrate both the extraordinary courage – 'press on regardless', taken quite literally – and also some of the dodgier items of lore – running engines on coarse pitch to induce failure before the point of no return, opening parachutes inside the fuselage (in theory a Captain had the discretion to turn back if any member of the crew had a defective parachute), and so on.

His covering letter to Sissons was very different in tone: combative and critical, demonstrating how he liked doing things his way, to be in total control. 'I must admit that I am a little stuffy about the way that this has been conducted, because if you look back you will see that the first approach was made through you by Falkus last November ... we had a meeting, Falkus agreed that this was the sort of book he was looking for

... and, hey presto, I am asked to submit a "letter of intent" on the basis of which a contract may, or may not, be agreed. In other words the tables have been turned right round and I am now put in the position of a supplicant trying to sell an idea. This not just a question of amour-propre, but I now foresee great delays in settling the contract, various conditions imposed and so forth. I want to write a book, just as I wrote *Aces High*, from my own personal standpoint ... There is no question of being pre-empted by anybody else and these ideas, being personal, will keep indefinitely. That is why I welcomed Weidenfeld's approach, but do not at all like the way I have been turned on the ropes.'[16]

Sissons did his stuff, spoke to Falkus and established that Alan's 4 March letter was exactly what he needed. On the matter of Alan's criticism of Falkus, a considerable editor and publisher, Sissons was robust in his reply: 'I think you're being a little unfair on him. You remember that at the meeting in January he said he was quite prepared to make an offer there and then but that he wanted to get as much up front as possible; he'd need just a very short statement as ammunition to bring in an American publisher ... Anyhow he's prepared to commit himself now to a world rights offer of £5,000 split more or less as convenient to you, and without a commitment from an American publisher.'[17]

Now it was down to the small print. The key was delivery – 31 December 1976. Weidenfeld wanted it for their autumn 1977 publishing list, and, no doubt, an American publisher would wish likewise. To Alan, though, money, as ever, became crucial. He would not start until a cheque had cleared his account. 'How's my contract going?' he asked of his agent on 13 April. 'I really ought to do some work in the Easter recess.'[18] Sissons responded next day: 'You can certainly go ahead in the confidence that the contract will be ok.' Falkus was out of the country, but Sissons needed to discuss a number of details for an improvement on the terms that Alan had received for *Aces High*.[19] By the beginning of May, when the contract had been signed, Alan's impatience once more showed itself. 'I want my cheque for the money due on signature. Could you please send it to the Westminster Bank at 10 Market Place, Devizes.'[20]

Whereas with the *Diaries* nearly two decades later Alan would have the raw material of his manuscript volumes to quarry, and his journalism was often top-of-the-head stuff, *Bomber* was original: both in research and writing. Was this the sticking point? Had he lost the aptitude? On hearing of a new film called *Aces High* he told Sissons, 'I understand from those who have seen the film that it is considerably dependent on my book and they recognise many similarities in incident and presentation. Certainly the posters advertising it are almost identical in theme, if not in form, to the cover of the Ballantine [American] paperback. Personally I think we are in a potential *Oh What a Lovely War* situation here.'[21] Not so: the film's makers drew on R.C Sherriff's *Journey's End* and Cecil Lewis's memoir, *Sagittarius Rising*.

If Falkus and Sissons thought Alan was now getting on with *Bomber* they were in for a shock. Early in August Alan confessed in a letter to Sissons, but also copied to Falkus, 'When I met my old friend Anthony Blond, at the *Spectator* cocktail party a couple of weeks ago, and we were both in our cups, he commissioned me to do a book about the various conspiracies of the leading Nazis in the closing six months of the war. And since then, to my great amazement, he has actually stumped up a hefty advance.' The book was to be called, according to Alan's synopsis, *The End Game: Conspiracies of the Nazi Diadochi 1944–5*, and Blond's advance was \$40,000.[22] Alan added that no time limit had been agreed for its completion, 'but I feel I ought to let Christopher Falkus know immediately as my dabbling in this is bound to affect the schedule on *Bomber*'.

Alan then went into self-justification mode. 'In fact, as you know, there were considerable longueurs between the verbal agreement concerning *Bomber* and then, still further, between that time and the payment of the advance. So it would be running behind the original schedule in any case. I still like the idea of *Bomber*, and have got a lot of notes for it, but I think I ought to offer to repay some (hopefully not all) of the Weidenfeld advance on signature as it will not be possible for me to make delivery of a completed manuscript by March 1977 which I think was the original optimum date. We are just off on holiday but when you get back I would be grateful if you could have a brief word with Christopher Falkus about this.'[23]

Sissons was furious. 'I do think your letter of 9 August is pretty extraordinary. I can't operate as your agent on the basis that you call me in when it's convenient to do so, and not when it's not. This makes particularly little sense when you are asking me, it seems, to unscramble a contract, which I've made for you, and to which I assumed you to be fully committed, in favour of a subsequent commitment, which I haven't. Second, while I like Anthony enormously, our view of his publishing operation these days is that it's virtually invisible, and I simply can't understand how it could be more worthwhile for you to be published by him than by Weidenfeld in this case.'[24]

Of any response from Alan there is no sign, although a Saltwood file

includes not only the draft proposal for the book but also a draft bibliography. In fact *The End Game* was never written. Alan received $6,000 on
signature and signed a contract that paid him $1,000 a month for the next
two years, the remaining $10,000 to be divided between delivery and
publication. The dollars were important as Alan instructed that all payments should be sent c/o the Union Banque Suisse in Brig, Switzerland.
Seven years later Anthony Blond Ltd, which had become part of another
small publisher, Frederick Muller, in 1978, started chasing Alan for repayment of the advance. Blond himself wrote to Alan: 'I'm under serious
pressure so it's either a book or writsville. That said, it would be jolly to
meet. How about lunch sometime at your club?'[25] Alan quickly responded.
'I wish you would not keep talking about "writs". If you want the money
back all you have to do is ask for it. I have already made this plain in earlier
correspondence and, indeed, had a very pleasant letter back from a man
at Muller who said that he did not want the advance returned. One day
there will be a book – but I am just as ready to reclaim my freedom if you
so desire.'[26] Blond replied with a two-line: 'I'm frightfully sorry, but there
has been a policy change this end – please reclaim your freedom.'

In the end lawyers were instructed and the solicitors Harbottle & Lewis
weighed in with a writ dated 1 June 1983. Did the prospect of an election
a fortnight later hasten Alan's repayment? The last thing he wanted was
bad publicity as he faced the electors of Plymouth Sutton. He sent
Harbottle & Lewis his cheque for $11,899.62 drawn on his UBS account
and, to confuse matters, made out personally to Anthony Blond (that took
some untangling). His accompanying letter was typical: 'I am a little
surprised that Mr Blond who from time to time lays claim to friendship
with me, and has enjoyed hospitality at my houses in England and Switzerland, should authorise you to include a demand for interest. However if
Mr Blond is in financial difficulties I wish him no ill.'[27]

This habit of Alan's of using publishers' advances as an overdraft facility
had also occurred with *Bomber*. By the spring of 1977 Weidenfeld &
Nicolson were no longer biddable. Alan was ignoring letters. Sissons tried
the jocular approach in February 1977: 'I think if I want to get a reply
from you I had better masquerade as one of your constituents. May we
please resolve this?'[28] To which Alan responded with apology, but nothing
firm on delivery. Falkus, however, had had enough. 'I think we ought to
cancel Alan Clark's *Bomber* and get our money back.'[29]

Alan appeared laid-back, even though he had other, serious matters on
his mind. He had just lost £800 at backgammon ('appalling punishment'),[30]
he was uncertain where his political career was going, James, his elder son,

was about to continue his schooling at Le Rosey in Switzerland, and his father was rewriting his will. To Sissons he wrote: 'If they are really anxious to get their money back and cancel the contract then, of course, they must have it.'[31] And there the matter lay. Alan and Jane were now living at Saltwood where, thanks to its enormous running costs, they had huge financial worries. The summer passed. Falkus wrote to Sissons: 'I seem to remember a hundred years ago that Alan Clark said he had no immediate plans to write *Bomber in World War II* and was willing to repay our money. I also seem to remember agreeing that this was a good idea (!) but no word since then. Can you let me know the current position?'[32] Sissons added another of his marginal notes to Alan: 'may we clear this up?'.

With cash flow at Saltwood at crisis levels Alan did not reply about what was in his circumstances a paltry sum. Falkus knew nothing of Alan's financial woes; he was simply under pressure from the Weidenfeld management: 'I'm sorry to have to write in this way, but I have been trying in vain to get a response about *Bomber*, a book which is overdue by ten months. I now have no alternative but to pass the matter to our solicitors.'[33] Alan adopted the hurt tone of which he was the master. 'I am sorry that you should feel that I have been ignoring your approaches – I have looked in the file and cannot find any letters from you on the subject since 24 September 1976 – and that only refers to the subject tangentially. I enclose my cheque for £1,800 (A.D. Peters took the balance on the way through).[34] Is someone else writing the book for you? Otherwise perhaps we could start again with a new contract and I could ask not only for the initial advance but also for the additional £1,000 payable on evidence of work in progress.'[35]

But no more would be written until the *Diaries*. Politics were increasingly to monopolise Alan's professional life.

TWENTY-TWO

Into Politics

In October 1968 Alan paid his first visit to a Conservative Party conference (in Blackpool), but having prepared a speech was disappointed not to be called. He wrote that Enoch Powell[1] 'spoke terribly well, but probably on the wrong subject, referring to racial "problems"'. Alan left before questions, but 'realised that even the conference were divided and so with the shadow cabinet united against him (boorishly non-clapping him during his speech) and with so few friends in the Parliamentary Party he hasn't got much of a chance. It will need a crisis to get a "call" going, and even then, look at the Tories refusing to clap Winston when he entered the Chamber on 10 May [1940].'

In Jane's recollection Alan became truly serious about a political career on hearing Powell speak at Bath late on the morning of 8 November 1968. They had proposed that Powell and his wife join them afterwards for a meal at Seend, but Powell politely refused, saying he had to go on to south Wales in the afternoon.[2] He did, though, accept an invitation to Saltwood in 1972. It was not Powell's racial policies (he had made his 'rivers of blood' speech at Birmingham in April that year), but his anti-European views that particularly appealed to Alan. Powell to him was 'the prophet'. Having only seriously embraced politics in his fortieth year, Alan's enthusiasm was that of a convert. He rushed headlong, his sympathies – unlike those of his father – being of the Right. He joined the Monday Club, then at the height of its political influence, in the belief that it would be easier to rise in its ranks than in a traditional Conservative association.

In late November 1968 a second significant meeting took place. Alan's initial diary entry is succinct: 'Valerie Harkess at the Monday Club annual dinner, and two meetings since.' The following month, 'Going up tomorrow to the Harkesses buffet party ... interesting to see what Jane and Valerie think of one another. Courtship of the latter proceeds favourably with possible seduction scheduled for this week.' Just before Christmas he reported the calamitous result. 'Total impotence in bed with VH – how ironic! There she was blond, voluptuous, fabulous and I could do nothing, a tight knot constricting my prostate, the cock a stubby piece of candle-wick.' Subsequent liaisons were more successful, as Alan confessed on meeting her in 1992, nearly a decade after the fourteen-year relationship ended. 'I said to her (which is true) "I have never felt the same degree of sheer physical desire as I did with you with any other human being".'[3]

Early in 1969, and not long included on the Conservative candidates' list, Alan had an unexpected first constituency interview. The sitting Member at Weston-super-Mare, David Webster, had died suddenly aged only forty-three in January 1969. Alan enjoyed beginner's luck, making the shortlist and being interviewed. His father, however, was not in favour. Alan had now proved himself as an author. Why change to an even riskier calling?

In February 1969 Alan, approaching his forty-first birthday, wrote to his father from Zermatt in a revealing credo about his attitudes.[4]

I can't say I am asking for advice, as you have already given this, and every word is borne out by my experience so far. Really, I suppose, I am elaborating on my motives and clearing my own mind. It is a curious thing, but even such slight contact as I have already had with the political world, suggests that it is, to me, highly addictive. While one is intoxicated all other interests and certainties seem unimportant. Also, there is the double fact that those practising it seem stupid, over-cautious and generally incompetent to the power and office which they dispose; and the curious mirage-effect surrounding the route or routes in. Sometimes it seems very cosy and exciting, sometimes arduous and boring. I got my score-sheet from Weston-super-Mare, I was third, ie two people away out of 850 – yet a break like this may never come again, as I am only too painfully aware.[5]

Why do it at all? I am completely happy with everything I could possibly have asked for. *Deep gloom* of course is something apart from this, tho' almost a synthetic (in the Hegelian sense, not meaning 'false')[6] ingredient of happiness. But at my age (I suppose) one has just crested a wave and for the first time (tho' some considerable distance after and only visible when the light is right) can be seen in the valley the open grave where one will eventually be rested.

If I just sit back, write a bit, do the things I like, travelling, vintage cars, mobbing around with the boys, I think I'll just age-along; come out of the mist some long time after with the boys grown-up, a ledger of small, cumulative disappointments and the grave is *right there*. I'll never write a book as good as *Barbarossa*, and anyway what if I do? – it's not enough, still just descending that same easy valley. I feel I must strike through, upward not down. Of course (and the odds must be on this) one can have a nasty fall, or get stuck. This will be fully cushioned by the fact that at that point the routes will still be parallel, ie I will be writing as well, but its effect will be final – a slow decline into the status of 'dear old boy' (and by then badly in need of the £note which Mama is wont to hand out to those embraced by this definition!)[7] What I can't yet assess is whether the overt disappointment which will follow will outweigh the satisfaction of having tried. I think it probably will (outweigh it).[8]

Michael Briggs recalls Alan seeing this as a watershed. 'When he went into politics he said to me, and I think to Euan, we won't see so much of each other unless you also go into politics.'[9]

In the new year of 1969 Alan and Jane decided to buy a second house at Seend which they knew as 'Miss Usher's', but which was actually named Seend Park. The price was £28,000. Alan called it 'a nice little estate with stabling, two service cottages, a new farmhouse [called Broomhayes], a copse and some respectable arable land'. In the Queen's Birthday Honours that June K received a life peerage. Alan would not have objected if it had been the hereditary model, but Harold Wilson's Labour government were only giving life peerages. Alan wrote in his diary of 'a brief fracas' when his father felt he ought to refuse, 'but I – I like to think – persuaded him'. Alan also knew the form: 'So Jane can be the Hon Mrs Alan Clark, which will be nice'.

In August Alan wrote a positive *tour d'horizon*, encouraged by his and Jane's new home, even if they were 'hugely overwhelmed with tasks, immediate and long term, but think it could be wonderful here once order is established'. However ... 'I am not going to move again (deo volente). Col can have Saltwood provided it's left to the boys and I get half or third of the contents.' (That idea was not mentioned again!)

James was now due to become a boarder at his first preparatory school. The Clarks had chosen the Wiltshire prep school Hawtreys, which had been founded a century earlier as a feeder for Eton. However, even when they went to look at the school Alan was in two minds, remembering his own time at St Cyprian's. 'I felt a horrible gloom for poor little Jamie ... those awful corridors and changing rooms, the other boys, unpleasantly menacingly peering.' On the day that term began, Alan recalled James controlling himself 'with great dignity – almost over-confident and optimistic poor little chap, he had been getting especially and – for him – unusually affectionate these last few nights as he felt his time drawing near'. A fortnight later he related his and Jane's first visit for a weekend exeat and James's 'frightful stories of violence in the dormitory, the sadistic "Sgt-Major" at PT etc'. Alan writes that James recounted them 'with a laugh and giggle (though they were anything but funny)'. But later there were tears, with Alan believing James to be too proud to say 'take me away'. He also got angry when told that James, although he had the reading ability of a thirteen-year-old, had only an average IQ – 'manifest nonsense'. After one more week, Alan was still at his 'wits end'. 'Really I can hardly write of my sick tears and worries.' They took James home for one night – to the disapproval of James's housemaster. Alan and Jane rowed, Jane blaming him for being soft on James.

Despite a Conservative Party conference, his ongoing affair with Valerie Harkess and a Jaguar car rally at Beaulieu, he found it impossible to keep James from his mind. The inevitable denouement came on Sunday, 23 November. 'Took James away from Hawtreys. I think his (protested) misery justified it, although of course I personally longed to have him back and had, ultimately, brainwashed darling little Jane into agreeing.'

The truism that troubles never come singly was amply illustrated. 'A most creepy and worrying thing. As we drove into the gates I said "oh, there's Mrs Yeo [the housekeeper], what *is* she doing?" – she had come out and was staring up the road. My mother also wandering in the drive (she had been staying the weekend) and Andrew out, without a jersey. Apparently Mrs Scott had rung through to say that "a labrador had been knocked down in the village" and also (it turned out) Jason was missing. I still didn't believe it. Jane took the car out, but hardly was she through the gate and in less time than it takes to write she was back saying "Jason's dead". Everyone was in tears. Jane and I dug a grave at once and buried him in his blanket while the others ate the jugged hare lunch.'

Jane's psychic abilities had played their part. That morning she had a premonition that something terrible was going to happen. It transpired that Jason had been run over by a milk lorry. Alan reported James as saying, 'I'd rather go back to school if it could make Jason alive again.' Alan thought he went 'straight to the point. There is more than coincidence here, but I don't understand it any more than I like it. Jane of course was absolutely shattered. She said he was almost like a lover to her, and it was true. They loved each other. He went shopping with her, sat on her cushion in the car, sat on her lap while she drove, slept on her bed while I was away. She talked to him while she was alone in the kitchen. It is terrible that she, and he, should be punished for something that is my fault. What now? We are still on the run, I suppose. It hasn't been a good year starting with Jamie's skiing accident [he had broken a leg at Zermatt], and the disastrous near-miss at Weston, and how they inter-acted. It's "decision-year", but I feel the decisions are going against us.'

Weston-super-Mare was but one of a lengthy list of Conservative seats to which Alan applied over three years. For some time afterwards he lamented failing to gain the nomination, not least, one suspects, because at the by-election the Conservatives secured a majority of over 20,000. But the political bug had definitely bitten. Evidence of just how serious he was in securing a candidacy survives in folders at Saltwood: Aldershot, Chertsey, Cirencester and Tewkesbury, East Surrey, Erith and Crayford, Hartlepool, Knutsford, Nottingham Central, Romford, Newcastle Central among others. To these he sent a carefully worded CV. In the May 1970 version he exaggerated his military service with the Household Cavalry training regiment into a second year, and he majored in 'specialist knowledge' of health thanks to being an 'executive governor' of St Thomas' Hospital. Most constituencies wrote him polite, often cyclostyled letters of rejection ('we regret it has not been possible to include you in our shortlist') and he became resigned to not finding a seat for the June 1970 election. Did it matter? He was convinced that Labour under Harold Wilson would be voted back for a third successive term. However, he and many others were mightily surprised when the Conservatives, under Edward Heath, overturned a Labour majority of 99 into a Conservative majority of 31. Alan and his Monday Club friends immediately began to plot. Might an Enoch Powell coup over Heath be a possibility with the Common Market as the issue? But that unlikely event was soon overtaken in his thinking by what he called 'the rigging up' of a constituency at Portsmouth, where boundary changes were in the offing.

Ian Lloyd had been Conservative MP for Portsmouth Langstone since 1964. A South African by birth, he had a superior manner that irritated many, as his obituarists were not shy of saying on his death in 2006. That he was pro-Europe and supported the abolition of capital punishment did not help, nor that some thought him 'an intellectual snob' and that he failed to devote enough time to his constituents'.[10] By late 1970, with the constituency being carved up in time for the next general election, a faction among the local Conservatives – some with Monday Club connections – decided it was time to make a move; otherwise, they feared, Lloyd might simply walk into the new adjacent constituency of Havant and Waterloo.

Efforts to deselect sitting MPs are inevitably divisive. A decade earlier, further west along the south coast, Nigel Nicolson, Tory MP for Bourne-mouth East, had been ousted by his constituency following a vitriolic campaign over his views against the Conservative government's Suez adventure of 1956. In the move to deselect Lloyd, Alan was seen as the Langstone rebels' secret weapon when the moment was ripe. Here was a Monday Club official – he now chaired the Wiltshire branch – he was anti-European, he had a celebrated father, was good-looking with a charming wife and two young sons, and it surely did not harm him that he was a historian who had not long before published his highly praised and readable account of Nazi Germany's Barbarossa campaign. Whether he was the 'constituency MP' they craved was a matter to which neither officials nor Alan gave thought.

Alan had already been in touch with a key player in the saga, Alan Warner, deputy chairman of the local Conservative Association, who ran the family holiday business. Warner was a keen skier, knew Zermatt and, as Alan said in one letter, 'our families are close friends'.[11] Contact between them also owed something to Alan's relationship with Valerie Harkess, whose second husband, James Harkess, had stood at the 1970 election as Tory candidate at Brixton, south London, where he espoused the Monday Club line on immigration, but failed to unseat the long-standing Labour MP Marcus Lipton.[12]

Although Alan was all but unknown, Warner took the opportunity in November of introducing him to local Conservatives as a last-minute substitute speaker at a constituency dinner. Alan enjoyed describing what happened. 'I shaved, changed, put on my Michael Fish silk shirt, blue suit and we were off. In the back of the Bentley (it was a long way) I was about to faint with nervous tension. Revived a bit before the meal, but sagged at dinner (hospital food). Ludicrous little solicitor chairman made monstrous introduction speech about my "looking for a seat . . . boundaries revision . . . shadow of a famous father etc". Then I rose. Spoke perhaps a little too fast, was conscious of crazy-nervous swelling between the fingers, but no bad gaps or stalls. Reasonable applause. Dealt with one question, then a man got up. "I wonder how many people shared my disappointment at having a second-rate speaker foisted on us" – I didn't much like this – "and instead found we were listening to one of the best political speeches I have ever heard in my life." What a moment! Then it was followed by another man who said he "did not wish to anticipate a vote of thanks, but was sure we all feel that the sooner Mr Clark is at Mr Heath's side in the House of Commons the better" !!! I was really devastated. If I can pull it off here, then anywhere.'

Ideally the Langstone rebels hoped to persuade Lloyd to stand down on the grounds that his business interests in shipping left him with insufficient time to put into the constituency – a familiar complaint at the time about Conservative MPs. He had also been appointed by the Prime Minister to the Council of Europe and Western European Union, which meant more absences abroad. But in a letter to the Association's chairman, Charles (known as Fred) Johnson, he made it clear that he stood by his record (his majority had doubled at the 1970 general election). The Langstone Executive Council finally met and voted on the issue in October 1971 – only eight were in favour of his readoption as Tory candidate, with thirty-five against. For Alan the moment seemed ripe, and yet for all the work he put in behind the scenes, his candidature failed to move forward with the speed that he wished. The next stage was the selection meeting early in 1972.

Lloyd did not 'lay down his sword' as requested in a letter from Warner. It was not until February 1973 that Lloyd's selection was finally endorsed by 480 votes to 336. He won the new Havant seat at the February 1974 election with a majority of over 9,000, thereby disproving the rebels' original assertion that the seat was marginal. Alan by then had long since moved on.

Back in government following the 1970 general election the Conservatives had substantially culled their list of approved prospective candidates to around 250. But there were also political motives. Before the election, Heath's private secretary, Douglas Hurd, told a young political journalist, Hugo Young of *The Sunday Times*, of his own 'private and unproven theory' – that the 'further you get from London, the more the selection tends to be controlled by a small group of people. It is much easier there to effect some kind of putsch, if you have the alliance of the local chairman. Nearer London, the press pays more attention, and also the centre has more of a grip.'[13]

Alan suspected that the Prime Minister, determined to rid the Party of its Powellite, Monday Club supporters, saw this as a way of ensuring that fewer constituencies would select right-wingers. Alan always maintained that Heath had also been getting at him personally and put him on a candidates' blacklist. Whatever the reason, Alan learnt by letter on 17 May 1971 that his name had been dropped from the revised list. This was not only a blow to Alan, it also upset the Langstone rebels' plans, leading Fred Johnson to write to Central Office. He could hardly say that Alan was their preferred candidate as Lloyd had not been dropped, but he did judge that Alan was 'good Parliamentary material that a Party such as ours needs' and that 'he has always supported Mr Heath'.[14] Alan had also fought back in a letter the previous month. He admitted that he was chairman of the Wiltshire branch of the Monday Club, but 'would like to emphasise that I have been at all times most scrupulous in confining the Club's utterances and activities within the limits of Party policy'. On 10 August he heard from Sir Richard Webster, Central Office's Director of Organisation, that his name had been restored.

Having for so long talked about leaving the castle and handing it over with many of its contents to Alan and Jane, Papa and Mama had finally decided. They had a new house, a bungalow, built on Saltwood's kitchen garden, and moved across in April 1971. Jane and Alan, though, were in two minds. 'We weren't keen – we had just moved the boys into new schools,' recalls Jane. 'And we loved Seend. At one point we even thought of coming to Saltwood just for weekends.' That April Alan observed that the castle, standing above Hythe and in sight of the English Channel, once again cast its spell on him. 'I always feel strangely randy there' – was it the effects of the sea? 'Jane now won over (better than "resigned-to") to the concept of a total move with beagles, peacocks, Mrs Yeo. But our style there still not settled.' Jane viewed Saltwood, as they received it, as 'really quite sad. My mother- and father-in-law just walked out after twenty years.' If they had moved to another part of the country it might have been different, but the Garden House, as they called their new home, was only a few hundred yards away. When K wanted to work he would return to his study in the library, not actually in the castle, but in the Great Hall on the other side of the Bailey.

Alan wrote in his diary (May 1973) of an incident that was one of many.

I am concerned that relations with my parents may be deteriorating.

They were standing on the lower terrace. My mama *exceedingly* dreamy, of both tone and deportment. She swayed at a lavender bush. Then, turning to Jane, 'I never told Cradduck [the gardener] to cut that back'.

'But I employ Cradduck now, Mama'. I spoke very gently. In fact the shrub had barely been cut back at all.

'It's all wrong; all wrong'. Pulling at my father's cardigan (it was a very hot afternoon but he was wearing a cardigan) she set off back towards the bridge. He, sensing this was something not to be drawn into, smiled and mumbled.

That was yesterday. This morning we were in Canterbury. When we returned Mrs Yeo said that they had both been over and 'gone upstairs'.

This has happened a great many times since my parents moved out. They lie awake in the Garden House and brood on the various items of 'contents' that they left behind. I think, but cannot be sure, that there was even a sort of verbal protocol agreed at the time of the conveyance that they should reserve a right of selection for items for which a 'need' became apparent. At the time it would have been graceless, as well as ill-judged, for me to turn this down. Already quite a few things, mainly books, they have retrieved.

Sometimes Lindley [the Garden House butler], who fancies himself as an *antiquaiere manqué*, is sent over in the car to collect objects, which whenever practicable, he does without referring to us.

Anyway, this morning my father apparently made off with a very nice early XIXc whalebone box about a foot in diameter which carried charming ink-engraved Eskimo drawings of seals and hunters. Jane loved this box, and was very upset. I found myself getting cross. I telephoned to the Garden House. My mother answered.

'So sorry we missed you this morning.'

'Papa had to come over and find a book.'

'He appears also to have taken the whalebone box which was in the dressing room.'

'Papa has always *loved* that box.'

'In that case why did he leave it behind when you made over the contents?'

My father took over. 'Oh God, God, don't say you are really making a fuss about the box?'

'No of course I'm not making a fuss. If you want the box, you must have the box. Jane is in tears, that doesn't matter at all. But ... ' (I must *not* be so icy in tone, it's only one stage off bellowing in rage.) ' ... mightn't it be a good idea if we worked out exactly what is left here which still belongs to you?'

'I'll bring it straight back; I'll bring it back over now, immediately. Take, take, take ... '

Then Mama came on. 'How can you do this to Papa? All he wanted was that box ... '

'Keep the bloody box. I just would like to know what else he must have ...'

Saltwood turned out to be hugely expensive, as Jane remembers. 'We were broke. It was lovely to be given the castle, but we had nothing to run it with.' Whereas the senior Clarks had eight indoor and outdoor servants, Alan and Jane made do with their housekeeper, Mrs Yeo, and Nanny Greenwood. The castle had been heated by coke; the boiler, as

Alan wrote, was like something in a Cunard liner from the 1920s, with two men deputed to keep it stoked. Alan and Jane switched to oil, and then the price doubled and went on soaring.

They sold Seend Park, but kept Broomhayes farmhouse and some of the land. Even before settling in at the castle, Alan had looked at the assets and decided that the adjoining land used by the local cricket club should be viewed as 'a development opportunity', providing funds towards a much-needed 'make-over'. But it was not to be. The local council threw out proposals for a housing estate, as they had forty years previously when a consortium of local businessmen bought the Saltwood estate from the Deedes family in the hope that they could use the land for speculative building. The year before his death Alan managed to repurchase the cricket field land, which he gave to Jane as a fortieth wedding anniversary present.

By 1980 Alan was forced to type a letter to his father. 'This is bad, I'm afraid. We are in financial difficulties. I don't mean we are going to be wiped out or anything like that, as the banks will always lend me money. But I cannot go on paying their interest. What I would like to do is sell one of the pictures in Mama's Trust.' He then went on to spell out the figures. His income as an MP, from a family trust, literary activity, from car- and share-dealing was 'not enough to keep up Salters (which seems to cost an additional £48,000 every year), pay all the insurances, rates, fuel, taxes, gardeners' wages and support the boys and, as it were, live'. He added that Jane was in despair, never going out, buying any clothes or having a holiday; she also knew the financial situation intimately as she 'does the books'. The picture he wished to sell was a Cézanne still-life drawing (not water-colour), 'partly because it is not one of my favourites'. He added in manuscript: 'I've never asked you for money . . . I hate doing so now.'[15] K responded, 'I can never understand how you got along so well for so long. The only question is which picture to sell.' His one reservation was over the Cézanne. 'I like it more than you . . . and would rather wish that you sold the Seurat.' But in the end it had to be his son's decision.[16]

There were pluses, not least in the amount of space, with Alan and Jane enjoying the luxury of separate bathrooms. Outside, but hidden from view from the castle, they built a line of garages for the ever-growing fleet of cars. The garden, which had been Mama's preserve, was taken over by Jane. A gorse bank, which they called Gossie, became a challenge. Alan's best time for the ascent was two and a half minutes, but James and Andrew easily broke the two-minute barrier.

★

In May 1972 Alan confided to his diary that 'a situation of considerable promise' had arisen in Plymouth. The new Sutton constituency was created out of boundary changes. Just as at Langstone he had Alan Warner, so at Sutton his contact, or spy as he called him, Graham Butland, was a member of the constituency Conservative Association who had identified Alan as the candidate Sutton needed. How much speedier it proved than the drawn-out and ultimately unsatisfactory saga of Langstone. Butland was an enormous help, leaking him the questions that the Sutton selection committee had prepared, and asking if there was anything he wished posed. Returning to Bratton before his interview Alan was reminded 'how lovely and soft and restful the West Country is! And how evocative of those early distant happy days with Jane and the babies and the blue Oldsmobile. Now we hardly have time to breathe, but I can still get a great draught of peace when I am at Bratton-Clovelly. Whether it would still be the same if I was an MP down there, I don't know.'

On Friday, 12 May he recorded events while overlooking Plymouth Hoe from a bay-window table 'with a tea tray in front of me' at the Duke of Cornwall Hotel, where the interviews took place. For Alan here was the opportunity to write a set-piece diary entry:

> I am clean-shirted and in a light tweed suit. My features are composed, set you could say, into an expression at the same time fresh and obliging.
>
> A big chap, fifty-ish, balding, spectacles sat about three tables away. He too appeared to be waiting. Was he the Chairman? Practically anybody could be the chairman at this stage, it seemed. Or at least the Treasurer, or the Vice-chairman. Silently ingratiating, I endeavoured to radiate good will.
>
> Several times I caught him looking at me. Curiously, but *cholerically*. Finally he lumbered over – 'Mr Fowler?'
>
> 'No.' Some sixth sense told me not to identify myself.
>
> Scattered about the room sat other candidates. Two of them greeted each other with braying declarations, plainly false, of affection and respect. Standard Party Conference templates; i.e. not very big, not very masculine. Spectacles, new-looking suits, tightly-knotted ties. For much of the time I looked at the ceiling – but *intelligently*, like Richthofen's dog, Moritz.
>
> Only one of these characters was actually seen back down stairs by an escorting bigwig. I recognised Michael Howard, much plugged in the broadsheet press as *thrusting*, a barrister, a high-flyer certain to enter the new Parliament, etc.[17]
>
> The bigwig held him in 'politician's grip'; one hand holding his, the other on Howard's elbow. Not necessarily a good sign, more usually an

indicator of impending betrayal of some kind. However – 'Well done', I overheard. 'You'll be hearing from us very shortly . . . '

That's that, then. All sewn up. Except, who the hell is 'Mr Fowler'?[18]

Afterwards he wrote that the interview had been 'a great success', and that he thought he 'might even have carried the whole thing on the spot'. But not everyone on the committee was a pushover. The next step was a cocktail party, with wives present, where each candidate – the other front-runner, David Hunt, was a leading Young Conservative[19] – made a speech and answered questions. Alan drew on a phrase that would become familiar in his diary: 'anything-can-happen in backgammon/politics. Throw 4x4, 1x1, 6x6; Fowler gets adopted elsewhere etc. I must press on – that special elation I felt on the Plymouth train after the interview, one is quite charged.'

Alan showed that he knew how to use the press to his advantage. In advance of the next meeting, with the candidates reduced to three, he orchestrated 'some shrewd publicity' in *The Times* Diary column; next he conferred secretly with his supporters. When it came to the meeting, he thought his speech a flop, but next morning learnt that the voting had been so close (10 for Fowler, 11 for Hunt and 9 for him) that all now depended on a full Association meeting on 30 June, again at the 'Duke'.

The night of the final meeting was 'the most memorable of my life with the exception of James being born'. He reflected next morning that it was 'easy enough now to look back and say that I knew I'd get it. I can only say that the moment when Tom Bridges [Association chairman] gestured to Doc Mac and Howard Davies [committee members] to console the other two – well! Like a Miss World contestant for a few minutes I couldn't believe it was actually happening to me, and didn't what you might call "come to" until the Press were taking pictures and data. Then there was the "repeat convivial" down in the bar.' This was followed by a post-mortem in the street with Graham Butland and another of his supporters, David Holmes. 'At last up to darling Jane who received one in triumph, a *nuit grise* from *sheer elation*.' The following morning, 'my mind just went over and over the wonderful fabulous fact that I had been adopted for a safe seat. Confidence totally restored in myself and in God's help – if you deserve it. It was the God question that won it for me, that clinched it. Before I had my turn, on arrival in room 24, I had opened the bible for a snap quotation, got the miracle of the loaves and fishes.'

What kind of Conservative were Sutton getting? 'Yes, you could say I am a Powellite,' he told the London *Evening Standard*, 'but like many members of the Tory Party, I feel he goes over the edge from time to time. I don't think men are any more equal than racehorses ... I believe in privilege, but it can be abused' – and here he referred to *The Donkeys* – 'as it was by the blimps.'[20] Alan was adopted formally as prospective Conservative parliamentary candidate on 17 September. Typically, he 'left the speech-making/learning a little late and had a demi-panic at lunch in the hot enclosed front lawn at Bratton. However recovered, washed my hair and did my stuff in the Duke ball-room.' He had to use a microphone, which he hated. He was criticised afterwards for his speech, which concentrated on violence, but, as he noted, 'all the publicity went to my answers on the Asians afterwards'. The *Western Morning News* quoted him next morning as saying, 'The Tory Party should capitalise on the public outcry against the coming influx of Ugandan Asians and ban all further coloured immigration.' Alan wrote that this caused gloom among many on the platform, including the chairman, but the response from the hall showed that he had struck a popular chord.

Here, though, was 'a *real* turning point'.[21] At forty-four a new career beckoned.

Part Two

TWENTY-THREE

Mixed Emotions

On New Year's Day 1974 Alan had forecast that the year would not be good.[1] And yet by the end of February he was a Member of Parliament.

Alan wrote little of the campaign, but made notes in a W.H. Smith appointments diary. He reported that constituency supporters were confident, but he didn't like talking about 'when you are in the House . . . '. He worried about the Liberal threat, and a week before election day became convinced he would lose. He remembered exactly where he was – 'I went quite faint and dry-mouthed' – crossing a Plymouth car park. He need not have worried. His majority: 8,104, ahead of his best expectations.

Victory was sweet. 'Must be reckoned the pinnacle so far.' Arriving at Westminster the following week he wrote of 'fabulous day of lingering euphoria and luxuriation' in being Alan Clark, Member of Parliament. His close friend, Euan Graham, Principal Clerk of Private Bills in the House of Lords, was there to greet him and show him around. 'Collected huge bundles of (miscellaneous) mail and through to Euan's office where he got me *monstrously* drunk; then drifted around the Palace of Westminster peeping and pottering, and observing massive available perks; drink in Strangers Bar and to (quite good) lunch. Hailed in Strangers dining room with incredible hurrahs by Jeremy Thorpe, more guardedly by David Steel.[2] Then spent rest of afternoon "walking off" drink going round various Sergeant-at-Arms type offices drawing vouchers etc.' Thirty years later Graham recalled Alan quickly demonstrating that he wished to make his mark and that he wasn't going to be a 'quiet as a dormouse' new Member.[3]

His father had a practical form of expressing his congratulations, offering him use of the B5 apartment at Albany. He wrote him a welcoming letter. 'I am absolutely delighted you are prepared to try sharing it with me. I could not bear to part with it, and yet I would find it hard to resist Mama's arguments if she found she would never go back there. It is such a marvellous property that I would hate to see it pass out of the family. It is convenient and will save you money.'[4]

The Parliament to which Alan was elected was in an unusual state of flux. More than two decades later Alan related events in his history of the Tory Party: Edward Heath, as 'the Prime Minister in possession' and leading a party boasting 1,200,000 more votes than Labour (but five fewer seats), had spent 'five painful days' attempting to 'form' an administration.[5] Jeremy Thorpe, leader of the Liberals (6,000,000 votes, but only fourteen seats), demanded nothing less than proportional representation; Heath offered no more than a Speaker's Conference to examine the question of electoral reform. The coalition did not happen, Heath resigned and Harold Wilson became Prime Minister, leading a minority Labour government.

As a backbench MP for the party now in opposition after four years of power Alan quickly realised that the Labour government was unlikely to last. The press widely assumed that if the Tories were in disarray, Wilson would go to the country at the earliest opportunity. Alan's euphoria turned to depression (not helped by Andrew's bronchitis and Jane's anger on discovering an invitation from a girlfriend). Only ten days had passed since his election, but he was already writing of 'the inevitability of Labour victory in next election'. He was, though, looking ahead, recording Margaret Thatcher's name 'concepted as possible successor to Heath'.

Alan had kept up his connections with *The Sunday Times* and, feeling that he had nothing to lose, three weeks after the election he rocked the boat with a leader-page article headed 'Tory Party needs a rethink, but where are the thinkers?' For a new backbencher it was brave if foolhardy to be highly critical of the Party machine and its reliance on the findings of opinion pollsters in formulating policy. Drawing on his own experience, he attacked Tory Central Office for its condemnation, 'amounting in the later years almost to a witch-hunt', of all expressions of dissent, particularly those who supported Enoch Powell's views.[6] When the *Western Morning News* reported on his article, eyebrows were raised in Plymouth. As for Alan's political standing, he quickly became more mainstream if still right-wing in his Conservative views. In a letter to David Butler, who was compiling his study of the February 1974 election, he suggested that at the time he had been looking for a seat it had been useful to be 'much more closely identified with Monday Club/Powellite sympathies' than he was to become once at Westminster.[7]

Soon after his arrival he fell in with the MP for Gillingham in Kent, Frederick Burden, a 'feisty old backbencher' who told him he was already causing 'a certain amount of resentment . . . don't push it too hard, lie low for a bit'. He was not yet part of any group, whereas his fellow Old Etonian, Douglas Hurd, was one of about a dozen of the new Conservative

Jane soon became caught up in Alan's car mania. Here they have been taking part in a hill climb in their Volkswagen.

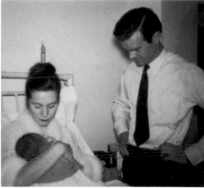

Jane and Alan's first son, James, was born on 13 February 1960 at the London Clinic. The christening (LEFT) took place at the Grosvenor Chapel when James was two months old.

After Trevor-Roper, another of Alan's mentors was the military historian Basil Liddell Hart, who visited Alan and Jane at Bratton-Clovelly in Devon in 1961.

Kenneth and Jane Clark in the late 1950s, a picture taken on a visit to New York. They had lived at Saltwood Castle since 1952, their lavish entertaining aided by a retinue of eight servants.

By 1965 Alan, Jane and their sons had moved to Wiltshire, in the first of two houses at Seend. James was five and Andrew three.

The photographer also caught Alan off guard.

Seend Park in 1969.
When Alan and Jane were
offered Saltwood in 1971
they were in two minds
about leaving Seend. The
boys were settled into
schools, and at one point
they contemplated using
the castle just at week-
ends.

Alan reading the *Sunday Times*, which he had begun writing for in 1961 following publication of *The Donkeys*.

Mama in the early 1970s. On her coat lapel is a brooch that was left to Jane.

By 1971 Alan and Jane had moved into Saltwood Castle with their sons. This photograph with Papa was taken not long after Mama's death in 1976.

Kenneth Clark with his second wife, Nolwen, outside the Garden House, built on Saltwood's kitchen garden. The family was not surprised that he remarried, only that his bride was someone Alan and Jane had not previously met.

Alan with the John Lavery portrait of his father as a young boy.

After the death of his father in 1983, Colin disputed the ownership of the Turner Seascape of Folkestone (shown hanging behind Kenneth Clark). On the eve of the painting being sold at Sotheby's the following year, he went to court to try and stop the sale, but withdrew his action at the last moment. The brothers were reconciled as can be seen from the auction photograph (RIGHT). Jane accompanied Alan to the auction which ran across two days. The Turner fetched more than £7 million, a record for any painting at the time.

ALAN AND JANE AT SALTWOOD

Outside the castle: on the battlements; Alan swimming the moat as he did early each summer; Jane cleaning the swimming pool; and ready to wield the scythe; and the trusty Mehari, a little plastic truck with a light foot-print – what Alan called 'a mobile wheelbarrow'.

MPs who had already worked in some capacity for the Party – in Hurd's case since the 1970 general election as political secretary to Edward Heath. They called themselves 'the office boys', after a 'contemptuous epithet', wrote Hurd, flung at them by Alan, 'who had already set himself apart by arrogance'.[8] Meanwhile George Gardiner, who also entered the House at this election, as Conservative MP for Reigate, recalls a party given by Alan where 'countless of my new colleagues were complaining of the "abysmal" election campaign Heath had just fought'.[9]

For his maiden speech Alan seized on the opportunity presented at the end of April 1974 by a debate on the Channel Tunnel. This had nothing to do with his constituency, as he explained, but if the tunnel were ever to materialise, the English end would inevitably surface close to Saltwood. He was, though, mainly concerned with the defence question, the country protected down the centuries from invasion by the English Channel. Any future attack would be by 'blitzkrieg, a lightning strike', and its most likely form would now be a parachute landing 'to seize the tunnel head and defend it for a short enough period for the invader to pass through the tunnel and completely bypass our natural protection'. And, he added, if the tunnel went ahead a fail-safe system should be installed allowing for its instant demolition.

Becoming an MP was Alan's first full-time salaried employment. 'At the age [he was forty-six] when most people start "slowing up", I suddenly gain a job, having been in retirement from the age of twenty-seven.' Retirement? He was still dealing in cars, he still had Saltwood to finance and run, and he now had his constituency more than two hundred miles from London. Sutton could not be ignored, particularly if another election was in the offing. On a personal level Jane was mainly based at Saltwood, the boys, both now in their teens, were at schools nearby, but his mother's increasing ill-health was a concern. With the Commons occupying him four, even sometimes five, days a week he was basing himself more and more on B5, Albany (with the lights in his favour he could make the Commons car park in ten minutes). Albany also became the base for his extracurricular activities.

His diary shows that despite the joy that becoming an MP had given him, he was still capable of recording 'depression so acute that great long uncreative periods supervene when the mind just rambles'. Andrew Roberts, who got to know him well in the last decade of his life, believes that 'Depression and pessimism are an absolute integral part of his psychological make up. Depression is a fascinating side of him ... And indeed of all Tories, Samuel Johnson, Lord Salisbury, Winston

Churchill among them.'[10] In another entry Alan writes of waking to unpleasant thoughts slotting into place including mounting backgammon losses. Two paragraphs on: 'Given up b'gammon ... statistical analysis shows it is too expensive.' Elsewhere 'long periods just brooding – cutting out birds, drink and backgammon should have helped'. The 'birds' still included Valerie Harkess, but at this moment, he wrote, 'out of my life'.

The Clarks' finances were in a dire state. Money borrowed at various banks and on different accounts meant interest charges now totalled £20,000 a year. 'Must stop the drain and can only do so by selling cars,' he writes. And yet the life he was able to enjoy meant much to him, as he summed up in mid-June, writing in the Commons library: 'From time to time, as I drive about in my blue Bentley – to which I am very attached, "MP's car" – I think about what a personification of privilege I am. Silk shirts, beautiful suits, write a cheque or sign an Amex for anything you want; chambers in Albany, castle in Kent, chalet in Zermatt, credit accounts everywhere, the Parliamentary pass to flash. Press the button, the machine will respond. Total confidence. How easy to be pleasant – that calm inner assurance of superiority (like I have sometimes noticed with people who are very good at Judo, the way they move quietly and confidently in crowds). Well, could it be in jeopardy? I got the aerial photos of Saltwood today, thought God what a wonderful place, worth hanging on to, and preserving for the boys.'

Parliament was exhausting. He was lucky, he wrote in midsummer, to be getting five to six hours' sleep a night, thanks to late whipping in the House (and, he admits, too much to drink). For a time adrenalin kept him going, and he was grateful when he could undertake constituency duties while based at Bratton – 'delicious, tranquil. What a place to recharge one's batteries.' Yet as the first summer recess approached he seemed near breaking point with bills accumulating and no sign of any car sales to relieve them. As a solution his mind turned to Zermatt, which he described as the Bavarian Redoubt – not the first time he would draw on a Second World War analogy. Perhaps he could move across some of the Saltwood treasures he was so lucky to own? A Degas, some Henry Moores and Graham Sutherlands, for instance. 'But how would one live in the long term? On reflection, must preserve Saltwood, so it can be run as a business.' Later that day – it was a Monday in August – he asked himself the big question, 'Am I a Renaissance Prince, a philosopher, or a big ageing dud?' At that point one suspects there was only one answer.

Was he no good at property deals? Alan admitted having 'totally mismanaged his one last great get-out deal, namely the sale of the cricket field' (and here he blames 'optimism, *folie de grandeur*, total lack of Scotch canniness, gross miscalculations of economic symptoms and also sheer inability, or at least unwillingness to *count*'). He looked back at what he called 'those lost opportunities of money-making'; he had squandered that first £15,000 given him by his father in 1948 when he was at Oxford; he had failed to capitalise on properties in Rye when they were going for next to nothing, and what about the Torridon estate in the western Highlands of Scotland – £40,000 in 1964, now half a million, he supposed? 'And yet when I go and plump for something like Newton [in north Cornwall], it becomes a lemon at once.'

September came quickly, and soon news of the second general election of the year. But before campaigning could begin Alan was summoned to see his bankers. Hoare's in Fleet Street were still a family firm. They had been good to him but, on their terms, the collateral for the loans had meant handing over the Saltwood deeds. He had six months to get his accounts in order. He came away and wrote, 'Everything happening at once' – financial collapse and the election. 'Waking early with all these worries.'

Jane joined him in Plymouth to canvass. She drove the Land Rover while Alan shouted through the megaphone the Conservative slogan – 'Firm Government – but Fair Government'. At one point in a near-empty street Jane accelerated and Alan 'affected a Devonian accent'. Jane jammed on the brakes. 'What *are* you doing? You just make yourself utterly ridiculous.' On the final Sunday of the campaign he wrote to his father. 'Outlook here is very poor – place absolutely crawling with Liberals who will split the Conservative vote disastrously and may even take the seats themselves if they get enough Labour converts. Last night I thought we were done, this morning (after a good night) I shall say a very close thing. Jane is being simply marvellous. Never flags or falters, always sweet-tempered, aborts all my nervous cursing and has many times "saved me from myself". I dread her tears when we lose. Somehow satisfying that politicians should have to take this punishment every four years or so. Now back to the trenches (and please no telegrams or messages/DON'T stay up, results won't be out till after 2 (or 3 if a recount)).'[11]

Across the country the Conservative campaign was not going well. Alan noted a phone conversation with Bernard Weatherill, the deputy Chief Whip and better known as Jack (and later Speaker in the Commons), who, when Alan voiced his doubts that the Tories could win led by Heath, responded, 'Later. That comes later. Leave it for the moment.' To Alan this could only mean one thing – a new leader. 'And that will be one of the exciting things about the new House. Getting a real change.'

The Conservatives did lose: 276 seats to Labour's 319, with Liberals down one at 13. Alan's vote fell by 1,192 votes and his majority from 8,104 to 5,188. He worried that as a 'safe' seat he had done less well than many a colleague elsewhere. 'It undermines my personal activities as a right-winger and also, of course, in the Association itself,' where he knew he had enemies. He and Jane returned to Saltwood and, as the towers loomed up in the headlights, Jane said, 'what a wonderful place'. Alan, however, admitted that he dare not tell her how much in peril it was. To get himself to sleep he devised a formula of selling the plot next to the Zermatt chalet – for £90,000 – and did not wake for nearly thirteen hours. He sold pictures, and opened negotiations with the Tate for David Des Granges' great seventeenth-century painting *The Saltonstall Family*.[12]

In February 1975 Margaret Thatcher took over the Party leadership from Edward Heath. Alan had been asked by Airey Neave, who ran the Thatcher leadership campaign with 'a military precision you would expect from someone who had escaped from Colditz', to talk to the October 1974 intake of new Conservative Members and find out 'how they were going to vote'. Alan remembered Neave as saying: 'Tell them she hasn't got a chance. They must vote for her because if Heath wins by a landslide we'll never get rid of him. And anyway if she gets no votes it will look bad for the Party with her being a woman.' In private Neave thought differently: 'My filly is going to win.' She did – by eleven votes on the first ballot.[13] Alan did not reveal in his diary how he voted, but it is the impression of Graham Stewart (his researcher on *The Tories* in the 1990s) that he wanted William Whitelaw.

A year had gone by since Alan had become an MP and only now was he writing up political events at Westminster. The first occasion was what he called the last day of the Common Market (Approval) debates. It was a free vote and Alan voted against, although he confessed that if Margaret Thatcher had told him to vote 'for' he would. The Heath and Thatcher factions were still at odds with each other. When Heath rose to speak, Alan reported one Heathite asking 'Where's Margaret? He listened to *her* speech.' To which Alan added, 'But wasn't very polite.' Enoch Powell, 'tortured, baleful, intense . . . spoke well, gestured pointedly . . . very good and moving and made me feel *all right* about voting anti'. Next day in the tearoom queue he told Dennis Skinner – despite their diametrically

opposing political views, they were to have increasing respect for each
other − 'I'd rather live in a socialist Britain than one ruled by a lot of
fucking foreigners.'

He used 11 May to look at himself. 'An evocative date, the great
German offensive across the Low Countries in 1940, Churchill gets the
premiership, the die is cast in the country's fight to the death. And five
years later, VE Day, with its illusions that took so long to disperse.' He
reckoned he had 'ten − *tennish* − more years active, eight as "an active
buffer", the remainder as a sage'.

Thanks to some judicious picture sales his finances were looking up,
and even though he had missed Hoare's original 1 April date, he now sent
them £18,000, which brought his overdraft down to the agreed level.
'More to follow,' he promised himself. 'The magic moment when the
deeds are returned to me not so far away.' But he worried about the state
of the nation, its 'terrible decline'. He pondered his own position: 'In the
train the other evening I thought perhaps I should go the whole way,
stand as National Front candidate, and switch if the Plymouth Association
kicks me out.'

With the summer proving blissfully hot he complained of being stuck
in the Commons into the first week of August. Hardly had the recess
begun than Sutton pestered − his word − him to pay more attention to
the constituency, and say when his next surgery would be. Bored by it all,
he decided in September that the answer was to stand down; he even
composed a press release, saying his resignation was for 'family reasons'.
His general disaffection with Sutton would continue on and off for the
rest of his time as its MP. Alan desperately wanted a political role. Defence
being his strongest suit, he was disappointed at failing to become vice-
chairman of the Party's Defence Committee (he did later get on its Home
Affairs Committee). At Westminster he at last began to make a mark. In
May he was pleasantly surprised to read *The Times* columnist George
Hutchinson tipping him for inclusion in the Shadow Cabinet.[14] In June
The Guardian published a piece of his in its 'Grassrooting' slot: he had
done some calculations on political stamina, and pointed out that in the
past year he went 37,000 miles by train, another 18,000 by car.[15] His
breakthrough came in November when, on behalf of constituents who
worked at Devonport Dockyard, he raised the question of compensation
for the two hundred employees there who had died of asbestosis. The
answer came from the Secretary of State for Employment, Michael Foot,
who had represented Devonport as its MP (1945−55), but who now said
that asbestosis was not a notifiable disease.[16] Alan did not drop the issue,

which gained him national press coverage so essential to a backbencher determined to make his mark.

His mother's health had been a cause for family concern for some time. After a stroke in December 1973, which left her left side paralysed, she had eventually returned to the Garden House in spring 1974 as an invalid. Some two years later, on Remembrance Sunday 1976, one of the Garden House servants banged on the front door of the castle to give the news that Lady Clark had died during the night. Alan and Jane dressed and crossed the grounds to find K '"in tremendous form", wiping mouth with back of hand having just eaten brown egg and grapefruit, little tray in library'. Of his mother, Alan wrote, her face was 'composed, determined, rather beautiful, not in any way distorted'.[17] He and Jane started to cry. Jane recalled, 'She looked very beautiful. She hadn't given up.' Or had she? Eighteen months later, Alan wrote that he was depressed by something he had learnt that day from Dr Rowntree about Mama's 'awful last illness' – and realised 'she had committed suicide – hence all the notes and the tidy way it was done. Presumably got the medicine to do it via Kathy [a nurse] or what, I don't know.'[18]

To Sue Lawley on BBC Radio 4's *Desert Island Discs* in 1994 Alan revealed: 'My mother was a terrific lip curler. I remember her saying to me when I was thirty, anyone who isn't married at my age had to be a pansy, and that was just monstrous and she knew very well that I wasn't a pansy ... She was often very cruel. I didn't have any standard to compare her by until I sat round a cabinet table with Mrs Thatcher and then I saw again a woman being as cruel to men as my mother was. That was quite a useful grounding in a way. Those are the women you want to prove yourself to.'

Mama had had a rotten final few years. Jane believes Alan was ultimately very fond of her, whatever the problems when he was a child. 'He used to go and see her after her stroke. I think my father-in-law was by then slightly irritated by her. He wanted to go on writing. She refused to try and walk because after the stroke she realised she couldn't walk. Her mind was still there, but she couldn't speak very clearly. She was very sweet really. I think she was very lonely. All the books around her had been approved by my father-in-law, but all she wanted were a few trashy magazines.' Jane remembers how one evening she staggered all the way up to the top of the house to say goodnight to her grandchildren, and fell into Andrew's cot.

Like K, Mama kept rewriting her will, making different dispositions on each occasion. In the version lodged at the Clydesdale Bank, and to his father's astonishment, Alan proved the beneficiary, 'a tremendous liberation for me,' he wrote, but he added, 'the way in which she died fills us with grief and affection'.[19] Celly and Colin were surprised, too, that she left nothing to either of them, as they both admitted to the publisher Naim Attallah. Celly said, 'She wrote the most beautiful letters to us and devoted half her will to saying that Sammie, my son, must be treated in exactly the same way as her other grandchildren, as if he were legitimate, but in fact she didn't leave him anything.'[20]

Alan's new year resolutions for 1977 were mainly political, asking questions, attending Question Time, endeavouring to get Speaker Thomas to notice him. 'This is last chance for "impact". Pretty bullish year, three books to write, and Saltwood to improve. Something's got to give and I suppose it will be b'gammon and sex – with the blondes [as he now called Valerie Harkess and her daughters] away.' But he was certainly not depressed, thanks to successful car-trading, having a big win – for once – off Charles Howard at backgammon, which continued to hold him in its thrall into the 1980s – 'it's an addiction and a destructive one,' he wrote.[21] The picture market was looking brighter and he had even been offered £27,000 for a house in Woodfall Street, Chelsea, which he had originally bought for Jane. She, though, never set foot in it, or saw the proceeds!

Politically his stock was rising. He took a stand against proportional representation – very much a Liberal cause to which Labour, whose majority of five had disintegrated at by-elections, were now listening – and took the opportunity of a tea with Margaret Thatcher – their first – in April to raise the matter. He found her attractive, particularly her ankles. He recalls half getting going on defence, but was interrupted.[22] In May 1977 he was widely noted when raising the case of special pay for Dartmoor prison officers. In June he had his first Commons triumph, as he noted in his diary: 'getting both sides to laugh at my "quip", as the *Telegraph* called it, about "anyone who has been to Eton ... has already served the equivalent of five years in gaol", to which Merlyn Rees, the Home Secretary responded, "There is one difference – in prison they learn to read and write."'[23]

Like all backbench MPs Alan found late and sometimes all-night sittings a trial. On one occasion in July 1977 he reported pushing curved leather armchairs together in Committee Room 7 to give him somewhere to sleep. Alan, though, had more serious concerns: as he recorded in the final entry of his 1977 diary, an Association member had called for a special meeting of the Executive Council to '"question me about my attitude to the National Front." Gach!'

Alan and Jane were determined that their sons would never suffer the neglect that Alan had experienced from his parents. When James reached eighteen – in 1978 – and began to assert himself, Alan noticed and wrote about it. 'Rang "Boy" and not too happy about him. He was talking "yeh man" to such an extent that I had to reprimand him – "don't use that 'y'know' interjection ..." etc. For the first time, particularly when signing off, his voice lacked that special spontaneous affection – "God bless you too" ... Rang Jane immediately, and of course she remembered it too from *her* conversation with him last Sunday. The gulf had opened. "We've become parents", I said, instead of family, elder bro or sister.'

A fortnight later Alan's thoughts on James had matured. 'This year he's suddenly discovered his independence, all in a total rush ... He wants to go back there [Zermatt] and then to South Africa where he thinks he will make his fortune, and so one has accepted this – I don't, can't, any longer allow myself to fuss all the time that he's out and away and so on. I mean at this moment he's driving up to London in the Datsun, and formerly I'd have been scared stiff; now I'm just numb.'

In politics in 1978 increasingly only one question mattered. Would James Callaghan call the election in the autumn or would he go for the full five-year Parliament and leave it until the following year? Everyone had an opinion.

Alan had now been an MP for four years, and Jane asked him 'for how much longer ... You work frightfully hard at it, you don't seem to be getting anything out of it.' To his diary, Alan wrote, 'I dissimulated. How could I confess that to give up would be to discard my perennial obsession, the vision that has been with me always, the certainty that I would be called to lead.'[24] At the start of the recess he wrote in his diary that, although loathing Plymouth, 'I just adore the Commons. I am seduced by its gossipy, club-like regimental atmosphere and love also the delicious karate-type confidence that being an MP gives me.' James Callaghan finally ended the election speculation, telling Cabinet on 7 September – and surprising even his closest colleagues – that it would be spring. Alan, though, barely referred to what became widely known as 'the winter of discontent'. Meanwhile, Alan had his own problems. In May he had worried that 'outgoings continuing to accumulate at Saltwood'. Were further picture and car sales the solution? Only time would tell. By October he was once again writing that he had 'forsaken b'gammon (presently owe Brooks's £888)'. He had also been 'chucked by the blondes'. And he was increasingly irritated by his constituency – 'when will it be possible to escape?'

By March 1979 his finances were at last in better shape. He delighted recording in his diary, 'Savoured today the first pleasure of writing a "surprised-not-to-have-heard-from-you" note to C. Hoare & Co who I had written to a week ago asking for exact figures with which to pay off my overdraft. Dropped it in by hand on way back from cigar-plus lunch.' And two weeks later, 'Getting deeds back from Hoare's *is* within my grasp now.'

In his diary he wrote little about politics even though the election was in prospect. In a column surveying the field, *The Guardian*'s Michael White described him as 'the elegant Plymouth reactionary'.[25] The Tories were ahead in the polls and Alan expected to win with an increased majority (although he suffered inevitable moments of uncertainty). If that was achieved he would then concentrate, he wrote, on finding a constituency in the south-east.

On the day before the election *The Guardian* published a light-hearted piece on his personal rules for canvassing: 'don't slam the car door. Shut the gate on your way in as well as when leaving; don't kick the empty milk bottles; use the bell rather than the knocker; don't ring more than once; don't look up – if they're peering from the first floor it's because they don't want to come down. Chimes are Tory; shrill bell old-fashioned Liberal; none at all, usually Labour.'

He concluded on a serious, if rose-tinted note: 'In the evenings when I look out over Plymouth Sound and imagine the Grand Fleet riding at anchor, with a thousand coaling stations around the globe within its fief; and when I reflect on the ideals that led me into politics, romantic and reactionary as they are and impracticable of fulfilment or even expression in contemporary politics, then I yearn for the days of the great public meetings ... today even Cabinet names can barely draw an audience of a dozen people. I would like to exclude for the duration of the campaign not only opinion polls, but the television camera itself, and see crowds of many thousands gather on Plymouth Hoe so that they can listen to Michael Foot or Enoch Powell or Keith Joseph and respond, as in ancient times, to the direct flow of oratory and argument.'[26]

3 May: election day. Alan need not have worried. His majority was up, to 11,287 over Labour; the Tories returned to government with seventy

seats more than Labour. A few days later he reported: 'Mrs Thatcher (or Mrs Carrington, as Papa amusingly – muddledly – called her) has announced her Cabinet, and I'm not in, anywhere.' He quickly identified a silver lining. 'Lovely to have freedom of the Commons, consolidated at Plymouth, and the summer before us.'

TWENTY-FOUR

Falklands and Papa's Death

Alan was never slavishly a Thatcherite. He did, however, identify with Nigel Lawson: 'The wrong definition is "whatever Margaret Thatcher herself at any time did or said". The right definition involves a mixture of free markets, financial discipline, firm control over public expenditure, tax cuts, nationalism, "Victorian values" (of the Samuel Smiles self-help variety), privatization and a dash of populism.'[1]

The return of the Conservatives into government under Margaret Thatcher in 1979 made Alan sit up and attend. If he was going to become a Minister he had to be noticed – for the right reasons. Here he is early in 1980 when, following a BBC interview with Robin Day, she was brought into the Commons cafeteria by Ian Gow, her parliamentary private secretary. 'Goodness, she is *so* beautiful; made up to the nines of course, for the television programme, but still quite bewitching, as Eva Peron must have been. I could not take my eyes off her and after a bit she, quite properly, would not look me in the face.'[2] Alan had indeed been noticed.

Alan's friendship with Ian Gow helped. As Thatcher's PPS from 1979 to 1983 Gow was extraordinarily influential; it was said they would have nightcaps together at Number Ten when Gow brought her up to date on what was happening at Westminster. Alan was one of his contacts. Not that all Tories, however, believed in her as the Party leader and, now, the Prime Minister. Thus in November 1979, not seven months after the election that returned the Tories to power, Alan reported a tough summing-up by Tony Royle, Richmond's Tory MP, 'eminently sensible, never seen him in a flap (ex SAS, I think). But he can be very forthright, no words minced. "Look at the people round her", he said. "Carrington – hates her; Prior – hates her; Gilmour – hates her; Heseltine – hates her; Walker – loathes her, makes no secret of it; Willie [Whitelaw] – completely even-handed, would never support her against the old gang; Geoffrey Howe – no personal loyalties – durable politburo man, will serve under anyone. The only people committed to Margaret are Angus Maude, John

Biffen and Keith Joseph and the last two are so tortured intellectually as to cast doubt on their stability in a crisis."'[3]

Looking back at Thatcher's decade as Prime Minister it is hard to recall that, as Alan put it in *The Tories*, two years into her first Parliament she was 'already cruelly beleaguered. Polls showed that she was more unpopular than any previous Prime Minister. Scarcely one person in her Cabinet had a good word to say of her.'[4] With riots in Toxteth and Brixton and unemployment well into three million, 1981 was a tough year to lead the country. But she survived, Alan believed, on 'willpower, founded on an extraordinary sense of uniquely being *right*'.

What saved 'The Lady', as he soon referred to Margaret Thatcher in his diaries, was the Falklands War – 'a battle of almost designer perfection to enhance the standing of its commander'. It was also the making politically of Alan Clark. When on 2 April 1982 Argentina invaded the Falklands, Alan remarked to Jane, 'We've lost the Falklands. It's all over. We're a Third World country, no good for anything.' This apocalyptic view was brought on by what he described as 'the shuffling and fudging, the overpowering impression of timidity and incompetence' which he had heard that day at Westminster.[5]

Before Margaret Thatcher attended the emergency Commons debate the following morning – a rare Saturday, which demonstrated the import-ance of the occasion – Alan reminded readers of *The Tories* that as she left Number Ten she was booed by the large crowd assembled in Downing Street (this was before security considerations made it a no-go area). Where was the bulldog spirit? Alan quoted the shouts, 'What are you waiting for?', 'Nuke them', 'Go on, Maggie, get them back'. He had helped arrange an immediate joint meeting of the Party's Defence and Foreign Affairs Committees where feelings ran high. Something had to be done.[6]

Alan revelled in the crisis, although in his memoirs Richard Luce, Minister of State at the Foreign Office, accused him of 'putting vanity before the national interest' by talking to the media out of turn, saying that Luce had told the Foreign Affairs Committee that Britain was sending submarines to the Falklands. Luce denies he said any such thing.[7] Alan meanwhile recorded a private meeting with James Callaghan, 'as always compos. Amiable and clear-headed', observing of the former Labour Prime Minister, 'it is in one's sixties, isn't it, that one starts to draw dividends from not consuming alcohol in middle age'. Callaghan was not sanguine about a full-scale amphibious assault with all the casualties that might accompany it. He was, though, critical of the Foreign Office and

Ministry of Defence. Alan endeavoured to bolster his confidence and agreed to offer advice on what Callaghan – 'from a position of objectivity as a senior statesman' – should say in the forthcoming Commons debate.

As matters progressed, slowly at first as the Task Force assembled and set out on its journey down the length of the Atlantic, Alan's deep knowledge soon made him an automatic choice for radio and television. His engagement diary got fuller and fuller: BBC this and that, News at Ten, Anglia, London Weekend, the local Plymouth Sound, uncountable numbers of foreign broadcast companies – 'every single day' he did at least one television or radio broadcast. There seemed no end. By the beginning of May he had been hailed as man of the week in the *Daily Express*, by the end Alan Watkins (in *The Observer*) had called him 'the leader of the war party'; he was even interviewed for *The Guardian* by Terry Coleman (not that Alan warmed to him – 'didn't thank Jane for tea, or me for a silver mug of ice Pol Roger – or my time, come to that'). He also found himself doing what he hated most, flying. He had been invited, in his Defence Committee capacity, to Washington, along with Francis Pym, the new Foreign Secretary, and a score of others. The Americans under Reagan, but personified by Alexander Haig, the Secretary of State, were opposed to the British efforts, 'a combination of jealousy and commercial interest', wrote Alan later.

When it was all over, with the Falklands back in British hands, Alan quickly noted the significance of Margaret Thatcher's words to the Commons, that the government was negotiating 'a surrender' (not a ceasefire). 'Trust her. She has led from the front all the way.' Following dinner with Norman St-John Stevas, Leader of the House for two years in the first Thatcher government and now a backbencher, Alan wrote that 'The Lady's autocracy was complete. She could make any policy or break any individual. At the moment, I said, she is completely fire-proof.'

He summed up the aftermath in *The Tories*. 'The war was short, heroic and, against hugely superior numbers, victorious. The return of the troopship *Canberra* was marked by celebration as prolonged and uninhibited as the relief of Mafeking in 1900.' It also brought home to him the importance of family relationships. A decade afterwards he recalled how Plymouth's local evening newspaper 'opened its pages free of charge to Task Force families so that they could send personal greetings to their loved ones. To this day I cannot tell how far those messages, heart-rending in their affection and simplicity, were spontaneous – the result of pent-up fear, of emotions constrained by years of repression, and now released by war.'[8]

For Alan there was a postscript. He may have hated flying, but in October 1982 he did not refuse a trip to the Falklands with an all-party delegation of MPs. As he wrote on his return in a note of thanks to Michael Jopling, the Tory Chief Whip, 'it was "without a doubt the most memorable and invigorating experience of my entire Parliamentary career"'.

You can see K's decline in his handwriting. As the 1970s turned into the 1980s and K approached his eightieth birthday, so he began writing fewer letters and those that survive show increasing evidence of a less steady grip.

Within a year of his first wife's death in 1976, K had married again. His choice was a twice-married Frenchwoman unknown to the family, Mme Nolwen de Janzé-Rice. 'He was going to be snared by someone,' believes Jane, who remembered walking with her father-in-law when they saw one of his ladies coming across the lawn. She told him: '"No good Papa, she's seen you!" He was like a bull with a ring through his nose. No, we didn't expect Nolwen. He was madly in love with Janet Stone.'[9] Jane says her father-in-law loved women, 'like Al'. 'And she believes that 'Al would have married straight away if I'd died before him'.

Nolwen was a Catholic, with a son and daughter from a failed first marriage, whose second husband was an Englishman, Edward Rice, a Kent farmer, who had not long died from cancer. After she and K married in November 1977 they divided their time between the Garden House and her farm at Parfondeval in Normandy. Alan and Nolwen 'did not enjoy good relations'[10] but as an MP his life was busy and he managed to see little of her. He and his father corresponded, which K still found the easiest and least confrontational form of communication. Jane says that her father-in-law was increasingly unwell. Did Nolwen hasten his end, as AC suggested in his diary? Lindley, his butler, told Jane, 'He was perfectly all right when I was looking after him.' Alan brooked no argument: 'Nolwen is poisoning him,' he concluded when his father was admitted for 'colonic lavage, to "clear up" his diverticulitis (which he hasn't got of course)'.[11]

Bad turned to worse. K fell out of 'the impossibly high hospital bed' and broke his hip, then suffered a blocked urinary tract. Within a few days it became clear that he would not survive much longer. Alan and Jane were in Plymouth for the May 1983 general election. Following a phone call from a nursing home at Hythe, Alan returned in time to see his father the day before he died on 21 May. In his diary he recounted taking hold of his clammy wrist, and saying 'Papa, I think you're going to die very soon. I've come back to tell you how much I love you, and to thank you for all you did for me, and to say goodbye.'[12] He held onto the wrist for a while before leaving the room. K died that night. Alan recounted his immediate feelings in his diary: 'I am sad, though not as sad as I used to be, that I never really made contact with him. And as I think about it, I suppose I'm sorry that I reacted away from the world of "Art", because that shut off a whole primary subject we could discuss together. The world of *Civilisation*. I must have been very crude and rough in my teens and early twenties (still am, some would say).'[13]

Reflecting on this ten years later Alan wrote about the inability of fathers and sons to say 'I love you' to each other. 'My father never managed to say this,' he confessed. 'I used to think that this restraint, like much else that is unnatural, was one of the mores of the English upper class.' One weekend at Eton when parents were visiting, Alan was walking in the street with a friend. 'Suddenly he caught sight of his father and rushed up to him, leaping into his arms: "Daddy, how lovely, how wonderful to see you ... " How odd, I thought. Of course, his father is not English. I felt superior. But inwardly a little disconcerted, and wistful.'

Perhaps he was thinking of his own pre-war experience of St Cyprian's, where children 'mercilessly bullied at their boarding school' would, 'when asked by their parents how they are enjoying it, bite their lips and say "all right"'. He saw this as 'a deliberate tourniquet on the emotions, so that parts of them atrophy'. Writing in 1994 with his own sons in their thirties he thanked God that this was, he believed, 'on the wane. Perhaps I am over-affectionate to my own sons. Does it embarrass them? In their early teens we were just like brothers, used to fool around, do wheelies, swap locker-room jokes. We still kiss each other, like Russian generals.' But 'When they wanted to confide they would speak to Jane – and still do.'[14]

In the Conservative landslide of 1983 they had an overall majority of 144. Alan's was his highest yet, 11,687 over the Liberal/Alliance candidate, with Labour coming third. Within a few days he was appointed as a Parliamentary Under-Secretary at the Department of Employment under Norman Tebbit. He had Ian Gow to thank, who, as Michael Jopling recalls, was his great supporter: 'Within half an hour of my ceasing to be Chief Whip he was in Government.'[15]

His appointment got off to a shaky start when he was called to Downing Street to see Sir Robert Armstrong, Secretary of the Cabinet. He told Jenny, his new ministerial secretary, 'He's a friend of my sister. They're both Trustees of Covent Garden. She's probably told him to be nice to me.' 'I don't think so,' she replied. At the Cabinet Office Sir Robert brought forth, 'like a conjuror,' Alan recalled, two files, one red, the other orange. One related to being spoken of with approval by the National Front – 'not at my solicitation', responded Alan; and the other 'certain matters of personal conduct . . . which could quite possibly leave you open to blackmail'. Girls! 'No, no. Perfectly all right,' said Alan. 'They've all married into grand Scottish families by now.' And that, as Alan related it, was that.

How does Lord Armstrong recall the occasion? 'There is no positive vetting for a Minister and when he was put forward for this appointment I don't think anybody had any reason to suppose that he might have needed to be positively vetted. The reports that we had drew attention to the fact that he had been quoted with approval by the National Front, the British National Party and of course to his extra-marital affairs. With Profumo, Jellicoe, Lambton very much in mind we had to think what we did about that. I discussed it with Margaret Thatcher, and she said, "well Robert, you had better see him".'

Lord Armstrong remembers that Alan came in and sat down at a table, where there were indeed two files. 'The first thing I turned to was the National Front business and I said that the PM needed to satisfy herself that he was not linked to the National Front.' Armstrong says Alan's account was accurate, but added 'that he said he had nothing to do with them, that he was not a member and did not associate with them. I had no reason to disbelieve that, it had the ring of truth.' Lord Armstrong now moved to the other file. If Alan said 'Oh shit!' (as in the *Diaries* and in the television adaptation), 'He didn't say that out aloud. I said that the fact that he had these affairs was a matter of some knowledge, and the PM had asked me to ask about that. What I remember him saying was that as far as he was concerned, he never made a secret of them, that he didn't conceal them, he didn't conceal them from his wife. She mightn't like it but she knew about them and if anyone said if you don't come to heel we'll publish he would have said "publish and be damned". I believed that, and so did Mrs Thatcher, which was more to the point.'[16]

Meanwhile letters of condolence over his father's death poured in. Alan devised a standard response to which he added a personal note. That to James Lees-Milne, fellow diarist and long-standing acquaintance of K, was most revealing, with Alan writing how sad it was that his father did not live long enough to see his elder son finally make it as a politician. Even in death Alan was still wishing to gain his father's approval.

Given his background, K's estate was, not surprisingly, huge: £5,315,170. At least, having handed over the castle to Alan and Jane in 1972, eleven years previously, K avoided any further duties beyond the capital transfer tax that had been dealt with in the mid-1970s. But it was clear to the Clark family that a sale from the Clark collection would be essential to meet the tax bill. Any thought that this might prove straightforward had to be quickly dismissed.

K's will, dated 22 December 1982, left detailed instructions. Celly received the Garden House and some of its contents, books in Italian before 1820 and furniture; Colin the single most valuable painting, K's Turner *Seascape: Folkestone,* dating from around 1845; Alan gained the Albany apartment, a cottage and some land at Saltwood, several paintings, including a Degas, *Woman Washing,* and William Orchardson's *The Last Dance,* a Michelangelo drawing, *Virgin and Child,* the Torres Strait tortoiseshell mask (that was said to have been owned by Picasso), and the royalties from his father's books. Nor were Jane, James and Andrew forgotten. Additionally a number of museums and galleries also benefited. 'I have tried very hard to be fair,' wrote K to Alan, in an undated letter, probably from the late 1970s.[17] The will further allowed K's three children to select paintings, drawings and sculptures not otherwise listed. In the opening round, Alan had first choice (and selected a Henry Moore drawing, *Crowd looking at tied-up object*), followed by Colin and then Celly; in the second Colin came first followed by Celly and Alan; in the third it was Celly first, with Alan next and Colin third. Then the routine started all over again.

In theory the future of the Turner should have been straightforward. In 1950 K purchased the painting from Agnew's, who had acquired it the previous year from D.J. Molteno, the grandson of the nineteenth-century shipping magnate Sir Donald Currie, its first recorded owner and a major collector of Turner's work. One critic described the *Seascape* as 'an audacious, almost abstract masterpiece . . . The greatest work by Turner in private hands',[18] K himself considered it 'the greatest picture ever painted'.[19] Now it was to be sold on the open market for the first time. But was it Colin's to sell? Colin was regularly short of money. K had summed it up in a letter to Alan. 'But what can I do if he continues to reside in a state where the wife gets half of everything?'[20] He added, 'I think Col now understands that no more can come from this source.'[21] By March 1982, again desperately in need of money to meet debts, among them the upkeep of Paco de Gloria, a seventeenth-century palácio in northern Portugal, Colin made a deal with Alan.

Colin had found it difficult to raise money on the Turner before his father's death because the will could be changed at any time. With the help of Sotheby's a valuation was made of £850,000. Next its experts computed, on the basis of actuarial tables, Kenneth Clark's expectation of life, assuming he was reasonably fit (which he was not) and discounting the value by the appropriate number of years. In the agreement Colin now assigned to the purchasers, who in the document were named as James and Andrew Clark, a fifty-one-per-cent share for the sum of US $90,000. K countersigned the agreement. Colin also agreed an additional clause whereby following K's death he would accept the instructions of the purchasers regarding the sale of the picture. The proceeds would then be divided fifty-one per cent to the Clark boys and forty-nine per cent to Colin.

The sale of K's paintings and works of art at Sotheby's New Bond Street galleries was due to begin on Wednesday, 27 June 1984 and to continue into the following week, with the Turner as the final of the 200 lots. Colin remained determined to have control of the Turner and took the route of last resort by starting a High Court action to stop the sale. At the beginning of the week he gained an interim injunction prior to a full hearing on the morning of 27 June, with the sale timed to start that afternoon at 2.30 p.m. His case was on the basis that ownership was disputed. His counsel stated that if the painting was vested in Colin and sold then there would be reduced liability for capital gains tax as he was domiciled abroad – thus all parties would benefit. In the end Colin did not pursue the action and the sale went ahead. Photographs show the brothers sitting close together in the Sotheby's saleroom with no apparent acrimony. Colin was quoted as saying that he and his brother 'often failed to see eye to eye'. 'But he had dropped his court action because 'we always agree in the end'.[22] The pre-sale estimate was £900,000. Bidding swiftly soared into seven figures.

One American bidder remembered that day a little ruefully. The Getty Museum, who had been lined up by Colin, were still determined to acquire it and hired Richard L. Feigen, a New York dealer, to act on its behalf. He told the auctioneer before the sale that he was not to look at him until he was ready to knock the painting down. His prearranged signal was to blink at the auctioneer. He later recalled: 'And it worked so well that Hugh Leggatt' – a prominent London dealer who actually landed the work for an anonymous client – 'was sitting right next to me, and we bid all the way from $4 to $10 million against each other. Afterwards, he turned to me and asked who the underbidder was.'[23] What turned out to be Leggatt's winning bid (including buyer's premium) was $12.4 million, or at 1984 rates of exchange about £7.37 million. Only later was the buyer revealed: David Thomson, grandson of Lord Thomson of Fleet, the Canadian newspaper proprietor and former owner of *The Times* and *The Sunday Times*. The sale was an auction record at the time for any painting, but in itself attracted capital gains taxes in addition to helping pay off the taxes due on K's estate.

Nor was the saga of K's art collection over. To Alan's annoyance at the time, not until December 1987 was agreement reached for K's Henry Moore drawings (valued at £450,000) to be taken by the British Museum in lieu of estate duty. Meanwhile Celly chose to sell much of the contents of the Garden House as well as the house itself, which Alan eventually acquired. He also tried to buy back items that Nolwen removed from the Garden House and took to France, in particular a Cézanne originally bought by his grandfather Kenneth McKenzie Clark, but when Alan inquired he was told it had been sold. She also took to Normandy some plates decorated by Duncan Grant (which should have gone to Celly) and the original sketch by Charles Sims for a portrait of K as a boy by the River Alde. They, too, never returned to Saltwood.

Alan and Jane achieved a long-term ambition after Papa's death: buying the Eriboll estate in Sutherland, thereby restoring the Clarks' Scottish connection which had ended when Shielbridge was sold early in the Second World War. Alan put Eriboll into a trust, with the asset objective 'a million Swiss francs, a million dollars, and a million Coats'.[24]

With Papa's death, relations between Alan and his siblings declined. When Naim Attallah interviewed Colin and Celly for *The Oldie*, what Colin was quoted as saying astonished Alan and Jane because the opening premise was demonstrably, as K's will shows, not true: 'People often ask why my father left everything to Alan, and the answer is very simple: it's because Alan told him to leave everything to Alan. He visited my father all the time when he was old and said, "I'm the eldest son – you've got to leave everything to me," and so my father, who was very obedient in a strange way, did just what he was told. On the other hand, it was a little bit of a surprise that my mother left everything to Alan, and nothing to either of us.'[25]

When Colin published his memoirs, *Younger Brother, Younger Son*, in 1997 he made no mention of the court case or the sale of the Turner.

TWENTY-FIVE

Tired and Emotional at the Dispatch Box

Fool Clark. Fool, fool, fool. Euan Graham remembers this Alan Clark catchphrase from Oxford. 'There was always that element of going over the top and regretting it.' Never was there a truer case than at the beginning of his ministerial career and described in a July 1983 diary entry which Alan blandly titled 'AC presents the Equal Opportunities Order to the House of Commons'.[1]

In the years succeeding Alan's death it became popular to suggest that the *Diaries* were often unreliable memoirs. Alan sometimes exaggerated or fantasised in them, but in this particular case he drew on the Hansard record.[2] What remains unresolved is Alan's state that evening: was he actually drunk at the dispatch box? Or was he cocking a snook at the impenetrable Civil Service English that made the order all but unintelligible? Or perhaps he objected to the very order which he was asked to lay before the House?

Alan had gained his first ministerial appointment early the previous month: Parliamentary Under-Secretary of State at the Department of Employment, where his Secretary of State was Norman Tebbit, known to many as Mrs Thatcher's rottweiler. Six weeks later, with the long summer recess only days away, the formalities of the government's Equal Opportunities Order were entrusted to Alan. It should have been a straightforward piece of parliamentary business – but the words were not Alan's. He was given a departmental script. Worthy, but dull.

Equal opportunities had not been high on the Conservative government programme, even with a female Prime Minister. The regulations that Alan found himself reading came about because British law was in breach of the Treaty of Rome. Brussels now demanded that the UK fall in line with other Community countries.

The day before he had answered his first Commons Questions on behalf of the Department, with Tebbit by his side giving him 'the gist of an answer' from the corner of his mouth as he rose to his feet. Frank Johnson, the parliamentary sketch-writer and a friend of Alan's, was there, emphasising that although his father was the recently deceased Lord Clark, Alan 'decided to make his own way in the world. So he did not join the family business, civilization, but he went into Conservative politics instead.' Johnson pointed out that Alan's expertise was defence, 'so, when he was finally brought into the Government after the general election, he was, of course, sent to the Department of Employment'.

With his first Question Time over Alan recorded in his diary, to his 'great delight', that Archie Hamilton, a junior Whip, complimented his performance in the Whip's book. This and other praise made him over-confident, he admitted, 'amazingly, suicidally overconfident'. He now wrote about the following day:

> I was booked to dine with Christopher, for a *wine*-tasting.[3] . . . That fucking text! I'd barely looked at it . . . It seemed frightfully long. So long, indeed, that I would have to excise certain passages. But which? And yet this didn't really seem very important as we 'tasted' first a bottle of '61 Palmer, then 'for comparison' a bottle of '75 Palmer then, switching back to '61, a really delicious Pichon Longueville. A huge Havana was produced, and I puffed it deeply . . . [4]
>
> The Chamber was unusually full for an after-ten event . . . As I started, the odiousness of the text sank in. The purpose of the Order, to make it more likely (I would put it no stronger than that) that women should be paid the same rate for the same task, as men, was unchallengeable . . . But give a civil servant a good case and he'll wreck it with clichés, bad punc-tuation, double negatives and convoluted apology. Stir into this a directive from the European Community, some contrived legal precedent and a few caveats from the European Court of Justice and you have a text which is impossible to read − never mind read *out*. I found myself dwelling on, implicitly, it could be said, sneering at, the more cumbrous and unintelligible passages. Elaine Kellet-Bowman [Conservative MP for Lancaster], who has a very squeaky voice, squeaked, kept squeaking, at me, 'Speed up.'

Hansard records that at one point Alan said that he might have to deal with certain legalistic passages 'at 78 rpm instead of 33', and later, 'In deference to the express wishes of my right honourable friend, I will accelerate my delivery for this particular passage.'[5] In Alan's own account he galloped through the text, which had, he said, 'no shape', 'No linkage from one proposition to another. The very antithesis of an Aristotelian pattern.' He would have gone on, but from the Opposition benches came the words 'Point of Order, Mr Deputy Speaker'. Alan sat down.

A new Labour member [for Birmingham Ladywood], whom I had never seen before, called Clare Short, dark-haired and serious with a lovely Brummie accent, said something about she'd read that you couldn't accuse a fellow member of being drunk, but she really believed I was incapable. 'It is disrespectful to the House and to the office that he holds that he should come here in this condition.' Screams, yells, shouts of 'Withdraw', counter-shouts. General uproar ... I sat, smiling weakly, my lips as dry as sandpaper ...

On and on went the shouting. 'ORDER,' kept bellowing dear old Ernie Armstrong, the Deputy Speaker. Soon, wearing an uneasy half-smile, definitely *not* catching my eye, appeared the figure of the Leader of the House, John Biffen, to sit in his appointed place. Now this was a bad sign. The Leader only attends business after ten o'clock when there is a *major row*.[6]

The minutes ticked by, with Alan fearing the government might 'lose the business' which would have been an indelible black mark on his record. Speaker after speaker had their say. Midnight approached. The Division was called. All was well.

Newspaper coverage next morning was thankfully brief: *The Daily Telegraph* a quarter of a column inside the paper, *The Times* in its final edition a front-page paragraph that gave only the barest account of the events of the night: 'A Labour MP was forced by the Deputy Speaker in the Commons to withdraw an accusation that a minister was not sober'. But if he thought the occasion had gone unremarked, he was forgetting *Yesterday in Parliament* on Radio 4. In its key slot on the *Today* programme that morning extracts were broadcast to an audience of several million. Thus when he reached Westminster Alan was challenged as to what had occurred and was forced to issue a statement. He admitted nothing. 'Miss Short's allegation is completely baseless, as anyone who knows me would testify.'[7]

Twenty-five years later Jane Clark remarked: 'I never remember Al drunk.'[8] But the legend has lived on. In Alan's own recollection it was 'an after dinner performance. I was kind of inviting people to laugh at some of the absurd phrases, which they did – it went very well for the first four– five minutes.' But he got carried away. 'I just thought I could do anything with the House. Very salutary to find out early on that you can't.'[9]

Having waited nine years to gain the bottom rung of the ministerial ladder only the month before, was it all now going to end ignominiously with a vertiginous plummet down the resignation snake? Alan's boss, Norman Tebbit, remembers 'very clearly' that he and Alan shared the same view on the legislation, but 'we were nonetheless committed to taking it through'.[10] That evening he had told Alan: 'I'm sure you don't need my help.' But he offered one piece of advice: 'Don't play it for laughs.' Next morning before leaving home for Westminster he turned on Radio 4. As *Yesterday in Parliament* relayed what had occurred, he thought 'oh shit!'. Alan had clearly not taken his advice. When he saw Alan at the Department later that morning he asked him straight out, 'Alan – were you pissed?' He recalls that his most junior Minister denied this 'absolutely flatly, saying he'd had a drink or two. As far as I was concerned I wasn't going to go over the top whether he was or whether he wasn't.'

Many of those in the Chamber that July evening remember the occasion. Matthew Parris (at that time Conservative MP for West Derbyshire) wrote in his memoirs: 'I'm a little ashamed to say we all thought it amazingly funny. Alan got away with this because he was handsome, charming, lived in a castle and did subtly crawl to Mrs T – but in a way he was clever enough to disguise. In his place I would have sunk.'[11] Peter Brooke (then Conservative MP for Cities of London and Westminster South) did not find Alan's performance 'in any way embarrassing'.[12] Robert Rhodes James, fellow historian and Conservative MP for Cambridge, noted that Alan, in the *Diaries*, related 'this catastrophe accurately, fairly, very amusingly, and with no self-pity'.[13]

Norman Tebbit says that the only department Alan craved as a Minister, no matter how junior, was Defence or Foreign Affairs, 'but he got me'. Alan, he said, had 'a somewhat flexible attitude to realities. You would sometimes find that there were two versions from Alan about the same matter.' As for the evening of the ministerial order: 'I think he may have been better for a drink, but I don't think he was worse for it.'

Although no daily newspaper wrote up the occasion, Hugo Young, who was beginning to make a reputation as a political columnist, used Alan's performance as the basis for his Inside Politics column in *The Sunday Times* under the heading 'Alas he was sober'.[14] Alan immediately wrote to Young: 'Thanks for confirming that I wasn't tight.'[15] Young had a more serious point. 'Arrogant, facetious and brimming with self-amusement, Mr Alan Clark was actually introducing a set of regulations on equal pay for women, in the name of the government to which someone, possibly taking leave of her senses, had lately appointed him an under secretary at the Department of Employment. So ridiculous did he make them sound and so divorced from anything a rational person could hope to understand, that inebriation might well have appeared the only

explanation.' As for the regulations forced upon a reluctant British government, wrote Young, 'For a man of Mr Clark's stamp the push for
greater equality offends just about all his primeval instincts. For a start, it
comes from the EC, a body he's never been much in favour of. It involves
the government in fixing pay levels, another sin against the Decalogue.
Worst of all, it gives rights to those most risible creatures, working women,
just at the time when some Tory thinkers are pondering deeply about
how to keep more of them at home.'

Readers of the *Diaries*, when asked for their favourite passage, divide
equally between shooting the heron that was stealing fish from the moat
at Saltwood and presenting the Equal Opportunities Order to the House
of Commons.[16] But as Rhodes James also wrote: 'How he recovered from
this fiasco was a mystery. Every other prime minister I have known (with
the possible exception of Harold Wilson) would have fired him on the
spot, but The Lady spared him, and he went on to become a successful
and respected minister, although a highly unpredictable one.'[17]

Alan spent two and a half years at the Department of Employment,
which he saw as a kind of imprisonment, before being moved to another
prison – or discharged. James Naughtie, then political correspondent
on *The Guardian*, remarked that he brought to the Department 'a
Waugh-like mixture of grumpiness and style'.[18] Later, there would be
much tut-tutting over several diary entries from the period. One such
came soon after his appointment, when he fantasised about standing on
the tiny *balcon* outside his office window eight floors above Victoria Street,
and relieving his bladder 'splattingly on the ant-like crowds below'. He
wondered if it was a sackable offence. 'Probably not. It would <u>have</u> to be
hushed up ... Certainly it would tax the powers of Mr Bernard Ingham
[Number Ten Press Secretary]. I might do it on my last day.'[19] Norman
Tebbit he admired and thought 'truly formidable. He radiates menace, but
without being overtly aggressive. He seldom smiles, but goes straight to
the heart of a subject, never gets diverted into detail, always sees the
political implications.'[20]

After four months Tebbit became Trade and Industry Secretary in a
minor reshuffle brought about by Cecil Parkinson's resignation following
revelations that a former secretary with whom he had had a long-term
relationship, was expecting his child. If Tebbit was 'Mr Nasty', wrote
Alan, his successor, Tom King, was 'Mr Nice'. Working at Employment
was good experience, but the Department's work did not engage Alan's
mind, unlike subsequent appointments. He learnt about committee proceedings and made a hash of his debut, but later acknowledged that he

had managed 'to impose acceptance of my own style, getting (both sides) to laugh occasionally. It is a totally different ambience, and requires an adapted technique, to the floor of the Chamber.'

By the end of 1983 he and his chief friend in the Commons, Ian Gow, another February 1974 entrant, began cooking up a plot which, if it worked, would allow Alan to escape 'the drudgery of the DE'. What the Prime Minister needed, they agreed, was her own department with perhaps a Lord Privy Seal (or Paymaster General) sitting in Cabinet, and a couple of PPSs, the senior of whom would be a Minister of State. That, Ian implied, was where Alan might come in ('whoopee!'). Alan even went as far as to put his thoughts on paper. Next the notion was leaked – what Alan called 'constructive leaking . . . to condition minds' – to a compliant journalist.[21] But the scheme, despite further rumblings, failed to materialise. Ian Gow's period of influence on Margaret Thatcher was on the wane. Towards the end of 1985 he was to resign in protest at the Anglo-Irish Agreement, and in the summer of 1990 he was killed by an IRA car bomb. Alan mourned: 'My closest friend, by far, in politics.'

The fortieth anniversary of D-Day in June 1984 allowed Alan the opportunity to flaunt his military expertise in *The Daily Telegraph*. In reviewing *Overlord*, a major new account by Max Hastings, Alan highlighted the key question: 'How was it possible that German troops, facing overwhelming fire power, outnumbered, drawn from an army that had been bled to two millions dead in three years in the east, could mount such a formidable resistance against the flower of British and American armies?' He expressed admiration for the German army, whereas 'whole British units collapsed under pressure'. From a Conservative Minister this was strong stuff, but was remarked only by *Telegraph* readers. Twenty-five years later Charles Moore, writing in the *Telegraph* and prompted by Antony Beevor's new account of D-Day, says that the fact that this caused so little fuss at the time, 'seems incredible,' Today 'our 24-hour media would have had Clark out of office that morning. He was let off, perhaps because the press liked his indiscretion, and thought that his sympathy for the Nazis was a sort of tease.'[22]

In September 1984 Alan survived another of the Prime Minister's reshuffles – despite being tipped for the sack by *The Daily Telegraph*. This brought a letter from Julian Amery, which particularly pleased Alan. 'You stick out like a red poppy in the hayfield of mediocrities surrounding you,' wrote this *éminence grise* of the Tory Right. 'It is very offensive to them to be original, intelligent, courageous and rich.'

October, as ever, was Party conference time, that year at Brighton. Following the Employment debate, Alan related how he and Jane decided to quit. Alan settled the hotel bill and by the evening they were back at Saltwood. Next morning, while Alan took the dogs out, Jane turned on the radio to hear news that a huge bomb (later identified as being the work of the IRA) had gone off and demolished the front of the Grand Hotel, always the heart of the conference. Margaret Thatcher survived, saved, as Alan wrote, 'by good fortune (von Stauffenberg's briefcase!) as she was in the bathroom. Had she been in the bedroom she would be dead.' Norman Tebbit and his wife were badly injured, as was another Minister, John Wakeham (his wife Alison was killed). One Old Etonian and Oxford friend of Alan's, the MP Anthony Berry, did not survive.

Alan was critical of what happened afterwards, all covered by television. 'Keith Joseph (indestructible), wandering about in a burgundy-coloured dressing-gown, bleating. The scene was one of total confusion, people scurrying hither and thither, barely a police "officer" to be seen. But what a coup for the Paddys. If they had just had the wit to press their advantage, a couple of chaps with guns in the crowd, they could have got the whole Government as they blearily emerged – and the assassins could in all probability have made their getaway unpunished.'[23]

Alan's ministerial career was never free for long from gaffes. In April 1984 he had been rescued by the Prime Minister from an inopportune remark he made over defence procurement on the BBC's *Question Time* (see Chapter Thirty-two). That was soon forgotten, but not the Bongo-Bongo land affair. Tom King remembers 'that we managed to pull him through, that was a difficult moment, although he didn't know it at the time. He was silly, the Whips were frightfully angry about him.'[24] Alan in the *Diaries* wrote that according to Tristan Garel-Jones, then a Whip, he was being defended 'vigorously' in the government's higher echelons by William Whitelaw.

The *Guardian*'s account began: 'For a son of *Civilisation*, it was an embarrassing affair. For a minister with responsibility in the Department of Employment for race relations, it was worse.'[25] The magazine *Searchlight* claimed that in a departmental meeting about black protests over ethnic monitoring, Alan had said: 'You mean to say that they don't want us collecting their names and addresses because they are afraid we'll be going to hand them over to the immigration service so that they can send them all back to Bongo–Bongo land.' The Opposition seized on this and two members of the Shadow Cabinet signed a Commons motion complaining about the allegation and denouncing him as unfit to hold office. *The*

Guardian reported that Alan was 'uncharacteristically silent' and that the 'nearest thing to denial in Whitehall yesterday was that the remark might have been said at a private meeting and such leaks were always regrettable, however unimportant'.[26] The affair dragged on in the press. When, the following year, he was made Minister for Trade, the Prime Minister told him that 'someone' (in the *Diaries* Alan said Douglas Hurd) thought his remark would make him unacceptable to, say, the Nigerians. Margaret Thatcher was at her most beguiling. 'But of course you will be, *perfectly* acceptable, won't you?'[27]

Alan later reflected that his time at Employment was 'a let down, so boring, so time consuming and so pointless'. He had the 'miserable job of announcing every month what the unemployment figure was. Our role was to get people out of the figures, by devising schemes: job release schemes, enterprise allowances – get them off the register. It was dodgy.' He could measure achievements of which he was proud both as Minister for Trade and as Minister of Defence. 'But as junior Minister for Employment I cannot tell you a single thing I did that made the country, the government, the people of this country any better than wouldn't have happened if I hadn't been there, if no one had been in that job.'[28]

For the Love of Animals

Robert Rhodes James could hardly have been a better choice to review the *Diaries*.[1] As the editor of 'Chips' Channon's diaries – Alan's favourite reading with EMT – he was struck by the 'soliloquies on mankind, and nature, and beauty, that raise this from political tittle-tattle to something very different'. A typical example comes on 15 June 1988, when Alan has suffered a galling defeat by the Prime Minister over his attempts to introduce a Fur Labelling Order. He returned to Albany feeling 'utterly dejected'. At that moment 'the cock blackbird started up, on the dot of four ... So clear and beautiful, as he went through the whole repertoire, he passed to me a lovely message of Nature's strength, her powers of continuity and renewal. And I drew some small consolation from this. Nature's timescale is so different from ours.'

Alan loved all animals and birds. Saltwood was a lung, little more than ninety minutes from Westminster; he wrote of the 'soft and restful' peace of Bratton; the open spaces of the estate at Eriboll with the crystal clarity of the seas that fringed its coastline – these natural pleasures were so often his salvation when the pressures of a working life threatened. Even from 35,000 feet up in a 747 on a Trade mission in 1987 he found himself looking at the airline map, spotting 'Ben Hope 927m' and the two stretches of water, Eriboll and Hope. 'Within these bounds is my beloved property; the gimmers and the peregrine falcons and the pine martens; the great tawny badgers, the stags, the little musquat deer and the sly peat foxes. I think fondly, sadly, of them all.'

In his teens he had taken Tor, the Clarks' West Highland terrier, on a walking expedition in north Wales; when Jane first saw him on the beach at Camber in 1956 he had had Big Dog with him. And throughout their married life together dogs were a part of their lives. Often in pairs: in the 1960s and 1970s the beagles Gangster and Grandee, for instance, and in the 1990s the Rottweilers Eva and Lëhni, and Hannah. Alan and Jane were in Zermatt when Gangster was put down. 'I'm sorry that I couldn't be there to bid him goodbye,' wrote Alan. 'But he's buried next to

Grandee. And I will always remember the Beagles and their period of great physical prowess.' On one occasion Alan recalled losing Grandee on Dartmoor, on the twin boggy ridges that stretched out towards Meldon. They drove home, with Gangster howling the whole way. Back at Bratton while Alan went to bed, Jane and Janet, the au pair, returned to the moor (it was now dark), but to no avail. Jane recalls the drive back to Bratton, and suddenly on the Okehampton side of the village, the car headlights lit up a dog ahead – it was Grandee making his way home.

Wildlife too. Alan's diaries are full of stories of blackbirds and jackdaws usually reared by the Clarks after falling from their nests as chicks. Alan claimed there had been jackdaws at Saltwood since King Henry II. In September 1978 there was George, a jackdaw, not the first, or the last, to adopt Saltwood. His saga ran across several diary entries. It all began the day before Alan and Jane departed for Zermatt. He had been missing since before breakfast, with Alan privately convinced that he must be dead. That evening he was reported as being down at the garage by the Military Canal. However, on arrival at the chalet they rang Saltwood to hear that George had been found and brought back by someone who had a little boy called 'George' they had called for him that evening and George, the jackdaw, had appeared! Nor was the story over. On their return to Saltwood the following weekend, Alan wrote that he was 'extremely shocked' that George had 'gone on Friday . . . Livid with James . . . I suspect not having nurtured George as he should.' Next morning – no sign of George. Five weeks went by before Alan's 23 October entry read: 'Last night George came back via a call from the train-driver's house after he had been trying to get into their children's window (his wife, as I always suspected, being extremely pretty). Althou' sleek he is very subdued and today was hardly off his "perch" on top of the open kitchen door all day.' Another was Max, who most mornings enjoyed digestive biscuits on their bedroom window-sill. The Saltwood kitchen also contained a cockatiel in a cage, who could whistle the theme tune from the comedian Benny Hill's television series.

His views on animals put him at odds with many of his fellow Conservatives. He loathed blood sports, forbidding hunts access to his land. He fought against the transport of veal calves across the English Channel. At times he even had to make unpalatable decisions that involved using his gun. It gave him no pleasure, as in June 1990.

This morning I killed the heron.
He had been raiding the moat, starting in the early hours, then getting

bolder and bolder, taking eight or nine fish, carp, nishikoi, exotica, every day.

I had risen very early, before five, with the intention of getting a magpie who has been pillaging all the nests along the beech hedge. But returned empty handed. They are clever birds, and sense one's presence.

Suddenly Jane spotted the heron from the casement window in my bathroom.

I ran down and took the 4.10 off the slab, cocked the hammer. He was just opposite the steps, took off clumsily and I fired, being sickened to see him fall back in the water, struggle vainly to get up the bank, one wing useless.

I reloaded, went round to the opposite bank. Tom beat me to it and gamely made at him, but the great bird, head feathers and eyes aglare, made a curious high-pitched menacing sound, his great beak jabbing fiercely at the Jack Russell.

'Get Tom out of the way', I screamed.

I closed the range to about twenty feet and took aim. I did not want to mutilate that beautiful head, so drew a bead on his shoulder.

The execution. For a split second he seemed simply to have absorbed the shot, then very slowly his head arched round and took refuge inside his wing, half under water. He was motionless, dead.

I was already sobbing as I went back up the steps. 'Sodding fish, why should I kill that beautiful creature just for the sodding fish . . .'

I cursed and blubbed up in my bedroom, as I changed into jeans and a T-shirt. I was near a nervous breakdown. Yet if it had been a burglar or a vandal I wouldn't have given a toss. It's human beings that are the vermin.

In February 1988 he wrote about a badger caught in a snare. A farmer tried to pinion the unfortunate creature's neck and head, but Alan realised that it would be better to use sacks as a muffle, and concluded: 'he went quiet, knowing I was a friend'. Elsewhere he conveys brilliantly what went through his mind when 'one of The Four Worst Things happened – I LOST TOM'. Tom, the Jack Russell, and a genuine character, goes on appearing in the diaries and often stealing the show until his death at not quite twenty.

In these instances Alan was off-duty, but sometimes politics and his views on animals were in conflict. If he had still been an MP early in 1995, he would have used every opportunity to raise the issue of the export of veal calves to Europe, a trade he found despicable: young animals who had known life for only a few months, bundled together in what he saw as appalling conditions and sent for slaughter across the Channel. Alan joined the protests. Then a leading protester, Jill Phipps, a thirty-one-year-old mother, died after being run over by a cattle truck that she and other demonstrators were trying to prevent from entering Coventry airport. Alan became irritated at the press attention that centred on him – 'Alan Clark to "mourn" Jill Phipps', ran the headline in *The Sunday Telegraph*. He was convinced that his Conservative friends – were they still friends now? – Tristan Garel-Jones, Richard Ryder, Jonathan Aitken, thought him unhinged on the subject. In May Alan reported a call from Garel-Jones saying he was being considered a 'loony' for his animal rights activities.

He attended Jill Phipps's funeral in Coventry Cathedral in February 1995. Another in the congregation was Brigitte Bardot, not that Alan mentioned the French actress in his diary, even though Bardot was now a passionate believer in animal rights. Some newspapers wrote of a packed attendance; Alan reported differently. 'I had hoped for a pilgrimage, a Mecca, a mullah's funeral. But although the Cathedral was respectfully full, it was nothing like at capacity. The Sutherland altarpiece is incredible, magnificent, and one of the most impressive works of art I have ever seen. The size of Saltwood towers' inner façade, perhaps even a bit under. The lady priest (deaconess?) was lovely, attractive and with a lovely clear voice, looked not unlike Presiley Baxendale.'

Seven years previously, when Margaret Thatcher was Prime Minister and Alan was Minister for Trade, he had a rare run-in with The Lady. Trouble is first hinted at in March 1988, when he learnt via the journalist Bruce Anderson (who got it from John Wakeham) that the Prime Minister 'will have him in the Cabinet if she can'. But Alan described his situation as 'precarious. I fear I may be heading for an unwelcome passage of arms.' His mission was to put through Parliament his 'personal *chef d'oeuvre*', a Fur Labelling Order. Alan's particular concern was for animals who suffered terribly when caught by leghold traps, but the principle of killing animals, whether farmed mink or creatures in the wild, was also alien to him. He had first raised the issue in 1982, but nothing had happened. Whispers were reaching him that 'she has a lot of furriers in Finchley [her constituency]', and she had, he feared, 'very little empathy indeed with the animal kingdom'.[2] Not long afterwards *The Guardian* reported that the fur industry was in uproar at his proposals.[3]

His fears were borne out three months later. Called to her room in the Commons on 14 June 1988 after Questions, it was clear that all the

enormous energy he had devoted to the Fur Labelling Order, threatening
and cajoling lawyers, ambassadors, senior civil servants in several Departments, Eskimos, furriers and 'small shopkeepers', was about to disappear
into dust. The Prime Minister would have none of it; she was about to
visit Canada – a major source of fur – where pressure would be applied
not to interfere with the status quo. It was also suggested, but unconfirmed,
that Mrs Thatcher did not wish anything to interfere with her ambitions
to sell nuclear submarines to Canada.

Alan's description of the interview is masterly. Feminists hated him for
saying that 'it was a prototypical example of an argument with a woman –
no rational sequence, associative, lateral thinking, jumping rails the whole
time'. Except of course that this was Margaret Thatcher, the Prime
Minister, who continued, 'why not labelling of battery hens, of veal who
never see daylight, of fish which had a hook in their mouth – what about
foxes? Do you hunt?' Mrs Thatcher was jumping rails with the best of
them. 'Certainly not,' Alan replied. 'Nor do I allow it on my land. And
as for veal, I'm a vegetarian.'[4] 'What about your shoes?' Charles Powell later
commented that here was one of the few instances where he challenged the
accuracy of Alan's *Diaries* account. As he recalled it was Mrs Thatcher,
not Alan, who indicated his immaculate Lobb's footwear and asked 'with
quivering sarcasm, "And I suppose those are *plastic*, Alan."'[5]

On and on they battled. Alan was not winning the argument if, as he
put it, such 'a confused, inconsequential but ardent gabbling' can be
dignified by that Aristotelian term. He then erred, about this being 'the
first step. In enlarging man's sense of responsibility towards the animal
kingdom.' The meeting had lasted fifty-five minutes rather than the
scheduled fifteen.

'"I hate quarrelling with you, Alan."

'I snarled. "I wouldn't do it for anyone else", and went out of the door.'

The aftermath was instructive. Alan took a call from Powell. The PM
was anxious to help him 'out' on this. The order could go up to a Cabinet
committee, the Attorney-General and the Foreign Secretary would give
a legal opinion, 'which would stop it in its tracks'. Alan would then have
his get-out. In his diary he mused 'Should I pre-empt? It would be the
first time that a Minister will ever have resigned on an issue concerning
the welfare of creatures that don't have a vote.' He rang Jane, who was, as
ever, 'wise and calming, though sad. Said, don't do anything hasty.'

The denouement came in the Commons a week later. In answers to
written questions on the subject Alan stated, 'Legal difficulties have been
raised, and I have regretfully come to the conclusion that it would not be

practicable to proceed in the way originally envisaged. I have therefore decided not to proceed with the proposed order and to defer further action on the matter.'[6] To his diary he wrote: 'But my relations with the Lady are damaged – perhaps beyond repair.'

This was not, however, the end of the story, although Alan makes no mention in his diary of a conspiracy that followed. When Stanley Johnson, then a senior official in the European Commission's environment department,[7] learnt that Mrs Thatcher had put the kibosh on Alan's plans he got in touch with him proposing a crafty move, that he would draft an EU rule instead. Johnson recalls a secret meeting with Alan in the Holiday Inn, Luxembourg, where they were both staying for an EU meeting – and plotted. All went well, and the Commission actually proposed not a labelling measure but a total EU ban on the import of fur coming from animals caught in leghold traps. This measure, duly approved by the European Parliament and EU Council, was due to enter into force after the statutory delay. With about two days to go Leon Brittan's officials – Brittan was EU Trade Commissioner – suddenly got cold feet about the trade implications. Quite unconstitutionally, they wrote to HM Customs and Excise and their equivalents in other member states saying don't implement the ban.

Alan was ahead of much world opinion. It took some twenty years, but in August 2007 the state of New York introduced a law requiring all real fur and fur-trimmed clothing sold in the state – the nation's largest fur-buying market – to be labelled as 'real fur'. The law goes further than anything Alan Clark or Stanley Johnson had in mind, requiring all garments made of or trimmed with fake fur to be labelled 'fake fur' so that customers may make an ethical choice.

TWENTY-SIX
Reviewing Defence

'I have just returned exhausted, but triumphant, from the Chequers CFE Seminar', noted Alan on 30 September 1989. Behind that announcement[1] lay a thrilling saga that led Alan to convince himself that the long-desired seat in the Cabinet would be his reward.

As he showed during the Falklands campaign, Alan had kept abreast of the state of the Armed Forces. 'I know all the weapons systems specs off the top of my head,' he had written in July 1989 at the time of his appointment as Minister for Defence Procurement.[2] His younger son Andrew, who was serving in the Army, kept him informed on morale and current Service thinking; James flew helicopters over the North Sea which gave him additional specialist knowledge. But perhaps more important, he could hold his own intellectually within the Ministry of Defence where 'The cleverest civil servant in Whitehall', Michael Quinlan, was Permanent Secretary.[3]

Alan's period at Defence coincided with the collapse of the Soviet Union, Iraq's invasion of Kuwait and the first Gulf War. At the same time the Conservative government conducted Options for Change, a review for the restructuring of Britain's Armed Forces. These were heady times at the MoD. Short of being at the Foreign Office, no other Ministry appealed so much to Alan's interests and his sensibilities. Tom King was Alan's Secretary of State second time around.

In his *Diaries* he records, at the time of the July 1989 reshuffle when Margaret Thatcher offered him the job, that he thought King 'an appalling prospect'. 'I'm sorry Prime Minister, but I can't work with Tom. I went through all that when I was at DE, I can't do it again. He's too ghastly.' She responded, 'Alan, you've always wanted to go to Defence. You can't let me down by refusing.' King himself, who was back in London after a long stint as Northern Ireland Secretary, remembers the call from the Prime Minister.[4] '"Would I have him?" I said yes; I don't know why, perhaps because I had him at Employment.' It was known that several other Cabinet Ministers had made the Prime Minister aware of their less than favourable views on Alan. King admits now that 'Maybe I wasn't quite au fait as to what Alan had been up to while at Trade. There had been a four-year gap. If you're in Northern Ireland you have a pretty heavy time where you lose a bit of contact with the Parliamentary Party.' But King recognised the points in Alan's favour. 'In many ways he knew much more about defence than I did. Therefore I thought he could be very useful.' His particular strength was 'on the strategy of defence. He had been taking a serious interest.'

Bruce Anderson, often close to Alan, wrote in *The Daily Telegraph*[5] that his pairing with King 'could prove the only mistake in this reshuffle. Clark is a defence expert with strong original views. He is a Gaullist. He disapproves of the Rhine Army. He is not pro-American. Above all he is no respecter of persons. He will enjoy asking sharp questions of generals and admirals and if he thinks their replies inadequate will tell them so. Some Ministers are overawed by stars and scrambled-egg. Not Clark.'

The Conventional Forces Europe seminar took place on Saturday, 30 September, little more than two months after King moved to Defence with his new team. With the Cold War out of the freezer, the need to reappraise the role of the UK's Armed Forces was paramount. As King recalls, Britain had 100,000 troops in Germany and 'the Germans were just beginning to get a bit scratchy about having training exercises and tanks beating the place up. We were going to have to make some changes.' Seminars appealed to Margaret Thatcher, who liked drawing on experts, academics such as Professor Sir Michael Howard and retired soldiers such as General Sir Nigel Bagnall (a friend and colleague of Jane Clark's father). 'She was very good at picking lots of other brains and bringing them in, kept all Ministers on their toes.'

Unsurprisingly King's account of what happened that Saturday at Chequers differs from Alan's in the detail and the telling. King remembers it as 'quite a gathering'. Alan referred to the 'heavyweight military men present', but how after 'an awful lot of balls was talked' discussion moved on to the kind of equipment that was going to be needed in 'the new scenario'. The Treasury representatives, Nigel Lawson (in his last month as Chancellor, although no-one knew that at the time) and Norman Lamont (Chief Secretary), were thinking of how much money might be saved. According to Alan, after an hour Lawson turned to the Prime Minister and said, 'could we hear on this subject from the Minister of State?'

Alan, as he put it, 'set out his stall, named and costed a number of programmes which could be eliminated without any risk'. From some of the military, among them General Sir Martin Farndale, outgoing C-in-C of British forces in Germany, there were '*slow* intakes of breath', but Lawson and Lamont beamed their approval. Mrs Thatcher, briefed by Charles Powell, wrote Alan, 'started on a quite well informed summary of the approach to equipment problems, and the need for "inter-operability" across Nato'.

When the Prime Minister said 'further work was needed', Alan jumped in. It was now or never. 'Prime Minister, may I have your instructions to draw up a schedule of our equipment requirements over the next five years, in the light of anticipated progress in the CFE negotiations?' According to Alan's record he looked across to his Secretary of State, Tom King, 'jaw dropped open, saucer-eyed'. King recollects it less theatrically. 'As we were breaking up, people putting their papers away, I think Alan slipped in, can I put a view? He did that without asking me.' In Alan's account, Mrs Thatcher responded, 'Yes. We must be able to make some savings now. But . . . (going dreamy-voiced – I know this – it is a defensive tack) . . . I want particular attention paid to inter-operability.'

Alan was exultant. 'What a coup!' But nothing would be plain sailing. When he phoned Julian Scopes, head of his private office, Alan reported that at first 'he couldn't really believe it'. After Alan gave him the details, he was immediately practical, 'Minister, you *must* be identified in the Meetings note, otherwise S of S's office, or the Permanent Secretary, or both, will take the whole thing over, and smother it.' Achieving this required all Alan's ingenuity, but it would have been nothing without the goodwill of Charles Powell, who remembered fifteen years later: 'I had a healthy respect for him. I thought he was a man with many original ideas even if his fundamentally cavalier attitude to the proprietaries did him down.'[6] In the Clark account, when Alan telephoned, Powell reacted as a civil servant: it would be most unusual for Alan to be identified; he could only name heads of Departments.

'If you don't identify me, the whole thing will be stillborn.'

'Oh surely not. Tom was there. He heard what the Prime Minister said.'

'Come on, Charles, ha bloody ha.'

'Well, I don't really see how I can.'

'Will you please ask the Prime Minister? Will you please tell her of this conversation?'

'If you insist. But I must warn you of my opinion that she will take the same view.'

'Even if she does, I'm no worse off. Please tell her.'

'All right.'

Alan ended his note: 'Fingers crossed!'

In the end Alan, thanks to his indulgent Prime Minister, got his way. It took a few days, but at the end of the Conclusions paper were the words, 'Minister, Defence Procurement, to take the Lead.' He also wrote of Tom King's reaction on being called in a day later:

'I just want to get one thing straight,' said King.

'Uh?'

'I'm in charge.'

'Well, yes.'

'I've talked to her. I've talked to Charles. I'm handling this.'

'Quite.'

'If we're going to work amicably together, which I'm sure we are, we've got to trust each other.'

'Quite.'

'I cannot have you passing notes to the Prime Minister down the chimney.'

'No'

Thus in the Ministry two defence reviews were under way: the departmental one, Options for Change, masterminded by Michael Quinlan, the Permanent Secretary, and Alan's, which he wrote with Julian Scopes.[7]

Scopes remembers 1989 as the moment that the whole *raison d'être* of Britain's defence of the previous forty years was disappearing into history. 'In a sort of very institutional way the MoD was quite flat-footed about this. Understandably you don't rush to make great policy decisions when you are faced with great uncertainties rather than the certainties you were used to before. You may sensibly take a little time and analyse what is going on.' He characterised Tom King 'as a rather cautious traditional thinker, not prone to making great leaps of faith'. Alan, on the other hand, was 'the guy who saw that this really was the trigger for very, very fundamental change, that the initial signs of the Wall coming down and the Warsaw Pact dissolving itself were undoubtedly just the start of a trend that would lead many years into the future.' As for the outcome of the Chequers meeting, 'for a Minister of State to get an authority to have a go at writing a paper, to get that sort of licence was extraordinary'.

A key figure was Peter Levene, Chief of Defence Procurement, who had been brought in from industry in 1985 by Michael Heseltine during his time as Defence Secretary. Alan quickly came to trust Levene and to listen to him. That was crucial as Levene was, as he recalls, 'the accounting officer for kit – anything Alan wanted the Department to buy had to have my signature'.[8] He thought Alan intelligent, full of ideas – 'yes, some barking mad, but some very interesting'. Alan's Defence Review he thought 'very clever, with hindsight some of it was right'.

The work on Alan's Defence paper encompassed 'a very intensive few weeks'. Alan wrote that Scopes was 'wonderful. Helpful, tactful, assiduous; he warns me when he thinks I am going too far. Though sometimes even he can be made to look slightly pop-eyed and startled.' Scopes says Alan's approach was 'very top-level looking down, but trying to make sure you could bounce opinions off people and try things out on people all within the structure he was going for. I remember at one stage he was getting very frustrated about who he could bounce things off and he was reaching outside the Department all the time. I said, look, I know enough about this Department. Whatever crackpot idea you come up with I'll find somebody in this Department who agrees and certainly someone who doesn't and get them into the room and in all but one particular issue I think I succeeded.'

Essentially Alan believed that in the 1990s the Royal Navy would be the key force – 'swift, flexible, hard-hitting'. With the Soviet threat no longer existing, Britain's forces in Germany (on land and in the air) could to all intents and purposes be spoken of in the past tense. He thought that hundreds of millions of pounds would be saved (that proved an underestimate). Alan's version was, he wrote, the only way Britain could 'keep military clout and not go bust'. Personally he enjoyed the adrenalin the review created. It was what being a Minister should, he believed, be about.

Work on both Options for Change and Alan's Defence Review should have been completed before Christmas 1989. On 21 December Alan wrote, 'It's all a bit awkward. I live dangerously.' In his account, he 'followed the two guiding principles in such matters – keep it short (five pages and an annexe) and get it in first'. Calling it, presumptuously, 'The 1990 Defence Review', he beat the deadline, immediately lodging it with Charles Powell at Number Ten. By being first 'on the table' his review would be in 'pole position against which all else is judged.' In this case 'all else' was the Department's own huge report. Scopes advised Alan to ensure that copies of his own Defence Review were in the hands of both King and Quinlan just before an early evening meeting called to discuss the departmental paper. Alan recorded, 'Unusually the meeting started on time. When I got in everyone was reading, avidly and urgently.' He wrote that no-one bothered about the Department's paper, indeed it was hardly referred to. 'Tom waved mine in the air. "This is pretty drastic stuff."'

The nub of the meeting for Alan was the moment when King, eyeing him closely, said, 'What we have to ensure is that this does not get into the hands of the Prime Minister. She'd get hold of completely the wrong end of the stick.' He felt it needed to be 'cleaned up a bit ... We must hold on to it until after Christmas.'

Said Alan: 'I am showing it to you.'

'Well, that's agreed, then. We'll all keep tight hold of this until after Christmas.'

'Yeah.'

In his diary he added, 'I could *just* say that, I pretended, because I hadn't handed it to her, but to Charles.' Alan returned to his office and immediately phoned Charles Powell to make sure that his earlier delivery of his paper would not leak. He was too late. King's office had already rung Number Ten to excuse the delay in submitting the departmental paper because the Minister for Defence Procurement had written something to which the Department needed to give consideration.

'So am I,' Powell had answered. 'It's on my desk now.'

Alan recounted breaking into 'an instant sweat. *So* embarrassing.' What should he do now? 'Leap into the car, drive down to Saltwood, hide for a week or so'? Scopes advised Alan to go straight to the Secretary of State and apologise. Minutes later he was in King's office. 'Tom was seated at his desk in I'm-in-charge mode.' For Alan it was his schooldays, called in front of the beak, 'with a chair directly in front, ready for a pre-caning homily'. Pretty galling for a government Minister not long turned sixty-one. 'I'm most frightfully sorry. I just couldn't own up in front of all those people.' King waved Alan's explanation aside, saying 'something about you should always feel free to let me see everything, it makes it so much easier for both of us'. Would any other Secretary of State have reacted so magnanimously? King had already spoken to Powell, who had agreed that the Prime Minister should not see this paper before Christmas – 'otherwise, ha-ha, she'll be making all our lives a misery over the holiday'.

Alan's 3,500-word Defence Review, as finally typed, had the prosaic title, 'Defence Policy and Defence Procurement Needs'.[9] The word 'SECRET' appears twice on every page. Alan addressed his review to the Prime Minister. By way of introduction, he explained that it was an 'entirely private document, which does not carry the broad endorsement of the Department – although I am showing it to the Secretary of State and to Archie Hamilton'.

In his narrative sections the language was unusually vivid for a defence review. 'The world remains a cruel, greedy and deceitful environment in which the Hobbeseian philosophy, that in the last resort only a sovereign state will advance and protect the interests of its own people, and alliances will not endure unless they are grounded on a mutual recognition of self interest, is paramount.' He set out the United Kingdom's role as a sub-stantial economic and military power: he believed that defence policy 'has to be able to guarantee such diplomacy a minimum level of force projection in all and any theatre of operations. Satellite communications and inflight refuelling have shrunk the globe so that there need be no such concept as "Out of Area".'

He felt it was important to avoid becoming obsessed by the European balance of power, 'but by the *world* balance'. He amplified his view that 'in a world context it is not the business of the UK to offset the dominion of one power by siding with the weaker (nearly always a recipe for disappointment) but to align itself with the strongest in each bloc and exploit the advantages of such close association'. In his summing-up he allowed himself only two underlined passages: 'Such bi-lateral under-standings are better served when both partners can share, even if unequally, the deterrence of military threat to trade or territory.' In his general conclusion he wrote: 'unless we are prepared to open our minds to the scale of probable change we will not adapt speedily'. He likened the vested interests – military, industrial, and political – to molluscs, dislodged by the high tides of autumn, which will 'find new rocks to which, limpet like, they will attach themselves'.

In the second half of his review, Alan proposed maintaining a strategic nuclear deterrent; air defence was a top priority in all directions; but 'most radically' he would move towards a 'very high degree of amphibious and/or airborne flexibility'. Among the Services Alan saw the Navy as future top dog, reverting to Britain's 'historic (up to 1914)' role of 'amphibious flexibility'. To Alan 'the maintenance of a standing Army on the European continent is a most unnatural posture for Britain without precedent since the time of Catherine of Aragon'. Here is the historian in him again: 'Its origins in military thinking can be found in the com-mitment of millions of soldiers to the Western Front in the first world war. But the victory in 1918 was a result of blockade by the Royal Navy; the four year haemorrhage of talent, life and hope in Flanders was the principal factor in our enfeeblement and loss of will in the Thirties.'

In the air, the Tornado (he would soon be standing up in the Commons to announce a cutback in production) was a back number, but he saw a case for continuing to support the European Fighter Aircraft (what became known as the Eurofighter). 'It should have a long expectancy as a dominant machine,' and he added, remembering his work at the Department of Trade, 'with good prospects of export sales'. As for the Army, he went into detail: he outlined increasing the Parachute Regiment, adding a second intervention brigade and upgrading the Territorials. Overall Army numbers would be reduced by 25–30,000, 'which should, incidentally, solve growing problems of recruitment, retention and quality'.

Nor had he forgotten the Prime Minister's call for 'particular attention to be given to Inter-operability' which he decided meant equipment which effectively could be deployed in widely different theatres instead of being confined to one particular role and area. Although the Navy was the future as far as Alan was concerned, it 'remains completely obsessive about anti-submarine warfare and' – here he remembered the Falklands experience – 'has done very little to correct those vulnerabilities to air attack learned at such high cost in San Carlos Water'.

Alan, in his second underlined paragraph, offered his conclusion: 'the purpose of this Review is to use the savings arising out of a role transfer both to support an enhancement of our amphibious flexibility and to produce a large enough overall surplus to secure both Treasury and electoral acceptance'. His grand total of net savings was £15 billion.

In the spring of 1990 the MoD was, not surprisingly, all abuzz. With the Departmental Defence Review reaching its conclusion, a major problem arose over the Eurofighter, for which the Ferranti company were supplying the radar. It became Alan's job to resolve matters when the Germans began worrying about Ferranti's commercial viability. Alan knocked heads together and encouraged GEC, run by Arnold Weinstock, to acquire the radar part of Ferranti's business. 'I ran the whole thing at breakneck pace,' he wrote, adding that a senior MoD civil servant commented to him afterwards that it was 'a wonderful feeling, to get hard decisions and clear instructions'.

That was not so easy with the Defence Review, where the Prime Minister was increasingly involved. Alan recounted at one point going head to head with her, with Britain exploiting German reunification 'while they still needed our support'. She shook her head, 'friendly, but implacable'. Alan hadn't finished. 'You're wrong,' he said. 'You're just wrong.' Ministers, junior Ministers, did not speak to Margaret Thatcher like that, but during a coffee break Alan kept up the attack, telling her, 'These are just a re-run of the old Appeasement arguments of 1938.' 'Yes,' she said, eyes flashing and as Alan reported ('she's in incredible form at the moment'), 'and I'm not an appeaser'. Alan added that John Major, 'whom I like more and more' and who had become Chancellor of the Exchequer the previous October, said, *sotto voce*, 'You're a military strategist. Oughtn't you to be sending your tanks round the flank, rather than attacking head on?'

Although the recommendations of what was seen as a 'secret' paper were partially leaked in January 1990 to Michael Evans, Defence correspondent of *The Times*, an internal inquiry by Michael Quinlan exonerated Alan from blame.[10] King went on television and argued forcibly to David Dimbleby on *Panorama* that 'Alan helped me very much with the review we did, Options for Change. He did this original paper for me, all this nonsense about secret papers; I sent it over to No. 10 ... valuable contribution to the debate ... then went round the chiefs of staff, major item in energising the debate about change, a very stimulating document indeed.'[11]

As Alan would tell Michael Cockerell in his film profile, *Love Tory*, 'I thought it was all going to plan and I'd be Secretary of State in the autumn.' Two events changed this. In November 1990 Margaret Thatcher was ousted as leader of the Conservative Party and therefore Prime Minister. Then a week later allegations appeared in *The Sunday Times* that Alan, when Minister for Trade, had advised the machine tool manufacturer Matrix Churchill how to get round the government's embargo on selling arms-making equipment to Iraq.[12]

Alan's Cabinet ambitions died on the vine.

The heading in *The Times* of 2 August 2005 read: 'How Alan Clark's vision for Forces became a reality'. The by-line was none other than 'Michael Evans, Defence correspondent', who opened his report: 'The late Alan Clark proposed swingeing cuts of £15 billion across the three Armed Services in 1989, according to a secret and highly prescient document ... The notorious unofficial defence review ... caused a political uproar at the time'.

Evans added of the review now being released under the Freedom of Information Act, 'Clark's ideas for cutting the defence budget may have been controversial sixteen years ago and were largely dismissed, but were he alive he might have good reason to say "I was right".' Only one of the predictions was off-beam: his view that China and Japan might annex former Soviet territory.

Not bad for an entirely private document that did not carry the Department's endorsement.

★

Tom King may have felt Alan failed to 'rally to the team', but one group
of Ministry of Defence employees thought him marvellous, as Peter
Levene recalled.[13] Before the honours system was made less class-ridden
by John Major's government in 1993, the lowest grade of award was the
British Empire Medal. Unlike other honours it was seen as a working-
class award and not presented by the Sovereign or senior member of the
royal family.

At the Ministry of Defence, the Secretary of State usually made the
presentations to the recipients, drivers, office staff, 'salt of the earth types'.
The ceremony took place at Admiralty House, with the recipients' families
invited. On one occasion Alan did the presentation. Levene thought him
brilliant. 'Really sincere, he told the recipients that Defence couldn't do
without people like them. He spoke not because he had to, but because
he believed it – it made them giants. They walked out ten feet tall. He
was outstanding.'

TWENTY-SEVEN

Reporting the Lady's Fall

Alan's accounts of the Tory Party during the governments of Margaret Thatcher and John Major have become a major source. While in the diaries he is, with few exceptions, in thrall to Margaret Thatcher, in *The Tories* he uses the benefits of hindsight in his criticism. He does not deny her 'three extraordinary victories' – the Falklands, the shattering of militant trade unionism and the winning of three consecutive general elections – but in his analysis of her personally, of the way she operated and even some of her policies – not least the poll tax – he is not shy of identifying what he saw as her weaknesses.[1]

In retrospect, in *The Tories* he recorded the early signs of internal discontent, beginning with the celebratory lunch at the Savoy Hotel in May 1989 to mark Mrs Thatcher's tenth anniversary as Prime Minister. At Alan's table was her bodyguard. 'On leaving the dining room [he recounted] I fell into step beside a friend from my schooldays, not long since a member of the Cabinet, and told him, "We had a man with a gun at our table." "Oh really," came the reply, "why didn't he use it?"' Alan did not identify the speaker in *The Tories*, but from his diary it is clear that this was Ian Gilmour, an arch wet, who had served in Margaret Thatcher's first government as Lord Privy Seal.

A week later rumours started that Geoffrey Howe was to be dismissed as Foreign Secretary. As Howe recalled in his memoirs, 'a disarming note' arrived from Alan. 'I know I irritate you from time to time,' he wrote – 'it's part of the fun, but I remain a staunch fan.' Alan told Howe to 'hang in there' for two reasons. He was 'the only person with enough cross-faction support to block Michael [Heseltine] if/when "something should happen"'. Alan did not want that option closed off. His second reason was based on his favoured theory of Hegelian tension. 'Thesis and antithesis are necessary to bring about a benign synthesis' and 'your role is crucial', at least for as long as Margaret Thatcher remained Prime Minister.[2]

In July 1989 Howe was moved, after six years as Foreign Secretary, to become a reluctant Leader of the House, Lord President of the Council and

Deputy Prime Minister. Four months later Nigel Lawson, the Chancellor, resigned, having told Howe a few days earlier that he was 'close to the end of his tether'. The Prime Minister had imported Alan Walters as her financial guru and Lawson found this unacceptable. The increasingly slippery slope that ultimately led to Margaret Thatcher's departure now included a stalking-horse challenge to her leadership in November 1989 by the little-known Tory MP for Clwyd North-West, Sir Anthony Meyer. Although Meyer secured only 33 votes against Thatcher's 314, a further 27 MPs abstained. 'The scale of the dissent was a significant warning for the future,' wrote Howe.

'By the early spring of 1990,' Alan wrote in *The Tories* of what he called 'the Year of Discontent', 'the concept of *changing* the Leader of the Party for another (displacing, that is to say, a sitting Prime Minister and installing in her place a former Cabinet colleague) was assuming a gradually widening acceptance among Conservative Members of Parliament.' John Major, who had come from nowhere to Foreign Secretary in three years, was the Prime Minister's latest favourite as heir, but realistically the enormously popular Heseltine (thanks in the main to his bravura Party conference performances) was seen as the principal claimant, even though he had not been a Minister since his resignation in 1986.

The departure on 1 November, 1990 of Geoffrey Howe from the government ('the death blow', wrote Alan)[3] set the balls in motion. Alan phoned the Prime Minister at Chequers the following Sunday afternoon, 4 November, and tried to cheer her up by telling her to hold tight. 'Geoffrey', she told him, 'was past it by now.' Alan added that she did not realise 'what a jam she's in. It's the Bunker syndrome. Everyone round you is clicking their heels. The saluting sentries have polished boots and beautifully creased uniforms. But out there at the Front it's all disintegrating. The soldiers are starving in tatters and makeshift bandages. Whole units are mutinous and in flight.'

That Sunday afternoon he also spoke to Hugo Young of *The Guardian*, who wrote up their conversation. Alan was on Thatcher's side, 'but with reservations'. He had no hesitation in telling Young that he thought Heseltine 'synthetic, appalling, cowardly. A terrible man, whom everyone should see through.' He also added that if the Tories lost the next election under Heseltine, and it could 'in the slightest degree be attributed to him, he would be finished . . . Unless he can guarantee to win, he cannot really run.' To which Young added a tart comment – 'which rather gives the lie to the cowardice point'. At this stage Alan was of the view that a good outcome would be for her to quit quietly with Douglas Hurd as her successor. Hurd confirmed this in his memoirs, reporting that on 29 October, two days before Howe's resignation, Alan had visited him in his room at the Commons to say that Margaret Thatcher must go and that he should take her place.[4]

Young also noted Alan's views on Charles Powell, whose role is 'ever more important. He does more of the "day-to-day" stuff than used to be the case ... Rather than it being a case of Charles second-guessing her, it's quite often Margaret second-guessing Charles. Also, at cabinet committees, he almost sits as a member of the committee. He interrupts if not mid-sentence, then certainly in mid-paragraph. Four years ago, he was quite different, sitting silent, as civil servants are meant to do. But because he is so good, this is all right'.[5]

A week later, after his Remembrance Day obligations in Plymouth, Alan confided to his diary on 11 November that it looked as if 'Michael is going to get forced into a position, whether he likes it or not, when he'll have to stand'. Next day he wrote, 'wild rumours are circulating about the leadership "contest" for which nominations close on Thursday'. But will there be a contest? he reported people as asking, Was it too close to a general election? 'This has to be balls,' was his reaction, but he thought the fact that the Whips had clammed up a bad sign. 'Already they have gone into "neutral" mode. Secret policemen burning the old files, ready to serve.'

Howe was to make his resignation speech on the afternoon of 13 November. That morning Alan thought the Party 'virtually out of control. Mutinous.' He reported the received wisdom that Howe's speech would 'finally tear the whole thing wide open'. At a midday meeting on Defence matters with Peter Levene, the Chief of Defence Procurement, he learnt that the previous evening the Prime Minister had been greeted with almost complete silence at the Lord Mayor's Banquet. Howe's speech included the memorable cricketing analogy of 'being sent into bat for Britain ... only to find that before the game the bats have been broken by the team captain'. He ended his speech, 'The time has come for others to consider *their own response* [Alan's italics] to the tragic conflict of loyalties with which I have wrestled for perhaps too long.' The way was now clear for a challenge from a Tory big beast. Enter Michael Heseltine.

'I change my own mind by the hour,' wrote Alan on 13 November. 'In some ways it would be better for her to go completely than to hang on mutilated'. He didn't think she had the nature to do a de Gaulle, and make a withdrawal to Colombey, 'for that course it is now really too late'. He listened to Norman Tebbit, who was against the idea of a compromise candidate. 'We must fight all the way to the death.' This appealed to Alan. 'Leonidas at Thermopylae. But we don't win. It's the end of me.' Over the next fortnight Alan kept his diary by his side, writing a day-by-day, even at times a moment-by-moment, record of the events that led to Margaret Thatcher's downfall. Not that those involved accept his every word as gospel – did he, they ask, allow his own bias to show through? However, whatever its failings, his account is the first everyone turns to.[6]

In the week that followed Howe's resignation the Heseltine bandwagon rolled. The press (with the exception of *The Daily Telegraph*) quickly tipped him to succeed and it became Alan's main aim – and that of many of his friends – to ensure that he did not. The rules for the leadership election were complex. In the first round a candidate needed a margin over their nearest rival of fifteen per cent (56) of the total electorate (379). In the two-horse race with Heseltine the Thatcherites refused to believe their leader was seriously threatened. As campaign manager the chief asset of Margaret Thatcher's parliamentary private secretary, Peter Morrison, was his loyalty: what she believed in he believed in. He had been a junior Minister, and almost anyone else might have seen the role of becoming her PPS as demotion, but Morrison, a man of considerable independent means, was happy to serve her. Morrison had been praised by Norman Tebbit when they worked together at Central Office.[7] However, in running her leadership campaign his organisational skills deserted him. He was meant to be counting his leader's supporters, convincing the doubters. Instead, according to Alan, he was 'useless'. After lunch on the day of the leadership election Alan found him in his office, asleep in a leather armchair, snoring slightly and his feet on the desk. When challenged he said, 'Do you think I'd be like this if I wasn't entirely confident?'[8] He boasted that she would get 220 to 240 votes, more than enough. On the first ballot that afternoon she was ahead, but her 204 votes to Michael Heseltine's 152 were four short of the 56 necessary for victory. Both candidates announced they would stay in for the second round. Would their votes stand firm?

Norman Lamont recorded Alan saying to him in the Division Lobby that evening, 'It's magnificent. She is a kamikaze pilot. She is not just going to crash the plane, she is determined to sink the battleship.'[9]

A key meeting now took place at Tristan Garel-Jones's house in nearby Catherine Place. Alan described it as 'Blue Chips' wall-to-wall. The attendance was impressive: Cabinet Ministers – Waldegrave, Chris Patten, Rifkind, Newton, Lamont and Lilley – and a string of junior Ministers. Alan noted that only Waldegrave was sympathetic to Margaret Thatcher's plight, otherwise she was not mentioned. As for Heseltine, there seemed to be wide agreement that he wasn't mad (Patten); they could serve under him; Norman Lamont shocked Alan by saying 'he could conceive Michael as being quite "effective"', although Lamont in his memoirs says Alan misinterpreted his liking for Heseltine as implying he might support him as leader; he was a John Major supporter from the beginning. Alan recounted his own contribution, that whoever replaced her was 'the one most likely to win the Election'. What was needed was a Baldwin, 'someone to reassure rather than stimulate'. But when he named Tom King, Chris Patten laughed out loud and John Patten said, 'I presume you're joking'. Alan then mused in his diary that winning the election was not uppermost in their minds. They had their careers to think about and wanted to identify with the new winner. He expected Garel-Jones 'to rig it', he wrote, for John Major, but as the evening wore on the consensus built up for Douglas Hurd. Alan was doubtful – he saw Douglas as '*too* much of an Establishment figure'. He concluded: 'I'm not sure the Party wants that. It's very risky, unless there is another candidate from the left who will peel off a tranche of Heseltine's total.' Was John Major that man?

The second ballot was a week later. Who would now throw their hats into the ring? While people gossiped and plotted Margaret Thatcher announced, 'I fight, and I fight to win.' But after the ignominy of not winning outright first time, Alan remarked that the priority was to find a way, 'tactfully and skilfully', to talk her out of standing a second time. At the House he kept his door open. People came in and out. John Major, he was told, wouldn't make a move while Margaret Thatcher remained in the field. Alan now shut his door, cleared his head and wrote: '1) If she fights head on, she loses. 2) Therefore, the Opposition vote has to be diluted by a candidate from the left – preferably Patten ... 3) Try and talk Patten into standing. QED.'

If Alan gives the impression that he was listening at keyholes, with his ear tuned to every rumour, every nuance, Michael Portillo, at the time Minister of State at Transport, wonders just how true this was. Ministers abandoned their Departments and took up residence in their Commons offices. His – on the lower ministerial floor – was next to Alan's. 'At various times during the day news would reach me ... Alan was – I supposed – an ally, but who knows? Anyway I would rush next door each time I had news and knock, and each time there would be a sort of stirring and fumbling inside the room and Alan would come to the door. Clearly he had been asleep on his sofa. The room smelt of sleep. Breathlessly I would give him my news, and he would thank me very warmly, but with that suave and lackadaisical manner that made me feel like a teenager telling him about my first kiss. That happened three times, and it all had a touch of Gethsemane about it.'[10]

Not only Cabinet Ministers visited the Prime Minister. Peter Morrison found room for Alan, too.

'You're in a jam,' he recorded telling her.

'I know that.'

'They're all telling you not to stand, aren't they?'

'I'm going to stand . . .'

'That's wonderful. That's heroic. But the Party will let you down.'

'I'm a fighter.'

'Fight, then. Fight right to the end, a third ballot if you need to. But you lose.'

There was quite a little pause.

'It'd be so terrible if Michael won. He would undo everything I have fought for.'

'But what a way to go! Unbeaten in three elections, never rejected by the people. Brought down by nonentities!'

'But Michael . . . as *Prime Minister*.'

'Who the fuck's Michael? No one. Nothing. He won't last six months. I doubt if he'd even win the Election. Your place in history is towering.'

Outside, people were doing that maddening trick of opening and shutting the door, at shorter and shorter intervals.

'Alan, it's been so good of you to come in and see me . . .'

Less than a month after John Major defeated Heseltine and Hurd to become Party leader and Prime Minister, Alan dined with his *Telegraph* friends, Frank Johnson and Peregrine Worsthorne. They discussed *The Book* (he italicised every reference), how important the Thatcher account would be. Alan recorded his response on learning that it would be ghosted by Conservative journalist John O'Sullivan. 'Ghost! Good God! The greatest political story of the century and they are looking for a "ghost".'

That night he thought 'why shouldn't I write it? She would trust me, I'm sure . . . As a Privy Counsellor I can get access to Cabinet Office records. I am trained as a historian, and she has often said (in public) how much she admires *Barbarossa*.' Having convinced himself, early the following morning he tried out the idea on Peter Morrison, who was enthusiastic. 'Said the present situation was "a mess", "too many cooks". He promised to speak to her, and this time I think he is going to.'[11] Alan wasted no time and, with the help of his agent Michael Sissons, prepared an outline, what he called 'The Thatcher Legend'.[12] He pointed out that for the legend to flourish it required 'strategic handling if it is not to be depleted'. He also anticipated a 'considerable reaction' against her memory, that it was in the interests of her successors to play down her record 'in order that their own conduct should not suffer unfavourable comparison'. He stressed the importance of the Thatcher Archive: keynote speeches and her papers.

The Book, he said, is 'the most important of all the instruments you have at your disposal'. He was adamant. 'You simply must resist the temptation to come up with an "instant" work (whatever persuasive formula may be suggested to you).' What he proposed was unlike any Prime Ministerial record. Here would be 'the far reach of History itself'. The literature, he said, was 'crucial. It has *got* to abjure any hint or suspicion of the polemic. I mean, we are dealing with one of the great heroic tales of politics; where the expectations, the so-called inevitabilities of the period are overturned by the constancy and resolution of a single human spirit.'

Margaret Thatcher took his proposal seriously enough to arrange an immediate new year meeting, as Alan related in his diary.[13] She began promisingly. 'I want *you* to do it, Alan,' but the rest of her sentence missed Alan's point, 'because you are a believer.' The exchange continued:

'It shouldn't be a "believer's" book. It doesn't need to be.'

'How can you say that?'

'The facts speak for themselves. They illustrate the scale of your achievement.'

'But look how it ended. The treachery . . .'

'Margaret, these aren't Memoirs. You don't want to get into that game. This is your *Biography*. Where you came from, how you got there, what you did for the Conservative Party, and for Britain. A major work of political history. It will go into every university library in the World.'

This, though, was not the book that Margaret Thatcher wished. Alan detected as their conversation developed that she was having second thoughts. He tried the tack of saying he would 'pay proper attention to the strange and disreputable circumstances of her ousting'. He turned to money (Sissons estimated a total take of about £8,000,000, but her son Mark had been, in Alan's words, 'winding her up' and was talking of twenty million). What finally tore it, he decided, was the format: no ghost – 'The Official Biography *by* Alan Clark'. However, he feared that what she wanted was *Margaret Thatcher. My Story*.

That in effect was the outcome.[14] On 21 February he wrote that instead of the biography Margaret Thatcher had gone for 'the big mechanistic technique of researchers and capable hacks'. He concluded, 'She's got no sense of art or scholarship at all, really. And has always been unreliable, loses her nerve and goes conventional.'

When he came to publish *The Tories* in 1998, it was clear that the love affair was over.

TWENTY-EIGHT

A Fit of Pique

For most of the final four years of Alan's time as MP for Plymouth Sutton his secretary was Alison Young. During that time he became infatuated by her, to the extent that at one point he even contemplated leaving Jane and 'starting again'.

With a general election in prospect in the spring of 1992 Alan made a decision that changed his life in more ways than one. He decided to resign his parliamentary seat. His constituency agent told the press that he was standing down from Plymouth Sutton for 'personal reasons'. Not so, riposted Alan, that usually means a scandal, 'and I can assure you there's nothing of that. It's just time to go.' Michael White in *The Guardian* reported that Alan 'dismissed two instant conspiracy theories: that he was making way for Dr David Owen to fight Sutton (majority 4,013 over the Alliance)' and that he was to be 'the fall-guy for Whitehall's widely-suspected complicity in embargo-breaking sales to Iraq when he was junior trade minister'.[1]

In fact he had been pondering resignation for more than a year, and by July 1991 was writing: 'This time next year I have *no* idea what I'll be doing or where. But I do know that I will no longer be a member of the House of Commons.' Just before Christmas he discussed with Jane the 'finality of "standing down"'. Confessing to his diary was one thing, but Jane believes he told no-one around him. Thus the surprise when he resigned on 24 February, just six weeks before the election (and therefore giving his constituency only three weeks to choose a replacement candidate).

Newspapers covered his departure with huge space, *The Times* adding a leading article headed 'The Spark of Clark'.[2] 'In a grey and conformist House of Commons, Alan Clark has been one of the few dashes of colour and originality ... he has not accepted the usual political cant. He has been witty, indiscreet and candid. He has often been wrong. His reasons for leaving the Commons now are honest, and mistaken. Sensing that his nine-year ministerial career is near its end (unless it continues in the

Lords), he wants to leave in his prime and not follow the example of elderly colleagues whom he describes as "self-important with the residual pomp of past achievement or declamation. Heavy watch chains glinting, they shuffle about, ancient mariners waiting to catch your eye or snoring for hours in the tearoom armchairs."' *The Times* went on to quote Alan's confidence in the government, that John Major's personality was ideally suited to today's politics. It referred to his remark that he saw no special role for a troublesome backbencher, 'and trouble, in its various forms is really the only solace left for a backbencher'. With Thatcher-era Ministers retiring, the utterances of those left 'vanish in a haze of un-memorability', continued *The Times*. 'Nobody forgets the utterances of Mr Clark.' And it concluded, 'Mr Clark's virtues are those of the aristocratic politician: independence of mind backed by personal wealth. These are unusual and close to being anachronistic. They should be valued the more for that . . . The back benches or the front ones, are not intended for the comfort of prime ministers. The Parliamentary Conservative Party will be the poorer.'

At past elections Alan often invited his secretaries to Plymouth as back-up, while he (usually accompanied by Jane) toured the hustings. Jane says that on this occasion he told her he intended asking Alison to stay at Bratton. She, though, would not countenance that. Bratton had been the first home they bought together; it was the first home of their children. She wasn't having Alan take another woman there to live under its roof. Was Alan unused to being told no so firmly by Jane? In what looks like a fit of pique he said to her, in effect, that if she forbade Alison to stay at Bratton, then he wouldn't stand at the election.

Alison Young has different memories.[3] 'I don't recall any discussion about that,' she says. Although she had visited Bratton on two occasions in the past, 'I wouldn't have stayed there'. As for the timing, was it the last moment? Had he not told anyone? In his diary (December 1991) he wrote of his '*dread* of telling Alison, the admission, that for both of us, our professional relationship is over'. The first she knew that he had finally made up his mind came not from him direct, she says, but on opening his office post one morning. She found a letter from David Owen thanking him for advance notice rather than hearing it elsewhere. 'I was furious. I was really cross, because I had been doing a great deal of work, for example, trying to improve his profile with newsletters.' Four years later he recorded parking outside the entrance to Plymouth's main post office with his letter of resignation in his hand, 'Alison begging me not to – as she had in the train coming up'. Her fury was compounded by the close proximity of the election. 'I wanted to work on an election campaign,

that's the whole point of the job really, to be out and about and to see
what impact your work has been having over a certain number of years.'
In place of Alan she volunteered to help a Conservative candidate on the
other side of the country: Henry Bellingham was standing for re-election
in North West Norfolk.

As for Alan's infatuation with Alison, his departure from the Commons
would prove the beginning of the end.

Alison had succeeded Peta Ewing as Alan's constituency secretary in
October 1988. Alan recorded the fact in his diary: 'Peta is leaving to get
married. Tedious. Her name is Alison Young. She was not Peta's preferred
candidate, but at the interview she showed spirit. I noted that her hair was
wet, for some reason, although it was a fine day.' Wet? 'Too much
hairspray,' recalls Alison.

Working for Alan was only her second job. In those days MPs' secretaries' offices were widely spread; the desk allocated to Alan's secretary
was round the corner from the Commons in the Cloisters, Dean's Yard.
There were ten desks in open-plan quarters. Alison sat, as she recalls,
between two Labour Members' secretaries. 'I don't think you'd have that
now – everything is segregated, everything then was quite relaxed and
old-fashioned.'

When Alison first worked for Alan he also had an office in the Department of Trade in Victoria Street, where she often had to go. When he
changed jobs in July 1989 to Defence, her trek was longer, but Alan's
driver would sometimes act as her chauffeur. Alan, like other Ministers,
also had a second office in the Commons. It was never a 9 to 5 job, more
10 to 6 or 7. She remembers that some old-guard Members still dictated
every letter. Most, though, and Alan was one of these, expected their
secretaries, once they had learnt the ropes, to generate the appropriate
replies which they would sign. Alison was keen, unlike one secretary she
worked with, who if a letter came at the end of the week would re-
envelope it before posting it back to the MP so she didn't have to deal
with it that day. By January 1989 Alison was regularly accompanying Alan
on his constituency visits, using the three-hour train journey to Plymouth
to catch up on correspondence. Alan thought her 'more efficient than
Peta, and more fun to be with'. He had also noted the colour of her eyes –
blue-grey.[4]

When did the relationship change? Alison thinks it must have been the
Trade and Industry departmental Christmas party in 1988. For Alan's part
this is confirmed in a chart like a graph which he devised towards the end

of 1990 – the year and months across the top, each point of significance to him numbered with a key alongside. December 1988 – DTI Christmas party; February 1989 – 'says yes to Bratton trip' and through the next two years he identifies significant moments by place names such as Lew-trenchard,[5] Albany, December 1989 MoD Christmas party and in October 1990 – 'too much of everything'. By Christmas 1989 he confides to his diary from Albany on the day he, with Alison's help, completed the 'great Defence Review'; their reward: 'A glass of champagne in the Pugin Room, came back here ... she was resistant ... We talked a bit ... she cried, which was dear of her ... today is the anniversary of the Christmas party. It's always a low point. I don't know what's going to happen.'

Alison says it was not a physical relationship, just a very intense friend-ship. Searching for a word she uses 'companion' as an appropriate descrip-tion. At the best moments she called him 'Dearest M.C.' (the initials derived from Mr Clark) and wrote to him either at Albany or at Brooks's in St James's. He called her 'Aly'. In June 1991 Alan wrote on the back of a sheet of Sotheby's notepaper, 'I bear you no ill-will my darling. Nothing but love and gratitude for everything you gave me – even the pain.' On more than one occasion Alan wrote in his diary that they would talk for hours on the telephone, often into the small hours, she from her flat, he from Albany – on 20 February 1992 he recorded three and a quarter hours.

For more than a year Alan led a double life. 'It's preposterous,' he wrote in February 1991. 'I'm actually ill, have been for months, lovesick, it's called. A long and nasty course of chemotherapy – but with periodic bouts of addiction therapy when I delude myself that I may be cured without "damage".' Jane knew Alison only as Alan's constituency sec-retary. 4 March 1991: 'Darling Jane is looking a wee bit strained. She knows something is up, and is quiet a lot of the time. But she doesn't question me at all – just makes the occasional scathing reference. I do want to make her happy – she's such a good person.' His confusion is frequently apparent. In the same diary entry he writes that he must get rid of Alison. When Jane eventually learnt of his feelings for Alison it was a body blow.

She noticed Alison was deliberately dressing like her, using the same hairstyle, something which Alison firmly denies. Where Jane and Alison were in agreement was over Alan's state of mind. Jane recalls saying to him: 'You are infatuated' and in one row suggested he look up the word in the dictionary. Alison says she tried to use his infatuation to get what she wanted, 'which was for him to settle down and do the job. If that didn't work; I would try different techniques. Sometimes being cross, sometimes being nice.'

She thought Alan was in mid-life crisis, had been, she said, since he was thirty – he was actually sixty when she went to work for him.[6] 'There were times when I probably had to be nasty just to try and get back on an even keel, a professional relationship. Afterwards you think when you've been purposely nasty to someone to force an action you want then that wasn't very nice. I would feel guilty that I'd been particularly unkind or cruel.'

Alison remembers how fed-up she became. Here she was in her early twenties with a career to think about. Looking back nearly twenty years later she recalls: 'I appreciated I worked for somebody interesting, and that he was a Minister. In terms of career progression, you either worked for an MP or you worked for a Minister. So I already had one of the best jobs in that sense. I really liked the job, and all I wanted to do was to do the job and to do it well, learn more about politics, how it all worked. I worked for someone interesting, who gave me freedom to do lots of work on my own.'

Alan, though, wanted more, as Alison relates. 'A by-product of all this was a certain amount of being chased around the filing cabinets. I suppose being quite naïve, or stupid, or unhappy, pick a variety of reasons why, at times I sort of relented because it was easier than just carrying on fighting, which didn't seem to make any difference and which seemed to encourage him more. I couldn't win either way. I didn't particularly want to give up the job, because I enjoyed it. I didn't see why I should be hounded out of a job for that sort of reason. But there could never be a balance with Alan. I would say, "Stop all that! and let's work." But then in a way that would be a bit dull, because it wouldn't be quite as much fun. It was interesting to accompany him to places or some event. But it was trying to find a balance between these two extremes. But there couldn't be one. You only know these things in hindsight really.'

Alan thought Alison had political potential. She recalls that 'one of the problems working for someone with a personality like Alan's, if they say things often enough you tend to believe them'. When he said she should stand as a candidate she responded that she was far too young and had not done enough preparation. Alan, however, thought that an upside. She was already working for the Party where she lived and had attended a women's conference where she met Baroness Seccombe, a Party vice-chairman with special responsibility for women, who told Alan that 'she has great potential and a very pleasing personality ... I am sure that she will be a great asset to the Party as the years go by'.[7] At the 1991 Conservative Party conference, with Jane accompanying him as usual, Alan records running Alison through the ladies' cocktail party, to provide her with 'some good "contacts"'.

A significant handwritten exchange between them appears on the back of a daily ministerial engagement sheet (the size of a bookmark and dated 9 July 1991), which opened with Alan asking Alison:

> Will you marry me? (please)
> Why?
> Aly PLEASE don't be cross. I can't bear it.

To which Alison has written: Tough shit.[8]

Not that marriage was ever on the cards. Alison wanted a long-term relationship with someone who would never be unfaithful. With Alan she knew that was impossible. She also knew he would never leave Jane.

Alison was setting off for a long holiday to South America, which caused Alan to write a lengthy diary entry, dated 23 July, on a separate sheet. It was full of fears. 'Last night I was so dejected. When I actually face up to the fact that it is over I feel quite ill and weak and yesterday, quite blithely, she was talking about arrangements for Sarah to do the mail; wouldn't even tell me when she was coming back (serve me right for asking – what does it matter anyway?) Later on, she rang. Instantly I felt incredible. Just her voice saying hello, sweet and friendly. I said as much. But we never broke the ice. It's crazy, isn't it. Every night this month we just go back to our separate empty flats, then talk for up to one and a half hours on the telephone. Why aren't we talking side by side in bed? I've held on for so long because, as the stars foretold, I'm emotionally enslaved, but I must summon some strength now. I'm consumed, ema-ciated by jealousy. How in hell do I exorcise it? Perhaps someone will smile at me? I'll just steer the Porsche onto the yellow roads. It'd be fun to drive really fast and recklessly, and on my own. Yet I know that if I do meet someone it won't do any good. I'll pine always for my Aly and her sweet waist and hips and quizzical expression and changing moods.'

The ongoing professional problem for Alison, a major cause of their fighting, was the way Alan neglected the Sutton constituency. In Sep-tember 1991 she wrote in permafrost mood: 'As from today it will only be necessary for you and I to meet twice a week for an hour. I suggest Tuesdays and Thursdays. Any other business can be dealt with over the phone and Pat [driver] can bring your signing. Please do not contact me

unless it is to do with the constituency.' She followed this up the same day
with an itemised list:

1. We have no links whatsoever – except that I am currently in your
employment.
2. I would gladly return 'the stone' [a gift] to you – particularly as it is
another symbol of all the lies and hypocrisy you stand for. You said it was
worth a lot of money (and all that bullshit about it being meant for me) –
but it is valueless. I resented having to pay good money to have it set and
buy a chain (just to shut you up) and so I am only keeping it because of the
value of the setting. Even an amateur gemmologist could tell it was of poor
quality – like its donor.
3. I won't ever want you. You must understand that. There is nothing and
never was anything of meaning. I don't want to see you because basically
I am sick of those pathetic scenes – schoolboy gloating, crude manhandling,
the simpering and begging which is all an act.

We could never be 'mates', as you say, because the two things that you
value most – your ego and your money – mean nothing to me.

My future lies with someone else who has a surfeit, unlike your poverty,
of principles. I am sad that you wore away some of my own, and lowered
me in some respects to your level, but I, at least, am young enough to change
my ways, and do not suffer from the debilitating insecurity which you have.
4. Please return the stone I gave you or throw it away.
DO NOT REPLY

Alan ignored this admonition. Alison tore up his next letter, clipped her
own note 'unread' on it and returned it to him. If this had been one item
he might have been expected to destroy, it was not so.

At another point that autumn Alison wrote that she hoped Alan and
Jane would make things up. 'It was never my intention that this whole
thing should get so out of hand – but I don't feel as if I can be to blame
entirely. I know she thinks it is all my fault, but she shouldn't have put up
with being treated so shittily for so long – and it was inevitable that after
years of your infidelities it would all come to a head at some point. [Alan
added his comments on the letter, here, specifically: 'yes. Because at last
I fell in love.'] I wanted you to make a sacrifice for me – but you didn't –
and if you want her to stay you will have to sacrifice all the other women
too, including me. Please let's be sensible and do the dictation properly.
I know you want me to leave, but it isn't fair. [Alan: 'please don't'. Alison:
'what is the point if you are being so difficult?'] We could be professional
about everything on your return in October. [Alan: 'never'. Alison: 'we

were in the beginning'.] You always promised me (for what it was worth) that you would keep business and personal separate. If you only ever keep one promise to me let it be that one <u>now</u>. [Alan: 'I'm terribly, truly, sorry that I broke the important one. Please forgive me.']. Always, Alison'

Two months later, with Alan behaving very much as before, she wrote: 'I said I would tell you how things would have been on my return ... I won't write it – and you will probably never know if you keep acting as you do – always talking and presuming – never listening and learning. Late now. But remember <u>you</u> changed things. You disturbed the fine balance which was beginning to go in your favour – and now we lurch from side to side. You betrayed me once (that I know of) and there is no reason why you wouldn't do it again. You will always have my respect, admiration and tender feelings of affection – or do I mean love? A xxx'

If there was a truce, it did not last for long. One day Alan took Alison's diary from her handbag, leading Alison to fume on 10 December 1991: 'How dare you read my diary? Particularly when you <u>do not</u> let me look at yours without supervision. So how dare you read mine? If you wanted to read bits of it – I would read them to you if you <u>asked</u>. You lock yours away from me – I can't believe you can be so obnoxious. You say your diary needs explanation – well, so does mine. Now you are all cross, hurt, and being petty ... and precisely because it is one rule for you (ie invade someone else's privacy, read their personal notes – but they can't do it to you because it is full of secrets of bonks with other women etc) and another for someone else (ie I can't look at yours). If you are upset by what you read you deserve to be. You don't let me look at yours on my own – so why should you read mine without me being able to explain?'

In his diary during spring 1992 Alan's confusion of emotions is clear. In February he wrote about the prospect of 'the pang of a final parting' from Alison. Ten days later Jane accompanied him on a ministerial trip to South America, leading him to reflect, 'she is really so good and sweet. That's what makes the situation so impossible. I mean what do I want? Certainly not to leave her and cause her pain. And yet as she herself admits Alison's appearance has revived our sexual tension by all the jealous cross-currents it arouses.' Although he was to make other references in his diaries to the end of the affair, appropriately it was the eve of the 1992 election and the chance to pray in the church at the top of Brentor that led him to write, 'The wonderful, excruciating, highly dangerous Alison "affair" has burned itself out and, to my utter nostalgic depression we are now only, and I fear never again can be more than "good friends".'

At the general election in April the Conservatives under John Major were returned for a fourth term, albeit with a substantially reduced majority.[9] Two months later Alison wrote to Alan, 'I do hate it when we part at railway stations. I hate it when we are apart too much – but we both have things we have to do and I have to explore the world a bit more while I have the chance. You are so sweet to me in many ways, but we can be so cruel to each other as well. I know I'll think about you when I'm away – and because the imagination can be so fertile and unpredictable, sometimes I'll be cross + jealous, and other times serene and content. Either we will remain attached, or we will grow apart, but either way we will always be special to each other. I know I've been rotten and cruel to you sometimes and that it is very difficult for you at the moment (particularly this week) – but what are we to do? Look forward to a good chat soon. Take care. Love Aly xx'

Occasional cards reached him via Brooks's, some from overseas. On reading that he was publishing his diaries she was concerned at what they might contain. 'I hope you haven't forgotten that you said I could look at the parts of the book where I am mentioned and decide if I agreed. You even said you would make it a legal agreement. So I trust you will keep to it.' On publication in June 1993 Alan dispatched a copy to her. She thought the references to her appeared harmless, and hoped now that the press would stop pestering her. Alan tried to revive the relationship, but Alison was firm. 'There has never been any point trying to explain things to you as you always make up your own story and interpretation anyway. All I can say is that we have been over all the arguments hundreds of times – and nothing has changed, and it never will. And it is for the best that way. You know that, too. I'm about to begin a new life, in many different ways, and you should too. Beginning with taking care of those in your charge. Take care of yourself, always.' But she found this dis-engagement difficult, as a later postcard demonstrates: 'You nearly made me cry this morning – you can be so disturbing. I just don't know what to do, which is why I keep running away abroad.'[10]

In August, Alan and Jane were at Eriboll. 'I hardly think of Alison any longer,' he wrote. His diaries testify that was untrue, but the infatuation was over. Later in 1992 Zermatt beckoned. It proved the beginning of the renewal of his marriage to Jane. 'We started again out here,' he recalled a year before he died. 'Absolutely delicious, never been sexually happier with Jane.'

TWENTY-NINE

Behind the Actualité

The Old Bailey joust between Alan Clark and Geoffrey Robertson QC on Wednesday, 4 November 1992 was surprisingly little reported at the time, but had ramifications for government and the Civil Service so diverse and unsuspected that they rumbled on through much of the decade. For Alan it ended several of his closest political friendships. It also ensured that he did not receive a peerage.

Alan was giving evidence in the trial of three former directors of a Midlands engineering company, Matrix Churchill, who were accused of selling machine tools to Iraq that could be used in the manufacture of munitions between July 1988 and August 1990. During part of this period Alan had been Minister for Trade and particularly concerned with encouraging exports. Not surprisingly, he considered any government guidelines that restricted his mission 'irksome, tiresome and intrusive',[1] not least because between 1980 and 1988 Western interests were 'well served by Iran and Iraq fighting each other' and the revolutionary Iran was now considered by Britain very much to be the enemy.

That Wednesday, during cross-examination by Robertson, who led for the defence, Alan admitted that he had advised machine tool companies early in 1988 that when applying for export licences they should concentrate on the peaceful uses of their products. Asked by Robertson why civil servants suggested that nothing should be said about the equipment's possible military uses, Alan agreed that it was 'a matter of Whitehall cosmetics to keep the record ambiguous'. Robertson challenged Alan that therefore an earlier statement attributed to him – 'that the Iraqis will be using the current order for general engineering purposes' – could not be correct 'to your knowledge'.

The exchange that followed would swiftly gain wide currency.

AC: Well, it's our old friend being economical, isn't it?
GR: With the truth?
AC: With the *actualité*. There was nothing misleading or dishonest to

make a formal or introductory comment that the Iraqis would be using the current orders for general engineering purposes. All I didn't say was 'and for making munitions'.[2]

In court the following day Alan went further, saying to Alan Moses QC, counsel for Customs and Excise,[3] that his job was to assist British firms in selling their goods abroad even if they had told him that their customers would use them to manufacture munitions. His one reservation would have been if their products had nuclear, chemical or ballistic missile applications. On Friday, 6 November Moses surprised the court by seeking an adjournment.

After the weekend all became clearer when Moses rose on the Monday morning and told the court that Alan's admission had, in effect, scuppered the prosecution. Customs and Excise, which had brought the case, with little encouragement from Whitehall, were dropping all charges. Thus Judge Brian Smedley QC[4] had no alternative but to tell the jury to find the defendants not guilty; they were free to leave the court. All were swiftly photographed in a pub close to the Old Bailey, with smiles across their faces and their hands wrapped around obligatory glasses of champagne.

As *The Guardian*'s extensive coverage next morning made clear, the case had opened a huge can of worms. The trial was but one act in a drama that 'exposed a litany of ministerial and Whitehall lies and double-dealing through which the true nature of government policy towards Iraq's Saddam Hussein was kept from Parliament and the public'.[5] Was this, as *The Guardian*'s leading article said in the same issue, 'Britain's Iraqgate, which had finally thrust itself into the public eye despite all efforts at evasion'? *The Guardian* argued trenchantly that the government cover-up 'almost served to put three innocent men in probable jail. It is scandalous that no fewer than four current ministers of the Crown should have sought to gag the defence by signing "national interest" certificates to bar secret documents from disclosure'. As for Alan Clark, *The Guardian* said he could be thanked 'for admitting last week that Western interests were "well served by Iran and Iraq fighting each other" and acknowledging that "Whitehall cosmetics" were employed to promote sales of "dual-use" equipment to Iraq. (But we should ask why he did not admit it two years ago when instead he denied giving a "nod and wink" to the industry.) Yet in the end the case fell less because of Mr Clark's admission than through the sheer weight of damning evidence against the Government in the disclosed documents.'

The trial itself had been ignored by the majority of the media (with the exception of *The Guardian*, the *Financial Times* and Channel 4 News), but its outcome was now splashed by the press across every front page.[6] And was Alan Clark to blame, as the Attorney-General, Sir Nicholas Lyell, immediately implied, in the House of Commons that afternoon?

> Counsel for the prosecution in the Matrix Churchill case informed the court yesterday that, in the light of the evidence given by Mr Alan Clark in cross-examination, he had concluded that it would no longer be right to seek a conviction in the case; and that the prosecuting authority, the commissioners of Customs and Excise, had accepted that conclusion. Both he and the commissioners were satisfied that during the course of cross-examination Mr Clark had given evidence that was inconsistent with a written statement that he had made in 1991 and with what he had said in an interview with an officer of Customs and Excise in September 1992.[7]

The Prime Minister, John Major, now found himself under enormous pressure. Already it was being suggested that successive Conservative governments from the mid-1980s had been less than honest where arms sales were concerned. Major and Lyell moved quickly, announcing an independent judicial inquiry, the time-honoured political route of legitimate delay in such circumstances. To chair it they selected Sir Richard Scott, a senior judge with a reputation for robustness. In 1987 he had found against the Thatcher government's attempts to ban *Spycatcher*, the memoirs of Peter Wright, a former MI5 officer. Not until February 1996 would he publish his Matrix Churchill report.

For Alan the Matrix Churchill affair had its innocent origins when Margaret Thatcher moved him to the Department of Trade from Employment early in 1986. He was now a Minister of State, one leg up from the Parliamentary Under-Secretary role at Employment, his first government posting. On his appointment Margaret Thatcher told him that Trade 'was the second most important Minister outside the Cabinet after the Financial Secretary – but don't shout that around'.[8] As Minister for Trade she said his job was to promote British exports ('negotiation is the key'), a role that he found congenial. Alan delighted in the realisation that every previous Trade Minister had made it to the Cabinet, and he was determined to be the next.[9] His appointment surprised many Conservatives. Chris Patten called him 'a protectionist, anti-American, anti-European lover of Hitler and Stalin. A joke maverick charmer.'[10]

Arms sales had long been a moral issue, but where jobs in the UK are at stake protests tend to be muted. In Plymouth Sutton Alan had substantial numbers of constituents whose livelihoods depended on the neighbouring Devonport dockyard. After quitting Sutton, and while the Scott Inquiry was under way, he was interviewed by the journalist John Pilger in 1994 about the British links to the death of 200,000 people in East Timor which was occupied by Indonesia, much of whose weaponry, said Pilger, was supplied when Alan was Trade Minister.

> Pilger: 'Did it bother you personally that you were causing such mayhem and human suffering?'
> 'No, not in the slightest,' Alan replied. 'It never entered my head.'
> 'I ask the question because I read you are a vegetarian and are seriously concerned with the way animals are killed.'
> 'Yeah?'
> 'Doesn't that concern extend to humans?'
> 'Curiously not.'[11]

The Arms to Iraq affair, as it became known, revolved around four government departments: Trade and Industry, Defence, the Foreign and Commonwealth Office and the Board of Customs and Excise. Their ambitions were not necessarily the same. At the DTI, where the businessman Lord (David) Young succeeded Paul Channon as Secretary of State in 1987, the task overseas was to maximise British exports, but Defence, headed by George Younger, was concerned about arms sales to countries that might use them against British forces or their allies. The Foreign Office, meanwhile, under Sir Geoffrey Howe, had the broad diplomatic picture to consider. Customs and Excise policed the licences.

When Iran and Iraq were at war, Britain's attitude was simple: no arms sales of a 'lethal' nature should be made to either side. Iran had, in the days of the Shah, been a considerable customer of Britain, but since the Islamic revolution of 1979, and in particular the fourteen-month siege of the US Embassy in Tehran, Western attitudes had changed. Meanwhile, Iraq, once under Soviet influence, but now ruled by Saddam Hussein, was seen as a stabilising force. With increasing oil revenues it was a ready customer for British exports, particularly arms. The Conservative government of Margaret Thatcher did not wish Britain to lose out to other nations.

In 1985 the FCO had drawn up a specific set of guidelines to cover Iran and Iraq. Following some minor amendments these received the blessing of Margaret Thatcher. The key clauses turned out to be (iii): 'we should not in future approve orders for any defence equipment which, in our view, would significantly enhance the capability of either side to prolong or exacerbate the conflict', and (iv): that additionally Britain 'should continue to scrutinise rigorously all applications for export licences for the supply of defence equipment to Iran and Iraq'. By the time Alan reached the Department of Trade in January 1986, the guidelines to consider export licence applications (ELAs) had generated a Whitehall bureaucracy. In the Scott Inquiry further acronyms were revealed, among them the Ministry of Defence Working Group (MODWG) and an inter-departmental committee for licensing exports (IDC).

If Alan had had his way he would have cut a swathe through the system which involved three Ministers of State, officials in Trade, FCO and Defence, and, in the event of a failure to reach agreement, the relevant departmental Secretaries of State. As a last resort it was possible to appeal to the Cabinet. Alan maintained, with good reason, that the bureaucracy made it all the more difficult for British exporters to gain approval for orders. Invited by the Scott Inquiry to supply written evidence, he was unsparing over the guidelines: 'The closer you approach the more does their similarity to the Cheshire Cat become apparent. They were an ideal Whitehall formula: imprecise, open to argument in almost every instance, guaranteed to generate debate, if not dispute, between different depart-ments (thus generating much paper, sub-committees and general bur-eaucratic self-justification). They were high-sounding, combining, it seemed, both moral and practical considerations, and yet imprecise enough to allow real policy considerations an override in exceptional cir-cumstances.' Those final words would prove of the greatest significance.

Alan was also closely involved in a project in the summer of 1989 to sell kits of British Aerospace unarmed Hawk trainer aircraft for assembly in Iraq. Professional advisers in the MODWG maintained that the Hawk would not significantly enhance Iraq's military capability and did not constitute the supply of 'lethal' equipment. Alan, representing the Depart-ment of Trade view, agreed. Here was a major export deal for Britain, with the additional merit that 'the project was a long-term one' (22 June).

William Waldegrave at the Foreign Office did not have to represent the salesman's view, but nevertheless wrote a realistic assessment for the Foreign Secretary, Sir Geoffrey Howe, of what the decision was really about. 'It is a horrible situation. Iraq's regime is one of the most vicious in the world. They are aggressive; use torture and repression; have used chemical weapons widely against Iran and the Kurds; and their diplomats have behaved intolerably in the UK.' Waldegrave then got to the nub of the arms sales conundrum. 'Are we strong enough as a trading nation to spurn their market on the grounds of morality? If we were, we should. On balance, I judge that we are not, but we should recognise that our decision to sell Hawk will do us damage in the UK with serious and honest commentators.' Not surprisingly, Sir Geoffrey decided that this hot potato should be raised at Cabinet level, which practically meant the Cabinet's Overseas and Defence Committee (20 June). Separately Waldegrave told Lord Trefgarne[12] that the argument that the Hawk sale would not break government guidelines 'would carry little weight in the media' (26 June). Scott later commented that approval 'hinged, therefore, on political factors'.

With what Alan called 'the very favourite date in a Parliamentarian's diary'[13] fast approaching – the long summer recess – the matter was propelled upwards and swiftly reached the Prime Minister. On 27 July 1989 and following advice from her private secretary, Charles Powell, it is clear from the papers published in the Scott Report just how uncomfortable Margaret Thatcher was at the idea of selling Hawks to Saddam Hussein. The Hawk order failed at the final fence.

Alan did not enjoy being thwarted, even by Margaret Thatcher. A fellow Tory MP, Jeremy Hanley, witnessed a practical manifestation of Alan's feelings. Hanley, who in a future John Major government would be Armed Forces Minister at Defence, recalled the scene. In an otherwise empty Commons Tea Room (one of his favourite Westminster locations), Alan bought six rock cakes (insisting to the waitress that they all should go on a single plate) and then proceeded to release his frustration by throwing them one by one with great force against the wall.[14]

The firm of Matrix Churchill probably first entered Alan's radar in November 1987, from a MI6 report, which as a Minister he would have seen. This referred to British machine tool companies (Matrix Churchill included) selling equipment to armament factories in Iraq.[15] Its managing director, Paul Henderson, was one of a deputation which visited the DTI and saw the Minister for Trade with his officials on 20 January 1988. He and other members of the Machine Tool Technologies Association (MTTA) were concerned at how their businesses were suffering either from licences being frozen (following an Intelligence report about Iraqi arms production) or from increasingly interminable delays when the granting of licences was being considered. Alan was bullish at the meeting, as Henderson related in his account of the Matrix Churchill affair:[16] 'We walked into the street thinking, what's the problem? Clark was going to clear the licences. We should stress the peaceful aspects of our business on future applications and we could go on selling to Iraq. Not only would the current orders be filled, but we would also be able to supply orders for the future.' Such optimism proved short-lived. As Henderson told the court during the Matrix Churchill trial, it then took the best part of two years for one group of licences to be approved. To do so required a meeting of the three Ministers of State.

Matrix Churchill and its managing director had an interesting back-ground. The company had originally been part of the TI Group, an engineering concern once known as Tube Investments. Only four months before, in October 1987, the company had been sold. The buyers were Iraqis. Henderson was not alone in wondering if they were purchasing the company not merely for its manufacturing expertise, but to milk it for its technological know-how which would be exported back to Iraq. Henderson himself had, like many other businessmen who travelled over-seas, for close on twenty years also been providing information to MI6 gleaned from his journeying within the Eastern bloc and Middle East. It became clear during the Matrix Churchill trial that British Intelligence knew the dual nature of some of the company's products, there being more to a lathe than its general engineering capability. (Henderson's knowledge of Saddam Hussein's military manufacturing muscle and its whereabouts would prove extraordinarily valuable to the US and UK Armed Forces in the first Gulf War.)

The first substantial public exposure of the Arms to Iraq saga came on 2 December 1990. *The Sunday Times* ran a front-page story about Alan Clark's meeting, as Minister for Trade, with the MTTA in January 1988 and the advice he had given about licence applications that stressed the 'general engineering' aspect of the exports. With Iraq now the enemy, having invaded Kuwait four months before, it was no wonder that the 'exclusive' appeared on the newspaper's front page; its weapons in the forthcoming Gulf War would, no doubt, include those made with British machine tools. The Editor of the *Sunday Times*, Andrew Neil, wrote in his memoirs that Alan first denied the story, and 'then changed his tune and admitted it was true'.[17] Publication hit Downing Street at a particularly awkward moment. John Major had been Prime Minister for less than a week.

Alan was in Oman the previous week at a conference of the *Cercle*, an Atlantist Society of right-wing dignitaries. While there he learnt that the new Prime Minister was reshuffling the government, but Defence would be unchanged. He recognised that with Thatcher's passing 'my greatly reduced (abbreviated indeed) access to No. 10 also threatens greatly to reduce the quality of life. The only mild consolation from the government changes is Richard [Ryder]'s placing as Chief Whip.'[18] The conference also allowed him to see his son Andrew, now a Major in the Life Guards, who was serving as Second in Command of the Armoured Force of the Sultan of Oman. His briefing was valuable and prescient, as Alan observed: 'Oman is a long way from Iraq, and their traditional apprehension is of Iranian muscle, their principal irritant is South Yemen. But the men, many of them, think privately of Saddam as a hero, who is leading the West a dance.'[19] With the first Gulf War about to happen, Alan now wrote as a father: 'I suppose I am relieved to be en poste in the war and to protect Tip.'

Although Alan's report of the visit occupies several pages of his published *Diaries*, he chose to skip his account of what happened on his return the evening before *The Sunday Times* piece appeared. 'Lovely to be home,' he wrote. 'Very late the phone rang and it was the Chief Whip – now dear Richard – he said that *The Sunday Times* shall tomorrow run "very objectionable [story]". "But don't worry!" he repeated, "Don't worry." What a charming thing to do. No other Chief would have done that.' On the Sunday, with the Insight story now public, he was surprised that the only call came in the evening from his journalist friend Bruce Anderson, who said, 'could be bad. I'll do what I can in the *Standard* if you need me.'

Of the two versions of what happened the next day, one emerged from the Scott Inquiry, the second – Alan's – in this hitherto unpublished account from his diary.[20] Leaving Saltwood before dawn, he wrote, he took the early train to London and, 'after some resistance got myself inserted on the 9.45 meeting at No.10 to discuss the topic'.[21] He was kept waiting for an hour outside the Cabinet room – 'What were they talking about?'

Alan recorded that he finally saw the PM 'in the little blue study on the first floor where I last recall discussing aid to Poland with Margaret Thatcher and – curiously – John Major when he was Financial Secretary. I got a kick out of calling him "Prime Minister", but got a faint feeling that all was not well behind the scenes. He wanted the Trade Minister, Tim Sainsbury, to make an immediate statement.'[22] On Alan's return to the MoD 'Archie [Hamilton] appeared, supposedly delighted, told me the Whips' office, PM, Cabinet office were all discussing how I could be "dropped" gracefully'. Alan was having none of that. '"The PM's perfectly all right," I said. "I am entirely unrepentant." I was, just, but uneasy nevertheless.'

At lunchtime Alan went over to Trade and Industry to get the form of the statement. 'Usual DTI panic scene – over a dozen officials round a table in my old office. Statement far too tame, shifted by implication blame onto me. Peter Watkins [Alan's private secretary] was helpful in sorting out rogue phrases. Tim Sainsbury was of course feline and sibilant in his pleasure in defending (v half heartedly) a situation for which he was not responsible and a colleague for whom he has no liking.'

The events of the day had a totally unexpected denouement when he reached the Commons. His driver handed him a note from his office, saying a letter from the Prime Minister awaited him. His mind raced, was he for the chop after all? In fact quite the reverse. The PM '"had it in mind" to recommend Alan as a Privy Counsellor and would he let his office know immediately!!'. Nevertheless, and 'half wondering if it might be withdrawn – a mistake, following events etc' – Alan rang the extension at Number Ten – 'sweet and charming voice said "congratulations". In spite of all adversity I had booked a sensible advance. Nice, too, to have got it from John, and not from Mrs T when it would have been depicted as favouritism.'[23]

A second version of that day emerged the best part of four years later, thanks to the disclosure of documents brought about by the Scott Inquiry. According to these Alan's meeting with John Major was attended by Sir Robin Butler, Charles Powell's successor as Cabinet Secretary, who drafted a minute. The first version stated that Alan told the Prime Minister that 'he was in effect advising them [the MTTA companies] to downgrade the specification of the machine tools ... *so that they could not be used for military purposes*'. Alan, however, disagreed with this report. His version said: '*so that they would not be seen as suitable for military purposes*'. As one subsequent account observed, 'It was a subtle but important difference, more consistent both with the impression the MTTA was given and with Clark's subsequent testimony at the trial.'[24]

If the new Prime Minister was sufficiently satisfied by Alan's explanation not to sack him as Minister of Defence Procurement, senior officials did not let the matter rest. The Cabinet Office organised a meeting that same day to look at the effects of the *Sunday Times* disclosures. A note was kept by Sir Robin Butler's secretary, Sonia Phippard. This led to questions at the Inquiry, and Sir Robin was recorded as observing of Alan's explanation that it was 'ambiguous'. In a secondary and substantial follow-on from this meeting, as Scott observed, officials had 'serious misgivings' about Customs and Excise's prosecution, not that they passed on their concerns. Indeed Alan Moses was extremely critical of the fact that the draft and the amendment ('significant') were not brought to his attention well before October 1992 (the trial date) – 'it should not have been left midst the vast array of documents in the hope that I might discover it and read it with sufficient care so as to note the change'.[25]

Following the *Sunday Times* article, and with the Matrix Churchill directors charged two months later, it did not take long for politicians and journalists to begin speculating as to what the trial might disclose. It was not, however, until a little under the month before the Prime Minister announced that the general election would be held on 9 April 1992 that Alan was first mentioned publicly as the 'fall guy' among Conservatives who needed someone to receive the blame.[26]

With the 1992 election over and the Conservatives returned to power, Whitehall's widely suspected complicity in embargo-breaking sales to Iraq became increasingly common gossip. Although ostensibly about his forthcoming *Diaries*, an interview Alan gave to Graham Turner in *The Sunday Telegraph* in August fanned the flames.[27] Turner asked, Was it true that he had tipped off British machine tool manufacturers as to how they should frame their export applications to get round guidelines for trade with Iraq? 'Yes,' replied Alan, 'and I did it for two reasons. First, I was Minister for Trade, so it was my job to maximise exports despite guidelines which I regarded as tiresome and intrusive. Second, Iran was the enemy – it still is – and it was clear to me that the interests of the West were well served by Iran and Iraq fighting each other, the longer the better.'

The Scott Report fills in what happened next. Customs and Excise were gearing up for the trial of the Matrix Churchill directors. Counsel for the prosecution, Alan Moses, was on holiday when the article appeared. His number two, Gibson Grenfell, said that the article might have 'a considerable effect' on the prosecution case. 'Whilst it did not attack the base of our case which involves deliberate deception, the inconsistency of Clark's statements to us and those attributed to him in the article do reduce his credibility as a witness.' Douglas Tweddle from Customs minuted Sir Brian Unwin (his chairman) as saying that if Alan confirmed the article 'we will not be able to proceed with the prosecution against Matrix Churchill'. Grenfell told the Inquiry that if Alan confirmed the accuracy of the article he would have advised the prosecution to be discontinued.

Moses on his return asked for inquiries to be made of Alan. They were unsatisfactory. Alan was at Eriboll and when reached by a Customs official, Cedric Andrew, he declined to discuss the matter in a face-to-face meeting, as Moses had asked. In a witness statement Andrew reported that Alan had suggested that Customs subpoena the journalist. He also said it would have been quite improper to help people fill in licence application forms. Anyway senior officials of the DTI were present when he met representatives of the MTTA – the only time he met them – and the official minutes of the meeting were accurate. Alan suggested that perhaps the journalist had transposed what was said during the interview, adding 'it is balls that I would have said that'.

Moses decided that despite all this the prosecution could properly proceed without any further interview with Mr Clark.

Curiously for someone who used his diary as a confessional, Alan's mentions of the Matrix Churchill trial and the Scott Inquiry are few and modest in length. Perhaps the reason for this was, as he commented in a statement to Scott a year later, that he 'regarded [his] role in the affair as only marginal, because the central point at issue was whether there had been a substantial deception by the defendants in relation to the capability of the tools.'[28] Jane, however, recalls his apprehension before both the trial in November 1992 and then again the following month when preparations were under way for the Inquiry.

Being no longer a member of the government or even an MP contributed to his certainty that he would be blamed. Yet when the time came to appear before Scott, as Richard Norton-Taylor, *The Guardian*'s specialist on security matters, remembers, Alan never seemed less than confident.[29] In March 1994 he complained of Tristan Garel-Jones 'quite openly trying to shift the Scott blame on me' as the 'direction of the Inquiry's finding starts to emerge', even though Scott was still hearing evidence and would not publish his findings for another two years. In March 1995 he wrote that it was useful to have heard from Max Hastings (Editor at the time of *The Daily Telegraph*) that on Scott, 'the Prime Minister was trying to persuade people to accept me as a "burnt offering"'.[30] Early in 1996, with the official publication of the Scott Report imminent, he noted, 'Various clouds on the horizon. Scott: ought to be all right and am steadfastly refusing to comment.' But what if Scott criticised him? 'Occasionally wake in the night and think of the ultimate nightmare – Henderson (and all the other Matrix C directors) suing me.'[31]

On 15 February, the day of the release of the Scott Inquiry Report, hysteria reigned at Westminster and outside when the government refused to allow the Opposition more than the briefest sights before it was published. That Scott did not offer a chapter of conclusions helps explain why every politician involved was able to take comfort from the findings, however selectively. No single individual was considered culpable. As for Alan, Scott was clear. 'I do not subscribe to the simplistic view that all that went wrong was that Mr Alan Clark gave evidence which was in certain respects inconsistent with his witness statement and was fatal to the prosecution. That was undoubtedly so, and was the immediate cause of the collapse of the prosecution, but there were also, in my opinion, a number of other factors which, independently of Mr Clark's evidence, undermined the prosecution.'

Alan was satisfied. He felt he had been exonerated and flew off the following morning to Mexico to stay with James Goldsmith on his estate at Cuixmala. A few days later, though, his conscience bit him and he wrote 'are papers bothering Jane?'[32] He returned to hear amazement among many Conservatives that he had 'got away with it'. His last diary entry on the matter was written on 13 March. He had been to the Temple to hear Scott give a talk (one of a series to lawyers and at universities). 'He is a splendid man – cool, clear-headed and witty. He was interesting – it was by and for lawyers – on case law. Lambasted discreetly Tristan Garel-Jones and the whole deception of the "response" document in the House of Commons Library.'

For Alan Clark, Matrix Churchill and Lord Justice Scott's Report changed his life. Although refusing to believe it at the time, it is clear that it wrecked any chance he had of a life peerage. Some political friendships ended, and even with the balm of time several former parliamentary colleagues chose not to discuss the matter when this book was under way. Alan kept a memento of the Inquiry: the complete five-volume set of the Scott Report signed by the full Inquiry team. He also enjoyed being portrayed on stage at London's Tricycle Theatre, by Jeremy Child in *Half the Picture*, a dramatisation of the Inquiry.[33] On his selection as Conservative candidate for Kensington and Chelsea little more than a year later Matrix Churchill and Scott were barely mentioned.

A few days after Alan's death in 1999 Hugo Young wrote a column in *The Guardian*. They had often talked, Hugo benefiting from Alan's informed comments, particularly on the downfall of Margaret Thatcher and the first Gulf War when he was a Defence Minister. 'The Clark philosophy was, in reality, the British philosophy, uncluttered by paper rules and regulations which try to make the official version seem more respectable. The premise is that this is a rough old world, in which Britain must defend the jewel among her exports. The presumption is that every arms sale is good, unless proved otherwise. The pre-condition is a high degree of secrecy, in the name of commercial and diplomatic confidence. The result is Britain's chronic entanglement, from time to time highly visible, with some of the most corrupt and cruel regimes in the world.'

Young summed up: 'Alan Clark's most enduring contribution to politics, apart from his ripping diaries, was as the only serving minister to express the truth about the arms industry.'[34]

THIRTY

The Making of the Diaries

When in spring 1992 Alan retired so suddenly from the House of Commons it did not take him long to realise that among his assets was one that combined three passions – politics, writing and making money. Alan had been keeping a diary since his twenty-seventh birthday in 1955. Rather than memoirs, why not follow the example of his parliamentary forebears, 'Chips' Channon and Harold Nicolson, and capitalise on the decade when he was a junior Minister in two of Margaret Thatcher's governments?

Michael Sissons, his agent of long-standing, had first raised the possibility six years before. A profile of Alan in *The Spectator*[1] on his appointment as Minister of State at the Department of Trade and Industry had mentioned in passing his diary-keeping. Sissons was quick off the mark and prescient: 'I read with interest that you keep a diary which I have no doubt will be the publishing sensation of the 1990s. In due course you must let me sell it for you for a fortune.'[2]

Alan had brought little business to Sissons since the highly praised and commercially successful *Barbarossa* (1965). But Alan was never shy of whetting his agent's appetite. As early as June 1973, he had written to Sissons: 'All publishers have got one great prize to look forward to and that is my witty, revealing, salacious and enlightening memoirs.' These would draw on his experience identifying a seat and being selected as a Conservative candidate. 'I already know enough about the internal workings of the Conservative machine to write a really appalling book.' And he was still eight months away from becoming a Member of Parliament!

A passing reference in the press in 1991 to Alan and his diary-keeping when he was still an MP and Defence Minister led the publishing house of Hodder & Stoughton to take an interest. The firm, where I was then publishing director, had previously had great success with *The Fringes of Power*, the diaries of John ('Jock') Colville, secretary to Winston Churchill during the Second World War and again in the early 1950s. Alan Clark's diaries, if they also offered an insider's view of the Thatcher years, could at the very least prove to be another Channon or Nicolson, or even, from a different direction altogether, another James Lees-Milne.[3] Michael Sissons, responding to my inquiry, said 'there's no way he could publish it while he is still a government Minister. I'll keep your letter on file.'

When Alan announced shortly before the April 1992 general election that he would not be standing again, the moment seemed opportune. Alan brought to Sissons' office some volumes of the diaries of the Thatcher years, saying that no-one had read them, not even Jane. Sissons had them for the weekend and as he dipped in and out his enthusiasm soared. Politics, yes, but so much more, all superbly written. Alan knew how to raise interest and in his lengthy interview with Graham Turner in *The Sunday Telegraph*[4] offered some tantalising glimpses of the contents. A full-page trailer followed in the *Daily Mail*.[5] Within days Sissons' in-tray bulged with letters and faxes from publishers. No well-known imprint was missing: Faber, Hutchinson, Cape, Michael Joseph, Macmillan, HarperCollins, Hodder (again), and Weidenfeld & Nicolson (where I had recently moved).

Alan now produced for Sissons one hundred pages of extracts from what he tentatively called 'Memoirs of a Junior Minister'. Sissons was euphoric. 'They're all I hoped for, and more, and I look forward enormously to having a lot of fun with you on this project. I have one suggestion. I'm sure it would enhance the value and make my job easier, if I could have one important political matter dealt with in extenso. What have you on the events of November 1990 for example?' He enclosed for Alan's approval the confidentiality letter – 'here's what we'll ask the punters to sign in our boardroom (with a warden in attendance)'.[6] Alan obliged with a page on the events leading to Margaret Thatcher's downfall as Prime Minister.

Sissons first asked potential bidders for the newspaper serial rights to come to his offices, then by the Thames at Chelsea Harbour, where editors would be given the opportunity to read for an hour – no note-taking and with Sissons' assistant, Fiona Batty, as 'warden'. The two *Mails, The Sunday Times* and *The Sunday Telegraph* each took part. The *Mail on Sunday*'s Editor, Jonathan Holborow, was top bidder, with £200,000.

Meanwhile the publishers had been visiting Chelsea Harbour to read by the same rulebook. Each publisher was given an hour. I recall speed-reading the hundred pages and then going back and reading particular passages again. When the hour was up I left Sissons' office and sat down on a bench overlooking the moored yachts and wrote down as much as I could remember. Back at our offices, Anthony Cheetham, chief executive of the newly formed Orion Group, which had acquired Weidenfeld & Nicolson, asked me to justify our taking an interest.

'Is it well-written?' – 'Yes.'
'Is it revealing about Thatcher's government?' – 'Yes.'
'Has it lots of gossip?' – 'Yes.'

And with that he authorised me to offer up to £150,000. This was before publishers demanded putative profit and loss sheets, with sales departments sounding out the book trade prior to any offer being made. 'And come back to me', said Cheetham, 'if that isn't enough.'

Alan was not then a familiar name outside Westminster. At the Weidenfeld editorial meeting next day, half those present said they had never heard of him. Nevertheless everyone was asked to put down on paper what they thought the first printing should be. Only Cheetham and I went to five figures. Our guts told us that here was something remarkable, politically valuable and commercially a potential goldmine.

Many of the documents relating to the progress of the auction for the book have survived. Faber, whose managing director, Matthew Evans, was hugely enthusiastic, made the running with an opening offer of £80,000. This went up to £130,000, which was topped by Weidenfeld & Nicolson (£140,000, then £150,000) and Hutchinson (£150,000). By then other publishers had faded away. At this point Sissons asked for marketing plans from the surviving trio and promised a viva with Alan. The Weidenfeld marketing plan ran under the heading 'In the great tradition of diarists from Pepys to Channon'; Hutchinson quoted Graham Turner's 'as different from the standard Tory Minister's memoirs as *Tropic of Cancer* is from *Pride and Prejudice*'.

In his diary for that date Alan makes only passing mention of the auction. '2 October 1992: Next week, agreeably, all those hardback contenders of 150k are going to make "presentations" to ingratiate themselves.' For the viva I took along Orion's new marketing colleague Caroline Michel, who had that week joined the fledgling group. It was one of the ironies of publishing that her husband was Matthew Evans, chairman of Faber. Caroline put job before marriage, and, knowing Clark's propensities, she donned a mini-skirt with the emphasis on 'mini'. We were the last in. It was not the shortness of her skirt that won us the book. Nor was it because he and I discovered a shared admiration for another diarist, James Lees-Milne. Our winning move was to take along a book 'dummy' produced by Weidenfeld's long-standing production director, Richard Hussey; this used creamy paper of a thickness that Alan found sensual to the touch.

'You mean,' he said, looking me straight in eye, 'you will print my book on this paper?' I nodded. Several days of impatient waiting went by before Sissons telephoned on 9 October 1992 to say that Alan had decided to go with us.

The contract took some organising, not least because Alan became concerned about libel and asked about insurance. Publication was set for May 1993, being the first anniversary of the election. This put Alan under enormous pressure as, apart from the hundred pages transcribed for the auction, the remainder of what would become *Diaries* (as it was quickly agreed to call it) was still handwritten in a succession of A4 volumes. Alan kept them in an office off his father's former study in the Garden House at Saltwood. He had marked likely passages for the published volume with a star. But transcribing them proved tough. Even Alan could not always read his own writing, made more difficult still by his decision many years before to write in a particularly crabbed and often minuscule hand, in case the current volume which he carried around with him at Westminster fell into the wrong hands.

He also had other things on his mind. The Matrix Churchill trial was progressing at the Old Bailey. When in early November his evidence stopped the case and the three accused were found not guilty, everyone was after him for an interview. But for only the second time in his writing career Alan kept to the delivery date in the contract – mid-February 1993. With the full print run of the *Diaries* required by early May, it was all systems go on editing, the design for the book, the legal reading by Alan Williams.[7]

In the short preface Alan noted: 'They are not "Memoirs". They are not written to throw light on events in the past, or retrospectively to justify the actions of the author. They are *exactly* as they were recorded on the day; sometimes even the hour, or the minute, of a particular episode or sensation.'

He kept expurgation to a minimum. At the time of editing he justified calling political colleagues such as Kenneth Clarke a 'pudgy puffball', Roy Hattersley 'just a slob' and his dismissal of Douglas Hurd with the line 'Might as well have a corncob up his arse' by adding the comment: 'My friends know me, and know that I love them, and that my private explosions of irritation or bad temper are of no import.'

Comparing the originals with the published version brings some surprises. In the preface he maintains 'Much of course has been excised. But of what remains nothing has been altered since the day it was written.' He adds: 'Is this conceit – or laziness? A bit of both, I suppose. But I found that when I attempted to alter, or moderate, or explain, the structure and rhythm of the whole entry would be disturbed.' This, however, is not strictly true. Alan would have made a splendid editor, he knew where improvements might be made – and made them! – and he also filled in the gaps in entries that for whatever reason remained incomplete at the time. But the spirit of an entry is invariably maintained.

At the eleventh hour before going to press the Cabinet Office pointed out that as much of the *Diaries* concerned his time as a Minister, they must vet the contents. Alan resisted, but then gave in, being sympathetic only to the point that names of the spouses of diplomats he often derided should be deleted and their identities blurred, because they were in no position, unlike MPs, say, to answer back.

A major decision during the editing concerned the women Alan called 'the coven'. In the *Diaries*, after taking advice, their first names only were given, and a footnote was added: 'three girls related to each other by blood whom AC had known for many years'. Alan expected some public response from them, but how and when it eventually came was a surprise. At the same time Alan agreed that Michael Cockerell, who was gaining a considerable reputation at the BBC as a maker of original and distinctive political documentaries, should use the *Diaries* as the basis for a television film. It was called, at Cockerell's suggestion, *Love Tory.*

The publication of Alan's *Diaries*, orchestrated for Weidenfeld & Nicolson by Caroline Michel ('definitely attractive')[8] and the publicity director Diane Rowley ('*very* sexy, legs and figure'),[9] was rapidly being viewed by the media as an event. The *Mail on Sunday*'s serial purchase the previous autumn was seen as a snip. But when the first of four extracts appeared in advance of publication disappointment was huge and widespread. Nothing wrong with their choice of opener on what they called 'The mugging of Maggie'. On six tabloid pages the *Mail on Sunday* chose to reduce Alan's sometimes languid cadences into what, presumably, they thought their readers wanted and would understand. But the overall result was catastrophic. They no longer sounded like Alan Clark. That first Sunday's extracts led Alan's former parliamentary colleague, the historian Robert Rhodes James, who knew about diaries having edited 'Chips' Channon's, to complain of Alan's reporting of Mrs Thatcher's downfall that 'alleged lengthy conversations with colleagues ... read like Jeffrey Archer on an off day'. He concluded: 'And on this first evidence, he is no Chips Channon.'[10]

In the meantime all was not lost. Peter Stothard, only recently appointed

Editor of *The Times*, had been allowed early sight of the *Diaries* under strict confidentiality terms; he quickly realised the quality of the material – as written by Alan, not as serialised by the *Mail on Sunday* – and acquired second serial rights for £3,000 on 1 June. The contract specified no more than 1,500 words 'and subject to your not running those parts of the books that deal with "girls"'. When these began to appear, billed as 'unexpurgated instalments' with Alan's sentence structure retained, the early enthusiasm was renewed.

The *Diaries* were eventually published on 30 May. Day after day the press kept raiding them for ever further anecdotes and gossip. Alan was widely interviewed, he and Jane were photographed. *The Times* Diary summed up the metamorphosis. In the autumn of 1992 Alan may have appeared to be 'yesterday's man. Since then he has been a central player in the Matrix Churchill drama, endorsed Charmley's biography which poured scorn on Churchill's wartime role, and has been outspoken about Maastricht. Then came the Newbury by-election and Clark's name was widely mentioned.'[11]

The *Diaries* sealed his celebrity, helped by almost entirely ecstatic reviews. From the political journalists: 'Absorbing . . . staggeringly, recklessly candid . . . tells the truth as he saw it without fear or favour' (Anthony Howard, *The Sunday Times*). 'These diaries combine the naïve candour of an Adrian Mole with the imagination of a devil and an angel' (Matthew Parris, *The Sunday Telegraph*). 'Compulsive reading' (Simon Hoggart, *The Observer*). 'The most brilliant political book I have read in years' (Simon Heffer, *Evening Standard*). 'In a hundred years' time it will be opened as Pepys is for ten minutes at a go, by anyone seeking the sheer pleasure of which it is a deep well' (Edward Pearce, *London Review of Books*). From politicians: 'Malicious, lecherous and self-pitying' (Julian Critchley, *The Daily Telegraph*). 'Unputdownable' (David Mellor, *Mail on Sunday*). From a most senior civil servant: 'Diaries are the raw material of history and these are elegantly and pungently written' (Charles Powell, *The Times*). Powell, though, confessed one disappointment. 'As for the rude bits, his scoring rate is well below that of Samuel Pepys.' The one that delighted Alan most came from Robert Harris (*The Independent on Sunday*). It was not simply his praise – 'the most compelling account of modern politics I have ever read' – but that Harris was the first to recognise that the endpapers of the hardback, which reproduced manuscript pages from the diaries, gave the reader some tantalising extra material not actually in the printed text.[12]

To Alan's relief, Robert Rhodes James, whose views he respected, now recanted, opening his review in *The Guardian,* 'One of my father's dictums was that "first impressions are always wrong", but I know of no case in my life when it has been proved so spectacularly right as in the case of Alan Clark.' He was not thinking only of the *Diaries,* but these, he now wrote, 'are infinitely more interesting and better written than the serialisations would imply'. He had some criticisms on historical accuracy – 'Historians are rightly wary about diaries', particularly where they rely on hearsay. However, he judged Alan's account of the 1990 leadership crisis 'quite brilliant, but obviously written only from his particular vantage point'. He thought 'the sheer fun of politics shines through ... His deep love of all animals is one of his most endearing traits, and results in some of the most moving and beautifully written heartfelt passages in his diaries ... Where he is so strong is on capturing atmosphere, and none better than in the extraordinary November 1990 crisis.'[13]

Weidenfeld's first printing of 20,000 copies – on the creamy paper that had so attracted Alan at the viva the previous autumn – was rapidly sold out and the firm raced through a series of reprints. But the creamy paper was a special making and supplies were swiftly exhausted. Weidenfeld's production team replaced it with something similar, but not as sensual to the touch. Alan immediately noticed. 'Hoy!' he called up. 'What's this?' He remained convinced that the firm had simply gone for a cheaper alternative.

Love (S)Tory

Television played its part in the promotion of the *Diaries*. Not that the BBC's Michael Cockerell saw it as promotion. On hearing that Alan was going to publish, Cockerell approached him and recalls Alan's enthusiastic response, 'it would be an honour'. His visit to Saltwood in November 1992 to discuss how it might be done coincided with Alan's evidence at the Matrix Churchill trial. 'It seems as if there were hundreds of journalists all outside Saltwood. I was the only one allowed to walk in. They all thought I had a scoop.'

He was introduced to Jane and to their dogs, Hannah and Lëhni, and soon felt they were getting on well. Alan, though, had a problem over giving Cockerell the manuscript, as he explained. His publisher, Ion Trewin, was 'absolutely protective', insisting that he must not show it to anyone. Alan was, however, not going to lose the chance of fifty minutes of prime-time television. 'What I propose to do is not to tell him, make photocopies and give them to you.' Cockerell responded that he thought his publisher would be pleased when he heard about the film. 'No, no! He is very protective, doesn't want anything to get out.' In fact, in practice, the Saltwood photocopier was not up to dealing with several hundred pages.

Making the film with Alan was not easy. When the BBC crew, under producer David Pearson, arrived early in March 1993 for the first day of shooting at Saltwood of Alan there was no sign. They found Jane. Cockerell recalls the conversation, which Jane confirms.

'Is Alan around?'

'Oh, no, he's not here. He's up in London, *seeing his publisher*', saying it in a voice like that, meaning nod, nod, wink, wink we know what that means. 'He may be back at lunchtime.'

'But, but, we've arranged to do the first of the interviews today.'

'Oh well, he said he may be back at lunchtime.'

'Do you know where he is?'

'No, I don't.'

'Can we ring him at Albany?'

'Well, you can try.'

We then said to her, 'Can we film you?'

'Really, I don't want to be in this, this is Al's show.'

'Can we film anything that you might be doing?'

'I suppose I couldn't stop you.'

It was a sunny day. Cockerell settled back to wait. After about an hour Jane emerged from the castle with a cocoa tin full of grain to feed the peacocks. They filmed her sprinkling the grain on the lawn of the Bailey. Jane saw the cameras and said, 'Peacocks are upper-class vandals. Al's got all these cars which he keeps highly polished, sometimes the peacocks see the reflection of their tail feathers and fly at a car so all our cars get covered with blood and feathers. If anyone asks us, I just make a joke about it and say we have driven through a charity cycle race.' Cockerell remembered thinking, 'Black sense of humour'.

He then suggested, unsubtly as he now admits, that Alan had certain peacock-like qualities himself. 'And that's when it all came out; she sat on the edge of the well and looked into the middle distance and then talked. She had been married for more than thirty years. I don't think anyone had ever asked her what she thought about Al, no one had ever asked her that question. All the best stuff in the film was her talking about Al.' What they were getting from Jane was dynamite. 'Al's always saying I should be more French. French men have mistresses and girlfriends, why can't you be like that? But I'm not French. I did throw an axe at him once. A chopper. When I threw it, when I picked it up to throw it I meant to hit him, but when it left my hand I was quite glad my aim was very bad. He's a bit of a S H one T, but I do love him.'

Alan eventually appeared, 'swaggering out with that funny walk of his', as Cockerell recalled. 'I hear you've been talking to Jane.' Cockerell nodded. 'Good, good, I'm glad she's been talking to you. Now, what do you want me to do?' 'An extraordinary moment. He had no idea what Jane had been saying.'

Cockerell had a sufficient budget to allow him to follow Alan, to Scotland, to Switzerland, wherever was necessary. Early filming at Eriboll in the new year had been trouble-free, giving Cockerell five minutes of valuable footage. He recalls particularly 'an amazing bit, about this being "where he'd like to have his heart attack"'. He also had another memorable moment talking of how the solitude and magic of the Highlands were a reminder that 'we're just grains of sand'. Cockerell found him good and relaxed. 'We had fun at Eriboll, that was the start of it. So then later the problems when we were going to do the formal interviews came as rather a shock.'

On several occasions Alan's attitude was high-handed, to say the least. Cockerell wished to show his love of cars and decided to film at Good-wood. The car was his powder-blue C-Type Jaguar. Alan wore his goggles and did two laps: 'That's it. Fucking boring. I'm stopping now.' Cockerell said he needed to go round at least five times for different shots. 'We've only got the one close-up. That's all we've got.' 'No, taken too long. That's it.' 'Pity,' remembers Cockerell. 'We had planned a nice sequence around the racecourse.'

Next stop was to be Zermatt to film him skiing. When they arrived he said, 'I've changed my mind.' Cockerell was understandably appalled and asked him why. 'Unless you're a really good skier you look terrible. Any amateur looks terrible because people are used to seeing the professionals on the television. I am not going to show myself up.'

Cockerell was not going to give up that easily. 'Would you at least talk to Jane about it?'

'Yes, ok, I will talk to Jane about it.'

Cockerell rang up Jane. 'He's playing silly buggers. Won't do it. Talk him into it.'

She was understanding. 'Of course, you've gone over. I won't let him get away with it.'

That evening they all had dinner at a posh Zermatt hotel. Alan rec-ommended 'a wonderful Swiss wine which was really good, but it was £30–£40 a bottle. He would say "Waiter, waiter, more, more." He kept ordering it – on our bill!'

Next morning they met. Alan said, 'I'm off now.'

'Oh, we had hoped that we might be able to film you. Have you talked to Jane?'

'Oh yes.'

'What did you say?'

'No, no, I'm not going to change my mind.'

On the train back, Cockerell asked him, 'What did Jane say to you?'

'I didn't talk to her.'

'What!'

'It was easier to lie to you and say I'd talked to her.'

Cockerell had to abort at considerable expense. The BBC spent £4–5,000 for one interview on the mountain that in the end was not used. The only Swiss shot that made the final film appeared briefly behind the opening titles, where it said, 'A Film by Michael Cockerell'. As he says now, 'A long way to come for that.'

One of the characteristics of Cockerell's films is to show his subjects watching film of themselves and how they react. For *Love Tory* this was set up in Saltwood's Great Hall, against the backdrop of Kenneth Clark's library. Here was footage of K talking about his obsession with the passage of time – he was, he said, 'the original white rabbit of *Alice in Wonderland*. "Oh dear, oh dear, I shall be too late." Several of my lady friends have told me they never knew anyone who looked so often at his watch – not the right temperament for a fisherman, or a lady's man one would suppose.' Alan observed that this was his father 'absolutely at his best, relaxed and funny, a hint of much wisdom that is unsaid.' The reference to his lady friends in such 'an easy style' suggested it must have been done after Alan's mother died.

Cockerell's team had unearthed a cinema newsreel of Alan and Jane's wedding made by Movietone titled 'Kenneth Clark's son marries'. Neither had seen it before. Alan thought he looked 'an incredible prat'. Of Jane, he said, 'great waist ... beautiful girl'. She had 'hardly changed at all in her appearance, in her face'. And yet his had been 'corroded by misdeeds and self-indulgence over time'. The matter of the crowded honeymoon was raised, with Christina, one of Alan's girlfriends, turning up at Positano. Jane mused on this: 'Actually she was nice. I have to say she was the nicest one; the others have been pretty good rubbish since. Christina was lovely. We could have had a Buñuel situation you know, done away with him.' Was she tempted? 'I have been plenty since.' And Alan now? 'I still think he's super.' Jane then came out with a marital acronym: 'ABL, as he keeps saying – Al's bloody lucky.'

Love Tory was a revelation, screened in mid-June 1993, just as the *Diaries* were becoming general currency. Until that point Alan had been interviewed mostly about political matters; Jane not at all. Here he talked frankly about Margaret Thatcher – more so than in the *Diaries;* the Matrix Churchill case – an ongoing matter as the film was being made; and what he thought about fellow politicians. Cockerell also challenged him about women and whether he was ever concerned as a Minister that his affairs might become public. Alan was in justification mood. 'Not the slightest, I haven't done anything wrong.' Cockerell wouldn't let him off the hook, reminding Alan that many political affairs had become sexual scandals. 'No, I don't see anything scandalous in that. What is wrong with two human beings of the opposite sex feeling attracted to each other? I don't see how that could be scandalous.' When Cockerell went on to refer to Ministers who had had to resign as a result of their extra-marital liaisons, Alan shot back, 'They've just handled it badly. They've allowed it get into a ludicrous "ooh ahh, phew! look at this" kind of situation.'

After Margaret Thatcher's downfall in 1990, which had kept him in London, Alan returned to Saltwood to find that Jane had, as Cockerell put it, 'taught him a lesson'. She had left the castle, left him. Now two and a half years later Cockerell was filming in the Saltwood kitchen with Alan sitting at the head of the table and Jane with her back to the Aga. It is immediately obvious that Alan was not enjoying the exchange, whereas Jane usually smiled when she interspersed her comments.

'Yeah, she has been away occasionally; she left about a year ago, she walked out.' Before he can continue, Jane butts in: '– twice in thirty-five years; it was only for two days and it was incredibly boring'.

'That was bad ... I prepared the meals. It was a very ascetic bachelor existence.'

Jane laughs. 'I should have stayed away longer.'

'I always laid her place for every meal, in case she turned up, and sadly had to clear it away again.'

Cockerell now slides in a question to Alan: 'Why did Jane go away for two days?'

'She went away because she' – and before continuing Alan turns to Jane, 'I'm answering this, not you.' The camera cuts to Jane, who will not be cowed '– well, let's hear your version.'

'She thought I needed, um, to be, er, punished.' Jane starts to speak. Alan looks firmly at her. 'Objectionable behaviour covers it.' A momentary surprised, even peeved reaction crosses Jane's face, as Alan goes on, 'It was one of those things ... like all rows the great thing is to keep them from breaking out.'

Jane then adds another phrase that would be much quoted: 'All girl-friends are like bluebottles aren't they, but this one was a little harder to swat.'

His body language shows just how much he is hating every moment. He is squirming. But the camera is running. He can hardly storm out.

To complete this section of the film Cockerell included another exchange, filmed on a different occasion at Saltwood:

'How do you think she's put up with you all these years?'

Pause. 'It is easier if you know the person loves you, I suppose.'

Cockerell now cut to Jane, but filmed when she was feeding the peacocks. 'I think it is rather Greek, really. In fact his career was brought to an end by women; he would like that I think. Destroyed by women, as well. Mrs T didn't have the courage to give him the job [in the Cabinet]; all his affairs and things a nice little twist, a Greek twist really to it. Women have been the problem, you could say.'

With a complete film ready to broadcast, Cockerell invited Alan and Jane to a private showing. He reminded them that they had 'no rights whatsoever over it'. If the press, who would also be shown it in advance of transmission, rang, Cockerell advised, 'You can either say "No comment" or "I haven't seen it", or you can say what you want. Unless you wish to slag it off completely which is a risk we obviously take.'

Cockerell, producer David Pearson, the film editor and a woman from the BBC press office assembled early in June with Alan and Jane (Cockerell had particularly wished Jane to be present). The lights dimmed in the viewing theatre. *Love Tory* came on the screen (the idea for the title, with an 'S' before 'Tory' immediately slipping off the screen, was Cockerell's). Fifty minutes later the credits rolled against a shot of the sun setting behind the Saltwood towers, with Cole Porter's 'As Time Goes By' tinkling on the sound track. Finally the screen darkened and the lights went up. Cockerell will never forget what happened next.

'No-one said anything, and we all knew that it had to be Alan who said the first word so none of us were prepared to say anything, we wanted to know what he thought; and we sat there in silence for eight minutes, I know, I looked, surreptitiously looked; eight minutes is a fantastically long time. His first words were real bathos: "Have you got a pen and paper? So many thoughts are going through my head, I want to get them all down." Another two minutes as he was putting his thoughts down.' Cockerell remembers that Alan was 'totally astonished and gobsmacked by Jane's role. "She had never said this to me in thirty years. I never knew she thought that. I never realised . . . Like watching yourself naked on the screen for an hour. She was the hero, not me."' To his diary he wrote of 'Jane's attractive performance . . . relegating me to "best supporting actor"'. And Jane? Said Cockerell: 'She was rather glad she had had the opportunity of telling him what she thought. She had been trying to for a long time, but he wouldn't listen.'

Reaction in the media to *Love Tory* was huge, and quickly concentrated on Alan and Jane's marriage. Cockerell remembers what women said. 'Was Jane a doormat and a milksop? Or was she making the best of a bad job? Here was a man she clearly still loved and in his own way he clearly loved her still. She lived in the castle and in the end he would always come back to her, so hang on in there was one view. The other was what about allowing yourself to be treated like this? I found that reaction all the time among women friends of mine – and they were quite divided. Down the middle on that.' Within the BBC Will Wyatt, the Corporation's managing director, said it was 'a TV event' and within two months *Love Tory* was given a repeat broadcast. By then the *Diaries* was the book everyone was talking about and top of the bestseller lists. No-one would now admit not to having heard of the Clarks.

THIRTY-ONE

Jane and the Diaries aftermath

With Alan and Jane talking openly on camera, Michael Cockerell's film more than the *Diaries* themselves made public the matter of Alan's infidelities. And yet he always insisted he loved Jane, as the *Diaries* often bear testimony.

Jane made clear her own distaste for his womanising. But she also believed in her marriage vows. She had married him in 1958, 'for better for worse'. She stuck with him despite times of considerable unhappiness, which Alan himself recognised and alluded to in his diaries. Jane had so often remained at home, at Bratton, at Seend, at Saltwood, while Alan got up to no good elsewhere, particularly in London. Simon Hoggart remembered one occasion.[1] Researching a profile on Margaret Thatcher for *The Observer* in the early 1980s, he contacted everyone who worked for her on a daily basis, particularly people who might have something interesting to say, which of course included Alan, by now a junior Minister, as 'he invariably had insights other politicians never noticed'. Hoggart wrote to him at the Commons 'so that civil servants wouldn't get their hands on it'. A letter came back on Department of Employment notepaper. 'Very sorry I can't do lunch as you suggest. I am usually engaged in Ugandan discussions at lunchtime. I will be happy to see you in the evening.' Hoggart thought this extraordinary, to write in this way to a journalist on departmental notepaper. They agreed to go to Wilton's a few days later. 'I have a guest arriving at eight o'clock. We'll meet at seven, drink a bottle of wine and I'll tell you what I know.' A bottle of Puligny Montrachet was ordered, 'way above what I would expect *The Observer* to pay for a dinner for two including a bottle of wine,' as Hoggart recalled. 'He was very helpful, full of great lines. At 8 p.m. a stunning girl whose surname ended on the letters 'lla' turned up. Al rose: "Nice talking to you, bye, bye".'

Jane, however, says she was true to her marriage: she never slept with another man. Inevitably, in the course of researching and writing this book our conversations turned to the subject. How did she feel?

I absolutely hated it. All these journalists who say well she only stayed for the castle. Come on. How long was I married to him?

There were moments with Al when I hated him, I really, really hated him. I just felt – always looked at things much, much longer, not the immediate thing. And I knew that in spite of everything he loved me, loved the boys. You can't really wreck their lives just for your convenience. He wasn't actually making everyone's life a misery except mine. I just had to look at it like that. I did actually feel that all these ladies – not one of them could have coped with him. If I had moved out someone else would have moved in, but not one of them would have understood. They only saw him, his glamour. If you were living in London ... The country and London are so different. I thought there was more to life. I was desperately unhappy at certain periods. I did wonder was it worth it.

You get particularly bad bits. We had a terrible row – about Alison? Went into my bathroom, shut the door and said I'm going to pack. He had a complete breakdown outside the door. I was lying there laughing. Little did he know. I threw out the odd remark. I was rather enjoying this.

He was amazingly selfish. I remember going for a walk. We always used to lean on Lord Clark's Gate with a view of the sea. Why don't you come closer? I thought ... You just don't get it, do you? Why should I move closer to you, let's have a cuddle or whatever. It's your job to woo me. He never got that. He never seemed to understand. I don't know if he did understand how much he hurt me. I think he probably did before the end. He used to say I have ruined your life. But I don't know; I don't know.[2]

Alan could be petty over such matters. In an undated letter, but almost certainly at the time of his infatuation with Alison Young, he complained to Jane, who had driven him from Saltwood to catch the London train, 'You never turned round at Sandling. I had my head out of the window and I saw you walk all the way along the platform and then the train started to move and you went up the passage and still didn't turn.' He wished to restore good relations. 'I thought things had got better. But they are worse, I suppose.'

Once launched, nothing could stop the success of the *Diaries* on its hardback publication in May 1993. After a first week when it was only second in *The Sunday Times* bestseller list (the key indicator) to *Some Other Rainbow*, the John McCarthy and Jill Morrell account of McCarthy's incarceration with Terry Waite and Brian Keenan in Beirut, it swept to number one position (with 'Jill and John', as Alan referred to them, at number two). *Diaries* remained in the list for more than six months. Alan recorded an audio version and, with mutterings of protest, promoted his book nationwide. At one point he told Weidenfeld that he found some of the customers at book-signings as irritating as his former constituents.

Certain phrases, certain stories, acronyms even from the *Diaries* swiftly entered common parlance. EMT (early morning tea), 'the coven', at the time an unidentified trio of related girlfriends. Everyone quickly had a favourite moment, often a set piece of which Alan himself was fond. Columnists and telephone phone-ins seemed to debate little else. As for Michael Heseltine's furniture ... in the *Diaries* Alan made it clear that he saw Heseltine as an 'arriviste' who 'in Michael Jopling's damning phrase, "bought all his own furniture"'. This rapidly became, in the hands of reporters, a phrase of Alan's minting. In fact Jopling denies that he created the remark. 'It had been around for some time.'[3]

The *Diaries* made Alan famous. He wished to be remembered as a Parliamentarian but, having never reached Cabinet, his political career was more likely to be consigned to footnotes (even Margaret Thatcher's memoirs give him only one entry) whereas his *Diaries* made him a Famous Person (or FP in Alan's argot). It was not long before celebrity led to unexpected references. Matthew Parris, who, on ceasing to be a Conservative MP in 1986, became first a television presenter and then in 1988 a noted parliamentary sketch-writer for *The Times*, recalls having fun at the expense of Tristan Garel-Jones's Blue Chip supper club on a visit ('in the club charabanc') to Saltwood. 'This was easy to find,' said his note. 'The gate was easy to spot, and we would immediately see that the drive up to his castle had at the appointed time been lined in our honour with naked black eunuchs, their heads shaven bare, each inclining towards the road an outstretched palm on which there would be a line of cocaine of the finest quality, to sniff as we passed.'[4]

Alastair Goodlad, who entered the Commons at the same election as Alan, produced what Max Hastings called 'a peerless unpublished parody' of the *Diaries*: 'on the way back from White's chatted up a girl outside St James's Piccadilly ... she made some pathetic excuse about the time of the month ... got back to Albany and rang Jane. Poor darling, she is so tired after cleaning out the moat all day.'[5]

Alan's delight in the success of the *Diaries* was tempered by two matters: the lack of an American edition ('I find it odd that you should not be able to interest any [New York] publisher in a book that has had so much attention, and been on the top of the list since publication day', he wrote to Michael Sissons)[6] and what he saw as a contractual dispute that would sour his relationship with Sissons' agency, Peters, Fraser and Dunlop. His agent had patiently explained what he had been asking other authors to do – countersign the firm's terms of business, at the insistence of their brokers and lawyers. Alan would have none of it. 'I'm sorry, but I can't possibly sign "the contract" which you requested. In fact I'm quite surprised that you should have asked me, after working together for more than thirty years.'[7] With what sounded like exasperation, Sissons responded, 'It is not a contract, it's a terms of business. But if you feel unhappy with it, then so be it.'

His agent moved on to something new. What about 'Big Book', Alan's long-term ambition to write a history of the Conservative Party? Weidenfeld were also pressing him about a further volume of diaries. As for America, Sissons reported 'a curious resistance among certain American publishers who we thought would be very strong potential customers but who clearly find your vivid prose something of a culture shock. I am sure we'll prevail.' Alan responded, reiterated his disappointment and added, 'I quite see that it is not to the taste of all those East Coast wankers who are terrified of being incorrect.'[8] Sissons enclosed a rejection letter from a doyen of New York publishing, Michael Bessie, who wrote that he had read it 'with mixed emotions. I am probably the number one sucker for British politics in this country and Lord knows I've published a lot of them.' However, he went on to say, 'Alas I find Clark such an egomaniacal and repulsive character that I simply don't enjoy it enough in the end. Indeed, I think it is superbly the kind of book that one can have a glorious time with in England, but not in the provinces.'

Towards the end of November 1993, in reply to his agent's question about the future, Alan wrote: 'I have not made any decision or even given much though to the subject of my next book. But a number of different publishers are bothering me, and I know this is a small world where rumours ignite and spread, fast. For this reason I am writing now to tell you that I will not be asking you to handle any negotiations that may, in the fullness of time, get under way. We have had a jolly association over many years and I hope you will accept my assurance that it is not rancour which underlies my decision.'[9]

Sissons, wisely, let it percolate for a few days before responding. 'I simply don't understand your letter of 25 November. It's thirty years since we went down to the East End to see *Oh What a Lovely War* on your behalf, and we have not had a serious cross word during this time. I've looked conscientiously after your published books, but we've never had a major success together until now. We then have an enormous success together with your diaries, and now this. Surely at the very least you owe me a proper explanation. I sincerely hope there is no rancour, because I can't imagine how there could possibly be any ground for it. The only conceivable cause for complaint, when I've been getting backlist titles into print again, is that we've so far been unsuccessful in selling *Diaries* in New York. Can we not meet in a constructive fashion to get to the bottom of this? We will in any case be continuing to represent all your existing titles and I can't imagine who will do a better job on your behalf than I will.'[10]

A telephone conversation followed in which a lunch was fixed for before Christmas. There was, however, some background. Eddie Bell, the ebullient chairman of the British end of HarperCollins (proprietor, Rupert Murdoch's News Corporation), wanted Alan's future business and made an all-out assault, deploying flattery and money, to see if he could acquire the sequel to *Diaries* and his long-talked-about history of the Tory Party. They met and talked, as Alan recalled, 'of huge sums of dosh'. (In addition to six-figure 'advances' for each book, Bell mentioned a £75,000 'signing-on' fee, as well as a guarantee of £200,000 against serial rights.) Bell also said HarperCollins would be happy for him to write a life of the Amery family (Alan had long been enthralled by this political dynasty, most recently represented in the Commons by Julian Amery, who had served in the governments of three Conservative Prime Ministers).

Whether Alan saw this as simply a way of gingering Weidenfeld to come up with more money for his next book, or whether he was seriously prepared to move to HarperCollins is unclear. But Sissons was not pleased. He now drafted a fierce rejoinder to Bell, but in the end thought better of sending the letter. Meanwhile Alan, who was at the beck and call of the Scott Inquiry, was forced to cancel lunch. Had they moved into calmer waters? Sissons now wrote: 'I am sorry to miss our lunch today but I quite understand the onerous demands of Scott. I'd like in any case to set out my view of the publishing situation. I can see no sense whatsoever in selling Collins a second volume of diaries. Second volumes of memoirs, diaries and letters are notoriously difficult in publishing terms. But if it's going to happen, and I hope it will, then a very important part of the long-term marketing strategy would be to have in due course handsome boxed hardcover and paperback sets of both volumes. That of course goes out of the window if another publisher is involved in the second volume.' Sissons then went on to postulate getting an advance of £100,000 for the Conservative Party history with an option for a further volume of diaries for another £100,000. He closed his letter, 'I hope that Scott wasn't too draining.'[11]

One of the bonuses for Alan from the *Diaries'* success came in the new year when Jonathan Holborow of the *Mail on Sunday* offered him a weekly column, with seven weeks' holiday, for £8,500 a month plus expenses. That was followed by word that one of the most distinguished of New York publishers, Roger Straus, the founder and chairman of Farrar, Straus and Giroux, had been given the *Diaries* for Christmas by Weidenfeld's New York scout, hugely enjoyed them and wanted to publish in the United States. He offered an advance of $10,000, which was accepted just in time for Sissons to tell Alan over lunch the following week.

The correspondence which followed shows two masters at work. 'I am afraid I must now return to this question of our relations,' wrote Alan. 'It has to be put bluntly. What do I actually get for my money? Negotiations with Fleet Street – fine, I can't or don't want to do that. But why should I lose £25k out of a book(s) contract simply to have you set it up. Orion have done everything for me in the last year, they act as PR agency, a diary office and a cuttings collection service. I am barely aware of the existence of Peters. The only contract they have produced is the TellTapes. Why don't you vary your commission scales in relation to the size of the earnings?

'If I sell something for more than £100,000 at Sothebys or Christies they don't charge <u>ANY</u> commission. I know we've been friendly acquaintances for years, and the rewards have been slight up until now. But you haven't actually lost money, have you? I still get a royalty cheque for *Barbarossa* (and *Crete)* under the old contracts. Anyway business is business etc. And in business I should be separating the tasks for which I need the services of an agent from those which I can do (handsomely rewarded if I take the commission instead of him) myself. What irks me is that whatever figure is agreed I actually only get half. "I'm bust, virtually."'[12]

Sissons had ammunition aplenty, and deployed it. 'May I deal with our relationship first? I suppose the answer in equally plain terms is swings and roundabouts, which has some force when I see our relationship goes back to 1961. The only book on which conceivably we've made a profit is *Barbarossa*, but you forget a great deal of unpaid work over the years on other matters. In fact there were more cancelled contracts than books! Do you recall such unwritten masterpieces as *The Yalta Conference* and *The Bomber in WWII*, on both of which you asked me to refund you our commission when the books weren't written? I put a lot of work into the Thatcher business, including the detailed briefing you asked me to write, and of course didn't expect to be paid unless it happened. The nett commission which you pay us is 6% and I am surprised that the issue gnaws at your vitals when I remember your very strongly expressed and much appreciative satisfaction at the way we set up the *Diaries*.'

Sissons went on to explain the difference between an author's agent and Sotheby's. 'We undertake on every business that we handle a responsibility which lasts for the full term of copyright, and there couldn't be a better example than *Barbarossa*, which I have looked after very carefully over the years and which is now about to come back into print on my initiative. Publishing has become very volatile. Who knows where Ion, or indeed Weidenfeld will be in five years time? We stay put. If it really bugs you then I suppose I would offer to do the serial negotiation for the new book on a commission of 5%. But obviously I don't like to do so when we handle the fortunes of many authors who are both successful and sophisticated who earn large sums of money year in and year out and feel that they get good value from the nett commission that they pay us. I'm glad that Weidenfeld give you good service. So they should. On a bestseller such as yours they make considerably more profit than you do, and probably many times our return.'

Alan was immediately disarming. 'I always enjoy a duel and was pleased by the often specious arguments that you deployed, thinking that the need to resort thereto was an admission that your own case is probably no stronger than mine. As for those authors "who earn large sums of money", they can't be all that successful and sophisticated if they allow you to trouser away their earnings as you say "year in, year out". However I appreciate your suggestion of a compromise and we'll settle for 10% on volume, 5% on serial.' Next he recounted a story from a lunch the day before with Jeffrey Archer, bestselling novelist and former Tory MP.

He was full of 'I sacked my Agent.[13] Saved me a million pounds on my last contract. I just got the best lawyer in NY to read the contract, paid him $50,000 ... ' (he can't have been the best at that price, I thought).

'So, Alan, who's your agent?'

'Michael Sissons'

'Oh. Him Well, he's big stuff. Could be tricky.'

'How glad and content I am that you are my agent, Michael."[14]

The saga ended with a return fax from Sissons to Alan. 'I am delighted we can move forward. I know you won't take it amiss when I say that had I to rely on trousering away your earnings all those years ago I would have been done for indecent exposure many moons (geddit?) ago.'

The *Diaries* were to have a lusty commercial life beyond the original hardback, helped in an unexpected way. By the time of paperback publication in May 1994 the hardback had had a bookshop sale in the UK of over 50,000 copies and appeared for more than twenty weeks in *The Sunday Times* bestseller list. In those days the supermarkets had yet to catch on to the notion of selling anything more literary than cookbooks at heavily discounted prices. Today, the *Diaries* might have sold more like 250,000 hardback copies over the same timescale.

With the paperback now on display in every airport, every bookshop, *The Times* – in a rare move – devoted a leading article to the *Diaries*. However, it was not this, not the reviews, not the publicity that ensured the success of the paperback. What catapulted the *Diaries* to the top of the paperback bestseller list was 'the coven'.

In the original *Diaries* 'the coven' (also known as 'the blondes') made their first appearance in 1983, on the evening Alan was appointed a junior Minister at the Department of Employment:

> In London I collected the coven and off we went to Brooks's for dinner. At intervals Joei said, 'Gosh, Al, are you really a Minister, zowee.' Valerie was less forthcoming. Ali sulked and sneered . . . Driving away we went past the Ritz and Joei said, 'Gosh, is that the Ritz? I wish I could go in there.'
> 'Why?'
> 'To go to bed, of course.'
> I was thoughtful.
> I have always been culpably weak in such matters.
> And when I got home I thought to myself – a new life, a new leaf.

In a footnote Alan added his explanation, which as it turned out was a masterly understatement: 'Three girls related to each other by blood whom AC had known for many years.'[15] He did not reveal their surname.

There the matter of the 'three girls' might have rested, but for the talents of Max Clifford, with, as his memoirs put it, 'his unique ability to protect and expose individuals'. By his account[16] the publicity that the *Diaries* attracted had raised the indignation of at least two of the three: Valerie Harkess, whom, as we have seen, Alan had first met in Wiltshire under Monday Club auspices in 1968, and her younger daughter Josephine (known by Alan as Joei). Alan, said Clifford, had broken 'a gentleman's agreement' by referring to his sexual relationship with them. The Harkesses, who now lived in South Africa, also particularly disliked the epithet 'the coven'. However, as in the *Diaries* Alan had not used their surname, who, apart from themselves, would make the connection – unless they blew their own cover?[17]

Clifford says that thanks to the *Diaries* 'the family faced humiliation and rejection from tight-laced South African white society'. (*The Daily Telegraph* relegated their social standing to 'South African white suburbia', and drawing on the 'coven' metaphor referred to the Harkesses 'plotting a ghastly revenge'.) Valerie Harkess' second husband James, who had been a barrister and retired deputy circuit judge in Britain, and was now endeavouring to make a career as an author, approached Clifford. If it was a question of getting their own back, by hiring Clifford there was a price to pay: Harkess, his wife, and his step-daughters would now be identified to the world at large. A few days later they arrived in London from South Africa. (Alison, the elder daughter, known by Alan as Ali and now married to a Russian, Sergei Kausov, the third husband of Christina Onassis and already living in Britain, stayed out of what followed.)

Clifford, a master in handling scoops and scandals involving celebrities, introduced the hitherto unknown Harkesses to the press, before selling Valerie's story to the *Sun* and Joei's to the *News of the World*. Valerie Harkess confessed to an affair with Alan over fourteen years. This she regarded as a 'celebration of life'.[18] She also said that Alan had seduced her daughters and was quoted as calling him 'a depraved animal'; Joei claimed that Alan had exposed his erect penis to her and her sister Ali when collecting them from school in his car (a claim Alan repeatedly denied). James Harkess said that given half a chance he would horsewhip Alan (and was shown by a tabloid newspaper with riding crop in hand), although he later retracted this, saying he had meant it only metaphorically. For a week or more the story was a number one sensation. And yet to whose advantage? Clifford says the Harkesses made over £100,000.[19] But it was not for the money alone, surely? James Harkess maintained, 'It is the most important thing in all our lives to tell the truth about him, something of the background of a man whom I consider to be lecherous and arrogant and deceitful and a poor leader of men which he has aspired to be.'[20]

Alan, however, despite palpable embarrassment, had little to lose publicly, whereas several other scandals during the Conservative governments of the period led to high-profile resignations, including one that followed the revelation of an alleged affair involving the National Heritage Minister David Mellor (another exposé in which Max Clifford played a part). This was said to have damaged John Major's only recently launched 'Back to Basics' campaign for the restoration of family values. Yet Alan, as he made clear in the *Diaries*, did not deny his philandering.

If Jane appeared 'unruffled' by the revelations, as *The Guardian* suggested, she was certainly 'ruffled by their social standing'. 'Quite frankly, if you bed people that I call "below-stairs class" they go to the papers, don't they?' Jane was quoted as saying, inaccurately as she wrote two days later to *The Daily Telegraph*. 'Below stairs as a category no longer has anything to do with social class.' And as her authority she cited Dame Barbara Cartland, 'who defined it succinctly as "Really Appalling People".' And she added, 'I am going to support Alan. This is hardly going to split us up. Our marriage is stronger now than it has been in the past.' Nor was Alan shy of talking to the press: 'I probably have a different sense of morality to most people. I have changed my ways and am a reformed character now.' He did not want to get involved in a slanging match, but said the Harkess visit was 'clearly a set-up job'. He thought his diary entries were 'perfectly innocent, just a few light-hearted references', and he was very surprised at the Harkess family's reaction. 'I don't feel any malice to them,' he said. 'I don't blame them particularly – good luck to them.'[21] Later, when the unfounded allegations included a love child called Billy and Alan flashing at gays (this latter inspired by his friendship with Christopher Selmes, who had died of AIDS aged forty-two in 1988), Alan exploded. He described the latest salvo as 'desperate'. He said: 'These are not even charges. They're just running at the wire of a colossal damages settlement. Of course there is no "love child".'[22]

Newspapers and their columnists had a field day. *The Daily Telegraph* found it hard to take the matter seriously. In a leading article it remarked that 'Great cads of cinema and fiction from George Sanders to Flashman would defer humbly to a former minister of the crown who admitted to dalliance with a mother and two daughters, if only out of fascination as to how he found the time.'[23] Next day, also in *The Telegraph*, Alan's friend Frank Johnson treated the spectacle as if he were writing a parliamentary sketch. 'Like many people, I am shocked that the wife and two daughters of a judge should have used their privileged position to have taken advantage of Alan Clark. It is quite clear they were interested in him solely as a sex object. They only wanted him for his body. It is said that there was hardly any conversation. They did not even ask him to talk to them about the Eastern Front in the Second World War – a subject about which he had written a book.'[24]

Historical precedents were raised, not least from the nineteenth century. Lord Palmerston, nicknamed 'Lord Cupid' as a young man, was taken to court aged seventy-nine for allegedly seducing a journalist's wife. He resisted the claim and, according to Palmerston's biographer, Jasper Ridley, although he stood 'vindicated and innocent in the eyes of the non-conformist Liberal voter, the naughtier elements of the population believed the worst about Lord Palmerston and loved him all the more for it'.[25]

When the Harkesses scuttled back to South Africa they could show little else but substantially inflated bank balances, as could Max Clifford, but in the war of moral judgements they must surely have hoped for a more positive response. Alan, meanwhile, reported a substantial mailbag running 14–1 in his favour.

THIRTY-TWO

The Wilderness Years

Alan quickly regretted quitting the House of Commons at the 1992 election. Until he returned to Westminster in 1997 these years were for him a political wilderness. The success of the *Diaries* gave him a wider public recognition than ever before, but although making him, with his love of acronyms, a FP, this was no substitute for the cut and thrust, the gossip and the inside track of politics, which had been so much part of his existence for the best part of a quarter of a century. His professional life now lacked focus. As Jane reminded him on more than one occasion that first summer out of Parliament, he needed discipline. Westminster had provided that, unlike even the deadlines for weekly journalism or the mounting paperwork at Saltwood, as he complained to his diary; 'the flat surfaces indoors ... impossibly congested ... the sheer scale of the task',[1] which could always be put off until another day. Alan was a master procrastinator.

He realised that in resigning his seat he had made a terrible mistake. Within a fortnight of the election, with the Conservatives somewhat surprised at being returned albeit with an overall majority of only 21, he wrote in his diary, 'I am doomed now in the wilderness, to awaiting "tidings of men and events"'. His hope, which he held onto as his salvation, was being elevated to the Lords; surely as a former and senior Minister of State he deserved nothing less? The fantasy continued; he could even be a Defence Minister there. 'I still think – perversely for one usually so realistic and cynical – that if I were there as a Minister of State I would inevitably get S of S – *even though as a peer.*'

He quickly became depressed, deserted, he felt, by most of his political friends (he specifically named Richard Ryder), although was pleased 'by a nice note from Soames'. By the end of April he remarked that 'notification for the Dissolution Honours' had passed and so, too, for the Birthday. (With John and Norma Major staying at the Garel-Joneses in Spain that summer Tristan said he would put in a word for a future list.) The Dissolution Honours, when published in June, made him still further depressed – a list of six working peers that included Barney Hayhoe,[2] 'how ghastly and mediocre – the archetypal safe Tory politician – can you get?'

It was a miserable summer – invited to Chris Patten's farewell party in the Durbar Room at the Foreign Office on 1 July, he turned up on the wrong day. He fed off rumours: that he was to be the next Editor of *The Spectator*, that he was to be Literary Editor of *The Sunday Times*. When in July he was asked if he missed Westminster, he responded 'Yes, dreadfully'. And in a separate entry, 'I feel the biggest mistake I ever made was to "walk away" from the Commons.' At his doctor's, where he'd gone for a check-up, he was told that his blood would be sent for a prostate cancer test as well as a testosterone count. Grrrh! But the results were fine.

Behind the scenes preparations were going ahead for the Matrix Churchill trial, not that Alan or anyone else at that point realised its significance. Alan was beginning work on editing sample material from his diaries for Michael Sissons to read and, he hoped, sell for publication. This would solve his current financial crisis. When that autumn his evidence at the trial led to its abandonment and the government's announcement of the Scott Inquiry Alan found himself back in the news. More pleasing were the publishing and newspaper serialisation deals for his *Diaries*. But first his views as a historian were called into question.

Shortly before Christmas 1992 Alan was asked to review *Churchill: the End of Glory* by John Charmley, a thirty-seven-year-old history lecturer at the University of East Anglia.[3]

The jacket blurb referred to a well-researched 'reappraisal' of 'the Churchill myth'. Alan was intrigued; perhaps Charmley's view coincided with his own – that Churchill's judgements during the Second World War were often flawed? He suspended completion of the transcription of *Diaries* ('I am under *such* pressure')[4] and his summation appeared in *The Times* on 2 January 1993.

Timing, as ever, had much to do with it. *The Times* ran Alan's piece on an otherwise quiet Saturday and made sure that the media as a whole took notice by previewing it in a front-page news story. 'Churchill war role under fire' ran its heading – 'Mr Clark argues that by refusing to make peace with Hitler in 1940 and 1941, Churchill betrayed the Commonwealth, lost the Far Eastern empire and shattered the British social order.' It quoted Charmley as probably the first historian to come to Churchill without the baggage of memories (he was born in 1955). 'What I'm trying to do is get behind the hagiography and do a Churchill on Churchill, who was one for warts and all.'[5]

Alan was no stranger to historical controversy. Now, however unintentionally, he hijacked Charmley's case. In the core of his review he argued:

The defeat of Hitler was [Churchill's] raison d'être ... There were several occasions when a rational leader could have got, first reasonable, then excellent, terms from Germany. Hitler actually offered peace in July 1940 before the Battle of Britain started. After the RAF victory the German terms were still available, now weighted more in Britain's favour.

In spring 1941, following the total defeat of the Italians in Africa, Britain had recovered its military poise and not yet paid over all its gold reserves to America. Hitler wanted to secure his flank before he turned on Russia. Hess, his deputy, flew uninvited to Britain with terms. Churchill, who saw the domestic dangers, would not talk to him, and repressed (in conspiracy with the whole establishment) the documents.

This was the real watershed, because if Britain had made peace in April 1941 the fleet and the Spitfires could have been moved to Singapore. The Japanese would never have attacked and the Far Eastern empire would have endured. But Churchill did not attach as much importance to this as to defeating Hitler; and he realised that total defeat was only possible if the United States entered the war. Only the Japanese could cause this to happen. Why deter them?

Who was right? The war went on far too long, and when Britain emerged the country was bust. Nothing remained of assets overseas. Now set out in a most scholarly work of some 700 pages, is probably the most important revisionist text to be published since the war. It is a sad tale.

As one newspaper put it, since Charmley's thesis 'came to the critics through the prism of Clark, it was hard to tell them apart',[6] and predictably it was upon Alan that the wave upon wave of abuse was aimed via the weekend press. Unlike *The Donkeys* and his attack on Haig, where he had the support of the then influential Beaverbrook press, he now stood almost alone. Professor Donald Cameron Watt, of the LSE, did not mince his words: 'He is an arrogant, self-centred man who talks bollocks ... He seems to think that Hitler was a rational man and that clearly was not the case.' Meanwhile *The Sunday Times* quoted Alan's reaction. 'A lot of people may well be offended by what I am saying, but I honestly couldn't care less.' The argument raged into the new week and beyond. Martin Gilbert, the official biographer of Winston Churchill, commented, 'You can't argue that the Nazis were not as bad as was thought at the time. If anything they were worse. Given what was known then, which was pretty comprehensive, there was no way a British government could have made peace with Nazi Germany without being overthrown.'[7]

Andrew Roberts, biographer of Lord Halifax, the wartime Foreign Secretary who backed the idea of negotiating peace with Hitler, was the one historian with something good to say for the Charmley-Clark argument, but even he had reservations. 'This is a very important revisionist book, but I don't think [John Charmley] has made the connection that he is trying to make. The verdict must be "not proven".' He added that it was a beguiling concept to argue that peace might have prevented Bolshevism and saved Britain's assets, 'but I don't think it actually ties up in terms of the military and political situation that existed at the time'. Roberts always felt the theory self-defeating. 'If we hadn't gone to war in 1939 we would have ended up losing the war in 1947 or 1949 or 1951 or whenever they got the nuclear bomb.'[8]

The Guardian published a nicely judged review by Norman Stone, Professor of Modern History at Oxford. 'Clark is rather good at controversy – of saying things that resonate somewhere in the national subconscious. There are times when he has been courageous and right – for instance over the Matrix Churchill affair. But in this case, in the words of a French diplomatic phrase, I must find another occasion upon which to manifest my esteem.'[9]

Charmley-Clark tested their theories before an audience that July when *The Times* organised a debate at Church House, Westminster, with Alan's former mentor, Robert Blake (now Lord Blake and Provost of Queen's College, Oxford) and Andrew Roberts opposing them. Before a packed house the Blake-Roberts view won the evening, with one heckler in the gallery having to be ejected for shouting 'traitors' at those who argued against a negotiated peace. As one member of the audience recalled, 'A rare example of popular support for that view – fifty years too late.'

Despite this almost total antipathy, the idea that peace might have been negotiated in 1941 remained tagged to Alan, the historian, for the rest of his life, just as the notion that he was a closet Nazi and that First World War generals were donkeys.

How does the Charmley-Clark thesis look in the twenty-first century? Graham Stewart, who wrote a well-received study of the Chamberlain-Churchill rivalry in the run-up to the war,[10] and who worked closely with Alan for three years on *The Tories*, recalls that this was the one question on which he and Alan could never agree. 'I remember he once told me how relieved he thought the country would have been if it had been announced that we had negotiated peace in 1941. Where did he get this notion from? This was certainly not my reading of the popular mood.'[11]

With his transcribing and editing of the diaries nearly complete Alan's ambitions were seduced by a by-election. Judith Chaplin, former political secretary to John Major, had won Newbury for the Conservatives at the 1992 election with a majority of over 11,000, then became ill and in February 1993 suddenly died. Immediately the press started speculating that this would be the seat for Alan to sail back into the Commons. But would it? He was immediately uncertain, writing in his diary that it was a 'very bad seat'. Since the general election ten months earlier the government's standing had plummeted, thanks in particular to sterling's ejection from the ERM the previous September, when interest rates rose, briefly, to fifteen per cent. However his desire to return to Westminster was such that he was persuaded to take it seriously.

Richard Ingrams, erstwhile Editor of *Private Eye* and now a columnist on *The Observer*, felt readers should be reminded that Alan did 'everything he could to provide arms for Saddam Hussein, turning a blind eye to all the deceptions involved and all the dirty tricks'. Ingrams was stern. 'Mr Clark subsequently defended this as "realpolitik". Judged simply by that criterion, his policy was a disaster. We never got our money for the weapons and we helped to arm a dictator we subsequently had to fight. I suggest that Mr Clark should remain in his castle and get back to writing books.'[12]

In the end Alan's ambition came to nought. There was also a moment when he was tempted to stand as the Referendum candidate, but Jane told him, 'You can't really stand against your own party.' Alan was fortunate not to have been selected as Newbury's Conservative candidate – he called it 'a lucky break'. At the by-election on 6 May the Party was mauled, the Liberal Democrats overturning the Tory majority by over 12,000 votes. As for Referendum/anti-Maastricht candidates, together they polled fewer than 700 votes.

No longer being an MP did allow him that summer to drive his Silver Ghost S1914, otherwise known as 'The Antique', on the Rolls-Royce Enthusiasts' Club's Alpine Commemorative run, about which he wrote at length in his motoring diary. 'Goodness knows what will happen. A challenge, of man and machine. Is this my last solo adventure? I hope my dear "Antique" holds up. Strange, a bit of catharsis, almost.'[13] The Antique, with expert mechanical assistance, completed the journey.

At Nicholas Soames's 'end of term' party on 29 July, Alan recorded a conversation with Jonathan Aitken, who 'so thoughtful and wise, asked me what I would say if Faust offered me a miraculous translation straight back into the Commons – Government or back benches as you wish – at the price of surrendering the *Diaries*. Initially, I suppose, one says "no". But always there is the heavenly recollection of the sword, now on the floor of the lake's bottom.' But overall he sensed, as he wrote afterwards to Richard Ryder, 'the "gossamer curtain" between those in power and those who are OUT'.

Financially, he admitted in October that as 'earnings won't cover everything owing – anywhere near' he would have to sell something. Not cars, he decided, 'they are a collection – bit of "Applied" rather than "Fine" – Art'. But what about the Torres Strait tortoiseshell mask thought to have once been owned by Picasso? He had been tempted in 1985 to accept an offer of $450,000 for it, but now he resisted even £350,000. 'It must work spells for me because I saved it, will have to make other sacrifices.'

Alan had shown an interest in music since a child, when his family went regularly to Covent Garden. He had learnt the piano, and still enjoyed playing a tune or two. Now the presenter of *Desert Island Discs*, Sue Lawley, wrote to him asking him to be her guest on the BBC Radio 4 programme. He makes no mention of this in his diary. With the benefit of hindsight one recognises how under Lawley's questioning he fudges the truth and allows his fantasies full rein. The programme was recorded for transmission on New Year's Day 1995.

Lawley had had a clash with Alan ten years before, on the BBC's *Question Time*. Since making his broadcasting reputation at the time of the Falklands War two years earlier he had become something of a regular on the programme, which was usually chaired by Robin Day. Being new to *Question Time*, she recalls being extremely nervous. In a nod to Robin's sartorial preferences she wore an outsize, floppy black silk bow-tie.[14] She and Alan did not hit it off. In his account, 'she, an "attractive woman" spotted at once that I have lecherous tendencies, but did not actually fancy her. She thought to put me in my place in her introduction by saying, "*He* went into politics because he thought it would make him more attractive."'[15]

Earlier in the day the government had decided to purchase an American surface-to-surface missile, 'Harpoon', in preference to the British Aerospace 'Sea Eagle'. The question – 'must have been planted', wrote Alan, 'as the news only broke after the audience had started assembling' – was on the lines of 'Does the Panel think it right that we should always be preferring American weapon systems to British ones?'

Sue Lawley turned to Alan, as the Conservative on the panel, and he, as he wrote, did not simply 'nibble at the bait. I swallowed, and most of the line, the float, the rod, the fisherman's waders, the lot. Sod it, I knew as much about this subject as anyone, a bad decision had been made – say so.' And he did, taking a swipe in passing at the Secretary of State for Defence, none other than his antagonist of long-standing, Michael Heseltine – 'It takes a very strong Secretary of State to resist recommendations from civil servants even though these are often quite narrowly founded.' In the chair Sue Lawley was appropriately quick-witted – Alan referred to her in his diary as 'still bitchlike' – and said, 'Well, since the Minister isn't prepared to defend his own government, is there anyone in the room who is?'

Not surprisingly his remark made the headlines next morning and was spun against him – 'another gaffe by Mr Clark', and 'the accident-prone Mr Clark'. Alan expected to be sacked, and, sure enough, he had hardly reached his office before being hauled in front of his Secretary of State, Tom King, who said 'We'll do our best to hold the line.' Alan reflected in his diary, 'What the hell? I was almost elated. At least I would be dismissed for something that related to my own subject, a hero in my own eyes.' But Number Ten's briefing to journalists took a very different line, 'no reason why he should resign'. Bernard Ingham, the Prime Minister's press secretary, was bare-faced, issuing a statement that said 'what Mr Clark meant to say was . . . '. Alan closed that particular entry, 'Dear good kind sweet Lady.'

Sue Lawley had been 'slightly, surprised, though pleased' when Alan accepted her invitation to appear on *Desert Island Discs*. With a colourful story to explore, he 'easily qualified as a castaway'. On the day of the recording she remembers fetching Alan herself from Broadcasting House reception, little more than a couple of hundred yards from the Portland Place house where he spent his pre-war childhood. She saw him before he saw her – standing, with one hand on hip, which held his jacket away from its natural fall and showed off his perfect flat stomach. Was it, she wondered, a pose?

She anticipated he would come along 'in punchy mode'. In the event – and she listened again to the programme before we talked – 'I thought *I* was too punchy with *him*. He, in fact, was in *gracious* mode and took my mentions of his philandering or political failures rather gamely. The result: I sounded as if I was being tougher than he deserved. I should have spotted his game – for game it surely was?' On the other hand, as she reflects, 'even *he* wasn't cleverer than the old formula: *Desert Island Discs* worked its magic again. For my money, helped of course by the honesty of his record choices, there was a lot of the real Alan Clark in that broadcast.' It also showed what Alan was thinking, aged sixty-six, out of Parliament, but with a sensational bestselling book just behind him. Was one more important than the other? Sue Lawley asked the same question as Jonathan Aitken eighteen months before. In a Faustian bargain, would he dump the diaries if it meant getting into the Cabinet? This time he sat on the fence: 'I can't just really decide, but I expect I'd make the wrong decision as I have on many previous occasions.'

Sue Lawley asked him how close he thought he had come to a seat in the Cabinet; would Mrs Thatcher eventually have delivered it to him if she hadn't lost her own? Alan had no doubts. 'Oh yes, I was going to be Secretary of State for Defence in 1990, but then two things got in the way. First of all Saddam Hussein attacked Kuwait and that meant you couldn't change half way through a war; it would have been done in the autumn of that year; and then she herself got into the most frightful jeopardy and she lost her Chancellor and she lost Geoffrey Howe and so on; she was in such a jam that she couldn't think about secondary appointments.'

Had it not occurred to him that by cleaning up his act and toeing the line he might have got the job he wanted? 'It should have done, and I was no good at that, spoilt I suppose. I thought I had a very good relationship with Mrs Thatcher and she would do for me in the end what she did for me when she made me Minister for Trade, which she did against great advice.' Her departure, he added, was the key to his decision to quit. 'And now you miss it?' – 'Tremendously.'

To introduce his first record, part of the 'Leonora' Overture, Lawley asked: was this the first time he fell in love? – 'No, I'm a soppy old thing; always falling in love.' And the exchange continued: 'Really in love? Or is there a difference, fancying people or falling in love?' 'No, no. Fancying, no, no, way beyond that.' And then came a typical Clark remark, delivered, she recalls, with Alan looking her straight in the eye, 'I'm reluctant to share my views on love with a stranger, Sue.' The questioning moved on to Jane and the remark by Alan's father in his memoirs that in Jane Alan had found his natural protector and that he was a lucky man. 'Yes, it's true. God knows where I'd be if I hadn't been married to Jane. I think I said in the *Diaries* at one point, I'd be locked up, locked up for long stretches at a time.' For what? 'Oh you know, brawling and breaking the law and you know ... She controlled my worst side.' 'Saving you from yourself?' 'I'm afraid there's some truth in that.'

When Lawley asked him about his ambitions on coming down from Oxford, Alan was less than truthful. He replied: 'I intended to go into politics and become Prime Minister and I regarded that as a perfectly natural outcome of everything else that I was doing. I'm not unique in that. A very large number of people who go into politics actually think they've got the answer.'

They talked too about the enjoyment of Westminster. What gave Alan 'the buzz'? – 'Going through the door marked "members only", a colossal latent charge of static electricity that pervades that place; it is so redolent of history and circumstance in such a concentrated way that any little incident can ignite it; you see and you can draw strength from this electric charge in the chamber and in the members' lobby – all that absolutely marvellous.' Would he stand again, make a political comeback? Alan was slow in his response. 'I just don't know. I still yearn for that ring-side seat, of course, you can't not; I honestly think that no-one who is honest would say that they didn't miss it terribly. Most people leave politics and Parliament in far more humiliating circumstances than I. Either sacked or turned out by the electorate or whatever. I suppose as neither of those things happened to me it is much easier for me to pretend that anything is still possible.'

Lawley wondered what he felt looking at a photograph of himself and seeing folds round the corner? 'Absolutely, it is dreadful. Today a photographer comes round and takes say fifteen pictures, it is like Hitler with his photographer, only two are acceptable; if the public see the others your stature would be diminished.'

'You're lucky to find two,' Lawley responded. 'Do you pine for your youth? Do you have a more serious problem than most?'

'I suppose if I start actually making a fool of myself I have got a problem, but right now I'm not aware of that.'

'I suppose some people might already say you've done that.'

'Well no. If you tell me why they think that, then I may suggest to you that they are just jealous.'

As the end of the programme approached Lawley asked how he would cope with being a castaway all on his own. 'I am quite used to solitude, yes, so I would enjoy it, but I wouldn't want to stay there until my bones whiten, I don't think. But a period of detachment and contemplation is what a lot of people say I need, so who am I to say they're wrong.' For his book he wanted one 'that gives variety, but stimulates the mind –

Bertrand Russell's *History of Western Philosophy*'. And his luxury – a piano 'without any doubt, I might leave the island actually quite good at playing the piano which I'm certainly not at the moment. I don't really even play ... What I do is I roll the bass, as it is called in New Orleans language, I straddle two octaves with my right hand and really half the time I'm just treating it as a xylophone.'

To which Sue Lawley remarked, 'But "Sentimental Journey" or "Candy Kisses" comes out the other end?'

'And "Stormy Weather".'[16]

'Alan Clark, thank you for letting us hear your Desert Island Discs.'

'Thanks, I've enjoyed it.' And he had.

THIRTY-THREE

The Making of The Tories

For Alan the reception for what turned out to be his final history, *The Tories*, was an enormous disappointment. Where did it go wrong?

As a project it had been percolating for some time and the years in the political wilderness proved valuable as he worried away at it. By May 1994 he contemplated 'a full switch, into historian, and to the Tory Party book'.[1] In January 1995 he finally made a move, after interviewing a possible researcher, a young Cambridge academic, Graham Stewart, who was completing his PhD on the Tory Party of the 1930s. Alan 'took to him almost at once; good mind, sympathetic attitude'.[2] With Stewart's appointment, there was no turning back.

In fact it was Stewart who made the initial move, offering his services as a researcher having read in *The Times*, in November 1994, that Alan was at work on a history of the Tory Party from 1922 to the present day. Stewart recalls that the interview took place at Saltwood over 'quite a Spartan lunch of pulses' while they talked about aspects of British history. 'We tended to see things in a similar way. By the end of the day he was taking me round to the Garden House – "you will live here. I hope it isn't too much above the shop."' Stewart moved into the Garden House just after the end of the summer term at Cambridge, 1995.[3]

On his arrival he was warned by Alan about the Clarks' two Rottweilers, Lëhni and Hannah. '"It is very important that you don't do anything to excite them, because if it got reported that you had been bitten by them, I mean Jane would just be distraught." What he was basically saying was, if you have your head bitten off just don't complain about it!' Stewart found himself made to feel immediately part of the family, joining Alan and Jane for an al fresco supper the first evening. Was it too good to be true? Stewart reflects how his 'gilded time at university had just seamlessly moved into another even more eccentric system'. Whereas most of his friends were now burning midnight oil at Morgan Stanley or Goldman Sachs, 'here I had found a sympathetic employer who just wanted to spend our days discussing the politics of the twentieth century'.

Until Alan set to work, the standard history of the Party, by Robert Blake, took Robert Peel as its starting point and ended with Churchill.[4] His book, as he told Hugh Trevor-Roper in an undated letter, would be 'Blake with the warts'. To Alan, though, as he wrote in his preface, 'for eighty years of the twentieth century, from its underwriting of the Lloyd George coalition in 1916 until it was put to rout by New Labour in 1997, the Conservative Party was the dominant political force in Britain – even when, for short periods, it was in opposition'. And the dominance as a party in its own right, not as a coalition partner, began in 1922 – at the Carlton Club in St James's, which Alan was later to call 'the up-market works canteen for senior Conservatives'.[5] (Hence the importance of the 1922 Committee, in representing the Party's back bench.)

His intention was to show how the Party had conducted itself. Its duty was simple: 'the nurturing, protection and advancement of the British nation state'. Over the eighty years it was not always possible to be so single-minded, but in his view, 'the interests of the British nation state are best served by contriving the perpetuity of a Tory administration whatever *apparent* sacrifices of principle or policy this may entail'. Hence his book's subtitle: 'Conservatives and the Nation State, 1922–1997'. Having appointed Stewart, Alan initially did very little. Health was once again a preoccupation. 'I rose very early and looked at some texts for Big Book over EMT. Later I said to Jane $\frac{1}{4}$ of my stress derives from not properly addressing Big Book; I can feel the level easing off as I get near it. So much twist (or "spin" as it is called) to put on this subject.'[6]

Stewart saw his task as less than a ghostwriter, but somewhat more than a researcher. 'In some areas of the book I had no almost input whatsoever, the last quarter of the book was almost entirely his work – much of it directly from his own knowledge and experience.' Alan's way of using Stewart was to ask him: 'Prepare me a paper on the Gold standard', not 'I need to find a fact that shows it was a bad idea.' 'This would take perhaps a better part of the month to do. By the end I'd have prepared a semi-academic treatise; he would then read it through, take the bits he liked, discard others, then weave it in. I did all the primary sources research. He would spend his mornings on the secondary sources – reading books, formulating his ideas. It was never "I want that paper by yesterday" kind of attitude. He had a very good sense that if you want good work then you had to let me go off to the Bodleian, and if you don't see me for the next five days you have to assume I am in the Bodleian and not at Newbury races. To me he was the perfect employer.'

Stewart, though, was able to use the time well, also working on his own book, *Burying Caesar: Churchill, Chamberlain and the Battle for the Tory Party*,[7] which proved an invaluable aid to Alan's understanding of the politics of that era. By November 1996 Alan reported in his diary that Big Book was 'potentially terrific. I am devoting more and more hours to it, and recovering confidence (and shape).'[8] He and his researcher did, however, disagree 'over Churchill whom Alan greatly disliked, and the policy of a negotiated peace in the Second World War'. Stewart had to defer to his opinion, and he was worried that the book as a whole might be sidetracked into a hobby horse. But ultimately the balance of the book righted itself. Thinking back, Stewart says: 'To me one of the interesting things about him was that he had a very romantic sense of British history, but unusually for people with this romantic sense he was also very hard-headed about it: first of all the Tory Party was power, the purpose of power is to do the best almost regardless of any particular principle. The leaders he tended to admire were the hard-headed ones.'

As a writer he was, says Stewart, 'the equivalent of a one-take actor. He would arrive with a sense of presence and majesty. As he'd come through the door he would already be talking as if his amanuensis would be ready to take down the words as he moved seamlessly from the Garden House entrance to the office at the back where he had set up his computer.' His strange way of walking, walking with his hips, 'added to this sense of regal procession. He would then sit down and just type. He wouldn't even read it through.' After an hour and a half or so he would ask Stewart to make sure the piece had been saved – technology was not his strong suit – and then more often than not wander off. He wrote with great self-confidence. 'The upside of this was that his style had freshness and immediacy – if there isn't a verb in the sentence it doesn't matter. The downside: sometimes he wrote things where a more academic approach might have been more appropriate.' Stewart did, however, note that – as with *The Donkeys* some thirty-five years before – Alan wasn't against quoting people selectively to make them look bad.

Although *The Tories* was conceived as a book, early on in the writing it also became a television series, called *Alan Clark's History of the Tory Party*. In 1994 Alan had been invited to take part in a BBC *Timewatch* programme, *Memo from Machiavelli*, where the lessons of *The Prince* were applied to contemporary British politics. Nicolas Kent, who made the programme, recalls going to Saltwood. 'I think Alan was a sort of armchair Machiavelli and he loved talking about the gossip and strategy of politics and knew Machiavelli back to front like most politicians do know him, or at least did then.' When Kent learnt that Alan was currently at work on *The Tories*, it immediately seemed obvious to him as a television series. 'He was now so famous as a politician. He had a unique position in English society, almost a national treasure, an Alan Bennett of politics. He was almost outside politics ... he obviously loved it, but a bit like Machiavelli himself he was better at writing, talking about politics than he was at practising it.'

Alan leapt at the opportunity, even if, as with most BBC series, it took time to set up and was not finally commissioned until the spring of 1996. But once under way he found it hard to multi-task. As the series, made for the BBC by Kent's Oxford Film and Television, involved many other people, script conferences and commitments to film on specific dates, it began to come first. With his unexpected selection as Kensington and Chelsea's Conservative candidate to be added to the mix in January 1997, and the general election following in May, it was obvious that something had to give. His publishers, Weidenfeld & Nicolson, had paid a substantial six-figure advance, for which they expected to be rewarded with the publication of the book coinciding with the screening of the series that September.

In his diary Alan preens himself at learning from the series' director, Clara Glynn, that he is 'so good on television'.[9] Kent does not demur. 'He had the ego and vanity of a natural showman' but proved 'a terrible interviewer, particularly when interviewing other politicians. Basically he was not terribly interested in what other people had to say; he was much more interested in holding forth himself.' But Alan would ask questions which would virtually incorporate the answer. As getting Alan to interview people was 'really a cast-iron way of sabotaging the interview', Kent and his team did further interviews themselves off-camera.

Kent found him 'fantastic talking about history', although surprisingly tentative about the Thatcher-Major years. 'He was quite timid. He wasn't as outspoken as you would have thought him to be. He didn't really talk about Margaret Thatcher with the same resonance that he wrote about her in the diaries. He was a little bit nervous about offending people; probably less nervous about writing it. Perhaps this was because while we were making it he got back into politics?' Although the series was not nearly as outspoken as Kent had hoped, he recognised in Alan 'an excellent performer, a bit like his father. Making the series we were very aware of this extraordinary legacy from *Civilisation*. He was very good at doing pieces to camera. He had a beautiful voice. A very confident, charismatic man.'

Again, like K Alan was a writer first. Kent found that for television purposes he had a fairly short attention span, a couple of hours at best. He felt that 'the book was always more important to him than the television series; the book was what he was spending his time writing'. However by the summer of 1997 and back at Westminster, he managed only to approve final revisions to the television series, which was transmitted over four weeks in September and October (but without the accompanying book). Although well-received, the timing – through no fault of Kent's or the BBC's – was problematic with the number of Conservative seats, at 165, smaller than at any time since 1906, and Labour now back in government with a majority of 179.

When Alan resumed work on the book in the spring of 1998, his enthusiasm for it had dimmed. The final quarter, from the advent of Margaret Thatcher's leadership to the loss of the 1997 general election, was, however, 'the best quarter' in Stewart's view, even though it was the least researched. 'It is much more personal ... Alan is almost freed from the sense of responsibility, he just pushes for the line.' This certainly separated it from Blake's history, but in the writing it was rushed – and it shows.

On publication in October 1998 he was, though, pleased – and relieved – that Robert Blake reviewed it warmly in *The Sunday Times*. *The Tories* was 'a wonderfully entertaining book, as one would expect from his hilarious diaries ... he is a serious historian and he has a case, though I have doubts. I am not convinced that Britain has declined as much as he seems to believe.' Otherwise the reviews were widespread, often generous, but lacked that spontaneous enthusiasm which separates the alpha mark from the beta. 'Unquestionably a disappointment,' was Alan's verdict,[10] and later, 'BB, which should have given me status, hasn't really'.[11]

After it was all over Alan and Stewart hardly referred to it, as Stewart recalled: 'You give a lot of your time to a subject that is going to be one of your memorials, then it comes out and doesn't work. In some ways it came out at the right time, the end of one phase in the history of the Tory Party when it needed to re-establish itself. In many ways it was the right moment. But it was also the wrong moment. In 1998 one thing the British public didn't want to hear about were the Tories who they had kicked out the previous year. Commercially the wrong time. He couldn't help that. He never reproached me. He never suggested that it's all your fault.'

THIRTY-FOUR

Back into the Commons

The itch to get back into the House of Commons did not diminish with time. Alan hired a professional adviser to smarten up his CV and began writing to Conservative associations in constituencies regardless of their suitability. In the winter of 1995, when he had been absent from Westminster for close on three years, he spotted the perfect billet, as he recorded in *The Last Diaries*. 'Lately I have – I just don't know why – been thinking about Chelsea. Albany resident, garden parties at Saltwood, safest seat in the country, etc. ... I know Chelsea are considering their vacancy ... I am still driven. I just feel that something may happen ... I popped over to the Great Hall and said a prayer at the long table where I composed my speech for the Sutton selection twenty-three years ago'.[1]

Following boundary revisions the liberal-minded but Conservative-voting Chelsea (MP Sir Nicholas Scott) and the southern Tory-leaning part of Kensington (MP Dudley Fishburn) were merging to become the new Kensington and Chelsea constituency, 'the safest, wealthiest Conservative seat in the country'.[2] Thus its Conservative candidate was to all intents and purposes guaranteed a seat in the Commons at the next general election. When Fishburn announced that he would not stand, it seemed as if Scott might walk it.

Alan's pursuit of the seat over the next two years was not without its tribulations. He also put in for others, including Sevenoaks. But Chelsea was the prize, 'a destination constituency. A place people dream about moving to rather than getting away from,' in the words of A.A. Gill.[3] His single-minded determination to return to Westminster was not shared by Jane, who did not want the parliamentary treadmill to begin once again.

In the summer of 1995 Scott 'crushed' a pushchair when reversing his car after a 'party' in his constituency, then shambled off 'to a friend's house', but was pursued, breathalysed positive, and arrested. This incident was hardly conducive to automatic election as Conservative candidate. Meanwhile Alan had been invited to speak at a Conservative Association garden party in the constituency. He took a taxi for a reconnaissance and recorded a chat with the cabby, who 'got going' on the state of the Tory Party and, somewhat embarrassed, said he thought Alan should replace John Major as Tory leader.

Paul and Marigold Johnson recall a summer party they gave – their house being in the northern part of the new constituency. There was some discussion over whether Alan and Jane should be invited. Paul says that in the end he secretly invited them, 'and all the sort of dutiful honourable upper-middle-class ladies of the party would come up and say, "Alan Clark's here, I would very much like to be introduced"'.[4]

By September 1995 K&C, as everyone now called it, was preparing its selection process. Alan submitted his CV. He was not confident. Relations with Jane were at a low ebb. 'I begged Jane to come on a long walk with me and help me think things through. It was a failure. We started by bickering; she just didn't comment at all on my dilemma except to say things like "you've had your chance". Never far below the surface the "you've been undone by women" accusation. A good deal of stuff about how absolutely impossible I am to live with. I suppose I am only making her unhappy (still).' He compounded matters by leaving the Barbican gate open – where were the dogs? They hadn't in fact wandered. 'We sat in total silence all through tea.'

The ladders and snakes of his emotions were no better illustrated three days later when he spoke to the 'perky-sounding' K&C agent, Barbara Lord, about its aim to get the longlist of potential candidates down to twenty by the Party conference in a fortnight. He was cheered, but then depressed: 'if I'm not in the twenty I will be thoroughly out of sorts (again)'. He wondered whether or not his status might work in his favour. 'But it helps me to become philosophical. If I lose at Chelsea then I will become a sage.'

His prayers were answered, but despite what he thought was a good interview before the selection committee, he reflected more on the agent's remarks. 'I think ... [hesitation] what will tell against you is your age ... If they do decide to replace Nick it will be with someone much younger'. When no call had come by 8 p.m. he knew it was over. Scott, it transpired, had been recommended for reselection. Next morning, 23 October, he set off for 'a great walk' and pondered that if age was the cause of his rejection 'that is a condition that worsens every day'. He closed the entry with a question, 'Can the mind overcome this reversal?' and answered himself with a remark that one day he would wish he could make true. 'The mind can do anything, even reverse a malignancy, if it is properly programmed.' And added what might be read as a PS: 'Only consolation is that Franko is back as Editor of the *Spectator*.'[5]

He was also thinking again of journalism ('I am not yet finished'), after an approach – however unlikely this sounded – by the *News of the World* to write a column (the precedent being Woodrow Wyatt, another independent-minded former MP, in his case Labour). Jane was 'totally opposed . . . Alastair [Campbell] said "grab it"'. He did.

By mid-November Nicholas Scott had been formally selected as the K&C Conservative candidate, but by a tiny margin: twenty-nine votes. The end of that particular road, but not of Alan's political ambition. In his frustration he wrote: 'What I hope, quite firmly now, is that the Tory Party is smashed to pieces and a huge number of people lose their seats. Then, at last perhaps, my particular brand of radicalism can grow.'

With Alan now at work on the television series *Alan Clark's History of the Tory Party*, a camera crew was dispatched to the K&C Conservative Association summer garden party where Alan was to speak. With hindsight the occasion has peculiar poignancy. Some unedited footage has survived showing Alan, standing at the top of a wrought-iron staircase, looking down to a crowded gathering, and being introduced by the ward chairman, who mentioned that they would be seeing a stage version of the *Diaries* – 'No you won't!' interrupted Alan, to general laughter. He spoke briefly about the current state of the Party and politics generally. Sir Michael Craig-Cooper, the constituency's Conservative Association chairman, was impressed; here was Alan working for the Party even though without a seat.[6] He was not alone. What Nicholas Scott said by way of thanks was eerie to say the least: 'I personally hope very much between now and the next general election he will find a seat'.

Relations with Jane now took a significant downturn. She left Saltwood, explaining her departure with a note:

6 August 1996

What <u>are</u> you
doing – London today
when you have no time
to spare or so you tell me.
Well I've gone too –
don't know when I'll be
back – to feed dogs, water
things, iron things, tidy things

cook things, find things –
the 'things' wives do –
we have so much and yet we
don't have time for each other.
Well make it, or lose it you
selfish genius. It's been
one moan all these past
weeks. If it is my fault say so.

Alan reflected in December the following year, having stapled the actual message into his diary: 'I suppose at that time I was ghastly to live with.' Jane, however, did not stay away for long, having found it boring to be away.

Filming for the television series continued at the Conservative Party conference at Bournemouth, where, as he wrote, his performance – fraternising with parliamentary friends and the Party faithful – was bogus. 'I have no standing. Am I famous, or infamous?' He was, however, noticed. Sarah Baxter, 'looking very attractive', wanted to interview him for *The Sunday Times*. What she wrote pleased him: her phrase 'busy reinventing himself' he thought a perfect formula.

On 16 October 1996 Alan and Jane's first grandchild was born, a boy. Andrew and his wife Sarah, who were living in the constituency, named him Albert and the following year he was enrolled as the Conservative Association's youngest member. In the same entry Alan wrote: 'I did privately notice that Nick Scott had barely improved his position by being "found" collapsing face-down in a side-street in Bournemouth, and saw he had been summoned to his Executive Council.' He added that his friend and parliamentary colleague Nicholas Soames had rung, 'claimed to have been told that people in Chelsea who had voted for him once now going to vote for me. "But don't do *anything*, Alan. Promise me you will say *NOTHING*" etc. Largely fantasy of course, but fun. I mustn't think about it. But no doubt I am on a roll at the moment.' On Monday, 4 November the Executive of the K&C Conservative Association met and recommended the deselection of Nicholas Scott. On 2 December the full Association met and confirmed Scott's deselection.

In his end-of-year review Alan was gloomy. 'The likelihood of my going back to the House, even being interviewed for Chelsea does seem quite remote.' The following day he pulled himself together, and sent off his application. Once into 1997, K&C moved quickly. In fact they had no choice as constitutionally the government had only four months left.

'What an exciting House it is going to be! If I go back in there I will die, or at least become impossibly infirm in harness.'

On Monday, 13 January he received a call from Barbara Lord. He was to be interviewed. 'A huge wash of adrenalin *surged* through me.' He got on well with the journalist Dean Godson, vice-chairman of the Conservative Association, who promised to tell him the questions for the first round of interviews (shades of Sutton a quarter of a century before). He learnt afterwards that the selection committee was enthusiastic, with every member voting for him. Next came the Association's Executive, but beforehand he wrote of 'darling little Jane. I am putting her through this ordeal. She is loyal. Doesn't of course want me to get through. And she is right, but I am driven by the sword ... I thought, too, that if I win I will immediately write Jane a long letter, not just telling her of my love, and my gratitude; but setting out my commitment to her.'

Alan dreaded the Executive, a difficult audience. With 150 members present he had to use a mike, which he hated. Jane accompanied him and made 'a conquest' of their minder, an 'initially un-twinkly battleaxe'. He was convinced he 'underperformed ... So although I came out top it was done not by conviction, but by allegiance.'

The final scenes in 'the last great offensive', as Alan called it, were played out in Kensington Town Hall on Thursday, 23 January. Andrew Roberts, a member of the Association, was one of the 1,200 people who packed the Town Hall that evening.[7] The atmosphere was 'very much a sense that it was going to be a great evening – completely free and much better than anything on in the West End'. Alan remembered the 'hateful paparazzi and brutal reporters with mikes' who mobbed him and Jane as they arrived. 'Aren't you even worse than Sir Nicholas Scott?' asked one journalist. The candidates were confined to an underground '"green room", windowless, tableless with four bottles of mineral water (three of them fizzy, so liable to induce a burp when answering questions)'.

In the view of Simon Hoggart in *The Guardian* Alan was the most left-wing of the candidates, 'which gives you some idea about the rest of the field'.[8] But Alan felt the others all had something. Patricia ('Trish') Morris – 'nice-looking, long copper-curled hair, vivacious, had wowed conference earlier on the ERM'.[9] Daniel Moylan – 'outrageously camp, but a former president of the Union and with a high-profile record in local government'; and Martin Howe, nephew of Geoffrey, '"the Eurosceptic QC" with a pretty wife and a portentous manner'. Moylan went second (after Patricia Morris). It was widely felt by others who attended that no-one else was on top form, which helped Alan; Jane was also an enormous asset – indeed Roberts says that without her presence, which demonstrated how vital she was to him as his wife, he would not have gained the nomination.

Before Alan went upstairs to face the membership, he rehearsed in a make-up room in front of a mirror. 'I was demi-transcendant, the space-craft was on course – collision, burn out, or triumph. Jane quite rightly came and fetched me out, knowing that I would be unsettling myself.' Roberts recalled what happened next. 'It was quite clear that his policy of being entirely unaffected by any sense of embarrassment for anything he had done in the past was going to work, K&C being a very different kind of constituency from 90 per cent of the other Tory constituencies in the country, indeed 99 per cent. It is much more sophisticated and it doesn't take infidelity to be an absolute bar to be chosen.' As has been shown by Alan's successors representing the seat – Michael Portillo and Malcolm Rifkind – its Conservative electors believe that its MP should be a serious and significant figure. Roberts agrees that there was a very strong snobbish element in it, which did Alan no harm at all: Eton and Oxford; that his father was Lord Clark 'of *Civilisation*'; that he lived in a castle; that he had an apartment at Albany (no-one seemed to worry that he did not have a home in the constituency).

People were expecting a dazzling performance from him – and they got it. When someone asked if he had skeletons in his past, his response, 'I've got whole cupboards of them', gained him a huge laugh and an ovation. Roberts doesn't think the question was intended in a hostile way, but more of a joke. 'The way he dealt with it was superb.' On political issues he did not alienate the strong liberal nature of the Chelsea mem-bership, which had always been in favour of Nicholas Scott. That he adored Margaret Thatcher worked in his favour, as did the fact that he was a loyal Majorite. Beforehand some members thought that the question of the Harkess family – 'the coven' – might prove a problem, alienating women and angering men – possibly out of envy? 'However,' says Roberts, 'the exact opposite happened. It amused women and impressed men no end.'

Although Alan did not win on the first ballot or the second, amongst the 900 who were eligible to vote, on the third he gained a 'fairly substantial majority', says Sir Michael Craig-Cooper, 'by an intoxicating mixture of guile, charm, flirtation and chutzpah', explained *The Guardian*.[10]

Outside, the press – British and foreign – were assembled and hungry for news. To ensure that no reporters or camera crews gained access to the Town Hall, Conservative Central Office locked the doors – doubtless against all fire regulations. This also meant that no-one inside the hall could get out. Pleading desperation for the loo, Roberts slipped between the arms of an official who was holding back the door into the foyer. With the outer doors into the street still locked, Roberts wrote on a scrap of paper from his wallet, 'It's Alan!' and pressed it against the glass. 'All the hacks were outside – even if we'd have shouted they wouldn't have heard us – there was absolute general jubilation on behalf of the press and the guy from ITN who I had known and been interviewed by beforehand, mouthed, "Promise, promise?" They ran with the story. By the time the official from Central Office went out to rather grandly and pompously announce the result to the waiting world, the waiting world already knew.'

Alan reflected afterwards: 'I was incredibly happy. But also got a hint of "all my life has been but a preparation for this hour . . . ".* Now almost at once, it seemed generally preordained. We went up the stairs to a loud cheer. I made a few anodyne remarks of gratitude; then congratulations, including lovely ones from Sarah and Andrew – and out to a battalion of flash bulbs and that most incredible sense of euphoria. Finally we were hauled away, followed Barbara to Jeanie Craig's house (all I wanted, desperately, was a pint of beer. I couldn't/didn't drink the champagne).'

In the aftermath W.F. Deedes, whose family had once owned Saltwood Castle, recalled in his *Daily Telegraph* column the case of Sir Patrick Spens, who returned from India after independence – he had been Chief Justice – and at the age of about sixty-five put in for the South Kensington seat. 'On the night of selection, he came dressed for a dinner, resplendent in white tie, tails and medals. The meeting was enchanted by this elderly grandee with parliamentary experience and picked him. It became a habit.'[11]

Alan's selection had an unexpected benefit when, on 29 January, Sir James Goldsmith's Referendum Party withdrew its Kensington and Chelsea candidate, Robin Birley, Sir James's stepson. Birley urged his supporters to vote for Alan, 'a proud and brave Englishman'. Alan, dubbed 'a Eurosceptic', attended the meeting and said there had been no deal on the question of a European referendum, but he thought it valuable that the Referendum Party had raised the level of debate on the issue.

Hardly had Alan got used to being a candidate again than John Major announced the general election for Thursday, 1 May. Alan was no longer optimistic: 'We are on the verge of annihilation it seems', he wrote on 18

---

* Winston Churchill's phrase on becoming Prime Minister in 1940.

March. 'Polls this morning show Labour 26 points ahead and the *Sun* has turned.' As for himself, 'I haven't had a normal pulse for ten days.' Four days later: 'I hate elections. This one hasn't yet started but already I want to fast forward ... My own majority is far from secure because of a personal anti vote ... and my fan vote is fickle.' He and Jane spent Easter at Eriboll, where he mused, 'Am I relaxed, confident, beautifully turned out, one of the few "real" Conservatives, historian, authoritative, high-profile media figure: to be returned smoothly to the new "difficult", "interesting", etc House of Commons? Or am I shaky, nervous of crowds, with incipient prostate, bowel and basal cancers; demi deaf in one (right) ear, completely non-functionally impotent with a limited lifespan and an enormous crowd of ill-wishers waiting for me to fall over? The next month is critical. But it is April; my "lucky" month.'

Alan's election campaign attracted enormous and positive media interest, but his confidence was undermined when on 15 April Carol Midgley of *The Times* reported to him that Max Clifford, mastermind of the Harkess furore three years earlier, was preparing something big, 'but won't tell us what it is'. He also had to cope with a rumour – perhaps connected? – that James Harkess was flying from South Africa to campaign for Robert Atkinson, the Labour candidate, on the grounds that Alan was 'not deserving of becoming an MP'. When Harkess arrived two days later he was barely noticed.

Simon Hoggart from *The Guardian* followed Alan round, noting that 'it is a seriously rich constituency. Some of the voters may even be richer than Clark himself.' Jane accompanied him everywhere, bringing, as Alan said, 'a uniform goodwill wherever we go, dispelling some of the cloud of suspicion which hangs over me'. Hoggart, a veteran of these walkabouts, remarked, 'It's not really canvassing at all, except in name. For the safest Tory seat in the country it is vital to be seen, to prove that you're not taking your constituents for granted. So every vote has to be stacked up one by one. An opponent said how impressed he had been at Clark "coming into the lion's den". "It's your cross we need," said Clark.'[12]

On election day *The Sunday Times* dispatched A.A. Gill to Chelsea. He and Alan had links, Gill being the son of Michael Gill, the producer of *Civilisation*, and married to Amber, daughter of Alan's Oxford friends, Tony and Ethne Rudd. In his view Alan was 'a bespoke candidate for a constituency that understands tailoring'. Gill did what many reporters have done – describe his walk, 'the first thing you notice. It's a sort of louche, pelvis-gyrating swagger, as close as an English public schoolboy gets to a New York pimp's jive roll.' He also observed, the second thing, 'that everyone else notices him, too. Women famously treat him as though he were Mr Darcy with a bus pass.' Sir Michael Craig-Cooper commented that he was the 'same to everyone – duke or dustman'.

Clark was, Gill added, 'touchingly and naively pleased at every brief encounter ... A tall, incredibly cool and handsome black man saunters past and does a double take. He stops, strikes a pose and points two index fingers: "Yo! You're a bad man." Clark smiles and replies: "I doubt if I'm as bad as you." "I learnt it all from you, man, I just copy you. You got my vote." They jive-roll away from each other like fighting cocks. "Now you see, isn't that extraordinary, a homosexual black drug dealer being nice to me?"' Even after Gill told Alan that he shouldn't tell him anything he doesn't want his constituents to know, 'the blue gossip and hot opinions flow without let or hindrance on the leadership race: "You don't know how the party really loathes Patten. Hague would be a disaster."'[13]

That night when the votes were counted, Alan (19,887) had a majority of 9,519 over Labour (10,368). After five years in the wilderness Alan was once more a Member of Parliament, albeit of a party that barely recognised itself: only 165 MPs whereas in 1992 it had 336.

When the House of Commons reassembled following the Conservatives' rout by New Labour, Alan could hardly wait. This was the moment he had been waiting for. But, as he related to his diary on 8 May, what an anticlimax! 'Yesterday I was up at the Commons. The whole thing should have been too delicious for words – but I was haunted by apprehension, and also a curious sense of hostility from colleagues.' Matthew Parris, in his political sketch of the new Parliament in *The Times*, could not resist mentioning Alan. 'One [new Labour MP] sat with Tony Benn. Had Peter Mandelson not warned him not to talk to strange men? ... On the Opposition side, gingerly testing their new benches, sat the remnants of Margaret Thatcher's once-proud parliamentary army. Virginia Bottomley, equally reckless in choice of companion, sat beside Alan Clark.'[14]

The Conservative membership of the Commons was decimated; many old friends were no longer in the House or had been elevated to the Lords, where in successive honours lists after the 1992 election he had hoped to find his name. But all thoughts of a life peerage were now forgotten. In the Commons the first task for the defeated Tories was to elect a new leader as John Major had resigned on the morning after the defeat and taken refuge at the Oval, where he was photographed watching Surrey play a British Universities XI.

The Conservatives of Alan's generation found themselves forced to give way to comparative youth. Tony Blair, the new Prime Minister, was forty-four years old; the Tories now went one better. If the voters of Enfield had not rejected Michael Portillo[15] all might have been very different. Alan wrote on 5 May that Portillo was 'probably the strongest' candidate, before going on to sum up the others: 'Ken [Clarke], supposedly, the most genial and experienced – won't get past the hard right. Little Hague – my aphorism about "the guy's a golf ball" has already got currency, I'm glad to say. Redwood is fluent in today's *Times* – but I don't like him. Lilley is cerebral – should be the leader, but hasn't got the oomph – white rabbit in the teapot at the Mad Hatter's tea party. Michael [Howard] presents me with a problem. I ought to support him, but I'm hesitating.' Ultimately the Conservatives selected Hague, aged thirty-six and an MP for only eight years. Whereas Blair had no easily identifiable accent, Hague's Yorkshire burr was immediately recognisable. Hague, who had famously been seen on television as a sixteen-year-old making a Thatcherite speech at the Conservative Party conference of 1977, had a keen intelligence, he debated well. In short he seemed ideal.

Alan's diaries for the next two years show a steady decline in enthusiasm for the new young and inexperienced leader, culminating in these sentences of vintage Clark commentary on 7 May 1999: 'little Hague, in his "Bruce Willis" haircut (whatever that is) and his dreadful flat northern voice. I find it just awful, skin-curdling, that the Party – our great Party – formerly led by Disraeli, Balfour, Churchill, Macmillan, Thatcher (even) could be in the hands of this dreadful little man who has absolutely no sense whatever of history, or pageantry or *noblesse oblige*. The whole enterprise to be conducted on the basis of a Management Consultancy exam tick-box, and the "findings" of a "focus group". Is not the 1922 Committee a valid "focus group"? as Eric Forth, justifiably, complained.'

Much else would change as New Labour with its huge majority realised that power could be exercised in Downing Street and Whitehall. Matthew d'Ancona, writing a few days later in *The Sunday Telegraph*, picked up the prophecy of a Labour acquaintance that this would be the 'last real Parliament', Tony Blair's immediate decision to reduce Prime Minister's Questions to a once-a-week joust being indicative. However, the government's decision to impose the change immediately without prior consultation infuriated Tory MPs. Alan was in the vanguard, asking the Speaker to intervene against this 'encroachment on the rights of Members of Parliament by Government'. D'Ancona particularly pleased Alan. 'This is what one would expect of the party of Robert Peel, Enoch Powell and Alan Clark. Parliament has long been the Conservative obsession, the party's mythic focus. The Tory candidates I know who stood ten days ago all wanted desperately to be part of this mystical elite.'[16] Not least Alan. His anger at the Prime Minister's apparent contempt for the House continued to erupt intermittently. On 2 September 1998 he remarked in a Commons debate, 'We are being used simply as a rubber stamp. The news is released by leak, by briefing, so that ordinary members of the House read about it for the first time in the newspapers as they are on the way to the House ... We are simply not being consulted.'

It should have been fun, but for the first few weeks being back in the Commons proved a frustrating period, disappointing at just about every level. As a senior Conservative, in experience as well as age, the obvious office for him was the 1922 Committee, possibly the chairmanship. But he admitted playing his hand badly, in his word he 'bogged' it, lacking strong support (he had been unable to reach Jane on the phone at the crucial moment and wrote that if he had he felt sure she would have said 'Balls, go for it, lead from the front'). The Party leadership election was proving fractious, with talk of tactical voting at each stage between Right and Left, leaving Alan to remark to his diary that if poll figures plummeted by the autumn, he might even put himself forward in November, although more likely in 1998.

Before the final leadership vote on 19 June he reported a chance meeting in New Palace Yard with his arch-enemy from the past, Michael Heseltine, still an MP, but in his last Parliament: 'I never thought I'd find myself saying this but I wish you were in the running.' Alan says Heseltine, now an Opposition backbencher, responded on the lines, 'I could never understand, you were taking the wrong briefs, we could have worked together.' David Davis, to whom he related the incident, gave him an answer: 'You're opium now, he had to have some. He's aching with withdrawal. No, worse, you were a still-smoking stub on the pavement which he picked up for a last drag.' To which Alan added his own brief comment, 'The delicious irony of it.' Perhaps being back at Westminster wasn't so bad after all. And early in July he was elected to the 1922 Committee.

With the summer recess following almost immediately, it would be autumn before the Tories could begin working out how to be the party of opposition after eighteen years as the party of government. Alan and Jane left for Eriboll. But on the morning of Sunday, 31 August, having just returned in the dinghy from a visit to the island in Loch Eriboll, their daughter-in-law Julie, James's wife, drove up in the Range Rover with shocking news. 'Diana and Dodi have been killed in a car crash pursued by the paparazzi.' For Alan this also had a strange significance. Three weeks earlier he had written a piece for *The Spectator* headed 'Death by press gang',[17] in which he criticised press harassment, journalists out to 'stand-up' gossip about someone's private life'. The piece was picked up by the national press, not least because of his final paragraph: 'And still elusive, though occasionally one must assume in the telescopic sight of every editor is the ultimate trophy, the most brightly plumaged of all. To accelerate, and then to be the first in capturing, the sudden death of Her Royal Highness in "unexplained circumstances".'

Alan wrote, 'We felt a great rage. Nothing will change, except that a lovely icon has been destroyed. Most fortuitously it was the Eriboll service that afternoon – in the Gaelic – and Donny [the incumbent] adapted beautifully. (Unlike, I was horrified to note that evening, the service at Craithie [Balmoral's church].)' With the royal family much criticised for their initial lack of response to the tragedy, Alan was completely in sympathy with the 'brave utterances' of Diana's brother, Charles Spencer, in Westminster Abbey. Five years later Spencer, in an interview in *The Guardian*, said that Alan had written saying he agreed with his every word, but added: 'Just watch now. The press and the royal family are two of the most powerful institutions in the country and they will make sure your name is dragged through the dirt.'[18]

Jane had her own crisis, what Alan called 'the strange sadistic ordeal of the case against their rottweiler, Lëhni'. They were facing a prosecution at Folkestone magistrates court over allegations that a BBC cameraman had been bitten during filming at Saltwood. Jane was warned that in giving evidence she might have to be in the dock 'for AN HOUR'. Alan became convinced that the BBC were out to get him and tried unsuccessfully to intercede with John Birt, the Director-General. Eventually the magistrates found for Alan and Jane, but it was not an experience they wished to repeat. In his day diary Alan noted that Jane 'almost fainted'. However, on the family front they were delighted by the birth of a second grandson – James and Julie's first-born, Angus.

William Hague's endeavours to modernise the Conservative Party included an MPs' bonding session at Eastbourne. It was not wholly successful, revealing, as Rachel Sylvester in *The Daily Telegraph* remarked,[19] 'a gaping new split in the party over style'. The dress code was casual. Alan was noticed immediately when he turned up in a tweed cap – 'dressed for the country in this year's hot fabric "knobbly tweed"', whereas John Gummer wore a suit, Bernard Jenkin sported jeans and the orange-haired Michael Fabricant a grey sweatshirt. Jumpers were also much in evidence. But Nicholas Soames refused to attend 'on principle' and other absentees included John Major, Michael Heseltine and Sir Edward Heath.

More serious was Alan's contribution to a fringe meeting event organised by *The Guardian* at the Party's annual conference (this year at Blackpool). Already viewed by Hague's men as a dinosaur, he made what Michael White described in *The Guardian* as 'an unguarded comment', a remark inspired by the opening of all-party talks in Belfast. 'The only solution for dealing with the IRA is to kill 600 people in one night, let the UN and everyone else make a great scene, and it's over for twenty years.' White reported 'a few gasps in the audience but little or no sign of support'.[20] Alan himself said that his IRA remark was but a 'jocular aside' of black humour: 'I was not even on my feet'.[21]

Back at Westminster Alan was appalled that Hague had agreed to dispense with hereditary peerages. 'I think the Party has had it,' he wrote in his diary. 'Our grip was ephemeral while Labour, even in the low, low times post-1983, had its hard core of TU and urban support. Now the hard core remains – "it has nowhere else to go" – but the whole sticky-crap consumerist adspeak culture has seduced our centre.' Journalists used to wait for the outcome of 1922 Committee meetings; now in December 1997, after ninety minutes discussing 'party reforms', the door was opened and there was not a single reporter in the corridor. The Commons ceased to matter, as tiny attendances demonstrated. On 5 February 1998 Alan articulated his view: 'Our great party, its historic roots dependent on rural dwellers and walkers in the countryside – and we don't even turn up, still less illuminate the Debate.'

Just before Christmas 1997 Alan suffered the added, if self-imposed, pressure of a High Court appearance where he was suing the *Evening Standard* over a parody of his diaries, which he saw as 'passing off' (see Interlude, 'Not Amused'). The stress did not help his sleep, but over Christmas at Eriboll it was Jane who became ill, was sick and collapsed unconscious. In the local hospital she was placed under observation. 'I thought how catastrophic if she died. I had to see it in personal terms. I would withdraw utterly. "In mourning." Instantly become a recluse (and a pretty scrawny one. All I have eaten today is bread and butter!)' With Jane absent no-one knew where she had put the plum pudding.

As 1998 sped by so Alan's opportunities to raise a storm multiplied. Early in June he tackled the plan to build a memorial garden in Kensington Gardens in memory of Princess Diana 'unnecessary, wasteful, unwanted

and hazardous'. He wrote in his capacity as the local MP, but the combination of Alan and Princess Diana was irresistible. Letters – both for and
against – poured into the press.[22] Inevitably the memorial was built,
although both its architecture and engineering were widely criticised.

With the World Cup under way in France, football hooliganism was
another subject guaranteed to draw blood. Alan remarked on BBC Radio
4's *Today*[23] that football punch-ups – English fans had rioted after the
England–Tunisia match in Marseilles – were a substitute for medieval
tournaments. With widespread 'prejudice' against the English abroad,
violence was inevitable. 'It's perfectly natural that some of the fans should
be obstreperous.' This was not a popular view at Westminster. Nor had
Alan finished. He amplified his *Today* remarks in support of an *Evening
Standard* reporter, Alex Renton, who had been knocked unconscious
during the riots: 'If you are English you are targeted, particularly if you
are English and tough-looking, and are wearing an English flag. And why
shouldn't you? In a sense it is a kind of compliment to the English martial
spirit I suppose. But they really haven't got a chance, these guys, everyone
is out to get them. There is absolutely nobody to speak up for them.'

Early one March morning in 1998, Alan drove down to Bratton. It was
getting on for forty years since he and Jane bought Town Farm for
£2,600 – he even remembered the vendor, the estate of Leroy Fielding.
But on ceasing to be MP for Plymouth Sutton in 1992 it had barely been
used. They decided to sell. 'The whole place very scruffy indeed.[24] Only
the "studio" is pleasing with Campling's door, and the giant (and, as it
now turns out, not invaluable) Duncans for the Queen Mary.'[25] His visit
caused him to reflect – perhaps a touch maudlin – 'It's strange, for ages
I was sad and calm and nostalgic about Bratton. It was monstrous of my
father to keep us so short of money that I had to sell the fields – "the
cream of Bratton" for £500. I recall walking up the "dump" road, looking
over "Bennett's" gate and feeling immensely content. Not much later
came "Jollyboy" and "more run" in the white pushchair.'[26] Typically, he
also recalled a trip over the Tamar and 'the magic afternoon with the girl
from Bray Shop'.

In the second drawer of the 'Rye' desk he found his diaries from the
early sixties. 'Somewhat mannered writing.' Written, he felt, more 'for
publication' than subsequently. He saw them now as 'a time-warp, when
we were pushed for cash, and made-do-and-mend'. This reminded him
of how, when an MP, he 'never really got it *up*, although a lot of "2nd
house" allowance money went on it, in my last Parliament'. '"My last

Parliament." Hm.' This set him musing. 'Everything seems to be collapsing. The Tory Party really doesn't *make any sense* at present. Just
running behind, fetid, panting. Now I read that the Queen is cutting
down as fast as possible – on ceremony. How crazy to get rid of the coach
and uniforms!' He felt 'pretty low. Of course I can say fuck them, fuck-
you-all. But I am sent back to have one more try at the sword. At present
I am lost in the undergrowth. I say, keep calm and concentrate on BB.'

Bratton was sold for £186,000. Visiting it with Jane, he reflected, 'I have
practically no pangs. It is peaceful, on a sunny July afternoon, because
there is no background noise, no M-way roar.' With the West Country
traffic, it took five and a half hours to drive from Saltwood; they returned
via Seend, a round trip of more than 600 miles in a day, 'absolutely
knackered'. Then a hiccough – the buyer welshed, but, as Alan put it,
they were 'very clever to have pouched the deposit'. Before Christmas it
was finally auctioned and sold to a man 'who hadn't even been inside (saw
it that morning) for £167,000'.

In spring 1999 Alan became one of the few supporters at Westminster of
the Serbs in the conflict that engulfed the former Yugoslavia. His attachment, sentimental perhaps, went back to 1949 when he and his Oxford
friend Malcolm Napier drove there on holiday in an Austin Sheerline.
Half a century later, in what *The Guardian* called 'his last hurrah',[27] he was
vocal in opposing American and Nato intervention in Serbia. In his diary
in early April he wrote, 'I am hugely depressed about Kosovo. Those
loathsome, verminous gypsies' – as he described the KLA (Kosovo Liberation Army), the Kosovar Albanian terrorist group – 'and the poor brave
Serbs'. He thought the crisis 'media-driven' and clashed with his friend
Alastair Campbell, Tony Blair's official spokesman. He was 'howled down'
in the Commons, as Matthew Parris noted, for 'the indiscretion' of
'venturing praise for the Serbian people ("brave Christians")'[28] and in
particular the former Serbian President, Slobodan Milosevic, having earlier
spoken in a Commons debate (25 March) and followed it up by writing a
passionate defence of the Serbs in *The Observer* (28 March 1999). 'The
assertion that human rights within the boundaries of a sovereign nation are
best defended by a sustained bombardment of its own civilian population is,
to put it most kindly, Orwellian.' He attacked 'the credulity of the Left,
and of progressive thinkers', and asked them how they had 'swallowed
whole the CIA-funded propaganda that demonises the Serbs?'. As so
often, he drew on history, reminding readers that the US Ambassador,
William Walker, in charge of monitoring forces in Bosnia, had been

On the road to the House of Commons.
Campaigning with Jane in Plymouth Sutton.

'The Lady' –
Margaret Thatcher
seen in 1987, when
Alan was Minister
for Trade.

At Trade in early 1986 Alan was involved in agreeing a long term Anglo–Soviet economic co-operation
programme, but he found many of the formalities of ministerial life tedious.

On the Government front bench during a Defence debate, 9 January 1990, Alan sits next to the Secretary of State, Tom King. Later he is seen answering a question from the dispatch box.

FAMILY WEDDINGS

James marries Ju
at Eriboll, a sem
derelict church
which they resto
for the ceremon
and (BELOW)
Andrew marries
Sarah in 1993 at
Saltwood church
The Life Guards
provided
the guard of
honour.

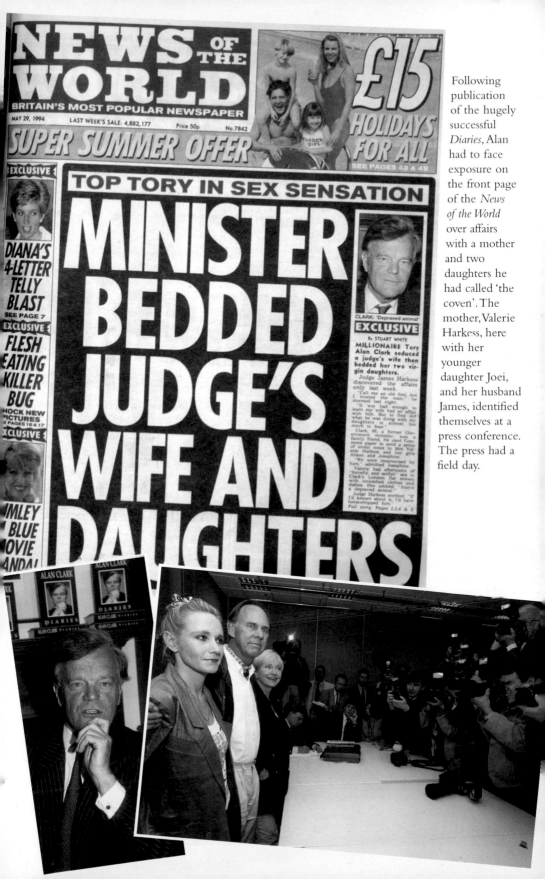

Following publication of the hugely successful *Diaries*, Alan had to face exposure on the front page of the *News of the World* over affairs with a mother and two daughters he had called 'the coven'. The mother, Valerie Harkess, here with her younger daughter Joei, and her husband James, identified themselves at a press conference. The press had a field day.

NEWS OF THE WORLD

BRITAIN'S MOST POPULAR NEWSPAPER

MAY 29, 1994   LAST WEEK'S SALE: 4,882,177   Price 50p   No.7842

£15 HOLIDAYS FOR ALL
SEE PAGES 48 & 49

SUPER SUMMER OFFER

EXCLUSIVE

DIANA'S 4-LETTER TELLY BLAST
SEE PAGE 7

EXCLUSIVE

FLESH EATING KILLER BUG
SHOCK NEW PICTURES
SEE PAGES 16 & 17

EXCLUSIVE

...MLEY BLUE ...OVIE ...ANDAL

TOP TORY IN SEX SENSATION

MINISTER BEDDED JUDGE'S WIFE AND DAUGHTERS

CLARK: 'Depraved animal'

EXCLUSIVE

By STUART WHITE

MILLIONAIRE Tory Alan Clark seduced a judge's wife then bedded her two virgin daughters.

Judge James Harkess discovered the affairs only last week.

'Call me an old fool, but I trusted the man,' he stormed last night.

'It was bad enough to learn my wife had an affair with him. But to find out what he was doing with my daughters is almost too much to bear.'

Clark, 66, a former Government minister, was a family friend. He used Commons paper to send a series of erotic notes to Mrs Valerie Harkess and her girls Alison and Josephine.

'We were mesmerised by him,' admitted Josephine.

Valerie had afternoons of 'forceful and selfish' sex in Clark's London flat strewn with unwashed clothes and dishes. She sobbed: 'Alan's a depraved animal.'

Judge Harkess seethed: 'If I known about it, I'd have horsewhipped him.'

Full story: Pages 2,3,4 & 5

TWO FAVOURITE LOCATIONS

With Jane at Zermatt high above the tree line. He had first visited Switzerland as a child. In the early 1950s he built Chalet Caroline on an old pigsty. Scotland was in the Clark genes, although the family links had ended when his grandmother died in the 1940s. After the death of Papa in 1983 Alan (seen here with Tom, their Jack Russell) and Jane acquired the Eriboll estate in Sutherland, now owned by their elder son James.

THE RETURN TO THE COMMONS

Newly selected as Tory candidate for Kensington and Chelsea in January 1997, Alan appeared on the *Breakfast with Frost* programme with the Chancellor, Kenneth Clarke. Their views on government policy on Europe and the single currency did not coincide.

Canvassing at the 1997 general election where he was elected with the second highest Conservative majority.

Alan's final appearances in the House were in support of the Serbs during the Kosovo conflict. On 13 April 1999, his seventy-first birthday, with the Hoare-Belisha watch in his top pocket, he makes a point from the back benches, with David Davis sitting next to him, and Peter Tapsell behind. Six weeks later he was in King's College Hospital, London, being operated on for the removal of a brain tumour.

LAST SUMMER AT SALTWOOD

Alan made his final public appearance at the XK rally at Saltwood on 18 July 1999. He told James on the phone: 'Fitting, somehow, that my impending departure should be attended by this huge retinue of XKs.'

A few days later, with Hannah, who knew instinctively that her master was unwell.

involved in the financing of the Contras. 'Have you no recall of that "Free World" crap that embraced Battista, Noriega, Syngman Rhee, Bao Dai, Nguyen Van Thieu and Sukarno?'

He was without a good word for Tony Blair. 'British soldiers are not mercenaries where there is no threat to our citizens. The safest rule in such circumstances is, stick to humanitarian aid. What do you imagine so far is the cost? How much aid might this have funded?' He saw this as a 'US-driven operation ... and the US never intervenes objectively. It may be that the pressures of domestic politics oblige the President, as a distraction, to order the obliteration of a pharmaceutical plant in the Sudan. Or it may be that considerations of oil brokerage, the "Seven Sisters" and projected pipeline routes, prevent attention being paid to, or even mention made, of the genocidal Turkish campaign against the PPK. It is certain that the continuing infringement of human rights in China is a complete irrelevance weighed against monopoly trade concessions to US-based multinationals. There are risks as well as humiliations in Britain doing always what the US instructs.'

Alan was not alone. As Andrew Rawnsley noted in *The Observer*, 'Rarely in the field of human conflict has there been a stranger pro-Serb coalition.'[29] Denis Healey and Tony Benn, historians Norman Stone, Correlli Barnett and John Erickson, feminists Germaine Greer and Julie Burchill, and the United States contingent included none other than Henry Kissinger. Alan was pleased at one personal response. Erickson wrote that Alan's *Observer* article was 'the most stringent and searching exposé ... the propagandist prating that we are embarked upon a "just war", merely by so characterising it, betrays woeful ignorance on the part of messrs Clinton and Blair'. His article, he concluded, will 'continue to resonate, above all as a demonstration that none will profit from remaining witless or heedless, passively bemused or actively suborned by "Orwellian speak"'.[30]

As a result his unlikely friendship with Tony Blair's chief press secretary, Alastair Campbell, was placed under temporary strain. They had known each other since the early 1990s when Alan was a Defence Minister and Campbell a journalist on the *Daily Mirror*. Their connection, wrote Alan, was 'a source of considerable irritation within the Tory leadership and I have in the past been hauled over the coals ... for saying that a problem with the Conservative Party was that we didn't have anyone like you'.[31] Campbell himself would write on Alan's death, 'he was a journalist's dream and a [Tory] spin doctor's nightmare. No matter how hard he tried (i.e. not very) he couldn't help telling you what he thought.'[32]

On a Saturday evening in May 1995, Alan and Jane were invited by Campbell and his partner Fiona as last-minute dinner guests in place of Neil and Glenys Kinnock. Campbell's fellow Hampstead residents, Melvyn and Cate Bragg, were also there. According to Campbell in his diaries Melvyn was 'absolutely horrified. He said he loathed Alan.'[33] Bragg remembers it differently. 'I don't recall loathing him at all. I was surprised when he said Alan was going to be at dinner because Alan seemed to be so very Tory and Alastair seemed to be so very Labour. I've got Tory friends, but I didn't think Alastair had. A bit of journalese ... I might have said "Christ, Alan Clark!".

Campbell recalls that the Clarks arrived in one of his Bentleys, which could barely squeeze through the two lines of cars parked in the narrow Victorian street close to the south side of Hampstead Heath. Alan left the car parked outside with the engine running and asked Campbell, 'Where does a chap park his charabanc round these parts?' Bragg recalls that it was 'a very good dinner and we got on extremely well. I remember Alastair teasing him about leaving his huge car in the street and what the local lads might do. Alan actually went out to check that the tyres were OK.'

Bentleys had already figured in their friendship. Early in the 1990s Alan kept in the Commons car park a dark blue Bentley bought with the number plate AC 1800.[34] On one occasion when they lunched Campbell mentioned that it always seemed to be in the same spot. Alan responded, 'You can have it if you want? You know AC – AC.' Alan was as good as his word, sending Campbell the keys. If Campbell was even momentarily tempted he quickly 'decided that the image of me running round in the Bentley was not quite right'. He returned the keys.

The hospitality was reciprocated. Campbell enjoyed visiting Saltwood. He recalls Alan showing him 'a seriously vicious-looking sword', which had been a gift of the Chilean dictator, Pinochet, and asking him to imagine 'the damage it could do to some dissident's throat'. He thought that Alan showed off his Hitler relics to see how his guest responded, hoping he might be shocked. Alastair, however, enjoyed saying, simply, 'oh yes, interesting'. Less threatening were the bagpipes Jane had given him when he stood down as an MP. She thought it would give him something to do, but Alan confessed that he 'couldn't get a note out of them'. Campbell, being a bagpipe player, was not surprised. Alan's pipes lacked the essential reeds.

Alan saw Tony Blair, believes Campbell, as the Labour equivalent of Margaret Thatcher. 'He thought Tony was absolutely the business. She was different for all sorts of reasons, she was a Tory and a woman and she was his sort of Tory and she had this talent, this ability to reach people. I think he felt that Tony was very bright, very different. He'd say it absolutely full of admiration, not you dirty rotten bastards.'

Who was joking when Alan recorded a particularly poor performance by William Hague at Prime Minister's Questions in December? 'Hague walked into an ambush which (as it turned out) he had set up for himself.' This was the occasion when Lord Cranborne did his deal with Tony Blair over the future of hereditary peers. The talk of the Lords between the two ACs led their conversation in a direction which Alan enjoyed recounting: 'Gratifyingly, Alastair C[ampbell] came on the phone for 35 minutes on Friday night (twice offered me a peerage, incidentally). In the end we were cut off. I assume that the Downing Street switchboard were changing the tape.' When reminded of this exchange, Campbell laughed.

Alan, though, was serious about the Serbs. During a Commons debate on the war in Kosovo, he was among those who criticised the way Nato briefly imported Campbell to handle its presentation of information. Those who knew of Alan's friendship with Campbell particularly enjoyed his remarks on 19 April 1999. 'Members have told us that the war is about Nato's credibility. Few things are more likely to reduce its credibility – what is left of it – than sending the head of the No. 10 press office to process Nato communiqués. Mr Campbell would be better advised to stick to coaching the Prime Minister on how to respond. At present that response consists simply of waving his hands about and repeating the name "Milosevic" at every possible opportunity.'[35]

The following day Campbell responded. 'I couldn't normally care two hoots what Tory MPs say about me, as you know, but as I don't see you as the run of the mill Tory, but a very intelligent man and a friend, I wanted to set out the position. This is not a "spin" job.' He went on to explain that he had been asked to boost 'the strategic capacity' of Nato's communications effort, and get better co-ordination. 'We have already worked to very good effect, not least because of the talent and enthusiasm of the civil servants who have been seconded from the UK.' Campbell concluded: 'I know you disagree with what we are doing, but we are doing it, and the media is a vital part of the conflict. It requires the kind of experience and commitment that I and others outside Nato HQ can bring to the operation.' And he added, 'I've not seen a journalist for days – bliss.' Typical of the relationship was his final line. 'I still think you're wonderful, whatever your alleged views.'[36]

Not Amused

As the 1997 election rolled towards its increasingly inevitable conclusion Alan had found himself the subject of a parody of his *Diaries* in London's *Evening Standard*. During the campaign he confessed that 'Alan Clark's Secret Election Diary' was on occasion 'very funny'.[1] Once elected as Kensington and Chelsea's MP, he might have expected the diary to end. But Max Hastings, Editor of the *Standard* and a long-standing friend of Alan's, had other ideas.

The *Standard*'s parodist, Peter Bradshaw (otherwise one of the paper's leader writers), had been on top form, having actually begun his alternative diary in the run-up to Alan's election as Kensington and Chelsea candidate:

Kensington Town Hall, midnight   *Thursday, 23 January 1997*

Victory!

I have been taking congratulations all evening. Happy days are here again! Suddenly Jane came through the crush of admirers, holding my mobile gingerly. 'It's Margaret,' she hissed. I snapped to attention, but the signal was faint. 'Alan . . . ' she quavered, 'you must carry on the flame . . . '

And then the line went dead.

During the election campaign, as Bradshaw recalled, 'the running joke was that Alan was thrilled by the idea of being on the verge of a fantastic victory, because of course the Tories were on the verge of anything but, but Alan was in fantastic self-obsession and would talk of a thrilling Wagnerian victory'.[2] This swiftly became a favourite with readers. Hastings had earlier been talking to Alan about his becoming a regular columnist in the paper. Alan showed interest, but as ever the money mattered. Hastings offered him a fee of £60,000 a year. Alan, however, thought that 'measly' as his current billet, the *News of the World*, was paying him around £130,000 a year for a weekly piece.

Hastings was 'amazed that anybody as rich as Alan cared so much about the money, preferring highly paid bondage at the *NoW* to dignified literary contributions to the *Evening Standard* (that's how we purported to see it, anyway)'.[3] The fact of this offer became central to what followed. The first sign of trouble came during the election. Early one morning the telephone rang in Bradshaw's office – 'the unmistakable voice, "This is Alan Clark"'. Bradshaw remembers saying something fatuous, 'Oh you mean the real Alan Clark.' 'Yes, yes. Listen you must stop this ridiculous column – effectively it is a counterfeit.' Bradshaw said with hand on heart that it was just a joke for the general election. The conversation ended 'perfectly amicably' and Bradshaw was especially delighted when Alan 'very flatteringly' read out a passage from the spoof diary in his own voice.

Seeing Alan's call as a shot across the bows, Bradshaw told his editor, '"I think we can't keep running it." This was completely the wrong thing to say to Max, because he sensed blood in the water. "He said that to you?" Roars of laughter. "Oh, don't worry about Alan. He can't really be upset. If he'd been really upset he'd have spoken to me." I had no ego to bruise. "That's probably true." "He's just blowing off steam. Don't worry about it."'

The *Standard* kept up the column, with Hastings enjoying what he saw as the seemingly impossible – getting under the Clark skin. As for lawyers, as Bradshaw recalled, journalists usually think of fire-proofing their articles against libel and only libel. But his column was parody and on that basis fine, surely? On the verge of the election Bradshaw wrote what he thought was his final article, and Hastings lunched the literary panjandrum Andrew (A. N.) Wilson (a former Literary Editor of the *Standard* and 'a king of mischief'), who told him that the Clark columns were so funny he should keep running them. Bradshaw recalled his editor returning 'in a high good humour, kicking open the leader writer's door and bellowing across the room, "Bradshaw, consider yourself chained to the oar"'. Next morning Bradshaw received a call from Alan 'Now you have stopped doing this, haven't you?" My heart sank and I said, "well ... not really ... no ... we have a piece in today's paper.' And at that moment you could sense the froideur.' Not long afterwards Bradshaw remembers reading in *The Times* Diary that Alan was suing the *Standard* for 'passing off'. Its item quoted the ending of that day's Bradshaw Clark: "Later this afternoon, despite a stinking hangover, I sparkled in the House, demanding an end to little Blair's edict abolishing Prime Minister's Questions. I really was on tremendous form and I even caught the eye of dear Claire, the young new Labour Member for Watford. Her rosebud lips pursed adorably and I'm certain I received the ghost of a coquettish smile! Steady, Clark ...!'

The Times Diary pointed out that despite an explanation accompanying every column, alongside Clark's photograph, that this was Bradshaw imagining how Clark might record events, 'the parodies ring remarkably true. Michael Winner, the film director, is said to have voted Labour because he thought the Bradshaw diaries, which he found so distasteful, were by Clark.'[4] Bradshaw can think of nothing similar. 'In its own way it was quite absurd; that's what made it so hilarious because a satirist being directly sued by his victim was also legally unprecedented.' Reflecting back a decade on, 'I sort of sensed because of the audacity and the strategic military brilliance with which he, as it were, came right round the Maginot Line I thought he's going to win; we're going to put up a great fight, but I had an awful feeling he was going to win, by virtue of making the attack in the first place.'

Why did Alan take the spoof so seriously? Clive Thorne, of his solicitors Denton Hall, believes he was 'genuinely upset'.[5] Although he showed a good sense of humour throughout, 'he felt that the *Standard* (and Max Hastings) had gone far too far. They had transgressed beyond isolated acts of parody and were now ridiculing Alan on a daily basis. In particular the nature of the spoof articles suggested that Alan was a buffoon, a caricature and an empty-headed sex fiend determined to rampage through ranks of nubile "babes". The joke had long since passed.' Might publication of the parodies also damage his own diaries, both in reputation and in sales? And was there an issue where Alan, having been offered and turned down £60,000, was now miffed that the *Standard* was using his name, as it were, for free?

If those at the *Standard* thought 'passing off' was unusual, Thorne, in advising that Alan had a claim for 'passing off' and for the statutory tort of false attribution of authorship under Section 81 Copyright Designs and Patents Act 1988, was more precise: it had been the subject of only one reported case since the end of the Second World War. 'In Alan's case,' says Thorne, 'the basis of the claim was that he was a serious, successful and respected political diarist, commentator and also a military historian of some renown.' The legal team at Denton Hall needed to find witnesses who had read the spoof diaries and been deceived into believing that the articles had been written by Alan when in fact they had not been. Thorne recalls that Alan was not particularly helpful in this exercise, but ultimately some thirty witnesses were assembled, including several Tory MPs, although none from Labour. Alan did, though, produce a caretaker from Albany.

At the *Standard* no-one seriously thought the case would ever go to trial. The decision to defend the action was in the hands of the late Sir

David English (editor-in-chief of Associated Newspapers) and the late Lord Rothermere (the company's chairman). Bradshaw believes that they decided to draw on the *Standard*'s promotional budget to fight the case. They were aided in their decision by Rothermere's son, Jonathan (the paper's managing director), who was 'a huge fan of the column and absolutely behind taking it to the high court and turning it into an outrageous, hilarious courtroom trial'.

Although now on opposing sides, Alan kept in touch with Hastings and they even lunched together (at Hastings' invitation) at Alan's favourite restaurant, Wilton's, although the conversation was more about the Tory Party in opposition than the forthcoming trial. Hastings also sent Alan a postcard, inscribed 'May the best man win!' Publicly Hastings expressed his feelings forcibly.[6] He believed that Alan, as he approached seventy, fancied recognition as an elder statesman of the Conservative Party, and to be 'mocked by Peter Bradshaw ... as an ageing right-wing roué* jarred intolerably with [this] self-image'. The Bradshaw diaries 'played with piercing skill upon the absurdities in his own Diaries'.

The hearing itself spread across three days before Christmas 1997. Commentators wrote in advance that it was about press freedom, with Hastings believing it was necessary to defend the right to satirise a politician, 'especially one with such a mania for self-publicity'. In fact those who attended the High Court remember it more now for the cross-examination of Alan by Associated Newspapers' QC, Peter Prescott. By the afternoon of the second day Prescott made his strategy clear: 'I will be suggesting [he told Alan] that your real purpose is not to prevent confusion or damage to your reputation as a serious man of letters. I am going to suggest that it is rather to hamper or prevent an effective form of criticism of you as a politician and as a man, indeed in your case the only really effective form of criticism, namely ridicule.' And he continued: 'I will be suggesting that it is criticism which you richly deserve. A further reason, a true reason, for bringing these proceedings ... is because these spoofs have injured your personal vanity which is colossal. Do you understand?' Alan responded with aplomb: 'I understand what you are saying, yes, certainly.' He paused. 'Please do not take my silence as concurrence.'

Thorne recalls that Prescott set out to show that Alan was disreputable and held unflattering and unfashionable political views. He also attempted to demonstrate that he was anti-Semitic. He thought Alan was 'most

---

* In the trial transcript 'roué' proved too much for the stenographer, so that Alan was described as 'an ageing ruin'.

unpleasantly cross-examined about his interest in the German war machine and the fact that he had been entertained by David Irving the historian. This was a dangerous road to take for Prescott, who in the event was found to have shown a lack of judgment.' With the trial judge, Mr Justice Lightman, being well-known as a leading member of London's Jewish community, Thorne felt that Prescott was 'playing with fire'.

It was no surprise to many in court that after having given Prescott his head for some time, Lightman took a strong line. At various points during Alan's cross-examination he interposed with comments such as:[7]

'I hope you will take very, very great care to make sure that you ask no questions which are not strictly relevant.'

'I will let you proceed, but make it clear that if there is no justification for this, I shall take a very serious view of it.'

'I think, Mr Prescott, we are coming to the end of this.'

Mr Justice Lightman raised a final complaint in his judgment. Prescott's cross-examination, he wrote, 'took the form of a totally uncalled for personal attack'. He concluded, 'The cross-examination elicited nothing of any value whatsoever save as copy for the press (and in particular the *Evening Standard*). The only consolation is that the Plaintiff stood his ground and survived the onslaught unfazed and unbowed'. Indeed he did, as demonstrated by the following examples. When Prescott asked Alan, 'Would it be fair to say, Mr Clark, that you are somewhat obsessed with your personal appearance, physique and sexual attractiveness', Alan responded, 'Self-assessment is difficult enough in dealing with one's income tax. I think in relation to character it is quite valueless.' Prescott quoted a newspaper article that alleged Alan had been unfaithful to his wife on their honeymoon. Alan explained that although it was 'totally untrue' he did not sue for libel on the basis that 'I prefer not to go through the courts and have counsel taking things out of context and quoting them to me in the sort of manner that you have recently been doing.'

Bradshaw summed it up succinctly: 'Our guy made a complete hash of it. Max was expecting our team to do a lot better. We were pretty much steamrollered. I don't remember Alan being the smallest bit discomposed.' Hastings recalled that as he and Alan walked out together after the Prescott cross-examination Alan turned to him and said, 'Your man made a pretty fair cock-up of that, didn't he?'

In his judgment on 21 January 1998, Mr Justice Lightman found for the Plaintiff on the matter of 'passing off' and also that his reputation and goodwill were placed at risk, thereby entitling him to damages. Associated Newspapers considered an appeal. Thorne recalls 'an unnecessarily gloomy conference in the early spring of 1998 to review the position. I told Alan that in my experience I would anticipate an early offer. Alan was very dubious that they would wish to settle.' To everyone's surprise next day Associated Newspapers made their offer, withdrawing their appeal, with Alan receiving a fixed sum for costs (£200,000). As a result Alan dubbed Thorne 'mystic Clive'. No offer was made for payment of damages (which would have been limited anyway). 'This essentially represented everything that Alan had been seeking. He felt fully vindicated in the actions that he had taken.'

However, in Hastings' view Alan's was a pyrrhic victory. The judge allowed the parody to continue as 'Not Alan Clark's Diary' with it clearly stated that Peter Bradshaw was the author, and a thick black band obscuring Mr Clark's eyes on the accompanying photograph. The *Standard* gained publicity of a magnitude that millions could not buy, and made a virtue out of defeat by giving 'Not Alan Clark's Diary' front-page billing:

> The moment of ultimate triumph has an ineffable sweetness, an almost sexual discharge of energy. A dashing and well-planned raid, completed with dazzling success. Was this how Montgomery felt at El Alamein?
>
> I shall now call for the offices of the *Evening Standard* to be razed to the ground, like Rose West's house in Gloucester, so that it does not become a grotesque shrine and place of pilgrimage for undesirables.[8]

Other newspapers commented on the outcome. *The Independent*, then under the editorship of Andrew Marr, was unhappy. In a leading article, headed 'Laugh where we must. And we must at this judgment', it took aim at Mr Justice Lightman for making a judgment which, 'if it stands, will damage the public life of this country', adding that the judgment diminished 'the public space within which we conduct our collective and political life and so threatened our capacity for honest self-government', and for good measure implied that 'newspaper readers cannot understand, let alone take a joke'.[9]

The Times was far less po-faced, producing a leader in the style of Alan's *Diaries* under the heading: 'In Victory, Magnanimity? A moment for suitably Churchillian grace from Mr Clark'. It opened: '*Der Tag* has arrived, victory is mine – total, crushing, sweet. My defeat of "Hitler" Hastings is as complete as the Allies' in 1945, and as just . . . ' and ended, 'Perhaps I might hope that Mr Justice Lightman is *gentle* with Hastings and Bradshaw. A nominal sum might be sufficient . . . And if they found out, in due course, that I had spared them, might they think me a kindly Caesar? The laurels are mine, I should wear them lightly.'[10]

THIRTY-FIVE

Worryingly Ill

In the year following his much desired return to the House of Commons in May 1997, Alan began to notice that his health was playing up – really troubling him, not just hypochondriacally, as he might have put it. To his diary he complained of problems with his eyesight, being unable to defocus. 'I am somewhat blighted by my head (eye) ache. I have sat here at the kitchen table for nearly 40 minutes pressing my temples with fingers and trying – very occasionally succeeding – to defocus.' Alan was quick to see the worst. 'A brain tumour would be moving faster than this, surely?'

Alan's memory, he noticed, had become atrocious, 'almost pre-Alzheimer'. But health worries had been put to one side with his unexpected selection in January as Conservative candidate for Kensington and Chelsea. He was now on a high for the best part of two months before anxieties once again rose to the surface. His moods see-sawed.

He returned to the Commons for the first time in five years. 'The whole thing should have been too delicious for words – but I was haunted by apprehension,' he wrote a week later. He soon realised how he had aged, which had unforeseen side-effects, not least nodding off in the Chamber. Matthew Parris's description of him in a defence debate ('His eyes were shut, his head had dropped forward and one hand spread across his famously chiselled jaw, covering his mouth. Mr Clark looked profoundly at peace')[1] made him furious. At the Conservative Party conference later that October he threw oaths at Parris in public and had to be restrained by Jane. In the past he would have ignored Parris's sketch-writing fun; was his inability to do so now a manifestation of the symptoms of something seriously wrong? A session with the Hythe reflexologist, Mrs Frowd, helped him relax. In mid-November, after over-eating too many Belgian chocolates, he dozed and woke 'feeling sinister – worried about brain tumour . . . and slumped back feeling "far from right"'. Alan's diary entry that day concluded, 'And now, even writing this, my glaucoma headache has returned.' His eyes tended to trouble him most and as

Christmas approached he became concerned that they might seize up and wreck his reading at the Sloane Street church carol service. Although he had written nothing at the time, he now confessed in his diary that it was thirteen months since the ophthalmologist in Hythe told him to go for a hospital examination. On 12 December he admitted to having had a 'slight frontal headache and inability to defocus' for over twenty-four hours. His doctor, Nick Page, advised him to see a specialist. When Alan remarked that he was terrified of cancer of the optic nerve, Page reassured him that it was rare and usually diagnosed only in infancy and old age. The reassurance lasted only until he found in the papers that day that the actor Walter Matthau (at seventy-seven) was going blind for this very reason.

Alan's visit to the specialist coincided with the stress of his High Court case against the *Evening Standard*. The specialist, David Spalton, was consoling. 'Stuttery, amiable and bespectacled (naturally) oculist ... Said the optic nerve ok etc. And I really haven't had a headache of any kind since ... ! Defocusing, and periodic lights and "flooders" of no consequence. This is such a relief; I clap my hands in prayer and thanks a lot of the time and when I wake up at night.'

Over the course of 1998 Alan's health shows an intermittent decline, but how much of his diarising is his hypochondria speaking? When in January he found a pulse, off and on, in his upper palate, he became convinced he had 'jaw rot (for want of a better word)' under his dental bridge. ('What does one do when the teeth go?' he wrote later that year. 'Like the king elephant in *Babar*, it is the end. No more photocalls either.') He wondered if it was related to an occasional shooting headache on the right side. He was creaky in joints, 'erection a total loss' and his arms were weak 'and look it'. Viewing himself on an American television documentary he felt 'put out by how *old* I looked.'

Exercise and relaxation helped. One midsummer weekend in 1998, the hottest day so far of the year, he walked to Sandling station to meet a ramblers' group. His pulse was erratic, rising to 130+, but at Saltwood again as soon as he had swum, it was back to 78. A month later, sitting outside and sipping a delicious new Riesling, he felt he could be at a café table beside a *place* in Normandy, '"putting the world to rights". If I was also sexual I would be completely happy. With this one exception, my good fortune is so TOTAL that it makes me apprehensive – both as to possible reverse, and also regarding my debt to "put something back in".'[2] Three weeks later he observed 'a nasty frisson walking in the old family garden this evening. How many more times will I see it, in its August fullness? Two or three (with luck) in my present condition; then perhaps another four or five as a buffer, or demi-buffer.' He noted another manifestation of his decline in August. 'No press-ups by the pool this year, or weights.' By October he calculated that he had done only 'three sets of two press-ups this whole year'.

In September in Zermatt he had difficulty sleeping. 'I tinkled five, finally six times quite copiously. In the morning Jane found blood on my pidgy bottoms. How? Why? Unsettling. I am absolutely desexualated. A nullity. Up until only two years ago I would always wake with a sleepy erection at 5.30.' The bad times were in the past. Notes to Jane included a Valentine which began, 'I don't think I've ever loved you more, than today.' An undated card from the same period: '. . . you are *unique* so good and special and magic.'

Back in London at Westminster he indulged himself with an evening at Shaun Woodward's Sybil dining club.[3] He drank copiously, smoked a Havana, walked back to Albany after asking Woodward's butler to feed the parking meter in the morning, and woke in the night with 'bitter vomit in the upper throat'. Back to sleep, woke again, tinkled and 'immediately and strongly came over Norwegian embassy.* Only just got back to bed; a bit worried about cerebral haemorrhage.' The cause was, though, more obvious. In the morning: 'This symptom is now definitely linked to (far) too much drink.'

Enduring 'a very long "cold", now in its twelfth day', with his voice still croaky, he attended his constituency Remembrance Service and spoke to Dr Jonathan Munday, Mayor of the Royal Borough. Alan told him that he had been feeling shaky for eight days and had lost his voice. 'Feeling ghastly for ten days, eh?' Munday cross-examined him. 'I trailed the idea of getting throat cancer from "straining" the voice. He spluttered. Spoke reassuringly about the vocal cords.'

With Christmas 1998 approaching his health report was mixed. The good news was that a leg 'ulcer' had healed to a tiny pink spot, half the size of the original 'lesion'. But he remained what he called '"throaten" – now seven weeks intermittently. Especially in a.m. and when voice is "tired" in the evening. I must say, though, that practically everyone in the House of Commons is mildly, or totally, throaten at the moment. We are, though, getting into "see your doctor" territory.'

New year 1999 showed signs of worse things to come. 'A *nuit cassé*. Awake from 11.45 till past 3 on and off. After I came back from tinkling second time (2.30-ish) Jane said, "are you ok?" "Not really," I said. I felt

---

* A Clarkism for 'weak at the knees'.

illish and sub-prostatic. I sweat hugely at night. During the day I am feeling incredibly tired. Yesterday we went out to the Garden House and while Jane and Eddie [the Saltwood groundsman] were wrestling (from time-to-time literally) with a tap in the kitchen I sat at the desk feeling utterly exhausted. Jane, when I said I felt illish, said again, and rightly, "you're trying to do too much".' Would this, he wondered, be the year of setbacks, when (at last) although not feeling his age he would show it? His prostatic-urethral symptons were now more or less constant, 'quite an acceleration from, say, December when they were intermittent. A fairly constant strain always in the groin after peeing, plus a hard to define feeling that all is not quite right.' In the end he realised he must have blood and, significantly, PSA tests, although if the results were bad, he mused, 'what do I do? I certainly don't want to be cut up and mucked about. I dread the leaked (as it is bound to be) publicity signifying the end of the old Al – the Clarkson Show prancer. Can't do it. Can't do it quietly because (a) an MP, and (b) the constituency. Have I got time to be still compos while I consolidate the wills, and get everything in order (ugh!)?'

Now convinced he was 'a condemned man', he made an appointment for the following Thursday, Nick Page's first day back from holiday – no doubt, he forecast, 'bronzed and youthful'. The sheer act of seeing Page – his first appointment – helped. Once more he thanked the Almighty. 'Before the consultation I whispered to God that if it can be done this will be the *year of dedication*. If it fails then spectator, or buffer.' That evening he slept eight hours uninterrupted for the first time since Scotland. He concluded, 'I do like life, and am eternally grateful even if it stops tomorrow – or today.'

Jane too was seeing a specialist, and returned to tell Alan that she needed to have a mammogram. 'Poor darling! This made her low, but very sweet and quiet.' It prompted him to think about their life. 'I suddenly realised that I felt terribly homesick. I miss Janey at these times, and am sad that effectively we only get one holiday a year – a long period when we can plan things and go on the wing. And only two days, if we are lucky, out of each week. Which means that each year out of 365 we only have 130-ish to each other. So how many days have we got left – a thousand? Perhaps far fewer.'

On the following Tuesday at the Commons, having heard nothing from Page, he called him himself 'using the little door-phone in the Library corridor and, briefly, thinking that I might faint if the news was really bad. In fact it was ludicrous: nought-point-five. My health *in the clear*; the sheer, total delight of daffodils and birdsong and lengthening days; the

relaxed enjoyment of planning jaunts and trips and going "on the wing".'
His *joie de vivre* lasted four days.

An upper respiratory infection led to 'Willie's eye',[*] and the eye specialist
prescribed chlorophormical drops. Then his voice started to go, particularly untimely as he had to speak at a ward AGM, attended by leading
Conservative lights. '"Where's the bright, ebullient Alan Clark?" asked
John Major at dinner. I announced my "flu" and was pleased to note that
both he and Tom King moved away to more distantly laid places.'

Reading accounts of SAD [Seasonal Affective Disorder] cheered him
up. On 8 February he went to another of Shaun Woodward's Sybil dinners.
The evening itself was enjoyable enough, but next morning's events made
him wonder whether it was not a question of drinking too much, but that
wine itself was now a problem brought on by something organically
wrong? 'I had Positano steps[†] coming down the B staircase [Albany], just
controlled it, then halted and spat at the 4 St James's Street Island and
realised I had to go to Brooks's and essay a vomit. I am not myself the
morning after Shaun's dinners.'

Even when things were going well, as at the Kensington and Chelsea
constituency AGM early in March 1999, the pleasure was short-lived. 'A
straight victory. Virtually no opposition ... I drank a glass of delicious
iced white wine in the kitchen and was effusive. I have really no excuse
now not to achieve this year. Health, wealth, seemingly.' And the entry
closed, 'But was exhausted, listless.'

His eyes had not bothered him since visiting the specialist in January. But
in early April he complained that they were giving him 'a bit of trouble –
blurry, intermittent inability to defocus leading to periodic headache'. This
affected his diary writing for the first time. 'I have an antipathy to the crabbed
scrawl in the blue Banner notebook.' Outside he had mowed the lawns,
humped sacks of wet grass and stretched and strained to turn a case of wine
on its side so as to read the label – perhaps for a man only a week away from
his seventy-first birthday it was no wonder that he asked himself, 'Have
I been *herniac* these last few days?' The Easter recess over, he phoned Robert
Rhodes James. The historian and former Tory MP for Cambridge had
cancer of the colon and was undergoing chemotherapy. 'Brave he was, and
calm-sounding though just a little weak of voice.' News then broke that
Cardinal Hume had 'inoperable' cancer, but was 'carrying on'. This led him

---

[*] 'Willie's eye' named after the Conservative MP and Minister, William Whitelaw, whose
eyes so often looked rheumy and tended to weep.
[†] A Clarkism for unsteadiness that leads to nearly going headlong downstairs.

to ponder, 'I am not particularly frightened of death, but I do not want to die as I am enjoying life.'

In May Alan's health took a distinct turn for the worse, the progress downwards from one shelf to another that his father had written about. But it began deceptively. 'I am more tranquil, I don't (it seems) have glaucoma after all. Spalton wrote today. My hernia less obtrusive; my weight back to 11.4 (+) and reasonable $\frac{1}{2}$ erection in the morning.' Next day, though, he started 'to feel *odd*. Almost like dropping off (before "lights") when different reasons and evocations move across the consciousness. I had been contemplating a glass of Puligny Montrachet, but thought first to go down to the Long Garage. But by the time I got there I was feeling peculiar. Headache by side of skull, v livid. Half "Hungarian embassy", almost sickish.* Sat on the seat by the VW axle and started a sub-panic sweat. I worried about a possible stroke. Just about pulled out of it. But had no appetite for a salad of prosciutto-melone, which Jane concocted. Felt, and continue to feel, incredibly sleepy, almost as if v late last night (which we weren't) and/or jet-lag. May be linked with o/d-ing of sunlight which is affecting my blood count. I daren't (although Jane urges me to) put up my feet and drop off for fear of how I may find myself when I awake. Boring, and rather frightening also.'

His appetite was non-existent, he had gone off alcohol. 'Am I heading for cancer? And if so, where?' A bath, and a hairwash from Jane, cheered him up until, catching his face in the mirror, he saw that the bags under his eyes were 'very pouchy'. Later that day he felt 'stree-ange; almost light, as with a high fever – indicating some body out-of-balance factor. I am being eaten by stress.'

Returning home on 6 May from Westminster, he described himself as 'Depressed Prince Enters Clinic'. 'I am not myself; and particularly *put out* by the non-performance of alcohol. Last night a pint of beer in Pratt's† – made no impact whatsoever. I seem to remember Cindy [Frowd] saying that this is an incredibly bad sign. At one point (middle of January) I said, "something-something-cancer-of-the-spleen". Nick did, I think, hear it. But made no attempt to "pick it up". How do I get out of this? Saltwood is no fun without sex or wine. Calm discipline and thought. But my self-confidence (due to its link to testosterone, perhaps) is down. Do I see my way?'

---

* Yet another Clarkism, meaning light-headedness and dating back to a journey he made to Hungary in 1986 as Minister for Trade.

† Pratt's – club owned by the Duke of Devonshire, at Park Place, SW1.

Just how prescient was Alan? On 7 May he writes, 'I feel now as if I may be about to die, possibly quite soon, "nearing the end of my life". A huge sadness, as if I am/may be looking at so many things for the last time. Somehow I am going to be cheated of my chance to get hold of the Tory Party, and this realisation, coming on top of the accumulated stress, will do me in.' After lunch he dozed off in the Pavillon, overlooking the pool. 'Trying to calm down and de-stress. Now going in to dinner, but afflicted by a particularly unwelcome symptom – the absolute non-effect of alcohol. Normally this is a time when wine inspires the mind. Not at the moment.'

Was he descending another level? He wrote of not wishing to get up in the morning, of depression, 'in many ways extending out into a "Nervous Breakdown"'. A day later, 'I am really "poorly". I wake utterly demoralised and so low that I want only to drop back asleep. I don't want to do anything in particular, no zest. Not even a delicious anticipation at going up to the House to see what "unfolds". On the walk with the dogs I no longer brighten at the thought of coffee and a fried egg and bacon.' Now he found he had lost his 'palate for cars, and to some little degree for the heritage; but also for politics, at present; even for political gossip. It is a Sybil tonight, but holds out no promise.' He was not encouraged by the news of the sudden death of Foreign Office Minister, Derek Fatchett, at fifty-three, and then, that evening, that Margaret Thatcher's influential PR adviser Gordon Rees was in a Texas hospital with cancer and waiting to have his tongue removed. But he did record 'one pleasing development ... Stirrings this morning. And in the tearoom I suddenly realised that I was enjoying *looking at* that waitress, what's her name? (who I have long in the abstract – in her striped blouse she is *exactly* like the cutie in a 'Careless Talk Costs Lives' poster of the 1940s – fancied) and I still get testicular writhings, tho' mild. Perhaps another next week before Whitsun in the Highlands?'

The good moments were getting briefer. That afternoon he again felt ill. 'I am so down on energy. This has always been my most precious asset. How is the whole thing going to end? I can't even look forward to the Scottish May-week jaunt; or the summer hols – *enfin le clef*. Before then, though, certain vicious *hurdles*. Most daunting, the Saltwood Garden Party. Invitations, lists, coach reservation, crockery, cheap (huh!) champagne.' He was maudlin when sitting in the doorkeeper's chair by the Chamber entrance, remembering a passage in *Chips* of Winston Churchill occupying one or other of these chairs (when actually Leader of the Opposition) and making jokes with, and waving at, passers-by, while puffing at his cigar.[4] He was, he confessed, still feeling awful.

On a practical level, his and Jane's wills were a total mess and had to be redone – 'everything to each other, and no legal gobbledegook'. To back this up he decided to 'write to darling Janey – a real text of love, and commiseration at all the frightful things, paper-mess, "How-do-I?", "Where-is?" etc that I bequeath to her. Investing and private values. Car values and historian. Also something of "a note to my literary executors". Increasingly his diary is less about politics. Briefly feeling a little improved, he talked to his younger son Andrew about looking after Jane if he were to die before her ('always ring her every Sunday'). 'If I get my affairs – Trusts, inventories, bequests – in then I *can* take the risk of dying, or inducing death (on, say, the Creaggan or the Schonbulweg) in order to evade misery.'

On 16 May they went for dinner with Bob and Margaret Worcester at Allington, a sister medieval castle to Saltwood, which some years before Alan had helped persuade the Worcesters to buy and restore. But just before leaving, Alan felt 'decidedly odd. Full Lenin-Stadium. This did not abate in the car, was aggravated, indeed, by being unable to find the place on the road map, where-do-you-leave-the-motorway etc. Jane, though, brilliantly sleepwalked on to both the exit and the route. On arrival I remained uneasy, though. Felt that I might have to absent myself at some point to go and sit in the car. Was some kind of cerebral occlusion building up? Something had told me to get page 1 of my new will signed and witnessed, or perhaps even bring it so that, gaspingly, I could have signed at the scene – drama! The fact that I hadn't added to my anxiety.'

Having lost TC the jackdaw two weeks before, Alan was now saddened by the death of the Clarks' grey cockatiel in his cage in the kitchen, 'the second intrusion of Death in two successive weeks. Bad-things-come-in-threes, all that. I don't like to think about it.'

Often in his diary now he wrote about his love for Jane, but 'a premonition of parting soon, made me terribly sad'. In the train to London on 19 May, 'I really dread, dread (almost as a child must) dread being parted from her.' 'I love Janey so much now. It is terrible how I miss her. I long for contact – it is almost like a child, waking in the dark in fear and calling out. I need the mummy to come in. It is a physical reassurance, and she is so reassuring and willing in the things she says and her lovely giggle. It was partly grounded, of course, this melancholy, in reminder of how horridly I treated her; it is ironic indeed that now I *really* can't do without her, even for a little while, and salutary also that I should be punished for my callousness in former times.' He did not delude himself about his diary. 'I write these dreadful entries, partly as a kind of exorcism, partly for the fun (can tell myself) of turning back to them when I am "better".' At the end of the week he had an appointment with Mrs Frowd, 'who might, ought, to *therapise* me'. And then the following week was a major event in his calendar, being the local MP: the Chelsea Flower Show. After that he looked forward to driving north to Eriboll. 'Providing no more setbacks. I must talk to God.'

He had not said much if anything to his sons about his ill-health, but on the phone that evening Andrew asked him what was the matter. 'The more I talked about it the more "anxious" I found myself becoming. I am having a bad time at the moment. Tip, very splendidly, could hardly understand. Looking back I don't think I would ever have envisaged it being "like" this. Or indeed "it" taking place at all. What a waste.' He wondered if he should resign his seat – or announce that he would not contest the next election.

When Jane spotted on 21 May Dr Stuttaford writing on depression in *The Times*, Alan rang him. Thomas Stuttaford had been a Conservative MP in the early 1970s, but lost his seat (Norwich South) at the February 1974 election, when Alan entered the Commons. 'He v splendid, quick and almost reassuring. Said I could be dosed (there is a school of doctors who think in these terms) remedially with Serotonin. "Replenishes" (sic) the brain. I don't hugely like the sound of this.' In a letter to Stuttaford, Alan expanded on his symptoms, which included losing the taste for classic cars, walking the hills, even a good debate in the House or a 'crisis' meeting of the 1922 Executive; and also an all-pervasive sense of foreboding, not least that for a lot of the time he felt himself to be mortally ill.[5] That same day, 22 May, he read the obituaries of his old friend Robert Rhodes James. 'Too many deaths at the moment.' He spoke to Angela, his widow. 'Made me worse because Robert, it seems (after coming back from Australia and another "go" of chemo), walked into his house and simply went upstairs to bed (he was feeling terribly weary, "because I think his liver was packing up") and just lay down – and died.'

On the morning of 22 May Alan had woken with an awful headache. Jane dispatched him to bed, but he was 'afraid of doing that; too much of an admission' so he sat in the Pavillon with his feet up, wrapped in the brown cashmere rug. 'Mrs F had told me that we must go abroad for two and a half (!) months. No. Not Scotland. *Abroad*. Would that we could. Well, it would be lovely, and probably therapeutic, to go to the châlet ... But if we do go to Shore sitting in the wheelhouse, or walking the

Creaggan should be pleasing. Although the Highland melancholy is never far away. We'll see.'

That evening he phoned Mrs Frowd: 'If I had liver cancer would you have picked it up? "I didn't pick up cancer anywhere ... You are still carrying a virus around." (Hey, just a minute, I thought I was suffering from deep depression?) She wants to see me as soon as we are back, clearly expecting an "improvement". But I am not looking forward to the trip as much as I would be normally. No point in going to Gleneagles, and the treat of eating in the conservatory, and their excellent *carte de vins* – if you can't *consume*. Must try not to be too much of a wet blanket for Janey.'

On Sunday, 23 May he based himself at the Pavillon, and wrote, 'I sit here (ironic how often I seem to find myself getting like my father, with cashmere rug, writing pad/text on the knee) and am feeling awful and apprehensive, having woken with a headache, then uncontrollably retch-vomit.' He wondered again about jaundice '(was it vaguely like this at Eton, when it started, in 1942?). Utterly without appetite, have indeed an aversion to food (couldn't even eat a didgy with EMT). Just thinking about releasing PA statement – "Alan Clark to 'rest'. The MP, 71, suffering from strain, has been advised by his doctors to 'take a complete rest' and has cancelled all public engagements." This will obviously affect my position in the constituency, and also in the House, itself.' By the early afternoon he had been persuaded by Jane to go to bed in the Summer Bedroom. 'The full sickroom, pad [electric blanket] on, teddy [hotwater bottle] warmly dutiful. I feel as if I am dying, as indeed I have for several months. There doesn't seem to be any escape from it – except to "pass away" ... It is strange up here, and creepy, as the wind blows the rose branches against the window. The blackbirds, though, sing "goodnight" enthusiastically. I am more depressed, I think, than I have ever been.' He confessed to feeling fussed over the following day's Chelsea Flower Show. Later he asked himself, 'How do I get out of this? It is, literally, incurable. Jane, with some truth, said, "I couldn't drive north in this condition." And of course it is so true that driving on the A1 adds to the strain. Don't want to miss the trip. Train or plane? I need the hills, but I am very, very weak now.'

Jane remembers every detail of the day of the Flower Show on Monday, 24 May. But first Alan's account, made the following day from the Summer Bedroom, 'where I am behaving exceedingly like (because, I fear, I am) someone "with" cancer in the '20s or '30s'. It was brief. He had longed for an excuse to cancel, but Jane told him, 'You have to attend', reminding him that as the MP he had to show the Queen around. After driving up with Jane in the morning, he walked to Nick Page's consulting rooms, and from there to Dr Muncie, 'who is attractive. She ran the ultra-sonic scanner over my abdomen. Images linked to a screen nearby. At the conclusion she claimed to have noticed that "everything was all right". This cheered me massively and I made a triumphant entry to Simon Hornby's lunch tent. Shook little Nick Brown[6] by the hand, then flirted with the red-haired married lady on my right. Disconcertingly, though, a glass of Sancerre had only an adverse effect.' He wrote nothing about greeting the Royals or saying goodbye to them. But concluded, 'If anyone at that time had said "you are going to have to sit next to the Queen at tea" I would have protested quite literally that it would have "made me ill".'

Jane says he had been sick on the morning walk, that he was looking dreadful and they still didn't know what it was. The Mayor, Dr Jonathan Munday, turned to Jane and asked 'Is Al all right?' Jane explained her worries. 'They say he's got depression. But he's not depressed. No-one seems to know what it is.' Munday suggested a second opinion. Jane's views are as strong now as they were at the time. 'That's what annoyed me. You could see he was ill. As he was going to Nick Page that morning and said he wasn't coming to the lunch, he dropped me at the entrance. Then he turned up at lunch! "I've been told I'm fine," he said, sat down and had some lunch. I thought he's not all right, actually. He's not all right. He certainly wasn't Al. Showed the Queen around.' Alan wrote that Jane – 'darling sweet Jane, she does so much – drove all the way home. Ate a small amount of curry and naan.' Later, Jane sat on the bed. '"Are you going to blub?" She nodded. "Come over here." The poor sweetheart, her lovely grey eyes were full of tears. This is my real sadness. I just can't bear to be away from her – for so long.' Later that evening he wrote that he was woken 'by her pretty face against mine, she was distinctly wet with tears. I am so sleepy I suppose I just dropped back off; but was soon rewoken by her touching my cheek, and hair and face. Jackie Kennedy and Jack in the Dallas infirmary. Poor little love. "I don't want to lose you," she kept saying. I am so exhausted I couldn't respond properly. What made her wake up to do this? For us both this is a deeply unhappy time.' Alan also prayed. 'God; I am frightened. You have given me so much, everything really; and particularly my little love, whom I betrayed. How I wish I hadn't done so! The thing I fear most is leaving her. She is so good, so important. Please, please will you care for her also.'

On the Wednesday morning, he and Jane had to go up again to London for the annual Mayor-making ceremony. It was also Jane's birthday, but, as Alan confessed to his diary, 'I forgot – how could I? Only remembered when Sarah rang this morning.' This time they went up on the train. Jane recalled, 'He looked so awfully ill. I thought something was major-major wrong. I thought he'd had something like his mother. I thought he'd had a minor stroke, slightly dragging his foot. He just looked so ill.'

First they went to the Commons, where he risked a slice of apple strudel, before attending the 1922 Executive. He felt ill-ish when picking up Jane at the Family Room. On to Kensington Town Hall, 'where cheery black attendant thanked us for our Christmas cards. Improvised my way through both the ceremony and the reception.' Jonathan Munday, now the outgoing Mayor, made a point of repeating to Jane, 'He must see somebody else.' Jane decided they would not stay for the dinner. 'That went down very badly,' she says. 'He wasn't doing it intentionally.' Meanwhile Alan had, as he put it, 'most recklessly eaten a canapé. It had the miraculous effect of making me hungry! So on getting back I had a tiny Jane-2-egger cooked in oil. Slept pretty well.'

At one point during the day Alan heard the results of Monday's tests. Nick Page mentioned a coloscopy. 'Cancer of the colon is the second biggest killer of men after lung and (I would assume) prostate,' he said. And Alan thought of Robert Rhodes James. Page added, 'There is no evidence of any liver, kidney, pancreas or heart disease; and the second blood tests are all normal. This tends to confirm the clinical impression that there is no disease here and I suspect it may be the psychological factor that lies behind all this'[7] Alan was delighted. 'This *has* calmed me, and made me feel hungry. I'd like a yoghurt and cereal.'

He had started what he called 'a Saltwood note for the boys'. Then James and Julie rang 'and were compos and cheered us up – have now definitely decided to provisionally drive north'. With no further London engagements they were able to stay at Saltwood. Jane recalls that he really wasn't making much sense. 'Repeating himself. On the Friday someone came to look around because we were going to have the XK Rally here in the summer. I didn't want people to see him. Not Al. He went up to bed, he lay down on the bed with his shirt and trousers still on. He felt absolutely awful. He was being sick; he couldn't eat very much.'

It was an awful night. Suddenly light dawned for Jane. Sitting on the bed at two o'clock in the morning she said, 'I think you've got a brain tumour. I'm going to ring the doctor.' Alan protested, but Jane insisted. The Clarks had not met Dr Chandrakumar, from the Hythe group practice, but he arrived at the castle at lunchtime, following morning surgery. Jane remembers that after examining Alan he came down and said he wanted him to have a scan. Something in the brain. He should go to Ashford hospital, then come back to St Saviour's to have a drip, he was so dehydrated.

'We went back upstairs and told Al and he said I'm not going anywhere. Dr C looked a bit startled, I don't think he was used to this treatment. I said, don't worry, I'll make sure he was there. I had to help him downstairs into the car. He could walk but I had to help him. By the time we got to Ashford and I had driven round to the entrance, he couldn't walk. They had to come out with a chair. He disappeared up to the room to have a head scan and whatever. He was feeling so awful, looking really awful sitting in his wheelchair that he wanted to be shut away, these corridors being so busy. I opened a door of a cloakroom and put him there in the dark and I sat outside the door. A chap came out who had done the scan. He said I've sent for Dr C. I thought, that's funny I was told bring him here to have a scan and go straight back. He brought out the scans for me to see. Even as a layperson the "y" at the back of the head, I could see it bent right over.'

Alan required specialist surgery, which meant King's College Hospital in south London. Ashford, meanwhile, had to ring round for an ambulance. That weekend Alan and Jane had intended to drive to Scotland, which Alan refused to cancel, because he thought he was going to be all right. Obviously they would not be going now. When the ambulance eventually arrived, Jane remembered the driver saying, 'Sorry it wasn't one of your Bentleys.' She returned to Saltwood with tears coursing down her face and told Lynn, the housekeeper, what had happened. 'I had left the house wide open, the dogs there. I had thought I was simply whizzing him across and whizzing him back.' Next morning, when she arrived at King's College Hospital, 'Alan was shouting and giving orders because they'd given him things to reduce the swelling and he was feeling better.'

Jane met the young surgeon, Nick Thomas. Although it was the Whit weekend, the operation was arranged for the bank holiday Monday.

THIRTY-SIX

High Hopes

Alan's final diary entry before the operation was, all things considered, surprisingly buoyant.

> *Whit Monday, 31 May (pre Op):* Just woken and (a bad sign) thought I was in France. Actually in King's College, SE5 – quite nice private room. Jollier last night; boosted by talking to both boys, doctors and Jane. Watching TV. Fell asleep instantly 11pm. But head filling with putative engagements for today ... Woken, panicking, by drip alarm. V sleepy. In came nurse and changed reservoir. Slept totally till 6-ish. Then started looking at clock. Could easily have depressed you (no!). Is this a function of the tumour itself? Heaven knows what it will be like when coming 'round' from the anaesthetic.

Typically, though, political matters were never far from his mind:

> Last night the Registrar was charming, said I was the only person who could rival Blair combination of charisma and authority.

The operation took place later that day. By early Friday, 4 June, fewer than four days after surgery, he was back at Saltwood. In fact he had had two operations, one to remove the tumour, a second to stop excessive bleeding. To his diary he wrote: 'I am back from (in a sense) the dead. I nearly – sic, etc – died last week.' He was pleased to note that although his physique had taken 'a real battering', Nick Thomas, the surgeon, told Jane that 'biologically, he's young'. Late on Thursday and aided by blood transfusions he was pronounced fit enough to leave hospital; Jane packed him into the Discovery, arriving back at Saltwood in the small hours of Friday morning. 'Yow! Did I creep – first real slip-change down into old age/infirmity with the walking stick – through the Garden Entrance, up the front stairs, line of route in reverse etc. And the previous two days in hospital I could hardly straighten the legs out without setting the heartbeat knocking, the blood coursing.'

Now began convalescence and, he hoped, recovery. By Saturday he was walking outside, though he continued to use the stick. In the Bailey he crossed to the grave of Tom, his favourite Jack Russell, paused at the well and then on to the sundial in the rose garden. He felt 'so empty. I must be terrifyingly anaemic, $\frac{1}{2}$ panicky about the haemoglobin'. He was not shy in his diary at revealing the more personal results of his ordeal: the 'awful green, vile-smelling colonic cancer Thompson'.* At all costs he decided to avoid any kind of mental work, any kind of analysis, which he was convinced 'particularly does/did affect the brain. But quickly leads me into unwelcome little naps with observationalist dreams involving my father, which make me a little frightened.'

He worried about the chances of his recovery. Would it be 'George VI valet?'. Alan knew his history – on the morning of 6 February 1952 the King had been found dead by his valet at Sandringham, having died peacefully during the night. 'Certainly the best (least "controversial") way to go.' Colin left a message on the answerphone. 'I shall be so cross if you go ahead of him,' Jane said.[1] He was cheered by a shower of letters, including two from ex Prime Ministers (Margaret Thatcher and John Major) and a personal, handwritten letter from Tony Blair. 'We're all thinking of you. Get well soon so you can come back and give me a hard time. It is not the same without you.' Alan wrote in his diary that he was 'utterly delighted and moved'.[2] He never knew that Alastair Campbell inspired the letter.

That first Sunday was typical of his first weeks back at Saltwood, a mix of the good and the bad. Although pleased at 'getting (bounding, almost) out of bed a good deal', and to have helped Jane start the Jaguar C-type ('which she did brilliantly'), he felt 'catastrophically depressed' and asked himself, 'How is this all going to end?' He was not fooled by the optimists. 'Much fiction being generated about "recovery". "You'll be back" etc etc. But my objective simply to "get comfortable". Tie up ends that need it, and then calm down for George VI valet.'

Thomas, his surgeon, came to Saltwood the following afternoon and took out the forty clips. He reported his first 'reasonable' night – 'Unexpected, strangely, after being told, indirectly, that you've "got" cancer.' He had even got up and unlocked the padlock on the main gate. 'At present, watching brief. Must not get involved in office paperwork (neuro toxins etc). James may be here tomorrow, which I'm looking forward to. But I hope he doesn't come out with any of that bloody crap – I am over-active.' Outside he worried about the man cutting the grass, and felt quite ready to take over. Of himself he enjoyed his first bath, weighed himself

* Defecation.

and found he had lost a stone 'and look like a thin old man'. His special
worry was colon blockage, if not cancer. The anaesthetic, he thought,
must now be almost out of the system. He was firm, though. 'I will not
ever (DV) go into a hospital again. I am still quite composed about George
VI valet. But when it happens the transition must be smooth. There is a
hell of a lot of heavy-duty paperwork still to be put in place (the worst
sort of situation). I have now wound up a notch in imagery. It's recon-
structing Vichy after the fall of Paris. But I am doing too much admin –
the sort of thing I ought to be avoiding.'

He developed a habit of waking in the small hours and sweating with
worry. On Wednesday, 9 June, 'really frightened at about 1.30 a.m. I must
not sleep until I have seen "Boy". Sweet Janey blipped (the first time) at
EMT.' Ever one for making lists, he did not mind repeating himself and
wrote:

1. I am really ill.
2. Never going into 'hospital' again. I am now the chieftain at the Mains.
3. So it may be George VI valet.
4. Or I may go, doing something. Nothing anyone can do about it.
5. So diminishing I have got to force the pace a bit.
6. Potter about. Make free with the place. Reacquaint yourself with the
Long Garage, the Great Library.

Each day brought something new. 'I'm still a tiny bit worried about
visual co-ordination and have had a brief left foot-toe panic.' But he had
more energy that evening: 'drove and turned XK140!'. He felt 'less fearful
(spelt also with a "t") though still hate falling asleep ("naps") in bed'.
Regularly in these entries he would thank God and Jane – 'still incredibly
pretty and fresh-faced'. And a week after returning home, 'Her wonderful
remark – "now" it's all bonus.'

Energised, he started using the phone, including a call to *Classic Cars*
about his monthly column, 'Back Fire'. Indeed the idea of writing for the
press was once more proving attractive, at least in theory. Encouraged by
Robert Coucher, *Classic Cars'* Editor, he dictated to Sue, his secretary, a
piece about the Talbot Lago.[3] John Coldstream, Literary Editor of *The
Daily Telegraph*, and his principal patron for book reviews, asked him to
consider *Burying Caesar*, the first book by Graham Stewart. This was their
last contact and Coldstream noted 'a realisation that things were not at all
good with him. I remember remarking to a member of the team that
there seemed to be a "disconnect" in his conversation.'[4] There was also
talk of his reviewing Gyles Brandreth's political diaries (Brandreth was a

Tory MP from 1992 to 1997), which were being published by Alan's regular publishers, Weidenfeld & Nicolson, somewhat to his displeasure. He sensed a rival. But he refused to read unbound proofs, which was all that was initially available.[5]

Almost a fortnight after surgery he felt that 'God has given me additional strength. I am hungry'. He mowed lawns, and one 'blissful afternoon' played with his cars, starting Chev, Big Red, Barnato, and Jane got the Mehari going. 'I thank God for such happy times.' Next day he enjoyed a visit from Andrew, Sarah and their son Albert, who would be three in October. Saltwood's summer openings were in full swing. 'Irritatingly the garden is full of children.' He found the noise generated by a painting group from a school near Ashford difficult. 'I really love being out-of-doors. But decided to "overdo" things. Blonde babies crawling about on the grass while Saltwood "shop" was run by Lynn, Andrew and Jane. If it wasn't for eye trouble (defocusing v difficult) I'd be in the lead at still not quite two weeks. God is being marvellous to me.'

He continued to be amazed at his recuperative powers, grateful to God. He studied his engagement diary. The operation and its aftermath 'in many ways perfectly timed'. He could now put a line through 'Sunday, Church Service in Chelsea', and the impossibly demanding day-by-day meetings and events, with each subsequent weekend eaten into. 'For what? Image projection.' As for life at Westminster, the 'whole strategic position had altered with Tory "triumph" in Euro elections. "Hague walks tall" etc etc. Stuffing Shadow Cabinet with "young Turks". My position would have been greatly weakened, but the "engagements" would remain.' Instead, he added, 'I can devote myself, with a clear conscience, to Saltwood and the family. Every day is a day gained, and being put to good, satisly, or constructive use. Will I succeed in being the Renaissance Count, but still holding myself ready to do God's command?'

The apotheosis (so far) of his recovery, in his view, was Sunday, 21 June. 'Felt energetic, grappled paperwork, moved cars around. Cindy Frowd came and also did good. A lovely cheese and cauliflower dinner. I slept excellently – best yet.' Next morning, he and Jane rose early in time for the pool man. His mood changed later with the arrival of Dr Chandrakumar to take some blood. 'He let fall the dreaded word oncologist and his radiotherapy. Actually this depressed me dreadfully. It's strange, because I am feeling better and my weight has now crept up again to over 11 stone. I now realise that the great benefice of Nick's operation (excision) was the return of enthusiasm, almost of *joie de vivre*, so that last evening, e.g., I classified all the Coutts, C. Hoare statements.'

Next morning his spirits had plummeted – 'far my worst day from the point of view of morale and apprehension'. He and Jane talked at EMT, mainly about how, after his death, his spirits would always find her at 'the dogs' grave'. Next came Jane's remark that 'really chilled' him. 'I will be so vulnerable on my own, just an old lady with a couple of dogs.' Alan immediately thought that the moment his death was announced 'all the crooks will converge on the place'. But he was cheered by his surgeon Nick on the phone, saying 'no contra-indication for glass of red wine!'. Alan could never accept the word 'oncology' and all that it implied. 'Quite clear (as I have all along both suspected and know) that radiotherapy is both disagreeable and useless. "No cure, so don't expect one" etc.'

'Why am I so feeble? I seem to be worse than for a couple of days. I dislike the bright, hot June sun. I hate the bluebottles which buzz round me whenever I settle. Just back from Cindy Frowd. Jane drove me down and I felt slightly carsick. She didn't seem to do much for the eyes – unlike on Thursday. I wonder about my blood test. Chandrakumar is keeping himself to himself. Perhaps my haemoglobin is still down – but so what?' Later that day he sat in his father's study in the Great Hall. 'I seem to have done an awful lot today, but feel knackered. I swam (!) – in the $\frac{1}{4}$ full pool. Delicious. Should have done two circuits, and funked it. Then on the walk in the woodland at 6 p.m. I felt so exhausted I thought I might have to lie down.' He napped after lunch under the fig tree, and noted 'sweet Hannah' came over to see if he was all right. 'I love that dog, she is so quiet and devoted.' He felt awful again, so weak, 'and this is new. What I don't understand or like is why I am not so strong as I was 3–4 days ago.'

In the light of the above, Sunday, 27 June, the day of the Vintage Car Club members' visit, was unexpected. 'I must record a wonderful day (against all expectations).' He rose early, moved things, fussed. 'When the visitors and their rather boring brass-age cars were assembled I mingled, felt pretty amazing. Jane was pleased with the way everything went. Saltwood "putting on a show". Then I slept, went on the "w". But I still feel as if I am "getting better". Quite remarkable. If I didn't have radiotherapy and Chandrakumar's silent blood tests hanging over me I would be over-confident. Came over here after tea and said a prayer of thanks. It's lovely this kind of demo that God can do anything.' Alan singled out Brian Moore, who came in his red Ghost with 'Alpine' tourer. 'I remember how fast the car was the first straight out of Vienna and told him so. Later I reminded Jane how lovely and romantic was our meeting at the Monaco landing stage in Venice, then going on to Trieste, making love in the hotel room before dinner; and then the rest of the magical [Alpine] rally. I have this divine serenity at present. I do hope it lasts.'

That summer Alan visited Westminster once, when the Clarks parked their car in the Commons car park on the way north to Eriboll via King's Cross and Inverness. It was the last day of June, little more than four weeks after surgery. He went up to the tearoom, almost empty, he recorded, except for Cheryl Gillan, the Tory Member for Chesham and Amersham. 'She was nice.' But he lamented not doing as he should have done, tip-toeing round and standing briefly at the Bar of the House. Alan then added, 'It would have been my very last time.' Did that mean that at heart he knew he was dying, or, more prosaically, that he had no option but to resign from Kensington and Chelsea? Elsewhere at Westminster he was delighted to be 'lionised by many, especially by the policeman; and the taxi driver who took us to King's Cross'. He appeared, though, to have lost his taste for the political life, 'not in the slightest bit nostalgic. Because, with Hague consolidating there is absolutely nothing I could do.'

The visit to Eriboll had first been mooted on 21 June, 'before the decline sets in'. He thought of more reasons, the Creaggan, Tom's game bank, beaches and coves where he and Jane used to nude-bathe 'into which I have got to lock my spirit before the body gives up'. But he admitted to feeling feeble. On 26 June: 'I don't want to die until I have seen Eriboll and there I may be able to contrive it.' In the past he had even cogitated in his diary dying on the Creaggan Road, 'my last sight being of little Jane's face'.[6]

Much needed organising and the burden fell on Jane. 'Am I up to the journey?' he asked. His surgeon cleared him to go and arranged a prescription. They decided to travel by train. Finally, late on Wednesday, 30 June, they made it. 'It's incredible. At 8 p.m. I sit in the wheelhouse. Troubled only by a full colon (blocked, presumably, by a(nother) tumour). But what an achievement to be here! Came up on the day train yesterday from King's Cross. A lovely journey with attentive staff, although I became adversarial with the passengers including a man of my age who sat on the other side of the aisle and seemed to be observing us and listening to our conversation.' Alan was not shy in turning to irony. 'He did not, irritatingly, appear to have prostate trouble. (Nor did I come to that.)'

At Inverness Macrae & Dick, the firm which supplied them with Land Rovers, lent them the latest Discovery. Jane drove the remaining 150 miles to Eriboll, stopping only en route for a take-away curry at Bonar Bridge, 'one of the most delicious meals I have ever consumed'. They arrived at dusk, it was drizzling, but Alan could not resist walking, big stalking stick in hand, to the boathouse. 'On the shoreline I thanked God for getting us here 30 days after Room 17. Then a cup of Ovaltine and slept like a log, as did Jane.'

The five-day visit gave Alan's morale an enormous boost. He refers in his diary to 'a certain anticipatory elation' each morning as he dressed. This was the Eriboll magic. One day they managed the Creaggan; he did not mind admitting that he was helped for some of the way by lifts in the car, although it was with pride that he 'walked the last bit to the summit of the col and then across to the little knoll (which featured in *Love Tory*) and round it'. So tired was he that evening that he ducked out of dining at the Lodge but did manage to eat five oysters before retiring. He slept 'virtually without interruption for ten hours!'.

Alan was under no illusions as to his future, but first to his diary he combined thoughts on Eriboll and the Almighty. 'How I wish that I could stay up here and just cure myself by God helping me to regenerate (as he has done so brilliantly up until now).' Then reality. 'Tomorrow we return, for me to be slowly and systematically destroyed. But how wonderful to have come up here, and tasted its strengths and touched all the beacons.'

They managed the return journey to Saltwood in one day, Jane again driving 'heroically' from Eriboll ('Scotch mist started on the Moine') to Inverness, and after the train to London, from the Commons to Saltwood. Next morning Alan harked back, already 'homesick for Eriboll. The sweet oystercatchers all came in a flock, full strength, to say goodbye to us yesterday morning at 6 a.m., when we were loading the Discovery. I see always the beautiful view of the shoreline from boat house beach and hear the slap of the wavelets. That is heaven for me. But today I seem to be an awful long way from it; and it's very inaccessible. There I would gladly lie down and die. But the gulls and the hoodies [crows] would take out my eyes, which would be upsetting for Jane.'

Life back at Saltwood began promisingly. The Eriboll aura did not immediately wear off. The morning after their return: 'I am serene, having been to all those lovely places where God could at any time take my spirit if he chose. I am now back at the Mains and must look to Him for strength.' One day he managed a length of the castle swimming pool, the first of the year, the next, two lengths, 'just like the old times with Lëhni waiting aggressively on the steps'. Once more he wrote, 'Thank you, God.' But he was lowered by the sight of chits that awaited about oncology appointments, by the accidental drowning of a little pea-chick.

The following day, 6 July, even a visit to Canterbury hospital did not depress him. He looked back at the month since surgery. 'My progress is really incredible. I dare not even write down what God could do if he chose so to do. I am happier now than I was in those days. Partly I suppose my recuperative powers. Partly, also the impact of the wonderful Eriboll memories.' But he confessed to a lack of appetite, feeling muzzily headachy after a nap. Chandrakumar, his doctor at Hythe, reported that his most recent blood test was completely satisfactory. He worried, though, about another car matter, a forthcoming visit by the Jaguar XK club. But Saltwood, once again, wove its magic. 'Here I am in these lovely rooms, still acquiring strength and confidence.'

He mused on how death would come. If not George VI valet, perhaps the press would report his death with 'all those lovely things' around him, 'suddenly at Saltwood'. He also reported a forthcoming visit that would have significant ramifications: 'The Catholics are coming. "Guild of the Divine Sacrament" on Saturday. I hope I'm up to it.'

THIRTY-SEVEN

Beliefs

Alan's view of God's work was often combined with the Arthurian image of the sword in the lake. In politics the sword was a seat in the Cabinet. At Eriboll the summer that followed his decision not to stand again at Sutton, he was driving in the dark and realised, 'almost with panic, just what I had thrown away by "standing down". I suppose I should have continued to trust in God, that He would give one the opportunity for the sword in the lake. Essentially it was selfish, opting for a quiet and comfortable life; sidestepping humiliation. God has given us self-determination, too, and of course if we are determined we can reject his gift.'

If Alan's parents showed few obvious signs of being 'religious', Celly says her mother and father had from childhood knelt and said a prayer when they entered a church. As adults they were much more likely to be there to look at the architecture. That notwithstanding, all the children did end up Christian. Canon Reg Humphriss, who knew the Clarks as Saltwood's Rector, wondered if God was the father figure Alan lacked as a child, someone who didn't answer back, an idealised picture of what a father could be.[1]

Alan sometimes prayed at St Leonard's, Hythe's parish church, asking for the key if it was shut. Canon Norman Woods, its long-standing Vicar, thought it was easier for him to be anonymous at Hythe, whereas, as Humphriss put it, to do so at Saltwood 'he would have to come across the fields'. In Woods's view Alan's God was a compassionate figure whom he made in his own image. He saw prayer as a way of 'referring things upstairs – when he was remorseful'. He was also convinced of God's forgiveness, perhaps even a little presumptuous.[2] In the midst of his infatuation for Alison Young he recorded a visit to St Leonard's. 'I knelt and reflected on "it" all. I almost asked Norman to hear my confession, but didn't/couldn't, though afterwards Jane said he would have. I was rather shocked to find how I prayed so selfishly. It was quite an effort to *focus* on the real purpose and to release darling Jane of her pain and sense of betrayal. She's going through exactly what I did in February – and I know what it's like – total hell. Only feebly did I give thanks for this wonderful life and all my blessings. Disgraceful.'[3]

In his diary Alan records several occasions during this volatile period when he prayed in the twelfth-century church at the summit of Brentor on Dartmoor, close to Bratton. Was there a sense of self-flagellation in making the long, steep climb? Thus in early 1991: 'I had a long, long prayer. Should make me serene. And it does while I'm talking to God . . . Like all addicts I can vividly remember the incredible rush of vitality and well being that comes from a good "fix".'[4]

As with his political beliefs and the Conservative Party, Alan was not prepared to follow one church without question. In his ideal world he would take a little of this and a little of that. Language, which meant so much to him, attracted him to the Church of England and the 1662 Book of Common Prayer. In August 1984, visiting Seend, he was appalled by the lack of a 'proper Bible, or King James Prayer Book'. This led him into a diatribe: 'I am completely certain that this degradation of the ancient form and language is a calculated act, a deliberate subversion by a hard core whose secret purpose is to distort the beliefs and practices of the Church of England.' Nor had he finished. 'Every time – usually by accident – that I attend a service where "Series III" used, and suffer that special jarring pain when (most often in the Responses) a commonplace illiteracy, straight out of a local authority circular, supplants the beautiful, numinous phrases on which I was brought up and from which I drew comfort for thirty-five years, my heart sinks. All too well do I understand the rage of the *Inquisitadores*. I would gladly burn them, those trendy clerics, at the stake. What fun to hear them pinkly squealing. Or perhaps, as the faggots kindled, they would "come out", and call on the Devil to succour them.'[5]

Alan's feeling for language influenced the form of baptism service for his grandson Albert, which took place in March 1997 at Saltwood church, where Andrew and Sarah were married. At a meeting beforehand, Humphriss explained they could use the Prayer Book service or the Common Worship version, which he said was now the more usual, and Andrew decided on that. Back at Saltwood Alan intervened. 'In the kitchen last night, horrified by the "alternative" form, printed on a cling-film-coated card which Reg had handed the young, I went upstairs and fetched the little white parchment-bound prayer book, inscribed by my father for Jane at the time of our wedding, and read to them the true form of service. I don't know what Andrew did, but most pleasingly Reg intoned the age-old phrases while the little prince was humped and jigged by me, fretting just a little, on and off, but easily distracted by the stained glass. Afterwards we posed, the three males in line, beside my father's gravestone.'[6] 'One of the loveliest of baptisms,' recalled Humphriss, 'it showed Alan in the best possible light.' It was also the only occasion he remembered when Alan, who was not known for contributing regularly to Saltwood church's funds, made a cheque out in the church's favour.

In Alan's religion confession played its part, and was one attraction of Roman Catholicism (Jane told him that all he wanted to do was say Hail Marys for his sins). However she also recalled that 'he didn't go along at all with the notion that animals hadn't got souls, which Catholics say'. He also remarked in a 1992 interview that he would have converted 'long ago if the Catholic Church itself hadn't changed so dreadfully'.[7]

In July 1999, little more than five weeks after surgery, the long-arranged visit by members of Westminster Cathedral's Guild of the Divine Sacrament was, he thought, just what was needed to lift his spirits.[8] Two days beforehand he wondered who else might join him and telephoned Number Ten. 'After tea (always the best time) I got a good adrenalin fix,' he wrote. 'Rang Anji Hunter[9] to inquire if Blair would like to come to the Mass on Saturday.[10] Long chat. Felt "tons better" at once. The combination of female admiration and political inner loop.'

Alan and Father Michael Seed of Westminster Cathedral had first been in contact in the early 1990s about animal rights, but that barrier to Roman Catholicism Father Michael was unable to overcome. In early 1995 Lord Longford, the Labour politician and Catholic, had 'in the strictest confidence' shared with Seed, 'in the position of a priest', Alan's interest in Catholicism. Longford was himself a convert, thanks, believes his daughter Lady Antonia Fraser, to the influence of Evelyn Waugh.[11] Shortly before Easter 1995 Alan joined Longford and Seed for lunch, after which Father Michael wrote, 'Dear Alan (if I may call you Alan, I feel as if I can). I hope the lunch was not too much like the Spanish Inquisition ... the Franciscans were only the judges to it, we never burnt anyone!! We left that to the Dominicans!'[12] Father Michael recommended that Alan read some Cardinal Newman. Alan was sceptical, but wrote in his diary that day: 'I don't wholly dismiss all that, and will read Newman over Good Friday.' In May news leaked of 'another Papist plot' with Alan, it was said, about to follow his Conservative colleagues, Ann Widdecombe and John Selwyn Gummer, on the road to Rome. Father Michael wrote apologetically to Alan, 'I would not blame you should you wish to just give up on the whole thing. I pray you will not and that we can meet very soon, if just to put my mind at rest on this.'

In August 1995 Alan and Jane gave a dinner party in Saltwood's Great Hall and invited Seed, with Michael and Sandra Howard, Nigel Nicolson, Algy and Blondel Cluff, Jonathan and Vivien Holborow, Selina Scott, Jeffrey Archer (joined at the last moment by his wife Mary, who, Alan recorded, 'asked herself *en supplement*')[13] and also their son Andrew and his wife Sarah. Seed wrote an ecstatic letter of thanks. 'Many many thanks indeed for ALL the trouble and care last Saturday, from door to door you looked after me! . . . what company for dinner – we almost had a vacancy for Home Secretary [Michael Howard] with that walk along the castle wall! Sadly, I had 3 glasses before !!! We friars are trained well for the missions!! I would like to take you up on your kind offer of a visit . . . it would do me good and perhaps when sober will walk the castle wall! Might also help our "spiritual" conversations! PS: how lovely Selina Scott was.'

After Alan's return to Parliament at the 1997 general election, Seed encouraged him to attend Mass at the Cathedral, invited him to address the boys at Ampleforth on military history (he did not go) and in return was invited by Alan to tea on the Commons Terrace. Conversations between them continued, but Alan did not take the plunge. Graham Stewart recalls passing on a message from Father Michael in 1999 before Alan's health took its final turn. Alan made it clear to Stewart that he appreciated his conversations with Father Michael and Lord Longford, but said he had no intention of becoming a Catholic.

Following surgery, in his first post-operative entry on 4 June, Alan wrote 'Tried to get through to Father Michael'. Interestingly, at this moment of crisis he chose not to turn to the Church of England. A month later Father Michael wrote about the arrangements for the Guild's visit on 10 July. 'Alan if we do not see you on the day, we will more than fully understand. Your health is what counts. We will offer the Mass for you and we will also offer the benediction for that intention as well. Thus, you will be back to health one month before you should! Our prayers and those of the Guild of the Blessed Sacrament are very strong indeed.'

The day itself was sunny and hot and, reported Alan, by 4 p.m. the Inner Bailey had the appearance of a garden party. 'Father Michael came up trumps. He produced the Marchmain case out of *Brideshead*, gave me sacrament for the sick, oil, holy bread etc.' *Brideshead* was among Alan's regular bedside reading with EMT. He would have remembered the scene of Lord Marchmain's final hours ('The priest took the little box from his pocket . . . touching the dying man with an oily wad').[14] If Alan recognised life imitating art, one wonders if he knew that in Waugh's novel art was imitating life, as Waugh drew inspiration from the conversion not long before the death of his friend Hubert Duggan?[15] Alan, in his 10 July diary entry, concluded, 'For a few minutes I felt cured. But it soon reverted. No appetite, or energy, headache. At periods I am back to May – which is particularly lowering.'[16] But no mention of going over to Rome.

Father Michael paid one further visit to Saltwood, the day before Alan died. Jane recounted the visit in her diary, that prayers were said and Father Michael anointed Alan with oil, but in particular her shock when Father Michael told her over tea downstairs that 'Al *was* a Catholic. He had made him one on 10 July.' He handed over some notes he had made of that day. Jane felt hurt that Alan had not confided his conversion to her, but Andrew, when she showed him Father Michael's notes, was unconvinced. He did not think that Father Michael *had* given his father last rites. Jane commented, 'This was very much a Catholic priest saying something for someone *not* a Catholic . . . I do *not* think he was fully received.'

Father Michael's thank-you letter over the Guild's visit tried to be practical. 'You are both very much in my prayers and thoughts, the whole family. I realise the pain and suffering that is there and you are both holding up well. Alan, the things we spoke about in private are very close to my heart. They are deeply in my prayer, please know that. I would be happy to go to Scotland for that which we spoke in a little time from now. This must be when things are more calm for you and Jane and family.' He added a PS: 'I have time off in August and would be happy to pop down for an hour or so.'[17]

THIRTY-EIGHT
Hopes Shattered

If Alan's mind had been boosted by the visit of the Catholics, his body now took a downturn. He complained almost daily in his diary of headaches, usually eye-related. He stopped swimming. Over in the Great Library one day with Jane and Lynn he had to sit down. All he wanted to do was rest. But Cindy Frowd, the reflexologist at Hythe, actually thought him much better. On another occasion Jane practised reflexology on his thumb to ease the head pain, which did the trick and sent him to sleep. He was, though, impatient, remembering the deaths of Mark Boxer, cartoonist and editor, and his fellow Tory MP Jock Bruce-Gardyne, both of whom had brain tumours. 'But how does it end with cancer of the brain?' he asked. 'Do you lose your faculties, vision, speech, balance? I wish I could conceive of an escape route. It is just so difficult to get to Eriboll. And anyway I must, I suppose, give the treatment a chance. I fear, though, that now I am degenerating into an invalid.' He dreaded the inference that another tumour lurked. On 8 July he had been X-rayed at Canterbury. 'My eyes complain if I do any kind of paperwork, like, e.g., even writing this note' or studying Jane's share certificates to see how they might be consolidated – 'quite a nice little list'.

On 12 July he wrote of continuing deterioration, including a 'little turn' in the Green Room. 'Sweet Janey cried, heart-rendingly, after "lights". "I don't want to lose you ..."' The laughing, the chatting, the strength.' Alan now spoke to his surgeon Nick Thomas, who was 'unwelcomingly grave'. The most recent X-ray had shown up a cyst, which could be removed surgically. He also authorised 2mg of D/M [Dexamethadone] per day to help with the headaches. 'I am so depressed', wrote Alan, who likened it to 'the stagehands fiddling about with the curtain(s)'. He 'took a D/M, and slept pretty well, though immediately on waking unease and pain starts to come through the eyes. I remain very, very exhausted and sleepy. I don't see how this can end now, except with my dying. I do not look forward to the gravediggers clumping about. God, please help to keep Janey's morale up.'

Each day brought a new sign of decline. On 14 July he 'Couldn't even manage EMT (a new low).' His appetite was decreasing, with consequent weight loss. In a note to Jane he placed what he called his 'tea order'. The rock cakes of the Commons tea room were in the past. Now it was '1 cup of tea and slice lemon (no milk) plus tiny brown bread spread with honey (no butter).' His outpatient appointments at Canterbury gave him little encouragement. His headaches were now combined with feeling sick. By Saturday he was 'Feeling simply dreadful,' and mused, 'Is this how Death approaches?'

Alan had been forecasting his own death a long time before. In December 1983 he recorded a premonition that, thanks to overwork on Part III (Financial Contributions) of the Employment Bill, he was perhaps vulnerable to a brain tumour. Two years later he estimated a life expectancy of fifteen years. He is, though, inconsistent. In November 1996, following 'a filthy flu-cold', he wrote, 'Usual answer − "20 years"', but quickly realised that this was unrealistic. 'Ten, then? But I will/would be the same age as my father when he became doddery and feeble-voiced. And anyway, *ten isn't enough*. How can I say this? I am so fortunate, so much for which to thank God. It just is I would like three completely free, but still with some vigour, to enjoy myself with Jane.'

As July wore on tempers frayed. One breakfast the smell of bread frying made him nauseous, and as he started leaving the kitchen Jane snapped at him, 'why?'. He wrote that he 'tried to explain, but was, I recognise, soft-spoken in the extreme'. Jane was quick to respond: 'Your problem is that you want to die; but are frightened of dying.' He worried further about Jane − 'so exhausted. Poor Jane is so exhausted. Can one wonder? She does so much.' At that moment she brought him a glass of cool sorrel tea.

Sunday, 18 July proved altogether more cheering when the XK members turned up in force. Alan recorded that Andrew was 'extremely competent in coping. The blue, the white and the grey cars all "won" awards. (So there!).' Afterwards Alan spoke to James on the phone and remarked that it was 'Fitting, somehow, that my impending departure should be attended by this huge retinue of XKs.' You must think positively,' he replied. 'Useless advice,' wrote Alan, 'although well meant.'

He wrote Jane a note.

Darling
    I think I'm going . . .
    The divide between giving up life and *being sick* is a narrow one.

You must not forget how much I love you, and regret having caused all this 'aggro'. Talk to Fr Michael. He knows.

Also get a message to the oystercatchers. And to Tom [their dog who had died], also.

I will always be *for you*.

A x x x x

He no longer wished to see anyone or indeed talk even to old friends on the telephone. He knew he was dying, but even admitting illness was, to him, as Jane had noticed many times before in their married life, 'a sign of weakness'.[1]

Alan worried that he was not using his time properly. He had done what he called 'a certain amount of contract note work to clear the decks for Janey, and all'. He was thinking, 'well at least I'm still living. But the actual end is very nasty to contemplate.' The phone rang just as he was going downstairs. It was Nick Thomas. He had looked at the latest scans. What he said next was bleak: 'There is really nothing more that surgery can do'. This was a body blow. 'I really don't know what I should do next. I am scared at losing my faculties and dying without dignity.' His thoughts suddenly moved to the political succession, how he wished he could hand on K&C to Andrew. 'He would be so good there.' He summed up the day. 'I still don't feel very well, but what is really horrible is the knowledge that you can't "get better". God could help, by why should he? Still, I might, I suppose, have died already like JFK.' In his diary the writing, which had become more difficult to read as he grew older, now grew smaller, more minuscule

His interest in politics had for the moment dimmed, but he did register 28 July, 'The very favourite date in a Parliamentarian's diary. All over. The great long recess is finally under way. For me the delicious feeling of relief is irrecoverable.' He looked out from the Green Room towards the pool: 'The Bailey in July at 1 p.m. was full traditional Saltwood. Beautiful, sunny, warm, hollyhocks burgeoning. I suppose that I should just have stripped and plunged in. The shock of the cold water ... what a way to go! A nice irony after all my earlier physical exultations there.'

A new stage was about to begin. If his surgeon could do no more, Canterbury's oncology department still had a role to play. His radiotherapy began on 27 July. His daily visits there were debilitating. On the last Wednesday in July he returned and wrote, 'Oh dear, I am down! Actually I do not think that I have ever been worse.' July 31 was the forty-first anniversary of his marriage to Jane. Alan had two weeks earlier written her a letter, and entrusted it to Lynn for safekeeping, just in case he wasn't there to give it to Jane on the day.

> Just back from a visit to Kent & Canterbury,
> not a very good day ...

Hello, my sweet Janey!

I am reminded that only 41 years ago I was somewhat apprehensively sharing digs with Celly and Caryl in Victoria Road, Westminster – a short distance from Grey-Coat Gardens [where Jane's parents were living]. At that time I was already bonded, and would soon formally be *pledged*, to the sweetest, kindest, most percipiently intelligent human-being I would ever encounter. What a union that would prove to be!

Those lovely 'fair-heads', of every generation! And all the sympathy and knowedge for *plants* and *animals* that has radiated out from you and transformed the whole ambience of the family seat. (Am I getting a bit illegible? If so, damn, and apologies.)

For every minute of the day you have worked for me, us and the family. Worked *too hard* ... A hundred times I ask myself how I could have been so cruel to you. Fool Clark, fool. *Nasty* fool, also! What's the use of my saying you are, will always remain, the only true love of my life? If you should ever need me, I will, I hope, be possibly at certain known localities in the grounds (of each property, even Zermatt).

Love, love, love from

A xxx

A new month, and 1 August was a Sunday. He now wrote what was to be the final entry in his diary, a true 'last', although he did not know it at the time, in a sequence that had begun forty-four years ago on his twenty-seventh birthday.

> Fact is, I've got brain cancer. And it is fairly disagreeable. My body realises that there is no hope. I mean what is the next stage? The next (local) demon with which to wrestle? My wrist shakes – why? Shades of little T.O. I could not eat, even put into my mouth, any of the delicacies prepared at lunch time today. Or even the 'accompanying medication' which hourly makes Jane very depressed. I am afflicted by a kind of despair, also. The Amazings[2] coming in tomorrow. What can I say to them? The house is like an oven now, excepting the rooms on the north side.

Although Alan would write no further entries, Jane now started a diary. She began on 2 August, the fifth day of radiotherapy at Canterbury. 'Al got dressed and so wobbly – came downstairs on his bottom, me placing his feet on each step. He is really bad.' He began to fight like a baby over taking pills or eating even the minutest piece of toast. 'I long for a meal that I don't have to get up every few minutes for some whim. I long for Al to take the pills without having to yet again explain what each one is for (more than twice, it's 4 or 5 times).'

For Jane the journal was a confessional, as Alan's diary had been for him. Early one morning 'EMT in bed writing this with Al sitting on the edge of the bed trying to be sick and soft-spoken. I feel ill with the struggle ahead – long for a dark, warm place that is silent, snug and I can sleep.' And each day she drove Alan across to Canterbury, manoeuvred him into a chair, then rushed back to park the car. Back at Saltwood she dug out his mother's wheelchair, which Lynn gave a good wash. 'It is jolly good,' wrote Jane. Only at weekends with no trips to Canterbury could she indulge herself with a 'lovely lie-in' and a swim.

She worried that he ate so little. One afternoon, on returning from walking the dogs, she found him on the floor by the banisters, bruised quite badly and with small abrasions on his right arm and elbow. 'It seems to have had the effect of completely unhinging his mind. He mumble rambled – did not really notice anything. Seemed far away – on about a PhD and being on water. Quite frightening and he was so good in a.m.' Supper that evening was a banana whisked in half a cup of milk. 'He had 2 spoonfuls v reluctantly and then pushed it away saying it was going all round his head. Told him he was a b fool of course.'

Next day he stayed in bed all day. 'He just lies there making bizarre zany muddled sentences or mostly just saying nothing, but lying looking miserable.' Nor was it just looks. 'Peed not in pot so changed pyjamas. Have got wheelchair upstairs to take him to loo.' Her routine now revolved totally around Alan. She bathed him, cut his nails, filed rough skin, brushed his hair, which made him look 'so much better'. But then he was sick. 'Damn, damn. Not a lot, says it is the vitamin pill so they're out.'

The radiotherapy routine was particularly tough on Jane, as it meant leaving Saltwood for Canterbury by 8.30. She had to rise at 6.45, which just gave her time for a swim, do the hens, make breakfast, porridge, tea and coffee for Al (if he wanted any). One morning she was so rushed she didn't have time to do the hens – 'oh dear, oh dear'. On another occasion she came in from the Pavillon, overlooking the swimming pool, as Alan wanted to go to the loo. It was not easy, as Jane's account makes abundantly clear. 'I had a breakdown as first couldn't negotiate the small rise by yard door, then hit a lot of things in outer lobby, and ended by kicking everything to right and left hurling boxes of papers, chairs etc. Shouting at poor dog (Lëhni) whose paws were slightly in the way. Broke down in tears in Cork bathroom with Al on loo.' By 9.40 that evening Jane still had not had a proper meal and was desperately tired.

By the second week in August Jane had to face the possibility that Alan was now incontinent. On a morning when she was pleased to have got Alan and herself into the car in good time, she found she had left it switched on the previous evening. 'Battery *totally* flat.' Fortunately Saltwood was not short of alternatives; transferring Alan into S16, an old Volkswagen Golf, she sped off to Canterbury. This was Day 11 of 20. But when Jane saw Stewart Coltart, the consultant, he gave her 'the shattering news that it was pointless to go on with R – unkind to Al and the family. He shouldn't be like he is after 11 doses, bladder going, no balance, lack of appetite etc. Very bad sign.' Jane was in tears – Alan had gone out of the room for a blood test. 'In my heart I *knew* it wasn't right although trying to look positive. We went to find Al, me with tears pouring down my face past all those people waiting – Al didn't really seem to have taken it in – has he? I don't know – although I was in tears he made no sign of compassion which isn't him at all. A gloomy drive home in suitably torrential rain, which stopped at M20.'

Jane reflected on the situation. 'It's strange I feel numbed by this news ... I love God, but this is such a cruel way to demolish such a brilliant brain – I dread to think what lies in store.' She talked to Andrew, Sarah, James and Julie, who were 'equally shattered. Amazings will be here Thursday and James as well. How long we have got only God knows – but miracles sometimes happen. It is the eclipse tomorrow. For us it was going to be a turning point – but now the beginning of the end.' Wednesday, 11 August, the day of the eclipse, also saw the arrival of the district nurse, Sister Angela Rourke, to 'assess' Al and offer Jane advice. Walking the dogs she met Eddie, 'who was terribly upset at the news'. That evening she rang her elderly mother in Spain – 'she poor darling is v ill too. I should be *there* as well as here.'

In addition to the district nurse Jane now had help from the local hospice team. At one point Saltwood became so crowded, '*so many* people – meaning well I know, but I'm not so sure they don't make you worse'. But she needed them, as she wrote, for making Alan's life pain-free and for access to commodes, sheets, waterproofs etc. He had also developed a rash. The arrival, though, of Andrew, Sarah and the boys was another matter. Andrew 'brilliantly mowed Bailey and dealt with battery problem – it was totally flat, wouldn't take a jumpstart at all. He also

shaved Al and helped move him from Cork to bed, while I ate lunch.'
But Jane closed her entry that evening in gloomy frame of mind. 'If this
is a game of snakes and ladders we have met the biggest snake – a veritable
pit of them.'

With the family around her, the kaleidoscope of her routine changed.
It was 8.30 the following morning. 'I must get up. We are lying side by
side. Al completely silent and looking so vulnerable and *young*. Not an
old person at all. Tup saw him, said how much he had lost weight from
Thursday's visit. It's lovely having everyone about, but I feel I am more
with them and *cooking* than with Al. We had a Sunday lunch of roast
venison, Yorkshire pudding, spinach, beans and spuds. V good for me as
I ate well! I took my tea up and lay in the bed with him for 2 hours talking
and weeping. It is so hard, he does not really respond as if a river was
between us, and he can't/won't hear and can't/won't respond. But I know
he hears as when I queried God's role in this he stopped me and said
I mustn't blame God. I don't, but why does God think *I* need proof of
his powers – what is he trying to say to me, to us both?'

It was now only a matter of time, as Dr Chandrakumar told Jane, James
and Andrew on 16 August. Jane liked him, not least because he did 'not
go for the make-him-eat-drink-and-force-his-bowels-open stuff. Is really
quite spiritual in that way – agrees the most important thing is to make
sure there is no pain, which, thank goodness, is the situation now.' And
yet, what about a miracle? 'I still keep hoping for someone to say it's all
ok.' Jane now felt able to discuss practical matters with Dr Chandrakumar.
What should she do when Alan died? Jane felt all the calmer for knowing
everything. Nor did she forget her mother in Spain. 'Rang Mummy
whose legs are still v bad – she goes tomorrow to have stitches out.'

Jane's journal is both reportage and reflection. She noted that while
James did not want to be left to get his father onto the commode, Andrew
was a carer, 'just like Al would be'. But watching her family, sons and their
sons playing on the lawn she 'cried tears for a future that Al was not to
share. It is like a terrible dream and you wake and it's real and oh how
I long for it to be not so. Al is not aware of my crying whereas tears would
have upset him before – that too is hard – we are already apart yet still
both alive and close. Strange.' When she cuddled Alan 'he was not really
here – a strange faraway look on his face. He had left me and I must realise
this will happen more and more. He has always been my other half, but
the branch is nearly off and the scar will take time to heal over. It is strange
to see and feel him and yet know he is fading away from me.'

What Jane called 'Another cruel quirk of this awful cancer – another "up" to give us hope before a steeper decline again to despair?' came on the morning of 23 August, when he said 'You have been crying – so have I.' To Jane he seemed 'quite different again, more on the ball and not so muddled. He had coffee and noticed today I had put sugar in it! Liked the idea of grapenuts and had 3 spoonfuls (teaspoons) and then two small pieces of brown toast and marmalade – and more coffee (nearly 1 cup of coffee). Drank nearly $\frac{1}{2}$ Redoxon. I stayed with him – carpet swept the room and polished about, talked.'

Politics had been forgotten. Of his Conservative friends David Davis continued to be a regular caller with the news and gossip that was so much part of Alan's Westminster life. On 25 August Michael Howard, a friend and their MP, telephoned. Jane wrote that he was shattered by the news.

Each day now Jane could see a fresh deterioration. On 26 August she wrote that 'He has now lost so much weight he looks like a PoW.' When Helen, the hospice nurse came, 'he was monstrous and grimaced crazily when I tried to lift him and then flatly refused to speak to her at all'. Over tea Jane asked if he'd like Reg Humphriss or Michael Seed, but he did not answer 'and when he did much later on being re-asked said no'.

Jane was getting organised for the inevitable. But even though Alan was now barely speaking when Jane kissed him and told him she was there, he half smiled, 'which is lovely'. He slept and after tea woke and asked Jane for a kiss 'so that he could remember my taste'. They talked about it all. 'He said he knew what I was doing for him and thanked me. Stayed until 7-ish – half asleep holding each other's hands.'

His temperament kept changing. While Jane took the dogs out, James showed him a 'lovely picture of swimming pool. J said he was very lucid and loving so I should go up and be with him. Told him I had been there all afternoon and he was just pretty non-speakers to one and I was bloody fed up with him. He was not loving and friendly so I left him and came down after changing for lovely dinner of squid. Bed 5 to 10. Al asleep, covered him up and kissed him goodnight – (no response).'

Jane recorded that James sat with him for forty-five minutes, 'came down and was quite rude when we said supper – he said he was going out for a fag. I then said don't worry I'm going up to bed and went out to get dogs. Dear J came out too and totally broke down in tears: "I'm nearly 40 and I'm crying. I love him so much." We both agreed it was absolutely vile to watch someone you love so much being destroyed by such an awful thing. He had his fag and we went in, both calmer.' Jane wrote that evening, 'Oh dear, darling Al. Oh God how I will miss you. I dread the future without my soul mate. I dread being really alone without his wisdom, strength, fun and companionship. For 41 years we have been together, through ups and downs. Can I live without him? For the children's sake I must remain strong – the "Dowager Empress" he said I would be. I must not let him down.'

Helen from the hospice and Dr Chandrakumar worried about Jane. Alan, they said, should have twenty-four-hour nursing now. But Jane said no, 'I simply wouldn't, not while he still is aware of what's happening and although sometimes he looks through me and glares he will suddenly smile and say "I know what you're doing and you are incredible" – or tonight he said he loved the gentle look I gave him. How could I just let a stranger take over? It is my job and I will go on.'

On Thursday, 2 September Jane woke before 6 a.m. to strange noises, put out her hand, 'but no response at all'. She panicked. He was 'drowning' in his phlegm. She tried, not very successfully, to put another pillow under his shoulders. 'By 6.15 I thought it was the end. Terrible noises and looking v v bad. I rushed down with dogs to see if Tup and Boy there – no sign. Back up, caught Tup going down so asked him to fetch James, who rushed out of room to "go for a pee" the minute he came in. Poor James, he is only making it harder for himself.'

With no sign of Reg Humphriss on the telephone, Tup drove to the rectory, but it was obvious that he was away. Tup 'brilliantly' suggested Norman Woods, the Vicar of St Leonard's, Hythe. Jane wrote that 'He is *so* nice, a truly good, holy man. Both boys came in and we said prayers and he was anointed with oil. Felt so much better for it, and in a way I was glad fate had decreed it was Norman. Although I like Reg, we have known Norman longer and he has been a good man to know. Feel *so* much better that someone came in time; I would have felt guilty before God if I had failed to have him blessed. Waves of calmness are there now.'

The final stages of Alan Clark's life had been reached. The evening of 3 September a syringe-driver was inserted – Jane left the room while it was being done, feeling it somehow wrong to violate the body. She wrote movingly of her thoughts.

Al had been in a coma, but could squeeze your hand until about lunchtime – his breathing so rasping through the mouth, eyes open, but not aware. Oh dear God what a waste, what a waste! It is this I mind so much, not just the fact I shall be losing my soul mate of 41 years, my lover, my friend, my companion, my dearest husband – oh *how* I shall miss him! What an empty horizon stretches ahead, so frightening I cannot think of it, so am blocking it out.

It is now 20 to 10. I am lying on the bed beside him. I talk to him of what I will do, the office, the woodland walk, the brambles on the cistus bank as well as the woodland. Keeping the paperwork in order, the bank statements in order, my life in order, a Lady Dunn minus Beaverbrook. We were always such a good team and now I shall be leaderless. Still the faith he always had in me will be my inspiration. I must not let him down. The Dowager Empress shall reign.

On Friday Jane recorded that she sat or lay on the bed beside Alan most of the afternoon. She became paranoid about flies settling on him. 'Do they sense he will shortly be dead? Finally went for a walk round the garden while Andrew sat with him. Several scares, but tonight (10.20) he sleeps ok, head slightly on one side. Sarah and Julie both come in and boys a lot. James (and Tup) really worried about *men* bothering me – how *dear* of them. I simply do not see it at all.'

Jane found sleep difficult, but not Alan, who, one or two hiccoughs aside, slept peacefully. At four she talked to him, sure that he knew. Shortly before six Hannah got on the bed, plus Lëhni. 'I put Al's hand out so they could smell him and he opens his eyes and I *know* he senses they are there – a lovely moment. Later back from a bathe and making EMT I tell him I'm back and have bathed and I love him etc and he squeezes my hand. Oh such magic moments, but cruel too as you suddenly think perhaps it's stopped and all will be well.'

The post included a cutting from the *Express* saying Alan was thinking of standing down and Jane was going to support his decision. 'Furious, *hate* the papers. What untruths they can publish. I shall have nothing to do with them after it all comes out.' Jane stayed in the room all day on and off. Lunch came up, 'lovely cauliflower cheese'. That night Jane slept fitfully. She awoke at 3.20 when Alan's breathing changed – 'shorter, tighter rasping breaths – with sighs every so often. Lay awake beside him. He is incredibly hot, "muck sweat", but his arms are very cold and body temp ok. V hot hands and face.' In the morning there was no change; Jane managed a bowl of cereal. Then the washing machine flooded.

Lynn, the Clarks' Yorkshire housekeeper, came back from holiday. Jane suggested she go upstairs and tell Alan she was back. She kissed him on the forehead. Shortly after returning downstairs Alan's breathing changed. Where were James and Andrew? 'Luckily, really luckily they were both outside in the courtyard and came running up. Within 5 or 6 minutes Al

had died. Silence, then gasp and a little breathing. More gasps and pulse
now weaker. He just looked so peaceful and you really felt his soul and
spirit had left on their journey, a wonderful calm feeling entered the room.
We all stroked him and talked and kissed him. It was such a lovely ending.
Then we all hugged each other. The end of an era.'

The decision had been made some time earlier to bury Alan at the castle,
and in a shroud, not a coffin. Father Michael had taken her aside on his
visit the previous day and said he would arrange a service 'very quietly',
but Jane knew precisely what she wished. When Reg Humphriss arrived
in the afternoon, Jane found him 'very nice and calming. Quite happy to
bury Daddy and will ask Norman to help. Rang the gravedigger who can
do it and will come tomorrow, at one o'clock.' Dr Chandrakumar also
came, checked Alan, but was also 'very kind and concerned' about Jane.

She walked the dogs and felt Al was above 'going towards Roman
tower'. On her return she talked at length to Celly. The funeral, it had
been agreed, would be on Tuesday. No announcement would be made in
advance. The press would be told only when Alan had been buried and
Jane and her family were ready. Just when it seemed like plain sailing,
suddenly a stumbling block. To bury Alan in the castle grounds required
the permission of Shepway, the local council. For Jane this seemed like a
last straw. 'I am quite shattered. Fear they will say no. I do pray that we
can bury Al as a family without pressure and where we wanted to, *when*
we want. Delay will inevitably mean he will have to leave to go somewhere
cooler. Julie very kindly came in and had a chat.'

Jane had a so-so night. 'No worries about Al beside me. In fact it was
lovely as I could talk to him still. Much nicer than an empty space, which
will come tonight, perhaps?' Next morning by 6.20 she was making 'the
first of many LISTS!'. Soon after 9, Reg Humphriss phoned with the
name, Sandra Francis, and number to call at Shepway. Jane dialled, 'a really
nice woman answered and it was Sandra. She was so sympathetic and
I cried, but wonderfully . . . she doesn't see any problems at all. Oh *what*
a weight lifted off my shoulder. Had got myself in a terrible state if the
answer had been "no, not possible".'

Jane recorded in detail what happened next.

Immediately wheels set in motion. James doing base for shroud (wood base).
Andrew organised to collect death certificate and have it registered. Sarah
has gone back to Broomhayes with little 'fair-heads'. Gail [nurse] came and
took syringe away. Julie and I bought flowers at farm shop in Sellindge. Back

and then Reg and Michael Marsh and his son arrived to dig grave. Reg very calming and we discussed placing of chairs and bier. Grave was dug in record time and looks very pleasing. Walked dogs and fed hens on return. Saw Graham [Stewart] who is coming, and Eddie, who is still terribly distressed. Picked bay and wild clematis and a few white sweet peas. Did some flowers for the Red Library – organised curtains for table after tea.

Andrew dressed Daddy, who, I must say, had made our room a tiny bit high and window had to be shut because of flies. We have prepared him in his Cuixmala t-shirt, white silk shirt, his favourite battered cords and his suede shoes, his blue neckerchief. He looked very nice. Tup had re-shaved him as well and sprayed him with Roger & Gallet. Downstairs with Tup – he seems to have got heavier somehow. Have all helped to wrap him in his shroud, beautifully done by Julie and Sarah, and he has taken with him a lot of softies: pricklepins, heart stone, Creaggan early heather, seaweed, markies for dogs, digestives, fruit cake, H of C miniature, Zermatt rock, 2 Swiss francs, his armband, his racing vintage goggles, his H of C pass and a travel warrant, 1 handkey.

Supper omelette in kitchen. James insisted on lasagne.

Bed very late 11.30, but feel so much better.

THIRTY-NINE

Last Rites

Alan Clark's funeral took place on Tuesday, 7 September. As Jane and the family wished, only those closest to him knew that he had died forty-eight hours before. The morning was overcast. Jane rose 'quite early and bathed and made EMT, took it and a bowl of cereal back upstairs to bed'. When she finally got up at 8 she kept herself busy, making a cake 'as nothing to offer people, then organised everyone and saw Al out of the house on to the Mehari and round on to the table in the Knight's Hall. A white damask tablecloth of Great Granpa's with Albany gold curtain over and then the shroud on its wooden base. Did the flowers, 2 large bowls. The white urns inside the blue pots – full of chrysanths, lilies, bay, rosemary, old man's beard and Russian vine and hops. We put our individual posies on Al – peace lilies from Hannah and Lëhni, mixed little bunches from all of us. Very pretty it looked.'

The service was due to begin at 11. Jane just had time to wash her hair and change. 'Felt very shaky, but hope I looked ok for Al, black plain linen dress, black stockings, black shoes, hair clean and loose. Only jewellery my diamond cross Al had given me, and my sapphire rings.' Only a dozen attended this very private funeral. The family, Jane, James and Julie, Andrew and Sarah, and Celly and Colin, were joined by Lynn, Eddie, the groundsman, and his wife Peggy, Sue, his secretary, and Graham Stewart, who had continued to use the Garden House after *The Tories* was completed. Canon Norman Woods and Canon Reg Humphriss, 'resplendent in flowing robes', conducted the service. The press were not there; they had not even been told.

Jane wrote about it afterwards. 'Julie looked lovely, and so did Sarah and both boys very dashing. I was so proud of them. It was the nicest funeral I have been to, intimate and personal and I do hope Al would have been pleased with me. Sue dear and kept saying how proud he would have been of you. The first part of the service over we went across the lawn to the grave. Reg blessed the grave and consecrated it and after a short prayer we lowered Al into it and I threw or rather shovelled 2 spades of earth on to him, the first one rather splendidly landing on his tinkey. All then to the Red Library for sandwiches, gossip and coffee/tea.'

The initial imagery that occurred to Graham Stewart, perhaps unsurprisingly given Saltwood's medieval origins, was of 'a fallen Crusader knight at the gates of Jerusalem'. He recalls doves fluttering overhead and the service itself, which naturally used the Book of Common Prayer. Graham was a pall-bearer with Colin, James and Andrew. 'An extraordinary day. I didn't know what to expect. I was very touched to be there.' The day unfolded. 'There he was swathed, no coffin. I had a real sense of burying some Saxon or Viking warrior who had been felled in battle and was being honoured in death. Had this almost Dark Age feel to it. Seemed completely right.'

The memory of the day has remained sharp in Stewart's mind: 'Good lord, I thought he's going to be heavy; suddenly the mind switches to the practicalities. Let's get through this.' The pall-bearers moved slowly across the grass to the grave. 'Everyone was of course upset, but quietly thoughtful rather than hysterical. Afterwards we were all standing around and Andrew turned to me and asked if I fancied a lager? In one of those slightly incongruous moments that the tension of such occasions throws up, we went to the fridge and located a couple of cans and stood around in the Bailey looking over to where AC was in his resting place, refreshing ourselves. Frankly, felt much better for it! Thereafter we repaired to the kitchen where the message to the press was composed and phoned through (I assume) to the Press Association. There was a quiet sense of shared confederacy and triumph that only then were the press told.' Stewart remembers the great sense of pleasure among everyone present that his death and funeral had taken place without the Fourth Estate finding out, 'one last victory over the priers and the prurient'.

Jane kept to what Alan had wished – 'Suddenly at Saltwood on 5 September. He would like it to be stated that he regarded himself as having gone to join Tom and the other dogs.' Jane added: 'Good and zany. Informed the Queen first as he was a Privy Counsellor, then Press Association. Phones frantic after that and camera crews at the gate.' The broadcast coverage was 'absolutely fantastic. On and on it went.'

When Jane phoned David Davis, his loyal parliamentary friend, he was hill-walking with the theme from *Schindler's List* playing on his Walkman. He played the theme for the rest of the trek. One of Alan's mentors, Hugh Trevor-Roper (now Lord Dacre and aged eighty-five) saw a London newspaper billboard announcing Alan's death. He turned to his companion, Blair Worden (later his literary executor) and said, 'My God, I need a drink.'[1]

As a bizarre coda to that day came news that the new Land Rover Discovery ordered by Alan and Jane in the summer from Macrae & Dick in Inverness was about to be delivered. It had been brought south from Scotland on a car transporter, but the driver's tachograph reading forced him to stop at a M11 layby near the Dartford tunnel. The only solution was to go and collect it. But with press cameras still massed outside the castle gates, Jane realised that to drive out past them in her old Discovery on the day of her husband's funeral only to return an hour later in a brand-new machine was to invite trouble. Jane and James waited until early evening, when, with deadlines passing, the press began to drift away. By the time they returned with the new Discovery the castle gates were deserted.

The press next morning devoted column upon column to his passing. Someone remarked that there had been nothing like it since Princess Diana's death two years before. Alan would have enjoyed the analogy. The coverage in *The Daily Telegraph* was not untypical, opening with two news stories, one of which began, 'In matters of death, as in politics, Alan Clark loved intrigue. The announcement yesterday that he had already been buried at a private family funeral, before his death had been publicly announced, was the last example of his capacity for surprise.' There followed a selection of memorable Clark quotations that included 'There are no true friends in politics. We are all sharks circling, and waiting, for traces of blood to appear'. Charles Moore, the paper's Editor, wrote an appreciative column: 'A psychotherapist would make hay with Alan's relationship with his famous father. They had great difficulty communicating. Kenneth devoted himself to the study of civilisation, Alan to the study of barbarism. Yet they had, I think, an equally aesthetic approach to the world, a sense of the pain of life, and a romantic longing for everything that made it more noble and interesting.' The paper's lengthy obituary observed, 'an irrepressible free spirit on the Conservative benches with a habit for outspokenness that ensured he never gained high office ... renowned not only for frequent public rows, but also for the candid and outrageous content of his very readable diaries. He said things of a kind many readers kept to themselves.'

Edward Pearce in *The Guardian* understood Alan's contradictions better than most.[2] Having been a political sketch-writer he was familiar with Alan as a Commons performer. 'A lean figure standing just below the government side gangway in the Commons, legs apart, arms folded, head tilted back, asking a question – so very often a question disagreeable to his party, the Conservatives. And until 1983, and appointment to a junior post in Employment, Clark was seen as pure backbencher – eccentric, clever, no doubt, but not imaginable in office. He was rude, outrageous, on certain issues very right-wing. Even under Margaret Thatcher he would surely be one of those weird ultras, loyal to her but offensive to good taste, like the Quasimodoish intriguer, George Gardiner.' He saw Alan as 'literate, astringent and insolent. His manner, languorous and throwaway, and his accent, ostentatious old upper-class, suggested a gent chippily entertained by the resentful rest of us.'

Nor was he ignored by the tabloids. The *Daily Mirror's* headline ran: 'Farewell to the only Tory the <u>Mirror</u>'s ever loved.' It also ran an appreciation by Alastair Campbell. The *Daily Star* called him 'The Toff they couldn't Tame – Farewell to Boozer, philanderer, scholar . . . and man of principle.'

Much more from across the political spectrum followed. In his *Daily Telegraph* column Craig Brown praised the diaries for their strange intertwining of the solemn and the silly, and the way he found them grudgingly reliant on each other, like Siamese twins. He also referred to 'his camp chorus line walk' which had a passer-by at the 1997 general election declare, 'Look at that walk. Beautiful. I'm going to vote for you.'[3] Frank Johnson in *The Spectator* recalled the time just after he became Editor when he published a piece by Alan that included some exuberant abuse of Dominic Lawson, his predecessor. In the ensuing furore Alan said that the offending words were written in a covering note and that it was Johnson who put them in the diary. But, responded Johnson, he had taken care to retain the original manuscript. 'That's *frightfully* middle-class,' said Alan.[4] Robert Coucher, his Editor at *Classic Cars*, wrote an appreciation, just before his last and posthumous column, reporting that after surgery Alan had complained to him, 'I feel like someone has driven a fucking JCB through my head.'[5]

Two months after Alan's death William Hague gave his tribute to a packed House of Commons – 'brilliant, irreverent, passionate about many things, a book lover's dream and a Whip's nightmare. He described himself as Genghis Khan, only richer.' Hague imagined what Alan might have written in his diary that day: 'Another dreary beginning of the Session, and this time I was the subject of the usual sanctimonious tributes, especially from that dreadful man Hague. Mind you, the Speaker looked particularly fetching.'[6]

In death as in life Alan Clark proved irrepressible.

Epilogue

The thanksgiving service for the life and work of Alan Kenneth McKenzie Clark took place on 1 February, 2000 across the road from the Houses of Parliament at St Margaret's church, Westminster, which Alan had so often attended when politicians were being remembered. The form of the service, with readings from his favourite King James's Bible, was Church of England. Politicians inevitably dominated the packed pews: the Speaker, Betty Boothroyd, the leader of the Conservative Party, William Hague, with Sir Denis Thatcher standing in for his wife, who was abroad.

In the Bidding, the Reverend Robert Wright, St Margaret's Rector, described Alan not only as politician, but as historian and writer. His love of nature was reflected from the first hymn, 'All Creatures of our God and King', and from the first reading, by David Davis, 'In the beginning God created the heaven and the earth'. Andrew read verses from St Mark's Gospel, and James the poem by Wilfred Owen, 'Anthem for Doomed Youth'. Jane asked Euan Graham to give the address and his mention of girls had St Margaret's ringing with laughter. At the end came the skirl of the pipes with a lament over the beat of a snare drum.

Next morning the column upon column of press coverage demonstrated that death had not diminished Alan's newsworthiness. Alan Hamilton in *The Times* called him 'that sparkling old rogue'. Although Simon Hoggart, in *The Guardian*, thought it 'a strangely conventional service for such a determinedly eccentric man', *The Daily Telegraph* referred to 'a magnificent send-off'.

What had been a 'robustly Anglican' service, as described by Quentin Letts in *The Daily Telegraph*, was the reporter's signal that the message Jane had given out in the aftermath of Alan's death had been noted.

In life Alan had never been far from controversy. Following his death a line in the *Daily Telegraph*'s obituary on 8 September ensured headlines anew. It stated categorically, 'Recently Clark was received into the Roman Catholic Church.'[1] Jane was incensed. The following morning she spoke

to *The Daily Telegraph's* editor, Charles Moore, who is, incidentally, a
Roman Catholic convert. On 10 September, the *Telegraph* headline ran:
'Clark widow denies priest's Catholic conversion claim'.[2] In the report,
Victoria Combe, the paper's Religion correspondent, wrote, 'Alan Clark's
widow yesterday denied reports that her husband had converted to Roman
Catholicism and claimed that the priest behind the story had got "carried
away". Jane Clark insisted that Father Michael Seed was mistaken and that
Mr Clark had "died an Anglican and was buried as such according to his
wishes".' The 850-word coverage was given top-of-the-page display by
The Telegraph. Victoria Combe quoted Father Michael as saying that Mr
Clark had followed in the footsteps of his father and converted to Rome
'quietly and without any fuss' in his last days.

Jane added that although her husband had 'toyed' with the idea of
converting, he had told his family he had not. She had summed up her
feelings in her own journal on Wednesday, 8 September 1999: 'A fax from
Fr Michael. Long and rambling, sticking to his tale of Al's conversion, but
tonight while cleaning my teeth I spotted Al's Day Diary which reminded
me I had his journal in my drawer – how silly of me, I could look and see
what happened. As we suspected – only the sacrament of the sick. Do you
not feel Al would have written up at length such a major thing as being
received into the RC church? Of course he would. He didn't, because
he wasn't.' To Victoria Combe she emphasised that she 'would not have
minded at all if he had become a Catholic, but I am confident he did not'.

A decade later the family's view, backed up by his local clergy, Canon
Woods and Canon Humphriss, remains unaltered. With intimate thoughts
such an inherent part of his diaries, particularly in times of travail, they
agree with Jane that he would not have been shy in writing something
about 10 July if it were such a significant moment in his life. Also, they
say, having talked through with Jane aspects of his funeral, the hymns and
the readings he wanted, Alan would, surely, have made it clear if he wished
them to be set in the framework of Roman Catholic liturgy? Woods and
Humphriss were also puzzled by aspects of Father Michael's assertions. If
Alan had converted on 10 July, more than seven weeks went by before his
death; would not Father Michael, who also visited Alan the day before he
died, have asked to attend his funeral?[3] And what about the Catholic priest
and his team at Hythe? It is usual practice for the local clergy to be
informed of a conversion in their parish, which would have led, naturally,
to a request on their part to be involved in the funeral service.

When approached for his account, Father Michael stated that his contact
with Alan was entirely confidential, 'particularly as he approached his

death'.[4] According to his account, 'On the day in early July 1999 when I was alone with Alan for some time there was no one present when certain spiritual events took place – however, the circumstances would have been difficult to have another present; as you may know when he was feeling better Alan was minded to have been received into the Catholic Church around the time he died but at his estate in Scotland – this was his desire during my conversation with him before early July. I simply wanted you to know the facts – his desire was for the whole family to become RCs in Scotland. Alan did not do things by halves as you know. I would have hoped that on this he might well have shared this with Jane, James and Andrew.'

However, other than to Father Michael, it is the widely held view that Alan died according to the rites of the Church of England. As for the reference by Father Michael to the deathbed conversion of Alan's father in 1983, this also leaves its own confusion. Meryle Secrest, K's biographer, recounts that the night before K died in a Hythe nursing home in May 1983 he asked for a priest, and according to Nolwen, his Roman Catholic wife, received the Eucharist. Secrest reported Nolwen as saying that her late husband's religious commitment was of long-standing. Nothing, though, was said publicly.[5]

Like Alan's, his father's funeral was a Church of England service (at Hythe). His memorial service took place in London at St James's, Piccadilly (itself an Anglican church), but ended sensationally when an Irish priest stepped forward and announced that Kenneth Clark had become a Roman Catholic a week before he died. This, though, was news to the Clark children. Yet a decade later Alan referred in passing to his father's conversion in old age as a matter of fact and without comment, and added, 'I'd have followed him long ago if the Catholic Church itself hadn't changed so dreadfully.'[6]

The press had by now accepted both conversions as matters of fact. But without additional evidence in either case, it is impossible to know for certain. The Scots would say 'not proven'. Like father, like son?

Interest in the name and work of Alan has shown no sign of diminishing in the decade since his death. On more than one occasion after publication of his *Diaries* plans to mount stage adaptations were announced, although these came to nothing. Not only was Alan against it, but Jane objected to the inaccuracy of another script which had Alan turning frequently to a drinks trolley behind the sofa. A plan by the BBC to adapt the *Diaries* for television was, however, a different matter. Here, in a format devised by

Andrew Davies, certain scenes were dramatised, but the authentic diary 'voice' was used as a commentary. The series, in six parts, starred John Hurt as Alan and Jenny Agutter as Jane. Some filming took place at Saltwood, but Jane's kitchen was deemed too small and had to be recreated in a studio. The series, initially transmitted on the new BBC 4 digital channel, was well-received and attracted more than a million viewers. It has since been repeated many times.

The drama documentary format on television has also yielded re-creations of aspects of the Thatcher years. Here Alan's *Diaries* have proved a valuable source, particularly on Margaret Thatcher's downfall. In *Margaret* by Richard Cottan, the scene where Alan finds Peter Morrison, her campaign manager, asleep in his office with his feet on the desk owed much to Alan's account. In fiction, too, Alan's name has been used as a symbol, again of the Thatcher years. Sebastian Faulks, in his 2007 novel *Engleby*, included a scene in which his hero, a journalist, interviews Alan Clark in 'a swanky French restaurant' near the Royal Opera House. Faulks captures Alan's speech, but if Mike Engleby had known his man he would surely have taken him to Wilton's in Jermyn Street.

As well as the publication of two further volumes of Alan's diaries – a prequel, *Diaries: Into Politics*, and a sequel, *The Last Diaries* – Jane also encouraged Alan's publishers to assemble a collection of his extensive motoring writings. Robert Coucher, who had commissioned Alan to write a column for *Classic Cars* magazine, edited the volume under the title *Back Fire*. The mix of memoir, deep knowledge and enthusiasm ensured it a large following.

The unique qualities that this biography has endeavoured to portray help explain why even a decade after his death Alan Clark is not forgotten. The publication of other politicians' diaries – notably Chris Mullin's *A View from the Foothills* in 2009 – always provoked comparisons, with Alan's invariably emerging as number one.

It is hard not to agree with the *The Times* when it noted in 1994 that despite his achievements as a politician and historian it is for his diaries that Alan, like 'Chips' Channon, will ultimately be judged.

Appendix: Monetary Values

Value of £ sterling during the twentieth century
compared with value in 2007

1900	£77.58
1910	£73.15
1920	£28.80
1930	£45.32
1940	£39.13
1950	£24.69
1960	£16.59
1970	£11.15
1980	£3.09
1990	£1.64
2000	£1.21
2005	£1.08

Figures from the Economic History Services website
www.eh.net based on the Retail Price Index

Select Bibliography

BOOKS BY ALAN CLARK

FICTION
Bargains at Special Prices (1960); *Summer Season* (1963); *The Lion Heart* (1967)

NON-FICTION
The Donkeys: A History of the BEF in 1915 (1961); *The Fall of Crete* (1962); *Barbarossa: The Russian-German Conflict, 1941–1945* (1964); *Suicide of the Empires: The Eastern Front, 1914–1918* (1971); *Aces High: The War in the Air over the Western Front, 1914–1918* (1973, revised 1999); *A Good Innings: The Private Papers of Viscount Lee of Fareham* (edited) (1974); *Diaries: In Power: 1983–1991* (1993); *The Tories: Conservatives and the Nation State, 1922–1997* (1998); *Diaries: Into Politics: 1972–1982*, edited by Ion Trewin (2000); *Back Fire: A Passion for Cars and Motoring*, edited by Robert Coucher (2001); *The Last Diaries: 1991–1999*, edited by Ion Trewin (2002).

Charles Ameringer, *U.S. Foreign Intelligence: The Secret Side of American History* (Lexington, Massachusetts, Lexington Books, 1990).
Antony Beevor, *Crete: The Battle and the Resistance* (London, John Murray, 1991).
Anthony Blond, *Jew Made in England* (London, Timewell Press, 2004).
Brian Bond (editor), *The First World War and British Military History* (Oxford, Clarendon Press, 1991).
C. M. Bowra, *Memories, 1898–1939* (London, Weidenfeld & Nicolson, 1966).
Peter Bradshaw, *Not Alan Clark's Diaries* (London, Pocket Books, 1998).
David Butler with Dennis Kavanagh, *The British General Election, February 1974* (London, Macmillan, 1974).
Alastair Campbell, *The Blair Years, Extracts from the Alastair Campbell Diaries*, edited by Alastair Campbell and Richard Scott (London, Hutchinson, 2007).
Chips: The Diaries of Sir Henry Channon, edited by Robert Rhodes James (London, Weidenfeld & Nicolson, 1967).
Colin Clark, *Younger Brother, Younger Son* (London, HarperCollins, 1997).

Kenneth Clark, *Another Part of the Wood* (London, John Murray, 1974).

Kenneth Clark, *The Other Half* (London, John Murray, 1977).

Alex Danchev, *Alchemist of War: The Life of Basil Liddell Hart* (London, Weidenfeld & Nicolson, 1998).

George Gardiner, *A Bastard's Tale* (London, Aurum, 1999).

Sebastian Haffner, *Defying Hitler* (London, Weidenfeld & Nicolson, 2000).

Max Hastings, *Editor: An Inside Story of Newspapers* (London, Macmillan, 2002).

Paul Henderson, *The Unlikely Spy: An Autobiography* (London, Bloomsbury, 1993).

Michael Heseltine, *Life in the Jungle: My Autobiography* (London, Hodder & Stoughton, 2000).

F.C. Hitchcock, *Stand To: A Diary of the Trenches 1915–1918*. (originally published 1937; reissued Naval & Military Press, 2001).

Alistair Horne, *The Price of Glory: Verdun 1916* (London, Macmillan, 1962).

Geoffrey Howe, *Conflict of Loyalty* (London, Macmillan, 1994).

Douglas Hurd, *Memoirs* (London, Little, Brown, 2003).

Norman Lamont, *In Office* (London, Little, Brown, 1999).

Nigel Lawson. *The View From No. 11: Memoirs of a Tory Radical* (London, Bantam Books, 1992).

James Lees-Milne, *Beneath a Waning Moon: Diaries, 1985–1987* (London, John Murray, 2003).

Joan Littlewood, *Joan's Book: Joan Littlewood's Peculiar History as She Tells It* (London, Methuen, 1994).

Richard Luce, *Ringing the Changes: A Full Life* (Norwich, Michael Russell, 2007).

Brian Masters, *The Passion of John Aspinall* (London, Jonathan Cape, 1988).

Leslie Mitchell, *C.M. Bowra: A Life* (Oxford University Press, 2009).

Piers Morgan, *The Insider: The Private Diaries of a Scandalous Decade* (London, Ebury Press, 2005).

Andrew Neil, *Full Disclosure* (London, Macmillan, 1996).

Harold Nicolson, *Diaries*, edited by Nigel Nicolson (London, Collins, three volumes, 1966, 1967, 1968).

Richard Norton-Taylor, *Truth is a Difficult Concept: Inside the Scott Enquiry* (London, A Guardian Book, Fourth Estate, 1995).

Richard Norton-Taylor, Mark Lloyd and Stephen Cook, *Knee Deep in Dishonour: The Scott Report and its Aftermath* (London, Victor Gollancz, 1996).

Matthew Parris, *Chance Witness: An Outsider's Life in Politics* (London, Michael Joseph, 2002).

Lance Price, *The Spin Doctor's Diary: Inside Number 10 with New Labour* (London, Hodder & Stoughton, 2005).

Meryle Secrest, *Kenneth Clark: A Biography* (London, Weidenfeld & Nicolson, 1984).

Meryle Secrest, *Shoot the Widow: Adventures of a Biographer in Search of Her Subject* (New York, Knopf, 2007).

Roy Strong, *The Roy Strong Diaries* 1967–1987 (London, Weidenfeld & Nicolson, 1997).

Brian Thompson and F.F. Ridley (editors), *Under the Scott-Light: British Government Seen Through the Scott Report*, The Hansard Society (Oxford University Press, 1997).

Dan Todman, *The Great War: Myth and Memory* (London, Hambledon London, 2005).

Hugh Trevor-Roper, *The Last Days of Hitler.* (London and New York, Macmillan, 1947).

Letters from Oxford: Hugh Trevor-Roper to Bernard Berenson, edited by Richard Davenport-Hines (London, Weidenfeld & Nicolson, 2006).

Alan Watkins, *A Conservative Coup: The Fall of Margaret Thatcher* (London, Duckworth, 1991).

Evelyn Waugh, *The Ordeal of Gilbert Pinfold* (London, Chapman & Hall, 1957).

F.W. Winterbotham, *The Ultra Secret* (London, Weidenfeld & Nicolson, 1974).

The Hugo Young Papers: Thirty Years of British Politics, edited by Ion Trewin (London, Allen Lane, 2008).

Notes

Full bibliographical information about books referred to by short title can be found in the Bibliography.

All Kenneth Clark's letters, the diaries of his wife Jane, the originals of Alan Clark's diaries and family correspondence are at Saltwood Castle unless otherwise stated.

Introduction (pp. 1–5)

1 *The Times*, 2 June 1994.
2 *The Independent*, 13 May 2008.
3 AC to Sue Lawley, *Desert Island Discs*, BBC Radio 4, January 1995.
4 By evidence of the typewriter; it was certainly before he began using a word processor in the mid-1990s.
5 AC, *Diaries, In Power*, 14 April 1987.
6 Simon Hoggart, *The Guardian*, 2 February 2000. Hoggart spent a weekend at Saltwood during the Labour government of the late 1970s, when it was fashionable to tout dictatorship as the answer to all Britain's ills. Hoggart recalls how Alan interrupted John Aspinall, also a guest, with a stout defence of democracy – how it had many faults, but you only had to see how dictatorships worked out.
7 Charles Powell, *The Times*, 10 June 1993.
8 Simon Hoggart to the author.

CHAPTER ONE: *Origins and Influences* (pp. 9–14)

Kenneth Clark quotations are from his memoirs, *Another Part of the Wood*, unless otherwise stated.

1 Records are inconsistent. Spelt Mackenzie, MacKenzie or McKenzie.
2 KC to Mary Berenson; see Meryle Secrest, *Kenneth Clark*, p.78.
3 Meryle Secrest, *Kenneth Clark*, p.13.
4 The name came from a town in Australia's Blue Mountains, which he had visited in his teens.

5 Sudbourne was pulled down in 1953. Alan and Jane Clark visited its site in 1996 (see *The Last Diaries*, 19 October 1996). Nor does Shielbridge exist today.

6 Miss Lamont remained close to the Clarks for thirty years, acting as Nanny to their children in the 1930s before working at Chequers.

7 Maurice Bowra (1898–1971), apart from a brief spell in the Royal Field Artillery in the First World War, devoted himself to the classics and Oxford. He never married and was a regular guest of the Clarks, not least at Saltwood where he was invariably invited for Christmas.

8 KC letter, n.d.

9 The American-born Jacob Epstein had recently caused a stir in 1929 for his nude sculptures *Day* and *Night* above the entrances of what became the headquarters of London Transport at Broadway, St James's. KC letter to Jane, August 1932.

10 BBC Kenneth Clark documentary, 1993.

11 Colette Clark to the author.

12 Colette Clark in BBC Kenneth Clark documentary, 1993

13 Graham Turner interview, *The Sunday Telegraph*, 2 August 1992.

14 KC to his mother, n.d

15 AC, *Evening Standard*, 12 January 1994.

16 BBC Kenneth Clark documentary, 1993.

17 *Younger Brother, Younger Son*, Colin Clark.

18 KC letter to Edith Wharton, Beineke Rare Book and Manuscript Library, Yale University.

19 KC and Queen Elizabeth became firm friends; on 28 June 1957 she visited Saltwood and planted a tulip tree there. It thrives.

20 Jane Clark diary.

21 Child was the 2nd Baronet; it is uncertain at this distance precisely where he stood according to Colin's definition.

22 *The Times*, 29 March 1938.

23 Colette Clark to the author.

24 BBC Kenneth Clark documentary, 1993.

CHAPTER TWO: *Early Memories* (pp. 15–28)

Kenneth Clark quotations are from *Another Part of the Wood* and *The Other Half*, unless otherwise stated.

1 Alice Clark letter.

2 In his published recollection (written originally for the Rolls-Royce Enthusiasts' Club in 1977 and reprinted in *Back Fire*), Alan says 1934, but he has got the date wrong as his grandfather died in October 1932. He also says he was standing on the quayside at Inverewe – which is too far north.

3 KC letters.

4 KC in his memoirs gets hopelessly confused over dates, saying that the twins were born on 9 April, 'because a few days after they had entered the world my father left it'. However their birth certificates survive at Saltwood, showing the date was 9 October at a clinic at 18 Bentinck Street, London, W1. He also says they were christened at Trinity Chapel, Oxford; in fact it was St Mary Magdalene, Oxford.

5 Alice Clark letter.

6 AC, *The Last Diaries*, 26 June 1999.

7 Colin Clark, *Younger Brother, Younger Son.*

8 AC interviewed by Ginny Dougary, *The Times*, 12 June 1993.

9 AC interviewed by Sue Lawley, *Desert Island Discs*, BBC Radio 4, 13 December 1994.

10 Colette Clark to the author.

11 KC to Edith Wharton, n.d. Beineke Rare Book and Manuscript Library, Yale University.

12 Meryle Secrest, *Kenneth Clark*, Chapter 10.

13 Saltwood archives.

14 Eastbourne Local History Society; Miss Frances Muncey (honorary secretary) and article by Marie Lewis, pulished by the Society.

15 Sir Owen Morshead (1893–1977). The proximity of the Castle to Eton meant that he had close links with the college. Sir Alfred Beit (1903–94). His friendship with KC stemmed from art, Beit being on the board of the National Gallery of Ireland.

16 KC letters.

17 Jane Clark to Edith Wharton, June 1937, Beineke Rare Book and Manuscript Library, Yale University.

18 The wife of the Conservative MP and diarist, Henry 'Chips' Channon.

19 *Chips. The Diaries of Sir Henry Channon*, ed. Robert Rhodes James.

20 KC letter to his mother, n.d.

21 KC to Edith Wharton, 8 February 1937, Beineke Rare Book and Manuscript Library, Yale University.

22 Jane Clark diary.

23 This was typical of Alan's surviving school books. In a chemistry notebook from Eton, 'Lent 1943 AD', when he was fourteen, amid drawings of bunsen burners, and the separation of salt and sand, there are accomplished drawings of tanks and a twin-engined bomber.

24 AC interview with Ginny Dougary, *The Times*, 12 June 1993.

25 AC *Diaries: In Power*, 15 February 1985.

26 Jane Clark diary.

27 Philip Ziegler to the author.

28 Letter from Tim Tomlinson to AC, 16 March 1994.

29 Jane Clark diary.

30 Many years later Ziegler hoped to be given Alan's *Diaries* to review and had

already worked up in his mind an opening sentence referring to this episode and that Alan thereby demonstrated all the opportunism, unscrupulousness and indifference to popular opinion which Ziegler felt were to mark his public life. But his *Diaries* went elsewhere and Ziegler ended up that year reviewing Tony Benn's.

31 Letter to his mother-in-law, visiting Jane's brother Alan in New Zealand, 7 July 1938.

32 Half her library was left to Colin, as her godson. They were looked after by KC during his lifetime, who eventually bought them from his younger son. However on his death Colin claimed them a second time; they were sold to a London dealer. They were eventually acquired by George Ramsden, a book dealer, who was reassembling Edith Wharton's library of more than 2,000 volumes. This is now housed at the Mount, her home in Lenox, Massachusetts, where she lived until 1911.

33 Samuel Courtauld (1876–1947), another National Gallery trustee at the time of KC's appointment as Director; co-founded the Courtauld Institute with Arthur Lee.

34 *Dorothy*, an elegant motor boat, gained its name from the youngest daughter of Sydney Phillips, owner of the Moorings Hotel, which he ran with his wife Mary. Mud Island was behind the hotel, man-made from mud generated by dredging the Overy Staithe creek. Bernard Phillips, now of Wells-next-the-Sea, Norfolk, and grandson of Sydney and Mary Phillips, to the author.

35 AC, *The Last Diaries*, 6 May 1996.

36 Jane Clark diary.

37 Arthur Lee (1868–1947) was a trustee of the National Gallery. He had been a Conservative MP, gave his house Chequers to the nation for the use of the Prime Minister, and was created a Viscount in 1922. By the late 1930s he and his American wife Ruth lived at The Old Quarries, Avening, Gloucestershire. To the children they became an honorary uncle and aunt.

38 Jane Clark diary.

39 Jane Clark diary.

40 Colette Clark to the author.

41 15 October 1985. James Lees-Milne, *Beneath a Waning Moon: Diaries, 1985–1987*.

42 AC, *Diaries: Into Politics*, 3 June 1976.

43 *Eastbourne Gazette*, 17 May 1939; *Eastbourne Courier*, 19 May 1939; *Eastbourne Chronicle*, 20 May 1939.

44 Now Wispers School for Girls.

45 Jane Clark diary.

46 Lord Newall to the author.

47 Meryle Secrest, *Kenneth Clark*, p. 158.

48 Colette Clark to the author.

49 KC letters.

50 AC, *The Last Diaries*, 3 September 1994.

51 Here Alan's memory compressed events. *Courageous*, actually an aircraft carrier, was not sunk until 17 September 1939.

52 Jane Clark diary.

CHAPTER THREE: *Worlds at War* (pp. 29–40)

1 Colette Clark to the author.

2 Jane Clark diary, 7 November 1939.

3 Meryle Secrest, *Kenneth Clark*, p. 160.

4 Colette Clark interview, Meryle Secrest, *Kenneth Clark*, p. 160.

5 Graham Turner interview, *The Sunday Telegraph*, 2 August 1992.

6 Francis, 2nd Lord Newall to the author.

7 Susana Walton, *Behind the Façade* (Oxford, Oxford University Press, 1988).

8 KC letters.

9 Alan identified himself at the front as being a scout in the St Cyprian's Tiger patrol and gave three addresses, Tetbury, Lympne and his grandmother's house at Shielbridge, Scotland.

10 Kenneth Clark, *The Other Half*.

11 Quoted in Meryle Secrest, *Kenneth Clark*, p. 163.

12 Alexander Urquhart, *The Guardian*, 21 December 1990.

13 Kenneth Clark, *The Other Half*.

14 KC to Jane Clark, 11 September 1940.

15 Colin Coote (1893–1979). After the war joined *The Daily Telegraph*, where he was Editor 1950–64.

16 Oliver Lyttelton (1893–1972). President of the Board of Trade and soon to be a member of the War Cabinet. Created Viscount Chandos 1954.

17 No. 3 Judges' Walk, a pair of cottages knocked into one, overlooking Hampstead's west heath.

18 Colin Clark, *Younger Brother, Younger Son*. Colin was exaggerating. Alan frequently refers to Arthur in his 1942 diary.

19 Kenneth Clark, *Another Part of the Wood*.

20 Anthony Tennant, later a distinguished brewer. Knighted 1992.

CHAPTER FOUR: *New Home, New School* (pp. 41–49)

Jane Clark's quotations are from her diary, unless otherwise stated.

1 *The Streets of Hampstead* compiled by Christopher Wade (London, High Hill Press/Camden History Society, 1972).

2 Lord Kimball to the author.

3 Mrs Celia Charrington to the author.

4 AC, *Diaries: Into Politics*.

5 *An English Education: A Perspective of Eton* (London, Collins, 1982).

6 *The Spectator*, 11 September 1999.

7 18 September 1982.

8 In that same unpublished diary entry Alan wrote that 'I suspect he did his best to prevent me getting elected to Pratt's. He is on the Scrutiny Committee, but he did redeem himself in what he told me about the proceedings afterwards. "Well, Alan, I must tell you that there was a certain doubt about your candidature; but the general view was that you are a big enough shit to be fun to sit next to at dinner."' (18 September 1982).

9 Douglas Hurd, *Memoirs*.

10 *Eton Voices*, interviews by Danny Danziger (London, Viking, 1998).

11 *The Daily Telegraph*, 8 September 1999.

12 '. . . like getting reported in the *Eton Chronicle* as having got my House Colours (in 1944) even though I hadn't (though deserving it)'. AC, *Diaries: Into Politics*, 24 January 1981.

13 KC to Alice Clark, 3 April 1942.

14 Cyril Newall to AC, 5 November 1943.

15 AC to Alice Clark, n.d.

16 KC had not yet absorbed the Hampstead lingo. They are ponds, a Hampstead string to the west, with three Highgate ponds to the east.

17 Graham Turner interview, *The Sunday Telegraph*, 2 August 1992.

18 Kenneth Clark, *The Other Half*. The other comments about Upper Terrace House that follow are also from his memoirs.

CHAPTER FIVE: *Eton and Onwards* (pp. 50–59)

1 *Humpty Dumpty* was written and directed by Emile Littler, a leading producer, and also starred four of the Crazy Gang: Naughton, Gold, Nervo and Knox.

2 Colette Clark, 1944 diary.

3 Ivor Novello (1893–1951). Actor (mainly musical comedies, which he wrote) and songwriter; Sibyl Colefax, political hostess from her Westminster home in Lord North Street; Hugh ('Binkie') Beaumont (1908–1973), leading West End impresario who ran the firm H.M. Tennent from the mid-1930s.

4 In this instance, not the Arthur Ransome novel, but inspired by his books, as becomes clear.

5 This is Anthony Blunt (1907–1983), the art historian, who was making his way in the world KC knew best. It would be thirty-five years before the astonishing revelation that he had also been one of the 'Cambridge spies' working for the Soviet Union.

6 John Sparrow (1906–1992). Like KC a Wykehamist, and a friend of long-standing. Fellow of All Souls and in 1944 Assistant Adjutant-General at the War Office. After his death Alan bought many of his books.

7 Bernard Fergusson (1911–1980), later created life peer as Lord Ballantrae, had been a senior officer in the Wingate expeditions in Burma. AC, letter to the editors *The Daily Telegraph*, 3 August 1961.

8 AC *Diaries, In Power*, 15 May 1983.

9 KC to Alice Clark, September 1944.

10 KC to Alice Clark, 29 September 1944 from Upper Terrace House.

11 AC, *Alan Clark's History of the Tory Party*. Oxford Film and TV, BBC, 1997.

12 Nancy Mitford (1904–1973). The eldest of the six 'Mitford girls'. A talented writer, after the war she moved to Paris.

13 L.H. Jaques to KC, Eton College, 5 April 1946.

14 AC, incomplete diary.

15 James Clark, Foreword, *Back Fire*.

16 In some later journalism he wrote 1945, but his final half was in the summer of 1946.

17 AC, *Back Fire*.

18 Colette Clark, diary 31 July 1946.

19 However, Colette's diary, 14 August 1946, states: 'Al has driving lesson.'

20 KC to Alice Clark from Upper Terrace House, n.d.

CHAPTER SIX: *Oxford, Prague, Cars and Girls* (pp. 60–75)

For permission to use letters from Hugh Trevor-Roper, the literary estate of Lord Dacre of Glenton; for a letter from Lady Alexandra Trevor-Roper, Mrs Xenian Dennen (daughter) and James Howard-Johnston (son); for the letter to Charles Stuart, Mrs Susan Chater (daughter) and William Stuart (son).

1 Ludovic Kennedy, *On the Way to the Club* (London, Collins, 1982).

2 Paul Johnson to the author.

3 Colin Clark, *Younger Brother, Younger Son*.

4 Colette Clark to the author.

5 4 September 1946. Household Cavalry records, Combermere, Windsor.

6 Lord Ashburton's memorial address for Euan Graham, 2008.

7 KC to Alice Clark, letter from Upper Terrace House, n.d.

8 Euan Graham to the author.

9 Roger Pemberton to the author.

10 Norman Painting, *Reluctant Archer* (Cambridge, Granta Editions, 1982).

11 Euan Graham to the author.

12 AC, *Back Fire*.

13 Brian Masters, *The Passion of John Aspinall*.

14 Hugh Trevor-Roper, *The Last Days of Hitler*.

15 James Brodrick, 'Jesuits and Nazis', *The Tablet*, 21 June 1947, p. 316.

16 Winston Churchill, 'an iron curtain has descended across Europe' – address at Westminster College, Fulton, Missouri, USA, 5 March 1946.

17 HT-R, 22 January 1948. *Letters from Oxford*.

18 The author is indebted to Arnold Davey, honorary registrar of the Lagonda Club, for further particulars. Chassis number 14085; registration FXN 603. The car is in the hands of a club member in Illinois, USA.

19 Frank Pakenham (1905–2001), the son of an Irish peer, was created Baron Pakenham in 1945, and on the death of his brother became the 7th Earl of Longford in 1961.

20 HT-R to Charles Stuart from Prague, 31 January 1947. Dacre archive.

21 AC, Webster's Blue Diary, 1947.

22 AC diary, July 1964.

23 HT-R to AC, April 1948.

24 HT-R to Bernard Berenson, 29 February 1948. *Letters from Oxford*.

25 Correspondence of HT-R and Alexandra Howard-Johnston. Dacre archive.

26 Blair Worden to the author.

27 Shirley Hughes to the author.

28 Lord Ashburton, address at the memorial service for Euan Graham, 2008.

29 Alan remarked of this 'admirable institution' that 'I don't think I'd been in credit since'. AC, *Back Fire*.

30 Lord Parmoor to the author.

31 AC to HT-R, Thursday 13, probably January 1949. Dacre archive.

32 AC to HT-R, 2 September 1960. Dacre archive.

CHAPTER SEVEN: *America and Possible Careers* (pp. 76–83)

1 Richard Boston, *Osbert: a Portrait of Osbert Lancaster* (London, Collins, 1989).

2 Osbert Lancaster quoted in Bevis Hillier's *John Betjeman: New Fame, New Love* (London, John Murray, 2002).

3 John Betjeman to KC, 16 November 1949. *John Betjeman: Letters: volume one, 1929 to 1951*, ed. Candida Lycett-Green (London, Methuen, 1994).

4 AC to HT-R, n.d. (HT-R's acknowledgement, 10 April 1950). Dacre archive.

5 AC motor journal, 27 June 1973.

6 The entry is dated 10 January 1950. The dinner took place on 14 December 1949 at the Allies Club. *The Diaries of Cynthia Gladwyn*, ed. Miles Jebb (London, Constable, 1995).

7 AC interview with Ginny Dougary, *The Times*, 12 June 1993.

8 AC article, n.d., *Back Fire*. He had also told Trevor-Roper in 1949 (n.d.) that a mutual friend was contemplating driving a Lagonda in that year's Monte Carlo rally, 'very brave of him ... it must be uniquely reliable.'

9 AC to HT-R, 14 February, and assumed to be 1950. Dacre archive. Trevor-Roper's response has not survived.

10 AC to HT-R, Sarasota, Florida, n.d. Dacre archive.

11 AC to HT-R, n.d. (HT-R's acknowledgement, 10 April 1950). Dacre archive.

12 AC to HT-R, n.d. (HT-R's acknowledgement, 14 November 1950). Dacre archive.
13 AC, *Back Fire*.
14 AC, *Road & Track*, June 1953.
15 Charles Howard to the author.
16 Jane Clark, Afterword, *Back Fire*.
17 Anthony Blond, *Jew Made in England*.
18 Isabel Colegate to the author.
19 HT-R to Lady Alexandra Howard-Johnston, 12 October 1953. Dacre archive.

CHAPTER EIGHT: *First Love and the Law* (pp. 84–94)

1 Much of this chapter is based on the author's conversations with Pamela Hart, correspondence and papers at Saltwood.
2 AC diary, 13 April 1958.
3 Almost certainly Amis's second novel, *That Uncertain Feeling* (1955).
4 Lord Hoffman to the author.
5 KC to AC, June 1953.
6 Jane Clark to AC, Paris, n.d.
7 Telegram, Colin to AC, 14 January 1955; telegram, KC and Jane to AC, 15 January 1955; letters KC and Jane to AC, 15 January 1955 and n.d.
8 AC, *The Last Diaries*, 13 March 1996.
9 AC to Pamela Hart, n.d.
10 AC to Hugo Young, 28 July 1983.
11 *The Sunday Times*, 24 January 1983.
12 AC to Hugo Young, 28 July 1983.
13 AC, *Diaries: In Power*, 22 July 1983.
14 AC, 9 October 1970.
15 Pamela Hart to AC, n.d.

CHAPTER NINE: *Words, a House and More Words* (pp. 95–103)

1 From a note in AC's hand, probably 1954, but n.d.
2 3 October 1953.
3 Henry James, Rye's most celebrated resident, was already an established novelist when in 1895 he wrote this play. It was not a success, James having to endure boos from the audience on the first night.
4 In *To Exercise our Talents: the Democratization of Writing in Britain* (Harvard University Press, 2006), Christopher Hilliard writes that Walter claimed to have deconstructed more than 5,000 stories, distilling them into what Hilliard calls 'a universal grammar of plot', a concise outline on a handy card to be consulted whenever the owner stumbled across a promising story

idea. Hilliard reminds us that George Orwell asked the obvious question: 'If these people really know how to make money out of writing, why aren't they just doing it instead of peddling their secret at 5/- a time?' Walter apparently cried foul, but his system would be damningly immortalised in the novel-writing machines of *Nineteen Eighty-Four*. See also Orwell's column, 'As I Please' (*Tribune*, 8 December 1944) where he answers back at Walter, who claimed that Orwell had traduced. Him.

5 KC to AC, 17 January 1955.

6 Paul Bowles (1910–99), American novelist and composer who spent over half his life in Tangier. His best-known novel, *The Sheltering Sky*, was filmed in 1990 by Bernardo Bertolucci.

7 AC diary, 30 July 1955.

8 KC to AC, 17 April (no year).

9 AC diary, 1 June 1956.

10 KC to AC, 28 April 1956.

11 AC diary, 28 April 1956.

12 AC diary, 1 June 1956.

CHAPTER TEN: *Meeting Jane* (pp. 104–115)

1 Jane Clark to the author.

2 Jane Clark, Afterword to *Back Fire*.

3 Jane Clark to the author.

4 Pat Brooks, briefly an actress, appeared in *Reach for the Sky* with Kenneth More playing the legless Second World War air ace, Douglas Bader. She married Vere Harmsworth, later Lord Rothermere, in 1957.

5 AC diary, 4 November 1956.

6 Sir Jeremy Hanley (Dinah Sheridan's son by Jimmy Hanley) to the author.

7 Colin had a job with Olivier, as he told in *The Prince, the Showgirl and Me* (London, HarperCollins, 1995).

8 Mary Ure (1933–75) was the second wife of John Osborne (1929–94). They divorced and she married the actor Robert Shaw (1927–78) in 1963.

CHAPTER ELEVEN: *Moscow Nights and Days* (pp. 116–121)

1 Russian Musical Highlights of the Twentieth Century, 1957. RUVR, the Voice of Russia. www.vor.ru/century/1957m.html.

2 To assist the letter's passage to Britain AC adopted 'a rather plebeian style of address', for which he hoped his father would forgive him. Plain Mr, no 'Sir'.

3 Charles Ameringer, *U.S. Foreign Intelligence*.

4 AC diary, 22 July 1956.

5 Alan would only drink Malvern Water from glass containers. When he was

Minister for Trade thirty years later, Peter Ewing, his secretary, recalls his disgust when the Department for Trade and Industry sent round a case in plastic bottles.

6 Alan loved slang and phrases of his own invention. 'Lenin-Stadium' appears in his *Diaries* as a description of how he felt – extreme apprehension – but the glossary of 'Clarkisms' that he created at the front of the published *Diaries* is silent on the subject. After his death, readers asked what could he know about Moscow's Lenin Stadium? It was only as a result of researching this biography that it became possible to piece together the surprising answer. The phrase had variants. Faced with huge debts to his bank, a feeling he was getting nowhere as an MP, he wrote of 'Lenin-stadium type cramp-angst at so much to resolve'. *Diaries: Into Politics*, 31 October 1974.

7 By 1957 the MVD, the Ministry of Internal Affairs, and the lineal descendant of the Bolshevik NKVD, was responsible for internal security, while the KGB ran state security.

8 A Soviet-built limousine in production during much of the 1950s.

9 Thirty years later, when AC (with Jane) was visiting the Soviet Union as Trade Minister, his knowledge of Russian had its unexpected humour. He and Jane were in a limousine awaiting the arrival of their guide, Natasha. Alan leant forward and asked the KGB man who had been assigned to them where she was. The fact that he spoke to them in Russian caused consternation. Might they have been saying something indiscreet?

10 A decade later, when *The Times*'s Washington correspondent, Louis Heren, commented that there are no guards at the doors of the Pentagon, Alan wrote, in a letter to the Editor, 'there are no guards at the door of the Lubianka either. Admittedly, once inside the lobby, the ambience is found to be rather different from that of "a comfortable lady at an enquiry desk" – a fact to which I can testify from personal experience.' *The Times*, 19 May 1967.

CHAPTER TWELVE: *Courting Jane* (pp. 122–33)

1 At Brighton, Aneurin Bevan replied on behalf of the Labour Party National Executive to a series of composite resolutions that would have 'pledged the next Labour government to unilateral action by Britain in stopping production and testing of nuclear weapons'. *The Times*, 4 October 1957

2 Wagner's opera is based on a medieval German legend that also inspired the poet Swinburne and an erotic novel, uncompleted, by Aubrey Beardsley. Tannhäuser is a knightly minstrel who gives himself up to Venus, the Goddess of Love, before, in guilt, deciding he must seek a pardon from the Pope.

3 Alan had been borrowing from a money-lender in St James's, London.

4 With five James Bond novels already published (*Diamonds are Forever* had been the most recent, the previous year), 007 had become the most successful

fictional thriller character since the creation of Bulldog Drummond by 'Sapper' in 1920.

5 Chapter 15, *Middlemarch*. There is a certain aptness, at least in part, of George Eliot's description of Tertius Lydgate, the doctor, even down to references to furniture. 'Lydgate's spots of commonness lay in the complexion of his prejudices, which, in spite of noble intentions and sympathy, were half of them such as are found in ordinary men of the world: that distinction of mind which belonged to his intellectual ardour, did not penetrate his feeling and judgement about furniture, or women, or the desirability of its being known (without his telling) that he was better born than other country surgeons. He did not mean to think of furniture at present; but whenever he did so, it was to be feared that neither biology nor schemes of reform would lift him above the vulgarity of feeling that there would be an incompatibility in his furniture not being of the best.'

6 AC interview, *Love Tory*, Michael Cockerell's BBC TV documentary, 1993.

7 Bertie Beuttler to KC, 1 July 1958.

8 In July 1958 Coats shares stood at 20s, give or take a few pence.

9 *Daily Mail*, 31 July 1958.

10 AC interview, *Love Tory*.

11 Tony Rudd to the author.

CHAPTER THIRTEEN: *Marriage and a Son* (pp. 134–45)

1 Lesley & Roberts of Savile Row made suits for AC throughout his adult life (and for Charles Ryder in Evelyn Waugh's *Brideshead Revisited*), except for a period in the 1960s when he moved to Blades, then the height of male fashion, but Jane felt Blades did not match Lesley & Roberts for quality.

2 *Evening Standard*, 2 June 1961.

3 Jane brought the rusty wire back to Saltwood and its symbolism is such that it has on many occasions inspired her in her painting.

4 *UCH Textbook of Psychiatry*, ed. Heinz Wolff, Anthony Bateman, David Sturgeon.

5 In an effort to improve relations, the Prime Minister, Harold Macmillan, was visiting the Soviet Union – and wore a sheepskin hat, which proved a PR coup.

6 AC was much influenced by Evelyn Waugh's *Brideshead Revisited*, where Charles Ryder admits to being 'concerned with two emancipated American girls who shared a *garçonnière*' in Auteuil in Paris. Waugh knew the word to mean a bachelor apartment, but it had its origins as a place where boys were separated from girls.

7 AC's father was born on 13 July 1903, AC himself on 13 April 1928, his elder son James on 13 February 1960, and his grandson Angus on 13 November 1996.

CHAPTER FOURTEEN: *The 'Bargains' Affair* (pp. 146–52)

1 *The Sunday Times*, 7 February 1960.
2 Edgar Astaire to the author.
3 AC diary, 8 February 1960.
4 Anthony Blond, *Jew Made in England*.
5 Nicolas Thompson to AC, 9 August 1957.
6 AC diary, 24 August 1957.
7 KC to AC, n.d.
8 AC diary, 30 March 1958.
9 Nicolas Bentley to AC, 30 April 1958.
10 AC diary, 11 June 1958.
11 The imprint's record for backing talent included two authors who went on to be Booker prizewinners (J.G. Farrell and Stanley Middleton) and two others who were shortlisted, Beryl Bainbridge and Elizabeth Mavor.
12 RT to the author.
13 RT to AC, 9 February 1959.
14 RT's own books included *The Golden Oriole*, a history of an English family in India across two centuries, and accounts of Second World War campaigns in which he served, *Rome '44* and *The Fortress*, a diary of Anzio and after.
15 RT to AC, 16 February 1959.
16 G.L. Lazarus to AC, 9 April 1959.
17 RT to AC, 15 April 1959.
18 Robert Lusty to AC, 25 June 1959.
19 RT to AC, 8 September 1959.
20 RT to AC, 31 December 1959.
21 RT to AC, 5 February 1960.
22 Robert Lusty to AC, 9 February 1960
23 Robert Lusty to AC, 10 February 1960.
24 *News Chronicle*, 11 February 1960.
25 AC diary, 3 April 1960.
26 Coincidentally that day and on the same page *The Times* also reviewed Raleigh Trevelyan's *A Hermit Disclosed*, a true detective story of a former inhabitant of a house in Essex where Trevelyan lived as a child. It reminded *The Times*'s reviewer of A.J.A. Symons' *Quest for Corvo*. By further chance *The Times* also reviewed Sylvia Sprigge's life of Bernard Berenson and a selection from Berenson's diaries. *The Times*, 17 March 1960.
27 AC diary, 26 January 1960.
28 Robert Lusty, 15 February 1960.

CHAPTER FIFTEEN: *The Young Historian* (pp. 153–64)

Permission to use quotations from the Basil Liddell Hart papers given by the Trustees of the Liddell Hart Centre for Military Archives at King's College, London (LHCMA). Extracts from various letters from B.H. Liddell Hart to Alan Clark © the executors of Lady Liddell Hart, deceased.

1 Liddell Hart to AC, 22 June 1961. LHCMA, LH1/172/115.

2 On the title page of Alex Danchev's hardback copy of *Diaries* AC wrote that Basil Liddell Hart was the 'fondest remembered mentor'. Danchev interviewed AC at Saltwood when working on *Alchemist of War*, his biography of Liddell Hart.

3 AC, *Diaries: In Power*, 10 December 1990.

4 AC was lucky to find a copy of *Stand To: a Diary of the Trenches 1915–1918* (originally published in 1937) as it had been out of print for many years.

5 See Martin Middlebrook, *The Kaiser's Battle* (London, Allen Lane, 1978).

6 AC diary, 14 October 1958.

7 Quoted by Alex Danchev in *Alchemist of War*.

8 Rodney Forestier-Walker to LH, 25 June 1946. LHCMA, LH1/293/39.

9 AC diary, 7 November 1956.

10 Rodney Forestier-Walker to LH, 14 April 1953. LHCMA, LH1/293/80.

11 LH to Rodney Forestier-Walker, 12 February 1954. LHCMA, LH1/293/84.

12 Liddell Hart lecture, King's College, London, 10 December, 1990. Quotations taken from AC's typed-up copy.

13 General Heinz Guderian was one of the German generals Liddell Hart interviewed in 1945; Guderian – 'the prime minister of Blitzkrieg' – was grateful to Liddell Hart for interesting publishers in the UK and US in his memoirs, *Panzer Leader* (1952).

14 AC to LH, 21 October 1958. LHCMA, LH1/172/3.

15 LH to AC, 24 October 1958. LHCMA, LH1/172/4.

16 AC to LH, 28 October 1958. LHCMA, LH1/172/5.

17 AC to LH, November 1958. LHCMA, LH1/172/9.

18 AC, Liddell Hart lecture, 10 December 1990.

19 According to Leslie Mitchell in his biography of Maurice Bowra (Oxford University Press, 2009), Bowra suffered 'the real possibility of being defeated' at L'Attaque by Alan. The game became for Alan a motif for *The Donkeys*. In its prelude he wrote that in September 1914 'the French army marched into action ... men and officers dressed like pieces in l'Attaque'. To which he added a footnote, that the parlour game had first been put on the market in 1890.

20 Alex Danchev in *Alchemist of War* lists his kindergarten: Paul Addison, Correlli Barnett, Brian Bond, Carl Boyd, Alan Clark, Hans-Adolf Jacobsen, Paul Kennedy, James Leutze, Jay Luvaas, John Lynn, R.M. Ogorkievicz,

Robert O'Neill, Barrie Pitt, Donald Schurman and Peter Simkins as well as scholar friends, Guy Chapman, John Connell, Guglielmo Ferrero, Alistair Horne, Michael Howard, Ronald Lewin, Kenneth Macksey, S.L.A. Marshall and Peter Paret.

21 AC to LH, 8 January 1959. LHCMA, LH1/172/13.

22 LH to AC, 17 January 1959. LHCMA, LH1/172/14.

23 AC to LH, 21 January 1959. LHCMA. LH1/172/15. The siege of Badajoz, between 17 March and 6 April 1812, was one of the bloodiest in the Napoleonic Wars, when the British and Portuguese forces under Arthur Wellesley, Earl of Wellington – he only received his Dukedom in 1814– attacked the French garrison under General Philippon.

24 LH to AC, 29 January 1959. LHCMA, LH1/172/16.

25 KC to AC, 17 January 1959.

26 AC diary, 10 February 1959.

27 AC to LH, 16 February 1959. LHCMA, LH1/172/18.

28 AC diary, 1 March 1959.

29 AC diary, 30 April 1959.

30 AC diary, 30 April 1959.

31 AC to LH, probably May 1959. LHCMA, LH1/172/23.

32 LH to AC, 9 June 1959. LHCMA, LH1/172/25.

33 LH to AC, 20 August 1959. LHCMA, LH1/172/29.

34 AC to LH, 3 September 1959. LHCMA, LH1/172/30.

35 LH to AC, 20 August 1959. LHCMA, LH1/172/29.

36 AC to LH, n.d., presumed to be September 1959. LHCMA, LH1/172/32.

37 Alex Danchev '"Bunking" and Debunking: The Controversies of the 1960s', in *The First World War and British Military History* ed. Brian Bond.

38 Sir Alistair Horne to the author. Horne's *The Price of Glory: Verdun 1916* was published in 1962.

39 AC diary, 4 October 1959.

40 AC to LH, 2 November 1959. LHCMA, LH1/172/34.

41 LH to AC, 4 November 1959. LHCMA, LH1/172/35.

42 LH to AC, 3 December 1959. LHCMA, LH1/172/42.

43 RT to the author.

44 AC diary, 8 January 1960.

45 RT to LH, 16 February 1960. LHCMA, LH1/172/51.

46 AC MS note on envelope, n.d., LHCMA, LH1/172/39.

47 Report on *The Donkeys*. A pencil note suggests Robert Blake as the author. He was not. LHCMA, LH1/172/51.

48 *Cassino: Portrait of a Battle* by Fred Majdalany (London, Longmans, 1957).

49 LH to RT, 18 February 1960. LHCMA, LH1/172/52.

50 RT to LH, 22 February 1960. LHCMA, LH1/172/54.

51 LH to RT, 23 February 1960. LHCMA, LH1/172/55.

52 Robert Lusty to AC, 25 February 1960.

53 *The Donkeys* jacket blurb. LHCMA.

54 AC to LH, 27 February 1960. LHCMA, LH 1/172/69.

55 AC to HT-R (3 March, 1960) and HT-R to AC, 5 March 1960. Trevor-Roper was also masterminding the campaign to have Harold Macmillan (still Prime Minister) elected Chancellor of Oxford University – the other candidate was the academic and diplomat Oliver Franks (later Lord Franks), nominated by none other than Kenneth Clark. Alan in his letter referred to Trevor-Roper's 'anti-Tammany' operation, but had to admit that his negligence in taking his M.A. meant he could not add his vote in Macmillan's favour. In the close-fought contest Macmillan was victorious by ninety votes. As for the matter of the Regius Professorship, thirty-three years later (24 April 1993) Trevor-Roper wrote to 'confess an error of omission'. He had forgotten the letter of March 1960 and, reminded by a biography of A.J.P. Taylor (by Adam Sisman), he retold the story, adding only that Taylor 'probably, in his eyes, added insult to injury'; Taylor, he suspected, no doubt harboured resentment at Trevor-Roper's 'bad joke'.

56 AC diary, 3 April 1960.

57 AC diary, 20 April 1960.

58 AC diary, 29 May 1960.

CHAPTER SIXTEEN: *A Steady Nerve* (pp. 165–75)

Quotations from letters from Lord Beaverbrook held at Saltwood by permission of the Lord Beaverbrook Foundation.

1 AC to LH, 19 July 1960. LHCMA, LH1/171/83.

2 LH to AC, 1 August 1960. LHCMA, LH1/172/81.

3 AC to LH, August 1960. LHCMA, LH1/172/83.

4 RT to AC, 26 August 1960.

5 The crisis was in Berlin where East Germany sealed the border with West Berlin.

6 AC diary, 1 September 1960.

7 AC to HT-R., n.d. Dacre archive.

8 HT-R to AC, 31 August 1960.

9 AC to HT-R, 2 September 1960. Dacre archive.

10 Frances Phillips to AC, 19 September 1960.

11 HT-R to AC, 18 October 1960.

12 Alexandra Trevor-Roper to AC, 21 October 1960.

13 AC to LH, 30 December 1960. LHCMA, LH1/172/96.

14 AC to LH, 8 February 1961. LHCMA, LH1/172/98.

15 AC to LH, 19 February 1961. LHCMA, LH1/172/100.

16 LH to RT, 20 February 1961. LHCMA, LH1/172/57.

17 Received 27 February. LHCMA, LH1/172/63.

18 Michael Rubinstein to Iain Hamilton, 27 February 1961.

19 Robert Lusty to Earl Haig, 2 March 1961. LHCMA, LH1/172/107.

20 AC to RT, 6 March 1961.

21 AC to Lord Beaverbrook, 8 March 1961.

22 Lord Beaverbrook to AC, 14 March 1961.

23 KC to AC, 7 March 1961.

24 Soon afterwards AC did employ a secretary, but in a handwritten addition to a much corrected typed letter to LH (27 September 1961) he remarked: 'The filthy mess on the other page of this letter is the result of using a secretary, which you have so often urged me to do. She is useless.' LHCMA, LH1/172/130.

25 LH to AC, 16 June 1961. LHCMA, LH1/172/110.

26 AC to Robert Blake, 16 July 1961. LHCMA, LH1/172/122.

27 AC to HT-R. No date. Dacre archive.

28 AC, *Diaries: In Power*, 6 June 1984.

29 *Daily Express*, 15 July 1961.

30 Henry Williamson (1895–1977). His book *Tarka the Otter* (1927) won the Hawthornden Prize.

31 AC diary, 23 July 1961.

CHAPTER SEVENTEEN: *Facing the Music* (pp. 176–89)

1 17 July 1961. Erich von Falkenhayn (1861–1922); Max Hoffmann (1869–1927); Erich Ludendorff (1865–1937).

2 Lord Beaverbrook to AC, 6 July 1961.

3 Winston Churchill to Lord Beaverbrook, 20 July 1961.

4 In *The Great War: Myth and Memory*, a valuable study of how views have changed and become distorted.

5 *Evening Standard*, 17 July 1961.

6 Bernard Fergusson, *The Daily Telegraph*, 21 July 1961.

7 John Terraine, *The Sunday Telegraph*, 16 July 1961.

8 A.J.P. Taylor, *The Observer*, 16 July 1961.

9 Michael Howard, *The Listener*, 3 August 1961. Howard moved to Oxford as Professor of War Studies in 1963; he was later Regius Professor of History there and knighted in 1986.

10 *The Times*, 20 July 1961.

11 As a Fellow of Merton College, Oxford, Edmund Blunden (1896–1974) taught Keith Douglas, one of the Second World War poets most admired by AC. The final page of *Diaries* has a stanza written by Douglas in 1944, a few months before he was killed in action.

12 Field Marshal the Viscount Montgomery of Alamein to AC, 22 May 1966.

13 Meriel Richardson to Jane Clark, n.d.

14 Alistair Horne to the author. *The Price of Glory*.

15 *The Donkeys* was selling well into the twenty-first century. A paperback edition, published by Pimlico in 1991, was still in print in 2009 and had sold in excess of 70,000 copies.

16 *The Sunday Times*, 17 September 1961.

17 Robert Blake to HT-R, n.d. Dacre archive.

18 AC reviewing Marquess of Anglesey, *A History of the British Cavalry, 1816–1919*, volume viii, *The Daily Telegraph*, 24 December 1974.

19 *The Sunday Times*, 8 December 1996.

20 *The New York Times*, 28 March 1962.

21 *The New York Times Book Review*, 25 March 1962.

22 London, T. Werner Laurie, 1927.

23 LH to AC, 25 July 1963. LHCMA, LH1/172/191.

24 John Curtis/Hodder & Stoughton, 1989.

25 Evelyn, Princess Blücher, *An English Wife in Berlin*. Dr Stephen Badsey was my informant.

26 Published by Brassey's, 1995, p. ix.

27 *Joan's Book: Joan Littlewood's Peculiar History as She Tells It*.

28 A.D. Peters (1892–1973) also produced films, including J.B. Priestley's *An Inspector Calls* (1953).

29 There was rivalry between the brothers. Colin had been working for Laurence Olivier. After the film *The Prince and the Showgirl* (with Marilyn Monroe) he joined his theatre production company, L.O.P. Productions.

30 ADP to AC, 27 May 1963.

31 ADP to Gerald Raffles, 31 May 1963.

32 Gerald Raffles to ADP, 2 June 1963.

33 ADP to Gerald Raffles, 5 June 1963.

34 ADP to AC, 10 June 1963.

35 AC to ADP, 11 June 1963.

36 AC diary, 22 June 1963.

37 AC diary, n.d.

38 Oscar Beuselinck to ADP, 1 July 1963.

39 ADP to AC, 7 January 1963.

40 Nicolas Cooke to ADP, 14 January 1964.

41 Nicolas Cooke to AC, 28 August 1964.

42 Nicolas Cooke to Oscar Beuselinck, 28 August 1964.

43 AC to Nicolas Cooke, 14 February 1965.

44 Nicolas Cooke to Michael Sissons, 28 April 1965.

45 Nicolas Cooke to Oscar Beuselinck, 30 April 1965.

46 *The Independent on Sunday*, 6 October 2002.

47 London, Methuen, 1965.

48 Nicolas Cooke to AC, 13 May 1965.

CHAPTER EIGHTEEN: *Tackling the Second World War* (pp. 190–196)

1 AC to LH from Bratton, 29 May 1960. LHCMA, LH1/172/76,
2 AC to LH, 19 July 1960. LHCMA, LH1/172/80.
3 F.W. Winterbotham, *The Ultra Secret*.
4 Antony Beevor, *Crete: the Battle and the Resistance*.
5 Antony Beevor to the author.
6 AC, synopsis for *The Loss of Crete*.
7 AC to LH, 28 October 1960. LHCMA, LH1/172/92.
8 LH to AC, 7 November 1960. LHCMA, LH1/172/93.
9 Anthony Blond to AC, 2 November 1960.
10 Michael Sissions to AC, 4 November 1960.
11 AB to AC, 8 November 1960.
12 AB to AC, 25 January 1961.
13 Winston Churchill: *The Second World War*, volume iii, *The Grand Alliance* (London, Cassell, 1950).
14 AC to LH, 8 February 1961. LHCMA, LH1/172/98.
15 AB to AC, 31 January 1961.
16 MS to AC, 1 February 1961.
17 AB to AC, 6 February 1961.
18 MS to AC, 27 February 1961.
19 MS to AC, 7 March 1961.
20 AC to AB, 26 March 1961.
21 Charles Wintour to AC, 5 April 1961.
22 Charles Wintour to AC, 29 May 1961.
23 John Hall Spencer, *Battle for Crete* (London, Heinemann, 1962).
24 AC to AB, 16 August 1961.
25 Desmond Briggs to AC, 15 January 1962.
26 AB to AC, 23 February 1962.
27 AC to LH, 19 March 1962. LHCMA, LH1/172/152.
28 *The Observer*, 13 May 1962.
29 AC to HT-R, Zermatt, 19 February 1963. Dacre archive.
30 HT-R to AC, 23 February, 1963. C.M. Woodhouse, MP for Oxford City 1959–66 and 1970–September 1974, had been in command of the Allied military mission to Greek guerrillas in German-occupied Greece in August 1943.
31 AC to HT-R, n.d.
32 *The Times*, 7 June 1962.
33 AC diary, 3 May 1962.
34 AC diary, 3 May 1962.
35 AC to LH, 4 May 1962. LHCMA, LH1/172/154.
36 Geoffrey Cox to AC, 7 June 1962.
37 AC to LH, 6 June 1962. LHCMA, LH1/172/160.

CHAPTER NINETEEN: Barbarossa *and Family Man* (pp. 197–209)

1 Anthony Blond, *Jew Made in England*.
2 AC to LH, 26 December 1961. LHMCA, LH1/172/145.
3 LH to AC, 29 January 1962. LHMCA, LH1/172/149.
4 Jane Clark to the author.
5 Quotations from AC diary, unless otherwise stated.
6 AC diary, 18 February 1962.
7 AC to LH, 6 December 1962. LHMCA, LH1/172/174.
8 London, Macmillan, 1953.
9 Colin married his first wife, Violette Verdy, a French dancer, in 1961 (marriage dissolved 1969); in 1971 Faith Shuckburgh (née Wright; marriage dissolved); in 1984 Helena Cheung (one son).
10 Simon Raven, *Boys will be Boys* (London, Anthony Blond, 1963).
11 Alexander Werth (1901–69), Russian-born, naturalised British writer and journalist, spent much of the Second World War in the Soviet Union as the BBC's correspondent. He was one of the first outsiders to be allowed into Stalingrad after the battle. Post-war he represented *The Guardian*.
12 *Hitler's War Directives 1939–1945*, ed. H.R. Trevor-Roper (London, Sidgwick & Jackson, 1964).
13 Lawrence W. Hughes to the author.
14 Lawrence W. Hughes to AC, 30 July 1964.
15 Antony Beevor to the author.
16 I am grateful to Andrew Roberts for drawing my attention to this inconsistency.
17 Andrew Roberts to the author.
18 *The New Yorker*, 12 June 1965.
19 Michael Howard, *The Sunday Times*, 25 April 1965.
20 AC to Michael Howard, 25 April 1965. Via Sir Michael Howard.
21 LH to AC, 9 April 1965. LHMHC, LH1/172/236.
22 LH to AC, 11 May 1965. LHMHC, LH1/172/238.
23 HT-R to AC, 20 June 1965. Dacre archive. AC, writing in *Barbarossa* about the summer of 1941, and the Russian situation at Kiev, referred to the 'imbecile Budenny, a general in the worst tradition of 1914–18, whose malevolent fatuity has no rival – even among those competitive effigies of the Great War, Haig, Joffre and Nivelle'.
24 *The Guardian*, 27 December 1978.
25 New York, Quill/William Morrow, 1983.

CHAPTER TWENTY: *Changes in Direction* (pp. 210–20)

1 Quotations from AC's unpublished diaries, unless otherwise stated.
2 Unusually, the serial ran eight months before the book's publication.

3 Alan and Tony Rudd, with his financial knowledge as a City stockbroker, had been talking of a bid for Jaguar, as Sir William Lyons, Jaguar's founder and chairman, was shortly to retire. 'It is feasible if we can talk round Lofty England.' Frank ('Lofty') England had been manager of the Jaguar racing team in the 1950s when they won Le Mans five times. Alan had got to know England from his days as the British correspondent of the American *Road & Track* magazine. Alan added, optimistically, 'Hoping to see him next week, but so far he hasn't replied (!)' Alan saw this as a springboard for politics 'and the divinely ordained ascent'.

4 David Cornwell to the author. AC kept a copy of Waugh's 1957 novel. *The Ordeal of Gilbert Pinfold* (London, Chapman & Hall) by his bedside at Zermatt. Periodically during the diaries he quotes from it, including: 'everyone on board most helpful', at the time he delivered his maiden speech (30 April 1974, *Diaries: Into Politics*) and 'more in the tones of a nanny than a Master-at-Arms' when Geoffrey Howe announced plans to reduce interest rates by two per cent (25 November 1980). Waugh died in 1964. In due course AC would quote the Marchmain conversion to Roman Catholicism from *Brideshead Revisited*.

5 AC to Kathleen Liddell Hart, 11 November 1972. LHCMA, LH1/172/269.

6 Colin Clark, *Younger Brother, Younger Son*.

7 *Weekend Telegraph* magazine, 4 March 1966.

8 *The Remains of the Day* by Kazuo Ishiguro (London, Faber, 1989).

9 AC to LH, 12 August 1965. LHMCA, LH1/172/240.

10 Statement by AC on the jacket proof for a British edition of *The Lion Heart*.

11 He was less than honest in an interview (newspaper cutting unidentified): 'I went there [Vietnam] recently and it made such an impression, I felt I had to write a fiction documentary. The eeriest thing is that there is no frontline. The war's all around you. You hear the guns and see the planes as you sit on your hotel roof.'

12 *The Times*, 19 April 1968.

13 Lord Mancroft was her second husband. Previously she had been married to Richard St John Quarry: one of her daughters, Miranda, married Peter Sellers and later Alexander Macmillan, 2nd Lord Stockton.

14 *Chips: the Diaries of Sir Henry Channon*, ed. Robert Rhodes James.

15 Harold Harris, Hutchinson editor, to AC, 19 June 1970.

16 AC to Harold Harris, 16 June 1970.

17 AC to MS, 16 June 1970.

18 MS to the author.

19 MS to AC, 22 June 1970.

CHAPTER TWENTY-ONE: *Banking with Publishers* (pp. 221–9)

The A.D. Peters/Peters, Fraser & Dunlop archives are held at the Howard Gotlieb Archival Research Center at Boston University, USA. The John Murray archives are at 50 Albermarle Street, the firm's former offices.

1 KC to John G. Murray (JGM), 7 December 1968. John Murray archive.
2 KC to AC, n.d.
3 AC to JGM, 24 March 1969. John Murray archive.
4 JGM to William Hardcastle, 7 October 1971. John Murray archive.
5 William Hardcastle to JGM, 27 April 1972. John Murray archive.
6 JGM to AC, 10 May 1972, John Murray archive.
7 KC to JGM, 18 May 1972. John Murray archive.
8 Herbert Rees to JGM, 29 March 1973. John Murray archive.
9 AC to JGM, 30 October 1973. John Murray archive.
10 Colin R. Coote, *The Daily Telegraph*, 11 July 1974.
11 Kenneth Rose, *The Sunday Telegraph*, 14 July 1974.
12 Christopher Chant, Purnell's *History of the First World War*, 28 January 1971.
13 MS to AC, 30 December 1971.
14 All international rights in *Aces High*, being an integrated illustrated book, were held by the originating publisher. Weidenfeld & Nicolson sold US rights to Putnam, who bought 8,000 hardback books from W&N and licensed US paperback rights for £7,500. Under the traditional terms of the contract, Putnam took fifty per cent of the paperback income, passing over £3,750 to W&N. Before any of this was credited to Alan's account, W&N subtracted twenty-five per cent commission, leaving £2,812.50. As the book had already earned its advance in the UK this was paid to A.D. Peters, who now took its ten per cent commission (£281.25) and paid Alan £2,531.25, or just a third of gross American earnings. *Aces High* also earned Alan royalties in Britain, paying him £462 over its original W&N edition advance of £2,000. For the UK paperback rights Fontana negotiated with W&N an advance of £1,500, also on a 50:50 basis, and when this too earned out Alan was paid royalties of £138.
15 AC to MS, 4 December 1975. Boston University.
16 AC to MS, 4 March 1976. Boston University.
17 MS to AC, 24 March 1976. Boston University.
18 AC to MS, 13 April 1976. Boston University.
19 MS to AC, 14 April 1976. Boston University.
20 AC to MS, 19 May 1976. Boston University.
21 AC to MS, 14 June 1976. Boston University.
22 The Diadochi were, as Alan acknowledged in a footnote in the opening chapter of *Barbarossa*, the surviving generals of Alexander the Great, who quarrelled over the division of his empire. Several authorities (among them Hugh Trevor-Roper and Alexander Dallin) adopted the term to describe

the senior Nazi leaders.

23 AC to MS, 9 August 1976. Boston University.

24 MS to AC, 16 August 1976. Boston University.

25 AB to AC, 9 February 1983. Random House archive.

26 AC to AB, 15 February 1983. Random House archive.

27 AC to Harbottle & Lewis, 23 June 1983. Random House archive.

28 MS to AC, 14 February 1977. Boston University.

29 Christopher Falkus to MS, 10 March 1977. Boston University.

30 AC, *Diaries: Into Politics*, 23 March 1977.

31 AC to MS, 31 March 1977. Boston University.

32 Christopher Falkus to MS, 11 October 1997. Boston University.

33 Christopher Falkus to AC, 2 November 1977. Boston University.

34 On the basis that A.D. Peters had taken their ten per cent commission off the Weidenfeld & Nicolson advance of £2,000 before paying the £1,800 balance through to Alan.

35 AC to Christopher Falkus, 7 November 1977. Boston University.

CHAPTER TWENTY-TWO: *Into Politics* (pp. 230–42)

Quotations from Alan are from unpublished manuscript diaries, unless otherwise stated.

1 J. Enoch Powell, Conservative MP for Wolverhampton South-West since 1950. Ahead of his time on finance and defence policy, he stuck by his firmly held views even when they were at odds with his party and his leader. Although twice a Minister under Harold Macmillan, he refused to serve in Sir Alec Douglas-Home's government and was sacked as a Shadow Minister by Edward Heath for his views on race, following the 'Rivers of Blood' speech. From 1974 until his retirement in 1987 he was an Ulster Unionist MP.

2 AC to Mrs Enoch Powell, 20 October 1968, and Enoch Powell to AC, 24 October 1968.

3 AC, *The Last Diaries*, 4 November 1992.

4 *Evening Standard*, 4 July 1972.

5 Jerry Wiggin, who was selected, was also an Old Etonian and Monday Club member. He won the by-election with a majority of 20,472 over the Liberals. Although appointed as a junior Minister in 1979, he rose only to Parliamentary Under-Secretary at Defence. Alan related in his diary what happened when Margaret Thatcher reshuffled her government following the 1983 election. 'The phone rang at his home on Sunday night. "Jerry, hello, it's Ian [Gow] here ...". "Oh yes, hello." "Jerry, the Prime Minister would like to see you at Downing Street tomorrow." Jerry's spirits soared, but before he could even say Yes, Ian went on, "I'm afraid it is not very good news ..." and his spirits plummeted cruelly as Ian went on, "... so

would you mind coming to the back door."' *Diaries: In Power*, 21 June 1983.

6 AC went through a phase of quoting from the German philosopher Hegel (1770–1831), being particularly interested in the way he resolved the question of contradictions that ultimately came together.

7 It was something of a family joke that whenever someone had done Alan's mother even the most modest of good turns, she would say to K, 'Give him a pound!'

8 AC to KC, n.d.

9 Michael Briggs to the author.

10 Ian Lloyd obituaries, *The Daily Telegraph*, 30 September 2006, *The Times* and *Independent*, 2 October 2006, and *The Guardian*, 5 October 2006.

11 AC to Alan Warner, 20 November 1970.

12 In what was at the time a typically small inner London constituency, Lipton polled 13,033 votes to Harkess's 9,727, giving him a majority of 3,306.

13 5 November 1969, *The Hugo Young Papers*.

14 C.F. Johnson to Peter Thomas, Conservative Central Office, 9 July 1971.

15 AC to KC, n.d.

16 KC to AC, 16 December 1980.

17 Michael Howard had twice unsuccessfully fought Liverpool Edge Hill. In fact AC was wrong in his forecast. Howard did not finally enter the Commons until 1983, when he won the Folkestone and Hythe seat, thereby becoming the Clarks' Member of Parliament.

18 Norman Fowler, MP for Nottingham South since 1970, but his seat would be disappearing as a result of the boundary revisions. He had previously been a journalist on *The Times*.

19 David Hunt had fought Bristol South in 1970. His was a troubled road to the Commons. He was chosen as candidate at the neighbouring Plymouth Drake constituency but rejected at his adoption meeting after criticising Enoch Powell at the Party conference two weeks before. He did not finally become a Tory MP (for the Wirral) until a by-election in 1976.

20 *Evening Standard*, 4 July 1972.

21 AC, *Diaries: Into Politics*, 19 July 1972.

CHAPTER TWENTY-THREE: *Mixed Emotions* (pp. 245–56)

1 Quotations from *Diaries: Into Politics*, unless otherwise stated.

2 Thorpe was leader of the Liberal Party until succeeded by David Steel in 1976.

3 Euan Graham to the author.

4 KC to AC, 12 March 1974.

5 AC, *The Tories*.

6 AC, *The Sunday Times*, 24 March 1974.

7 AC to David Butler. David Butler with Dennis Kavanagh, *The British*

General Election, February 1974.

8 Douglas Hurd, *Memoirs.*

9 George Gardiner, *A Bastard's Tale.*

10 Andrew Roberts to the author.

11 AC to KC, n.d.

12 It was eventually purchased from Alan for an undisclosed sum with the help of the Friends of the Tate.

13 AC, *Alan Clark's History of the Tory Party.* Oxford Film and TV, BBC, 1997.

14 *The Times,* 8 May 1976.

15 *The Guardian,* 21 June 1976.

16 7 November 1976.

17 AC, *Diaries: Into Politics,* 14 November 1976.

18 AC, *Diaries: Into Politics,* 18 March 1978.

19 AC, *Diaries: Into Politics,* 14 November, 1976.

20 Colette Clark interviewed by Naim Attallah, *The Oldie,* July 1998.

21 AC, *Diaries: Into Politics,* 7 November 1978.

22 AC, *Diaries: Into Politics,* 28 April 1977.

23 AC, *Diaries: Into Politics,* 21 June 1977.

24 AC, *Diaries: Into Politics,* 2 May 1978.

25 *The Guardian,* 23 March 1979.

26 *The Guardian,* 2 May 1979.

CHAPTER TWENTY-FOUR: *Falklands and Papa's Death* (pp. 257–65)

1 Nigel Lawson. *The View From No. 11.*

2 AC, *Diaries: Into Politics,* 26 February 1980.

3 AC, *Diaries: Into Politics,* 27 November 1979.

4 AC, *The Tories.*

5 AC, *Diaries: Into Politics,* 2 April 1982.

6 AC had been elected vice-chairman of the Conservative Defence Committee in December 1980.

7 Richard Luce, *Ringing the Changes.*

8 AC, *Evening Standard,* 12 January 1994.

9 Jane Clark to the author. Janet Stone was the wife of the designer and typographer Reynolds Stone. She died in 1998.

10 AC, *Diaries: In Power,* 15 May 1983.

11 AC, *Diaries: In Power,* 15 May 1983.

12 AC, *Diaries: In Power,* 20 May 1983.

13 AC, *Diaries: In Power,* 15 May 1983.

14 AC, *Evening Standard,* 12 January 1974.

15 Lord Jopling to the author. In the reshuffle that followed the election, Jopling, MP for Westmorland since 1964, became Secretary of State for Agriculture.

16 Lord Armstrong to the author.
17 KC to AC, n.d.
18 The Art Wolf, www.theartwolf.com.
19 *Time*, 16 July 1984.
20 Colin and his second wife Faith had divorced.
21 KC to AC, n.d.
22 Colin Clark, *The Daily Telegraph*, 26 June 1984.
23 *The New York Times*, 29 November 1987.
24 In the mid-eighties/early nineties the shares in Coats, the lineal descendant of the Clark spinning company, had been selling at roughly 200p each, so the emotional link was fully justified financially. By 1998, when Alan added 100,000 of the company's shares into the trust, they had fallen to 25½p.
25 Colin Clark interviewed by Naim Attallah, *The Oldie*, July 1998.

CHAPTER TWENTY-FIVE: *Tired and Emotional at the Dispatch Box*
(pp. 266–73)

1 AC, *Diaries: In Power*, 22 July 1983.
2 Parliamentary Debates (Hansard). House of Commons Official Report, volume 46, 20 July 1983.
3 BBC2's *University Challenge* got it completely wrong. In a programme on 1 October 2007 Jeremy Paxman asked from a question card about who was tired and emotional at the Dispatch Box while delivering a ministerial order having been drinking 'with the Conservative MP Christopher Soames' – some careless question-setting here. As Alan related in the *Diaries*, his host that evening was Christopher Selmes, a financier, gay and some years younger, who often spent Christmas with the Clarks in Zermatt. Tony Rudd introduced them. He though Alan was 'kind of enthralled by Selmes', who was wealthy enough to employ his own chef (Simon Hopkinson) and provide him with unlimited funds for both ingredients and wines. Equally Selmes, 'A very amazing young thruster', recalls Rudd, 'in a way modelled himself on Alan. He started to buy vintage cars; he had already got into wine. Alan was a bad influence on Christopher, who didn't have the background to sustain all that, to handle it and reject some of it and take some of it with a pinch of salt, too innocent. Very sad.' He died of AIDS.
4 Selmes – and Alan – knew what they were talking about. Palmer was not at that time considered an obvious fine wine, being technically a third-growth Margaux. Alan never smoked cigarettes, maintaining even at Oxford, as Euan Graham recollected, that he was sure they were bad for one's health. But the occasional cigar ... He noted his father's enjoyment.
5 David Pannick, barrister and Fellow of All Souls, wrote that, as one observer pointed out, 'it is doubtful whether this enabled the House to grasp the point of a particular clause on which the Parliamentary draftsman must have

laboured for many months: it combined two negatives with "unless" in a phrase which would give pleasure to a postgraduate logician'. *The Guardian*, 21 November 1983.

6 AC, *Diaries: In Power*, 22 July 1983.

7 *The Times*, 22 July 1983.

8 Jane Clark to the author.

9 AC to Michael Cockerell, *Love Tory*, BBC, 1993.

10 Lord Tebbit to the author.

11 Matthew Parris, *Chance Witness*.

12 Lord Brooke of Sutton Mandeville to the author.

13 Robert Rhodes James, *The Guardian*, review of AC *Diaries*, 2 June 1993.

14 *The Sunday Times*, 24 July 1983.

15 AC to Hugo Young, 28 July 1983.

16 AC, *Diaries: In Power*, 22 July 1983.

17 Robert Rhodes James, *The Guardian*, review of AC *Diaries*, 2 June 1993.

18 *The Guardian*, 7 February 1985

19 AC, *Diaries: In Power*, 23 June 1983.

20 AC, *Diaries: In Power*, 5 July 1983.

21 AC, *Diaries: In Power*, 18 January 1984.

22 AC, *The Daily Telegraph*, 4 June 1984, review of Max Hastings, *Overlord* (London, Michael Joseph, 1984). Antony Beevor, *D-Day, The Battle for Normandy* (London, Viking, 2009). 'Fear and cruelty in sun-dappled orchards,' Charles Moore, *The Daily Telegraph*, 1 June 2009.

23 AC, *Diaries: In Power*, 12 October 1984.

24 Lord King to the author.

25 *The Guardian*, 7 February 1985.

26 AC maintained the leak came from a senior civil servant.

27 AC, *Diaries: In Power*, 31 January 1986.

28 AC, *Love Tory*, BBC, 1993.

INTERLUDE: *For the Love of Animals* (pp. 274–9)

Quotations are from *Diaries*, unless otherwise stated.

1 Robert Rhodes James, *The Times*, 19 May 1993.

2 AC, *Diaries: In Power*, 19 March 1988.

3 *The Guardian*, 7 April 1988.

4 Peta Ewing, his secretary at the time, says he told people he was a vegetarian, but he wasn't. 'He'd eat tongue.'

5 Lord Powell to the author.

6 Hansard, 20 June 1988.

7 Stanley Johnson to the author; he was MEP (C) for Wight and Hants E. His youngest son, Boris, was a Conservative MP (for Henley) before resigning on his election as Mayor of London in 2008.

CHAPTER TWENTY-SIX: *Reviewing Defence* (pp. 280–89)

1 AC, *Diaries: In Power*, 30 September 1989.
2 AC, *Diaries: In Power*, 24 July 1989.
3 John Smith MP, leader of the Labour Party 1992–4, quoted by Tam Dalyell in his obituary of Sir Michael Quinlan, *The Independent*, 28 February 2009.
4 Lord King to the author.
5 Bruce Anderson, *The Daily Telegraph*, 25 July 1989
6 Lord Powell to the author.
7 Julian Scopes to the author.
8 Lord Levene to the author.
9 What follows is taken from an unnumbered copy of the review.
10 AC, *Diaries: In Power*, footnote, 31 January 1990.
11 Tom King, *Panorama*, BBC, n.d. Excerpt, *Love Tory*, BBC, 1993.
12 *The Sunday Times*, 2 December 1990.
13 Lord Levene to the author.

CHAPTER TWENTY-SEVEN: *Reporting the Lady's Fall* (pp. 290–97)

1 *The Tories*.
2 AC to Geoffrey Howe, 5 June 1989. Quoted in Geoffrey Howe, *Conflict of Loyalty*.
3 AC, *Diaries: In Power*, 4 November 1990.
4 Hurd adds: 'This meeting is not recorded in his published diary.' Douglas Hurd, *Memoirs*.
5 Hugo Young, *The Hugo Young Papers*.
6 Three years after the publication of *Diaries* a separate paperback edition confined to this single event sold over 50,000 copies at 60p. *Alan Clark Diaries: Thatcher's Fall* (London, Phoenix paperback, 1995).
7 The political writer Alan Watkins recalls seeing Morrison one Sunday evening about this time at the Beefsteak Club with a young man he thought was 'his current fancy'. But Alan Clark, also there that evening, told Watkins the young man was Morrison's minder, to prevent him getting into trouble, rough trade and all that. Did Margaret Thatcher know? Watkins believes her to have been 'the most unworldly person in many ways'. Watkins to the author.
8 In the BBC drama documentary *Margaret* (2009), the author, Richard Cottan, drew on AC's *Diaries*, particularly over the Peter Morrison incident.
9 Norman Lamont, *In Office*.
10 Michael Portillo to the author.
11 AC, *Diaries: In Power*, 12 December 1990.
12 A copy of the proposal is at Saltwood.
13 AC, *The Last Diaries*, 4 January 1991.

14 Margaret Thatcher's output was prodigious, initially *Margaret Thatcher: the Downing Street Years* (1993), in which John O'Sullivan was involved, and where Alan is, incidentally, mentioned just once, in a footnote, followed by *The Path to Power* (1995), *The Collected Speeches*, edited by Robin Harris (1997) and *Statecraft: Strategies for a Changing World* (2002) – all London, HarperCollins.

CHAPTER TWENTY-EIGHT: *A Fit of Pique* (pp. 298–306)

AC's quotations are from *Diaries*, unless otherwise stated.

1 *The Guardian*, 25 February 1992.
2 *The Times*, 26 February 1992.
3 Alison Young to the author.
4 AC, *Diaries: In Power*, 25 January 1989. AC's opinions and recollections varied according to the occasion. Peta Ewing recalls his note with a reference when she left: 'I should have written you a letter of love immediately ... you were the perfect secretary. I will miss you dreadfully. Alison is settling in quite well now although I can't say she finds shorthand that easy.' Peta Ewing says he had tried to convince himself that if he said No often enough, it wouldn't happen. Her mementos of her time working for Alan include a handwritten note on Minister for Trade headed notepaper: 'What is this bloody machine doing? Letter spacing quite batty.' He also told her that he had once fired a secretary in the middle of the road, on a traffic island.
5 Lewtrenchard, a country house hotel on the Devon side of the county border with Cornwall.
6 AC himself noted at this time, 'a great series in the *Sunday Telegraph* on "the mid-life crisis" ... it's going to be hard to come to terms with this, particularly in the knowledge that it's my "fault"'. *Diaries*, 14 April 1991.
7 Baroness Seccombe to AC, 5 June 1991.
8 Alison recalls Alan saying he wanted a stamp with TS on it to respond to certain ministerial documents.
9 General election result: Conservatives 336 seats; Labour 271 seats; Liberal Democrats 20 seats; others 24 seats. In Plymouth Sutton, AC's successor as the Conservative candidate, Gary Streeter, had a majority of 11,950.
10 Alison Young, Mexico, n.d.

CHAPTER TWENTY-NINE: *Behind the* Actualité (pp. 307–19)

1 AC, evidence, 5 November 1992.
2 If AC thought he was offering an alternative to 'economical with the truth', a phrase made famous in contemporary parlance by Robert Armstrong, the Cabinet Secretary, during the Australian *Spycatcher* trial in 1976, his knowledge of French let him down. 'Actualité' means topicality or current

events. However, thanks to AC the phrase, with his intended meaning, has entered the language, however erroneously.

3 Alan Moses, QC, had been a Recorder since 1986. In 1996 he was knighted and became a High Court judge, Queen's Bench division.

4 Brian Smedley was at the time a circuit judge. He was appointed a judge of the High Court, Queen's Bench division, and knighted in 1995. He died in 2007.

5 Richard Norton-Taylor, *The Guardian*, 11 November 1992.

6 As *The Guardian* pointed out (2 November 1992), the lack of coverage highlighted the gap left by the Press Association's decision to save money by cutting back its court reporting. PA had played a crucial role in feeding detailed and reliable court reports to print and broadcast media. Not until the trial collapsed did *The Times*, for instance, offer coverage to its readers; then it lead with the story and with background pieces (10 November).

7 Hansard, 11 November 1992.

8 AC, *Diaries: In Power*, 31 January 1986.

9 Michael Cockerell, *Love Tory*, BBC, 1993.

10 Quoted in Hugo Young, *The Hugo Young Papers*.

11 John Pilger, 'On Her Majesty's Bloody Service', *The New Statesman*, 18 February 1994.

12 Trefgarne was Minister for Defence Procurement. On 24 July 1989 he became Minister for Trade, swapping jobs with Alan.

13 AC, *The Last Diaries*, 28 July 1999.

14 Sir Jeremy Hanley to the author.

15 For detailed histories of the Matrix Churchill trial, the Scott Inquiry and its aftermath, see listings in the Bibliography.

16 Paul Henderson, *The Unlikely Spy*.

17 Andrew Neil, *Full Disclosure*.

18 Richard Ryder, MP for Mid-Norfolk since 1983. Successively Economic Secretary to the Treasury and Paymaster General before his appointment by John Major as Chief Whip four days previously.

19 AC, *Diaries: In Power*, 28 November 1990.

20 Perhaps it is unsurprising that Alan left out his account of that day. He was in the midst of transcribing and editing this period of his diaries for publication as the Matrix Churchill trial was taking place.

21 AC, diary, 3 December 1990.

22 Timothy Sainsbury, successively Parliamentary Under-Secretary at the Ministry of Defence and the Foreign and Commonwealth Office before moving to the Department of Trade and Industry in 1990; he was currently Minister for Trade.

23 Secrecy now had to be maintained. The new Chief Whip was only finally able to write to Alan on the eve of the New Year's honours being published. 'I was so pleased about your PC. Pleased because, of course, you deserved

it and I am thrilled as a friend. You have shown great kindness to me over the past few years and I greatly appreciate the warmth and generosity of your friendship. This is the only post in politics I have ever really wanted to fill. I have no wish to graduate to anything else ... It is an advantage which I intend to deploy in the months ahead. Please let us keep in really close touch. We shall face a huge task and we cannot afford to take wrong turnings.' Richard Ryder, 20 December 1990.

24 Richard Norton-Taylor, Mark Lloyd and Stephen Cook, *Knee Deep in Dishonour: the Scott Report and its Aftermath*.

25 Alan Moses, QC, 18 March 1994. Written statement, Scott Inquiry. G9.2.

26 Michael White, *The Guardian*, 25 February 1992.

27 *The Sunday Telegraph*, 2 August 1992.

28 AC, supplemental statement, 13 December 1993. Scott Inquiry report. G8.8.

29 Richard Norton-Taylor to the author, 2008.

30 AC, *The Last Diaries*, 21 March 1995.

31 AC, *The Last Diaries*, 24 January 1996.

32 AC, *The Last Diaries*, 17 February 1996.

33 *Half the Picture* by Richard Norton-Taylor and John McGrath, directed by Nicolas Kent. Tricycle Theatre, June 1994.

34 Hugo Young, *The Guardian*, 9 September 1999.

CHAPTER THIRTY: *The Making of the* Diaries (pp. 320–326)

1 *The Spectator*, 8 February 1986.

2 MS to AC, 13 February 1986. Boston University.

3 *Chips: the Diaries of Sir Henry Channon* and the three volumes of Harold Nicolson's *Diaries*, ed. Nigel Nicolson. James Lees-Milne began the multi-volume edition of his diaries with *Ancestral Voices* (London, Chatto & Windus, 1973).

4 *The Sunday Telegraph*, 2 August 1992.

5 *Daily Mail*, 7 August 1992.

6 MS to AC, 18 August 1992.

7 Alan Williams, a media specialist at Denton Hall Burgin and Warrens (now Denton Wilde Sapte). Williams proved an invaluable adviser on subsequent volumes of the diaries following Alan's death; and when Alan decided to sue the *Evening Standard* in 1997, Dentons was the firm he chose to represent him.

8 AC, *The Last Diaries*, 10 February 1993.

9 AC, *The Last Diaries*, 4 June 1993.

10 *The Times*, 19 May 1993.

11 *The Times* Diary, 8 March 1993.

12 Alan enjoyed rewriting entries to fit the space. The second ended with a

cliff-hanger. He reproduced what happened when, on returning to Albany one May evening in 1989, he found the landing outside B5 blocked by builders' equipment. 'Livid and perspiring – it must still have been in the 70°s – I could hardly reach my own doorway. I threw the industrial Hoover down the stairs – it crash-banged satisfactorily, followed it with a huge sack of sundry carpet clippings and broken glass (ditto) and then a heavy sanding machine hired (or so it proclaimed) from a tool company. The secretary [of Albany], greatly to his credit, as it was nearly midnight, appeared in his shirtsleeves, alerted by the commotion'.

13 Robert Rhodes James, *The Guardian*, 2 June 1993.

CHAPTER THIRTY-ONE: *Jane and the* Diaries *Aftermath* (pp. 000–000)

1 Simon Hoggart, who knew Alan from the 1970s when on *The Guardian*, to the author.

2 Dr James Le Fanu, in *The Daily Telegraph* (7 June 1994) identified relentless male heterosexual philandering, satyriasis, or Don Juanism, as the 'Alan Clark syndrome'. There was no clear explanation, but many theories. He quoted statistics from the United States where male sexual promiscuity was seen as an addiction for which apparently no fewer than 300,000 people in America were currently 'in therapy'. He also stated that psychoanalysts, 'implausibly', attribute the syndrome to the Oedipus Complex – the many women loved and left are substitutes for the mother who was guiltily desired, but denied by the castrating father. He went on to quote analyst Adam Jukes in his book *Why Men Hate Women* (London, Free Association Books, 1993): 'every time he conquers a woman he is recreating his mother, bringing her back to life after destroying her'. And Le Fanu concluded that 'as with so many aspects of human behaviour, the real answer lies in a complex mixture of all of them. The last words on this matter undoubtedly belong to Mae West, who famously observed: "Too much of a good thing can be wonderful".'

3 Lord Jopling to the author. AC had twice referred to the remark in the *Diaries*, 17 November 1980 and 17 June 1987. Heseltine wrote in his memoirs, 'over the years, as someone once said, we had always bought our own furniture – and we enjoyed every minute of it. Come to think of it, *someone* always has to buy the furniture. Unless you have ancestors or parents who did it for you, at some stage in life you have to start for yourself. The rest of my family still had very good use for what they owned. Anne and I have spent many happy hours combing the junk shops of Portobello Road, wandering from antique shop to antique shop in the Cotswolds, bidding at auctions and searching art galleries together. We do so to this day.' In 2006 he was asked by a reader of *The Independent*, 'Did you buy your own furniture?' and responded. 'Yes, my father could not afford to do it. Alan

Clark's father could.' 19 June 2006.

4 Matthew Parris, *Chance Witness*.

5 Max Hastings, *Editor*.

6 AC to MS, 10 July 1992. Boston University.

7 AC to MS, 10 July 1993. Boston University.

8 AC to MS, 27 October 1993. Boston University.

9 AC to MS, 25 November 1993. Boston University.

10 MS to AC, 30 November 1993. Boston University.

11 MS to AC, 15 December 1993. Boston University.

12 AC to MS, 16 January 1994. Boston University.

13 Archer had been represented, most successfully, for his fiction by Deborah Owen, the wife of David Owen, Labour MP for Devonport. Her client list also included the Israeli novelist Amos Oz and the cookery writer Delia Smith.

14 AC to MS, 20 January 1994. Boston University.

15 AC, *Diaries: In Power*, 13 June 1983.

16 Max Clifford and Angela Levin, *Max Clifford: Read All About It*.

17 *The Daily Telegraph* published a letter from Mrs Rita Miller of London, N14 (3 June 1994) making the point: 'Readers of Alan Clark's book cannot possibly identify these people, so why assist their gallop into the limelight? They are involved in a sort of inverted blackmail: instead of the victim paying for silence, the tabloids pay for the gossip (true or untrue) and the superior papers are happy to repeat all the salacious detail. It all fills column inches but is it responsible journalism?'

18 *The Daily Telegraph*, 1 June 1994.

19 *Max Clifford: Read All About It*.

20 *The Daily Telegraph*, 1 June 1994.

21 *The Daily Telegraph*, 1 June 1994.

22 *The Sunday Telegraph*, 5 June 1994.

23 *The Daily Telegraph*, 1 June 1994.

24 *The Daily Telegraph*, 2 June 1994.

25 Jasper Ridley, *Lord Palmerston* (London, Constable, 1970).

CHAPTER THIRTY-TWO: *The Wilderness Years* (pp. 345–54)

1 AC, *The Last Diaries*, 29 December 1994.

2 Barney Hayhoe, MP for Brentford and Isleworth (and its previous incarnation) 1970–92.

3 John Charmley, *Churchill: the End of Glory* (London, John Curtis/Hodder & Stoughton, 1993).

4 AC, *The Last Diaries*, 3 January 1993.

5 *The Times*, 2 January 1993.

6 *The Guardian*, 5 January 1993.

7 *The Times*, 4 January 1993.

8 Andrew Roberts to the author.

9 *The Guardian*, 5 January 1993.

10 Graham Stewart, *Burying Caesar: Churchill, Chamberlain and the Battle for the Tory Party* (London, Weidenfeld & Nicolson, 1999).

11 Graham Stewart to the author.

12 Richard Ingrams, *The Observer*, 14 March 1993.

13 See *Back Fire* and *The Last Diaries* for full account.

14 Sue Lawley to the author.

15 AC, *Diaries: In Power*, 13 April (Friday) 1984.

16 His full choice of records: 1. Beethoven, 'Leonora' Overture No. 3. 'Absolutely bowled me over the very first time I heard it. I was sitting next to a most beautiful woman. I was very, very young, sixteen or seventeen I suppose. I shall always remember them together.' 2. Slim Whitman and 'Candy Kisses'. 'A song played on a juke box in Sarasota, Florida. It has always stayed with me, because of a particular line in it, "Candy kisses wrapped in paper mean more to you than all of mine do".' It reminded him of 'various high spots in his romantic life'. 3. 'Sentimental Journey' played by Joe Bushkin. 'A great Air Force song at the end of the war.' 4. 23rd Psalm – Welsh male voice choirs. 'A wonderful rallying hymn.' 5. Los Paraguayos and 'Bell Bird'. 'Conjures up a lot of escapist visions of great heat and white dust and mid-summer and almost deserted but brightly coloured village streets in Latin countries and very, very navy blue sky.' 6. 'The Dead March' from Handel's *Saul*. 'Played in the Abbey whenever a notable dignitary, particularly a Tory, dies.' 7. 'Scotland the Brave' – Scottish Pipe Band. 'Archetypal bagpipe tune. The pipes played men to their death across no man's land in the First World War, so you can allow your mood to swing from heaven to hell when you listen to the pipes.' 8. Tchaikovsky's 'Capriccio Italien'. 'One of the very first bits of what one would call classical music that I heard on my own.'

CHAPTER THIRTY-THREE: *The Making of* The Tories (pp. 355–9)

1 AC, *The Last Diaries*, 16 May 1994.

2 AC, *The Last Diaries*, 25 January 1995.

3 Graham Stewart to the author.

4 Robert Blake, *The Conservative Party from Peel to Churchill* (London, Eyre & Spottiswoode, 1970). Blake updated it to include Margaret Thatcher (London, Fontana, 1982) and John Major (London, Arrow Books, 1998).

5 AC, *Alan Clark's History of the Tory Party*. Oxford Film and TV, 1997.

6 AC, *The Last Diaries*, 21 April 1996.

7 *Burying Caesar* was eventually published in 1999.

8 AC, *The Last Diaries*, 3 November 1996.

9 AC, *The Last Diaries*, 7 June 1996.

10 AC, *The Last Diaries*, 4 December 1998.

11 AC, *The Last Diaries*, 30 January 1999.

CHAPTER THIRTY-FOUR: *Back into the Commons* (pp. 360–77)

1 Quotations in this chapter are from *The Last Diaries*, unless otherwise stated.

2 Luke Harding, *The Guardian*, 5 April 1997.

3 A.A. Gill, *The Sunday Times*, 4 May 1997.

4 Paul Johnson to the author.

5 Frank Johnson succeeded Dominic Lawson, who had been Editor of *The Spectator* since 1990, with Lawson becoming Editor of *The Sunday Telegraph* where, latterly, Johnson had been deputy Editor.

6 Sir Michael Craig-Cooper to the author.

7 Andrew Roberts to the author.

8 Simon Hoggart, *The Guardian*, 25 April 1997.

9 Patricia Morris, later Baroness Morris of Bolton, was already an authority on children's policies. The Exchange Rate Mechanism was at the time rarely out of the headlines when the European single currency issue was being discussed.

10 Luke Harding, *The Guardian*, 5 April 1997.

11 W.F. Deedes, *The Daily Telegraph*, 27 January 1997.

12 Simon Hoggart, *The Guardian*, 25 April 1997.

13 A.A. Gill, *The Sunday Times*, 4 May 1997.

14 Matthew Parris, *The Times*, 8 May 1997.

15 Michael Portillo, MP for Enfield North, was defeated by the Labour candidate by 1,433 votes.

16 Matthew d'Ancona, *The Sunday Telegraph*, 11 May 1997.

17 *The Spectator*, 8 August 1997.

18 *The Guardian*, 15 July 2002.

19 *The Daily Telegraph*, 22 October 1997.

20 *The Guardian*, 8 October 1997.

21 *The Guardian*, 10 October 1997.

22 AC, *The Daily Telegraph*, 3 June 1998.

23 *Today*, BBC Radio 4, 18 June 1998.

24 Bratton-Clovelly residents complained that the poor state of the house had wrecked its chance of winning a best-kept village competition. 'Clarkie', as they knew him, agreed to have the lawn mowed, the flower beds weeded and the gate rehung. To no avail; Bratton lost the 1988 competition to nearby Sampford Courtenay. *Daily Express*, 20 September 1988.

25 Robert Campling's painted door in the Bloomsbury style, now on one of the Saltwood tower office walls. Duncan Grant, Bloomsbury artist, had, on

the recommendation of Kenneth Clark, been commissioned in the mid-1930s by Cunard to paint a huge picture for the *Queen Mary*. It was rejected. Jane and AC bought it in the 1970s, dividing it into three separate pictures.

26 'Jollyboy', yet another name for the Clarks' elder son James, who so enjoyed being pushed at speed in his pushchair that he invariably asked for more. In clearing out Bratton they discovered the pushchair, *Rosebud*, named after the sledge in Orson Welles' *Citizen Kane*.

27 *The Guardian*, 9 September 1999.

28 Matthew Parris, *The Times*, 14 April 1999.

29 Andrew Rawnsley, *The Observer*, 31 March 1999.

30 John Erickson to AC, 31 March 1999.

31 AC to Alastair Campbell, 21 April 1999.

32 Alastair Campbell, *Daily Mirror*, 8 September 1999.

33 Alastair Campbell, *The Blair Years*, 13 May 1995.

34 The Bentley was later sold, but Alan kept the number plate, which is now on one of his son Andrew's cars.

35 Hansard, 19 April 1999.

36 Alastair Campbell to AC, 20 April 1999.

INTERLUDE: *Not Amused* (pp. 378–83)

1 AC, *The Last Diaries*. 29 April 1997.

2 Peter Bradshaw to the author.

3 Max Hastings, introduction, *Not the Alan Clark Diaries*, the collected Peter Bradshaw columns.

4 *The Times* Diary, 27 May 1997.

5 Clive Thorne to the author.

6 Max Hastings, introduction, *Not the Alan Clark Diaries*.

7 The quotes from the trial are all taken from the court transcript.

8 *Evening Standard*, 21 January 1998.

9 *The Independent*, 22 January 1998.

10 *The Times*, 22 January 1998.

CHAPTER THIRTY-FIVE: *Worryingly Ill* (pp. 384–96)

Quotations are from *The Last Diaries*, unless otherwise stated.

1 Matthew Parris, *The Times*, 16 June 1997. Also see Matthew Parris, *Chance Witness*.

2 Named after Disraeli's landmark novel, *Sybil: or The Two Nations*, although in his diaries Alan sometimes spells it after Sibyl Colefax, who lived at 19 Lord North Street, off Smith Square, Westminster, where she entertained famously. A particularly desirable home for a Member of Parliament, Alan lunched there on 11 February 1995 as a guest of Tory MP, former Whip

and Foreign Office Minister Alastair Goodlad. 'Something especially pleasing about entering Sibyl's house at lunchtime – although of course while remembering the geography I never (or did I once?) came as a guest in my own right?' The 'Sybil' met at the Queen Anne's Gate house of Shaun Woodward, since 1987 Tory MP for Witney.

3 'Winston smilingly made his way towards one of the Porter's chairs and asked for snuff, which the attendant handed him in a silver box. Then, surprisingly, Winston looked at the chair (which he must have known for 40 years) as if he had never seen it before in his life, got into it, and sat there for fully five minutes, bowing and beaming at other Members who looked at him through the little window. A boyish prank. How endearing he is, sometimes. A few minutes later, however, he was making what was to be one of his very greatest speeches ... to a crowded and anxious house.' *Chips*, 28 September 1949.

4 AC to Dr Thomas Stuttaford, 22 May 1999.

5 Simon Hornby, president of both the Royal Horticultural Society and the Chelsea Society since 1994. A former chairman of W. H. Smith, he had also twice been a Conservative parliamentary candidate. Nick Brown MP, Minister of Agriculture since 1998; (Labour) for Newcastle-upon-Tyne East and Wallsend since 1997 (Newcastle East 1983–97).

6 In a review of *The Last Diaries* in the *British Journal of General Practice* (April 2003) David Tovey wrote that this reminded him 'how difficult being a doctor is when we are offered such a small sub-section of symptomatology (and yet so much white noise)'.

CHAPTER THIRTY-SIX: *High Hopes* (pp. 397–404)

1 Colin died in 2002.

2 AC, *The Last Diaries*, 6 June, 1999.

3 It was not his final thought on cars. To Jane he later dictated a memorandum on his own collection and what to do with it, which was published posthumously in *Back Fire*.

4 John Coldstream to the author.

5 Gyles Brandreth, *Breaking the Code* (London, Weidenfeld & Nicolson, 1999).

6 AC, *The Last Diaries*, 12 January 1998.

CHAPTER THIRTY-SEVEN: *Beliefs* (pp. 405–9)

1 The Rev. Canon Reg Humphriss to the author.

2 The Rev. Canon Norman Woods to the author.

3 AC, *The Last Diaries*, 14 April 1991.

4 AC, *The Last Diaries*, 17 February 1991.

5 AC, *Diaries: In Power*, 31 August 1984.

6 AC, *The Last Diaries*, 8 March 1997.

7 AC to Graham Turner, *The Sunday Telegraph*, 2 August 1992.

8 The visit was arranged by Father Michael Seed, a Franciscan based at Westminster Cathedral, who was making a name for himself following a number of high-profile conversions to the Catholic faith.

9 Anji Hunter, special assistant to Tony Blair, as leader of the Opposition and as Prime Minister, until 2001.

10 Tony Blair was brought up in the Church of England, but married a Roman Catholic. In 2008 he was accepted into the Catholic Church.

11 Lady Antonia Fraser to Ginny Dougary, *The Times*, 5 July 2008.

12 Father Michael Seed to AC, 28 March 1995.

13 AC, *The Last Diaries*, 6 August 1995.

14 Evelyn Waugh, *Brideshead Revisited*.

15 Evelyn Waugh, *Diaries*, ed. Michael Davie (London, Weidenfeld & Nicolson, 1976), 13 October 1943.

16 AC, *The Last Diaries*, 10 July 1999.

17 Father Michael Seed to AC, 12 July 1999.

CHAPTER THIRTY-EIGHT: *Hopes Shattered* (pp. 410–21)

1 Jane Clark to the author.

2 Alan and Jane's name for Andrew and Sarah dating from the time when they would say everything was 'amazing'.

CHAPTER THIRTY-NINE: *Last Rites* (pp. 422–5)

1 Information via Blair Worden.

2 Edward Pearce, *The Guardian*, 8 September 1999.

3 Craig Brown, *The Daily Telegraph*, 11 September 1999.

4 Frank Johnson, *The Spectator*, 10 September 1999.

5 Robert Coucher, *Classic Cars*, November 1999.

6 William Hague, 17 November 1999.

Epilogue (pp. 426–9)

1 *The Daily Telegraph*, 8 September 1999.

2 *The Daily Telegraph*, 10 September 1999.

3 For the thanksgiving service at St Margaret's Father Michael did seek to be part of the family procession when it entered the church. Jane thought that inappropriate.

4 Father Michael Seed to the author.

5 Meryle Secrest, *Kenneth Clark*.

6 Graham Turner, *The Sunday Telegraph*, 2 August 1992.

Acknowledgements

The idea for this biography of Alan Clark came from his widow, Jane. She had been hugely supportive after Alan's death when I edited two volumes of his diaries; she also suggested the collection of his motoring writings, published as *Back Fire* (edited by Robert Coucher). Her aim throughout has been to ensure that the life and career of her husband would not dim. A biography was the natural next step. I am enormously grateful to her for asking me to undertake the task. Although requiring a year longer than I anticipated it has never been less than enthralling both in the research and in the writing.

My thanks to Jane are legion. From the start she encouraged me to roam throughout Saltwood Castle. Filing cabinets – one of which required a jemmy to open – yielded unsuspected treasures. In a box long hidden in the laundry room, in a tea chest in a tower attic, in desk drawers . . . I turned up discovery after discovery. Jane herself produced valuable papers from her own files. She introduced me to members of her (and Alan's) circle of friends who talked freely. I soon realised that she would not necessarily welcome the publication of some of the material that I discovered. But just as with *Diaries into Politics* and *The Last Diaries* I have had a freedom which many another biographer must envy. As the copyright owner of Alan's writings as well as those of parents-in-law, Kenneth and Jane Clark, she has allowed me a free run.

I also wish to thank her for the hospitality she has given me across the past decade. Conversations over numerous lunches have often provided me with unsuspected insights into her life and her forty-one-year marriage to Alan.

Thanks to the editing of Alan's *Diaries* and supervision of the publication of *Back Fire,* I have greatly benefited from the knowledge of Alan and Jane's sons, James and Andrew.

Alan's surviving sister, Colette, known to all as Celly, produced memories of the Clark children's early years for which I am particularly grateful. I also enjoyed two conversations with Colin Clark before his death in 2002.

For most of his career as a writer Alan was represented by Michael Sissons, first at A.D. Peters and then at Peters, Fraser & Dunlop. Not only did Michael tell me much about Alan's writing career, but he led me to the University of Boston, which holds the A.D. Peters and PFD archives, an invaluable resource. I have also been fortunate for this volume in drawing on Michael's skills as a negotiator and for his ongoing advice. His assistant, Fiona Petheram (née Batty), was in at the birth of Alan's *Diaries,* and it is good to have her continuing involvement. Let me also take this opportunity to thank Alan Williams, who has been the legal adviser on Alan's writings since the original *Diaries.*

A number of those who helped me in my researches also read drafts of relevant chapters. My thanks in particular to Antony Beevor, David Cornwell, Alex Danchev, Pamela Hart, Richard Norton-Taylor, Andrew Roberts, Gary Sheffield, Clive Thorne, Alison Young and Philip Ziegler. Graham Stewart, who worked for Alan as his researcher on his final book, *The Tories,* and retains links with Saltwood, read the complete script. I am in his debt. Adam Sisman, who is working on the forthcoming biography of Hugh Trevor-Roper (Lord Dacre), and I swapped correspondence between our subjects that went back to 1947. His knowledge and that of Blair Worden, Lord Dacre's literary executor, helped enormously over a relationship that knew both highs and lows.

Over the five years since I started work on this biography I have been struck by the generosity of those I have interviewed and those who have helped answer my questions. In addition to the people referred to above let me acknowledge with thanks:

Jonathan Aitken, Lord Armstrong of Ilchester, Lord Ashburton (John Baring), Edgar Astaire, Osman Azis, Lord Baker of Dorking, the late Anthony Blond, Peter Blond, Peter Bradshaw, Melvyn Bragg, Gyles Brandreth, Isabel and Michael Briggs, Peta Brough (née Ewing), Lord Brooke of Sutton Mandeville, Alastair Campbell, Robert Caskie, Celia Charrington, Anthony Cheetham, Algy Cluff, Michael Cockerell, John Coldstream, Basil Comely, Artemis Cooper, Sir Michael Craig-Cooper, Michael Crick, Judith Curthoys (Christ Church, Oxford), Iain Dale, Matthew d'Ancona, Arnold Davey (honorary secretary, the Lagonda Club), David Davis MP, Henry Deedes, the late Lord (W.F.) Deedes, Ian A.K. Dipple, Luke Dodd, Michael Evans, Julian Fellowes, Lady Antonia Fraser, Gavin Fuller, Peter Furtado, Lord Garel-Jones, the late Euan Graham, Penny Hadfield (archivist, Eton College library), Katie Hambly, Sir Jeremy Hanley, James Hanning, Ronald Harwood, Sir Max Hastings, Tim Heald, Simon Heffer, Peter Hennessy, Dick Hennessy-Walsh, Anna Hervé, Lord Hoffmann, Simon Hoggart, Sir Alistair Horne, Charles Howard, Michael Howard MP, Sir Michael Howard OM, Lawrence W. Hughes, Shirley Hughes, Bruce Hunter, Lord Hurd of Westwell, Richard Ingrams, Dotti Irving and the team at Colman Getty, the late Frank Johnson, Marigold and Paul Johnson, Stanley Johnson, Louise Jury, Nicolas Kent (Oxford Film and Television), Lord Kimball, Lord King of Bridgwater, Sue Lawley, Barbara Leaming and her husband David Parker, Lord Levene of Portsoken, Guy Levin, Andrew Lycett, Brian MacArthur, Patricia Methven (Liddell Hart Centre for Military History, King's College, London), John Miller, Lord Montagu of Beaulieu, Virginia Murray, James Naughtie, Richard Norton-Taylor, Lord (John Julius) Norwich, Robin Oakley, Lord Owen, the late Lord Parmoor

(Milo Cripps), Roger Pemberton, Andrew Pierce, Michael Portillo, Lord Powell of Bayswater, Michael Prodger, Renata Propper, the late Sir Michael Quinlan, Tim Radford, Richard Rhodes, Elisabeth Ribbans, Peter Riddell, Hugh Robertson MP, Stephen Robinson, Anthony Rudd and the late Ethne (Ena) Rudd, Julian Scopes, Simon Sebag-Montefiore, Victor Sebestyen, Meryle Secrest, Sebastian Shakespeare, Keith Simpson MP, Adam Sisman, Godfrey Smith, Nicholas Soames MP, Will Sulkin, Lord Tebbit, Nicolas Thompson, the late Burt Todd, Raleigh Trevelyan, Hugo Vickers, Lord Waldegrave, Brian Walden, Sheila Watson, Alan Watkins, Lynn Webb, Lord Weidenfeld, Michael White, Ann Widdecombe MP, Sir Robert Worcester, Mariam Yamin.

To all at Weidenfeld & Nicolson and the Orion Publishing Group, in particular Malcolm Edwards, who commissioned this biography, Ben Buchan, my inestimable editor, Bea Hemming who helped in so many editorial ways, including the photographs; Linden Lawson, peerless copy-editor, and Jane Birkett (who read the proofs as meticulously as ever). The knowledge of Douglas Matthews, who first indexed Alan Clark with his *Diaries* in 1993, proved once more invaluable.

The staff of the London Library were as ever most helpful, as were the staff of the Liddell Hart Centre for Military History at King's College, London. I am also grateful to the staff at the Howard Gotlieb Archival Research Center, Boston University, USA.

If I leave my family to last this in no way reduces my debt to them. My wife Sue has not only put up with my frequent absences as I researched and wrote, but often through her pertinent questions led me in directions I might have missed. I am enormously grateful to her. Our son Simon and daughter Maria (and their families) were, as ever, always supportive.

As an editor over more than a quarter of a century let me end with a sentence that I invariably advised my authors to include. The responsibility for this book ends with me.

Ion Trewin

Index

HON. ALAN CLARK MP

Jolly Jane (y)

Be
My
Valentine

Cheap card, but
special love,

JANE